# The Unlikeliness of it All
## Part 1

### An Insider's Perspective:
### A Small Maine Town's History of Resilience, Transformation, Collaboration, Immigration and its Global Singularity

**Phil Nadeau**

Published independently by
Phil Nadeau
Bradenton, FL 34202
Email: phil@philnadeau.com


Copyright © 2021 by Phil Nadeau


Published 2021
Second printing with corrections


ISBN: 978-1-7369505-0-0 (ebook)
ISBN: 979-8-7164324-6-8 (Amazon paperback)
ISBN: 978-1-7369505-1-7 (hardcover)
Library of Congress Control Number: 2021905176


*Notice*: The information in this book is true and complete to the best of the author's knowledge. It is offered without guarantee. The author disclaims all liability in connection with the use of this book.


All rights reserved. No part of this book may be reproduced or transmitted by any electronic or mechanical means, including information storage and retrieval systems, without prior written permission from the author except in the case of brief quotations embodied in critical articles and reviews.

*For my wife Marcia and son Tony whose love is all that matters,
my parents "Guy" and "Jackie" who let my free spirit find its own path,
and to educators Roland Roy, Dr. Marcus Pohlmann, Dr. John Nickerson,
and Dr. Josephine "Josie" LaPlante for seeing
something more in me than I could see in myself.*

# TABLE OF CONTENTS

**INTRODUCTION** ......... 1

**CHAPTER 1** ......... 13
**LEWISTON'S EARLY HISTORY: 1850S – 1980S** ......... 13
TEXTILES & EARLY IMMIGRATION ......... 13
POLITICS ......... 24

**CHAPTER 2** ......... 46
**FORGING A NEW PATH FORWARD: 1950S – 1990S** ......... 46
COLLABORATION ......... 46
TRANSITION ......... 68
THE CONJOINING ......... 84

**CHAPTER 3** ......... 106
**TURNING THE CORNER: 1990S – DECEMBER 2000** ......... 106
THE "OTHER" REFUGEES ......... 106
TURNING POINT ......... 119
NEW MILLENNIUM, OPPORTUNITIES, FAMILIES, AND A NEW KIND OF RENAISSANCE ......... 133

**CHAPTER 4** ......... 146
**WELCOME TO LEWISTON: JANUARY 2001 – AUGUST 2001** ......... 146
WHO ARE THE SOMALIS AND HOW DID THEY GET HERE? ......... 146
THE FIRST FAMILY AND NEW ARRIVALS ......... 154
MAINE HAS A PROBLEM AND AN OPPORTUNITY ......... 165

| CHAPTER 5 | 174 |
|---|---|
| FEAR, UNCERTAINTY, GRIEF, AND NEW BEGINNINGS: | 174 |
| SEPTEMBER 2001 – DECEMBER 2001 | 174 |
| THE UNIMAGINABLE—9/11 | 174 |
| THE LISBON CONNECTION | 184 |
| PROJECT QUALITY AND THE PHOTO FINISH | 195 |
| **CHAPTER 6** | **216** |
| BELIEVING, NOT BELIEVING, AND LISTENING | 216 |
| JANUARY 2002 – JUNE 2002 | 216 |
| THE WORKING GROUP | 216 |
| THERE'S A STORY BREWING AND A TOWN MEETING | 233 |
| THE GOVERNOR LISTENS | 246 |
| **CHAPTER 7** | **264** |
| DISCOVERY, CREATIVITY, AND OUTREACH | 264 |
| JULY 2002 – SEPTEMBER 2002 | 264 |
| THE SUMMER PUNCH LIST | 264 |
| JOCKEYING FOR POSITION | 280 |
| FULL COURT PRESS AND REACHING OUT | 291 |
| **CHAPTER 8** | **300** |
| THE CONVERGENCE | 300 |
| OCTOBER 2002 | 300 |
| JUST A COUNTRY LAWYER | 300 |
| THE MAYOR'S LETTER | 318 |
| TWO CITIES AND TWO TALES | 345 |
| **CHAPTER 9** | **351** |
| LA RÉPUDIATION | 351 |
| NOVEMBER 2002 – MARCH 2003 | 351 |
| HATE BOOKS A MEETING | 351 |
| DIVERSITY MAKES A STAND | 376 |
| "UNITED AGAINST HATE" | 389 |
| THE FADEAWAY, LARRY STAYS, THE CATALYST, AND THE CLOSER | 414 |

| | |
|---|---|
| **CHAPTER 10** | **428** |
| **PROGRESS, PEAKS, VALLEYS, AND THE UNEXPECTED** | **428** |
| **MARCH 2003 – DECEMBER 2020** | **428** |
| MARCH 2003 – 2008 | 428 |
| 2009 - 2014 | 438 |
| 2015 - 2020 | 446 |
| **EPILOGUE** | **462** |
| **ACKNOWLEDGEMENTS** | **465** |
| **NOTES** | **473** |

# Introduction

My memories of growing up in Lewiston, Maine are filled with images of my old neighborhood. I was the oldest and the only one of four siblings that would spend any part of their childhood living downtown. I was a little less than a year old when my parents bought their first house.

When we first arrived in our new house, the wooded area that bordered our neighborhood enveloped the space where the last of these mid-1950s new homes were built in that residential area. For the Nadeau's, our home was one of the last to be sold. Growing up, the dirt streets in this newly developed area were filled with little kids claiming the roadway as our personal playground. There were limitless opportunities to play just about any sport on those streets, or in the few remaining vacant lots that were close-to-home opportunities. These lots were 'real game' opportunities that were played on uneven, somewhat overgrown fields where bases and home plate only required pieces of cardboard, or a foot dragging in the dirt to start a game.

No other kids in the area ever used the South Avenue lot, and as neighborhood fields go, it was perfect for us. Our backyard ballpark was often no match for "Goose" Gosselin who could hit the ball a mile, which made him the 'all time' home run leader on that field. There was a pile of scrub brush left behind by a contractor on the outside edge of the outfield, the deepest part. It was too far for most of us to hit into, but Goose knew if he really caught 'a fat one' we would be looking for the ball.

Over time, we decided that any ball that landed 'on the fly' into the scrub was a home run (rolling into the brush was a ground-rule double). Although the home run ball was celebrated if Goose or anyone else could hit the ball that deeply, the plaudits were usually short lived, given the need for an immediate all-hands-on-deck effort to find the ball. The consequence of not finding the ball meant that someone would have to go home and find a replacement ball, or the game was over.

It's difficult to look back and remember every moment you had as a ten-year-old, but one Sunday afternoon on May 23, 1965 stands out from all the other times we played on our South Avenue lot. It was unusually warm for May in Maine and the baseball field was in great shape. The grass was growing and had not become so high that you could not find a ball hit into the outfield.

On this particular day, it was not Goose hitting another mammoth shot into the scrub brush that stands out in my memory. It was the number of planes filling the friendly skies of our city. They were flying in to see the Tuesday night, May 25, 1965, World Heavyweight Championship rematch between the new title holder Muhammad Ali and his opponent Sonny Liston, the man Ali defeated in Miami in early 1964.

One of the regular players on our field, Paul Labrecque, who was five years older than I was, had heard that the ABC network was going to handle the closed-circuit broadcast of the fight. They would be broadcasting from atop Applesaas Hill, up the street from where he lived and housed our precious ball field in his backyard. Paul "gathered some friends," all older than me, and made their way up to the ABC van hoping to watch the closed-circuit broadcast.[1] I was not invited and only found out about the opportunity 40 years later after I read the story in the Sun Journal. Not receiving an invitation was the cruel price one must pay for being the "kid" whose parents would likely have nixed watching the broadcast on a school night.

The Central Maine Youth Center in Lewiston was selected to host title match shortly after the Suffolk County District Attorney Garrett Byrne publicly announced that he and his office were prepared to do all they could to stop the fight from happening in the Boston Garden arena, according to Rob Sneddon's[2] book "The Phantom Punch." Liston's prior record as a convicted felon, and his association with individuals convicted of fixing a fight in Los Angeles (something that caught the attention of Robert Kennedy while he served as U.S. Attorney General in his brother's administration) certainly may have influenced D.A. Byrne who cited that Liston's criminal record and his desire to fight in Massachusetts would "not be in the public interest."[3]

Not explicitly stated by the district attorney, but well known publicly, was how the assassination of Malcolm X on February 21, 1965 might affect Ali's safety. Malcolm X was a student of the Nation of Islam's Elijah Muhammad and was also his lead spokesperson and recruiter. It was well known that Malcolm X had influenced Ali's decision to become a Muslim. Malcolm X separated from the NOI after Elijah Muhammad had received backlash from the public about Malcolm X's comments about the Kennedy assassination that resulted in his removal from ministerial duties. Malcolm X also had differences with Ali when he left NOI, approximately one year before they shot him. Many believed that there would be an attempt on Ali's life given suspicions about the Malcolm X assassination's connection to his departure from the Nation of Islam. "Multiple gunmen" took part in the assassination of Malcolm X and NOI member Talmadge X Hayer was arrested at the scene.[4]

Sensing that D.A. Byrne would not give up his attempts to stop the Boston fight, Sam Michael, then Industrial Development Director in Lewiston, Maine, took on the task of getting the fight to Lewiston. Michael was also well connected to the sport of boxing through his affiliation with a closed-circuit television company interested in developing boxing into a pay-per-view sport. This was visionary stuff in 1962.[5]

Michael's boxing connections kept him connected to what was going on in Boston. Once Michael convinced himself that the fight would likely not happen at 'the Garden,' Michael was certain he could persuade the promoters that Lewiston was ready to go and that they would not encounter the trouble they had in Boston. According to the Sun Journal's Kalle Oakes,[6] Doris Michael, the widow of Sam Michael, stated that "(w)hen (Michael's) found out that (D.A Byrne) refused it in Boston, he called people down there that he knew to get the word out that he'd like to have it up here (in Lewiston)."[7]

According to Portland Press Herald journalist Mark Emmert, fight promoter Sam Silverman was desperate to find a site that was available on short notice and willing to deal with the World Boxing Association who were upset that Ali and Liston had agreed to a second fight "before the first (fight) even occurred." Silverman had been in touch with facilities in Cleveland and Pittsburgh. Houston was "briefly in the running, but the Astros didn't want to give up a home baseball game against the Reds that night."[8] The promoters finally agreed on Lewiston. The fight would be hosted by "the smallest city to host a heavyweight fight in 42 years."[9] The bottom line for the promoters was that it would make the real money through their closed-circuit TV deal, broadcasted through that ABC network van that my friend Paul thought would give him a front-row seat.

The Central Maine Youth Center was a six-year-old structure, and the largest indoor sports complex in the state with a seating capacity of 4,000. Sneddon wrote that Lewiston Mayor Robert Couturier, who at 25 was the youngest mayor in the country, was looking to change the name of the facility. The former St. Dominic High School graduate wanted to reclaim the name "St Dominic's Arena," the original name. The facility was built by the Dominican Fathers in 1949 and destroyed in a spectacular fire in 1956. Couturier was never successful in renaming the building, but he and the promoter settled on having the name "St. Dominic's Arena" printed on all the fight tickets.[10]

The fight was over in the first round, at about one minute and thirty seconds into the round. The debate of how it ended would be the stuff of speculation to this day. Did Liston take a dive? Or was the "phantom punch" an anchor punch Ali had once described as some sort of secret weapon? Regardless, Lewiston was now at the center of pro-fighting folklore for the rest of boxing history.

Prior to this fight, the only other notable historic moment in which Lewiston found itself in the national spotlight was on the Sunday evening of November 6, 1960 when Senator John Kennedy spoke to a chilled crowd of 8,000 people, including my 13-year-old cousin Marc Nadeau, in Lewiston City Park (renamed Kennedy Park on December 3, 1963). After multiple delays in Kennedy's schedule, the future president would address a smaller crowd after arriving at 11:52PM and leaving around 12:19AM early Monday morning,[11] the day before his election. Kennedy would have seen a crowd of some 14,000 people had he arrived around the 8:00 PM start of his scheduled appearance. For many "shivering"[12] attendees who would not see Kennedy, the cold temperatures and almost four-hour delay were too much to overcome, particularly for parents who needed to get home with children who had to attend school the next day.

The Ali fight now stands on its own as a significant moment not only in Lewiston's history, but a significant boxing moment in Ali's history as well. A writer once stated that even when you are looking back at the extraordinary career and life of Ali, it is difficult for the casual fight fan to remember the many specific fight dates, opponents, or locations that make up the moments of his life. The Lewiston fight was the exception to that axiom. It was one of four fights that stand out as the most memorable fight locations of his career: the 1975 "Thrilla in Manila" in the Philippines to regain his title against Joe Frazier; the amazing knockout win against George Foreman in the 1974 "Rumble in the Jungle" in Zaire, Africa; the 1964 Miami fight when Ali won his first championship belt against Sonny Liston; and the 1965 "Phantom Punch" championship fight rematch against Liston. Truthfully, many will connect the "punch" with the famous picture of Ali standing over Liston, but not remember that it took place in Lewiston, Maine. We might say the same for the "rumble" fight in Zaire, which most people may only know as somewhere in Africa.

Although the fight in Miami was the first championship fight and victory for Ali, and the fights against Frazier and Foreman rank as some of the best heavyweight bouts in history, the Lewiston fight featured several moments before and during the fight that make it one of the most memorable:

- *The reported threats of potential harm against Ali from Muslims who opposed Malcolm X following his assassination in February 1965;*[13]

*the actions of the Suffolk County District Attorney to block the event at the Boston Garden;*[14]

- *the insistence by many in the public and sports media to address Ali by his old name (Cassius Clay) although his new name was used to introduce him publicly in the ring for the first time in Lewiston;*[15]

- *stories linking Liston to organized crime;*[16]

- *singer/actor Robert Goulet's struggle with the "Star-Spangled Banner" (whose mother was born in Lewiston)*[17]

*- and Sonny Liston's botched knockout count in the first round by referee and former heavyweight fighter Jersey Joe Walcott;[18]*

These events contributed, on their own, to Lewiston becoming one of the most memorable locations in boxing history. However, there is little debate about the one thing that makes Lewiston the place most closely associated with the Champ's storied boxing history — and that is 'the picture.'

Many consider Neil Leifer's now iconic photo of an angry Ali screaming "Get up and fight, sucker!" over a defeated Liston to be one of the greatest sports photos of all time. For sport and non-sport individuals alike, it is one of the most recognizable photos in history. The photo's composition and quality has given it a special place in sports and human history as the cover photo selected for the July 26, 1999 issue of Sports Illustrated Magazine's "The Century's Greatest Sports Photos" and selected for Time Magazine's list of the one hundred "Most Influential Images of All Time" spanning the years between 1826 and 2015.

As a child and later as an adult, I knew little about the fight other than when it happened and where it took place. That would change when I arrived in my hometown of Lewiston to become its assistant city administrator in 1999. By 2002, the arrival of Somali refugees in our city had grown into a national news story. Many of the national news media covering the Somali story also knew about the Ali-Liston fight, and would ask me questions the event.

Before the refugee relocations, the Ali fight had been the most covered national and international news story in our city's history. Once the national news arrived to cover the Somali story in Lewiston, the inevitable inquiries about the fight, and what might be available for them to see or photograph, were becoming so frequent that I made it a point to know more about it. Even as a near lifelong resident of the city, I was unaware of any artifacts or pictures on public display anywhere in the city.

How did such a historical moment in our history become so difficult to find in Lewiston? How could I know so little about the fight that took place a mile from my boyhood home?

My first inclination was to get into my car and drive to the location of the fight. It was literally right down the street from City Hall. I could not remember seeing any evidence of the fight in the building over a lifetime of playing hockey, and attending hockey games, boxing, graduations, and concerts in the building. It seemed obvious to me that it should be the first place to begin my search.

The Central Maine Civic Center building was rarely closed to the public during the day. Whenever locked front doors were encountered, anyone who frequented the building knew that the side door entrance would be unlocked, particularly during hockey season. I knew the owner Roger Theriault, who was in the building when I arrived, and asked him if there was any physical proof in the building that the fight had taken place on that site. To my dismay, he said there was not a single artifact of the Ali fight publicly displayed anywhere in the building. Privately, Roger showed me a painting (on velvet) that attempted to re-create 'the picture' but it looked more like someone's first artistic endeavor.

Believing that Mr. Ali deserved something more fitting to commemorate his fight, I broadened the search beyond the Civic Center. Unfortunately, this effort also came up empty as I could not find any pictures or memorabilia of the fight in our city buildings or public spaces. Regrettably, I did not know that Joe Gamache Sr. had a boxing program in the Lewiston Armory's basement with Ali boxing memorabilia pinned to the walls. It was hard to believe that both the Civic Center and the city had appeared to forget the fight ever happened in Lewiston.

Lewiston had not only overlooked Ali's fight in 1965, they also had buried any evidence of his return 30 years after the fight. One would think that when the city then invited Ali to Lewiston as part of its 1995 Bicentennial festivities, they would capitalize on the moment to properly recognize Ali's place in the city's history.

The bicentennial celebration commemorated the Pejepscott Company's transfer of a land parcel to Jonathan Bagley and Moses Little in 1795 that "became known as Lewiston and Auburn."[19] The featured speaker at the banquet launching the bicentennial festivities on February 18, 1995 was Senator Robert "Bob" Dole. It was unknown at the time if Ali would return to Lewiston, but the organizers convinced Ali to commit. It was a major coup for the organizing committee. Ali would come to Lewiston a second time in recognition of the 30th anniversary of his victory against Liston.

Ali arrived in Lewiston on September 22, 1995, accompanied by former world heavyweight champion Floyd Patterson.[20] Ali and Patterson started the evening's festivities at a banquet in Ali's honor at the Ramada Inn in Lewiston and a presentation by the city's first African American Mayor John Jenkins.

> That (Ali) wit was on display during the banquet. Lewiston did not have a Key to the City to hand out to dignitaries. The best Jenkins could find was a city lapel pin. "I handed him the pin," Jenkins said. "He looked at the pin. He looked at me. Then he looked at the audience. In true Ali fashion — the timing was perfect — he said, 'I came all the way up here to Maine for this pin(?)'...(while) holding this little pin in his very large hand. Everyone broke out laughing." Trying to recover, Jenkins apologized with a smile and then said the city did not give out keys because keys symbolized locked doors, which got Ali laughing.[21]

It was a wonderful celebration of Ali's return to Lewiston, which made it even more regrettable that the people of Lewiston once again failed to permanently recognize the historic importance of Ali's victory or his return.

I could not accept that every time someone came to Lewiston wanting to see or learn more about this famous fight, they would have to use the internet and a Google search of the event as we had nothing to show them in our city. Determined to do something about it, I took it upon myself to find something fitting that I could at least display in my office.

On a trip to South Portland's Maine Mall, I walked by a kiosk of sports photos and there it was—or so I thought. A black and white framed photo of 'the picture' with Ali standing with his arm bent over Liston stretched out on the canvas mat.

*That's it!* I thought to myself.

Finally, I could now display something that was at the very least a respectable attempt to have something available for journalists to see about this historic fight. I also believed that hanging the famous Ali picture in my office, a photo that had grown in stature as the greatest sports photo in history, would at least say to reporters that the city had not forgotten about the fight, or Mr. Ali.

Not too long after I purchased 'the picture,' someone came into my office and noticed it hanging on the wall. He commented about the photo and shared his thoughts about the fight. To my surprise, he also told me that the photo was not the actual Ali photo. In disbelief, I questioned why he would think that. It clearly looked like the photo, but I became concerned that I had chosen the wrong picture to hang in my office.

I began my Google search, something that by 2002 was already standard practice. To my surprise, and utter disappointment, I discovered that what I had hung in my office truly was not 'the picture.' It was in fact a black-and-white photo taken by Associated Press photographer John Rooney that looked very similar to the now iconic photo that was taken in color.

I also discovered that someone named Neil Leifer took the historic picture I was looking for[22]. The Leifer's were selling a limited number of prints produced from the original negative, and my wife and I decided to buy one. There would no longer be any debate about the authenticity, as it was not only 'the picture,' but it was also a limited color print from his original 1965 negative. I quickly replaced Rooney's photo with the real deal, which I hung up on my office wall until I retired in June 2017.

About a week after we purchased the print, Neil called our home. Both my wife and I spoke to him for about an hour. He was calling to share that he believed we were probably the first people in Lewiston, and possibly in Maine, to have purchased the photo. There was also some discussion about the fight and about his desire to return to the place, which in his words, will forever connect him to Ali and likely serve as the pinnacle of his very long and distinguished career as an award-winning and celebrated photographer.

To my surprise, Neil called me again in January 2005 to share that Sports Illustrated was sending him on his last assignment and worldwide journey to cover some of the biggest events in sports he had covered as a photographer. One of those stops would be Lewiston, Maine, to shoot the "St. Dominic's Arena" on May 25, 2005, the 40th anniversary of the fight.

Neil and I worked together on setting up the photo shoot for four months. The old St. Dominic's Arena was now owned by the city and renamed "The Colisée." That meant the city now had complete control of the facility, an important development as Neil wanted to set up a fight card on the anniversary date. I soon discovered that there was not sufficient time to get a boxing match organized through the Maine Boxing Commission. Knowing that we had control of the facility, Neil and I decided to replicate, as closely as possible, what the interior of the arena floor looked like in 1965 during the fight.

Neil quickly mailed me a great photo from his collection, taken from a camera he had attached to the catwalk above the arena to catch the action in the ring. The camera was connected to a manual cable allowing Leifer to take the photo while maintaining his position near the edge of the ring during the fight. The photo was one I had never seen before, and it was exactly what I needed. It not only showed Ali and Liston actively boxing, but it also provided a great interior shot of the crowd on the floor, the ring, and the lighting setup above.

With no scheduled events in the Colisée the week prior to the photo shoot on May 25th, people like Lewiston Police Officer Bill Brochu, Joe Gamache (father of Lewiston native and former Super Featherweight and Lightweight Title holder Joey Gamache), Richard Martin, Colisee Maintenance Supervisor Jeff Bolduc, and the Colisee staff helped me to closely recreate what the interior of the boxing ring area looked like in 1965. The staging of the photo shoot would include a full-size boxing ring, chairs and tables on the arena floor, and a lighting rig with operational lights above the ring. It was all set up to look as though time had stood still in the building for 40 years.

Just to make the entire experience that much more enjoyable, Neil's close friend Frank Deford[23] from HBOs "Real Sports with Bryant Gumbel" (who graduated from Lewiston's Bates College in 1970) interviewed Neil inside the ring replica on the day of the anniversary and the photo shoot. Two of Neil's Colisee photos taken on the 40th anniversary date of the fight were published in his 2006 book "A Year in Sports" featuring the other GOAT (Greatest of All Time) Tom Brady on the cover.

I should note that Neil very generously provided the Sun Journal with exclusive rights to all his photos as part of their coverage of his visit, and the 40th anniversary of the fight. The Leifer photos, including the now iconic Ali picture, were published in the Sun Journal's 40th anniversary edition of the fight. City Treasurer Paul Labrecque then arranged to frame poster-sized reproductions of the newspaper's multi-page photo layout that were hung in the Colisee food court area shortly after the photo shoot.

Finally, the city now had a fitting Ali boxing tribute on public display that everyone could enjoy and appreciate, 40 years after Ali's fight at the St. Dominic's Arena, the place that produced 'the picture' that immortalized Ali's boxing career and celebrated the art of Neil Leifer. All of this would not have occurred had it not been for the arrival of the Somali refugees into our city and the national news media's insatiable curiosity about the Ali fight.

I believe that the Somali story has now achieved the same level, and possibly more, of the national and international notoriety as the Ali-Liston fight. Our "new Mainers" continue to attract national, or international coverage some nineteen years after their arrival. Unlike the Ali-Liston story, the evidence of the Somalis' arrival and the refugees that followed is visible throughout the cities of Lewiston and Auburn. This book's purpose is to better understand the circumstances and the context of what was taking place in our community prior, during, and after the Somali arrivals in 2001, and to share how the city's immigrant history continues to shape our city to this day.

The Somali arrivals in our city also provided me the opportunity to get to know more about Mr. Ali, his Lewiston story, and the importance of a legacy that speaks to his desire for peace and equality for all humankind. It is noteworthy that this book begins with the story of Mr. Ali's impact on our city's history, and how the arc of this book will again involve Mr. Ali's impact on Lewiston some 48 years later. His 'return' to Lewiston and his words validate our community's actions and decision not to succumb to fear and hatred in the face of a possible confrontation with white supremacists.

Mr. Ali's unsolicited message of peace in 2003, and the outpouring of support the city received from people all over the world, continues to remind us that matters of race and equality still require everyone's attention. In 2020, the "Black Lives

Matter" movement and other issues about race continued to impact the national and international headlines. Our city's immigrant history is a story about fear of the unknown, the power of overcoming that fear, and how understanding and tolerance are often followed by unity, and collaboration. The community's resilience, adaptability and collaborative commitment influenced its historic challenges and successes. This book will reveal how those qualities prepared us for what would take place in 2001 and 2002, and how those events would change how we work together as a community to this day.

# Chapter 1

# Lewiston's Early History: 1850s – 1980s

> *"Lewiston, like any city, is a living organism; it is constantly changing. When change ceases, the organism is dead. The history of Lewiston, therefore, is the study of origins and of changes. If they are to be meaningful, it is necessary to understand not merely what has taken place, but why things occurred, who was involved, and what impact these developments had."*
> James S. Leamon

### Textiles & Early Immigration

Leamon's prophetic words from his 1976 book "Historic Lewiston: A Textile City in Transition"[24] perfectly illustrate the purpose of this book you are currently reading. Any undertaking about why various immigrant groups made Lewiston their home must also provide some context regarding the community's local, state and national socio-economic, political and cultural history prior to, and during, their arrival.

From the early 1800s, the direction of Maine commerce shifted away from an economy largely built on agriculture, lumber, shipbuilding and fishing. Maine's river water resources, funding, and large labor pool presented opportunities that attracted textile and shoe manufacturing industries. In his 1999 paper, Peter Temin[25] wrote that "(i)ndustrialization came early to New England because the industry that has led industrialization in many countries, cotton textiles, could use women who were available in New England" given that "(a)gricultural production in New England did not use women very intensively."

Temin also pointed out that many people in New England left their agricultural roots to live in cities where these industries were located. In addition to the availability of higher wages, the cities also offered lifestyles and other conveniences that typically were not available in the many rural and smaller communities throughout New England.[26]

In the mid-1800s, access to Boston capital and natural resources helped to support the aspirations of a few bold and wealthy individuals who saw New England's true industrial potential for textiles milling cotton and wool, and shoe manufacturing. Their enlightened ingenuity harnessed the energy and scale of abundant rivers for manufacturing on a global scale. Leamon stated that "(t)he ability of one dam to power many mills created conditions that economists describe as economies of scale. One could put a single water wheel in a large river and generate power for a single mill, as the Romans put water wheels in the Arno to grind flour."[27]

Lewiston, and its sister city Auburn, benefited from their proximity to the Androscoggin River and the "Great Falls" in between the two communities. In 1845, the locally owned Lewiston Water Power Company (later reorganized as the Franklin Company) envisioned the potential power of the falls and gained the legal control for land and water rights for the river and its adjacent properties. Their vision led to the creation of the "Great Androscoggin Falls, Dam, Lock and Canal Company," later called the "Lewiston Water Power Company" which was modeled on textile operations in Lawrence and Lowell Massachusetts.[28]

The locally owned Little Company undertook construction on the first mill and canals. Project costs were exceeding their funding capacity. In search of cash to realize their vision, the local owners went to Boston to sell stock in the company. That decision attracted the investors and architects of what was to become the foundation of Lewiston's textile economy for the next 100 years: Thomas J. Hill, Lyman Nichols, George L. Ward, Alexander Dewitt and Benjamin E. Bates.[29]

The underfunded structure and canal projects were eventually rescued and completed in 1850 by Benjamin Bates of the newly formed Bates Manufacturing Company and the Franklin Company. At about the same time, rail transportation to the area opened once unavailable commerce connections to Maine's seaports and the national and international markets to Canada and the west coast. Although ownership of the mills went through a number of changes, mill construction accelerated during the 1850s and 1860s: Bates Mill (built three mill buildings through 1863), Continental Mill, Lewiston Bleachery, Androscoggin Mill, Hill Manufacturing, Lincoln Mill, Aurora Mill, and the Lewiston Mill.[30]

To meet the growing demands for labor in these rapidly growing mill operations, the mills hired workers from Maine and throughout New England that were often women and children who came from the many farms throughout the area. "Young women were the majority of the workers in the mills from about 1815 until the 1840's."[31] This was not a permanent solution to the growing need for labor in the mills. By the 1850s, the Irish began to arrive in Lewiston and replaced many of the women.[32] "The mill owners found they could hire as many Irish workers as they wanted and did not need to recruit young women from the countryside. As the Irish families lived in Lowell, there was no reason to maintain the boardinghouse system in which the Yankee girls had lived apart from their families."[33]

The arrival of new Irish residents was "met with a good deal of antagonism"[34] by the largely Protestant population in Lewiston. In an interview with the Sun Journal, Leamon said that "(t)o many of Lewiston's Yankee inhabitants, the presence of the Irish represented a real threat to their social and cultural traditions."[35] Tensions occasionally resulted in violence against the Irish. In 1855, anti-Catholic Know-Nothing sympathizers burned the first Irish Catholic chapel on Lincoln Street. The attack on the Irish chapel certainly did not occur because of local concerns for job safety.[36] Locals held most of the better jobs in the new mills. In fact, Irish workers often performed labor in which many residents preferred not to engage, such as digging canals for new mill construction.

The lower wages paid to the new residents certainly helped mill owners generate profitable bottom lines, but they also contributed to levels of poverty that exposed native locals to new social challenges such as mass sickness, slum housing (then called "patches") and public welfare.[37] "In 1854 a cholera epidemic killed 200 (Lewiston) residents, most of whom were poor Irish immigrants that lived in the 'patches.'"[38]

The resentment of local residents did not deter the Irish from pursuing their own American dream, something that those back in Ireland could not do while they struggled to even survive. The Great Famine (aka The Great Hunger) from 1845 to 1849, produced famine and disease that killed one million Irish people. The hardest hit group were the largely impoverished Catholics who made up 80% of the population. Andy O'Brien [39] wrote that "(a)ccording to Irish historian James Donnelly, applicants for relief were means-tested and holders of even a quarter acre of land could not receive (welfare) assistance unless they gave up their land. (Donnelly) writes that in order for landlords to 'rid their estates of pauperized farmers and labourers' at least 500,000 people were evicted from their homes between 1846 and 1854."

Historians have always struggled with accurately estimating when the famine in Ireland specifically started and ended, and consequently have difficulty determining who may have died because of the famine. Most of the literature focuses on the period of the mid to late 1840s and into the early 1850s as the famine's peak. During that period, it is estimated that approximately 800,000 to 1,000,000 deaths were directly attributed to the famine. Some 1,000,000 more emigrated to other countries, including the U.S. and Great Britain.[40]

If escaping starvation and poverty were not enough, Irish Catholics soon learned that their presence was not welcome in many areas of the U.S. "The Irish were seen (by anti-immigrant and anti-Catholic groups like the Know-Nothings) as a different kind of immigrant from the 'traditional' English and Scottish people who had come to the US in earlier decades."[41]

It is likely that the Maine Irish were aware of violent events that transpired in nearby Bath and Ellsworth, Maine, before the 1855 chapel fire in Lewiston. "On July 6 (1854), a mob attacked the Old South Church (in Bath), which was being rented by the local Catholic congregation… of Irish and Acadian immigrants…

setting the building on fire." In Ellsworth, a group of Know-Nothing sympathizers called the "Cast Iron Band," led by the city's newspaper editor, kidnapped Father John Bapst, "took him to the town wharf, and tarred and feathered him. On the verge of hanging the priest, the mob was talked down into tying him to an iron rail and attempting (sic) to ride him out of town."[42].

It is possible that the combination of the Lewiston chapel fire, as well as the violence against Catholics in the prior year's violence in Bath and Ellsworth, were intended to 'send a message' to the new Irish residents throughout Maine. Although there is no evidence to prove that the actions against the Irish were coordinated statewide, the response from the Irish to the Lewiston chapel fire was clear. Their decision to confront the heartache, violence, and discrimination that they and other Maine Irish Catholics experienced, was to mobilize for a common cause. They would replace their lost chapel with another larger structure: a church big enough to accommodate 500 more Catholics in the future.[43]

It was common knowledge in Lewiston that the Boston capitalists had demonstrated their financial support for a number of Protestant churches in both cities. The priest of the burned chapel approached the Lewiston Water Power Company to seek similar assistance from the board but was repeatedly denied his requests. After some persistence, the priest found a sympathetic company agent who arranged to have the company board sign a lease, without their knowledge, as part of a normal corporate document signing. The agent, who had agreed to sell the parcel for an amount far below its market value, then presented the chapel priest a deed for a parcel of land considered prime real estate in Lewiston[44]. That Main Street parcel would accommodate Lewiston's first Catholic church, which was named St. Joseph's Church. The deconsecrated building remains standing to this day.

Around the same time of the new church's construction, thousands of French Canadians began their emigration to a number of New England towns and cities to work in the wool and cotton mills and the growing shoe manufacturing business. The relocations were driven by several factors that Damien-Claude and Claude Bélanger [45] characterized as those that "pushed" and "attracted" French Canadians to emigrate to the US.

The Bélangers believed that "poverty, overpopulation, debt and infertile soils pushed French Canadians off their land. However, external factors also attracted emigrants to the United States…(I)ndustrialization progressed far more rapidly in the USA" and industrial wages were often higher than they were in Canada. Better wages and the abundance of jobs were nearby in New England, and the growth of rail into areas with mills and shoe manufacturing made it possible for up to 743,000 Quebecois to relocate between 1840 and 1930.[46]

The Lewiston Historic Commission's 1974 pamphlet "Historic Lewiston: Franco-American Origins" [47] states that Lewiston's first Franco, George Carignan, settled in the city in 1860. Mary Rice-DeFosse and James Myall [48] wrote that the 1860 census listed a man named "Joseph Brooks" arriving in Lewiston from Quebec in 1845, returned to Quebec in 1855, and then returned to Lewiston where he enlisted in the Union Army to fight in the Civil War. By "1875…the (Lewiston Weekly) Journal counted 3,000 French-Canadians in Lewiston" and "unlike the Irish, (Francos) were actively recruited by mill agents with whom the French-Canadians had a reputation for hard work and docility… In 1880, 35% of Lewiston's total population was foreign born and during the next two decades that figure rose to almost 40%."[49]

The mill agent opinions of the French-Canadians, particularly their penchant for "hard work and docility," did not mean that the new arrivals from Quebec were immune to the ugliness associated with discrimination and stereotyping. There were reports of animosity between the Irish and the French-Canadians in the U.S. as early as the middle 1850s.

> Friction between French-Canadian immigrants and their Irish coreligionists… was reported as early as the middle of the 19th century… Though the French and Irish shared the same faith, their differences of religious customs, parochial habits, and temperament, as well as language, were so great that one Franco-American priest wondered whether God was going to separate them in heaven. [50]

The Irish, who spoke the native language and worked to assimilate themselves into American customs and culture, "tended to look down in turn upon the later French-Canadian immigrant because (they) spoke another language, refused to change (their) native ways, (their willingness) to work harder and longer for lower wages," and their insistence on establishing "foreign language... parishes and schools."[51]

In addition to the friction with the Irish, there was growing anti-Catholic sentiment from groups like the Know-Nothings in Maine and New England around the time the French-Canadian emigration accelerated. In 1860, the population of the city was 7,424 people. Lewiston experienced "a population explosion of over 80% in which her numbers swelled (to) 13,600 (in 1870). By 1880, Lewiston's population topped 19,000."[52]

The 1900 census revealed that the population grew to 23,761 people, and 70%, or approximately 5,000 employees[53] of its labor force, worked in its mills.[54] This 375% increase in population over less than 40 years was the fastest period of growth in the city's history. Although the 1913 city school department records show that there were "American, Irish, French, German, Italian, Greek, Jewish, Polish, Dutch, Belgian, Syrian, (and) Albanian" students in the school system,[55] the sheer size of the Franco immigration into Lewiston positioned them as the largest ethnic group employed by the mills and in the community. The friction between the two largest ethnic groups persisted, but there seemed to be little public evidence of direct violence (of the kind experienced by the Irish in Maine) against the growing Franco population over the first several decades.[56]

The growing numbers of Francos in Lewiston and around New England created enough critical mass for the Quebecois to fight the anti-Franco efforts of the Irish and Protestant elements that existed nationally, but also resulted in exposing divisions among French-Canadians on how they should assimilate as Americans.

According to David Vermette,[57] the French-Canadians who were under British control going back to 1763, had maintained their language, cultural identity, and believed that they could preserve their religion and their heritage in the United States. This French-Canadian desire to protect all things French-Canadian extended back over 100 years to the British Parliament's passage of the Quebec Act of 1774. The Act protected their religion, language, and expanded the geographic area of Quebec to include the Great Lake and Ohio Valley areas of American colonial interest.

J.D. Belshaw[58] said the Quebec Act was intended to garner the support of Roman Catholic, French speaking Canadians, but created conflict with Protestant colonials who saw the incursion into the Ohio Valley as another mercantilist power grab by the British and an increasing threat from the Catholic Quebecois. Historians believe this so infuriated the colonies, that they identified the British Parliament approved Act as one of several punitive British Intolerable Acts that led to the assembly of the 1774 First Continental Congress in Philadelphia, and eventually to the Revolutionary War in 1775.

Although over 100 years had passed since then, tensions between the Anglo Protestants in the U.S. and the Catholic French remained. In 1889, the New York Times published an article titled "The French Canadians" on what was needed to address the newspaper's uneasiness about the potential for a political and social uprising by the Catholic French-Canadians that were arriving in the U.S. According to the Times, "(t)he French Canadians mean to retain in this country, as for two centuries they have succeeded in retaining in Canada, the religion and the language of their ancestors, as distinctive badges of their separation from their neighbors."[59]

The New York Times published another article in 1892 which went a step further regarding the increasing number of Quebecois entering the U.S. The Times saw increasing French-Canadian immigration into New England as a strategic act, heavily supported by the Catholic Church, to assimilate into American life on their own terms. The Times quoted Egbert C. Smyth, who stated that the French-Canadian immigration was part

> of a priestly scheme now fervently fostered in Canada for the purpose of bringing New England under the control of the Roman Catholic faith. (Smyth) points out that this is the avowed purpose of the secret society to which every adult French Canadian

belongs, and that the prayers and the earnest efforts of these people are to turn the tables in New England by the aid of the silent forces which they control.[60]

The article finished by saying that this ongoing "conquest" of New England could only be stopped through the adoption of laws which would require solely English to be the spoken and written language taught in all American schools.

What is often lost in history about the Catholic French-Canadians was that the Quebec Act did not completely extinguish the Quebecois' desire to achieve the same freedoms gained by the Americans through their Constitution and Bill of Rights. The British refusal to let the Quebecois self-govern resulted in the Patriot Rebellion in 1837 and 1838. French-Canadian Freedom Patriots wrote their own "Declaration of Independence" seeking the same freedoms won by the American revolutionaries. The defeat resulted in the hanging of 12 Patriots, the deportment of dozens of supporters, the imprisonment of some 1,000 Patriots and countless others who fled to the U.S. Effectively, this episode of French-Canadian history began the first significant Franco exodus to the U.S.[61]

The remnants of the deep-seated, historic distrust of the North American Protestants regarding the Catholic Francos may certainly have contributed to the anti-Catholic fear mongering directed at the Francos in New England and in Maine in the late 1800s. Others sounded the warnings of the New York Times and other national publications about Catholic French-Canadian intentions to occupy New England. Egbert C. Smyth [62] wrote:

> (w)ith the parish and its church and presbytery come the convent and its parochial school...(s)oon the network of parishes spreading over New England will meet and unite with that which covers the Province of Quebec. There will be practically one controlling social and religious organization, whatever political distinctions may remain.

According to James Allen,[63] French-Canadians "felt that their language was inseparable from their religion, (and) that the

French language was a necessary bulwark for Catholicism. As long as a person continued to use French rather than English, he would remain a Catholic." Faced with increasing public suspicion regarding the French-Canadian parish expansion in New England, Francos forged ahead to construct parish churches, schools and their support systems.

As early as 1871, only 11 years after the first Franco arrivals, Lewiston had its first Catholic parish, St. Peter's Parish. It was Maine's third parish following the founding of the Diocese in Portland,[64] and the parish of St. Francois de Salles in Waterville in 1869.[65] By 1878, the Grey Nuns established Lewiston's first parochial school with 200 students. By 1883, the Dominican Fathers finished construction on a new five-story Catholic parochial school "still known today as the Dominican Block... on the corner of Lincoln and Chestnut Streets" in downtown Lewiston. The new school had an enrollment of 700 students, and also provided adult education classes for 200 young women and men who worked in the nearby mills.[66]

The construction of these parochial schools "was often the first concern of the pastor in a growing Franco-American community. In 1908 there were over 9,000 pupils in parochial schools in Maine, and two-thirds of these students were in French schools."[67] Maine lawmakers recognized the growth of the Franco parochial school enrollment, and likely knew about the kinds of fear mongering expressed publicly by organizations like the Ku Klux Klan and people like Egbert C. Smyth. In response, the Maine legislature passed English-only school legislation in 1919, requiring English as the basic language for all public and private schools. Although Maine had approved the legislation, many of the Franco parochial schools were producing a bilingual population.[68]

"In fact, until the 1950's, the state of Maine never really enforced the requirement that English be the basic language of instruction in all schools although, until 1969, the state officially prohibited the teaching of subjects other than a foreign language in a language other than English."[69] In my personal experience, I entered Holy Cross parochial school in 1960, where the eight-year elementary school curriculum was divided into two different sessions with French instruction for half of the day, and English instruction in the second half. All the instructors were nuns, and many spoke French while conversing among themselves and resorted to English only when necessary. Typically, most New England schools with this kind of curriculum would offer subjects such as catechism, history, French grammar, and cultural arts like music in the French session; while the English session would typically cover math, geography, social studies, and English grammar.

I remember one fellow Holy Cross student who spoke French as their primary language, although that changed when I later attended St. Dom's high school. Growing up in a neighborhood with many homes built only a few years before I entered Holy Cross, all my neighborhood friends came from predominantly Franco families, where the primary language in the house was English. I had first-generation Franco grandparents that owned a neighborhood grocery store and a second-generation father (the first of his seven siblings to be born in the U.S.) that operated a catering service in the back of their store and also used a kitchen on the ground floor of his Republican brother's social club, the Derby A.A. My upbringing revolved around first and second-generation Franco adults who reverted to speaking mostly French when they were among 'their own.'

There were exceptions, but most third-generation Franco kids around my age could speak French, but not fluently. We were 3rd generation Francos who most often limited speaking French with our families, but rarely if ever with our friends. We were also the last generation given the opportunity to receive our elementary education in French for half of the school day. When I graduated in 1968, Holy Cross school and its grade one through eight program may have been one of the largest elementary schools, both private and public, in the state. According to my younger siblings Greg, Monique, and Michelle, who also attended Holy Cross, the French/English half-day curriculum ended sometime between 1968 and 1970.

## POLITICS

Politically, only 20 years after the arrival of Lewiston's first French Canadian, the city elected its first Franco in 1880 when Emile Lefebvre won a seat on the Common Council.[70] At that time, elected officials made up two legislative bodies that included the Board of Aldermen. Shortly thereafter, Dr. Louis Martel became the first Lewiston Franco elected to the Maine Legislature in 1884 and served as Chair of the Board of Aldermen in 1891-92.[71] It took longer to elect a Franco mayor, which occurred in 1914 with the election of Robert Wiseman who was re-elected as mayor from 1925 through 1929. Franco Charles P. Lemaire served between the years 1917 to 1920.[72]

There is little doubt that the Franco population's early successes in elected office had much to do with the presence of its local French language newspaper. Like many Franco communities in New England, Lewiston's newspaper Le Messager, "the longest-running French language newspaper in the United States... from 1880-1968"[73] was an important part of communicating the news and opinions of the Franco community to its growing French speaking community.

According to the Lewiston Historic Preservation Review Board's "National Register of Historic Places Registration Form:"

> Throughout its existence, Le Messager did not limit itself to reporting news. In addition, the publishers and editors used the newspaper to advance issues such as the preservation of French language and culture; promoting the interests of the Franco-American community; demanding changes in the Catholic Church; and advocating for reforms to city government. In 1925, Le Messager wrote that Franco-Americans were 'entitled' to the majority of City Hall's 'plums.' The paper made an audit of the city's tax receipts and determined that two-thirds of the taxes had been paid by people of French origin. Thus, the

paper declared, 'we can... reply to those who would object to the large number of French office holders at City Hall: 'Representation in accordance with taxation'.' In the 1930s, Le Messager announced itself '... the Representative of the French Canadians of Maine.' Two major reform efforts Le Messager championed were an attempt to repeal the 'Corporation Sole' statute and the implementation of a new city charter for Lewiston.[74]

At the urging of the Diocese of Portland, the Maine Legislature approved the "Corporation Sole," law, making "(then Bishop Healy) of Portland sole owner of all church property in the state." Catholic Francos "with their custom of lay administration of parish finances, opposed the law."[75]

The Francos had a "warm" relationship with Bishop Healy but that all changed following his death in 1901 and the appointment of Bishop Louis Walsh in 1906. The Diocese made many changes that included the realignment of parishes by geography, as opposed to language. These changes were perceived by Francos as contrary to their independence and nationality. French language newspapers like the Messager led a highly public effort for Francos to regain what they had lost with a new administration in Portland.[76]

In 1909, Le Messager editor Jean B. Couture was one of seven men of Franco descent who, frustrated by the lack of French-speaking representation in and the pro-assimilation agenda of the Irish-Catholic church hierarchy in Maine, led an effort to have the "Corporation Sole" law overturned and thus return power to individual parishes. Couture used Le Messager to gain support for the protests and to demand that parishes regain control of their own finances. Le Messager also encouraged Catholics

25

not to donate to the Church until they met their demands for representation.[77]

Couture would continue to write editorials, as would the editor of Biddeford's "La Justice." Bishop Walsh was so incensed by the editorials he "placed an interdiction" on the two editors, "one step short of excommunication." Although the confrontation between Maine's French newspapers and the diocese did not result in the repeal of the Corporation Sole law, the Francos ultimately retained their parish "French-speaking priests and control of (their) parochial schools. As Couture outlived Bishop Walsh, the interdiction was lifted."[78]

## The Franco "Klan" Response

It is evident that the pro-acculturation, pro-assimilation movement directed at Francos in New England impacted French speaking and culture in Maine, and likely reinforced the negative ethnic image some people had about Francos. Although the Lewiston area Franco Catholics did not experience any direct violence from organized anti-Catholic or anti-immigrant groups, the Ku Klux Klan[79] was very active in Maine and in Lewiston.

The Klan typically supported Southern conservative Democratic candidates sympathetic to anti-Catholic positions. It also[80] saw itself as more closely aligned with New England GOP non-Catholics who would more likely support "(r)einforcing the supremacy of Anglo-Saxon Protestantism, in the face of an influx of Catholic 'foreigners'" and providing "the New England KKK's *raison d'être*."[81] This New England strategy resulted in their endorsement of the 1924 Republican gubernatorial candidate Owen Brewster who did not publicly denounce the KKK's support. "Although Brewster denied he was a Klan member," the Klan celebrated the victory by detonating a bomb at nighttime "to draw attention to a burning cross on a high point (in Lewiston on Mount David near Bates College)."[82]The Brewster victory and the Franco belief that he was a KKK sympathizer, actually helped to solidify Lewiston's Franco political unity among themselves and against the Klan, who had no real success in the Twin Cities of Lewiston and Auburn.

In response to the Brewster victory, many Francos enrolled as Democrats and focused on candidates that supported Franco political interests.

> The Klan sought to limit the culture and use of the French language by Franco-Americans on a local level through state legislation. The Klan backed politicians in the state who could pass the type of legislation they wanted, such as the amendment prohibiting public funds from being used in parochial schools. While the Klan seemed to hold power over local politics, Franco-Americans mobilized their numbers and educated themselves on how to combat this opposition. Franco-Americans in Maine became naturalized citizens, enabling them to act and vote for the politicians who best represented them.[83]

The Franco's renewed energy and attention to the positions of their candidates, produced a decision from their collective group to back supporting an anti-Klan U.S. Senate Republican candidate, Arthur R. Gould "who, after overcoming opposition from a once influential Ku Klux Klan, became the first of our Maine U.S. senators to have been identified with the Catholic Church"[84] in 1926. This victory served as a significant Franco victory against the Klan and the Republican candidate they supported.

During the 1930s, Lewiston's Francos saw significant gains in locally elected and appointed positions. Henry Paradis' successful mayoral bid in 1931 was historic as it marked the beginning of a succession of 21 Franco mayors over a 39-year period ending with John Beliveau in 1970 (other Franco, Irish, Greek, Polish and Anglo mayors were elected in future years).[85] "Since 1914,... (Francos) have held the majority of local municipal offices, as well as many at the county and state level"[86] and in many of the city's locally appointed positions.

For many Francos and other immigrant groups, working in the shoe shops and textile mills in Lewiston-Auburn was their first exposure to the business of union political activism involving their working conditions or supporting political candidates that would be sympathetic to their employment and family needs. "Because (the Francos) were slow to unionize, it does not follow that they were averse to strikes... In Brunswick, there were at least four strikes in the Cabot mill in the six years between 1881 and 1887."[87] The many shoe shops in Auburn and the textile mills in Lewiston became fertile ground for both unions and the Democratic Party in a state that was dominated by the Republican Party in the 1800s and early-mid 1900s.

The power of union activism in the Lewiston-Auburn area was on full display in the 1930s. Union efforts to seek better wages for shoe workers in Auburn and Lewiston's 20 shoe factories involved approximately 6,000 union workers walking off the job. Some 3,500 union strikers later assembled at Lewiston's City Hall to support a strike organized by leaders of the CIO (Congress of Industrial Organizations which later merged with the American Federation of Labor to create what is now the AFL-CIO). Weeks after the vote, 1,000 strikers met at Lewiston City Hall and made their way across the North Bridge (now the Longley Bridge) clashing with eight companies of the Maine Army National Guard on April 21, 1937. It was the first time in state history that tear gas was used in a labor dispute.[88]

Over the ensuing days following the strike, there were multiple reports involving non-strikers being victimized by strikers who burned cars, used slingshots used to break the windows of homeowners, and took part in assaults in both cities.[89] For one young Lithuanian boy who was on his way to his uncle's shoe shop in Auburn, what he saw happen to a shoe worker during the strike would change his life. His name was Bernard Lown.[90]

## Dr. Bernard Lown

Bernard's family left their home in Utena, Lithuania, in 1935 to escape the anti-Jewish sentiment that had grown with Adolph Hitler's ascension to power in Germany. Bernard's father Nison had previously visited the States and his brother Philip, who owned Lown Shoe in Auburn. Bernard's family would take up residence in Lewiston and Bernard was "enrolled as a sophomore in high school at age 14." His father soon became a director in his brother's company and would offer Bernard a job at the factory for $15 a week. Although Bernard's father worked at the factory, he did not know that a strike was imminent in 1937. What Bernard also did not know was that his father had hired him as a replacement worker.[91]

Shortly after being hired, he encountered some people on the picket line on his way to work. One striker screamed out "'scabs'" as he walked by, provoking a man that was walking alongside of him to hit the striker, rendering him unconscious. Lown remembered the incident. "'He fell in the snow. His nose was bleeding, his teeth were knocked out and the police came and arrested him'...Police didn't bother the strikebreaker who did the punching. Lown quit (his job)." Bernard's decision to leave his job was not well received by his father. Arguments ensued around the dinner table. "'That made a radical out of me,'" Lown said. He credited that moment as beginning his "'radicalism,'" and he was "'proud of it. If you don't have an experience like that, your life is different.'"[92]

Lown went on to the University of Maine where the dean of the college told him that if he worked hard, "he had C-student potential." He became an A student and even his father could not believe it asking "'(h)ow could you get an A when you were in Lewiston all the time?'" Lown went on to attend Johns Hopkins Medical School to become a cardiologist.[93]

At the Harvard School of Public Health and Peter Bent Brigham Hospital, Dr. Lown pioneered many life-saving advances in cardiology, including the direct current defibrillator. A lifelong peace activist and humanitarian, Dr. Lown founded Physicians for Social Responsibility, SatelLife, and ProCor. He co-founded International Physicians for the Prevention of Nuclear War (IPPNW) with Russian physician Dr. Evgueni Chazov. The two doctors received the Nobel Peace Prize in 1985 on behalf of IPPNW.[94]

The quotation above is inscribed on monuments located on both sides of the bridge between Lewiston-Auburn that was dedicated as the "Bernard Lown Peace Bridge" on October 17, 2008. It was a local elder German surgeon named Dr. Max Hirshler who had "inspired Lown to go into medicine" instead of pursuing a career as a "foreign correspondent." Lown credited both Lewiston and Auburn for "sharpening (his) moral sensibilities while (he) was still an impressionable youngster, and also thanked the community for "celebrating peace."[95]

The Lown family left Lithuania because they feared that their lives, as Jews were in danger because of a "well-founded fear of being persecuted for reasons of race, religion, nationality, membership of a particular social group or political opinion, is outside the country of his nationality and is unable or, owing to such fear, is unwilling to avail himself of the protection of that country," the definition now used by the federal government to define refugees entering this country.[96] The Lown family's decision to move to Lewiston and Dr. Lown's status as a former resident would, under today's refugee definition, recognize their entry into this country as refugees and likely establish Dr. Lown as the most well-known and accomplished former refugee in the community's history, and its only Nobel Peace Prize winner.[97]

## Lewiston Corruption, Auburn Charter First & Manager Conflict

Eventually, the power of shoe factory ownership, the jailing of some union organizers, and unfavorable labor laws proved to be more than the union and strikers could handle. The CIO voted two months later to end the strike leaving many to discover their jobs filled by others or to find their former positions left vacant because of an earlier recession that had affected the industry.[98]

The 1930s also served as a period of change for how local politics were influencing the governing of both Lewiston and Auburn. The Irish had made some notable inroads in both cities, and many Anglos made significant gains in Auburn with some elected successes at the local, state and national level. Other smaller immigrant groups, including the Greek, Italians, Polish, and Lithuanians, had some success at elective offices. During this period, however, things in Lewiston were far more volatile as residents were confronted by a city government in crisis, fueled by influence peddling and corruption.

> Politically, the 1930s also came with its share of problems for Lewiston. For some people graft had become an accepted mode of operation and they caused politics to become a dirty word. Control of the Police Commission was taken over by the state. Corrupt practices by the Board of Education led to state supervision in that department also in 1937... Teachers and janitors had been buying their jobs,... (and) free milk was delivered to the homes of the city officials involved... The mayor's salary was legally set at $600 per annum, yet for twenty years he had been paid more. The Mayor and Aldermen were in actuality selected by the party caucuses rather than by the democratic city wide(sic) election.[99]

According to Rice-DeFosse and Myall, the Lewiston Daily Sun reported that "six current and former members of city government were arrested and convicted of soliciting or conspiring to solicit bribes. Five of the six were Franco-Americans."[100] At the local level, there was interest to change the existing form of government but the advent of self-rule, or "home-rule" as it is referred to in New England, had not yet been approved legislatively for municipalities and consequently gave the state tremendous power over the governance of Maine's cities and towns (the state legislature eventually approved a home-rule statute in 1969).

In response to the corruption, an organization called the Association des Vigilantes that was comprised of "a group of prominent Franco-Americans"[101] pursued legislation creating a new city charter through the Lewiston legislative delegation. The state legislature passed the bill that allowed the charter to be voted on by Lewiston citizens. There was speculation that if citizens failed to support the new charter, the state would assume the responsibility of governing the city. On March 6, 1939, 60% of Lewiston citizens voted to support the new charter moving the city from a mayor-city council (then called aldermen)[102] form of government to more of a mayor-commission form of government most notably with a mayor, board of aldermen, fire commission, police commission (with members appointed by the governor), and a powerful five-member department of finance that was solely appointed by the mayor, who also appointed all board members.[103]

Although Francos achieved nothing near a majority of seats on their Board of Aldermen or future city councils in Lewiston's neighbor Auburn, the manner in which they governed it took a significant turn early in the new century. In 1917, Auburn voters approved a new charter creating a manager-council form of government where the authority to run government would lie with a professionally trained city manager.

It is often recorded that Auburn's 'council-manager' form of government was the first in the state. In fact, Auburn's new city charter made it the first municipality in New England to create a council-manager form of government where the manager hired, fired employees, and implemented the legislative actions of an elected city council. The distinction of being the first city manager form of government often belongs to Norwood, Massachusetts, that approved its charter in 1914, but the town had adopted what is more commonly referred to as a 'town manager' form of government (noted in the NY Public Library 1918 reference notes as a "manager *town*" government[104]) where budgets, legislative policies and major purchases were approved through a 'town meeting' vote of the citizenry and not through an elected representative body like a council or board of aldermen.

Auburn's decision to adopt a form of government with professional administrative management served it well. The city had the benefit of beginning a professionally developed city planning, financing, and hiring process and avoided any evidence of public corruption within its government. However, having a professional manager did not mean that the city would avoid conflict, including the tumultuous 1930s.

The power of Auburn's city manager was made clear in 1937. The decision to call in the National Guard to deal with striking shoe workers in 1937 was not made by Governor Lewis Barrows nor the Auburn City Council, or mayor; it was made by Auburn City Manager Frederick Ford. Ford went so far as to support a declaration of martial law in Auburn if it was needed to quell the union protests. Ford also stated that he would ask for more troops if the situation necessitated "declaring...a state of insurrection." [105]The City Manager's sentiments in the Lewiston Daily Sun were not supported or refuted publicly by any Auburn elected officials.

After a little more than 11 years on the job, a new city council replaced Ford, with David Walton on January 2, 1938, eight months after the confrontation between striking shoe workers and the Maine Army National Guard.[106] Replacing Ford created a furor with many of his supporters. Following the public announcement of Walton's appointment as manager, a group of Auburn citizens and businesspeople petitioned the Maine Attorney General who filed an injunction in the Maine Supreme Judicial Court. The Maine AG and the Auburn group believed that there were state law provisions that could challenge "illegal acts of a municipal corporation." [107] As a result, the court temporarily suspended Walton's appointment "pending a hearing on January 17." Ford told the newspaper that he had "absolutely nothing to do with it."[108]

The complaint by the petitioners and many of the former elected officials and citizens who supported Ford, claimed that the three newly elected Auburn Councilors who voted to appoint Walton had not provided due process to Ford before relieving him of his duties. On January 28, Justice Harry Manzer of the Maine Supreme Judicial Court lifted the restraining order against Walton that permitted the Council appointing him to stand. In the end, Manzer's opinion to keep Walton on the job was based on his analysis of the charter language stating how the city council bi-annual terms always began with the appointment of the city manager for the two-year period. In Ford's case, each newly elected city council had appointed him five consecutive times. Manzer believed that the charter's prohibition of dismissing the city manager without due process spoke only to a council's desire to fire the manager within the two-year period. Judge Manzer ruled that the action of appointing Walton by the new Council elected for the 1938-39 term, was consistent with the "ambiguous" charter language and past precedent allowing Walton to replace Ford as the Auburn manager.[109]

## The Ed Muskie Effect and Louis Jalbert's Rise to Power

As the decline of the textile and shoe industries in Lewiston and Auburn shifted the economic developmental focus in both cities, the power and influence of Lewiston's Democrats experienced a significant transition in the 1950s. The moment that underscored this historic Democratic Party shift occurred when Ed Muskie, the Polish Catholic from Rumford, won the governor's office in 1954. This victory was no small feat in a state that had been in Republican control seemingly forever.

Former Lewiston Mayor John Beliveau stated in a Muskie Archives interview that Muskie's victory "was a lot like the (Lyndon) Johnson landslide that impacted Maine and all of the Democratic Party."[110] According to Douglas Rooks, "Muskie was the first Democrat elected governor in twenty years, and just the fourth in a century."[111] All this happened while Lewiston was the home base for the state's Democratic Party. Lewiston's Frank Coffin, who would later become a U.S. Congressman and a Senior Judge for the U.S. Court of Appeals First Circuit, was a major force in Muskie's win and moving the trajectory of the state's Democratic Party in a direction that would ultimately gain them a majority in the state legislature some 20 years later.

Muskie's election generated excitement and success for Lewiston Democratic residents who supported Muskie and set their sights on state offices in Augusta. One notable Lewiston resident who wanted to move the Democratic needle in Lewiston and Augusta was Louis Jalbert who was elected to the State House in 1944. His 19 two-year terms in the State House earned him the moniker "Mr. Democrat"[112] during his tenure. Jalbert quickly rose through the Democratic ranks and became minority leader in 1946 but gave up the seat to Ed Muskie in exchange for a seat on the powerful Appropriations Committee in 1948.[113] Jalbert held the committee seat until his primary loss finished his term in 1954.

During Jalbert's tenure, he was admired, despised, and praised. Rooks writes Jalbert thought up an idea for a "reverse press conference... where Democrats asked reporters for ideas" that "intrigued" reporters covering the Muskie governor campaign.[114] Many also viewed Jalbert as intelligent and politically ruthless. He was convicted in 1965 on a bribery charge and for obtaining money under false pretenses, although that did not stop his re-election in 1966.[115]

Aside from his many character traits, he was the consensus leader of the Lewiston Democratic Party for several decades. While still serving as a legislator, Jalbert pursued his first campaign for municipal office in the 1954 mayoral election against the very popular former mayor Ernest Malenfant who had been beaten in 1952 by Roland Marcotte. The February 15, 1954 race resulted in a runoff between Malenfant and Jalbert, who came in second, only 342 votes behind the former Lewiston mayor.[116] The runoff election on March 1, 1954 produced a very different result. Malenfant beat Jalbert with 65.5% of the vote by an almost 2 to 1 margin. It was the largest margin of victory in a mayoral runoff election since 1939. Residents cast only 87 more votes for Jalbert than what he received in the February election.[117] It would be the last time Jalbert would ever run for any municipal office, but it would not mark the end of his political career.

Jalbert would come into the June 1954 Democratic primary with a record of five terms as Lewiston's state representative. He had organized a "political machine" in all the city wards "staffed with some of the city's veteran politicians." Although he had already assembled a very impressive legislative resume, this primary election was not an absolute certainty for him as he had "not led the (Democratic state representative) ticket...in recent years."[118]

The primary results of this election would not help Jalbert in recovering from the indignity of his March election drubbing. Not only did Jalbert lose in the June Democratic primary and not return to the legislature in 1955, Jalbert would lose again to Ernest Malenfant three months later. Malenfant would go to the Maine House of Representatives at a time when primaries were won by the five candidates receiving the most votes. The results of the June 21ˢᵗ primary would not only result in another Malenfant defeat of Jalbert, Malenfant would receive the largest vote majority of the five primary candidates. For Malenfant and the rest of the ticket, the absence of any Republican opposition meant that all the House Democratic primary winners would run unopposed and serve as state representatives in January 1955.[119]

Disappointing as it was for Jalbert to lose in 1954, he quickly returned to the State House in 1957. For some inexplicable reason, Jalbert requested that he not be given any committee assignments upon his return to the House of Representatives.[120] For this reason, Jalbert did not immediately return to his very powerful position on the Appropriations Committee until 1963 where he would remain until 1984, though never serve as chair of the committee.

What is also notable is that beginning in 1963 and continuing through Jalbert's defeat in the June 1984 Democratic primaries, the city of Lewiston maintained a seat on the Appropriations Committee, with Representative Greg Nadeau's appointment from 1985-1988 (Nadeau would serve one more term from 1989-1990 as the Chair of the Housing and Economic Development Committee); Representative Roger Pouliot 1989-1996; Representative Patricia Lemaire 1997-98; Representative Richard Mailhot 1999-2004; and Senator Margaret "Peggy" Rotundo from 2003-2016. [121] The 53 consecutive years of Lewiston representation on Appropriations would end with Senator Rotundo's departure from the legislature in 2016.

## Changing Political Landscapes and Mr. Democrat's Fall

During Jalbert's tenure, he exerted his influence on local politics through his position as the Chair of the Androscoggin Committee and his position on the House Appropriations Committee, which controlled funding for all legislation that required a fiscal note. In 1970, Jalbert was beaten for the minority floor party leader by the rising Aroostook County Franco Democrat, John Martin. At that point in Jalbert's career, Martin saw him as "an aging, widely resented Franco from (Lewiston)".[122]

Jalbert has been credited for leveraging his influence to secure Lewiston a badly needed third bridge over the Androscoggin River, the founding of the Central Maine Vocational Technical Institute (he claimed the title "father of vocational education in Maine"), as well as the establishment of a downtown state office (Department of Human Services) building.[123] Those accomplishments were not enough to fend off Aliberti's campaign against Jalbert in 1984, something that was possibly fueled by a new "wave of young Democrats, energized by their opposition to the Vietnam War." Candidates of this mentality, like John Martin, were entering state politics around 1970.[124] Whether Jalbert's defeat was connected to new wave Democrats or just voter fatigue with Jalbert, his 1984 June primary defeat was not technically the end for 'Mr. Democrat'.

Jalbert lost to the former schoolteacher, administrator, and School Committee member John Aliberti by 15 votes. Lewiston Daily Sun journalist Joe O'Connor wrote that "(t)he contest was also unique in that it saw the incumbent... opposed by some of Lewiston's most prominent Democrats including Pat Lemaire and Laurie Parkin, who served as co-chairwomen of Aliberti's campaign."[125]

Word got out that Jalbert's attorney had filed for a ballot inspection that was scheduled at City Hall for Wednesday, June 20, 1984. Lewiston Daily Sun journalist Glen Chase contacted Jalbert at his home for a comment about the recount request that unleashed a profanity-filled response. Jalbert, who likely read the article written by Joe O'Connor, was in no mood to respond to the question and fired back at Chase — "'F*** you and your newspaper. Don't you or any other reporter ever call me at home again... I'll never give anybody at The Lewiston Sun(sic) a story ever again.'"[126] From my own firsthand experience with Louis Jalbert, I can attest that he was never one to restrain himself, particularly when he was upset.

Following the inspection by the City Clerk's office, the formal recount process was moved to Augusta where the work done by the Secretary of State's Office was eventually moved to the next level of appeal with the Governmental Ethics and Election Practices Commission. Jalbert's attorney used several technical legal challenges on disputed ballots attempting to gain a numerical edge for his client. On June 18, 1984, the Commission "preserved (Aliberti's) Election Day victory over Jalbert, the state's most veteran legislator, by a final tally of 485-474."[127]

After one more appeal to Governor Joseph Brennan, who ruled on August 21, 1984 that Aliberti had won the election, the only remaining step left for Jalbert was to take his case to the Maine Supreme Judicial Court. On August 23, 1984, it was reported that Jalbert had accepted Governor Brennan's decision about the election outcome but announced that a write-in campaign, that Jalbert claimed was not initiated by him, was being organized for the November 1984 election in which Aliberti was running unopposed.[128] Aliberti won the election, and one of the most powerful, and combative legislators in Lewiston and Maine history would serve the remainder of the 1984 term confronting the fact that he had lost yet one more Democratic primary in Lewiston. Jalbert would not go quietly. There was still one more fight ahead for Jalbert, and for the supporters of L-A College.

## Union Politics

Lewiston's Franco 'Muskie' Democrats enjoyed a period of growth and influence at the city, county, and state level during the 1950s and into the 1960s. Lewiston Democrats, particularly people like Louis Jalbert, were known in Augusta for their success in focusing and succeeding on what Douglas Rooks called the "economic lunch-bucket issues that united Democrats,"[129] and not the divisive and incendiary social issues of the 1960s that occupied many Democrats in the rest of the country. Matters of importance involving the textile and shoe workers understandably drove much of the Lewiston Democratic focus party in Lewiston. Legislation involving working conditions and compensation, safety, wages, and other union concerns received the lion's share of attention that often drove the committee assignments for most Lewiston legislators. Obviously, Jalbert's insistence on holding onto his Appropriations Committee seat gave him significant power and influence on much of the legislation that was important to textile and shoe constituents.

For someone like Denis Blais who was born in Quebec and the youngest in a family of 12 children, his skills as a young TWUA-CIO textile mill union organizer in Rhode Island resulted in being assigned to Lewiston in 1947. His assignment was to serve as the bilingual manager for five union textile mills, but 5,000 of Lewiston's 9,000 textile workers were non-union workers (either non-paying or unregistered). Blais set out to get those workers registered as paying members.[130]

Blais' textile union experience made him uniquely qualified to understand "lunch-bucket" issues like wages, hours and working conditions. He also recognized that those issues were priorities for the significant majority of workers. Blais led a successful union strike in 1955 after Bates Mill ownership tried to implement a 10% wage reduction, which they had successfully accomplished in their southern mills.[131]

In Denis Blais' eyes, he saw union membership as more than just a vehicle for obtaining more favorable contracts for its members. He believed it was important for the union to "play a part in the community" and to identify needs that would improve the quality of life for members. Blais saw a community that was lacking in providing social opportunities for members and their families. He organized large entertainment events for all members including outdoor barbeques for each mill's workforce, an annual Christmas event that would attract 2,000 to 3,000 children, organized members to help donate community money, and to assist in the construction in a new St. Dom's Arena, which was destroyed by a fire in 1956.

Union activity could also become an entry point for aspiring politicians. From the ranks of union activism came people like Marie A. Dugas who became the first woman elected to the Lewiston City Council on February 17, 1958.[132] The mills also produced other public office holders including Leo St. Pierre who served on the city council and George Ricker who served both as a city councilor,[133] school board member and the state legislature.

Paul Couture was another example of a working-class Franco whose union membership launched his service in the Maine House and Senate and eventually on the Lewiston City Council. He had been employed in the mills and was a union leader.[134] Paul was also the brother of boxer Aurele "Shiner" Couture, the Lewiston native who fought nearly 300 professional fights and recorded the fastest professional boxing knockout in the sport's history.[135] His 10.5 second knockout remains a world record.[136]

Paul Couture served nine terms in the Maine House and Senate between 1951 and 1970. According to former Mayor John Beliveau, Couture also served on the city council while he was mayor and did much of his political work in some of the "social clubs" that filled much of the after-work down time for many textile and shoe workers in both cities. According to Beliveau, the "20M" club and "Le Montagnard" club were the places where Couture would meet with city councilors (called "aldermen" at that time) and state legislators such as Bill Jacques (former mayor), Albert Cote, Roland Tanguay (who owned "Le Montagnard") and Louis Jalbert.[137]

While Paul Couture was assembling a very impressive political resume in local Democratic politics, my father Guy H. Nadeau was a local business owner whose family had been doing business in Lewiston since the 1920s. His parents had emigrated to Lewiston from St. Ephrem, Quebec in the 1920s. They later opened Nadeau's Market on the corner of Bartlett and Walnut Street in 1936. The family business provided my father an opportunity to become involved in local politics as part of the 1956 re-election campaign for Governor Edmund Muskie.

As the oldest of four siblings and the first to work in the family business, my father's growing interest in getting involved in Lewiston Democratic politics provided me an opportunity to meet and know many of the elected Democratic officials who my father knew during the 1950s, 1960s and 1970s. These people were the 'movers and shakers' in local, county and state politics that included Louis Jalbert, State Representative Albert Cote, County Commissioner Roland Landry, County Treasurer Norm Labbe, U.S. Representative (later U.S. Senator) William "Bill" Hathaway, County Sheriff Robert "Bob" Bonenfant, City Treasurer Fred "Freddie" Plourde, City Controller Lucien Gosselin, State Representative Roland Tanguay, former mayors Emile Jacques, Romeo Boisvert, John Beliveau, Judge (and later Maine U.S. Attorney) Thomas "Tom" Delahanty II, Mayor (and later Maine Supreme Judicial Court Justice) Robert "Bob"

Clifford, and countless others who would do business with my grandparents grocery market, my father's catering business and deli, or stop by at my Uncle Yves "Babe" Nadeau's social club, the Derby A.A. (Athletic Association).

In time, my father's work with the Salvation Army, appointments with the city's fire and police commission (showing his Police Commissioner's badge[138] got him into the Ali-Liston fight but he never saw the knockout as he was getting into his seat), and catering events that were often connected to Democratic fundraisers like the Jefferson-Jackson fundraising dinner, as well as barbeques at the Montagnard Chalet, all influenced my father's decision to run for public office.

In 1970, he ran in the Democratic Primary for County Commissioner against the formidable Paul Couture who had garnered enormous exposure and influence with mill and shoe workers and was a familiar public figure in other parts of the county. After running a strong campaign, dad lost to Couture by 36 votes. He won in Lewiston, but Couture edged out a win in the outlying county communities. I got to see firsthand how exhilarating and heartbreaking a campaign can be. Eight years later, our family would finally experience its first political victory when my brother Gregory "Greg" Nadeau was successful in his first election bid for a seat in the House of Representatives in 1978. He would serve in that seat until 1990.

**Not Just Democrats Anymore**

Much of Lewiston's politics had been inextricably linked to its working-class textile and shoe manufacturing roots, and the social settings, activities, newspaper and radio station that served, celebrated, and supported their culture into the 1960s. Today's Maine sunshine laws that prohibit political officials to gather and conduct official business in social settings did not exist at that time. Numerous Lewiston elected officials were right at home conducting political business in many of the 'social clubs' that dominated the city's downtown, and in the churches, activities, and social organizations they supported. The presence of only one newspaper and radio station that provided French content, simplified what to read and listen to for the largely French-speaking population, and for the politicians who needed their support.

Democratic politics during the 1970s and 1980s looked and felt different both across the state and in Lewiston's own backyard. Muskie had established himself as a serious presidential contender at the beginning of the 1972 campaign year. Democrat Ken Curtis was having success restructuring state government, and Lewiston Democrats continued to control both City Hall and their own legislative delegation. The biggest change in Lewiston was the declining employment of people working in the mills and shoe factories. Reductions in mill industry employment eroded union influence among Franco Democrats who embraced the union's role in their social, political, and religious lives. Declining union influence also eroded the ability of Lewiston Democrats to connect with many of the people who once depended on the union-controlled information networks involving the social clubs, churches, schools and French language media.

One of the true marquee moments for Lewiston politics was 1974, and it involved a resident from Lewiston named James Longley whose gubernatorial victory as an independent rocked Lewiston Democrats and the entire state. His election also sent shock waves across the country as Longley became the first independent candidate in history to be elected as a governor. Longley's achievement occurred in the same year President Richard Nixon resigned from office. Longley's victory seemed to reflect the changing local and state public attitudes that appeared to place more focus on personal integrity, fiscal conservatism, and taxation concerns rather than the social issues involving the Vietnam war, civil rights, women's rights, and the environment that had dominated the previous decade's headlines.

This was not only reflected in Longley's election, but in the 1976 electoral victory of Lewiston's first female mayor Lillian Caron.[139] As a Democrat, Caron promoted herself as a person with the personal integrity and fiscally conservative values that were attracting more voters in Lewiston. Longley also recognized those qualities and appointed her to a variety of state committees and commissions.[140] Longley also recognized the independent disposition of another Lewiston Democrat named Georgette Berube.

## Georgette Berube

Georgette Berube had not been "groomed" by local Democrats for the opportunity to become the first woman to win a Lewiston legislative seat in 40 years. She was the involved in the family furniture business as a "co-manager" when she ran for the House of Representatives. Berube had also not received the blessing of the county Democratic Committee and who sought to consign her to the local "Women's Club." Berube advised local Democrats like Louis Jalbert that she wanted "to make policy, not coffee."[141]

Berube was a working-class Democrat who "seldom failed to mince words" and "expressed (a) conservative philosophy (that) was unusual for a (Democratic) woman"[142] in Maine, particularly since there were few Democratic women in the legislature to be compared against. The year that Berube would enter the legislature, only 8% of the House of Representatives were women (out of 154 members).[143] By 1991, Maine would have the "second-highest percentage of female legislators in the country."[144]

Berube would be elected in 1970 and would continue to serve in both the House and the Senate until Lewiston Mayor John Jenkins beat her in 1996. She would become the longest service woman in the state legislature's history.[145] Berube would also become the first woman in state history to run as a Democrat for governor losing to incumbent Democrat Joe Brennan in the 1982 primary.[146]

Berube developed a reputation as a fiscal conservative who did not support abortion but supported gay rights. She was also an advocate for education, but her fiscal conservatism caught the eye of Governor Longley who appointed her to his budget "Performance Audit Committee."[147] Upon her election to the state senate in 1984, except for the 1996-1998 legislative session,[148] Lewiston would keep a woman in the state senate until 2016, when Senator Peggy Rotundo retired.

Georgette Berube died in 2005. She was inducted into the Franco-American Hall of Fame in 2009.[149]

## The Lewiston Republicans and Other L-A Notables

Though Democrats continued to comprise most Lewiston's city councils and its state legislative delegations, being a Democrat no longer guaranteed you an office seat in Lewiston or in the Second District (Trump would win its single electoral vote in 2016 and 2020). Republican William Cohen was victorious in his first campaign for the Second District in 1972, and his first U.S. Senate run against Democratic incumbent Bill Hathaway in 1978. In both instances, Cohen did not win in Lewiston, but the Second District was becoming more accustomed to electing Republican candidates. That proved to be true again in 1978 when Auburn resident and Republican Olympia Snowe would fill the seat vacated by William Cohen. Snowe defeated the Democratic incumbent, Maine Secretary of State, war hero, and POW Markham Gartley[150] in the Second District. Her first federal office victory would launch a career that would end as one of the most influential women in the U.S. Senate.[151]

Over time, people like Republicans John Telow, Stavros Mendros, Paul Madore, Denis Theriault, Nelson Peters, Leslie Dubois, Robert Reed, and Robert MacDonald were also garnering successes in winning Lewiston seats as mayor, city councilor, or as legislator and would continue to do so to the time of publication of this book. What was clear is that the declining numbers of predominantly Democratic textile and shoe workers were having less of an impact on elections. A new generation of voters and elected officials were coming into the picture with an array of political philosophies that would range from fiscally and socially conservative to very progressive.

Lewiston would also elect John Jenkins, the city's first African American mayor in 1993,[152] the first African American state senator in the city's and the state's history in 1996, and Auburn's mayor in 2007 (making him the first person to become mayor in both cities).[153] Lewiston would also elect its second female mayor Kaileigh Tara in 1998, and another female, City Council President Kristen Cloutier, who would fill the position of mayor after the resignation of Mayor Shane Bouchard in 2019.[154] Over time, several female Republicans and Democrats from both cities would also be successful in pursuing offices on the city council, school board, state legislature, U.S. House of Representatives and the U.S. Senate. This new wave of elected officials would all play a role in shaping the community's transition from its aging and outdated industrial economy.

# CHAPTER 2

# FORGING A NEW PATH FORWARD: 1950s – 1990s

*COLLABORATION*

As far back as 1938, the focus of Lewiston officials had little to do with professionally managing a city for future growth. In the words of The Lewiston Daily Sun's Stanley Attwood, "(t)here is such a thing as city planning but it hasn't arrived here. Until it does, Lewiston will 'just grow'." [155] That optimistic view of Lewiston's future was short-lived as the "just grow" reality began to subside along with the unrelenting contraction of the mill and shoe industries through the 1940s and 1950s.

The decline of manufacturing in Lewiston and Auburn was taking place across the entire country. In 1953, manufacturing accounted for 28% of the nation's Gross Domestic Product (GDP). Manufacturing's share of GDP and employment in the sector then steadily declined with GDP dropping to 12% and employment plummeting from 32% to 8.7% in 2015. [156] Transforming a local economy would not happen overnight, or without its challenges. This was particularly true for Lewiston, which was transitioning out of an economy where 70% of its workforce was employed in manufacturing industries or their ancillary businesses only 50 years earlier.

New businesses were being recruited to both cities and were also attracting new homes, department stores, strip malls, banks, and other retailers. Lewiston and Auburn were also having some success in filling the vacant mill and shoe factory square footage.[157] There were few options available for either city in their individual attempts to arrest the agonizing decline of their once powerful industries and economies.

Collaboration between the cities of Lewiston and Auburn had its historic roots. According to a 2009 report published by the "Citizens Commission on Lewiston-Auburn Cooperation," two joint ventures that continue to this day originated in the 19th century. "In the 1880's(sic), the two cities established the Lewiston-Auburn Railroad Company, whose rail facilities continue to this day to be a dynamic factor in the economic development of the region. In the same decade, by legislative action, the cities worked together to share a common water supply, Lake Auburn."[158]

According to Douglas Hodgkin, the first recorded instance of a collaborative effort between the cities of Lewiston and Auburn was an act by the state legislature in 1849 creating the "Lewiston Falls Village Corporation." They created the special firefighting district to protect "the village that grew up on both sides of the river in Lewiston,[159] Danville and Minot."[160] The effort to create and raise tax revenue for a fire service eventually encountered public questions regarding efficiency and training. There were also jealousies about the operation coming from both sides of the river. The final blow occurred following a large fire that "burned much of downtown Auburn in August 1855," and the December 1855 burning of the Lewiston Irish Chapel that also produced local newspaper accusations of "prejudice" and "arson" "motivated by... another incident in which four Irish shanties were burned." They disbanded the joint effort in 1856.[161]

The undertaking to pursue the construction of an airport to serve both cities was another significant joint effort milestone for both cities. The area of interest had been referred to as the "Androscoggin airport" and was described as "a large tract at Marston's corner, Auburn (that was) taken over for port(sic) purposes (and continued) to lie fallow as far as air activities" were concerned in 1930.[162] The Auburn Chamber of Commerce believed that "something definite and tangible should be done about the airport." It was also known that Lewiston had a "more than luke(sic) warm sentiment... to match Auburn forces man for

47

man and team for team if the work will actually get under way there."[163]

The interest in that "Marston's corner" land led to the decision by Lewiston and Auburn to construct an airport in Auburn. Funds for construction were a part of the FERA (Federal Emergency Relief Act) New Deal program,[164] involving a component of (the) Civil Works Administration (CWA), a temporary agency established on November 9, 1933. Conceived in response to the need to put millions of unemployed people immediately back to work during the harsh winter of 1933–1934, the CWA created thousands of construction jobs for unskilled laborers. Projects mainly included building or improving roadways, schools, playgrounds, and airports; laying sewer pipes and masonry walls; or simply raking leaves and shoveling snow in public and national parks.[165]

By 1934, the building of the airport was underway[166] through some joint funding between the two cities and the WPA (Works Progress Administration).[167] As happens between many local government collaborative efforts, there were those that questioned the benefit of the jointly funded project and the financial obligations of the two cities. In second-term Mayor Donat Levesque's March 15, 1937 inaugural speech, Mayor Levesque expressed that

(t)he Lewiston and Auburn Airport, now nearing completion, has been the object of much controversy between both cities. At present, a facility of little value to these communities, it has nevertheless provided work for many needy citizens, and will of course, in years to come, be a great asset to Lewiston and Auburn, when transportation by air is more general in this part of the Country. Cost of lighting equipment for the Airport, has also caused some

48

> concern to some of our citizens, and I wish to point out the fact, I was opposed to Lewiston paying more of the cost than Auburn, as a joint agreement between the two Cities had been reached. Lewiston should have paid only fifty per cent of this contract and not sixty-six and two-thirds per cent as passed by the Lewiston City Government, over my objection.[168]

Mayor Levesque's comments reflect the complexities of joint agreements between governments, be they local, county, state or quasi-governmental. Despite the Mayor's unsupportive comments about the financial arrangements between the cities, the facility opened in 1937 [169] and would also see its first commercial flight on December 1, 1937. As part of a new airmail service for northern New England, the Boston-Maine Airways Lockheed Electra "Silver Albatross" landed at 10:08 A.M. to become the first commercial flight to arrive at the Lewiston-Auburn Airport. The historic moment also took on special significance as the Lockheed Electra was piloted by 1923 (Lewiston) Jordan High School graduate and Auburn resident Captain Sanford Chandler.[170]

Critical as he may have been only eight months earlier about the necessity of the airport, Lewiston Mayor Donat Levesque accompanied Captain Chandler on the first commercial "express" mail run to Bangor. Levesque reported that "he was greatly impressed with the trip and stated that the service will be of great benefit to Lewiston and Auburn."[171]

The new community asset also became one of 6 Maine airports considered important for national defense by the State Defense Commission in 1940."[172] The Lewiston and Auburn airport (now the Auburn-Lewiston Airport) would be temporarily taken over by the Navy in 1942 to establish a VS-31 scouting squadron to patrol the Atlantic. It officially became the "Lewiston Naval Auxiliary Air Facility (NAAF)... Site Number: D01ME0009" on April 15, 1943.[173] As many as 523 personnel were on location to train on a variety of Navy aircraft.[174] In 1945, George H. W. Bush (who would go on to become a US

President) trained at Lewiston NAAF after his airplane was shot down in the Pacific in 1944.¹⁷⁵

> On 2 July 1946, the entire 547.35 acres comprising Lewiston NAAF was declared surplus by the Navy to the Surplus Property Board... On 18 December 1947, the United States conveyed 401.5 acres of the site to the Cities of Auburn and Lewiston... A supplementary quitclaim deed for the remaining 34.5 acres was conveyed from the WAA... on 15 December 1948.¹⁷⁶

The airport has remained a jointly operated and funded enterprise of both cities and remains a vital and integral part of Lewiston-Auburn's economic development.

## Roland Marcotte

Any discussion of Lewiston's collaborative history during the 1950s and 1960s would not be complete if it did not include former Mayor Roland Marcotte, who served the city in 1952, 1953 and 1964. What is noteworthy about Marcotte is that he was the first city official to publicly endorse the virtues of cooperation between the two cities, as well as professionalizing city government. His obituary summed up his impact on the city:

> (H)e was instrumental in creating a full-time Industrial Development Office for Lewiston and encouraged the development of the Franklin Pasture, in later years known as Marcotte Park. As Mayor, he promoted and passionately advocated for initiatives that included unification of the Twin Cities, the hiring of a City Manager, and the building of a circumferential highway for Lewiston-Auburn. ¹⁷⁷ Prior to Mayor Marcotte, there is little evidence that unifying the two cities had any real public interest outside of

the collaborative effort involving the Lewiston-Auburn airport during the 1940s or 1950s.

The matter of professionalizing city management had been publicly discussed before Marcotte was elected in 1952. The December 11, 1948 Lewiston Evening Journal reported that hiring a city manager was considered but eventually dropped by the Lewiston Charter Committee. The article stated that (local businessperson) Frank Hoy shared his opposition to the idea of a city manager describing Auburn's manager-council form of government as a "'half-way(sic) city manager system'" and also "thought Lewiston was not ready to take up that form of government" asking "'(a)re we ready to sacrifice representation for efficiency (?)'"[178]

In 1949, Lewiston also explored hiring a "'salesman, so called, to act as agent for the City of Lewiston'... who State Representative Jalbert believed should be 'free to travel and seek out industries which might come to Lewiston.'" Jalbert went on to say "'(t)he South is not only bidding for our vacation business but for our industries as well.'"[179] The Lewiston Daily Sun opined about the merger of the Chamber of Commerce operations in the two cities. Their 1951 op-ed supported the idea and believed that "they ought not to be looked upon as rivals or competitors...The two cities' resources, combined, are so much larger than those possessed by either alone."[180] Publicly, there were discussions about professional management, economic development, and collaboration between the cities. No one championed these ideas until Mayor Roland Marcotte made them priorities in his administrations.

Marcotte likely observed how Auburn had been guided by a professional manager for 35 years. Whether he envisioned the same manager-council structure in the Auburn charter is unclear. What was clear was the front-page headline of the Lewiston Evening Journal's March 16, 1953 headline about Marcotte's second inaugural address: "Marcotte Assails Present Gov't(sic), Wants Professional Administrator." During the morning inaugural event at the City Hall auditorium, he spoke about the need for "'a full-time professional administrator at the top level'" of city government:

> (A 'full time' city administrator)... could plug the many leaks in the functions of our various agencies. Lewiston is a corporation that spends over 2½ million dollars annually, but our city, despite its big business status, lacks continuity in both routine matters and future planning. As a multi-million dollar organization, we should be beyond the dabbling of unqualified amateurs, and until the time we can all be made to understand this, and place aside political quibbling, we will struggle along with second-string direction of our municipal business and pay the extra costs of second-rate management.[181]

Marcotte's interest in taking a more strategic and professional approach to city government was also reflected in his support for the newly created Lewiston Development Corporation (LDC). Marcotte threw his support behind it with a $12,000 appropriation to support "industrial development and diversification" in the city. In his 1952 inaugural address, Marcotte stated that "'industrial diversification protects a community from the tragedies which accompany the failures of recessions in one or two industries.'"[182] Additionally, 1952 also marked the year when Marcotte created the Industrial Development Department (IDD)[183], which was the precursor to the city's current Department of Community and Economic Development.

Both the IDD and the LDC played an important role in the city's new vision for economic development. Their importance was underscored on July 1, 1959 when the largest project since the construction of the first mills in Lewiston, was publicly announced. The Raytheon Corporation would a new technology industry into the city and employ thousands of employees.[184] It was a seismic event, complete with a police-escorted caravan into the city. Given the challenges associated with convincing manufacturers of their size to relocate to Maine, this became a significant achievement for the city's two economic development entities and the State of Maine.

Raytheon's announcement to manufacture "transistors, diodes, and rectifiers," was front-page news and likely covered statewide and regionally given the company's significant presence in Massachusetts. The company would potentially generate an annual payroll of $8 million, employ as many as 2,000 people in a new 140,000 square foot, $2.5 million building described as "the most modern industrial structure in the State of Maine."[185]

The project was described as a "new industry" with statewide importance.[186] The size of the project, and the fact that Raytheon was a major national technology company, signaled to the city that the economic development work of the last seven years was clearly headed in the right direction. IDD Director Sam Michael [187] and the LDC collaborated with the company, community, and state government leaders to acquire the land, build the structure, and work out the funding.

In a speech during a luncheon at the DeWitt Hotel, Lewiston's Industrial Development Director Sam Michael reflected on Raytheon's choice in selecting Lewiston: "The Industrial Heart of Maine has added to its industrial family the largest single industry under one roof in the State. The Maine industrial renaissance has begun."[188] This project was seen as a seminal moment for a city coming to terms with its declining textile industries and how it would view its ability to change its economic development future.

In hindsight, that 'seminal' moment may not have been in how the city worked and collaborated to secure a major technology company like Raytheon to Lewiston, but how they reacted when the city received notice from Raytheon that it was leaving on March 1, 1963.[189] Although other front-page articles in the Lewiston Evening Journal issue said that the Mayor was "'dumbfounded'" and quoted Industrial Development Director Sam Michael's reaction as "'a complete surprise,'" the fact was that two days earlier, there was a fairly innocuous story on the back page of the February 27, 1963 Lewiston Daily Sun that reported the company was "halting (the) production of diodes" in the facility. The story also said that some "50 to 75 women and a few (male) engineers" would be impacted by the action. Officials at the company would not offer any comment about their decision to stop production.[190] Although the story mentioned nothing about any possible shutdown of the entire operation, in hindsight, it obviously served as a harbinger of what would happen over the next few days.

After officially opening the plant on June 19, 1961, and after only 20 months in operation, a Raytheon spokesperson stated that the reason for the company's decision to end operations was influenced by a "'(c)ontinued deterioration in demand and prices'" that would "'force the phasing out of Raytheon's Semiconductor operation in Lewiston, Maine within the next ten months." At peak employment, approximately 1,300 people worked in the semiconductor plant. On the day of the announcement, there were approximately 1,000 people employed at the facility.[191]

What Raytheon did not explain, was that 70% of their company's total sales involved military sales, primarily the Hawk missile. In a 1964 U.S. Senate floor discussion, it was noted that Raytheon had laid off 8,000 workers between 1963 and April 1964. That discussion on the Senate floor suggested that in a post-Cuban crisis world without a major war in the country's future (which was a pre-Vietnam view of the world) there was need for discussions of future defense spending cutbacks. Some said that nuclear stockpiles were adequate to meet national security needs,[192] and in doing so may have led Raytheon to believe that its future dependence on military contracts was at risk, triggering their sudden decision to leave Lewiston.

Raytheon officials also provided a sneak peek into the future of micro technology when they pointed out that the "'component devices'— ones in which several transistor-type devices all are combined in one tiny device, (were) forcing the transistor business down." That "tiny device" was likely the company's entry into the new integrated circuit/microchip business that would be manufactured in a smaller California plant.[193] Both the city and the state had done all they possibly could to make this a long-term relationship. In the end, it appeared that timing, more than anything else, resulted in Raytheon's departure. The opportunity to attract another company that could immediately provide almost 2,000 jobs under one roof would be difficult, but not demoralizing.

Lewiston city officials were clearly surprised and extremely disappointed about the loss of Raytheon. What was notable, however, was the messaging coming from City Hall. Sam Michaels, Mayor Donia Girard, City Controller Laurier T. Raymond (father of then District Attorney and future Lewiston Mayor Laurier Raymond Jr.), were all disappointed, but they all reaffirmed their belief that the city would put this news behind them quickly. They would all look forward to what could be done with the building, while simultaneously focusing on future development possibilities. The Lewiston Evening Journal editorial reflected the reaction of city officials:

> Twin city area citizens know without being told that the Raytheon decision is 'bad' news... It is our conviction that the cities of Lewiston and Auburn and the Androscoggin County area generally are capable of 'rolling with the punch' and of coming back undismayed. We are convinced that if they do this, the job loss situation created by the closing of the semiconductor division here will prove temporary.[194]

In 1963, Roland Marcotte won election to return to the mayor's office. In his January 4, 1964 inauguration speech, Marcotte embraced his ideology of thinking positively and progressively about government in terms of planning, regionalizing, professionalizing and once again returned to his vision of collaborating with the city of Auburn. With the Raytheon story only ten months removed from his inauguration, Marcotte never mentioned Raytheon's departure in his inaugural address. What he did was to once again advocate for the two cities to consider merging their growing water and sewer systems.[195] Marcotte also made another appeal for the outright merger of the two cities, or at the very least, more collaboration for the delivery of services:

> Every avenue should be explored in our attempts to improve ourselves and bring a secure future to our people. It is my personal conviction that we should open the door to

> closer relations with our neighboring City(sic) across the Androscoggin, Auburn. Experts in the field of Economics, tested leaders in government and others associated with important phases of our system have been pointing out the great strides and benefits which have come about through the consolidation, merger and other pooling of resources by two or more communities.[196]

Marcotte's desire for more collaboration between the cities was an uphill struggle but not without merit. Of the nine joint efforts between the cities going back to 1849, six were still in effect or operational (see the Appendix).[197] Although Marcotte could not forge the collaborative synergy he desired between the two cities, his legacy of advocacy would be realized in the not-too-distant future.

In some ways, Marcotte's vision for cooperation had already begun at the regional level when the Androscoggin Valley Regional Planning Commission (now the Androscoggin Valley Council of Governments) created in 1962 (see the Appendix). It would bring together Lewiston, Auburn, and 14 other towns from the surrounding area to work together on regional planning.[198] Before Marcotte left municipal office for the last time, and "faced with the collapse of Lewiston's textile industry," Marcotte would take action to save the remaining textile industry in Lewiston. "With the support of a four-citizen committee (Lewiston Enterprise Committee, a subsidiary of the Lewiston Development Corporation), (Marcotte and the LEC) negotiated the purchase of the Bates Mill to preserve the property for (another 26 years of textile operations, and) local community development that flourishes (to this day)."[199]

The other collaborative initiative involving the interests of both Lewiston and Auburn was the passage of a November 1963 referendum[200] approving Lewiston Representative Louis Jalbert's vision for a vocational school in the L-A area. Both cities were interested in siting the college in their respective communities, but development costs made Auburn the preferred site. Higher than expected sewage connection costs in Lewiston were estimated at $500,000 to $1 million, as opposed to Auburn's estimate of $40,000.²⁰¹ Representative Jalbert, Mayor Marcotte, and several Lewiston officials and businesspeople set aside their parochial interests to support finding the best location. Their goal was to select a site that would be both suitable and affordable for state taxpayers, and would benefit not only Lewiston but the entire L-A region.²⁰²

Even after Marcotte left office in 1965, his desire for the two cities to merge their water and sewer operations became a partial reality in 1967. The Maine Legislature approved a bill to create a charter for the organization that would eventually build a jointly funded sewage treatment facility in Lewiston. "The 'Lewiston-Auburn Water Pollution Control Authority' (LAWPCA) charter would oversee wastewater treatment services for the Cities of Lewiston and Auburn. The plant was operational in 1974 and was one of the first secondary wastewater treatment facilities in the State of Maine."²⁰³ Since its completion, the facility has been a leader in the sewage treatment industry for decades. LAWPCA's $15.5 million anaerobic digestion sewage treatment and co-generation facility became operational in 2013. Its process for wastewater treatment harnessed anaerobic digestion to reduce its bio-solids production, while also utilizing the methane gas byproduct to produce electricity for the plant.²⁰⁴ It was the first publicly owned facility of its kind in the state and one of the largest public sector projects in the community's history.²⁰⁵

## Collaboration Stalls

The Lewiston and Auburn government officials were spending enormous time and energy on new programs passed by the Johnson Administration to help cities deal with aging infrastructure and agricultural blight in the 1960s. Lewiston's selection as a Model Cities program, and its ongoing efforts around urban renewal initiatives, were understandably driving much of the city's political and financial interests.

Although both cities were involved in a number of 'urban renewal' driven projects to address their economic decline, the U.S. economic picture in the early 1970s was chaotic. Rampant inflation was affecting everything, with historic annual rates through the 1973-75 period of 6.2%, 11.1%, and 9.1%, respectively. Inflation rates like these had not been seen since the post-WWII years of 1946 and 1947. [206] Price increases were being impacted by oil and gas costs related to fuel shortages and price controls. For Lewiston, higher costs and revenue reductions in Model Cities and other federal urban programs, also challenged city budgets and residents. The Vietnam War was winding down, the country was living through the Nixon impeachment hearing, his eventual resignation in 1974, and both cities were continuing to experience declines in their industrial economies.

Resources were too thin to undertake more collaborative efforts or to find common ground between the cities. Between 1968 and 1975, there were two minor, but important, mutual aid agreements between the fire and police departments. There was also a more informal collaborative agreement between the two city libraries that would lead to the creation of the LA Arts organization that continues to operate in both cities (see the Appendix).

The federal funding coming into both cities was important and could not be ignored, particularly when the country's economy was struggling. That did not derail the interest of a few people in Lewiston and Auburn to get together and start discussing what more could be done to have their cities work together to deliver city services and reduce costs for its residents.

By 1975, the two cities were already jointly operating or involved in the airport, the sewage treatment facility, their chambers of commerce organizations, the Androscoggin Valley Regional Planning Commission, mutual fire aid, and transportation planning. It may have been two 1975 events that nudged the twin cities to explore what additional possibilities for collaboration could be pursued. One involved the privately operated transit system serving both cities, the other involved a weekend retreat.

## L-A Transit Committee

Like many cities, transit began as a rail system powered by electric trolleys or trains that in many cases were replaced with transit buses. The commonality with most transit systems is that few of them were profitable. Privately held Hudson Bus Lines purchased "the defunct Lewiston Auburn Transit Company"[207] in 1959. Profits declined after the first year of operation in both cities. By 1962, Lewiston officials awarded Hudson a school bus contract to provide services to all city schools in an effort to create more cash flow for the company. By the end of the decade, things for Hudson had not improved.[208]

As difficult as the 1960s were in the cities, the 1970s proved to be even more challenging. After a series of cost-cutting moves, Hudson announced on March 1, 1973 that subsidies were needed from both cities to avoid shutting down operations. Only last-minute temporary funding from the state saved the struggling system. By the end of 1973, the Maine Public Utilities Commission worked to negotiate a temporary measure where both cities would each pay a 6-month subsidy of $13,750. It would mark the first time in the history of the two cities where a municipal subsidy was paid to a city transit provider (the subsidies continue to this day).

Hudson's finances improved in 1974, and Auburn elected to continue paying a monthly subsidy, while Lewiston refused. By July of 1974, both cities agreed to pay $22,500 as a full-year subsidy.[209]

The two cities agreed in 1976 to create the Lewiston-Auburn Transit Committee (LATC) to oversee transit services. The two cities would jointly work with Hudson Bus to develop financial and ridership information that the LATC would use in formulating funding recommendations for the two cities.[210] Over time, the LATCs role expanded as federal transit funding created opportunities for the two cities to purchase fourteen of its own transit buses in 1981, at which time it negotiated its first transit management contract with Hudson Bus Lines to provide maintenance and driver services.[211]

The Hudson bus-ownership model continued to struggle and was replaced in 1998 by a LATC bus-ownership model with Western Maine Transportation Services (WMTS) providing the maintenance and drivers. Both cities would continue their financial support for bus purchases, drivers, administration (through AVCOG), and maintenance. The business model created by the two cities and LATC in the late 1970s and early 1980s has evolved. The bus system is now a federal funds "direct recipient" that is no longer dependent on the state to provide all the fiscal management and oversight regarding bus system maintenance and purchasing.

The value of transit and the almost two decades of work to keep transit operating could not have been a more valuable community asset in the 1970s. An increasingly impoverished group of people relied on public transport as an affordable option. The demographics of both cities in the 1979 Census necessitated that a largely federally funded fixed route system be in place to meet the transportation needs of two underserved municipal populations where incomes were in the nation's lowest 20 percent of families: Lewiston at 26.5% and Auburn at 22.7%.[212]

All the economic indicators statewide and nationally were simply going the wrong way going into 1975. Both cities likely understood that their options were limited in finding and creating the "scales of economy" needed to produce real savings in delivering city services. As Lewiston City Administrator Lucien Gosselin and Auburn City Manager Bernie Murphy's relationship became closer over years of working together, a conference organized by their Maine Municipal Association state organization, and a discussion in an Orono restaurant, would lead to an idea for how the two communities could improve their business relationship.

That 'idea' would involve an April 1975, three-day meeting at the Samoset-Treadway Hotel (now the Samoset Resort) in Rockport, Maine. Little did anyone know that what would happen in Rockland would launch a new era of collaboration between L-A and make the two cities a municipal partnership model in Maine, New England, and just possibly, in the United States.

## The Rockland Experience

Lucien Gosselin's connection with the city goes back to 1960 when he became a volunteer[213] with the "(Lewiston) CD (civil defense) Police Reserve," while also helping to create the CDs "Radiological Division" in that same year. Gosselin was then given the opportunity to be the unpaid "administrative assistant" to CD Director Alphee Ouellette in January 1961, moving up to the paid part-time position of Assistant Civil Defense Director in February 1963. In October 1963, he was hired as the Assistant to the City Controller Laurier Raymond Sr.[214] and later became City Controller in 1969.[215]

Beginning with his civil defense position in 1961, Lucien Gosselin was involved with many collaborative efforts. By 1975, six of seven proposed collaborative efforts (with the only exception of the L-A Chamber of Commerce) were approved between the city governments. All six of them were significant in that they all remain operational to this day (see the Appendix).

Gosselin was just one half of the equation of the collaborative success between the two city governments. The other half was Bernard "Bernie" J. Murphy, Jr. who had served as Auburn's Assistant City Manager beginning in 1966 and became its city manager in 1970.[216] Murphy had also been connected to several of those successful joint initiatives between the cities and also knew the L-A area and many of the Lewiston city staff. The partnership formed by Gosselin and Murphy (who would leave Auburn in 1978) to create the "Rockland Experience" would have a demonstrable influence on the momentum for all future collaborative efforts between the two cities after 1975. Of the 51 total joint efforts (43%) dating back to 1849, 32 in total remain active (62.8%) and of that active number, 22 were created after 1975 (see the Appendix).

In my interview with Bernie Murphy, he recounted that when he became Auburn's assistant manager, it did not take long for him to realize how good Lucien was at his job. Murphy went on to say that he "had a lot of interest in (Gosselin) and a lot of respect for him early on." Over time, they "made some sort of arrangement to get to talk to one another and get to know one another."[217]

Although Murphy believed that the relationship between himself and Gosselin became closer, and that the relationship between the two cities was "cordial" prior to Rockland, he also recollected that, "there wasn't a hell of a lot of cooperation between the two cities."[218]

At some point in 1974, Gosselin and Murphy attended a Maine Town City Manager Association Interchange seminar at the University of Maine Orono (UMO) campus. During the seminar, Gosselin recalled that he and Murphy went out to dinner at "Pats Pizza" in downtown Orono with James "Jim" Pritchard and Irving "Irv" Masters Jr. from the UMO Bureau of Public Administration (BPA), Division of Public Services and Research.

Both Masters and Pritchard had recently attended "a four-week 'Managing Change' program sponsored by the National Training and Development Service," and during that evening, they conveyed (to Gosselin and Murphy) what both had learned during the program.

Pritchard's paper on the experience stated that the evening turned into a "rap session" regarding the "potential management-development programs for each of the cities."[219] The evening's discussion had made an impression on both administrators. According to Pritchard, by the end[220] of dinner both Gosselin and Murphy exclaimed "why not (have) a (jointly attended) twin city program."

There were reasons the BPA, Gosselin, and Murphy were so agreeable to the idea of bringing the two cities together. According to Murphy, there was a competition and tension between the Lewiston and Auburn city staff, although it was rarely expressed publicly. Up to 1975, there was a history of 13 total collaborative city efforts (see the Appendix) over the course of 125 years, demonstrating that they could occasionally set aside their differences. Both Gosselin and Murphy understood they would somehow have to address "a kind of undercover seething on the part of local officials. On the surface, the heads of government in both cities (had) managed a correctly polite attitude toward each other, but behind the smiling facade (had) been much irritation."²²¹

Pritchard and the BPA staff understood that "efficient task performance and cooperative problem-solving both high on the agenda of Lewiston and Auburn officials – (were) not possible if relationships (were) cluttered with interpersonal problems." he prospects for success would depend on how well the participants could realize "their interpersonal and group processes—what they (did) well and what they (did) that thwart(ed) understanding and cooperation."²²²

The advance preparation for an April 11, 1975 start date at Rockland's Samoset-Treadway Hotel²²³ "was more thorough than any BPA had undertaken."²²⁴ BPA invested almost 200 hours of staff time through the months of January and February 1975 in meetings with many key officials in both cities. Mike Bancroft and Pritchard then met with all the prospective participants individually, approximately 10 from each city,²²⁵ to give them an opportunity to express their concerns about the upcoming seminar. Notes were not taken by either BPA trainer to allow for a more relaxed setting that produced the transparency and honesty that was achieved.

At the outset of the interview process with the prospective participants, the trainers emphasized that the usefulness of the openness and honesty they shared with them would be of no value if they were not capable of "rais(ing) those issues themselves during the (upcoming) team-building session (as) the trainers would not."²²⁶ With all the advance work completed, all parties appeared to understand their respective roles. "Despite the concern (expressed by the prospective participants), the trainers were convinced, after three days of interviewing, that they had a 'feel' for most of the critical issues and an idea of the kinds of personalities that would be involved. It appeared that 'all systems were go.'"²²⁷

Approximately two weeks before the Rockland seminar, an article in the Lewiston Evening Journal reported that Lewiston officials had decided not to take part.²²⁸ According to Pritchard:

> On March 26, Lucien Gosselin had called a staff meeting to go over last-minute preparations for the weekend portion of the team-building

program. He was met with an unexpected barrage of hostile feelings, mostly directed at Auburn. The Lewiston staff proceeded to run down the long list of intercity irritants. These were amplified by rumors and fantasies about what might happen in Rockland and assumptions about Auburn's 'lack of commitment.' A few Lewiston officials flatly refused to participate.[229]

After Gosselin went to Auburn to meet with Murphy and his staff to explain what led to the March 27th newspaper article, he paired up on April 4th with the Auburn Assistant to the Manager Kirsten Larson Turley in Lewiston for a four-hour conference call with Pritchard and some of his staff (Murphy was out sick that day). After much discussion, the trainers persuaded both city officials that delaying the planned seminar would only "'fan the flames'" of distrust between the parties and raise more suspicion with the press about the real value of the event.[230] Paul Pare reported that there were people who were already saying that "the taxpayer-financed ($4,000 from Washington and $1,000 from each city) conference was no more than a 'junket' for city officials.'" One of the city officials believed that the reports of tension between the groups would lead to "(a) closed retreat."[231]

Following the meeting between Gosselin, Bancroft, and the BPA trainers, there were two significant changes that were made to the weekend's program. The first was the elimination of an orientation for each group of participants two-days before the program, and the other was to dedicate Friday, April 11th to each city team that would "meet individually at first, in separate parts of the conference facility, and would come together if and when they were ready."[232]

On Friday April 11th, 15 city officials (eight from Lewiston, seven from Auburn)[233], five BPA staff, and the conference keynote speaker arrived as scheduled.[234] Everything was going according to plan until Paul Pare from the Lewiston Evening Journal arrived to cover the three-day event. Pare was invited by Gosselin who had not shared that he was inviting the press with anyone in the Auburn group or with BPA staff. This was not received well by either BPA or Auburn. "Some Auburn officials indicated they were wary about the press' presence, and one indicated his participation would, as a result, be reduced by 50 per cent(sic)."[235]

Gosselin explained he invited Pare, given the suspicions of the press and some in the public. The idea was unsettling to the BPA staff.[236]

> Openness in government was a value to which the Bureau subscribed; but the presence of reporters at the preliminary phase would be just one more inhibiting factor in attempts to build an open learning environment. Initial thoughts of disinviting the press for at least the first two days were disregarded in favor of a more prudent approach.[237]

All agreed that Pare would be permitted conditional access to the event. The first condition was to ensure that he would take part in the weekend's activities; the second would be that if participants asked him to leave or not attend an event that he would comply. Pare agreed to the conditions and his participation was recognized by the BPA for the "quality and accuracy" of his coverage.[238] From my perspective, Pare's coverage and Pritchard's case study are invaluable artifacts that provide invaluable insight and accuracy that helps preserve the historic importance of such events.

The weekend proved to be valuable in that the full range of what Pritchard called the "content issues" (e.g., solid waste, police, fire, etc.) and. "process issues" (government structures, trust, politics, etc.)[239] were all on the table for honest and open discussions. Misunderstandings were discussed, and some clarified. Trust issues were frankly and civilly discussed improving relations between some officials. The up-close-and-personal approach worked and the guidance that was provided by BPA proved to be the glue that kept it all together.

What may have been a moment of true enlightenment for the weekend's participants may have involved the keynote speaker, Frederick Fisher of the Washington-based National Training Development Service. This was the same non-profit agency that hosted the program attended by BPA's Pritchard and

Irving Masters Jr. before that pivotal discussion with Gosselin and Murphy in Orono.

Fisher spoke about the uniqueness of what the two cities were doing in its rarity in local government, particularly in places like Texarkana, Texas where they were awaiting the results of what the two cities had endeavored to accomplish. Pritchard told Pare that he did not "know of any place in the country where two cities have gotten together in this kind of fashion" and that in his "eight and a half years in the management building field involving governments he had never seen anything like it."[240]

What was accomplished on the weekend of the "Rockland Experience" was said best by Paul Pare:

> Most importantly, according to those there, there was agreement on a goal. 'Everyone stated they will make an attempt to be honest with each other, they will be candid and express how they feel about issues... Success came and will follow, according to Pritchard, because the participants were able to 'break through their roles' as chief of police, city manager, city engineer, etc., and 'started respecting each other as people.'[241]

Pritchard's report and its conclusions provided an honest assessment of the weekend's success. Both managers were very pleased with the results. Gosselin called it a "once-in-a-lifetime experience."[242] Murphy opined that the conference had "remarkably improved day-to-day communications, relationships, mutual respect (between the two cities)... to be contrasted with the suspicion, mistrust, (and a) what's-in-it-for-them attitude before Rockland."[243]

Murphy added that he was "fascinated" how close some relationships became during the weekend. He distinctly remembered that some people hugged each other and that "it surprised me." Murphy also commented that he developed at least one very close relationship from that weekend with Lewiston Public Works Director Roger Pruneau, and that the relationship remained close for years. Years after Murphy left Auburn, Pruneau visited Murphy while he was city manager for Sanibel Island, Florida.[244]

In the end, the real evidence of the impact of the "Experience" were the results. Following the Rockland meetings, the Appendix shows that 12 additional joint efforts were initiated during the administrations of Lucien Gosselin and Bernie Murphy/Chip Morrison between 1975 and 1987, only one shy of the same number created over the previous 125-year period.

## TRANSITION

On the other side of the Androscoggin River, Auburn's population and economy grew, fueled by a shoe manufacturing industry that quickly expanded during the mid-1800s. According to local Sun Journal reporter Steve Sherlock,[245] Joseph Roak opened Auburn's first shoe factory in 1835, years before the first textile mill opened in Lewiston. The factory eventually moved to the in-town area of Auburn and was joined by other shoe manufacturers attracted to the locale's proximity to rail and the Lewiston Falls. The shoe and boot industry ballooned to 25 factories by 1859 and fueled a population increase that tripled to almost 10,000 people by 1880. Auburn had quickly become the shoe capital of the state.

Population in Auburn continued to grow through the early part of the 1900s with the shoe industry's 12 Auburn-Lewiston factories in 1922 (with most in Auburn) employing 8,000 workers, and making 70,000 pairs of shoes per day. This level of production ranked Auburn as the fifth largest shoe manufacturing city in the country.[246]

According to John Rand in his book "The Peoples (Bank): Lewiston-Auburn Maine 1875-1975," "(for) a long period the mill owners had been content to reap profits instead of plowing the proceeds back into needed research and renovation. Technology had suddenly passed them by... Now, electric power was the driving force."[247] The South had more to offer for textile operations: cheaper labor, power, and newer machinery. It simply made more sense to build a new factory in the South than it did to retrofit older ones in the North. According to Leamon, between

> the period from 1930 to 1960 (Lewiston's population) increased from 35,000 to only 41,000. Well before the Crash of 1929 it was obvious to persons in the textile business that New England's mills were in the grip of a deepening depression that threatened the very economic basis of cities like fall

River, Haverhill, Lawrence, Lowell, Manchester, and Lewiston.[248]

Although Auburn saw a six percent increase in its population in 1960, population growth in both cities was slowing (Auburn's population would decrease 1.2 percent in 1970).[249] Anemic population growth coupled with increasing competition from other states and countries, and the relocation of industries, were wreaking havoc on the local economy. Auburn, once a shoe manufacturing juggernaut, was undercut by "(t)he widespread move to 'offshoring' for cheaper parts and labor in the 1970s and 1980s decimated the shoe industry in Maine and the United States."[250]

War World II provided a temporary surge in business in both cities, but changes in ownership of Lewiston's and other Maine textile mills proved to be the industry's undoing throughout New England. In 1947, approximately 9,000 people worked in Lewiston's textile mills.[251] By 1970, only 1,800 people worked in the three mills that remained.[252] Unable to pay its property taxes, Bates Mill, the lone remaining survivor of the industry that built the city, turned over the remaining portions of its property to the city. The city took action to acquire the land and buildings through the tax lien process.[253]

## The Lewiston Development Corporation

By the 1950s, city officials in both cities recognized that its economic dependency on the textile and shoe industries needed to be reassessed. Although fewer people were being employed in the area's shrinking textile industry, Bates Mill had nearly 6,000[254] employees, making it Maine's largest employer[255]. Nevertheless, city officials were cognizant of what was happening to the textile industry both locally and in New England, while also recognizing that they could no longer depend on the mature industries of both cities to drive the local economy. In response, the Lewiston Chamber of Commerce (that would become the Lewiston-Auburn Chamber of Commerce in 1963[256]) assembled "18 community leaders" in March 1951 for the purpose of "bringing new enterprises to settle in the city".[257] By the following year, that initiative would grow into a more formal organization when five Lewiston residents formed a "stock corporation" called the Lewiston Development Corporation (which remains active to this day).[258] In 1964, it would spin off a subsidiary called the Lewiston Community Enterprises committee (during the Marcotte administration), whose primary purpose was to do everything possible to preserve the mills that remained in operation.

With the formal organization in place, the Lewiston Development Corporation (LDC) sought the support of community organizations. According to the weekly Twin City Times newspaper, "the Lewiston Development Corporation (was) a private, non-profit corporation established through collaboration with the Junior Chamber of Commerce, (Lewiston) Chamber of Commerce, the Lewiston-Auburn Jaycees and L'Association des Vigilantes."[259]

The LDC and its partners had a common vision regarding the economic future of the community. The organization's efforts to leverage its influence and ingenuity, resulted in receiving the support of local banks to underwrite the construction of a building that was needed by prospective client Geiger Brothers of New Jersey. The LDCs first development venture was successful in raising the $200,000 needed for the building and in overseeing the construction of the project.

### Geiger Brothers Comes to Lewiston

Geiger opened for business in 1955 (and continues to operate at its original location in Lewiston).[260] Its genesis can be trace to former Lewiston Mayor Al Lessard inviting his old classmate, Ray Geiger, to Lewiston to consider moving his New Jersey based company[261] to Lewiston in 1954. At the time, the Geiger Brothers Publishing Company had been publishing the Farmer's Almanac for 137 years. Jere Clifford, one of the founders of the LDC, recounted that

> '(Lessard) was driving around to look at various parcels of land when he got a flat tire somewhere near the (Mt. Hope) cemetery. Ray got out to change the flat, looked around, and

> liked what he saw. It was farmland owned by Alphee Robitaille, and Geiger ultimately bought it. This company from New Jersey was moving its operation to Lewiston. That was a big deal.'[262]

When the news of Geiger's relocation to Lewiston "reached Wall Street... (Geiger) predicted to New York newsmen 'that Lewiston, and not the South, holds the key to the future for growing industry and business.'" Geiger went on to say that his prediction of success in Lewiston rivaled the predictions that his Farmer's Almanac made about the weather.[263] Geiger was a person who spoke with conviction. He was a Notre Dame graduate who joined his parents' firm in 1932, where he served as the Farmer's Almanac's editor for 60 years,[264] and became its president in 1951.[265]

When Geiger took over the company in 1951, "the company was in a serious (financial) slump." Geiger persevered and elected to search for "a more hospitable setting" for the company. When Geiger found his new Lewiston location, he and the LDC worked together to build a new 60,000 square foot building. Within six years, the company's newfound profitability allowed it to expand another 20,000 square feet. The success and the expansion allowed the company to increase its circulation from the 1960s annual output of 85,000 copies to "more than 6,000,000 copies by the early 1990s. As editor, Geiger tirelessly promoted the Almanac, giving by his estimate more than 18,000 interviews and traveling 5 million miles."[266]

Ray Geiger and his family were widely recognized for their commitment to Lewiston-Auburn. He served as a long-time member and chair of the Androscoggin Chamber of Commerce, chair of the local United Way campaign, and his company was frequently the top United Way fundraising business in the community. "In 1988, the Chamber created an award in honor of his dedication." The award recognizes local businesses that strongly commit themselves to the Chamber and the community.[267] Geiger Brothers epitomized the kind of business reflected in that award:

> Among the company's many well-known projects is the

Geiger/Montello Adopt-A-School Partnership, which was established in 1988 with the objective of raising the aspiration of every student at Montello Elementary School. 'It started with an art exhibit and Author's Night,' said Peter (Geiger). 'Over the years it has included dozens of initiatives and thousands of hours of Geiger staff time. Approximately, 60 percent of Geiger associates are involved in one form or another. Everything we do is a joint effort with staff and always with the student learner in mind.'[268]

When Ray Geiger died on April 1, 1994 at 83, his son Peter Geiger assumed the helm of editor for the Farmer's Almanac.[269] After 61 years in Lewiston, Peter's sibling and CEO Gene Geiger, announced in 2016 that the company was "recommitting" to Lewiston with a $12 million expansion that "would convert the old factory space into new offices...(and would) build a massive, 620-panel solar array, enough to generate more than 250,000 kilowatt-hours per year" and almost 90% of the energy load for the company.[270]

Boosted by the hearty industriousness of its workforce, Geiger's family business was reborn when a relationship between two friends led to the company's move from New Jersey to Lewiston-Auburn. Geiger Brothers' relocation represented the first in a wave of new businesses that helped L-As economy transition from textile and shoe production beginning in the mid-20th century. The project also proved to be the linchpin for the future success of the LDC that continues to play a critical development role in Lewiston.

Geiger's success has blossomed into a 65-year relationship between a company and community that exists in only a handful of municipalities in the United States. A new generation of Geiger's are now part of the company, and the people of Lewiston will continue to heed Ray Geiger's prophetic words about the city holding "the key to the future for growing industry and business." That key will always start with community engagement; the kind that Geiger Brothers have been embracing since 1955.

## The New Economic Development Wave

The Geiger project's success stimulated interest in other development projects in the area over the mid to late 1950s: the LDCs venture into building the Lewiston Industrial Park (1957); buying land, constructing a building, and leasing the property to the Raytheon Corporation (1959); constructing a 40,000 square building to house Paragon Glass in the Industrial park (1959)[271]; and other non-LDC projects, including the construction of the Central Maine Youth Center (1959) and the expansion of St. Mary's General Hospital (1958) all served new high-water marks for Lewiston's new effort to diversify its economy[272].

The late 1950s and early 1960s also made clear that transitioning from a mature yet declining textile-shoe manufacturing economy, to something less dependent on those established industries, would not go smoothly.

The first milestone event signaling dark economic clouds on the horizon was in 1960. The Maine Public Utilities Commission authorized the termination of passenger rail service into the city.[273] The decision to cease passenger rail operations appeared to serve notice that the Lewiston-Auburn area was no longer a passenger transportation priority for two of Maine's largest cities.

Passenger rail service was clearly declining nationally, but it remained the primary mode of transportation for most people in the L-A area who could not afford the higher priced air travel alternative. Many travelers turned to intercity-interstate bus carriers like Greyhound out of necessity, but soon discovered that buses did not offer the comfort nor the speed of rail. The 5-year-old high-speed interstate system was not yet fully developed and required the buses to use state roads and federal highways that added additional miles and stops for passengers. The federal interstate system would not be substantially completed until the mid-1970s.[274]

The rail announcement came in the same year that Continental Mill ceased its operations. In 1963, the Raytheon

Corporation closed its doors less than two years after its official opening in 1961. In 1962, the area's economic outlook would appear to improve with the announcement that Auburn's Dane-T-Bits Biscuit Company's plan to build "a unique mass production bakery" that would be "the most modern" facility of its kind in the eastern United States. They also hailed it "as the most significant development in the predominantly shoe-producing city in decades." In early 1963,[275] the facility opened its doors, but like the Raytheon Corporation, the promises it made to its host city fell short of expectations and it eventually closed in 1964.[276]

While the Lewiston Development Corporation worked to blaze a new economic strategy outside the city, Lewiston officials pressed forward to address the mill closings and job reductions through its newly formed "shell corporation" the Lewiston Community Enterprises, in 1964[277]. The entity's mission would focus on working with mill operators to assist them. That resulted in the group purchasing the financially troubled Bates and Hill Mill properties, and leasing the properties back to the owners for $1 while also allowing them to be relieved of their property tax obligations.[278] In 1977, the Bates Mill employees purchased the mill complex back, but according to Lucien Gosselin, who served as the LDC President from 1972 until 1974, the Hill Mill was not part of the employee buy-back which allowed the LDC to sell it outright. According to Gosselin, "the (city's) Hill Mill sale provided the first real opportunity to capitalize the LDC."[279]

Another economic investment that was beginning to impact commercial development in L-A was the completion of the new $75 million Maine Turnpike toll road in 1955.[280] The 60 MPH closed highway and its proximity in both cities was a significant asset to the new Geiger Brothers plant in Lewiston, and the tenants occupying the newly constructed Lewiston Industrial Park. Auburn was similarly well positioned with its municipal airport and industrial development locations within a mile of the turnpike.

Raytheon's departure in 1963 was a tremendous blow to the city's economic development momentum, but the city's dogged efforts to recruit a new tenant for the building proved successful in 1965. The RCA Corporation's purchase of the city property was a perfect fit for a building already designed to fabricate transistors and to employ 500 people.[281] This newest jewel in the city's economic development portfolio was special, but it also marked a major shift in how the city was now approaching its new economic strategy for job creation—by expanding its commercial business development focus outside of downtown Lewiston. Similarly in Auburn, what appeared to be a significant blow to Auburn's entry into the national cookie market resulted in General Electric's purchase and occupancy of the building abandoned by Dane-T-Bits. General Electric remains in that location to the time of this book's publication.

The economic development strategies were remarkably similar in both Lewiston and Auburn. The future of their mature industries was becoming bleaker by the year, and both cities had developable land that was in proximity to the new Maine Turnpike. In a new era of economic development with more dependence on trucking to accommodate shipping and receiving, city officials recognized that companies not only wanted sites to accommodate buildings—they also desired enough space for employee parking.

Most of the city's workforce was no longer walking to work, as young, post-war era families with automobiles and more income continued to move outside of the downtown to the newly developed residential areas in both cities. These largely single-family residential areas were becoming more desirable to a growing population of upwardly mobile families, and more attractive to retailers who saw opportunities to offer new amenities to customers including newer, larger stores with more selection and parking. For employers, they were now looking for new buildings to meet modern commercial needs, and to provide parking for the increasing number of employees who owned cars. There were efforts to save the aging and shrinking textile and shoe industries, but both Lewiston and Auburn were now focusing on new development opportunities outside of their in-town boundaries.[282]

## Aging Cities and New Federal Funding

As Lewiston continued to work on plans to transition out of their single-industry declining economy, the city was quickly aging relative to its municipal infrastructure, downtown commercial property, and housing stock. All of this contributed to its shrinking downtown population.[283] A review of the 1970 Census shows that the downtown was largely defined of Census tracts 201, 202, 203 and 204. The 1970 data shows that 76% of housing structures in those census tracts had three or more units (the significant majority were located within stick-built tenement structures), and 48% of the buildings had five or more units. Of the 7,617 downtown structures, 93%, or 7,288 of those tenement structures were built with three or more stories, with 76% of those buildings constructed in 1939 or earlier.[284]

In 1970, census data stated 2,860 people who lived downtown were still walking to work, almost exactly the same number as those who drove to work (3,007). When you added in the number of "passengers" that traveled to work in a car, that number increased the total number of people driving to their job to 4,441, 55% more than those who walked to work.[285] What was also notable in 1970 was the 8,081 females (44% of the workforce) now in the city's labor force,[286] indicative of a growing number of families that now had more two wage earners going to work (also possibly contributing to the number of people driving to work as the number of two-car families was also increasing—most of the homes in my parents neighborhood by 1972 were two-car families).

In the absence of adequate construction and building safety codes prior to 1960,[287] wages for many downtown owner-occupied tenement structures were so low that the owners were struggling to cover the cost of maintaining their buildings and still feeding their family. For many, the cost of owning a tenement property was outpacing the owner's wages (most were employed) and the rental income. A look at the median wages in 1970 provides some evidence of this income disparity. Lewiston's 1970 annual median family income was $8,065 (in real dollars).[288] That was 18% lower than the $9,870 for U.S families;[289] 9% lower than Auburn families, and 2% lower than Maine families.[290] The lower median family income may have been driven by the 42% of 18,390 [291] total eligible workers, or 7,723 total workers that continued to be employed in "manufacturing," a category impacted by lower paying textile and shoe manufacturing jobs in the 1960s.[292]

By the 1960s, the aging housing stock and blighted neighborhoods visibly needed redevelopment, or outright demolition. The city had undertaken efforts to reinvest in its downtown through the creation of the Lewiston Urban Renewal Authority (LURA) sometime around 1962,[293] with Auburn following suit.[294] Projects focused on the removal of blighted properties and the redevelopment of targeted areas of the city. The first extensive project involved detailing the scope of the work in the 12-acre,[295] 64-parcel, 47-owner[296] site[297] along Park Street using a $99,000 federally funded second phase to address "the planning and survey end of the program. Items include real estate appraisal, land reuse appraisal, marketability analysis, relocation plan."[298]

The LURA would be in existence until the late 1970s and numerous urban renewal initiatives would be developed during the Model Cities program years, part of Lyndon Johnson's "Great Society" initiative.

> The purposes(sic) of the (Model Cities) program (was) to rebuild or revitalize large slum and blighted areas; expand housing, jobs, and income opportunities; reduce dependence on welfare; improve educational facilities and programs; combat disease and ill health; reduce crime and delinquency; enhance recreational and cultural opportunities; establish better access between homes and jobs; and generally improve living conditions for the people who live in slum and blighted areas... The Department of Housing and Urban Development (HUD) selected 150 cities to participate in the program the District of Columbia, cities in 45 States, and a

city in Puerto Rico. In the spring of 1968, HUD awarded planning grants to 75 of these cities, which were generally referred to as first-round cities.[299]

In Maine, Portland was selected as a Model Cities funding recipient on November 16, 1967 and Lewiston was selected on September 6, 1968.[300]

According to former Lewiston Model Cities Executive Director Henry Bourgeois,

> it was a...five-year designation. (For) (e)ach year you were designated, we were designated two million dollars in discretionary money. But we were also designated a lot of other latitude to secure more federal money, and the rule about federal money is that you can't use federal money to match federal money. Most federal money that communities receive have to be matched locally, and if you're a(s) poor (of a) community as Lewiston is, ... you can't find the money locally, so Model Cities said, HUD said, that you could use Model Cities federal money to match federal money. So, the two million dollars a year leveraged another six or seven million dollars for housing and childcare and all kinds of programs like that... new housing, a lot of the housing was rehabbed. The (construction of the) multi purpose(sic) center was a Model Cities (project).[301]

My father, Guy Nadeau, bought his parents tenement/business building in 1969, located just several blocks away from City Hall. Like many commercial and tenement buildings in downtown Lewiston at that time, a number of properties had highly distressed exteriors and interiors with aging electrical and plumbing infrastructure. My father received a Model Cities loan to renovate the exterior of his newly purchased building with metal storm windows (to replace manually installed wood-framed storm windows used to cover the older "sash," single-pane windows), and aluminum siding to update the aging cedar clapboard exterior that had not been painted for what appeared to be decades. He also did a brick veneer facade on the first floor of the structure, which was not funded by Model Cities. This became a delicatessen (Friends Deli) in 1970, replacing his parents' business, Nadeau's Market, which had been in the family at that location since 1936.[302] Numerous downtown tenement owners pursued this kind of exterior investment (many buildings were owner-occupied in the late 1960s and into the 1970s). Certainly not everyone in the country was enamored with the program, but the investments made a visible difference in many Lewiston neighborhoods and for millions more around the country who "did benefit from it."[303]

In addition to the exterior improvement in many neighborhoods and the funding of new assets such as a school/community center (Lewiston Multi-Purpose Center), a new snorkel fire truck,[304] and partial funding for the new Central Fire Station,[305] the Model Cities federal funding programs also paid for new amenities in Kennedy Park (the city's largest downtown park) including an Olympic-sized swimming pool, wading pool, pool house, and basketball courts.[306] Lewiston also continued to pursue demolition in neighborhoods as part of their urban renewal plan to address blighted neighborhoods.

The most visible evidence of demolition activity in the 1960s and 1970s occurred in the downtown area bordering Park, Bates, Oak and Ash streets (part of the initiative that was launched by the LURA in 1962. Many properties were demolished; land was cleared for a new Park Street esplanade design; and a site was made available for a new central fire station that opened on August 23, 1973.[307] The 12-acre site also included a large parking area that was devoted to supporting parking for the downtown retailers that were already suffering a decline in their business as retail began its emigration out of downtown to the area's new strip malls and eventually a larger covered mall in Auburn. Former Mayor John Orestis[308] reflected on the federal funding impacts in Lewiston:

> The late sixties and early seventies for Lewiston were very banner years from a domestic (and)...federal

> domestic spending point of view. We used to shop the domestic programs catalogue, literally like we were going to WalMart(sic) and shopping for something. We'd look for programs that fit Lewiston and go after them. And I spent a lot of time back and forth to Washington both as city attorney and then as mayor sort of chasing these applications. And using (then Senator) Muskie's office as the pressure point to get some of these things done the best we could in a Republican administration, you know. But... we built a high school, a fire station, multi purpose(sic) center which is also an elementary school, a sewage treatment plant, hundreds of units of low income family and low income elderly housing.[309]

Most importantly, the Model City program was also a collaborative effort between the city and resident stakeholders. This was likely the first such program where both city officials and citizens worked together on city projects with this kind of funding and scale. Former Lewiston Model Cities Director Henry Bourgeois credited citizen participation as the reason for the program's success:

> I lived in the Model Cities neighborhood, the downtown area, and my first involvement was in getting the citizens organized and writing the proposal to get the money from the feds...(W)e had six committees, a committee for each topical area that we worked on. So there was a physical improvement committee, there was health and human services committee, and we had citizens running the committees. We had bureaucrats, state and mostly local government people on as well who were very committed people but the majority of the members were

> citizens...(a)nd the citizens kind of ran things. Our staff, we had twenty-five or six staff, managed the process and facilitated it and gave them information, but we really...put them forward to help them make decisions.³¹⁰

The 1960s and early 1970s heavily occupied both Lewiston and Auburn in urban renewal projects given the abundance of municipal domestic spending programs aimed at dealing with inner-city social and blight challenges. Changes occurred in the years of the Nixon and Ford Administrations that significantly reduced the Model Cities funding flow by some $7.7 million to Lewiston.³¹¹

By 1973, it was evident that the Nixon cuts were having a dramatic effect on Model Cities funding levels, particularly staff cuts to the Model Cities staff undertaken by Mayor Robert Clifford and his appointee Henry Bourgeois. Clifford understood that the federal funds were ending and directed Bourgeois to reduce staffing by ten percent each year. In 1971, the staff had "26 full-time and two part-time" staff on the Model Cities payroll. Bourgeois would have it reduced to 8 positions by the end of summer. Bourgeois was merely dealing with the reality of a new attitude to such programs in Washington. By the end of 1974, the program that had helped Lewiston with making the first significant investments in its downtown was over. This level of federal support for cities would not be seen again.³¹²

It became apparent to city officials, residents, and business owners like my family,³¹³ that Model Cities would not be the panacea to all of the city's housing and infrastructure challenges. The growing inventory of distressed downtown tenements continued to grow into the 1980s and 1990s and attracted investors looking for inexpensive opportunities to make short-term profits. An increasing number of individuals from outside Lewiston purchased many of these buildings at less than market rates. This real estate investment strategy succeeded through a combination of minimizing or not completing needed structural and utility repairs, neglecting general maintenance and upkeep, and delaying or avoiding compliance with city code requirements. The neglect produced a downtown filled with tenement structures that were blighting neighborhoods and threatening tenant safety.

Interestingly, many of these landlords would complain about the declining market values that were depressing rental prices but would also reject the notion that doing the necessary investment to make their buildings livable might attract tenants willing to pay higher rental fees. It was easier to just bleed a property and then abandon it once it became unprofitable. The result would often result in the LLC[314] owners (who were frequently not residents of the area) who could protect their personal finances while bankrupting their company, leaving their tenants and the city with the remnants of their neglect.

The aging and neglected housing stock and municipal infrastructure was also contributing to a declining resident population in the downtown census tracts.[315] A review of the 1970 data shows that 76% of housing structures had three or more units (tenements), and 48% of structures had five or more units. Of the 7,617 downtown structures, 93%, or 7,288 of the structures were 3+ unit tenement buildings with 76% having been constructed in 1939 or earlier.[316] The family business property owned by my grandparents, and later purchased by my parents, was built around the late 1800s and early 1900s, as were many others in that downtown neighborhood area. Many more were built before 1900.

The city increased its enforcement of building codes through the 1980s and 1990s, forcing many of the bad actors to sell or abandon properties that became unsalvageable. The ongoing deterioration of Lewiston's downtown tenements was recognized by the city as early as 1982 when Development Director Gore Flynn commented that "Lewiston's 80 to 90-year-old housing stock had led to problems with (code) enforcement and that many decrepit (tenement) buildings were now abandoned by owners when repairs became too expensive."[317]

The combination of taking action to enforce code violations with gentle persuasion, working agreements with owners to phase in improvements, as well as civil penalties and legal action for owners in violation, produced results through the 1990s into the new millennium. Hundreds of buildings would be demolished, burned in fires, or abandoned and sometimes repurchased and rehabilitated with federally funded programs that supported a combination of subsidized and/or market rate apartments (and in some cases, tenements with commercial space on the first floor).

Our family business that had been owned by my grandparents, where I spent the first year of my life, where my maternal grandmother lived for years, a building that had been in the family for decades, burned in a $1 million fire fought by "150 to 175" firefighters.[318] The conflagration on February 13, 1989 destroyed my father and mother's building and business, along with three other tenement properties. The fire also damaged five other buildings displacing some 55 people and forcing 16 families to require temporary shelter.[319]. The fire cut power to 2,100 electrical customers, temporarily closed two schools, and was considered one of the largest fires involving multiple apartment buildings in the city's history since the great New Auburn fire in 1933.[320]

My father, brother and I elected to rebuild the property with no city or federal assistance beginning in 1989, completing the project in 1990. The reconstruction of another tenement/commercial building on that same location also required that we purchase three other adjoining properties to meet new parking and building codes, the kind of building codes that would have greatly reduced or eliminated the significant destruction seen in our fire.

The combination of a poor economy, a regrettable partnership with two non-family members, and some poor decision making resulted in losing the property and new business only two years after the fire. To my knowledge, our new tenement/commercial property was the last three story (or more) tenement structure built in downtown Lewiston without any city, state, or federal assistance.

## THE CONJOINING

Lewiston's pursuit of a state university is a story that best represents the transition that helped to shape its trajectory over the last 70 years. How L-A College was supported, funded, and finally built in 1988 demonstrates how the influences of changing economies, demographics, governmental structures, partnership commitments, and a changing political climate all converged to create a collaborative community and political effort that took six years to realize.

The effort to establish a state college in Lewiston was not something that received much public discussion or press coverage prior to the 1980s. Lewiston's Bates College had a well-established reputation as one of the best liberal arts colleges in the country. As a Lewiston native and former Bates' student, I knew the history of our alumni including such notables as: former Secretary of State Ed Muskie, Bryant Gumbel (who was working for NBC Sports at that time), actor John Shea, and Robert Kennedy who completed his Navy V-12 officer training program[321] at Bates in 1944.

For many area residents, which included my parents, affordability was a significant barrier to entry at Bates College. I got accepted to Bates after finishing my Air Force tour of duty in the Pentagon in 1976. I worked with instructors like Professor Marcus Pohlmann, who believed I had earned his support for a Harry S. Truman Scholarship that I regrettably did not receive. After exhausting my savings and my G.I Bill [322] education allocation, my inability to secure additional financial assistance from Bates led to my departure from the college after only three semesters at the end of 1977.

That regrettable experience led me and many others in the area to believe that not having an affordable state university presence was unacceptable, particularly in the second-largest city in the state. There were campuses in much smaller municipalities like Gorham, Augusta, Farmington, Presque Isle, Fort Kent, and Machias. It was hard to understand why Lewiston or Auburn, two of the five largest cities in Maine, did not have a four-year state university college in a community whose demographics clearly demonstrated that a need existed.

Lewiston and Auburn's industrial history had taken its toll educationally and financially on numerous families in our community, many of them Francos. In 1980, the percentage of residents over the age of 25 not completing high school was 50.1% in Lewiston (down from 62.2% in 1970), and 36.3% in Auburn (down from 50.3% in 1970). The manufacturing industry (much of it textiles and shoes) had been employing fewer workers for decades. The trend continued into 1980 with 36.0% of workers in Lewiston (down from 42.1% in 1970) employed in manufacturing, along with 30.1% of Auburn workers (down from 39.1% in 1970). In 1979, measured against family incomes in the lowest 20% nationally, 26.5% of Lewiston "central city" households were in the lowest 20% of incomes, with 22.7% of Auburn's also fitting that profile. The overall percentage in the Lewiston-Auburn Metropolitan Statistical Area[323] was 24.1%.[324]

Mayor Paul Dionne, a lifelong resident with time away to attend college, and to defend his country in Vietnam, was first elected mayor in 1979.[325] He knew the history and the demographics of the city and understood the need for an affordable college education for area residents. The two cities had worked tirelessly with Representative Louis Jalbert back in the early 1960s to bring two and four-year post-secondary vocational programs to the area. Jalbert's success in resulted in the construction of the Central Maine Vocational Institute (now the Central Maine Community College) that was built in Auburn in 1964. Dionne believed a similar effort warranted his leadership in pursuing a University of Maine system college in Lewiston.

Lewiston officials also understood that achieving success in pursuing a state university campus in L-A would require a partnership with Auburn. Dionne and City Administrator Gosselin had a real understanding of the ability of both cities to coalesce around a significant need for their residents, and no one on the Lewiston side of the river ever believed that this college idea would be a success without Auburn. Lucien Gosselin had been connected to multiple joint city efforts, many of them with Auburn City Manager Chip Morrison, who had been hired in 1978.

According to Gosselin, who had been newly appointed as Lewiston's first City Administrator under the new 1980 city charter, the matter of seeking a university presence started in

1981 with a visit from the president of the University of Maine at Augusta to his City Hall office. The president "had stopped by... and talked about the fact... that (UMA was already) offering courses (in Auburn) and they needed more space and were looking for additional space in the Lewiston-Auburn area to offer more courses." Gosselin recollected that not long after that, the University of Southern Maine president also met with Gosselin to discuss similar space needs and the desire to offer more courses in Lewiston.[326]

Those meetings with the state university presidents prompted Gosselin to have a discussion with first-term mayor Paul Dionne about establishing a university in Lewiston. Gosselin recalled they were alone in the office one morning when he told Dionne, "'this is ridiculous. We're the second largest city in the state and we have no choice or (university) presence.'" He also said that there were "an assortment of courses being offered" but there was little being offered in the way of degree programs.[327]

Gosselin went on to say that the conversation about the college with Dionne had occurred shortly before the legislature's annual trip to the Quebec Winter Carnival in February 1982. Both Gosselin and Dionne knew that Governor Joseph Brennan would be attending, and Dionne would use the opportunity to broach the subject of a university presence in Lewiston with the governor at some point over the weekend.[328]

Dionne also confirmed that he believed that this first conversation with Gosselin[329] about a college in L-A may have occurred just after November 10, 1981, the day that the iconic 101-year-old Peck's department store announced it was closing its 4-story, 100,000 square foot store in downtown Lewiston.[330] Gosselin stated that the closing had nothing to do with the idea of a university in L-A,[331] but the Peck's building would play a significant role in a college proposal a year later.

Dionne and Governor Joseph Brennan met at the Quebec Winter Carnival in February 1982.[332] The governor knew Lewiston and its history. He also knew that Lewiston was still a Democratic stronghold. It was not the power it once enjoyed, but it remained a city that was historically important to anyone seeking to become governor. Brennan was intrigued with the idea of a state university campus in Lewiston. Brennan agreed to set up a meeting with the University of Maine System Chancellor

Patrick McCarthy that, according to Gosselin, was set up about a week or so after the Quebec Winter Carnival.[333]

The meeting with Chancellor McCarthy was not something the chancellor expected would happen. Those in attendance included Mayor Dionne, Gosselin, the vice-chancellor, and Dave Redmond who served as the chief of staff for Governor Brennan. The discussion with the Chancellor did not go well. "Chancellor Patrick McCarthy remember(ed) that first meeting." [334] McCarthy's recollection was that "'(t)he governor's office contacted us, and they asked us to come down and talk about (the Lewiston proposal),'" saying that he "'explained (to the Lewiston officials) that putting a campus in Lewiston was not a priority of the university's and would not be a foreseeable priority in the future.'"[335]

In Gosselin's opinion, McCarthy's assessment of the first meeting was not completely accurate. Gosselin shared that the meeting did not last for more than "five minutes" recalling that "Dave (Redmond) introduced the topic about the possibility of putting a university presence... in Lewiston-Auburn. About halfway through this whole conversation, the chancellor (interrupted) and said basically, 'look, I have seven campuses of the university (system) to deal with (and) I don't have any resources to build another university in Lewiston-Auburn'... (He) basically (said) that (if) the 'Irishman up there, Brennan... if he (wants) a university in Lewiston-Auburn, he (can) fund it.' And then chancellor and the vice-chancellor got up and left." Gosselin added that Redmond was so mad, he restated that this college was something that the governor wanted "whether (McCarthy) wants it or not."[336]

McCarthy's reaction was not completely unjustified. According to Douglas Rooks, the James Longley administration years of 1974-78 had not been kind to the university system budget. During his term, the relationship between Longley and the university had not been cordial. Longley "insisted on reducing funding to the fledgling seven-campus system, from which—by some estimates—it has never recovered."[337] McCarthy's reaction to the Lewiston proposal was disappointing but did not derail their enthusiasm for the idea. McCarthy noted the enthusiasm declaring that "'(t)he mayor and his people turned out to be very persistent."[338]

87

McCarthy was right. There was no shortage of persistence by the Lewiston officials. After the first meeting with McCarthy, other meetings followed, but the prospects for convincing the trustees to consider a new college in Lewiston did not improve. "Policy sub-governments, like the UMS Board of Trustees, are able to control the agenda in one of two ways. Either they can make the debate about policy issues unintelligible to outsiders and act as a barrier to broader participation in problem definition, or they can define the issues in ways that favor their interest.[339]The UMS Trustees did the latter."

Before the college was first discussed by Dionne and Gosselin, Dionne hired State Representative Greg Nadeau as a paid intern during the summer of 2001. Both Dionne and Gosselin understood the value of having Greg working in the mayor's office. Once Dave Redmond offered that the governor would be behind the city's efforts to bring a college to L-A, Greg was well positioned in Augusta to represent not only his constituents, but also the mayor's office. Nadeau assembled the support needed to work with the Lewiston legislative delegation and the Androscoggin County delegation [340] that was still a legislative force in 1982.

With Nadeau covering legislative outreach, Gosselin and the mayor could focus on handling the interactions with staff, the city council, the city of Auburn (largely through City Manager Charles "Chip" Morrison and Mayor Peter Whitmore who also pledged his support for the project), the LDC, and any other city departments, agencies, or constituents that required monitoring, support, and assistance. Nadeau and other Lewiston legislators like Paul Gauvreau could also handle direct interactions with the governor and his staff, Speaker of the House John Martin, and the legislative leadership.

Internally at City Hall, things were not making progress with the chancellor, and the system trustees, who remained concerned about another campus diluting UMS funding. In 1982, the city decided it needed to act on the vacant Peck's property, as well as another vacant and occupied property that Peck had on the market. Controlling those properties would allow the city to put together a schematic plan to provide a visual image of what a new college in Lewiston might look like. It would help to billboard how intensely interested the city was in this college project.

The Pecks' properties included buildings and land behind the department store, along with buildings and a large parking lot across the street that once housed the J.C. Penney and Sears department stores. The city had its sights set on not only trying to obtain control of the old Peck's department store as a possible site for the college, but it was also looking to preserve the Sears and J.C. Penney properties across the street that were leasing space to the state's Department of Health and Human Services. In November 1982, the city met with Brennan to present him a schematic proposal for all Peck properties, a kind of "urban campus"[341] that highlighted the value of these multiple parcels and buildings in the city's pursuit of a "state office and university complex in Lewiston."[342]

The Lewiston Development Corporation then demonstrated their commitment to the college project for the UMS trustees. The LDC paid $75,000 in December 1982 to secure an option on the Peck's building, and all buildings and land that were owned by B. Peck Real Estate Company run by President Sumner Peck.[343] The pieces were now in place for Dionne, Gosselin, Gauvreau and Nadeau to move forward with a location and a governor that was in locating a state university and state office complex in their community.

Exactly what kind of college it would become was still conceptual. Given the city's need for more technological training in a changing economy, the very first conceptual idea for a college was for an "electrical engineering school" that served as "the seed of a notion (for) a university." [344]Everyone knew that regardless of what they thought the university might become, it was the UMS trustees who would have the final say regarding what they built and what the curriculum would look like.

Without a firm commitment in hand from UMS Chancellor Patrick E. McCarthy, Governor Brennan featured the proposal to build a state college in Lewiston's former Peck's department store in his 'State of the State' speech before the Maine Legislature on February 22, 1983. Brennan had proposed $2 million for the project that would be, according to Dionne, "applied, in all likelihood, to the operational budget of the school itself."[345]

Not everyone was enamored with the proposal. Many Republicans, who were in the minority both in the House and the Senate, did not believe that the Peck's site was adequate given the lack of expansion opportunities. Republican concerns also reflected McCarthy's anxiety regarding the project's impact on diluting funds that would otherwise go to the system's seven campuses. The opponents also defended their opposition by underscoring the fact that Lewiston already had Bates College within its borders, and that people only needed to drive 30 minutes to Augusta or Portland to attend a state university.[346]

Criticism also came from a Bangor Daily News editorial which labeled Brennan's proposal as a "pork barrel's mother lode…(handing) Lewiston an outright gift of $2 million for a new campus."[347] Concern was also expressed by Chancellor McCarthy who was uncertain about how the new college would affect one-third of the University of Maine Augusta's students at its Lewiston-Auburn Center[348] in Auburn, an aging facility that was operating out of an abandoned Catholic parochial school.

The Lewiston-Auburn Economic Growth Council's Executive Director John Turner invited GOP legislative leadership to Lewiston in early March to respond to the GOPs opposition to the college project that was broadcast statewide on March 2, 1983. Questions were again raised by the GOP regarding the impact of the Lewiston college on other UMS colleges in cities outside the area. The GOP also did not address the paltry 36% of Androscoggin County's high school graduates, made up mostly of L-A students, who attended a college as opposed to the much higher statewide average of 50%.[349]

GOP statements that other colleges in the area reduced the need for a campus in Lewiston left out critical details.[350] In fact, Bates College and Brunswick's Bowdoin College had tuition rates that were some of the most expensive in Maine for their four-year liberal arts/professional study college degrees. That reality did not stop the criticism, even from some Democrats. Arguments against L-A College also came from the Democratic Senate Education Committee Co-Chair Senator Kenneth Hayes, who was also a University of Maine professor in Orono. His opposition was likely rooted to Chancellor McCarthy's lack of support for the project, and his parochial constituent interests in Orono.

Besides what was going on politically, the economies of Lewiston, the state, and the nation were still slowly recovering from the 1981-82 recession. According to the Census, the

Lewiston unemployment rate in 1980 was 7.0%,[351] compared to Maine's rate of 7.6%[352] and the national rate of 7.9%.[353] According to the Bureau of Labor Statistics, "(t)he (U.S.) unemployment rate, already high by historical standards at the onset of the recession in mid-1981, reached 10.8 percent (in Lewiston) at the end of 1982, higher than at any time in post-World War II history,"[354] although the numbers in Maine were lower (8.4%).[355]

Going into 1983, jobs and the economy would improve slowly. Unemployment in Maine for the year had decreased slightly to 8.3% and continued to decline significantly through 1989 (dropping to 4.0%).[356] For those seeking funding for L-A College in the early 1980s, ongoing high rates of unemployment and commercial/residential borrowing were likely also affecting legislative funding decisions. Mortgage rate borrowing averaged 14.91% between 1980 and 1983.[357]

After weeks of negotiations between the city and the governor's staff, Dionne publicly released the city's $5.1 million Peck's building proposal for a college supporting 2,500 students on March 7, 1983. The state would provide an annual $2 million appropriation that would be contingent upon the city's contribution of $3.1 million to purchase and renovate the property for the first year. The state's $2 million commitment would then become annualized to help cover operating costs. Any remaining costs to acquire and renovate the college would be the city's obligation. All of this would be contingent upon UMS trustee approval.[358]

With the Lewiston City Council's support to fund up to $3.1 million for the college in hand, some of the challenges ahead were covered in the two local papers. Councilor James Begert pointed out during council discussions that a state college presence in the city demonstrated that "'there is a correlation... between low income in this area and our not keeping up with the rest of the state in terms of our higher education.'" Councilor Denis Latulippe supported the idea but wanted assurances that county towns would be asked to contribute to a college supporting the entire region's population. Dionne stated he would pursue county-wide funding.[359] On that same day, the city's evening paper painted a different story. While Auburn officials appeared receptive to the idea, area towns in the county were less "enthused".³⁶⁰

Councilor Paul Couture disagreed that Lewiston would have to subsidize the project. He based his objection on the perception that the state had not required other communities with state colleges to do the same. Representative Nadeau responded to Couture sharing that Speaker of the House John Martin had told him that Fort Kent had contributed some "land and buildings to establish the UMFK campus." ³⁶¹ In fact, the idea of local contributions to support state colleges was not new. According to Governor Brennan, there were several more communities that had made some sort of local "cash, land or building" contribution for the establishment of their local college that included: Farmington, Orono, Presque Isle, Gorham and Machias.³⁶²

Dionne met with the UMS trustees on March 28, 1983 to present the city's paper outlining its support for the college project. In response, the trustees directed Chancellor McCarthy to conduct a study on the feasibility of a college in L-A. The Chancellor remained pessimistic and unsupportive but agreed to the study. City officials were certain that the study would support the project while others believed that the trustees and McCarthy "felt the study would kill it." With trustee support to move forward, the Cambridge firm of Arthur D. Little, Inc. was hired to conduct the study.³⁶³

During the Little study, Brennan's state budget with funding for L-A college went before the state's Appropriations Committee in April 1983. Although Rep. Louis Jalbert sat on the committee as Lewiston's legislative representative and the ranking Democratic member on Appropriations, journalist Tom Robustelli reported for the first time on April 25, 1983 that Jalbert was opposing the project.³⁶⁴ According to the article, Mayor Dionne stated that he "'heard (Jalbert) was opposed to the project but would not elaborate on his reasons.'" Although there was no comment from Jalbert in the article, his opposition was confirmed again in another Robustelli article on May 2, 1983.³⁶⁵ Recognizing that Jalbert would not support the project or publicly clarify his opposition to the project, Dionne and other city officials moved forward to testify before the Appropriations Committee in April, and to urge them to support Lewiston's $2 million college request.

In the June 2nd Robustelli article in the Lewiston Journal and a June 3rd Lewiston Daily Sun McDonald article,[366] Lewiston Democratic Rep. James Handy from Lewiston, and Auburn Democratic Rep. John Michael, both members of the Androscoggin legislative delegation, stated that they did not oppose the college project but did express their discomfort with both the research and the choice of the Peck's location. This meant that there were now at least two Democratic legislators from Lewiston and Auburn opposing the project. The appearance of dissension in the ranks of the Androscoggin delegation from Lewiston-Auburn was not a positive development for the legislative funding effort.

The initial June 14th vote of the Democratically controlled Appropriations Committee deleted the funding for the college with Jalbert voting with the majority. Five Republicans, along with Democrats Jalbert and Rep. Lorraine Chonko of Topsham voted against the funding, with the remaining Democrats voting to support. Old Town's Rep. John Linsk, who supported the project, was not present for the vote. It was now a matter of record that Jalbert opposed the project, but he continued to offer no public explanation for his opposition.[367] Jalbert's resistance, and Representative Handy and Michael's public expressions of uneasiness with the Peck's site, may have interrupted the L-A legislative momentum for the project, but all was not lost. Appropriations would not vote on the final budget proposal until June 21st. This newest development against the college funding concerned supporters like Representative Greg Nadeau who was becoming the recognized legislative leader of the initiative.[368]

On June 21st, the Appropriations Committee voted to support the state budget to include the $2 million for the L-A college project. It was a six-five vote, six Democrats, including the key vote from Rep. Linsk voting to support, five Republicans voting not to support, and two Democrats electing to abstain from the final vote—Democrats Louis Jalbert and Lorraine Chonko.[369]

Jalbert continued to not immediately reveal his reason for abstaining, but it was possible that he did not want his legacy tainted as the champion of a post-secondary vocational college in Auburn. It would not reflect well on Jalbert if the Lewiston legislator had stopped a state university college for his city from surviving a committee vote and never make it to the House floor. The story may have been similar for Chonko, who likely knew that Jalbert would abstain and may have also chosen to avoid the 'stain' of being the person who torpedoed Lewiston's efforts at the committee level. The abstention option would create the most distance between these two Democrats who abstained and those on Appropriations who believed in the project and its location.

His abstention vote did not derail his opposition. After the Appropriation's vote, Jalbert publicly vowed to fight the college appropriation on the floor of the House[370] and would save the reason for his opposition as part of the floor fight.

Jalbert's announcement to stop the college project on the House floor, would be followed by his eventual revelation that his opposition to the Peck's as an unsuitable and too costly project. Those concerns would be repeated, before any public statement by Jalbert, by other legislators such as Rep. Susan Bell, a Republican from South Paris. She stated that while she opposed the project because of the possible excessive costs of a separate university campus and its location in the Peck's site, she recognized the legislature's need to provide a collegiate alternative in the area, noting the number of students that did not "complete high school" and went on to "higher education." Bell went on to say that "Republicans 'respected' that(sic) Lewiston commitment… 'but $5 million (to fund the entire project) is not very close to (the unconfirmed report of) $15 million and the long-term implication in terms of funding requirements was another concern.'"[371]

Jalbert's opposition may also have given rise to the comments that were shared with Auburn City Manager Chip Morrison one evening in the University of Maine Augusta's L-A Center in Auburn. Chip could clearly recollect the discussion that he had shared multiple times over the years. He remembered the conversation and the location but could not narrow down the specific date or who the individual was. He remembered that it was a "high-ranking university official."[372] In our interview, Morrison said:

> We were the only two people in the classroom… (The 'university official') said 'c'mon, let's talk about this,' and

> he said 'ya know, there's this big push to have a university presence in Lewiston-Auburn, and I think that what we have here is enough because the people of Lewiston-Auburn really don't want to go to college.³⁷³

The official's statement struck Morrison and shared in the interview that he "probably was kind in telling (the university official) he was wrong" adding that "he was wrong, he was badly wrong." The statement so offended Morrison that he added "it stuck with me a lot and I used it with university people because it was inappropriate."³⁷⁴ Morrison knew what the demographics of the community were relative to its population of non-high school graduates and the low number of people pursuing post-secondary education. He also knew how difficult it was for many who were financially unable to make the trip to Augusta or Portland to pursue degrees that were not available in Lewiston. At that time, the Auburn UMA center featured only two four-year degrees: one in business and the other in public administration.

In the end, Jalbert's concerns about the Peck's site drove his public arguments against the college on the House floor. His efforts behind an amendment that would have removed the $2 million in funding for the college came up short in the House of Representatives on June 22, 1983. The ranking Lewiston member on the Democratically controlled Appropriations Committee, and the longest serving Lewiston legislator and Democrat in the city's history, was the only Lewiston or Auburn legislator to support the amendment against funding the college. The amendment was defeated by a margin of only six votes. The full budget won the support of the Senate and the approval of the governor. Jalbert would now publicly state that he opposed the project because "the aging Peck's building (was) not a proper home for a university" given that an unidentified Lewiston building inspector had told him that repairs in the building had not occurred "for at least 15 years," ³⁷⁵ a comment that likely fueled the prior speculation about the project's excessive costs.

The close amendment vote also triggered the first public mention of ethnicity creeping into the discussion of Lewiston's mission to have the state-built college in its community. Democratic State Senator Paul Violette, from Aroostook County, which was populated with many Acadian Francos,[376] shared something that I was feeling at the time of the debate (not knowing anything about the statement made to Chip Morrison)—that there were lingering perceptions in the heavily Anglo, English-speaking Maine Legislature about the value of investing in higher education in places with large Franco populations (no state university campus was ever built in Biddeford or Waterville, historically both two of the largest Franco communities in Maine).

Violette spoke from the floor of the House during the funding debate, citing that "'there had been a number of actions unfavorable to Franco-Americans in Maine'" over the years "'(w)hen it comes to places in which French people live.'" He said that there was also "'an increasing attitude on the part of this Legislature against my people... There has been a feeling in the Franco-American community that they want to attend an institution in their own community'" and added that "Lewiston, as the state's second largest city, deserves the opportunity to provide higher education for the people in the community."[377]

What was not being discussed publicly was the effort by Lewiston native and Franco Louis Jalbert to seek recognition for himself regarding the college project that he ended up opposing for the rest of his life. What neither Jalbert nor anyone else had ever revealed publicly, is that he had contacted Gosselin and Dionne with his conditional offer of support for the project prior to his April 1983 acknowledgement to the Sun Journal that he would oppose the college funding.

According to Gosselin, shortly before Governor Brennan's state-of-the state speech in February 1983,

> Louis called me and made it very clear what he wanted. He wanted to be given credit (for the) Lewiston-Auburn project and wanted the governor, when the governor made the announcement at the state-of-the-state address, to acknowledge Louis' role in getting the college established (in Lewiston-Auburn). I said I couldn't do that, obviously, I couldn't tell the governor what to do... There were a few choice words from

> Louis... After his tirade, he sort of hung up on me."[378]

Gosselin informed Dionne of his call with Jalbert. According to Mayor Dionne, Jalbert also met with him (confirmed by both Gosselin[379] and Nadeau[380]) in the mayor's office at City Hall. The meeting occurred sometime before the June Appropriations Committee vote[381] to discuss the college project with Jalbert.[382] Dionne shared the following details about that meeting:

> We had coffee and donuts... at City Hall in the mayor's office... trying to enlist (Jalbert's) support for the project... It was at that point in time that he indicated to me that he would not be supporting the project... (and in exchange for his support) wanted the public credit (for the college).[383]

I asked Dionne what he meant by "public credit." Dionne said that he believed that "(Jalbert) wanted to at least share in the initiation of the college for Lewiston-Auburn... and wanted to be noted by me, and probably the city council, that he was one of the prime movers behind it all." Once Jalbert understood Dionne was not prepared to meet his demand, Dionne "asked him to leave" his office.[384]

Jalbert had received an enormous amount of public attention and admiration for his role in leading a years-long effort in the 1960s to establish a vocational college in Auburn, often referring to himself as "the father of vocational education in Maine," as noted in Chapter One of this book. Jalbert had been advised of the L-A college project along with the entire legislative delegation in advance of its public release in the February 1983 Brennan speech,[385] but had never been invited to be part of the Lewiston team leading the effort. Jalbert's desire for recognition in his call to Gosselin, and his meeting in Dionne's office, may or may not have been in response to not being invited into the process. What is certain is that the results of the Dionne meeting were followed by his opposition to the project.

The city's price for denying his request likely served as Jalbert's motivation to fight the project until the end of his career and beyond. Dionne did not disagree and felt that if the city had been "a little more amenable to his request, (Jalbert) might have supported it." Former U.S. Attorney Tom Delahanty II. may have said it best about Jalbert's reputation as Lewiston's hard-nosed politico: "'You didn't want him with you but you didn't want him against you, either.'"[386]

Whether Jalbert's decision to wage open warfare on the city was an instinctual reaction to the rejections of both Gosselin and Dionne is unknown, but it is possible his decision to fight the college's approval may have contributed to an organized effort by Lewiston Democratic leadership to support candidate John Aliberti's decision to run against Jalbert in the June 1984 primary. Aliberti was not only a supporter of the college. He was also a teacher and a supporter of higher education in Lewiston. Aliberti's candidacy resulted in ending 'Mr. Democrat's' career in the same year that residents would finally vote on the new L-A College.

**The College Vote**

Following the approval by the legislature and governor for the college's funding in June 1983, there were concerns from residents and some elected officials. Questions remained about what type of university and curriculum would be approved for Lewiston. In response to those concerns, former Treasurer and mayoral candidate Alfred Plourde sent a September 13, 1983 letter to Dionne and to the Council. He requested that the November 8, 1983 referendum be delayed another six months to allow the city time to analyze the Little study and the UMS trustees' recommendations.[387] Plourde's letter, and the resulting public and council reaction, convinced Mayor Dionne to visit the trustees in late September. He shared that although ideas had been publicly expressed regarding the type of institution desired by the city, in the end "(w)hat (the city was) concerned about is more professors, more classes, more educational opportunities."[388]

The Arthur D. Little study and recommendations were publicly released in October 1983. Though the study confirmed that there was a significant need for "college credit courses,"[389] it also "concluded that demand for courses" was "overwhelmingly for part-time classes" with "about half of the prospective students (favoring) business courses with about one in 10 opting for computer sciences."³⁹⁰ The report also rejected the idea of an independent college that would have resulted in an eighth campus in the university system. The study opted to assemble a sizeable group of university system leaders, trustees, and administrators to create a program for the new college that would also incorporate a significant amount of public input.³⁹¹

Although Dionne said in our interview that the Little study "could have been a lot more positive," Nadeau believed that the study's findings spoke to an important need for "part-time courses" that was ahead of its time.³⁹² Lewiston was filled with working married and single adults who would benefit immensely from a college institution offering a diverse college curriculum with degree opportunities. In the end, that was precisely the direction the program would take.

In response to concerns voiced by Alfred Plourde, and the recommendations of the Little study, the Lewiston City Council voted to postpone the scheduled November 1983 referendum. Dionne also had assembled a special sub-committee to oversee the college initiative to its conclusion. The group included: Dionne, Lucien Gosselin, Greg Nadeau, local attorney James B Longley, Jr. (who according to Gosselin, initially opposed the project as a UMS Trustee), ³⁹³ local businessperson Roger Michaud, and City Councilor Denis Latulippe.³⁹⁴ It now appeared that all was in place to settle the issue at the polls, but the vote would not occur until November 1984.

From the very beginning of 1984, all efforts regarding the college were invested in Chancellor McCarthy's committee efforts to put together a proposal for the university. On the city side, much of the effort from staff revolved around recruiting funding interest from the county and area towns and to work with trustees to select a site.

On July 9, 1984, the UMS Trustees approved the Franklin Pasture nine-acre site next to Lewiston High School. According to a report produced by UMS Vice Chancellor for Facilities Richard Eustis and his staff, the University of Southern Maine affiliated college would "meet the requirements of a curriculum that represents a planned balance between liberal arts and professional study." University of Southern Maine President Robert Woodbury stated that the college would be a "'unique'" facility and an "'institution more appropriate to the needs of the region and therefore be more useable by the region.'"[395]

Lewiston officials were not making progress attracting other towns or the county to contribute funding to the project, but Auburn remained steadfast in its support for a $1 million subsidy that it would bring to the voters on November 4, 1984, an election with an expected high turnout given that it would also be a presidential election year. On August 20, 1984, the Auburn City Council approved sending the $1 million bond question for the college to the voters.[396]

The strength of the relationships between Lewiston and Auburn was on full display. The college collaboration was not the only partnership initiative occupying the time of the elected officials and staffs of both cities. There was also the matter of very complex negotiations involving the two cities, Central Maine Power, and two hydro-electric dams that were being proposed by CMP on the Auburn side of the Androscoggin River, and by the city of Lewiston on the other side.[397]

What was noteworthy was just how challenging the college and dam initiatives were, and how both cities rose above politics and parochial self-interests to do what was best for the entire Lewiston-Auburn community. On December 3, 1984,[398] both cities agreed to the ground-breaking hydro-dam deal characterized as "the most complex hydro project in the United States." It would allow both cities to share in the revenues generated by Central Maine Power who would build and own the dam.[399]

Following the Auburn City Council vote to send the college initiative to the voters, the L-A college initiative received significant statewide news coverage. In Lewiston, given that Reagan was the consensus leader in the presidential national polls, the most discussed item on the ballot in November may have been the college. In local polling, The Lewiston Daily Sun reported their polling reflected "solid support" for the initiative but estimated the number of undecided voters to be somewhere between 25 and 35%,[400] a very high number so close to the election.

On November 6, 1984, the day of the referendum vote, the local paper reported that there was organized opposition to the college referendum. Lewiston Taxpayer Association was a five-year-old organization that had originally organized around a failed attempt for a property tax cap initiative in Lewiston. On November 3, 1984, they began running newspaper ads opposing the college funding plan. There were reports that Representative Louis Jalbert, who lost his bid for another term in the June 1984 primary, had paid for the ad. The group refuted the claim, but an unnamed Jalbert associate reported he was "exulted over the ads and claimed they were his idea." The ads suggested city leaders had deceived the public, and that costs for the proposal exceeded the university system's ability to support it.[401]

A margin of 1.2% of the total vote defeated the UML-A proposal in both cities. The spread between the 'yes' and 'no' votes in Auburn was 52 votes out of 11,372 total votes. In Lewiston, the difference was 303 votes out of 18,787 total votes. It was a heartbreaking loss for those that had worked on the project for almost two full years. What went unspoken from city leaders was that voters were misguided. They respected their right to not approve the project, but they also felt that many were simply misinformed about its benefits. The real question for those who still supported it was 'what now?'

Governor Brennan was not ready to walk away from the project. Re-elected for his second term, the governor returned to Lewiston on March 12, 1985, and spoke with both city councils at a joint meeting. He urged both councils to send the question back to voters, something that was not unusual for elected officials to try, following a result that was not in line with their position.[402] Privately, Representative Nadeau did not believe that this was a good idea,[403] particularly so soon after the first vote. Nadeau was not going to publicly oppose a governor that had remained supportive of the college project from the moment Paul Dionne approached him at the 1982 Quebec Winter Carnival.

Another referendum vote was approved for June 4, 1985. The referendum had 13,343 voters—56% fewer votes than those casts in November 1984. The initiative lost by 60% of the vote although turnout for a special election in June was larger than usual. It certainly felt to me and others that we had lost our chance for an affordable college for "liberal arts and professional study" within the L-A city limits.

## Final Approval

Behind the scenes, the project was still alive. Following Jalbert's primary defeat in June 1984, Nadeau assumed Jalbert's seat on Appropriations in January 1985.[404] joining Rep. John Lisnik who had cast the crucial Appropriations vote for the college in 1983; Republican Rep. Sue Bell who had cast a vote against the college but expressed support for the initiative in 1983; and Democrat Rep. Lorraine Chonko who had joined with Jalbert to abstain from voting and avoided supporting the project on the Appropriations Committee.

During 1985, Lewiston Mayor Alfred Plourde, Administrator Gosselin, and Auburn Mayor John Cleveland met with Governor Brennan to explore options about L-A college. They also met with long time Democrat, former candidate for governor, and UMS Trustee Severin Beliveau who confirmed his ongoing support, and Helen Greenwood who had published a paper identifying the "(f)our models through which educational opportunities could be increased in the Lewiston-Auburn area to Chancellor Patrick McCarthy." [405] Nadeau was chair of the Androscoggin County legislative delegation, and multiple meetings between Brennan, the delegation, and college committee officials from both cities were conducted to "find a way to finance the project" without asking for a local contribution.[406]

Momentum was building through 1986, and much of it had to do with the leadership of the core group that was on board through the last two college referendums: Brennan, Nadeau, Gosselin, Plourde, Morrison, Cleveland, and USM President Robert Woodbury, who would become UMS Chancellor in August 1986.[407] An April 1986 effort by Nadeau and the county delegation was initially successful at including $5.1 million into the upcoming UMS capital funding bond. The bond request also produced a legislative resolution "urging the UMS Board of Trustees to establish four-year baccalaureate degree programs in Lewiston-Auburn." [408] After multiple meetings and proposals, rather than wait for the bond referendum and leave the issue once again to the voters, newly appointed Chancellor Woodbury put a funding proposal into the system's biennium budget in

September 1986 to support "a modest four-year bachelor's level program in Lewiston/Auburn... drawing on the resources and efforts of several existing campuses."[409]

The effort to finally fund L-A college gained serious legislative momentum in 1987 when the Appropriations Committee, led by its only Lewiston committee member Representative Nadeau, and with the support of committee member Representative Chonko from Topsham, voted to insert $1.1 million per year through 1989 for the L-A college into the UMS Part II funding request as part of its preliminary state budget proposal on June 11, 1987.[410] It was the first time that a specific line-item for the Lewiston college had been introduced into the UMS budget without a requirement for local funding. According to Nadeau, whose role in the legislature was critical in moving the initiative forward, the arbiter who delivered the last crucial elements of the college's budget success was Maine Franco, Speaker of the House John Martin,[411] who was[412] also an instructor at the University of Maine Fort Kent[413].

The Appropriations Committee approved the budget with the $1.1 million for L-A College and forwarded Republican Governor John McKernan's budget legislature for the final vote. Nadeau stated that in the waning days leading up to the final House and Senate budget vote, a budget standoff occurred involving the college funding. Democrats wanted money for the college to come from the tourism budget, while Republicans demanded that the money that Democrats put into the college not be removed from tourism. There were some other minor items in the budget that needed resolution but addressing tourism and college funding represented one of the larger hurdles stopping the governor from signing the final budget.[414] The deal to get the budget and the final, irrevocable, funding for L-A college was nothing dramatic, but it has never been shared publicly. According to Nadeau:

> We had recently created DECD (Department of Economic and Community Development) with (Governor) McKernan, and McKernan and I were pretty proud of it (Nadeau would become the first House Chair of the new Joint

> Standing Committee on Housing and Economic Development in 1988 with DECD in its jurisdiction). So, now the Democrats are trying to cut (the budget funding)... out of tourism (and)... effectively, McKernan's holding Lewiston-Auburn college hostage to try to get his tourism money. So, John (Martin) went across the street (to the governor's official residence the Blaine House) to cut the deal to fix all that by basically caving on his insistence that we cut the tourism budget (by finding other cuts to preserve both items)... I told John that I will forever refer to (him) as the grandfather of Lewiston-Auburn college... I've always considered Paul Dionne the father.[415]

On June 18, 1987, the 'below-the-fold' headline in the inside Metro section of the Lewiston Daily Sun read "State Budget Includes $1.1 Million in UMLA Funding." The five-year effort to place a state university with baccalaureate programs in Lewiston-Auburn was finally successful, and this incredibly challenging, collaborative, emotional and important achievement could be found on page 13 of the local paper.[416] Later in the day, the Lewiston Evening Journal would place the college story in its rightful position above the fold on the front-page edition of the Lewiston Journal.[417]

The new Lewiston-Auburn College of the University of Southern Maine and the University of Maine at Augusta was in an existing Lewiston building that was large enough and well suited for a quick renovation that allowed it to be open in September 1988.

Through 1993,

> LAC (had) 1,443 individuals taking courses. Collectively, they... enrolled for 8,676 credit hours. Women constitute(d) 74% of enrollment. The average student (was) 30 years old. The LAC offer(ed) five baccalaureate degrees through USM and one from

UMA, and four associate degrees from UMA. In addition, the UMS Board of Trustees (had) recently approved a new degree offering of Master in Occupational Therapy(sic). Over 100 courses each semester (were) offered in such diverse topics as computer science, business, literature, art, philosophy, management, genetics, psychology, chemistry and sociology. The college (was) linked to the Community College of Maine's interactive television system.[418]

In 1991, I was an out-of-work Lewiston resident and became a student at the Augusta University of Maine campus, seeking to finish the undergraduate degree I had pursued when I first enrolled as a non-matriculated student at the University of Maryland in 1973. I attended approximately half of my classes in Augusta and the other half at L-A College. I received my degree in Public Administration in 1994. I was appointed as the Town Manager in Richmond, Maine in May 1994. My professor, mentor and friend Dr. John Nickerson at UMA offered me the opportunity to teach one of his courses and to become an adjunct instructor at L-A College in 2002 and 2004. The opportunity of teaching at L-A College provided me with the distinct pleasure of working with another adjunct instructor, Roland Roy, my former high school teacher who wrote my letter of recommendation to Bates College in 1976.

Most importantly, I would not have been presented the opportunity to work as Lewiston's Deputy City Administrator had it not been for the efforts of the many elected officials, city leaders, businesspeople and residents who believed in the importance of having a college in Lewiston-Auburn, and the importance of working together as a community. Without question, L-A college had a profound impact on my life. I am certain that thousands more feel the same way.

I was unable to locate any evidence that Louis Jalbert ever publicly commented on L-A College's funding approval in 1987 or its construction in 1988. Jalbert died in 1989.

# CHAPTER 3

# TURNING THE CORNER: 1990S – DECEMBER 2000

### THE "OTHER" REFUGEES

The April 5, 1999 meeting organized by Catholic Charities Maine (CCM) and the St. Mary's Regional Medical Center involved approximately 40 area people "with strong ties to the community and its businesses."[419] City Hall had not been given advance notice of the meeting's purpose. Except for Portland, the meeting involved a subject that had not been experienced by the significant majority of other cities or towns in Maine. The meeting's purpose was to discuss the plight of refugees around the world when Belgrade (at the time part of Yugoslavia) was "in flames," and what that might mean Lewiston.[420]

The discussion would also involve "how the Twin Cities (could) prepare to accept refugees."[421] CCM and hospital officials were not specifying that the refugees would necessarily come from the civil war in the Balkans but suggested that CCM begin the process of expanding refugee resettlements in the state, and specifically in Lewiston. As the state's second largest city, Lewiston would become only the second of Maine's 10 largest cities that would be designated as a refugee resettlement community. Attending the meeting was Portland Mayor Thomas Kane, who shared how their refugee history had been enriched by the cultural and ethnic diversity of those who resettled in Portland. Kane added Portland was "not saying (the city could not) do this anymore. (Portland's) goal (was) to bring as many people as possible" as it was "the right thing to do."[422]

Although the Lewiston meeting would involve resettlements that would fall under the newer refugee resettlement provisions of the 1980 Refugee Act, the reality was that refugees may have resettled in Maine as far back as 1891[423]. If they had come to Maine, most had likely taken up residence in Portland. Although refugees had been seeking American refuge as far back as the 19th century, the best data available for refugee resettlement in Maine and in Portland begins in 1975,[424] the year the U.S. was ending its participation in the Vietnam War.

> In March 1975, communist forces in South Vietnam and Cambodia strengthened their military efforts. This led to the rapid collapse of government forces and a sudden flow of hundreds of thousands of refugees, many of whom ultimately sought rescue and safe haven in the United States. Preparation began in March 1975 in South Vietnam to move refugees from northern provinces to other areas… U.S. evacuation of Americans and Vietnamese from Saigon began on April 15, and evacuation flights ended on April 30 when the American Embassy in Saigon closed. A few hours later the Republic of South Vietnam surrendered to Communist forces.[425]

On Sunday July 27, 1975, Alleghany Airlines flew three times between the Pennsylvania and Portland airports with 50 Vietnamese refugee passengers on each trip. "The only fanfare surrounding the (150) arrivals was the appearance of Gov. James B. Longley, hobbling on crutches because of a knee operation and greeting the Vietnamese" at the Portland airport.[426] The refugee arrivals were organized by the Maine Office of Economic Opportunity (OEO)[427], the state government office that was effectively creating the state's very first organized refugee resettlement program. OEO officials traveled to one of several

U.S. refugee staging sites in Indiantown Gap, Pennsylvania, to interview refugees "about Maine and what opportunities for a new life might be possible in the Pine Tree State." [428] The interview and screening process assessed the "job skills (that) matched with available positions in Maine."[429]

Upon their arrival, the state provided the refugees temporary quarters at St. Joseph's College in Standish, Maine, who were assisting the refugee relocation following "reports indicating many Americans did not want the refugees brought to the United States." A "local deputy sheriff was stationed" on campus to screen people coming onto the campus as a precautionary security measure. He reported that threats against the refugees had not been received by his office, "but there were some questions about job displacement."[430] Expressing some of that concern regarding jobs was Congressman David Emery and other Maine employees, but the OEO assured the public that they had taken steps not to endanger anyone's employment. The state's screening process had revealed that many of the Vietnamese they interviewed were "middle class and educated."[431]

Maine confirmed that the resettlement was viewed as an opportunity to bring individuals into the state that could contribute needed skills to the state's worker pool. The OEOs Assistant Director Nancy Kenniston reported that "Bath Iron Works had openings for several special pipefitters, but the jobs were not being filled by Maine workers because of the complex skills involved." A Congressional Report stated that "more than 43 percent of (refugee) heads of households were previously in medical, professional, technical, managerial, clerical, or sales occupations" and that "75 percent of all (refugee) heads of households had completed at least a secondary education."[432]

Multiple state agencies were also involved with the new refugee population. In addition to the OEO, the state's Department of Education and Cultural Services, Department of Employment and Securities, and the Department of Health and Welfare would work with organizations like the Portland based Peoples' Regional Opportunity Program [433] and the Roman Catholic Diocese of Portland.

The $405.3 million in funding for the Indochinese resettlement was being overseen by the President's Special Interagency Task Force for Indochina [434] as part of the resettlement process driven by the Indochina Migration and Refugee Assistance Act of 1975, enacted on May 23, 1975.[435] "$100 million (from the $405.3 million in funding) was appropriated to the Department of Health, Education, and Welfare to provide cash and medical assistance, educational activities, and public health services to refugees."[436]

Over much of the long history of refugee resettlement in the U.S., volunteer agencies (VOLAGS) "worked primarily through their own resources"[437] around the United States. VOLAGS largely funded and managed refugee resettlement reception and placement services going back to the early 1960s.

> With the arrival of about 600,000 Cuban refugees during the 1960s and early 1970s, the U.S. provided grants to VOLAGs to assist them in their resettlement efforts. During the early 1970s, the Government contracted with VOLAGs to resettle refugees. In 1975, with the sudden influx of Indochinese refugees (and newly appropriated resettlement funds to handle the crisis), the Government again turned to VOLAGs. Their expertise and experience were needed, since the United States had never before experienced so many refugee arrivals in so short a time.[438]

The first Maine refugee resettlements would not be a VOLAG-driven process initially, but one where the State of Maine became the lead organization receiving the resettlement funding, coordinating the arrivals and placements, and paying all costs associated with the OEO program to assist the 'new Mainers.'[439] Maine was one of five states along with Oklahoma, Washington, New Mexico, and Iowa that opted to take on the primary agency responsibility for a program that they all viewed as an economic development opportunity for the state. The U.S. Department of State negotiated contracts with the states (similar to those contracted with the VOLAGS) that would provide $500 in funding for each individual refugee,[440] in addition to paying for all associated state funded costs including: Medicaid, welfare, bilingual or vocational training, and public health.[441]

It all changed when the Bangor Daily News reported on August 6, 1975, that OEO Director Timothy Wilson was curtailing the plan to bring in another 150 refugees scheduled to arrive on Saturday, August 9th "because of sponsorship and employment difficulties." The program recognized that family "sponsors were not as numerous as first believed." What appeared to be driving the apprehension of many sponsors was the belief that "orphaned children" would be involved in the resettlement, and that this had also occurred elsewhere in the country. Wilson also said that he believed that the "problems (could) be ironed out" for the remaining 150 refugees,[442] but that was not to be the case in 1975.

In a congressional report, the Maine refugee data showed that the Maine Division of Community Service (merged with the OEO in September 1975) had resettled 167 Vietnamese refugees in Maine by December 20, 1976. Other Maine agencies had settled an additional 209 Vietnamese refugees. [443] "As of December 19, 1975, other state government lead resettlement efforts (line those by the OEO) helped 4,663 refugees to resettle in the United States."[444]

Although Maine's OEO office had failed in its goal to resettle 300 refugees, that goal was exceeded by an additional 76 refugees through the work of what was the largest VOLAG in the country, the U.S. Catholic Conference (later to become the U.S. Conference of Catholic Bishops) and its affiliates including Maine's (Portland Roman Catholic) Diocesan Bureau of Human Relations Services (that would later become Catholic Charities Maine). USCC resettled 60,000 Vietnamese around the country between 1975 and 1976, more than any other VOLAG in the country.[445]

## The Chinese of the Eastern States

Catholic Charities Maine's refugee program representative Sandy Hollett came to Lewiston on August 12, 1999 to share that "sooner or later, refugees will be coming to Lewiston." Hollett believed that the advance work done in the city was progressing and that it was "close to being ready" for its first refugees. Hollett added that once the community told CCM it was ready, then it would likely take action to resettle a refugee family in Lewiston.[446]

Mayor Kaileigh Tara, who was also a St. Mary's Regional Medical Center employee, shared that people were not worried about refugee arrivals, but were focusing their concerns on how the arrivals would impact property taxes. Something Tara acknowledged was as a legitimate concern. The group that had been assembled by St. Mary's to assist CCM with any future resettlement, listened to Victoria Mares Hershey who worked with Portland refugees as an employee of the city's police department. Hershey shared that very often, a refugee's first public encounter upon arrival is with a police officer. Given the trauma many refugees have experienced, Hershey believed that officer training was needed and that it must be provided by local police departments. She also suggested that city police departments "should pay for classes just like they pay for computers and weapons."[447]

Lewiston Housing Authority Commissioner Peter Grenier was in attendance as a "concerned taxpayer." He responded to Hershey saying that he had "'no problems with refugees coming to Lewiston." but he believed that problems would occur if his "property taxes are going to go up to support" the refugees. Grenier added he thought CCM was "out of line to say our doors are open to anyone" arriving in the city who would not be self-sufficient upon arrival.[448]

What Grenier was saying was not an uncommon response to refugee resettlement, particularly in smaller cities and towns that had never experienced becoming a host community. CCM and St. Mary's were working to ensure that the necessary public outreach was done with the agencies and organizations who would likely be involved with the refugees once they arrived. It was likely that both CCM and St. Mary's also knew that historically, some level of anxiety about refugee employment, welfare, and financial impacts on communities had been expressed in Portland, and by many U.S. communities throughout immigration history.

A similar kind of public anxiety was on full display in the first significant piece of federal immigrant legislation involving ethnicity-based quota restrictions through the 1882 U.S. Chinese Exclusion Act.[449] This federal law "marked the beginning of the U.S. government's embrace of restrictive immigration policies and highlighted the different treatment immigrants received depending on their race and nationality."⁴⁵⁰ This law would also become a concern to Franco Americans.

Before 1882, immigrant movement into the United States was mostly unrestricted, a policy supported by Americans during that period. When California attempted to pass restrictions targeting Chinese immigrants following the Civil War, the U.S. Supreme Court in 1875 upheld a California U.S. circuit court opinion in Chy Lung V. Freeman declaring those restrictions unconstitutional "on the grounds that Congress had exclusive power to regulate foreign commerce and immigration."⁴⁵¹ This decision also corresponded with a downturn in the California economy following the decline of the gold rush from 1848 to 1855. Good-paying jobs for Californians were scarce, but not for immigrant Chinese who were willing to work jobs for longer hours and less pay. The railroads also recognized the affordability and willingness of the Chinese to help them build the railroad systems of the west. ⁴⁵² Although many residents saw the willingness of the Chinese to work for less pay as a threat to their economic well-being, some argued that

> it was by the application of Chinese "cheap labor" to the building of railroads, the reclamation of swamp-lands(sic), to mining, fruit-culture, and manufacturing, that an immense vista of employment was opened up for Caucasians, and that millions (were) now are enabled to live in comfort and luxury where formerly adventurers and desperadoes disputed with wild beasts and wilder men for the possession of the land. Even when the Chinaman's work is menial (and he does it because he must live, and is too honest to steal and too proud to go the almshouse), he is employed because of the scarcity of such laborers... You may as well run down(sic) machinery as to sneer at Chinese cheap labor. Machines live on nothing at all; they

have displaced millions of laborers; why not do away with machines?[453]

The "contributions of persons of Chinese descent in the agriculture, mining, manufacturing, construction, fishing, and canning industries were critical to establishing the foundations for economic growth in the Nation, particularly in the western United States,"[454] made no difference to many American natives with an immigrant family history. The Chinese were confronted with racism and violent assaults that included "attacks on Chinese immigrants in Rock Springs, San Francisco, Tacoma, and Los Angeles...(and) the 1887 Snake River Massacre in Oregon, at which 31 Chinese miners were killed."[455]

The first public mention of the connection between the Chinese and the Franco Americans living in the Northeast may have occurred in an article published by the New York Times on May 1, 1881, titled "The Chinese of the Eastern States[456]." The article involved a report in an annual document published by the "Massachusetts Bureau of Statistics of(sic) Labor" that included "a variety of investigation" that included commentary submitted by Carroll D. Wright.[457] Wright reported on "the results of extended inquiries into the expediency of a uniform adoption of ten hours as a day's work in the manufacturing establishments in the East."[458]

In short, the New York Times stated that Wright believed that limiting workdays to 10 hours would not impact product quality while also "materially benefit(ting)" the "physical, mental and moral condition" of employees who were currently working 12 to 14 hours or more a day. This proposal was made more complicated by the "French Canadians (who) worked for lower wages, and sometimes were used as strike-breakers. They were blamed for keeping wages low and for resisting naturalization."[459]

Wright reportedly also believed that because the Francos were "docile and indefatigably industrious, working any number of hours, and living on a beggarly pittance," that they were negatively impacting the mental and physical well-being of those not willing to do the same work for the low wages being paid out by the industry owners. According to the Times, Wright's opinion that "the Canadian French are the Chinese of the Eastern States" was attributable to the fact that, unlike the Chinese, the Francos were "ignorant and unenterprising, subservient to the most bigoted class of Catholic priests... (and chose) to live as meanly as possible, and ultimately return to Canada with their gains."[460]

It was easy to understand the Francos reaction to the New York Times 1981 article. "The comparison with the Chinese, when one understands the very unfavorable view that North Americans had of (the Chinese) at the time, greatly offended leaders of the French-Canadian community."[461] The Francos were not only offended; they became greatly concerned with the passage of the 1882 Chinese Exclusion Act. They had reason to be. The Chinese Act "prohibited skilled and unskilled Chinese laborers from entering the United States for 10 years... was the first Federal law that excluded a single group of people on the basis of race; and... required certain Chinese laborers already legally present in the United States who later wished to reenter to obtain 'certificates of return', an unprecedented requirement that applied only to Chinese residents."[462] It appeared to French Canadians as though a case was being made to make them the next target of an anti-immigrant movement growing across the U.S.

Although no equivalent anti-French Canadian immigration legislation was ever approved by the U.S. Congress, the anti-immigration movement against the Catholic French Canadians continued, as discussed in Chapter One of this book. The Know-Nothings, the KKK, English-only legislation, and the resulting discrimination and ethnic stereotyping of the Franco Americans continued well into the 1950s and 1960s. I would argue that Francos were still the target of the unspoken residual attitudes about Francos into the 1980s. In Chapter Two of this book, people like Van Buren's Senator Paul Violette voiced his concern about this 'unspoken residual' discrimination against Maine Francos from the floor of the legislature in 1983 He accused some legislators of their ongoing discriminatory attitudes towards Francos as the basis for their supporting a budget amendment deleting funding for Lewiston's college, a measure that failed to pass by only 6 votes.

Although Senator Violette's concerns about Franco discrimination may now feel to some like a thing of the distant past, the idea that some people may not approve of 'outsider' immigrants because of the impact they may have on jobs, or the local and/or state budget, has been part of the American immigrant discussion (and the 'unspoken residual' attitudes) for over 135 years. Recent history has shown us that arguments opposing immigration, particularly those about protecting "American" jobs, continue to this day.

## The Togolese

Catholic Charities Maine's Director of Refugee and Immigration Services Matt Ward and Director of Operations Sandy Hollett met Lewiston city councilors and school committee members from both cities to discuss refugee resettlements on December 20, 1999.. For the first time publicly, CCM announced that the refugees coming to Lewiston would not be Kosovo refugees that had been the focus of much news coverage over the previous year, but a group of refugees from Togo.[463] According to CCM, the "refugees from the West African nation of Togo" would likely be arriving sometime in January 2000. Ward was unable to confirm how many of these first resettled refugees would be arriving.[464]

Ward reported that there were "18 million refugees," and that "(f)ederal law require(d) each state to take some refugees," and that the United States typically resettled about 90,000 refugees per year with Maine accepting approximately "200 and 250 (refugees) a year."[465] A review of the ORR and U.S Census data between 1983-2000 reveals that all fifty states (in addition to the District of Columbia) did in fact participate in the resettlement program at that time. During that 1983-2000 period, Wyoming's resettlement of only 155 refugees and West Virginia's 387 refugees ranked them at the bottom based on per capita resettlements (0.0314 and 0.0214 respectively). With a per capita ratio of 0.3361, Maine's ranking of 35th was similar to Hawaii, New Mexico and Kentucky. It should also be noted that North Dakota, a state with a population half the size of Maine, had resettled more refugees in total than Maine (5,592 versus 4,285) and had a per capita ratio that was 259% more than Maine's (0.8708 versus 0.3361).[466]

CCM went on to say during the meeting that the Togolese[467] were "good fits" as their primary language was French. CCM also stated that although the U.S. resettlement program did not require the city's approval, they believed that the preparation work they had done for almost a full year made them believe that they "'were at the point'" where they believed their organization and the community had achieved that goal. Lewiston Housing Commissioner Grenier was also in attendance at the December 20th meeting and restated his concerns about the fiscal impacts on the city. The Lewiston resident did not think that CCM had been "'talking to the same people'" he had been in contact with, and that he didn't "'know of one person in the general public'" who supported the resettlement. The commissioner added "'(m)y objection is not having immigrants come to town,'" his objection was that he needed to "'foot the bill'" as a taxpayer.[468]

CCM went on to say that the U.S. resettlement program, under the supervision of CCM, would provide the necessary programs and services all paid for by the federal government for "up to eight months" and if the refugees are financially eligible, they would also qualify for "food stamps and Medicaid." Ward also said that it was his experience that "92 percent" of the refugees that are resettled are employed and economically self-sufficient "within the first 90 days." Several other attendants spoke in support of the program including Mayor Tara, Lewiston City Council James Carignan, and Auburn School Committee member Ross Bartlett. Their comments ranged from how refugees would make the city more culturally diverse and "alive," to defending the right of refugees to reside in the two cities, or anywhere else in the country, as a community could not stop a refugee or any person from residing in a community for fear that they "might increase the budget."[469]

The city held one additional January 2000 public meeting in advance of the Togolese resettlements in the basement of a Catholic church in Lewiston with approximately 45 people in attendance. "No one in the basement meeting… spoke against the resettlement plan. To the contrary, they wanted to know how to make their new neighbors feel more welcome."[470] Representing Bates College staff was anthropology Professor Elizabeth Eames, who spoke to the differences between the new African refugees and Americans. Eames pointed out that one difference was "that

Africans focus on duties to the group. Americans stress individual rights." Bates college students from Senegal and Gabon shared that the differences should be celebrated and reminded attendees that people back in Africa "have their own misconceptions of America." They added that though the Togolese may bring "different perspectives, 'we have common values with them.'"[471]

In the February 29, 2000 Sun Journal, an article inside the "City" section titled "Spreading the Word," reported about the public-school system's struggles with teaching English to the 27 students who spoke seven different languages. The school department's "elementary director said the two newest students are refugees from Togo" who were high school level students. This article appeared to be the first public report confirming the Togolese arrival in Lewiston.[472]

There had been enough coverage of the Togolese arrivals by the Sun Journal to attract a Maryland based anti-immigration group on March 23, 2000 to issue the city's first public statement regarding the resettlements. The "United Fascist Union" reportedly had a membership of 22 people. Someone from the Bangor area chapter sent the Sun Journal article to the group's national director, who responded with a letter to the SJ Editor. In the letter, the director wrote that "'(t)here's too much ethnic diversity in this bloody country as is.'" He also said that they accepted "'blacks... Jews, Asians, homosexuals, almost anybody but white racists,'" referring to them as "'garbage.'" Although he claimed that the organization rejected racism and white supremacy, he did state, "that the United States was never supposed to be a 'melting pot' of ethnicities, (and) that it was created by English and German settlers."[473] What he failed to mention was that the settlers from those two countries were overwhelmingly white and Protestant.

There is little record of any other anti-immigrant group activity in Lewiston during the remainder of 2000. The plans for the Togolese resettlement continued without any other reported incidents. Another Sun Journal article would appear on November 21, 2000 with CCM's Matt Ward confirming that four families had been resettled in Lewiston since January-February 2000, and that every able bodied adult member of those families "found a job within four months of moving in." Ward confirmed that more Togolese families would arrive during the year but would not confirm how many more families would be resettled.[474] Lewiston was now on its way to becoming a government approved resettlement community. The city's refugee resettlement story would add another chapter in 2001, almost exactly a year after the first Togolese refugees were resettled in Lewiston. The 2001 refugees would also trigger more discussion about refugees, immigration, race, religion, and diversity not only locally, but at the national and international level.

## Turning Point

While Lewiston grappled with its newly assigned designation as a refugee resettlement community in 2000, Lewiston was also dealing with other changes that it had not experienced for decades: success, transformation, recognition and a good economy. Countless articles had been written describing Lewiston as an "old mill town" but never referred to Auburn as the "old shoe town." Unlike Lewiston, Auburn had a noticeable absence of any old shoe manufacturing buildings in its city center, the product of aging and urban renewal.

The "old mill town" description of Lewiston was obviously influenced by the continued presence of these mill complexes that dominated its often photographed eastern skyline when entering the city from Auburn. They included Bates Mill, Hill Mill, Androscoggin Mill, Continental Mill, and the remaining remnants of the W.S. Libbey and Cowan Mills next to Great Falls. The properties housed some 3 to 4 million square feet, with approximately half of it occupied with any number of small companies. The reality was that large-scale industrial manufacturing activity in those buildings had long since passed, with Bates Manufacturing as the last holdout, and operating its equipment[475] with less than 100 employees.

The town was in transition and so was its economy and its urban landscape. I wanted to be a part of it, and I would start the year by visiting with Lewiston Assistant City Manager Peter Crichton early in January 1999. Peter was someone I got to know during my tenure on the Lewiston Finance Committee from 1989-1994, and through my position as Town Manager in Richmond, Maine from 1994-1999.

I was blessed with the opportunity to be appointed as Richmond's town manager. The Board of Selectmen took a chance on someone who had no prior experience managing a municipality, and it was a wonderful opportunity to work in my new profession. It also enabled my wife and I to live in a community we immediately loved. This town of about 3,000 people had its own village area with a large grocery store, convenience store, hardware store, florist, restaurant, electricians, plumbers, contractors, other small businesses, and a great town park on the Kennebec River where most of the locals would moor their boats. Our part of the river was tidal, allowing boat owners' direct access to the Atlantic, which was only 25 miles downriver.

It was also the town of the last remaining Etonic shoe company in the U.S. making high-end golf shoes by hand. Etonic eventually started phasing out operations and closed around 1998. The town also had its own K-12 municipal school system, something very uncommon in a state where most communities our size were part of a larger 'union' or 'SAD' (school administrative district). The town also had a public works department, police department, and 'volunteer' fire department where all firefighters were part-time per diem paid employees. It also had its own water and sewer district, also very unusual for a town of its size.

Most unique of all in this picturesque town by the Kennebec River, was its Russian heritage and community. According to the 2016 Richmond Comprehensive Plan (draft),

> Richmond was once the center of the largest Slavic-speaking settlement in the United States. People of Ukrainian, Russian, and Polish heritage immigrated to the United States during World War II to settle along the Kennebec Valley. In the 1950s and 1960s, there was also a large influx of White Russian émigrés who earlier fled the Bolshevik Revolution of 1917, and eventually came to Richmond both from Europe and from major US cities like New York. Many of these settlers were retirees, and their families often chose not to remain there. For this reason, the Richmond White Russian community has now largely disappeared. One of the churches that they built, the Russian Orthodox Church of St. Alexander Nevsky, continues to function to this day.[476]

As much as I loved working and living in Richmond, I was intent on finding out more about my hometown's job opening. During my visit with Crichton, he and I went to lunch at a small Italian restaurant around the corner from Lewiston City Hall. He was leaving his job to become the County Administrator for Cumberland County, the county with the largest city in the state (Portland), and the county with the largest budget and population in the state. I asked Peter if he believed that I might make a suitable candidate. Although I had only been in the public administration profession for five years, Peter believed that my experience in Richmond, and the fact that I was a Lewiston native, knew many residents, elected officials, people working for the city, served on the city's Finance Committee, and interned at City Hall in 1991 while in college, would all enhance my candidacy.

Working for a town only 30 minutes from my hometown was also helpful. The proximity to Lewiston allowed me to stay connected with my family and with what was going on in the community. Even from Richmond, I could see the progress being made in Lewiston on my frequent trips to the city. I would inevitably have with Lewiston officials like Peter and others through the network of committees, seminars, and other activities that typically filled a town manager's calendar. I could not have been better prepared for an interview.

Peter's insight was invaluable. We both returned from lunch and I immediately went into the City Administrator's office with Peter and turned in my application to the city administrator's assistant Dottie Perham-Whittier. I interviewed for the position in March and was presented the offer to be hired the next day. This was all happening during a time when someone in my family was seriously ill and would remain in the hospital for another seven months. It was all a blessing, and I was fortunate that I would be working with City Administrator Robert "Bob" Mulready who I already knew through my position on the Finance Committee, and as the father of one of my son's football teammates at Lewiston Middle School. Bob had much to do with my hiring as he had the final say on who would be selected. Both my wife and I will be forever indebted to Bob who passed away April 5, 2020.

## 1999

Down East Magazine had been a Maine staple my entire life. It was (and is) a wonderful publication that celebrated many of those things that are special about our state. Typically, articles focused on the protection and enjoyment of our state's abundant forests, mountains, fresh waters, and coastline, and its unique demographics and communities (coastal, western, northern and southern Maine). It also did a wonderful job of capturing the people who make Maine their home and those that love to vacation in Maine during all four seasons.

In 1999, Down East magazine did an extraordinary thing. It did something it had never done in its long and distinguished history—it dedicated its entire January 1999 issue to articles about one Maine community, and then doubled down on their first-in-history issue. They would reserve all of their monthly coverage to not one but both of the twin cities of Lewiston and Auburn. The banner on the cover read "The Heart of Maine: Lewiston-Auburn confronts the Future," with several articles including its two dynamic female mayors, Lewiston's Kaileigh Tara and Auburn's Lee Young, and the community's growing health care industry that coincidentally was also connected to Tara who worked for St. Mary's Regional Medical Center, and to Young whose husband was CEO and President for Central Maine Health Care, the parent corporation of Central Maine Medical Center in Lewiston.

The decision by Down East to take such a bold step with their publication had much to do with the transitional and economic development progress being made in the two cities. It was hard to overlook L-As collaborative efforts that had generated such impressive results. They included the two first-in-the-state revenue sharing agreements involving the jointly owned and operated airport, and the Central Maine Power owned hydro-electric dam, and other joint efforts such as L-A College, the 911 center, and the outreach efforts between Bates College and the two cities.

Down East was in many respects the harbinger of yet more exciting future developments for the two cities. If one were to review much of what occurred in 1999, it is difficult not to overstate the importance of how both cities arrived at this point. It was not just the herculean effort that was required to shift the community's entire economic and developmental trajectory following the rapid decline of their two primary industries. It was also the determination of their local and state elected officials, and their city staffs, to weather the economic and social turmoil of the 1960s and 1970s; to navigate the slow but steady economic recovery through the 1980s and 1990s; to persevere and commit to collaborate with each other whenever possible; and for both cities to maintain a continuity of purpose and policy to get it all done.

My argument about how L-As transformation was made possible has always focused on the unmatched ability of both communities to sustain long-term local, state, and federal legislative commitments to major projects. This enabled both cities to work through incredibly challenging but important long-term economic goals and development projects that had few equals in Maine and possibly in New England and beyond. The willingness for both cities to maximize the use of their limited resources, often through collaborative initiatives, in a coordinated and strategic manner was finally paying dividends to both cities. This all appeared to be coming together at the beginning of 1999.

Down East magazine in some ways helped to publicize the beginning of our 'tipping point' moment. We saw something special happening but getting that endorsement from another outside organization, particularly Down East magazine, meant that it was also being noticed beyond the borders of our community by one of the most respected magazines in and outside of Maine. The economic renaissance of the twin cities was underway. The two cities would adopt their very successful branding slogan "L-A It's happening Here!" [477] and 1999 served notice that it would continue to happen "here."

A few of the 1999 highlights during my first year with the city:

> ***Auburn:*** *ADAPT (Auburn Downtown Action Plan for Tomorrow) initiative began its public hearings and the City Council later approved the plan.* [478] *The ADAPT plan lead to millions in new downtown Auburn investment including the rebuilding of major arterials, a new city park (Festival Plaza), the renovation of an existing historic building, transforming it into a city*

government center that will house City Hall, the school department, and a new parking garage to support the government center and downtown businesses.

**Lewiston:** Lewiston rolled out its new Downtown Master Plan identifying major project areas in the "Southern Gateway," "Western Gateway," "Courthouse Plaza," and Main Street Medical District."[479] Over 10 years, approximately $100 million in new private investment happened in those areas.

**Auburn:** Local residents announced their intention to locate new 100 room Hilton brand hotel in Auburn or Lewiston.[480] The final location would be in Auburn in 2000, and it became the first major hotel to be constructed in the downtown area of either city in many decades.

**Lewiston:** The city assumed ownership of Bates Mill and its 1.24 million square feet for non-payment of property taxes in 1992. Mill #3 became the first fully renovated mill structure that permitted Peoples Heritage Financial Group (later purchased by Fleet Bank) to expand its workforce by some 200 people.[481] This project would eventually lead to the creation of over approximately 1,000 jobs and the presence of TD Bank (who purchased Peoples/Fleet Bank) for the next 20 years.

**Auburn:** Developers announced multiple plans to develop sites near retail operators Walmart,[482] BJ's and the future site of Home Depot. One site would become the new home of a Walmart supercenter that would spur additional retail development in the area.[483]

**Lewiston:** The city redeveloped a site for public open space that was once filled with old manufacturing, other businesses, and a railroad freight yard and passenger station. Railroad Park would open to the public in time for the third annual Great Falls Balloon Festival in August.[484]

**Auburn:** Planning began for increased traffic capacity expected with the new Whitholm Plaza development that would serve as home for the new 220,000 square foot Walmart supercenter,[485] and the expansion of 900,000 square feet in additional retail in the area.[486] Over the next 10 years, no less than twenty or more new retail outlets were built in that area. Auburn spent over $4 million on transportation improvements alone to support the increased traffic.

***Lewiston:*** *Developer Bill Johnson announced his plan to renovate two additional downtown properties. Both projects involved the preservation of historical buildings. One would house the state's new 40,000 square foot municipal district court with an estimated cost of $5 million.[487] Projected projects costs were approximately $11 million.[488] Cost would increase to approximately $15 million when the court project was finished.*

***Lewiston-Auburn:*** *The state agreed to fund overpass bridge projects over the two major arterials in Lewiston and Auburn that would finally allow a major east-west connector between the cities to be linked directly to the Veterans Memorial Bridge,[489] a connector corridor that had been discussed for 30 years. The state department of transportation required the construction of overpass projects in both cites before approving the expanded retail area. Both city councils eventually approved overpass projects in their cities. Lewiston's failure to approve project would have resulted in the Maine Department of Transportation stopping much of Auburn's retail expansion plans.[490]*

***Lewiston-Auburn:*** *Both cities agreed to sign a joint development and tax increment financing (TIF) agreement to eliminate inter-city competition for prospective development in the community. The policies would guide future economic development in both cities so that all development used the same TIF standards for development.[491]*

***Lewiston-Auburn:*** *CMMC hospital submitted application to the state in December to build a cardiac center. Both cities worked together to encourage the state to approve the application.[492]*

***Lewiston-Auburn:*** *After a multi-year process, the two cities were both chosen as potential sites for a new regional U.S. Post Office distribution center that was located in the Portland area at the time of the selection.[493]*

***Lewiston-Auburn:*** *Unemployment rates were at historically low levels[494] in the community and many employers were having difficulty filling vacant positions, something that had not occurred for decades.[495]*

## The Bates Mill Project

For the area, the acquisition and redevelopment of Bates Mill was perhaps one of the most important projects for both cities relative to its potential impact on the entire L-A area, and its prospects to generate new jobs. It was also viewed as an opportunity to create real momentum for downtown revitalization, and to reduce or eliminate the potential for acres of buildings and property to deteriorate, becoming a financial burden to the city over future decades. City officials understood how damaging it would be to have a prime downtown development area filled with blighted properties. The area occupied the equivalent of fifteen city blocks near the riverfronts of both Lewiston and Auburn, and this level of blight was both unacceptable and potentially damaging to the long-term stability of the area's economy and image.

Renovating and repurposing 18 mill buildings[496] of the Bates Mill complex would not be easy. No city in Maine had ever undertaken the redevelopment of 1.24 million square feet of textile mill space in its downtown.[497] This project would test the city's political and financial will, and most of all, its long-term commitment to what needed to be done to continue to move the city and the L-A community forward. It would not only test the will of the city's elected officials, it would also challenge the resolve of city staff and its residents. Six years of work since its 1992 acquisition of the building would either prove that the city was prepared to move forward, or confirm that there was no public support to assume the risks associated with the project. This would become the single largest municipal commitment to an economic development project in the city's history.

Lowell, Massachusetts had undertaken a similar project with its vacant mills, but it also had the help of the federal government when Senator Paul Tsongas convinced Congress to invest $40 million in 1978 to create the Lowell National Historic Park operated by the National Parks Service. Between 1978 and 1987, local and state government appropriated another $40 million in addition to the $240 million that was invested by the private sector.[498]

In testimony before a congressional hearing in Washington on January 24, 2012, Representative Niki Tsongas, wife of the late Senator Paul Tsongas, said "(w)orking together with the City of Lowell, the Commonwealth of Massachusetts, and many other public and private partners, the Lowell National Historical Park ha(d) played a vital role in rehabilitating over 400 structures, and... since 1978 helped spur an estimated $1 billion in private investment in the city."[499]

This project was revolutionary in that it was one of the first of its kind. For perspective, this project involved "the redevelopment and restoration of over 5 million square feet of formerly vacant mill buildings to productive reuse and leveraged nearly $175 for every federal dollar originally invested."[500] The Lowell Mill complex was four times the size of the Bates Mill complex with a 5.6-mile canal system that was 4 miles longer than Lewiston's.

Lowell's mill complex size and importance placed it in special company as "an important part of American history in the 19th century. The textile mills built in Lowell used advanced technology to build more efficient mills, hired young, healthy women to work in the mills, and marked the beginning of industrial transformation in the United States."[501] The size and historic importance of the Lewiston site simply would not have qualified it as a facility that was large enough to warrant its designation as a national park. The Bates Mill would eventually receive a designation as a National Historic Place, but if Lewiston wanted to redevelop the Bates Mill complex, it would do it without the assistance of the National Park Service.

Lewiston's fiscal relationship with the mills went back to 1964 when Lewiston Community Enterprises was formed and later entered into "hardnose negotiations between the owners of (the) Bates Mill (properties) and the city of Lewiston to provide some form of tax relief." Those negotiations permitted the owners of the mill buildings to transfer ownership of their properties to the LDC for one dollar, and permitted the LDC to lease the property back to the owners for one dollar. The LDC's ownership of the property would mean that mill operators would no longer pay property taxes, something that would immediately provide the additional financial relief needed to operate. The deal would also allow the LDC to sell the vacant Hill Mill property now owned by the LDC to another owner, providing the LDC with the capital it needed for other city projects. As stated in the previous chapter, the Bates Mill employees who were now the owners of Bates Manufacturing, Inc., purchased the property back from the LDC in 1977.

The city's position with Bates Mill and every other business in the city was to do everything possible to retain these businesses. For Bates Mill, they had been rowing against the tide of textile manufacturing decline in the U.S. since the employee purchase in 1977. By 1991, they only had 75 employees [502] working in what was then called Bates Fabrics. By the end of 1991, property tax payments on the real estate had come due and resulted in the city acquiring "(18 buildings) with 1.2 million square feet, the largest property in the city."[503]

Bates Fabrics had been experiencing financial problems since 1987, ten years after the employees purchased the mill from the LDC. Bates was also involved a contractual dispute with the labor union in 1987. The company shared publicly that they had lost "approximately $2 million during each of the past three years."[504] On April 3, 1992, the city took possession of 150 pieces of textile equipment to pay overdue personal property taxes totaling $365,000 over a three- year period. It then put the equipment out to auction, and then sold the equipment back to itself for $5,000 in the absence of other bidders being present on the day of the auction. That purchase was contested in federal court by the First National Bank of Boston in a lien fight with the city.[505] The city's purchase resulted in keeping the equipment on the mill premises in the event an agreement was reached with ownership.

In the end, Sun Journal reporter Martha C. Dumais reported on August 13, 1992 that Bates Fabrics and the city came to an agreement that would "allow the bedspread manufacturer to continue operating while making monthly payments on its back taxes." It was always the goal of both parties to keep Bates viable, and it took months of work to accomplish the task.[506]

While Bates Fabrics returned to the business of making bedspreads in Mill No. 5, the city returned to the business of figuring what it would do with almost 900,000 square feet of vacant mill space (Mill No. 5 had approximately 350,000 square feet). It took the first step on November 18, 1992 when "(t)he Lewiston Mill Redevelopment Corporation (LMRC) was incorporated as a nonprofit entity... to act on behalf of the City Council in the management of the... former Bates Mill Complex."[507]

The first order of business for the LMRC was to survey all the properties and note the condition of the structures, looking for the presence of asbestos, lead paint, industrial chemicals, signs of contamination, as well as what was left behind in terms of equipment, tools, raw materials, manufactured inventory, chemicals, etc. It was an enormous task. That process alone took almost a full year.

The city was fortunate that it had someone on board who was up to the task. Robert "Bob" Mulready was hired as its second city administrator on January 8, 1990. This was an important hiring for the city. For the first time under the new city charter, someone who had not previously worked for the city, and someone from out-of-state, would manage the city. Mulready would replace Lucien Gosselin who had worked for the city since 1963, had served as the City Controller from 1969 to 1979, and was then hired to become the city's first City Administrator in 1980 retiring in 1989. Bob knew he was replacing someone in Gosselin who was a 'legend' in Lewiston city government, and Mulready relished the opportunity to lead the city. Bob also believed in developing Bates Mill and was the city's most enthusiastic supporter. The eventual success of the mill's redevelopment would have much to do with his leadership.

"The... (LMRC), consist(ed) of elected officials, City staff (Mulready, City Economic Development Director Greg Mitchell, and Public Works Director Chris Branch) and appointed private citizens, (and) was created to shepherd the redevelopment (of the mill.)"[508] The LMRC produced a report in 1993[509] that identified projects that required immediate attention. Most of the projects addressed the immediate structural needs such as leaking roofs and creating a usable space in the mills, enabling the committee to develop rentable space for tenants. There were early successes with companies like Floor Systems, a retailer that sold and installed flooring products, and DaVinci's Italian restaurant. In the beginning, the city paid any expenditure that required attention with city funds or with federal or state grants.

By 1996, the LMRC soon realized that they did not have the expertise or the staff to do all that was necessary to redevelop the mill.[510] Tom Platz was hired to provide "design services" and oversee the "redevelopment plan" of the mill complex. Platz and Associates were interested in leveraging their professional services as architects with their in-house project development expertise. Platz was involved with development in Auburn and had already constructed a new seven story high rise in Auburn that also housed their offices. Platz believed they had the expertise Lewiston needed for the job. The contract would not only involve a fee for services, but Platz also negotiated a provision that would allow the firm the first option on any Bates Mill property.

Tom Platz was born and raised in Auburn. After graduating from Edward Little High School in Auburn, he attended Harvard, receiving both undergraduate and graduate degrees in architecture. His firm had been involved in the L-A College project, the redevelopment of the Peck's building to house a new telecommunications center for L.L. Bean, and a host of other big projects that included five years working in Boston.[511] Platz knew the area and had experience in the development of successful projects. The question for the city was, could this experience translate into success for one of the most challenging projects in the city's and, some would argue, the state's history given the scope, complexity, and size of the project.

There were many milestone moments once Platz was hired:

 1996 – Phase 1 Environmental Assessment application was completed.[512]

 1997 – Bates Master Plan released with recommendation to build a convention[513] center[514]

 1997 – LMRC was awarded $200,000 EPA Brownfields Phase 1 grant to assess on-site contamination.[515]

 1998 – Platz submitted a purchase request to city for two of the "11" mill properties. The city council rejected the proposal on August 11, 1998.[516]

 1998 – The Bates Community education and participation meeting on September 9, 1998 provided the public access to LMRC members and staff.[517]

 1998 – The Community group 'We the People' placed a non-binding referendum question on the ballot urging citizens not to support the project. The referendum failed with 44% of the vote but the group succeeded in also placing the same question as a binding referendum on the ballot for Nov 1999.[518]

With a defeat of the first Bates referendum in hand, the city council forged ahead with the confidence of knowing that they had 56% of the vote supporting that they continue with the Bates project. In response, the 'We the People' opponents threatened legal action[519] against any additional financial support for the project. On January 19, 1999, the city council ignored the threat and approved a $5 million bond to allow Platz to begin renovations of Mill No. 3. It would be the first full renovation of one of the eleven buildings that remained on the property (others were demolished or not suited for development), occupying over 1,000,000 square feet of developable space.[520] There were several tenants partially occupying Mills No. 1, 2 and 5 and both the LMRC and the city council agreed it made financial sense to focus on the vacant Mill No. 3 with its 161,000 square feet of space.[521]

The city council's decision to redevelop Mill No. 3 served as the catalyst for a significant part of the mill's redevelopment. Soon after the vote, Peoples Heritage Bank, who already had 250 employees in the Bates complex, announced that it wanted to lease all the space to be developed in Mill 3. The move would boost Peoples' total number of employees in the area to over 1,000. It also served as the first project where Platz would make a commitment to contribute his own funds to the development costs. The move by Platz was in reaction to the surprisingly quick request from Peoples, as both he and the city were expecting to develop and lease to smaller companies over time. The Peoples' development marked the moment when Platz announced his intention to buy Mills 3, 6 and 7.[522]

It may have sounded like hyperbole at the time, but Lewiston's Economic Development Director Greg Mitchell was right. The city was on its way to "'regaining its economic status in the state'" with the Peoples announcement. Mitchell's next statement bordered on the clairvoyant when he announced that the project was "'a turning point in the city's history. In 10 years, you will be able to look at this year and say '1999 is when the city turned the corner.'"[523] The list of projects and collaborative initiatives in this chapter serve as evidence that Mitchell's prediction about 1999 did mark the beginning of a perceptible economic and community renaissance in both cities.

It would not be easy, but with the ongoing support from the public and the city's elected officials and staff, the city continued to deal with both the difficulties and opportunities associated with the Bates Mill. Difficult decisions involving existing tenants needed to be made to raise lease rates that were kept at rock-bottom prices to entice them into a largely empty mill complex in 1992. The city also continued to work with Platz to complete the sale of the three mills that he initially wanted to purchase in 1999.

After more than a year of negotiating, the city inked the mill purchase with Platz in 2001.[524] He would purchase all the buildings, except for Mill 5, and would eventually sell Mill 3 to Bill Johnson who had also contributed to his share of milestone developments in the city. In 2018, the city would also negotiate a final deal to acquire the 1.5 miles of canals with Constellation Energy after ten years of negotiations with two different energy companies. The acquisition occurred with no city funding and permitted the city to keep all the water rights it had negotiated for the canals that came with the Charles Monty hydro dam revenue-sharing deal in 1984.

All of this was made possible because the city took that first step to commit to a project never duplicated in Maine, and to do it without $40 million from the National Park Service. The sheer will, courage, and determination of a community transformed a 10-acre mill footprint into an economic expansion opportunity that impacted development over some 100 acres around the site. The Bates project also influenced other development throughout the downtown areas of Lewiston and Auburn. Mitchell was right, the city's economic development efforts did happen in 1999, and it took a 50-year effort for the city to arrive at its destination and to turn that corner.

## New Millennium, Opportunities, Families, and a New Kind of Renaissance

There was no shortage of drama entering the new millennium. The "Y2K" headlines that often dominated the news in 1999 had produced none of the doom or gloom predicted by many technology experts. The information technology people in both cities were doing due diligence and were heeding the advice of the "experts" that certainly may have contributed to the absence of drama for our Lewiston community, and likely the rest of the world. I spent the evening of December 31, 1999 with the emergency management agency director Joanne Potvin in the county EMA office waiting for something to happen at the stroke of midnight. We both enjoyed the festivities that ensued after midnight, and the fact that we would not have to go into 'crisis mode' to handle whatever might have occurred had we all not prepared sufficiently.[525] Frankly, after all the Y2K drama, it was a great way to start the new year and the new millennium.

The resilience of both Lewiston and Auburn propelled the cities to a moment in time where the community no longer needed to be the sole messenger of a narrative expressing how things were changing in the community. There were now organizations, people from outside the community, and some media publicly communicating what they were witnessing about a new energy and vision in both cities. Some people from the outside could see a community renaissance had begun, and many wanted to be part of it.

The U.S. Post Office (USPS) decided in 1999 that it also wanted to join the twin cities renaissance movement. The search for a new postal distribution center had begun in 1994. After considering 40 applications[526] for prospective sites, the USPS reported they were dropping the city of Portland Rand Road site for their new distribution center scheduled to employ up to 1,000 people. USPS officials also reported that they were dropping the Rand Road site given plans for a new Maine Turnpike exit that might affect the building's design, and "because of neighbors' concerns regarding the size of the plant, its impact on residences, and intrusion on nearby wetlands."[527]

Lewiston and Auburn officials and the Lewiston-Auburn Economic Growth Council were elated, but realistic. Everyone believed both cities had an ample number of suitable sites, but some officials realized that moving the existing distribution center location north to Lewiston would have its detractors, and most of them would be the 800 postal union employees that lived in the greater Portland area. Auburn City Manager Pat Finnegan shared that the Portland USPS "'made it real clear they hadn't given up on (the Portland area) by any means.'" Lucien Gosselin, the former Lewiston City Manager, and now the President of the Lewiston-Auburn Economic Growth Council (LAEGC), thought that because of the center's significant economic impact in its new location, he did not "'believe for one minute (that) the Portland community is going to roll over and play dead.'"[528]

Although federal USPS search process was doing their due diligence through the LAEGC to choose the best site in one of the five cities under consideration (3 of them in the greater Portland area), selecting the final site appeared to drag on. On October 21, 1999, the USPS announced that it had narrowed the location down to two cities—Lewiston and Auburn. The original process had started years back with 40 possible sites. It then narrowed to five back in January 1999, and shortly after down to two locations. All that remained was to select one of two L-A sites that were both optioned by the cities for the center. USPS officials confirmed it would take approximately four to eight weeks to decide.[529]

The next day following the USPS October 21st announcement, Portland city officials and 800 USPS employees made certain that the public knew that they were not accepting the decision without a fight. The Portland Chamber of Commerce CEO said that he was "still waiting for 'the fat lady to sing.'"[530] That lady would sing on December 4, 1999, when the USPS announced it would reopen the selection process and look at other sites. The Portland political and union pressure that included picketing in front of the current postal center in Portland,[531] had been effective. The USPS attempted to qualify their new decision by denying that the new search announcement had removed L-As status as "front-runners" but for most of us that had been working on the project, we had mixed feelings about "front-runner" assurances following the news of a reopened search process. USPS spokesperson Steve Korker did not ease the community's ambivalence when he said that it was "'important for (USPS) employees to know that we're doing all we can, that no stone will be left unturned.'"[532]

I, along with many other staff and elected officials, were privately questioning why the USPS insisted on coddling us with their less-than-sincere assurances. We wanted them to just say what they really intended, so that we could move on and focus on organizations that really wanted to be in our community.

The USPS ended the suspense on May 25, 2000 when they announced they were selecting Scarborough for the distribution center.[533] Everyone who had worked on the USPS project in Lewiston-Auburn understood that not every opportunity that comes along may happen, no matter how initially attractive it may appear. It was and remains the reality of the economic development business. It is very similar to what most actors go through. If you audition, you might get a 'call back,' and if you are fortunate enough to be invited back, you also understand that most callbacks do not result in getting the part. Here, we had already been selected for the 'part' and understood that the 'call back' would not guarantee success. With numerous new 1999 projects already in development, we were looking forward to our next project 'audition' in 2000.

The irony of the USPS story, and the selection of Scarborough as their last site, was that what initially appeared to be our loss became an opportunity to attract one of the largest economic development projects in our city's history. The USPS center we believed would boost our local economy, would encounter several delays. On Saturday, July 8, 2006, the postal distribution center finally opened its doors. Scarborough Town Manager Tom Owens commented that the project might hopefully "someday stimulate more development that will be profitable" for the municipality, but that it would never "add any tax revenue" to town coffers given that the facility was "government run."[534] Tom was right, we would rather have the "tax revenue." That would become an unimaginable reality in 2001, and result in one of the city's largest projects in its history being completed before the USPS distribution center.

### Refugees and the Affordable Housing Crisis

The Togolese refugee resettlement had begun with little fanfare in early 2000. Although Lewiston's Togolese were receiving support from CCM, St. Mary's hospital, local families, and local organizations, much of what was occurring with the refugees was well under the public's radar in 2000. The Sun Journal reported that four Togolese families had been resettled by November 21, 2000 with expectations that more families would be resettled in 2001.[535] The newly resettled refugees involved 31 adults and children who arrived through 2002. Their resettlement in Lewiston was a resounding success.

The Togolese news coverage generated no calls at City Hall about the new refugees, and my elected officials were not seeking me out to discuss their arrival while I was serving as Acting City Administrator. I and many others were also not being advised during this time of what was happening with Portland's refugee population and housing availability.

Portland had been the epicenter for Maine refugee resettlement going back to the Indochinese refugees who were resettled throughout the U.S. in 1975. "Gerald Cayer, the city's Human Services director, said Portland had long been established as 'the gateway to Maine' for political refugees and others fleeing upheaval abroad." In the opinion of freelance writer Douglass Rooks "(a)s far back as the Vietnam War, Portland has welcomed the homeless and stateless, and they have become an increasing part of its identity as perhaps the most cosmopolitan city in the Northeast."[536]

When CCM resettled Somalis in Portland in 1998,[537] the city made a very favorable impression not only on those who had been resettled in Portland, but also on Somalis who had been resettled outside of Maine.

> Between 1982 and 2000, Catholic Charities Maine's... Office of Refugee/Immigration Services resettled 315 Somalis (starting in 1998) and approximately 3,500 other refugees in the greater Portland area. The gradual resettlement of these few hundred Somalis in greater Portland

most likely affected the relocation decisions of an additional 1,000 or more secondary migrant Somalis from other parts of the country. There (were) a variety of reasons why secondary migrant populations move from their initial communities of resettlement. Perhaps the simple explanation offered by the Office of Refugee Resettlement (ORR) (was) the most reasonable: '... better employment opportunities, the pull of an established ethnic community, more generous welfare benefits, better training opportunities, reunification with relatives, or a more congenial climate.'[538]

What could not be explained was the exceedingly large number of Somali secondary migrants[539] that were choosing to relocate to Portland. Portland's refugee resettlement history included a very diverse group of nationalities. "Through the eighties and early nineties refugees from the former Soviet Union and the Balkans comprised the bulk of resettlement (Bosnia, Bulgaria, Kosovo, Poland, Romania, etc.). African refugees (Sudan, Uganda, Zaire, Ethiopia, Somalia, Rwanda, Burundi, etc.) began coming to Maine as early as 1987."[540] None of the nationalities that resettled in Portland ever matched the rapid surge of secondary migrant relocations generated by the Somalis.

According to Cayer, when the Eastern European and Soviet Union refugees began to arrive in Portland in the 1990s...

'(t)he economy was bad, storefronts and apartments were vacant, and there was plenty of capacity,' he said. Landlords were more than happy to rent to natives of Latvia, Lithuania and Byelorussia, countries they may not have heard of a few months earlier. At first, there was room for the Somalis, too. However, by 2000 Portland's latest economic boom and an absence of new apartment construction was producing an affordable housing crisis.[541]

Cayer was not exaggerating. According to the Maine State Housing Authority "the squeeze (was) on. In the rental market, very few apartments were added during the (1990s). The vacancy rate ha(d) dropped from 8% to 1% (through 2001), rents (were) high, and at the current rate of rental inflation (18%), (would) soon top $1,000 a month for an average two-bedroom unit."[542] As secondary migrants increased into 2000, Portland's Social Services Department was forced to either house families in their city-funded homeless shelter or find significantly more expensive hotel accommodations that could not be sustained long term.

Catholic Charities Maine, St. Mary's hospital, and the city of Portland had all taken part in a very successful, albeit small, refugee relocation in Lewiston. Portland and CCM officials also knew that there was an ample supply of affordable rentals in Lewiston. There were few options available to Portland outside of contacting Lewiston. "In the early winter of 2000, the City of Portland Health & Human Services Department Division of Social Services together with the Lewiston Human (Resources) Department's General Assistance [543] (Services) office and the Elders(sic) in the (Portland) Somali community began to develop a plan to relocate secondary migrants to Lewiston."[544]

There was no reason for Lewiston to believe that this collaborative effort to accommodate Portland refugees, who were living in temporary quarters and unable to find permanent housing in the area, would produce subsequent refugee relocations of any significant amount. Lewiston had worked successfully with Portland and CCM to relocate the Togolese with no apparent difficulty, and there was no evidence of Togolese secondary migrants following the resettlement. Portland officials had no reason to believe that moving few Somali families could trigger many Somali secondary migrants. They had experienced Somali secondary migrant arrivals, but that was not an unusual in any established refugee resettlement community.

A community typically must achieve some level of 'critical mass' of a particular nationality of refugees before secondary migration begins, typically following a planned refugee resettlement. Variables such as: employment opportunities that complement the skills within a population, affordable housing, good public schools, healthcare, public safety, etc., are also important in the resettlement site selection process. With the resettlement of some 315 Somali refugees, Portland had enough 'critical mass,' jobs, services, and amenities to attract the additional 1,000 secondary relocations through 2000. What Portland could not anticipate was the low vacancy levels would literally fill their shelters with people who could not find or afford rents. The only option was to look north to the state's second largest city that had experienced success with refugee resettlements. The goal was to work with Lewiston and put a plan together to move some families to available Lewiston apartments in early 2001.

**The Cardiac Center**

Lewiston-Auburn was fortunate to have two major hospitals in their community. Both hospitals offered a range of primary, specialty, emergency and urgent hospital care. Examples included cancer treatment, trauma center, mental health, obstetrics, surgical services, gastroenterology, birthing centers, wound care, orthopedics, sleep disorders, neurology, and a helicopter ambulance service at CMMC that began in 1998.

What was not available in the twin cities, and required a 2-hour ride to Bangor or a 45-minute ride into downtown Portland's Maine Medical Center (assuming you did not hit traffic and there was a bed available), was "open heart surger(y) and coronary artery angioplasties."[545] On January 18, 2000, the Sun Journal front-page headline read "CMMC Seeks Heart Support." The hospital had filed its application for the cardiac center in December 1999, and was hoping for a strong showing of support from the community at large. It was seeking the state's approval for a cardiac center that would provide the services that were not available in either of the city's hospitals. CMMC estimated that "500 patients a year (were) sent to other hospitals outside the region." It was also seeking the support of both city councils and other local elected officials.[546]

According to CMMC President Bill Young, regardless of what CMMC or the twin cities believed, "a challenge from MMC

(Maine Medical Center)" would likely question whether the smaller hospital would be capable of performing "(cardiac) operations at the same skill level CMMC can." The cardiac center would get its first public support from resolutions approved by both city councils. The Androscoggin County Commissioners followed with their own resolution supporting the project.[547] There was also support from organizations like the Androscoggin County Chamber of Commerce, area organizations, and from the towns in Androscoggin County.

It was highly unusual for any greater L-A project to receive unanimous support from both councils and the county commissioners. The additional support from the county's smaller towns was also exceedingly rare. This may have marked the first time in the regions history where there was little to no opposition to an L-A project from anyone in the central and western Maine area. They all understood the project would not only benefit L-A, but many other communities more than an hour away from both cities. All this was happening as we awaited the delayed decision from the U.S. Post Office on its reopened search process for their distribution center. The people of L-A had not forgotten the fight that Portland had put up for the USPS project.

On April 1, 2000, both Finance Director Richard "Dick" Metivier and I assumed joint responsibility for managing the city as Bob Mulready ended his employment with the city on March 31st. Bob would undoubtedly be missed, but we were well prepared to assume the responsibilities of overseeing multiple new projects, the results of the USPS project, and the new cardiac center. It was not long before the next shoe would drop on the CMMC project, and we would see the value of our strong collaborative support for the cardiac center.

Almost immediately after the May USPS announcement that the center would be located just outside of Portland, the Maine Medical Center launched a month-long public ad campaign against the CMMC project with some questionable facts both about their cardiac center's track record. They asserted that another smaller cardiac center in the state would not "assur(e) higher quality that lower volume hospitals provide," a claim that CMMC refuted based on recent national rankings.[548] MMC did not hold back in its scathing rebuke of CMMC, questioning "the validity of conclusions reached by CMMC's independent consultant," and accusing CMMC "of including 'inaccurate and misleading' information in its application."[549]

The state's Bureau of Medical Need offered MMC an opportunity to air its grievances at a public hearing. MMC elected to submit its case against the CMMC project in writing and meet the August 25th deadline. The commissioner of the Department of Human Services could then make his final recommendation on August 26th, although more time could be taken if it was necessary. [550] Not unexpectedly, DHS Commissioner Kevin Concannon announced that his final decision would be delayed until October 1st. "(T)he state was waiting for the results of a $120,000 independent study being conducted by a Portland-based research group on the existing and future needs for cardiovascular services throughout the state."[551]

Chuck Gill, Vice President of Marketing for CMMC said "(t)he purpose of the study was to determine the need for catheterization labs...The definition broadened in the middle of the review of our application to include all cardiovascular services. It is unprecedented." The issue for both the city and for CMMC was that no one at DHS ever shared why the purpose of the study had changed before the delayed announcement. Chuck Gill voiced what everyone in Lewiston and Auburn believed, "this sure look(ed) like the post office all over again." [552]

Coincidentally, the Portland firm hired by DHS was conducting the study while MMC started their attack-ad campaign against the Lewiston center. For many of us, the added insult of not being advised about why the study had changed was only compounded by the same DHS officials whose objectivity was now in question. The optics of DHS hiring an "independent" Portland firm for a study that could potentially oppose our project to the benefit Portland's hospital, was less than ideal.

After significant public pressure from every corner of central and western Maine, Kevin Concannon announced the approval of the cardiac center in Lewiston on October 2nd, 2000. CMMC President Peter Chalke was right about his assessment regarding the community effort behind the cardiac center. The "heart center (was) on its way to CMMC because of the work of many, many hands...It was truly a team effort." Over the next 15 to 18 months, CMMC would spend $6.5 million on the new "16-bed unit that (would) perform both open-heart surgery and angioplasty." [553] The two cities, the county, all of Western Maine, and CMMC had fought the good fight, and everyone's efforts had been rewarded.

The community's success in assisting CMMC in their efforts to build the cardiac center was both an emotional and symbolic victory for an area that had mind-numbing experiences in losing major projects. The disappointments of the Raytheon departure in 1963, the closure of Dane-T-Bits in 1964, the end of the Bates Manufacturing in 2000, and the debacle that was the U.S. Post Office distribution center search process, were all interconnected in that they were highly motivating in their economic and emotional impacts. Great outcomes followed those events for the city. Raytheon's departure was followed by RCAs purchase of a property, and is now occupied by Liberty Mutual, and the Dane-T-Bits property was purchased by GE that has been operational ever since. As for the Bates Mill, except for Mill 5, it is now privately owned, redeveloped, and employs over 1,200 people (although many were working from home) in multiple businesses, and is home to loft apartments.

The CMMC cardiac center would signal that the momentum gained in the turned "corner" of 1999 would continue through 2000 and into 2001. As for the May 2000 USPS decision, their choice to reject Lewiston's site would result in an opportunity that few of us in the city would have ever imagined possible. In the interim, we were working with the city of Portland on their refugee housing challenge, assembling a community response for a new cardiac center, feeling the momentum of a hot area economy, and attending to other project developers that wanted to be part of our economic renaissance.

## The Economic Renaissance and Refugee Jobs

Eric Agonke and his family were living in Lewiston and making the adjustment to living in cold weather. Sister Jeanne Nicknair of St. Peter's and Paul's Church in Lewiston said that in February "(i)t was 45 degrees out and sunny, so I thought it was pretty warm for Maine, but (Agonke and his family) were absolutely freezing." They were so grateful to receive warm clothing upon arrival that they wore the clothing on the first day in their new home.[554]

The Agonkes were the third Togolese family to move into Lewiston since January. The small number and infrequency of family arrivals made working with the families much easier for organizations like CCM and St Mary's hospital to support the needs of the newly resettled refugees. As many adults were educated and literate in their native French language, it enabled the case workers to find translators who could speak the language and assist them with the day-to-day business of becoming acclimated to a new country and a new community like Lewiston. Finding work was always at the top of the list for refugee case workers given the Office of Refugee Resettlement's emphasis on refugees becoming economically self-sufficient:

> (R)efugee resettlement assistance programs, administered by the Office of Refugee Resettlement (ORR) in the Department of Health and Human Services' Administration for Children and Families (HHS/ACF), provides transitional assistance to refugees and other designated groups. These programs are intended to help the (refugees)... achieve economic self-sufficiency as soon as possible after their arrival in the United States.[555]

Finding work in the Lewiston-Auburn metro area would likely be less of a challenge for a limited or non-English speaker given the Lewiston headline on May 19, 2000 — "Jobless Rate Down." Employers faced with a small labor pool might be more inclined to work with someone's English limitations. The April unemployment rate was 3.0% in the area and 3.3% statewide. It was 4.0% back in April 1999 and was the lowest rate for the month of April since 1960.[556] Another August headline read "L-A Area Booming" and reported on the "record-setting economic pace in June" that added another 800 jobs to the areas workforce. "The number of people living in the region who (took) home a steady paycheck was higher from December to June than during any similar period since such record keeping started in 1960" according to the state's labor analyst Gerard Dennison.[557]

The jobs and income picture had been steadily improving as far back as 1997. In December 1999, Dennison had reported that the area had been below the national unemployment rate for 18 consecutive months. Androscoggin County's job growth was the third best county performance in the state; only the more southern and larger counties of Cumberland and York were better.[558]

The good news for newly relocated refugees was that they were arriving when the area's economic renaissance was fully underway, and when employers were looking to fill vacant positions. This surge of economic growth was not anything like the period of industrial expansion in the 1800s and the early to mid-1900s in both cities. During that period, the Irish, French-Canadian, and other immigrants were the workforce backbone of New England's industrialization. In many respects, had circumstances not been favorable for those immigrants to move into New England, L-A's economic history may have looked very different.

During this new economic expansion, many area residents descended from the generations of those first immigrant arrivals were now providing the capital, talent, resources, government staffing, political influence, and the labor to propel the community into its new economic renaissance. The new immigrants coming into the area had potential opportunities to build new lives if they had the language and work skills to fill vacant positions. For the community, new immigrants with the ability to be employed would be a timely development that could increase the labor pool needed in a city and a state that was losing its young people, growing older, and suffering from anemic population growth. These concerns were only in the early stages of being publicly discussed toward the end of the 1990s.

The more immediate concern for the city would be to learn more about Togolese levels of literacy in their own native language, their English-speaking ability, and their level of education. That would be important to understand in the community's new, and much more diversified economy, where most jobs required some level of high school education or better to be hired. While Lewiston-Auburn had plenty of jobs available, it was no longer a place with an abundance of entry-level opportunities, plus they mostly required English competency.

Most of the entry-level jobs had largely disappeared from the area with the near extinction of the of the textile and shoe manufacturing companies in the area. Some would argue that for the few jobs that remained in those industries, introducing new manufacturing equipment that often employed the use of artificial intelligence and robotics now required at least a high-school and often post-secondary vocational education, or certification.

Finding work for Folikoue Andre Teko was not a matter of speaking English, nor having an education. Mr. Teko held a Ph.D. and was a law professor from a university in Togo. "His first job in Maine was cutting up plastic bags, for which he was paid according to how many bags he sliced into small plastic pieces."[559] Though his English was "wobbly," his ability to obtain a teaching certification in Maine, or anywhere else in the U.S. would not be a simple task.

Rectifying Mr. Teko's problem would likely be hindered if he did not possess his education records from Togo. In the event that he had his records, Maine or other U.S. educational institutions would likely not recognize the documents. It was also possible that possessing the documents would still require testing to obtain his certification and academic status. Maine likely did not have any reciprocity agreement with Togo that would allow the state to recognize his academic standing.

The work that began in December 2000 with Portland to assist the city in relocating some Somali families was being organized based on Lewiston's limited experience with the Togolese resettlement. In Lewiston, we understood there would be a 'learning curve' regarding the Somalis. We would also learn that even the city of Portland or Catholic Charities Maine, with some 25 years of experience in refugee resettlement, did not understand just how different the Somali refugees would be relative to their desire to relocate to Maine from other areas of the country. The Somalis would soon demonstrate just how many of them would see moving to Maine, and to Lewiston, as an opportunity to be shared with many others.

# CHAPTER 4

# WELCOME TO LEWISTON: JANUARY 2001 – AUGUST 2001

## *WHO ARE THE SOMALIS AND HOW DID THEY GET HERE?*

During the initial discussions with Portland regarding the possibility of moving a few Somali families to Lewiston in December 2000, there were no discussions that either myself or Sue Charron, the Director of the General Assistance Office, could recall regarding the circumstances that triggered the resettlement of refugees from their homes in Georgia to Maine or from Africa to the United States. We had a very basic notion of how the refugee resettlement process worked at the local level from discussions we had with Portland officials and CCM staff. At that juncture, we projected that there were a handful of Somali families who we all believed would require the same level of resettlement help, similar to what occurred with the Togolese families after their arrivals in 2000. We certainly knew little about Somali refugee history, nor immigrant policy regarding Somalis in the U.S.

Somalis arrived in the U.S. in the early 1900s. "The first Somali immigrants came to the United States in the 1920s and settled in the New York area. Most were sailors, although some worked in steel mills, and most came from northern Somalia."[560] In the 1960s, students who were fortunate enough to be awarded scholarships from the "U.S. government or U.N. scholarships or (financial assistance) through the support of relatives who were living in the United States" were also entering the U.S.[561]

The history of what led to their displacement from their native country began is a complex blend of the fall of colonialism, authoritarianism, and the rise of the factional infighting between clans all leading up to the outbreak of civil war in 1991:

> Several powerful Somali states dominated the Indian Ocean trade from the 13th century onward. In the late 19th century, the area that would become Somalia was colonized by Britain in the north and Italy in the south. Britain withdrew from British Somaliland in 1960 to allow its protectorate to join with Italian Somaliland and form the new nation of Somalia [562] ... In 1969, a coup headed by Mohamed SIAD(sic) Barre ushered in an authoritarian socialist rule characterized by the persecution, jailing, and torture of political opponents and dissidents. After the regime's collapse early in 1991, Somalia descended into turmoil, factional fighting, and anarchy. In May 1991, northern clans declared an independent Republic of Somaliland that now includes the administrative regions of Awdal, Woqooyi Galbeed, Togdheer, Sanaag, and Sool. Although not recognized by any government, this entity has maintained a stable existence and continues efforts to establish a constitutional democracy, including holding municipal, parliamentary, and presidential elections. The regions of Bari, Nugaal, and northern Mudug comprise a neighboring semi-autonomous state of Puntland, which has been self-governing since 1998 but does not aim at independence; it

has also made strides toward reconstructing a legitimate, representative government but has suffered some civil strife. Puntland disputes its border with Somaliland as it also claims the regions of Sool and Sanaag, and portions of Togdheer. Beginning in 1993, a two-year UN humanitarian effort (primarily in south-central Somalia) was able to alleviate famine conditions, but when the UN withdrew in 1995, having suffered significant casualties, order still had not been restored.[563]

What ensued after the fighting began in 1991 was the displacement of hundreds of thousands of Somalis from their homes. According to the Office of Refugee Resettlement (ORR) FY99 annual report, between FY1983 and 1994, there were 7,921 Somali U.S. arrivals. Resettlements continued from FY1995 with 2,524 arrivals, peaking at 6,440 in FY1996, and followed by 4,321 arrivals in FY1999.[564] During the period between FY1983 and FY1999, there were 29,106 Somali resettlements in the U.S. There were no African refugee admissions recorded by the ORR until FY1980 with 955 arrivals.[565]

According to Dr. Jay Newberry, if you include the total number of asylees and non-immigrants requiring U.S. visas (what he refers to as "I-94" non-immigrants) along with the number of Somali refugees in the U.S. between 1980 and 2009, Somali arrivals totaled 108,000 people during that period. Newberry also noted that although Somali arrivals into the U.S. were not all refugees, 94.5% of all Somalis "legally admitted" in the U.S. during that period entered the country as refugees or asylees.[566]

Somali resettlements were taking place, like most of the refugee resettlements, throughout the U.S. after the passage of the 1980 Refugee Act.[567] Between 2004 and 2007, the U.S. resettled Somali refugees in over 40 different states in the country "with the largest number being settled in the metropolitan area of Minneapolis/St. Paul."[568]

The Somalis represented only a fraction of the new immigrants arriving in the U.S. going back to the 1800s. For most of the 19th century, the U.S. had always been a country with open borders for immigrants and a place of refuge for those who were being persecuted for their religious or political beliefs. According to the Department of Homeland Security, the number of "legal permanent residents" arriving in the U.S. between 1820 and 2017 totaled approximately 83 million people. Approximately 41% of that number arrived between 1820 and 1920.[569] The U.S. population in 1820 was approximately 9.5 million people. By 1920, it had grown to approximately 106.5 million people. Immigration to the U.S. produced one third of the country's growth, which did not include the calculation of immigrant offspring.

U.S. attitudes about their open borders changed with the passage of the 1882 Chinese Exclusion Act, which restricted entry for Chinese immigrants. New immigration law followed with the passage of the Immigration Act of 1917 which

> ...set forth qualitative grounds for exclusion of (all) aliens; (followed by) the Immigration Act of 1924 (that) established numerical quotas, primarily based on national origin, limiting immigration. With a few exceptions, refugees were indistinct from immigrants under these immigration laws. Millions of people were uprooted during or following World War II, which required extraordinary measures to reduce the human suffering and disruption it brought about. During the postwar years, the United States adopted a series of special refugee admissions programs outside the regular immigration law under which thousands of refugees and other persons displaced by the war became permanently resettled here. The United States continued a largely ad hoc approach to refugee admissions into the 1970's. Although some refugees entered the United States under normal immigration procedures, the bulk of refugee

admissions were authorized outside the normal immigration channels by special programs. This was true for the Hungarians in the 1950's, the Cubans in the 1960's, and the Indochinese in the 1970's.[570]

What started as an effort to codify U.S. law to better define the federal immigration and refugee admissions programs, resulted in a complex maze of individual legislative and executive acts, each trying to provide guidelines on how these programs would address the crisis of the moment. The following is a sample of that legislative timeline beginning after WWII and though 1979:

1. Presidential Directive of 1945: Truman announced procedures to handle displaced immigrants in compliance with existing quotas.
2. Displaced Persons Act of 1948: Truman cited difficulties of resettling displaced persons under the existing quotas resulting in the first "significant refugee legislation in U.S. history."
3. The Immigration and Nationality Act of 1952: These amendments to the 1924 Immigration Act merged numerous immigrant laws but did not provide for the admission of refugees. It contained a "parole provision" that allowed the Attorney General to use discretion in permitting temporary admittance of immigrants into the U.S. on a "case-by-case" basis.
4. The Refugee Relief Act of 1953: Addressed the expiration of the Displaced Persons Act. Congress acted in response to "Cold War" European displacements and authorized the refugee admissions ceiling of up to 214,000 persons over and above existing immigration quotas.
5. The Hungarian refugees, 1956: President Eisenhower authorized the entry of 21,500 Hungarian refugees under provision of the Relief Act and used the AG parole authority under the 1952 immigration act to allow 15,000 more resettlements. This was the first use of the AG parole authority. "By 1958, 38,000

Hungarian refugees had entered the United States, 32,000 of them under the parole provision."

6. The Refugee Fair Share Law, 1960: Many refugees remained in European camps and created the need for Eisenhower to turn to the parole powers of the AG once again. The U.S. would leverage this parole power with the new Share Law to ensure that the volunteer agencies resettling these "difficult to settle" displaced persons focused on refugee self-sufficiency and required family support. Although this covered all nationalities, the program was a temporary 2-year program.

7. The Immigration and Nationality Act as amended in 1965: For the first time, this legislation would create an immigrant visa system that would now have seven visa categories. It reserved one category for refugees creating a "permanent authority for the admission of refugees, the so-called conditional entry provision... that remained in force until its repeal by the Refugee Act (of 1980)." Initially setting a refugee total immigrant visa quota of 170,000 per year for only the Eastern Hemisphere at 20,000 visas per country, the act was amended in 1978 to include both hemispheres to create a universal ceiling number of 290,000 worldwide visas with a limit of 17,400 annual conditional entries from each country. The parole powers of the 1952 amendments would remain in place until the Congress eliminated them under the 1980 Refugee Act.[571]

It is important to note that the refugee resettlement numbers were occasionally misreported as a single number during the years between 1956 and 1979. The number of refugees who entered the U.S. under the *parole* provisions of the 1952 Immigration and Nationality Act between the years 1956 and 1979 was 1,027,407.[572] Under the *conditional entry* provisions of the 1965 Act, the number of conditional entry refugees that entered the U.S. between the years 1965 and 1978 was 126,288.[573] For a comparison, the number of paroled refugees entering the U.S. between 1965 and 1978-79 was approximately 900,000.[574]

The combination of the patchwork of immigration and refugee laws produced a significantly large number of paroled refugees: 707,219 Cubans (including Cuban prisoners and families) between 1962-1979; and 208,200 Indochinese between 1975-1979. The combination of both groups constituted 94.5% of all paroled refugees resettled in the U.S. between 1962 and 1979. This wave of refugee arrivals into the U.S. led to the amendment of the Immigration and Nationality Act and Migration and Refugee Act of 1962, and the creation of The Refugee Act of 1980.[575] The new 1980 act would codify the definition of a refugee for the first time with no reference to nationality or ideology:

> "... The term 'refugee' means (A) any person who is outside any country of such person's nationality or, in the case of a person having no nationality, is outside any country in which such person last habitually resided, and who is unable or unwilling to return to, and is unable or unwilling to avail himself or herself of the protection of, that country because of persecution or a well-founded fear of persecution on account of race, religion, nationality, membership in a particular social group, or political opinion, or (B) in such special circumstances as the President after appropriate consultation (as defined in section 207(e) of this Act) may specify, any person who is within the country of such person's nationality or, in the case of a person having no nationality, within the country in which such person is habitually residing, and who is persecuted or who has a well-founded fear of persecution on account of race, religion, nationality, membership in a particular social group, or political opinion.[576]

The 1980 Refugee Act was the first legislation to specifically address refugee and asylee admissions, and the most comprehensive refugee legislation in U.S. history that replaced the many existing refugee laws and processes. It created the new Office of Refugee Resettlement (ORR), which would oversee all refugee resettlements in the U.S, and would also: codify the definition of a refugee with no reference to nationality or ideology; define asylum in U.S. law; limit the use of parole for refugee admissions; fund ORR refugee resettlement programs; establish the system of using volunteer agencies (VOLAGS) in resettling refugees in U.S. cities; and codify the establishment of an annual ceiling number and maximum for refugee admissions by the President in consultation with Congress.

## THE FIRST FAMILY AND NEW ARRIVALS

The approaching new year in December 2000 would not be uneventful. The presidential race was in the throes of legal maneuvering as the Vice-President Gore and George Bush campaign teams worked through the process of making their case regarding which votes should be accepted. It would come down to a Supreme Court decision, with Bush as the victor. While the candidates fought it out in the Supreme Court, we were busy in Lewiston putting together the last details on another large development project to build an entirely new $3.5 million building for the new state Department of Human Services Region 3 center. We were also hanging on every word from Roger Theriault, owner of the Central Maine Youth Center, about the possibility of having a Quebec Major Junior Hockey League team in Lewiston, the first such franchise in the United States from a league that was producing many players for the National Hockey League.

Auburn was forging ahead with plans to develop the Mt. Auburn-Turner Street area. The Maine Department of Transportation decided not to permit Auburn's plan to expand retail in the area unless Lewiston built its overpass over Route 202. Maine DOT traffic engineer Bruce Ibarguen said that in his four years at MDOT, "the state had never denied a developer the right to build (a project)," but was prepared to do it. The road connecting the two cities over the Androscoggin River's Veterans Memorial Bridge required the construction of one overpass in Auburn and one in Lewiston. If one of the overpasses were not built, the ability for unimpeded traffic to flow between the two cities would not be possible and result in MDOT blocking the Auburn retail expansion project.[577]

Officials in Auburn approved their overpass, and the state was slated to begin construction during the summer of 2001.[578] However, the story was different in Lewiston. There was neighborhood opposition, and much of it came from Lewiston City Councilor James Carignan. Jim was also Dean at Bates College, which also bordered Russell Street, the same street involved in Lewiston's overpass. There was also support for the project from much of the public and most of the city council, something that did not necessarily guarantee success. Lewiston had already experienced a similar level of broad public support for a project in the mid-1990s. The project then encountered neighborhood opposition that stopped the development of a second Maine Turnpike interchange (Lewiston continues to have only one I-95 interchange, while Portland has four and the smaller city of Augusta has three). There was no guarantee that the council would approve the Russell Street overpass project.

Auburn Mayor Lee Young expressed how important it was for both cities to work together. The Auburn retail expansion project would be "Auburn's biggest development in more than a decade," and a new planned project for a Walmart superstore would be "jeopardized" without Lewiston agreeing to build its overpass. Young went on to say that "the two cities affect one another" and that "neither exist in a vacuum."[579]

After listening to Councilor Carignan's impassioned "all of the species" speech in opposition to the bridge on May 2, 2000, the Lewiston City Council voted 5-2 in favor of the overpass construction with Councilors Carignan and Marc Gousse voting in opposition.[580] Once again, the importance of focusing on the benefit of the entire community was underscored by the need for both cities to work together. Lewiston would get the MDOT funding to build and complete the overpass.

In Lewiston, we were also getting to know the new city manager, Bob Vitas, who had arrived in mid-November 2000 after working as a USAID deputy director. The entire management team was doing all that it could to get the 'new guy' up to speed, and he soon learned about the discussions between Lewiston and Portland to move some Somali families to Lewiston. "In the early winter of 2000,"[581] discussions between General Assistance Director Sue Charron and Portland Social Services officials began to focus on the logistics of relocating the families, as well as to discuss what levels of support we would receive from Catholic Charities Maine, who had a small satellite office in Lewiston, and from the City of Portland.

CCM would continue to support the refugee relocation to Lewiston and noted that the direct cash refugee support they currently received in Portland only lasted eight months under the existing federal program. In addition to CCM providing the eight-month federal cash support, they would also continue offering case management services that included employment assistance services.[582] I remember wanting to understand just how much "case work" would be required locally from our Social Services office, as our Social Services staff was not equipped to physically leave the office to assist people. The discussions with CCM and Portland officials suggested that help would be available, and that St. Mary's would likely assist as they did with the Togolese.

According to a June 2001 city of Portland meeting record document,[583] City Manager Bob Vitas and a representative from the Lewiston School Department met with Portland city officials from the Family Shelter, and the city's Refugee and Immigrant Case Manager, on January 9, 2001 to discuss the final details of the family relocations. Also in attendance at that meeting was a representative from the Lewiston Housing Authority, likely Executive Director James Dowling. There were at least three more meetings between Portland officials and Lewiston housing officials before Portland moved the first Somali families to Lewiston from the "Portland Family Shelter."[584]

According to the 2001 unanticipated grants meeting schedule, a meeting occurred on February 2, 2001 to discuss the "relocation of a family to a Lewiston public housing unit (Hillview Apartments)" operated by the Lewiston Housing Authority.[585] This conversation likely marked the relocation of the very first Somali family that was previously resettled in Lewiston. Although both Sue Charron and I were directly working with Portland officials on the relocations, neither of us could remember if we actually were told the specific date or names of the family being relocated to Hillview. It was unlikely that the Lewiston General Assistance office would see any of the families for services immediately, as they were receiving all their financial support for the relocation from Portland.

Daniel Hartill's Sun Journal story covered the first Somali family arrivals on February 13, 2001. How the story was picked up by the newspaper is also something that neither Charron nor I could remember.[586] I speculated that because we were prohibited from discussing the confidential names of General Assistance clients, and the circumstances under which they were receiving GA benefits from Portland, it was highly unlikely that the story came from Lewiston City Hall. Aside from how the SJ knew about the relocations, it was important that Hartill confirmed "a pair of Somali families" families had been moved to the city over the "past couple of weeks."[587]

Hartill also referred to Portland's predicament with housing the incoming Somali secondary migrants arriving in Portland. According to Lewiston native Portland Director of Human Services Gerald Cayer, there was "no room left in Portland." Rental prices for apartments had become unaffordable for refugee families, and family shelters in Portland were full. Some Lewiston building owners knew about the city's housing shortage as "landlords in Lewiston (had) solicited Portland (directly) with notices about available rents."[588]

Lewiston School Superintendent Leon Levesque confirmed in the SJ February 13th story[589] that a group of eleven new Somali kids had been enrolled in school and that the ESL (English as a second language)[590] program had "tripled to about 60 students... (with) one dedicated teacher and two assistants." I was asked in the story if these new families warranted the creation of a "formal plan." I responded that "there (was) enough policy to manage the issue within the current framework (of existing policy)."[591]

According to my interview with Fatuma Hussein,[592] her recollections about coming Lewiston for the first time, and her meetings with Lewiston's first families align, with the Portland meetings document and the Hartill story. The first Somali family arrivals clearly happened at the very end of January or the first day of February (likely driven by the need to give the families the full benefit of a full month of paid rent for the new apartment). News stories and my own discussions with people initially appeared to confirm that the first Somali family to be relocated into the city of Lewiston was Awil Bile's family, who took up residence in the Hillview Apartments complex.

Awil Bile confirmed in a Sun Journal story published on December 18, 2011, that he arrived shortly before Fatuma's visit to his home. "In late January 2001, Awil Bile moved to Lewiston with his family and two other families. There were no other Somalis in the city at that time, Bile says."[593] My ability to confirm if Awil's family did occupy the mantle of Lewiston's 'first family' of Somali immigrants may have been lost with my friend Awil's passing several years back. I did not remember ever having the conversation with him on the subject. My interview with Fatuma Hussein revealed that she believed the first families' identity could be confirmed but would not elaborate how that could be accomplished. Hussein did confirm that she had met both Bile's family, and two other Somali families at Hillview, on a trip to Lewiston days after her arrival in Portland on February 5, 2001.[594]

Although most of the public reporting suggests that Awil and the two families appear to be some of the earliest families relocated into the city, there is now irrefutable evidence to support that Awil Bile's family was not the first family. It was confirmed that the first resettled Somali family in Lewiston involved a woman and several of her children (something that Awil Bile may not have known) according to my interview with Regina Phillips,[595] the person who served as the Portland Family Shelter Supervisor from 1997 to 2005. In Phillips capacity as the family shelter supervisor, she was the person who physically transported the first Somali family (and other shelter families) to the Lewiston Hillview apartment complex.

Bile's willingness to speak publicly about his relocation from the Portland Family Shelter to Lewiston, and his openness in sharing this otherwise confidential information regarding his move with the public, makes it possible to eliminate his family as the first family as he was relocated with his wife and five children. It also strongly supports Awil's account of his arrival that may have established his family as the second family to arrive in Lewiston.

It is also important to note that all the relocated families from the Portland family shelter were confidential General Assistance (GA) cases. By definition, because their stay in the shelter was subsidized through GA funds, the information about their cases must be treated as confidential. In this case, the only way to identify the first Somali family in Lewiston is for the woman or someone in her family to come forward and publicly state that their family was the first family to be resettled in Lewiston. In the absence of that happening, what we know is that the first Somali family, and they will be called "Family A," was moved into the Hillview apartment complex sometime at the end of January 2001.

"Family A" will now join the Bile family as two of the first documented immigrant families to resettle in Lewiston. They will also join the French-Canadian families of either George Carignan or Joseph Brooks who 141 years ago became the first resettled French Canadian immigrant families of their respective era.

## Fatuma's Journey

Fatuma Hussein's arrival in Lewiston at the time the first Somali residents arrived in the city had much to do with her inexhaustible curiosity and courage to discover what was on "the other side of the hill." Fatuma's journey to the United States may or may not be like many other refugees that came into this country, but it is her story and explains why she is today perhaps one of the best sources of information regarding what occurred in those early months of 2001.

Fatuma was 13 years old when she arrived with her aunt in New York's LaGuardia Airport on July 23 or 24, 1993, on a direct flight from a Kenyan refugee camp in Africa. Leaving her family behind in Africa was driven by her desire to experience something more than living in a refugee camp. She wanted to pursue an opportunity to improve her life and the life of her family back home. The flight was filled entirely with Somali families, estimated to be at least 100 or more people. Many had never flown before, particularly a flight that was some 14 hours in length. She recalled how difficult this first international flight was for everybody on board.[596]

> People were throwing up, people were sick... These were people (including Fatuma) who were not used to a flight (of that length)... This was very traumatic (for people who had just lived in refugee camps, sometimes for years)... The food (on the flight) was different... everything was different... People were asking for goat meat... asking for rice... they were looking for things that we're used to.[597]

Fatuma, her aunt, and 18 other people from her "extended" family now had to board a flight from New York and fly to Atlanta's Hartsfield-Jackson airport. That flight was uneventful, but the walk through the airport was not. Their footwear on the "glassy, glossy floors" of the terminal were causing many of them to fall. Fatuma shared that some were injured, which made caring for one individual in a wheelchair and a 5-year-old child in the group that much more challenging. Local church sponsors finally greeted the exhausted group and would bring them to their first U.S. home in Norcross, Georgia. Fatuma and her aunt were now 'home' in their two-bedroom apartment.

The following morning, Fatuma ventured out of her apartment.[598]

> I got out into the neighborhood. You know when you are a child, you're intrigued and you want to know what your surroundings are, and for the first time in my life, I am seeing a Somali woman smoking!... I have never, never seen a Somali woman (doing that)... I run back home and I say (to my aunt), 'there's a Somali woman outside smoking!'... 'Oh my God!'... and we all rush outside (to see her).[599]

The newness of Norcross began to wear off. Disagreements and the tension of being away from home, as well as trying to get along with people she did not know, led to a decision to move to Clarkston, Georgia, in December 1993. This would be home for the next few years and where she would meet her husband Muktar while attending high school in Clarkston. Shortly after high school, Fatuma and Muktar moved from Clarkston back to Norcross, as Clarkston was not where they wanted to bring up a new family.[600]

According to Fatuma, there was simply too much tension between the Somali families and the African American community that lived in Clarkston. She understood racism and what it was like to be at the receiving end of a racist action or comment. What was driving her discomfort, and the discomfort of many Somalis in Clarkston, was the tension that existed between the Somalis and the African American community who made up much of the population in Clarkston. Fatuma believed local Somalis were making every effort to coexist with the African American community, but there was often pushback. "We

Africans thought that we were black people and so we were aligning ourselves with African Americans and they were like, 'no, we are African Americans. You are Africans from Africa.'"[601]

Fatuma recalled an encounter with an African American cashier in a Clarkston supermarket while shopping for groceries with her Somali friend. After buying a pizza, her friend noticed that there were food items on the pizza box lid. Fatuma's friend had limited English-speaking skill and did not understand American culture or product advertising. Confused about the image's purpose, she asked the cashier, "are you pork?" The cashier reflexively replied, "Are you calling me a pig?" The entire matter dissolved into a confrontation between the two people. Fatuma used the episode to describe what she saw as a "toxic" situation between the Somalis and African Americans in the city, which only fueled Fatuma's growing desire to leave the area.

The U.S. Census numbers support Fatuma's recollections of Clarkston's demographics. Although census surveys have a history of undercounting minorities, some data from multiple sources appear to suggest that the Somali and the African American population together made up the largest percentage of Clarkston's population. A 2005 Clarkston comprehensive plan states that the 2000 Census reported a total municipal population of 7,231. The "Black or African American" population in the city was 55.6% (4,025) of the population; the "White" population with 19.4%; and the "Asian" population making up the third largest group at 909 people or 12.6%.[602]

The comprehensive plan also states that 31.8% (2,301) of the population was foreign born. Some basic data analysis showed that 909 Asians, for the purpose of this analysis, were foreign born (it was possible that all were not foreign born). That would have left 1,392 people who self-identified as foreign born and not Asian. The difference may have reflected that the approximate percentage of the Somali population in Clarkston in 2000 was approximately 19% of the total population and 35% of the Black or African American population.

Of the 4,000 Somalis who resettled in DeKalb County between 1992 and 2002, 60%, or approximately 2,400 lived in Clarkston.[603] A conservative estimated number of 1,000 Somali foreign-born residents in 2000 would have equaled approximately 14% of the total population and approximately 25% of the Black or African American population of the city in 2000. Using Bouchard's numbers for 2002 and the 2000 city census, a Somali population of 2,400 people would have been equal to 33% of the total population of the city and approximately 60% of the Black or African American population in 2002.

By the fall of 2000, Fatuma thought about her family's future in the Clarkston area, but neither Lewiston nor Maine had ever been discussed. In Fatuma's orbit of experience and knowledge, she had never heard of anyone simply deciding to move to another state to start a new life. That was about to change. Unbeknownst to Fatuma, her husband Muktar had a sister whose sister-in-law Zamzam had moved to Portland, Maine and was living in a family shelter "at the end of 2000." During that period, Fatuma was on a shopping trip to Clarkston where she typically visited the Somali stores in that area. This trip was different, and "what was about to happen next (would change their) lives forever."[604]

> We are trying to do shopping and this guy, his name is Amin... says, 'hey!', he's an older man, an elder of the community, he says 'have you ever heard of Maine?,' and I said, 'no, what's Maine?'... He said 'it's a state,' and then he says 'you wanna go?'[605]...
> Do you want to go sahan?[606]

After some discussion about traveling to another state to explore and gather information about the area (sahan), Fatuma found herself next door with Amin at a travel agency run by a Somali woman married to a Muslim African American man. They proceeded to set up Fatuma's and Amin's "sahan" to Portland, Maine, via Boston. Fatuma and Amin connected with Khalis around February 5, 2001. Khalis had resettled in the Riverton apartment complex in Portland with his wife and family who had lived in Atlanta, and whose brother was a family friend of Fatuma's. Khalis' apartment would serve as their home base for the next week. Fatuma was already familiar with Khalis as he had been actively promoting the area to people back in Clarkston before her trip, and he was more than happy to help people with this sahan from people back in the Clarkston area. Although Fatuma and Amin were not Khalis' only guests, Khalis was doing what he could to provide shelter to newcomers. Fatuma said that is what Somalis do.[607]

While in Portland, Fatuma found out that Somali families were living at a shelter in Portland and discovered that her sister-in-law Zamzam (not Zamzam Mohamud who appears later in this book) was also living there with her children. Not knowing anything about the shelter, she and Amin went to the shelter. Fatuma got to speak to Zamzam who had been in the shelter for months and had time to recognize the need for Somali retail services in Portland. The city had a growing Muslim population with a need for halal[608] food items.[609] Zamzam's information would later lead to Fatuma and Amin's first business opportunity.

Zamzam also told Hussein that she and her family were scheduled to follow several other families who had already relocated to Lewiston. She shared her concerns about going to a community filled with "white people" almost an hour away. Fatuma explained Zamzam's trepidation about the move: "In (the Somalis) heads, people (in Lewiston) had machetes... have guns... and... they (thought) the minute they stop in Lewiston... nobody is ever going to hear from them, they are going to be erased."

Many in the shelter were terrified of going to a city filled with white people and no Somali population, particularly after many had just spent months, if not years, suffering through the challenges of living in a refugee camp and experiencing the many traumas and tragedies of a civil war. Fatuma and Amin helped to convince many shelter families that going to Lewiston, a place with abundant housing, was an infinitely better choice than waiting out the prospects for an apartment that may not become available for months.[610] According to Phillips, the shelter facility could not provide the Somalis housing indefinitely if they rejected other available facilities.[611]

Fatuma and Amin considered the trip to Portland and to Lewiston a resounding success and departed for Georgia. Over the course of approximately one week, they had put a deposit on a store, which according to Hussein, was the first Somali halal market in the city; convinced families in the shelter that working with the staff to be resettled in Lewiston was their best option; and connected with some of Lewiston's first families. They would share the news about Maine and this city that could truly provide Somalis with a place to raise their families; and had found a new state and area that would become her new home for the next twenty years.

## Maine Has a Problem and an Opportunity

Lewiston's population decline was prominently positioned on the front page of the Sun Journal with the headline "Census 2000: Twin Cities Lose People During '90s."[612] City Hall knew that the census population projections would show a decline. While the news was not surprising, we were not prepared to see that it would be the largest decline in the city's history—10.2%.[613] In that same month, a Sun Journal headline read that "Businesses, Jobs Rolling In" even though unemployment had "inched higher" the previous month.[614]

We were having success in diversifying our new economy. So much so, that we had not yet felt the effects of the 2000 'tech' bubble recession, the resulting inflation,[615] and the declines in employment[616] that had impacted other parts of the country. What the census news exposed about Maine's demographics had been under the public radar for years. The declining population problem was not related to the area's ability to be creative, inventive, or committed to preserve and develop jobs. Our local problem was systemic. For years, Maine's largest cities had difficulty holding onto their populations because of the ongoing out-migration to the smaller rim communities around the metro areas of Lewiston-Auburn, Portland, and Bangor.

Much of the migration to the rim communities were residents moving to nearby smaller towns where property taxes were lower, but allowed them to be close enough to the cities who provided most of their jobs. The Sun Journal quoted me at the time about resident "rising expectations" for the ever-expanding need to provide more services in the cities, forcing urban centers to be more dependent on property taxes for revenue. Very often, the declining ability for property taxes to produce sufficient budget revenues often caused reductions in service through the elimination of programs, or personnel. All of it was hurting our ability to preserve and expand our residential base[617] (and to keep up with service costs supported by revenues raised through our antiquated dependency on the property tax).

Another problem was that the Sun Journal, and people like me, were not talking about the 500-pound gorilla in the room that had significantly contributed to Maine's overall population problem for decades. There was an Associated Press story in the May 23, 2001 Sun Journal with the headline "Maine Becomes Fourth-Oldest State" [618] but there was little to no media discussion about its effect on our future economic health. I simply did not know the extent of the problem in 2001, nor did the Sun Journal. There was little 2000 census news coverage anywhere about the real problem—how Maine's inability to hold on to its younger people, its rising senior population, and how its lack of diversity would impact our state's ability to grow its economy.

While Maine's population problem was receiving little public discussion, there were publications available that spoke to the details of our state's population problems. According to the Maine Policy Review,

> Maine's population (was) aging. In 1980, the median age in Maine was approximately 30 years. By 1990 it had increased to 34 years. The median age in Maine in 1997 was estimated to be around 36 years. The proportion of the population in Maine age 65 years and over grew from 11.5% in 1970 to 13.3% in 1990. [619]

Maine's 1980 median age was the 12$^{th}$ oldest in the country; in 1990, it was the 8$^{th}$ oldest; the median age of 36 was the 4$^{th}$ oldest in the country in 1997;[620] and by 2000 continued to be the 4$^{th}$ oldest at 38.6 years.[621] By 2010, Maine would become the oldest state in the country with a median age of 42.7 years, 14.8% higher than the median U.S. rate of 37.2 years.[622] MPR also said that population growth in northeast states "was the slowest growing region of the United States." That was certainly true in Maine. The state increased its population by an average of 10,400 people per year in the 1970s and 1980s, but that number had dwindled down to an average of 2,040 between 1990 and 1998.[623]

According to MPR, the entire matter of population change simply came down to what drives population growth or decline—"births, deaths and migration."[624] In what was described as the "rate of natural increase (excess of births over deaths)," and "natural decrease (excess deaths over births),"[625] Maine had seen a declining rate of natural increase coming into 2000. Between 1990 and 1998, the rate of natural increase in the U.S. had been 5.7% while Maine's had declined to 2.3% in that same period. By 1997, Maine's birth rate had declined to its lowest levels "since records began in 1892."[626]

When former Maine Attorney General James Tierney spoke at the TIAA/CREF[627] "Distinguished Honors Lecture" at the University of Maine in 2002[628], the title of his speech was focused on what was our state's greatest need—"Maine Needs People." Tierney drove the point home on what he believed was the problem and the solution:

> We need people to move here - from other places in the United States and from other countries in the world. Now, you wouldn't know that by reading the newspapers. The northern half of the state says 'no way... we don't have enough jobs as it is! Immigrants and refugees will take our social services... save those jobs for our own kids'... (hold['s] up Bangor Daily News of 3/27/02 with headline 'Hundreds of Mainers to lose jobs.') The southern half of the state says 'no way... we have sprawl... our roads are packed... our schools are overcrowded and we need new ones we can't afford... we don't need more people!'... (hold['s] up Portland Press Herald of 3/27/02 with headline 'Winter a Hot One for Maine housing: Sales of homes surge 18% as interest rates and unemployment stay low.')[629]

Tierney admitted that his message advocating for bringing more people to Maine might fall on deaf ears for many people in his "baby boomer" generation. Many people around his age likely preferred fewer people clogging up roads, using up Maine's "pristine" land, and would support progress, but not embrace change. He went on to say that for the younger generation, recognizing Maine's 1.3% growth rate between 1990-1998; its national growth rate ranking of 46th in the country; and that our birth rate was the worst it had ever been in recorded history all required action sooner rather than later by the state.[630] Tierney went on to itemize some of what should have concerned everyone, but was certainly something his young audience should know about the population problem:

> Between (2002) and 2025, there will be a decrease in every category under the age of 45...
> 1995 to 2025, the percent of Maine people under 20 will drop from 27% to 22%...
> In 1995, Maine was ranked 42nd among states in its proportion of people under 20...
> In 2025, (our growth rate was) predicted to be 49th.[631]

When Tierney spoke to the UMO audience that day, he likely knew about Portland's history with refugee resettlement going back to 1975, and that the diversity, and population growth in the city, was primarily the product of its foreign-born population.[632] Tierney also knew about the Somali relocations and how they had grown since their first arrivals in February 2001. Comparatively in April 2002, the numbers were much smaller in Lewiston than they were in Portland, but it was likely that he saw the same opportunity for a city that had lost 10% of its population in the last census.

What was surprising was that growth in the foreign-born population in the Northeast had been declining through 2000. In 1960, the percentage of foreign-born in the Northeast was 47% of the population and dropped to 23.2% by 2000.[633] A look at the foreign-born data in the Northeast showed why the New England region's population growth benefitted from foreign-born in-migration. Of the six New England states, Maine, New Hampshire, Vermont, and Connecticut had declines in their foreign-born population percentages between 1960 and 2000. Massachusetts and Rhode Island were the only two states that saw higher foreign-born population ratios. Connecticut, whose foreign-born population was 11.3%, had never dropped below 8.2% since 1960 and saw its overall population grow in 2000 because of their foreign-born population in the state.[634] The three states of Connecticut, Massachusetts and Rhode Island had largely driven the foreign-born numbers and the increase of New England's overall population growth in 2000.

The suggestion that immigration may be one of the primary methods to address a community's or state's declining or stagnant population growth has been, and will continue to be, a politically charged issue. As far back as 1880s, native California workers targeted immigrant Chinese workers who they believed were taking away potentially good paying jobs. The 1882 Chinese Exclusion Act was approved because some native Californians believed that the hiring of Chinese immigrants, who worked more hours for lower wages, hurt them financially. Others believed these perceptions were unfair given the role the Chinese played in helping to build the railroads that contributed to changing the economy of the West.

The data has been and continues to be clear that Maine will have difficulty in changing its population trajectory without new policies that will require bold and creative political action. That action will likely require integrating more diversity into its population and into its economy. The real challenge will have much to do with the political will of its leaders and voters, on both sides of the political spectrum, to agree on what will work best to ensure Maine's economic future. Back in 2001, these discussions were simply not on our minds. New Somali families had arrived, and more were on the way. There would also be an historic event in 2001 that would occupy most of the attention of every U.S. resident in the country.

### Directly from Clarkston

For those of us that were working with Portland on relocating Somali families to Lewiston in 2001, there was no reason to look at what was going on between our two cities as anything more than one neighbor helping another. We saw the Somali experience as an extension of what could be done based on our experience with the very successful resettlement of the Togolese in Lewiston.

Fatuma and Amin headed back to Clarkston. Fatuma and her husband Muktar had decided to move their family, but he would remain back in Atlanta and continue driving for the cab company. Fatuma had put down a deposit on the store in Portland, and she needed to return to get that up and running.

In Lewiston, Sue Charron and her General Assistance office staff were largely in charge of working with Portland social services and family shelter staff to move more families out of the Portland shelter.[635] In Portland, Regina Phillips was trying to convince more Somali families that Lewiston housing opportunities would be a far better choice than to remain in a family shelter for months. The Portland housing crisis with the Somali families had been a recurring issue since 1999. The success of the first few families moving to Lewiston would hopefully generate more interest by those in the shelter to move into a community and a housing complex where other Somali families were living. Before long, Phillips believed the work that both she and Charron were doing resulted in some 20 or more families being moved either to Hillview, or to other Lewiston Housing Authority properties that also provided federal subsidies for housing Somali families and other eligible non-immigrant families.[636]

As the number of families moved from the shelter increased, people like Zamzam, Fatuma, other Somali families in Lewiston, were communicating to other Clarkston Somali families about the new home they had found in Lewiston. Phillips, who helped to relocate every Portland shelter family to Lewiston, could see that once they arrived in our city, the families began to see the possibilities of calling Lewiston their home. Phillips was not only helping to move the families; she and other Portland city staff were also providing the relocated families with some case management support. Phillips did not want Lewiston "to think that we were just dropping people off."[637]

The positive reactions of Somali families to their new Lewiston surroundings were likely being communicated back to Clarkston, along with the recommendation that it was no longer necessary to go to Portland, as the housing situation had not changed. Unless they wanted to be in Portland and were willing to wait it out in a shelter, it was simply more practical to come directly to Lewiston. According to Charron's interviews with me in 2001, the first direct Somali family arrivals from Clarkston began in April 2001.[638]

Charron recalled the first time when "(the families) started coming with their suitcases right off the bus (and) coming into the (General Assistance office) waiting room at City Hall... that's when we knew things were really happening and there (was) no more Portland in between Lewiston." [639] By April 2001, Lewiston's General Assistance office reported "that fewer than 100 Somalis had relocated from Portland to Lewiston." Phillips believed that the shelter moved approximately 20 or more families to Lewiston during the period between February and April 2001.[640]

Once the families began to arrive in Lewiston directly from Clarkston, both Phillips and Charron agreed that Portland shelter relocations to Lewiston began to decline. Portland also saw a corresponding reduction in their Somali secondary migrant numbers. Even with Somali secondary migrants moving directly to Lewiston, Portland continued to see secondary migrant Sudanese, Liberian, Ethiopian, and Iraqi refugees in 2001.

Most of Lewiston's relocated Portland Somali families were likely receiving General Assistance into July 2001 as GA staff continued to work with the state Department of Human Services office to move eligible families over to Medicaid (referred to as "MaineCare" in our state).

The combination of relocated Portland families, and those arriving directly to General Assistance from Clarkston since February 2001 (not including those that had never received General Assistance), was estimated by Lewiston officials at 38 new-applicant families. These applicants, who may or may not have qualified for help, represented approximately 250 adults and children.[641] A city administration practice that began in late 2001 or early 2002, would add 25% more to the total number of Somali GA first-time applicants to provide us with some idea of what the Somali population numbers were (this would not reflect how many would qualify for state GA assistance).[642] Using that methodology produced an estimated July 2001 Somali population of 300+ Somali residents.

Although the Portland-Lewiston Somali family relocation effort was experiencing some benefit in opening available beds in the Portland family shelter, the combination of continuing out-of-state secondary migrant Somali arrivals to both Lewiston and Portland concerned officials from both cities. Portland officials set out to seek funding that might provide the kind of secondary-migrant case management follow-up that would be helpful for the families in both cities who required additional support.

There were many needs and no federal funding to support secondary migrant refugees. Many had been in the country less than a year when they arrived in Portland and Lewiston. Becoming familiar with a new westernized lifestyle, complete with a language, healthcare/transportation/legal system, culture, and social and technological lifestyle was a daunting undertaking. Services for an "unanticipated," rapidly growing number, of relocated secondary migrants was not something that neither Portland, nor certainly Lewiston, needed before.

Portland's discovery of an Office of Refugee Resettlement "Unanticipated Arrivals" grant for precisely that purpose would become a critically important resource. Over the course of approximately 60 days in May and June, the staff from the Portland Family Shelter, Refugee and Immigrant office, Social Services office, Emergency Shelter Advisory Committee, and Lewiston's General Assistance office, Administrator's office, Housing Authority, Grants' Coordinator, along with the Maine Refugee Advisory Council, Catholic Charities Maine, Maine Department of Human Services, Faithworks, Lewiston landlords and Somali elders all came together to write a grant.[643]

The joint application for the "Portland-Lewiston Unanticipated Arrivals Secondary Migrant Program," filed on behalf of the cities of the new "Portland and Lewiston Collaborative Refugee Services Program"[644] (a.k.a 'Portland and Lewiston Refugee Collaborative'), was approved by the ORR in September 2001 for $250,000.[645] Portland would serve as the fiscal and administrative agent for the grant. Staff would be hired through a jointly coordinated process to work in both Lewiston and Portland with other staff floating between the two cities. All staff assigned to a particular city would work under the authority of that city and its personnel policies.

What was truly noteworthy about this partnership between Lewiston and Portland was ORRs approval of a first-in-the-country Unanticipated Arrivals program jointly operated by two municipalities. It was also the first partnership between Portland

and another municipality for refugee services. This program would feature

> multi-lingual staff assist(ing) new arrival Second Migrant Refugees(sic) in both Portland and Lewiston who are in need of immediate and short-term services... Services include(d) case management,... cultural skills training..., referral, case planning interpretation, understanding and accessing resources and crisis support... Case plans typically support(ed) the following areas: Housing location, employment assistance, education, mental and physical health issues or needs, family relationships, assistance securing financial support, and establishing and utilizing support networks. Cultural skills training include(d) use and care of living spaces, understanding and utilizing resources and services (including transportation, education and English as a second language, interpretation, health, mental health, financial, and support) and problem solving(sic) issues that arise.[646]

In December 2001, the Portland-Lewiston Collaborative hired two case managers and one cultural skills trainer. The end of the year would also see an increase to approximately 137 families,[647] representing 400 Somali individuals processed through General Assistance.[648] Adding an estimated 25% for the number of Somalis not requesting help, the total number of Somalis living in Lewiston was likely around 500 as of December 31, 2001. The Collaborative would be up and running by January 1, 2002, but the staff were unaware of just how many more secondary migrant arrivals would come to Lewiston, Auburn, or Portland.

# Chapter 5

# Fear, Uncertainty, Grief, and New Beginnings:

## September 2001 – December 2001

### *The Unimaginable—9/11*

I'm the kind of person who needs to stay in contact with the news, be it local, national, or international. In 2001, we had the internet, but it simply was not ready to handle the rigors of providing small towns with the bandwidth capacity or enable existing technology to deliver multi-platform live updates or broadcasts of local or national news. Our only option was to get live or breaking news from television. For some inexplicable reason, the entirety of our City Hall had only one TV connected to the local cable network, and it was located in the City Clerk's office. Its primary purpose was to provide up-to-the-minute information on local and state election results that were not yet available online.

Faced with that reality, I contacted the cable TV company to run a cable feed to our administrator's conference room located down the hall from our offices in late August. I purchased a small TV for the room and was now connected to the world. I could now see "breaking news" at any given moment. It was a small step for City Hall, but a bigger step for the only employee that wanted to be connected to the world without asking someone's permission to watch television.

On September 11, 2001, my wife called me shortly after I arrived at my City Hall office that morning. She had been watching NBCs "Today Show" when they broke into their regular programming to report that a 'plane' had hit the North Tower of the World Trade Center. I thanked her and went down the hall to view it on our newly installed television. My first reaction to watching the broadcasted images was 'those poor people' in the plane and in the building. My wife, son, and I had visited the North Tower in 1988, and I had some idea of just how big that hole was in the building. I watched for a few minutes more and then retreated to my office.

My wife called again about 15 minutes later. She sounded visibly shaken and shared with me that while she was watching the live television coverage, she saw a second plane that looked like a passenger jet hit the South Tower. Now we were both shaken, as we knew that this meant something far more insidious. We also recognized that this was no longer a random, horrible accident involving a plane colliding with a building in New York. The 'unspeakable' had happened. New York and our country were under attack.

I told her I would call her back after watching more of the coverage. About 30 minutes later, she called me back. Her brother had not felt well that morning after serving breakfast at his Michigan bed-and-breakfast inn. He told his wife that he was going up to the bedroom to rest. His wife went to check on him and found him dead in bed. He had died from a heart attack, his fourth. Officials estimated his time of death to be 8:45AM, a minute before the first attack on the North Tower.

The events of the day are well known, but they became more personal for me and my wife. She would lose her brother and the next attack that morning would occur on the Pentagon, the place where my wife and I had both worked in the 1970s. She was in the Navy and had worked for the Office of the Deputy Secretary of Defense. I was working for the U.S. Air Force. We had left Washington in 1976 and did not believe that anyone we knew were still working at the Pentagon, but the math still made it possible. We both had known people who worked at the Pentagon and would make an entire career of working in the building. They would simply transfer between departments, agencies, and joint agencies like the Secretary of Defense that had multiple divisions and offices. We could not rule out that someone we knew was a victim. At some point well after the attack, we located the list of 184 military and civilian personnel that had perished in the attack and did not find anyone we knew, but we grieved nevertheless.[649] It was unavoidable to think 'it could have been us.'

The unrelenting terror of the morning continued an hour or so later when a fourth plane was reported to have gone down in Pennsylvania. We had personally been in two of the three attack locations where thousands of people had perished, and my wife had lost her brother. Like most Americans, we will always grieve and never forget the events of 9/11/01.

The Sun Journal headline the day after the attacks said it all: "'An Act of War.'"[650] The newspaper provided many stories and perspectives on what had occurred the day before. There was the story of Alison King, the 26-year-old insurance clerk from Farmington, Maine who worked "on the 103$^{rd}$ floor of the World Trade Center's south tower until mid-July, when she inexplicably left."[651] There was also the story of Kevin Delahanty of Lewiston, who was in midtown Manhattan. "'Everybody just froze'" when he and others saw the South Tower collapse. He shared that television images could not convey the immensity of the carnage. "'The debris alone rises for 30 stories.'"

From my point of view, perhaps the most compelling and necessary piece in that Sun Journal issue was written by Executive Editor Rex Rhoades:

> As we struggle to comprehend and respond to this tragedy we must remain human even in the face of inhumanity.
> We are a nation of many colors, faiths and nationalities. We welcome and accept travelers, immigrants and refugees.
> We must reassure those in our midst who may be in fear. We have foreign students who live with us, we have people who have arrived here fleeing such mindless terror in their homelands.

> We must not lash out blindly or individually in response to this incident.
>
> There is evidence that our nation already is responding in a measured way to punish those responsible.
>
> We urge our government to act swiftly and decisively to punish these terrorists and the governments that support them.
>
> In the meantime, we should seek to console and reassure those among us who may have fear or doubt or loss.
>
> America must remain a place of justice, compassion and toleration. If it does not, the terrorists will have won.[652]

In the days to come, the national television media provided a torrent of coverage, and much of it was uninterrupted coverage without commercials. Locally, there were many stories having to do with Maine and Lewiston people connected to the 9/11 events. One victim was a former Lewiston native named James Roux. He was a Lewiston High School and Bowdoin College graduate and became an attorney who eventually opened his own practice in Portland, Maine. He was flying to California to see his brother on the morning of September 11th and was on board United Airlines Flight 175 when it struck the South Tower of the World Trade Center.[653]

There was also the story of Abdiaziz Ali who "(j)ust 12 hours before the first airplane crashed into the World Trade Center...had picked up his family at Boston's Logan Airport." Ali shared that his family "could have been victims too."[654] Ali also stated how upset the Somali community was and how they empathized with the victims, as they also had experienced the trauma and tragedies associated with war back in Somalia. Ali also reported that many Somalis feared that there would be reprisals given that most Somalis living in the community were (Sunni) Muslims.

Ali went on to say:
> Whoever did this, they are doing it for political reasons, not religious.

> This is not Islam, no matter what you hear on TV. This kind of horrific act is outside of what we believe...We are American. I am a U.S. citizen; I have been here almost my entire life and I have five children here. Many of us are citizens and we feel like any other citizens. But I share the fear of all Americans today. We are very saddened by this.[655]

This was a story with a global impact, but the story for many communities was also personal and local. Yet another local story appeared in the pages of the Sun Journal on September 14th covering a reporter that once worked for the Sun Journal in 1985. His name was U.S. Navy Commander Robert Allan Schlegel who was identified as one of the military personnel listed in the Pentagon as "missing and assumed dead in the crash." The Navy later confirmed Commander Schlegel's death. Also confirmed as a World Trade Center victim was Lewiston native Robert Jalbert.[656]

The articles covering the 9/11 attacks conveyed what many of us were feeling and may have been thinking about the terrorist acts. Grief, anger, fear, suspicion, sympathy, helplessness, hope, and courage drove much of the coverage by the media—some objective, some not.

In the issue covering Commander Schlegel was the story about the reaction of Bates College international students to the 9/11 attacks, and their "shock, horror and outrage" of that day's events. They also voiced "indignation at the presumption of Muslim involvement in the tragedy." One international student at Bates expressed how the immediate association with terrorism and Islam bothered him. "'There are extremists of all kinds'... it's not just Bates students who related Islam with extremism 'it's (all) westerners.'" Other students at Bates did not believe that most students felt those sentiments. One student claimed that he liked to think Bates students were "above that (kind of sentiment)."[657]

If public reaction showed how the city felt, the "1,500 people (who) gathered in Kennedy Park" on the evening of September 16th mirrored the area's desire to band together in a demonstration of community support and patriotism. There were messages of hope, prayer, unity, and optimism that the attacks would not undermine the spirit of the community.[658] The news was filled with these messages.

On September 17th, there was also a headline in the Sun Journal proclaiming that "Minorities Feel Backlash" around the country.[659] A Pakistani Muslim store owner located across the river in Auburn reported an example of that kind of backlash. He had received "harassing phone calls" following a television report showing people in Pakistan cheering the U.S. terrorist attacks. The owner believed some in Pakistan may have celebrated the attacks, but that he and many in Pakistan felt differently. "'I've read the papers, I've talked to my parents. They're sad. They're worried.'"[660] Bonnie Washuk also wrote a complimentary story to the Auburn incident about how local Muslims wanted to ensure that people understand that "true Muslim religion does not allow violence—and promotes peace." Washuk also quoted the store owner in the piece. He believed that Islam "'never teaches to take innocent lives or (conduct) terrorism like (what occurred in the U.S.).'"[661]

Understandably, stories of the horrific 9/11 tragedy and related events dominated the news. There were numerous reports about U.S. made plans to assemble worldwide support for a military action, along with ongoing efforts to recover remains at the World Trade Center, the Pentagon, and in Pennsylvania. There was work being done around the country to change security procedures on air travel and border security, and to hunt for those responsible for the attacks. The national coverage about the attack involved Maine communities as ATM camera footage in South Portland, and other security footage at the Portland (Maine) International Jetport, confirmed the hijackers had come through the airport to take a connecting flight to Boston. The two men then boarded American Airlines Flight 11 in Boston. It would never arrive in Los Angeles and was flown into the North Tower of the World Trade Center.[662]

On October 7th, the U.S. unleashed its attack on Osama Bin Laden and the al-Qaida, who were reportedly hiding out in Afghanistan. The October 8th Sun Journal was filled with headlines about the attack: "Target: Taliban;" "U.S. Brits Pound Terrorist Bases;" "Bin Laden: God Hit U.S;" and "Bush Assured Muslim Nations Osama Doomed." It also featured a full-page history about Afghanistan and "its troubled past and... uncertain future." The U.S. would eventually proclaim victory against the Taliban but ultimately remained in the country for years. As of this writing, some U.S. military personnel remain in that country.

Before the attacks in Afghanistan, something happened in Boca Raton, Florida, a community not initially considered by the press to have been targeted by a terrorist attack. The October 5th headline in the Sun Journal read "Florida Man Hospitalized with Anthrax." According to a 2010 Department of Justice report, "(h)ard evidence of the (anthrax incident) surfaced on October 3, 2001, when Robert Stevens, the AMI employee who worked in Boca Raton, Florida, was diagnosed as having contracted inhalational anthrax, an infection from which he later died (on October 5, 2001)."[663]

The Florida incident led to a number of other anthrax incidents and reports:

> October 9. After the CDC confirmed the first case of anthrax in a Florida man, Secretary of Health and Human Services Tommy Thompson suggested that he most likely contracted the disease through outdoor activities. This theory proved untrue when the origin was traced to a letter sent to his place of employment, American Media.
> October 12. NBC announced that news anchor Tom Brokaw's assistant tested positive for anthrax after receiving a suspicious letter.
> October 13. Two doctors notified New Jersey state health officials that their patients, both postal workers undergoing treatment for skin lesions, likely handled the letter.
> October 14. Another postal worker at the Hamilton plant that processed the NBC letter developed flu-like symptoms.
> October 15. Anthrax spores were found at a post office that handled mail for American Media. This

discovery did not prompt the testing of any other postal facility. Anthrax also was also discovered in a letter sent to Senate Majority Leader Tom Daschle. Public health officials acted quickly and decisively to address the contamination of the U.S. Senate. Forty members of Senator Daschle's staff were tested immediately. Over the next two days, testing and medication was offered to hundreds of members of Congress and Hill staffers.

October 18. Test results from two New Jersey postal workers with skin lesions came back positive for skin anthrax. The FBI and CDC began environmental testing at the plant at which they worked. The assumption was still that only those who touched a contaminated letter were at risk. Neither the state nor federal government assumed any responsibility for the medical treatment of the postal employees, suggesting they seek treatment from their own doctors.

October 19. The State of New Jersey Department of Health became increasingly concerned because of the outbreak at the Capitol and changed its recommendations. It urged all postal employees at the Hamilton and West Trenton facilities to take antibiotics. But the department persisted in stating that postal employees should seek treatment from their own private doctors or a nearby hospital.

October 20. Anthrax was discovered in the mailroom of another office building on Capitol Hill.

> October 21. Officials confirmed that one employee of the Brentwood post office in Northeast Washington, D.C., had been diagnosed with inhalation anthrax. In New Jersey, 13 of 23 samples taken by federal officials at the Hamilton facility tested positive for anthrax contamination.
>
> October 22. Officials announced that two postal workers from the Brentwood facility died of inhalation anthrax. The government abandoned its position that only those who touched mail would likely become sick.
>
> October 23. Federal health officials said that in the future they would more aggressively test and treat postal workers who may have encountered contaminated letters or packages. Postal officials then ordered the testing of thousands of postal workers.[664]

Anxiety levels only increased for many local Lewiston residents who read the headlines over that period. The Sun Journal reported the first local anthrax-related incident on October 12th involving a "white, powdery substance" found at a local Lewiston bank. Assistant Fire Chief Paul LeClair responded to the incident in the only way the department could—they had to treat every such call with the seriousness it deserved. Given the heightened state of concern about similar anthrax reports, LeClair said the department would respond to such calls as a "hazardous material incident" and that the fire department wanted to "err on the side of caution."[665]

News broke on October 13th regarding NBC news anchor Tom Brokaw's assistant being exposed. The Sun Journal emblazoned the Brokaw story[666] on the front page of the newspaper while local officials expressed concern about their preparedness for a bio-terrorism attack. Director of Emergency Management Peter Gagnon reported that, "local emergency officials (were) limited by budgets and training in what they can do." Gagnon said the level of preparedness needed for the anthrax attacks that had been occurring did "not exist in the Lewiston-Auburn area." According to Gagnon, Maine communities depended "on the state's Weapons of Mass Destruction Civil Support Team for dealing with terrorist threats." That dependency caused the Lewiston Police Department to shut down the local bank for six hours until the state's team could finish their work.[667] Reporting on these chemical attacks was taking its toll on the public psyche.

Bonnie Washuk reported resident concerns and anxiety associated with these anthrax incidents on October 17th. In the article, the Director of Maine's Bureau of Health Dr. Dora Mills reported on the fear that health officials were seeing across the state. "Doctors say people are coming to emergency rooms '"wanting something'" for their anxiety or wanting to be tested for anthrax when they had not been exposed. Dr. Mills stated reports like these were often seen during natural disasters, particularly when people are experiencing the sensation of not being in control of the situation.[668]

On October 18th, there were more headlines about anthrax and one more headline that was not particularly good news for the city of Lewiston. Bob Vitas, after less than a year on the job, announced his resignation to accept an international government management position in Belgrade, Serbia. The city council would meet on October 18th to map out a strategy to replace Vitas.[669]

The city and the country had been through some arduous weeks since the 9/11 attacks, but staff and the council took the Vitas announcement in stride. It would be just one more adjustment that we would have to make during a time that required flexibility and adaptability. When the mail had the potential to harm someone, we set up a process to handle it so that trained staff would do the initial sorting, allowing for containment in one room. We also had several city projects that were ongoing or in development. The incidents of the last few months would not derail our community. Good news was around the corner, and the public would certainly welcome some genuinely good news involving something called "Project Quality."

## The Lisbon Connection

The chaos, confusion, distraction, and emotion and news coverage of the 9/11 attacks made doing the 'other' things challenging and sometimes difficult, but our city staff was resolute in their commitment to just simply continue to get the job done. This was also the case for many other people in the community who still needed to work, educate their kids, take care of their elderly and sick, and to just simply do what they needed to do.

There was likely more anxiety within the Somali community about the attacks. Some of the horrible things that were being said to our 'new Mainers'[670] by some residents resulted in many Somalis keeping a low profile in the community. Women, often wearing the brightly colored abayas, guntiinos, diracs, and hijabs,[671] were simply not gathering with their children in the same numbers in Kennedy Park. This was one of the most visible areas in the city across the street from both City Hall and the police department.

At City Hall, many employees and I believed that the 9/11 attacks were going to have a noticeable impact on the number of secondary migrant Somali arrivals coming into the city. From the time of the arrival of the first family in February 2001, the General Assistance first-time applicant data revealed a very different story (numbers reflect accumulated totals since February 2001):

April 2001 – approximately 20 families and fewer than 100 individuals

July 2001 – 38 families and approximately 250 individuals

September 2001 – 76 families (no individual data available)[672]

December 2001 – 137 families and approximately 400 individuals[673]

Once the Somali families understood that other Somali families were resettling in Lewiston successfully, more families were traveling directly to Lewiston without the long stay in Portland. By September, the number of families doubled. Perhaps the anxiety of the 9/11 attacks in other communities was more significant and Lewiston was considered as "safer" in their eyes. At the end of December, the number doubled again, despite entering the colder part of the season. The ongoing growth of the Somali population increased the urgency to completing the staff hiring for the refugee collaborative project so that it would be up and running by January 2, 2002.

During that time, the city also had to deal with the Vitas resignation on October 18th. The city council and mayor elected to undertake a fast-track hiring process for Vitas' replacement before the end of the year. Mayor Tara was termed-out under the city charter, and city council members James Carignan and Marc Gousse would not be returning for another term. I was serving as the acting city administrator and elected not to pursue the vacant position for personal reasons.

I would continue to focus on the refugee arrivals, as both Sue Charron and I had been taking the lead in managing a still-developing situation for the city. City Finance Director Richard "Dick" Metivier would take the lead on managing the financial side of things for the city. Dick and I had known each other for over twenty years and our directive from the council was to collaborate on running the city. Economic Development Director Greg Mitchell also had his hands full. Many projects were either nearing completion or in development. It was a team effort with a highly confident and capable staff.

The process of seeking a manager went as well as we could have hoped for. After several interviews and some follow-up vetting, the mayor and city council chose someone who I already knew well. He was currently serving as the assistant city manager of Portland, Maine. Larry Meade was uniquely qualified given the responsibilities he had in Portland. Our contract negotiations went well and both Human Resources Director Dennis Jean and I worked on the final contract document into the late hours of November 21st, the day before Thanksgiving. With the last of the details double-checked by both of us, I sent Larry the contract via email, and Denis and I set out to enjoy the evening and the long Thanksgiving weekend.

On Friday, November 23rd, Larry called me with some disappointing news. He was not going to accept the position. Larry was a great candidate. Twenty-two years in municipal government with "a strong background in business and cultural development."[674] For Larry, it was a difficult situation that simply came down to a family decision. I advised the council and mayor by phone over the weekend that Meade had declined the position. It was decided that I would get together with the council on Monday, November 26th to discuss next steps. We had shared with the press that we would likely announce the new administrator that day, but it would now be used to discuss what the council and mayor wanted to do going forward.

Some members of the new incoming council and the new mayor (who had all taken part with the current council in the manager interviews) favored selecting someone from the "short list" of two candidates that were finalists along with Meade. Others, like newcomers Mark Paradis and Lillian O'Brien, said that they needed more discussion before making any final decisions.[675] In the end, the new incoming council decided to forego selecting anyone else from the "short list," turning over the responsibility for choosing the next administrator to the new incoming council and mayor.[676] The incoming council began advertising for a candidate by mid-December.[677]

At some point in December 2001, Councilor Bernier called Jim Bennett with an invitation to meet with mayor-elect Laurier "Larry" Raymond's law office in Lewiston to talk about his willingness to apply for the position.[678] Bernier was on the current 2000-2001 council (and re-elected for a second term on the 2002-2003 council) when they selected Vitas. She was also familiar with the circumstances that led to Bennett's decision to pull his application in 2000. Bernier knew that Bennett had been one of the candidates for the Lewiston position that resulted in Meade's selection.

The news of Bennett's interest in the Lewiston job had somehow leaked to the press in 1999. For Bennett, that meant the Westbrook City Council (and the rest of the state) was also aware of his interest as early as September 1999. After Bennett applied for the position, he and other candidates were interviewed. The city council and mayor then decided to extend the recruitment process and publicly announced in March 2000 that they would expand the manager search nationally.[679] After hearing the council's decision, Bennett chose to publicly announce that the extended search process would necessitate that he withdraw his application. Given the change in manager selection process, Bennett believed the uncertainty of an extended search was unfair to both the elected officials and residents of Westbrook.[680]

Jim had the qualifications for the Lewiston job. He had been involved in municipal government going back to 1982 when he became the youngest person to be elected as a Lisbon, Maine selectman.[681] He went on in 1986 to serve as a town manager in Dixfield, Maine and worked in three other communities before applying for the 1999 Lewiston job.[682]

When Bernier contacted Bennett to inquire about his interest in the position, Bennett stated he was not "overly convinced" that he wanted the position, or to put his "family or the community (of Westbrook) through (my pursuing the job) again" for a third time. He "needed to be convinced" that the city was serious about getting this selection process completed.[683]

There was no offer from Bernier to give Jim the job. He was advised there would be other candidates, but it was also clear that there was an interest to give him the opportunity to be interviewed and to get the search done quickly.[684] The city needed someone on board before the budget process began (the city's fiscal year started July 1st and ended on June 30th – the council typically began their work on the budget the first week of April).

Bennett did meet with mayor-elect Raymond who assured Jim that he and the council were serious about getting the search done. Raymond also did not promise what the outcome would be, but he and the council kept their commitment to move the process along. Jim stated in our interview that he believed the city had hired a firm to manage the entire selection process.[685] They set a deadline for all interested applicants to submit their resumes for January 31, 2002, and the new mayor and city council began interviews sometime after February 5th.[686]

Bennett made the final list of candidates during the last week of February 2002. According to Bennett, there was extensive testing and interviews. He remembered that there was another serious candidate in the running,[687] but Bennett was selected sometime during the week of March 4th.[688] Contract negotiations took some time[689] but were completed during the week of March 11th. During the week of March 18th, Bennett was splitting his time attending to business and attending city council meetings in both Lewiston and Westbrook. On Friday March 22nd, his Westbrook employees set up "an open-house going away party for him." On the next day, he and his family all traveled to Lewiston to help set up Jim's new office. Bennett wanted to "hit the ground running" for his first day at work on Monday, March 25, 2002.[690]

Jim knew what was going on in Lewiston. The city had been enjoying unprecedented growth over the last three years, but there still was much work to be done. The Bates Mill project was progressing but was far from complete. There were new projects, and there was a new population of refugees that were becoming more convinced by the day that Lewiston was a place they, and other Somalis from around the country, could make their home.

Jim was born in Lewiston but had grown up in the neighboring community of Lisbon, Maine. Many of Bennett's family members and close friends still lived in Lisbon. Lisbon was also the place where Staff Sergeant Thomas Field had lived. A section of Route 196, the major connector road between Lisbon and Lewiston, had been named after him. Staff Sergeant Field received his recognition after dying in the line-of-duty. He had been killed in the 'black hawk down' incident in Somalia in 1993, something that would take on a new meaning for some local residents in a post-9/11 world, and at about the time of Jim Bennett's arrival.

## The Black Hawk Tragedy

"Operation Restore Hope began as an Operation Other Than War, with humanitarian aspects and nation-building overtones. It rapidly became a straightforward combat mission that took place in Somalia, a nation situated on the Gulf of Aden and the Indian Ocean on the horn of Africa."[691]

> The main challenge to the smooth flow of relief supplies continued to be the rivalry between feuding warlords, particularly between the forces of General Muhammed Farah Aideed of the Habr Gidr subclan and Ali Mahdi Mohamed of the Abgal subclan in Mogadishu. Aideed, previously a general in dictator Siad Barre's army

and a former ambassador to India, now headed the Somali National Alliance (SNA) with pretensions to ruling the entire country. His opponent, Ali Mahdi, was a former businessman and farmer with little military experience and only an ad hoc militia. Their feud had led to open conflict from November 1991 to February 1992 and only added to the tragedy of Somalia by killing thousands of innocent Mogadishu citizens. Backed by overwhelming U.S. and allied power, Ambassador (Robert) Oakley effectively established a cease-fire between the two forces as a precondition to establishing a military and relief presence in the interior of the country. However, it was not in the UN charter, nor in the U.S. mission guidance, to disarm or attack either faction. Ostensibly, the UNITAF forces were neutral and there only to ensure that relief supplies flowed.[692]

Somalia's 1992 humanitarian crisis created an opportunity for the U.S. to position itself as the lone remaining post-Cold War world superpower and leader following the collapse of the Soviet Union in 1989. It was also an opportunity to promote multilateralism to deal with conflict by leveraging and strengthening the United Nations' role in addressing "prevention, peacekeeping and peacemaking" around the world.[693] "A successful UN operation in Somalia would strengthen the UN capacity to execute multilateral peace enforcement and reduce the pressure on the U.S. to respond unilaterally to crises around the world."[694]

Though President George Bush "called on nations to develop and train military units for possible peacekeeping duty and advocated multinational planning, training and field exercises to better prepare UN peacekeeping force," newly elected President Bill Clinton's plan for peacekeeping "looked very similar to President Bush's policy but with one major difference;

President Clinton signaled a willingness to deploy regular combat forces in support of peacekeeping operations."[695]

In order to address the increasingly serious humanitarian situation in Somalia in December 1992, "Bush immediately initiated Operation Restore Hope. The U.S. officially assumed the lead in what would be termed the Unified Task Force (UNITAF)."[696]

"Although the United Nations continued to play an important part in the politics within the country, especially in the delicate negotiations between rival Somali factions, its role was soon overshadowed by U.S. military and diplomatic power." [697]U.S. special operations forces arrived in Somali "in the early morning hours" of December 9, 1992 "with the first 1,300 marines coming in by helicopter directly to Mogadishu airport." Even with the news media covering the event in advance of the arrival of U.S. troops, there was no resistance from the Somalis. "Thereafter, Somali warlords (Aideed and Mahdi) quickly agreed to cooperate with each other (for the time being) and work with the U.S. troops."[698]

As difficult as it was to achieve civility under these very challenging circumstances, daily life in Mogadishu appeared to be returning to "some (comparative) measure of normalcy" with only a few "incidents of violence from February to May 1993." The economy showed evidence of this 'normalcy' when markets opened, and people began to feel that they could travel with some level of safety. Along with a measure of optimism about the future, "Operation Restore Hope succeeded in its goal of bringing an end to mass starvation," and bringing some level of security in various sectors of the city. If nothing else, "an uneasy truce kept the peace between the factions." Before long, "UN diplomats" pressured the U.S. to have its military confiscate weapons hoping to speed up prospects for peace. "(S)oon after, the United States turned over the mission completely to the United Nations in May (1993), (and) the situation began to unravel."[699]

Over time, Aideed demonstrated that there were Somalis that who were not prepared to accept any attempt to confiscate their weapons and did not want U.S. military forces in their country. "On 5 June 1993, his Somalia National Alliance forces ambushed and killed 24 Pakistani soldiers assigned to (United

Nations Operations in Somalia), (and) (a)nother 44 were wounded." The next day, this attack produced a U.N. resolution supporting a military response against Aideed and the SNA, and "more troops and equipment" from member states.[700]

"Aideed did not take this personal threat to him lying down. On 8 August his (SNA) forces detonated a mine under a passing U.S. Military Police... vehicle on Jialle-Siaad Street in Mogadishu killing four U.S. MPs." With the situation escalating, the UN Secretary General asked President Clinton for his help to capture Aideed.[701] Unable to find Aideed, more attacks on U.N. and U.S. military personnel continued. A "roadblock-clearing" U.N. Pakistani team was attacked on September 21, 1993 "and it lost an armored personnel carrier and suffered nine casualties,[702] including two killed. On 25 September a U.S. Black Hawk helicopter was shot down and three soldiers killed." Of particular concern to military officials was the helicopter being shot down with an RPG (rocket-propelled grenade), a military weapon typically used to "attack armored vehicles."[703]

The frequency and seriousness of the military encounters with the SNA, and their RPG weapons, led to a military operation (the 'black hawk down' mission) on October 3rd when TF (Task Force) Ranger launched its seventh mission,[704] code-named Operation Gothic Serpent,[705] that had the specific task of raiding Aideed's

> stronghold near the Olympic Hotel in Mogadishu, Somalia, seeking to capture two of his key lieutenants. Although the task force accomplished its mission and captured twenty-four (Aideed) supporters, Somali clansmen shot down the first of two MH-60L Black Hawk helicopters using rocket-propelled grenades. With the downing of the first of these MH-60Ls, the mission of TF Ranger changed from one of capturing (Aideed's) supporters to one of safeguarding and recovering American casualties... [706] Casualties were heavy. TF Ranger lost 16 soldiers on 3–4 October and had

another 57 wounded, with 1 other killed and 12 wounded on 6 October by a mortar attack on their hangar complex at the airport. The 2-14th Infantry suffered 2 Americans killed and 22 wounded while the Malaysian coalition partners had 2 killed and 7 wounded and the Pakistanis suffered 2 wounded. Various estimates placed Somali casualties between 500 and 1,500...(ending) one of the bloodiest and fiercest urban firefights since the Vietnam War.[707]

Back in Lisbon, Maine, the first public news about U.S. military action in Somalia involved headlines that read "New Hampshire Native Captured After Helicopter Crash in Somali" [708] and "U.S. Deaths Rise in Somalia, More Troops Ordered to Go."[709] Tim Hanson's October 6th Sun Journal story covered Sgt. Aaron G. Williamson of Carthage, Maine, who was shot while "rappelling from a helicopter," and wounded a second time when "he took a direct hit in the upper left shoulder fired from a grenade launcher."[710] In that same newspaper issue was the headline "Missing Man Was in Same Helicopter as N.H. Captive (Chief Warrant Officer Michael Durant)."[711] That "missing man" was Staff Sergeant Thomas Field from Lisbon, Maine.

On October 7th, the news of SSgt. Field being missing in action was widely known in Lisbon and throughout Maine. All of those killed, wounded, or missing in action was also national and international news. On the second day after the U.S. military had reported Field missing, Susan Johns wrote about how Lisbon High School students had banded together to tie yellow ribbons on the trees of the high school property. SSgt. Field was described by those who knew him as "a helpful, happy young man. 'Always nice, kind, friendly... happy-go-lucky... really neat kid, on the quiet side and pleasant.'"[712]

The Johns story also pointed out how many residents believed that this latest incident indicated the need for the U.S. to withdraw from Somalia. An English teacher from Lisbon High School expressed that "'(s)eeing the Somali kids kicking the dead bodies of soldiers'" did not demonstrate that Somalia "'deserve(d) our help.'"[713]

The article went on to say that the father of SSgt. Field could no longer watch the coverage given some of the images that had been broadcasted globally. He also shared a greeting card with Johns that was recently sent to him from his son saying that he was only sending it along to show his "appreciation" for both his parents, and that he wanted to send his "love to everyone" in the family. Mr. Field's repeated the town sentiment that it was time for the U.S. to "leave Somalia."[714]

For many Lisbon residents, the realization that SSgt. Field, one of their own, was the missing man in the news coverage was hard to fathom. One resident summed it up for many who lived in this town... "'(i)t hit too close to home.'"[715]

The following day brought the news that everyone feared about SSgt. Field's missing status. The Sun Journal front-page headline on October 8, 1993 read "Lisbon Soldier is Reported Killed in Action."[716] An Army military officer from Fort Campbell, Kentucky was at the Field's family home on the day his death was made public. The only comment from the officer was that he was in the home "to assist the family."[717]

The news of Field's death traveled quickly, and American flags were lowered to half-staff around the town, including the home of Sgt. Field's former next-door neighbors "Forest and Dorothy Jordan Sr." Mrs. Jordan said that her son used to play with Thomas expressing that she was "heartbroken" and felt like "it's happened to me." Jordan added that her grandson was in boot camp and lamented "'(i)t could happen to anybody.'"[718]

The local story about the tragic death of a local person killed in military action, like many others, would generate community interest to memorialize its favorite son and fallen hero. Lisbon recognized SSgt Field with a highly visible memorial assigning a section of state road connecting Lewiston and their town. In 1994, the "Staff Sergeant Thomas Field Memorial Highway"[719] would become a tribute to his courage and for the person who many knew as that "helpful, happy young man."

Mark Bowden would also immortalize the events leading to the deaths of the U.S. troops in Operation Gothic Serpent in his best-selling book "Black Hawk Down: A Story of Modern War" that was published in February 1999. The book would eventually become a nationally released movie in January 2002 and one of the more successful movies of the year.

The movie would also be released at a time where the conversation about Somalis and Islam in a post-9/11 world would intersect with the connector road from Lisbon to Lewiston carrying the name of SSgt. Field. For Somalis who were coming from Portland using I-295 and arriving at Lewiston for the first time, they had likely taken the memorial road into our city, ending a journey where many had escaped the very people who perpetrated the violence against them, their families, and friends in the 1991-93 Somalia civil war.

The Somali residents that took the memorial road likely would have not known anything about SSgt. Field or what he sacrificed for his country, but many of them may had also lost loved ones in the pre-civil war and civil war period in Somalia. "Overall violence within the atrocity period of six years (1988-1993) likely resulted in 50,000 to 100,000 civilian deaths as a direct result of violence or hostilities." During the same period, another 500,000 may have died from the famine, while another 500,000 may have been forced from their homes.[720] War and famine rarely spare the innocent from violence and starvation.

Some residents would go on to believe that the events of Mogadishu were an indictment of the entire Somali population, but nothing could have been further from the truth. The refugees came to the U.S. to escape the violence and the difficult living conditions of the refugee camps, not to embrace or condone the civil war in Somalia, or those responsible for all the death and destruction.

The story about the Somali refugees relocating to Lewiston remained a local and state story coming into 2002. By June 2002, that would all change with the first published national story about the Lewiston Somali relocations in the Chicago Tribune. Whatever local and state scrutiny the Somalis were subjected to in early 2002 would pale in comparison to what would eventually become a global story.

## PROJECT QUALITY AND THE PHOTO FINISH

While I worked with the council on the city administrator search process in November 2001, I received a letter from St. Mary's Regional Medical Center CEO James Cassidy. On November 6, 2001, Cassidy wrote: "As we were involved in previous refugee resettlements in Lewiston through our partnership with the Catholic Charities Refugee Resettlement Program, we would be interested in being helpful in the transition process for the recent newly arrived (Somalis). We believe that it would be helpful to convene individuals from State Government, the city of Lewiston, the Lewiston School Department, and Catholic Charities to discuss how we might work together to assist with the transition process for these (refugees)."

Timing is everything very often in life, and Jim Cassidy's letter had simply come at a very busy moment for me and our office staff. Bob Vitas was just about finished with the city, and the Sun Journal had just published a front-page story about the "mega-deal" we had been quietly working on for months. The Sun Journal was eager to find out what company was involved in this deal that journalist Doug Fletcher described as potentially occupying over 80 acres of city and private property. Fletcher also said that he could not get any city official to confirm the rumors about the "distribution center" that would be coming to Lewiston.[721]

Fletcher was right. We were operating under strict guidelines from the company's search consultant not to break the confidentiality protocols, something both parties had mutually agreed that upon. Any perception by the company that we were not complying would likely result in losing a project that would rank as one of the largest in our city's history. We did not initially confirm that it was a viable project to our own elected officials until the summer. When the council and mayor were given information, they were only told that it was a very large project with hundreds of jobs, worth millions for the city, that other states were also potential suitors, and that the prospective development opportunity would be called "Project Quality." At some point well before the story broke in the newspaper about the project, we confirmed the identity of the company to the mayor and the council, emphasizing to them that confidentiality was paramount until we were prepared to bring the project before the council for a vote.

As busy as we were, I would not forget about Jim Cassidy's letter about bringing the city and other agencies together to discuss the Somali relocations. I was excited about Jim's idea and would give it the time it deserved, but there was another thing that required my immediate attention. We were working with a Fortune 500 company to locate a large distribution center in Lewiston, and the company involved was looking to have this project done as soon as possible. We had been working on this project for months and Greg Mitchell, Linc Jeffers, Chris Branch, Dick Metivier and I were determined not to let down the company, the elected officials, or our city's residents.

**Project Quality**

At some point in early 2001, Joe Wischerath from Maine & Company met Mike Mullis of J.M. Mullis, Inc. at a conference or business development function, possibly in Boston, where they struck up a conversation about what was keeping Mullis busy in New England. During that conversation, Wischerath heard that Mullis, whose company did site consultation searches and other work for large corporations, was looking in southern New England for a large retail distribution center site and not getting the results he was looking for. Wischerath asked if he had any interest in looking in Maine. Eventually, the two agreed to assemble some sites to review, and the process worked its way into the Lewiston-Auburn area.[722]

In my interview with former Lewiston Economic Development Director Greg Mitchell, he shared that Wischerath's success in convincing Mullis to consider Maine basically resulted in a three-day aerial tour of potential development sites around the state.

According to Linc Jeffers, before the aerial tour, Joe Wischerath contacted LAEGC and asked them to send a list of potential sites and all other requisite information to Mullis by the end of the week sometime around May 2001.[723] Mike Gotto, the

President of Technical Services, Inc in Auburn, confirmed this timeline through his "job number" records that reflect the year and approximate time-of-year Lucien Gosselin hired him for Project Quality.[724] Gotto was hired to provide surveying and engineering expertise on the project. He prepared "graphics for both cities for the sites they had chosen" to send to Mullis.[725] It just so happened that both the Lewiston and Auburn sites rejected by the U.S. Post Office distribution center in May 2000 were ready to go with a "three-inch binder"[726] full of information about the sites, demographics, and other data originally developed by Gotto, but "adjusted (by Gotto)...as directed by each city for Mullis." For Lewiston, the old Post Office location would be the only site it would submit. Auburn officials, at their direction, had Gotto create plans "for the second site in Auburn," one that "was adjacent to the airport," and positioning Auburn with two potential sites.[727]

That statewide aerial tour narrowed the site selection process down to Lewiston and Auburn. During the three-day aerial tour, Mike Gotto contacted Linc Jeffers to let him know that all the other Maine sites were off the table, and that L-A would be the only remaining Maine location under consideration.[728] Jeffers passed that information along to LAEGC and arrangements were made for all the parties to meet with Mullis and Wischerath who would be flying into the Auburn-Lewiston Airport.

Things were happening so quickly that "(b)oth cities had no idea if they would be able to pay (Gotto)" right away given the speed at which decisions were being made. That included not having time to secure contracts that needed to be reviewed and signed. Both cities and the LAEGC had worked with Gotto many times and knew that he "understood the permitting process and had worked on most of the larger lots or projects on both sides of the river." Both cities also "wanted (Gotto's) experience to help them respond to site questions" from Mullis.[729] The speed at which decisions were being made would not have been possible without a high level of trust and respect all parties had for each other.

The night before Project Quality representatives Mullis and Wischerath would arrive at the Auburn-Lewiston Airport (according to Linc Jeffers, the name "Project Quality" was coined by Mike Mullis[730]), Lewiston's Greg Mitchell received the site selection criteria from Gosselin and forwarded the information to Gotto the day before the Project Quality group would fly into L-A.[731] Mitchell knew Gotto might find the information useful, as he would be part of the meeting with the Project Quality representatives in the morning. More importantly, Gotto was already familiar with all the potential Project Quality sites in Lewiston-Auburn, as they were produced by his firm.

One of the biggest project criteria hurdles was the need for over 100 contiguous acres of developable land for the project. Most people would think that a place like Maine had an infinite amount of developable land that was available for the project. The reality was that finding 100 acres of contiguous land that had no environmental issues, with a direct connection to Interstate-95, access to ample water, sewage, power and natural gas, and the labor supply to meet the needs of a one million square foot distribution center was challenging to find in Maine.

Gotto shared in our interview that "once I received the criteria (from Mitchell the day before), I knew that none of the sites (Auburn & Lewiston)(sic) would meet the criteria provided (by Mullis)."[732] According to Gotto, the next morning, he produced a worksheet for an alternate Lewiston site across the street from the proposed former U.S. Post Office location his firm had drafted.[733] "I had a taped-together(sic) worksheet from the City GIS maps showing the City pit and surrounding parcels (across the street from the Post Office site) that I created early that morning before my (TSI company) staff arrived. I only had a few minutes with staff (to instruct them on the immediate need for new site plans that morning) once they got to work before I left for the Mullis meeting (at the airport)."[734]

Armed with his "taped-together" alternative Lewiston plans, Gotto and the Lewiston and Auburn officials boarded their rented van and proceeded to meet Mullis and Wischerath (and possibly another person who was from the company Mullis was representing) who were flying in on a private jet into the Auburn-Lewiston Airport located in Auburn. According to Gotto, the delegation included himself, Lucien Gosselin, Greg Mitchell, and Roland Miller (Auburn Economic Development Director). Some members of the delegation went into the plane to discuss what they would do that day. During that discussion, the location of the first two sites came up as they would be the first sites visited given their location in Auburn. When Mullis learned that the first two Auburn sites were near the airport and rail services, he notified Miller that the Auburn sites would not fit the selection criteria.[735] According to Gosselin, the company had a prior experience with some sort of airplane accident involving one center. Gosselin could not recall why the rail system's proximity was also problematic, but it was to Mullis.[736]

Gotto commented that once Mullis and Wischerath decided they would not visit any Auburn sites, they would not get off the plane and proceed to Lewiston until the Auburn official departed. At some point, Gotto remembers Gosselin having to explain to Miller that Auburn was no longer part of the search process. Miller made his way back to Auburn City Hall. The group then departed for Lewiston to see the one remaining site on the list. The group met with general contractor Dave Gendron at his Lewiston office, which coincidentally also abutted the only Maine site now under consideration: the original Lewiston proposed site (also owned by Gendron) for the U.S. Post Office distribution center.[737]

Shortly after their arrival in Lewiston, Gotto was only a "few minutes" into his presentation when Mullis noticed a line on the survey map and "interrupted with a question... What's that?"[738] Mullis asked. "'That's a stream'" Gotto responded. Mullis immediately gave notice to everyone in the room that they would immediately remove the site from consideration. Mullis knew enough about Maine environmental law to know that any evidence of wetlands on a development site was never a positive development.[739]

Gotto knew he now needed to break out the other worksheet he had "taped" together that morning. He spent "40 minutes" speaking to the "Project Quality" representatives and the city officials in the room about the alternative site that was literally across the street.[740] Gotto was doing his best to stretch the new alternative "taped together" worksheet site presentation when his

> staff showed up with a polished GIS graphic with additional details of the (gravel) pit and surrounding properties to address the specific site selection criteria. That's when we

were able to start looking at how many lots may be required to make the site work. Most of the site was owned by the city, South Park Development and Gendron. That's why I knew the site could be assembled with these ownerships involved. The area was also a gravel pit and there were no streams anywhere near the properties. The site also met the length and width requirements for the project.[741]

Gotto's decision to create an additional worksheet with an alternate set of site plans for that morning's gathering with the Project Quality representatives effectively saved the project for L-A. Without the alternate site plan in hand, it is likely that Mullis and Wischerath would have boarded the plane and never returned to L-A.

It is hard to imagine what the odds would have been for two major projects being rejected within a year's time of each other, and both projected to occupy approximately 100 acres in the same neighborhood and employ around 500 or more people in Lewiston. Gotto received the 2002 "Economic Development Award" [742] from the LAEGC for his work on the Walmart project. What he did not receive, was the recognition for sacrificing a good night's sleep, and waking up early enough with an idea that likely saved one of the most important projects in the city's history from being lost before we could negotiate a single line of the deal.

Once Mullis supported Lewiston's location as one of Project Quality's viable sites in New England, the genuine work began for Gotto, LAEGC, Greg Mitchell and Linc Jeffers. The city knew that its "Project Quality" proposal would compete with other out-of-state sites. It was unknown to us how many other sites were involved, but a site in Connecticut appeared to be one of the more frequently mentioned potential sites. The Lewiston site was a complex undertaking. It would require assembling 17 parcels of land,[743] and negotiations needed to get underway to secure the parcels not owned by the city (or the Lewiston Development Corporation).

Additionally, the site would require the re-engineering of Alfred Plourde Parkway; additional investment in the water service for the project; more electrical and natural gas service for the areas; and the grading and movement of soil equal to 5.7 trillion pounds of earth.[744] According to Linc Jeffers, "there was a 100 (foot) grade difference between the eastern and western edges" of the 100 plus acre site. Jeffers also noted that the "amount of earth" that needed to be "moved to create a level site... large enough for the (distribution center)" would rival the amount of soil moved in the construction of the 300-mile Maine Turnpike.[745]

The Project Quality deal would also have to include city economic and state economic incentives; the purchasing of new property for another gravel pit operation; negotiating a land swap with Gendron for the newly engineered parkway that would ultimately lead to a new business park across from the development; and the ability to keep the Walmart name out of the project until the project was ready for a city council vote.

Lewiston was, and remains, a small town by most "city" standards. News of the possible project began to leak out into the public very early into the summer of 2001. Auburn-Lewiston airport staff eventually tracked the tail numbers on the planes that carried Project Quality out-of-state officials who were arriving and exiting with some frequency. The plane was registered in Arkansas, the state that houses the Walmart corporate headquarters.

We were sworn to secrecy but were being pursued by the Sun Journal (and many residents) for verification about rumors of it being a Walmart distribution center. The Sun Journal persisted. The city eventually agreed to provide the Sun Journal 'deep background' about the project in exchange for an embargo on printing anything about the project or the name of the company in the newspaper until the deal was ready for a city council vote.[746]

The Sun Journal agreed but became increasingly uncomfortable holding onto the story, expecting that the project would progress more quickly. In response to their growing unrest with the timeline, the persistent public rumors, and their growing discomfort to withhold information from the public, they believed they needed to print something about the story.[747]

The editors gave the approval to move forward with the Sun Journal's first story on the project on November 1, 2001. The article spoke to the "mega-deal" for a large "distribution center" that would add "600 jobs" for the city. The article said that "many officials privately acknowledge(d) the (project) effort" but would not "discuss it on the record."[748] The Sun Journal knew we believed if there was any disclosure from city officials, it would likely end the deal. We held our ground and the Sun Journal held onto the Walmart name until December 20th when the front-page headline read "City Offers Walmart Deal,"[749] and disclosed the "tax break" that the city council would vote on in the following week.

By this time, there were multiple parties and challenges involved in this deal. We were working with the governor's office for a package of economic incentives that they would make available as part of the deal; the city was looking to lock up the privately owned parcels for the project; one developer wanted to construct a new industrial park and wanted to barter a land swap for the city's re-engineered road for the project; the city needed to ensure that the electric and gas utility companies were prepared to support the needs for up to 1,000,000 square feet of building; and city staff and elected officials were working with the neighbors who had been living next to a well-hidden gravel pit for decades, and had concerns about a large-scale operation with trucks entering and exiting 24 hours per day.

We also had a city council that was justifiably concerned about the limited time that the project would allow for public process and constituent concerns before scheduling a final vote for the project. Having this all happen at a time when I was the acting city administrator did not make matters easier. Richard Metivier, Greg Mitchell and I were entrusted with the responsibility of assuring the public, mayor, and council that our economic development, finance, and public works staff, who had done a magnificent job in assembling this very complex proposal in seven months, would give them the information they needed to support this project. We had also done our best to work with the council and mayor through the process behind closed doors for months.

There were many last-minute complications with the package proposal that were pushing us to delay releasing the public documents as we got closer to the scheduled day of the vote, Friday, December 28, 2001. The full package of materials explaining the scope of the project and all the city and state economic tax incentives for Walmart, were not delivered to the mayor and council until Wednesday, December 26, 2001. Councilors were understandably annoyed about the delay. The stakes for the city were high, but this kind of delay was a departure from our normal practices and timelines with most projects. The Walmart clock was ticking to finalize the project, and some councilors were understandably uncomfortable with the compressed schedule. Jim Carignan's email to the mayor and the city council on December 26th reflected some of the frustration on the city council:

> I am sure that the Council will do this. Can't we just try to save some semblance of public disclosure—some sense that a democracy depends on the people knowing. This is Wednesday. I am being asked to vote on a major thing on Friday... It does not strike me as very democratic the way this is happening.[750]

The project was put before the city council on December 28, 2001. It was a Friday night, a highly unusual time for a city council to act on city business by any governmental standard, but the circumstances leading up to the scheduled vote were also highly unusual. One of the most frequent observations voiced by some members of the public, the press and certainly from Jim Carignan, was whether the city's call for urgency really existed with Walmart.

Our staff response to Jim Carignan and the city council was driven by Walmart's insistence that in their world, lost time was big money. The company had committed to Lewiston, and the time it would take to restart the process was simply not an option. The city needed to commit or not commit to the project at this meeting. Greg Mitchell added that this facility would also become the first food distribution center using "robotics"[751] that would result in the first "mechanized produce and refrigerated grocery warehouse(s)"[752] in the country and replicated in all other new distribution facilities. Walmart wanted this model distribution center up and running as soon as possible.

Before the evening's city council meeting, we all met privately in executive session with six city councilors (Councilor Gary Adams was not present for the meeting)[753] and the mayor to discuss the agenda that would include the Walmart vote and labor negotiations. Greg Mitchell, Richard Metivier, Linc Jeffers and I were inside the executive meeting room to answer any last-minute questions.

Councilor Carignan clearly remained undecided and shared some of his thoughts as to why he felt that way. Both Mitchell and I stressed with the group that a unanimous vote would send a powerful message validating our unity and support for this project. There was no 'straw vote' to see where councilors stood on the issue, but both Mitchell and I knew from the discussions in the room that we had the votes to get the project approved. We also knew that a project of this importance to the city would be greatly helped with a unanimous vote (we needed no less than four votes to approve the project and one city councilor was absent that evening).

After a brief executive session behind closed doors, we exited the conference room at the back of the council chambers and walked through a standing-room only crowd that was waiting patiently for the meeting to begin. Greg Mitchell opened the meeting with a presentation about the scope of the project: how many would be employed; when construction was scheduled to begin; what the city and state tax incentive package would look like; and when it would become operational. It would be smaller than originally reported in the press at about 480,000 square feet and Walmart would invest $45.5 million into the project.[754] The project would receive "$16.6 million, not including up to $360,000 more in state training funds" resulting in approximately $10 million in tax breaks from the city and about $7 million from the state.[755] The agreement would require Walmart to employ 350 people when it was projected to open sometime in April 2004.[756]

It became apparent as the evening went along that no one was speaking in opposition to the project, with the sole exception of one resident, who believed that the city should not be "providing such a large tax break to a large corporation." Most of the other concerns had to do with ensuring that the city would address what needed to be done with increasing traffic loads on the parkway, the landscaping that would be done around such a large facility, noise levels, and doing what it could to address the design of this type of building, which are most often "very ugly buildings."[757]

The city council was supportive, but Councilor James Carignan wanted to express his concern about a project that concerned him from almost the very beginning, even before it was identified as Walmart. During the meeting, Carignan said he was not "'convinced that (the project) into the future is a move that's positive and that's progressive.'" Carignan questioned what people would be paid and said that any project should reflect on Lewiston as a "'special place'" and he was not sure the distribution center met "'that criteria.'"[758]

Carignan also asked about the center's impact on the city regarding its "utility expenses, return on investment, environmental operations of the company... (the) possibilities of withdrawal from the project," and what ramifications that might have for taxpayers. Councilor Marc Gousse added he wanted to "make sure the City (was) able to get the best deal possible." Carignan also said that he thought it was "despicable that this company chose to avoid public disclosure... (p)eople can say that's not the way it works. Well, not in my world."[759] I know that at this point in the meeting, I was fully prepared for Jim to vote against the project. Both Jim and Councilor Gousse were very close, and I thought Gousse might support his colleague and vote against it knowing that the project had four solid votes from the other councilors.

When it came time for the vote, most of us in the room were preparing for a more muted celebration with an affirmative, but not unanimous vote. Under the conditions, and given some public concerns about the highly compressed timeline, the city would be fortunate to have a majority on the council, along with the mayor, supporting the project. Much to my amazement, and I am certain to the amazement of many others in the chambers that evening, the roll call vote produced a unanimous 6-0 vote to support the project. Carignan was "high-fived" by his city council colleagues, "(a)nd many in the audience of about 100 (who) rose to give (Carignan), the council, and the prospect of landing the deal a standing ovation."[760]

It was an extraordinary ending to a highly improbable project that was only made possible by a simple conversation between Joe Wischerath and Mike Mullis, and Mike Gotto's last-minute idea to produce an alternate site plan involving a gravel pit on the other side of the street.

Mike Gotto also shared a story about the opportunity he had been given to develop site plans for another large development parcel in Auburn, one that also required the excavation and grading of a very large site. Given the topography and land preparation requirements of the prospective site, Gotto initially believed that it would not be possible for the site to accommodate the kind of retail use the Whitholm Farm owners desired. The success in getting that project site developed led him to believe that Lewiston's gravel pit was a viable site alternative for Project Quality. That previous experience had involved developing a site that would accommodate a number of retail stores, including one of the state's first retail supercenters...and the store's name would be Walmart.[761]

The Walmart distribution center deal was officially announced on January 3, 2002[762] when Tony Fuller, a vice-president for Walmart's real estate division, told those in attendance, who included Governor Angus King, that the company chose a "'community where we can be a part of economic growth, a place we believe we can call home for a long time.'" Walmart's intended target opening of April 1, 2004 would be delayed as the city and the company continued to work through multiple complexities associated with its primary tractor-trailer entrance, and the need to purchase some additional property.

The ground-breaking ceremony occurred on a very chilly day in December 2004,[763] and the grand opening ceremony would finally happen on August 3, 2005. The project, now estimated at $60 million and delayed by some 16 months, would open with its dry-goods warehouse fully operational, 200 employees hired, and its phase-two refrigerated warehouse under construction with another 250 employees projected to be hired.[764] The company would meet all of its required targets to qualify for the tax incentives that were part of the original agreement.

## Pressing On

There is little doubt about where the Walmart deal's place in Lewiston's history belongs. When all the textile mills were built, no single mill ever had the number of square feet of the current Walmart facility, making it the largest single building ever constructed in the history of the two cities. As for employees, the Raytheon Corporation remained the community's single largest economic development project under one roof with 1,300 hundred employees at the peak of its 20-month existence (it was originally scheduled to employ as many as 2,000).

As busy as we were in dealing with all the complexities of the Walmart deal, the business of government never allowed you to work on one large project. As 2002 was quickly approaching, my staff needed to address several priority initiatives and continued to deal with the ongoing fallout from the 9/11 attack before our current city council and mayor were going to finish their terms in office.

As much as we tried to focus on the job at hand, we were still being impacted by the after-effects of the 9/11 attack. On the day before the unnamed "mega" Walmart project was announced in the Sun Journal on November 1, 2001, the city experienced another anthrax event on October 31$^{st}$, only one block from City Hall. The Ash Street Post Office center staff noticed a business-sized envelope that contained "a powdery substance" addressed to Mayor Kaileigh Tara. The letter caused the post office to call the E911 service who dispatched local police and fire to the scene and triggered a response from the state's Weapons of Mass Destruction Civil Support Team.[765]

The ensuing investigation and inspection of the post office facility meant that postal workers were stuck outside until the state made a determination about the powder. They were quickly given shelter by a law firm across the street from the center once the law firm employees saw the postal workers standing out in the cold. Law firm owner Bob Laskoff felt it was just the right thing to do sharing "(we) all have to stick together in matters" like these. Fortunately, the powder was found to be harmless. One woman commented that if she had children, "they wouldn't be (going) out to trick-or-(treat) tonight." Another woman at the scene commented, "'I've been saying, 'Well, it's not going to happen here, but I guess you never know.'"[766]

The post-9/11 anthrax attacks and scares would not dampen anyone's commitment to keep the city moving forward. The CMMC cardiac center that hospital officials and the community worked so hard so get approved started construction in late October[767], just about a year after it had received DHS approval on October 2, 2000. We were also making progress with the 40,000 square foot 1877 Music Hall[768] that was being transformed into a modern municipal district court building.

The Music Hall court project, like many that involve the renovation of historic properties, encountered its share of challenges. The project was first conceived back in January 1999 and estimated at $5 million.[769] When the state approved the project, that estimate increased to $7 million. The structural challenges that were encountered required unanticipated engineering services that drove up the project costs and to another $2.5 million. In order to complete the project, our legislative delegation, spearheaded by Appropriations Committee member Rep. Richard Mailhot, helped to secure funding to get the job done.[770]

While all of this was going on near the end of 2001, I was also trying to wrap up contract negotiations with several unions. Approximately 300 employees had been without a contract since June 30th. Negotiations were made a little more challenging given my instructions to have all the unions make their first payroll contributions to their health coverage.[771] We were seeking a monthly premium contribution of 7%. In my experience, any time you are asking for union employees to do something that will cost them money, and it is being done for the first time, neither you nor the proposal will not be received warmly.

Contract negotiations were making progress, but we still had a way to go. This was all occurring at the same time we suddenly found ourselves starting all over with the city administrator search process. The Human Resources office and I were spending a lot of time together, but we had little choice but to simply bear down and keep moving the ball forward.

In that same month, the Lewiston High School Civil Rights Team sponsored a "Diversity Day" event that featured "a series of workshops, performances and panel discussions focusing on different cultures." One student, who was a 1998 LHS graduate, said that although he had encountered very little discrimination while in high school, he still "kept to himself" and felt "sheltered" and saw himself as an "outcast." Another 1993 LHS graduate said that while she had also not experienced much discrimination from the school as a student of color, she had experienced one episode where someone had called her the 'n' word. She also shared that there were only "three or five blacks and two Chinese" students when she attended school and marveled at the "60 to 80 minority students" that were now attending LHS.

The staff of the Western Maine Community Action [772] organization in western Maine, along with staff from the Maine Department of Labor's Career Center, were also hosting their own November diversity event. They reached out to the new Somali residents with a casual event featuring a meal of "rice and beans and greens, spiced beef and lemon and orange cake... after sunset, ending another day of fasting during the Muslim holy month of Ramadan." Staff invited their guests to meet the newcomers in a more social setting and to learn more about Somali culture. The Somali guests expressed their appreciation for their new community and for people like Rose Hodges, one of the Career Center staff who worked with the new residents in their search for employment. Rose was referred to as "the queen" by one of the Somali attendees in deference to her dedication and commitment in working with the new Somali population. The "newcomers" also shared that they chose to live in Lewiston because they saw it as a "welcoming" community that was a "safe place to raise their children."[773]

I was also left with the unenviable task of working through the process of finalizing the purchase of a building called the Pillsbury Block, which the city partially acquired in 1995.[774] The city's library had been looking to expand for years. The last effort to expand the library was in 1991 and involved a joint effort to seek a mutually agreeable location for a new library that would serve both Lewiston and Auburn. Both public library systems had worked together for years. The Lewiston Library efforts to bring more cultural and artistic events to the city resulted in the creation of the "LPL plus" program in 1973. That program led to a joint effort with Auburn creating "LPL Plus APL" and the creation of LA Arts in 1988[775] that is still in operation as of the publication of this book. The effort to build one library was not successful but the need for a larger library in Lewiston was still something the city desired.

Before the city could fully acquire the building, a local businessman secured a 30-year lease for the remaining section of the building. After both sides could not come to an agreement over the value of the remaining space, both the city attorney and I believed that we needed to ask the city council if they desired to pursue acquiring the space by eminent domain. The action was brought before the city council on November 13, 2001 and would occur during my first meeting as the city's acting administrator.[776] The city council agreed with a unanimous vote that all reasonable measures had been pursued, but the difficulty with doing so was that the businessperson involved in the library property dispute was also Councilor-elect Norm Rousseau who would be in office in January. He would also be a city councilor at a time where we would either continue to negotiate the eminent domain action or pursue the matter in court.

I understood that this was really nothing more than a business transaction, as it did not involve an operating business or homeowner being displaced; it was merely a real estate matter where the two parties disagreed about the price. I was fortunate that Councilor-elect Norm Rousseau appeared to feel the same way and he and I never discussed the matter either while he was in office, or afterward. We actually became good friends and traveled together to California where we were both part of the effort to have our city designated as an All-America City[777] in 2007. Norm also became a potential buyer for our home that we sold back in 2018. In a small town, you always hope that your municipal job never produces an instance where you may disappoint someone or make them unhappy. That was not always the case, but I was fortunate in that it did not happen with Councilor Rousseau.

One of the more pleasant tasks that I had near the end of 2001 was to also serve on the first board of the newly created Franco American Heritage Center that was officially signed over to the Center on November 9, 2000.[778] Lionel Guay, had helped resurrect Lewiston's Franco American Festival and turning into a three day event shutting down a part of downtown on Friday night for a street festival. Guay was also the primary force in negotiating with the Catholic Diocese of Portland to sell the property to the newly created Franco center board with a commitment to do the necessary structural work that the church needed. Without it, the 73-year-old[779] church's stone face of the front of the building had the potential of collapsing onto the sidewalk and into the street.

The Diocese was willing to take the risk the renovating the old church but insisted on a narrow window of time for the renovations in reaction to problems the Diocese had encountered with another church restoration project in Portland. Lionel and our board members knew that failing would mean that the Diocese would have no alternative but to demolish St. Mary's Church. At the close of 2001, we were on our way to raising the funds to do the necessary façade repairs, to rent out the facility for community events, assembling historical Franco artifacts, pictures, and other materials for the historical section of the building, and to establish what would become one of the best performing arts facilities in the state. Without Lionel Guay, the Franco center would not have become a reality. Guay would go on to become Lewiston's mayor in 2003.

## James Carignan

For Bates Dean Emeritus and City Councilor Dr. James Carignan, the end of 2001 would mark his departure as city councilor with a true 'photo finish' at the end of his career. Elected officials with the kind of drive, intellect, and compassion that he possessed come along infrequently. In his position at Bates, "Carignan saw himself as an educator and teacher first, rather than a disciplinarian... Instead of simply doling out punishment when students ended up in his office, Carignan looked for teachable moments in the meetings." According to former Dean of Faculty Carl Straub "'Jim believed strongly that colleges like Bates had a responsibility to educate students in good citizenship.'"[780]

Jim also demanded much of himself and sometimes his students. "In 1985, one such moment might have led to

Carignan's being shot by a sniper while sitting at his kitchen table... The bullet lodged less than an inch from his heart. Carignan later told a Sun Journal reporter that he believed the damage (the bullet) caused led years later to his two heart transplants."[781] Undeterred, he returned to work, albeit a step or two slower. "Responding to a colleague's greeting after his return in 1986, he said, "'It is good to be here,'" then restated the sentiment with emphasis: "'I mean, it is good to be here.'"[782]

As a city councilor, Jim could be masterful and captivating, even in defeat. He had supported the renovation of the Bates Mill throughout his tenure and supported many of the major projects that had marked much of the city's economic success since 1999. Jim could also launch a formidable effort to oppose something that he did not believe was beneficial for the city. The matter of building an overpass over one of Lewiston's busiest state highways to connect to the Veterans Memorial Bridge and the city of Auburn was one of those projects. Jim fought valiantly, although unsuccessfully, against the overpass project connecting Russell Street that in his opinion, had the potential for increasing traffic loads and creating negative impacts on neighboring homes.

Like many other elected officials, Carignan had his share of failures and successes, but the approaching end of his tenure on the council appeared to energize him. He had an interest in the Lewiston Housing Authority's efforts in building a community center two blocks away from City Hall. When LHA received a $1 million earmark in November 2001 from a HUD bill to fund a new community center in downtown Lewiston, Carignan led the charge for the additional funding needed to complete the project. He not only fought and succeeded to have the city council add another $500,000 in city reserve funds, against the advice of City Finance Director Metivier, he also ensured that $385,000 would be obligated for the project from Community Development Block Grant Funds.[783]

He also led the council effort to protect the 160-acre Garcelon Bog from any future development, and to support the creation of a conservation easement that would protect the property in "perpetuity."[784] In a November 13, 2001 action by the Lewiston City Council to accept the Parsons Brinckerhoff Report, the city council effectively gave its endorsement to eliminate the city-owned bog parcel from any future building or road development.[785]

According to the Lewiston Planning Board minutes of June 25, 2002,

> (i)n the 1950's it was the original site of a highway going through Lewiston. The proposed route was to go through Garcelon Bog property backing out on to Webster Street. In the 1960's, this alternative was moved forward with additional studies on transportation network. In the early 1970's action was taken by the City to reserve the route from the Russell/Sabattus Street area all the way over to the turnpike exchange. That particular route was never moved forward...(B)ack 20 years ago, the City was still concerned about the connection of the Maine Turnpike Route 196 area, up into Route 126 and over to Route 100. A viable route is needed to move traffic...There was a long, drawn out two- (2-) year review of alternatives. Three (3) of the alternatives which were developed by the Public Advisory Committee impacted the Garcelon Bog in one way or another...(Public Works Director) Chris Branch said that he spoke with consultants regarding the viability of this project. Environmentally-damaging(sic) alternatives need to be looked at. Based on the recommendation from the environmental consultant (Parsons-Brinkerhoff), due to the wildlife habitat and wetlands in this area that would be impacted by these three (3) alternatives, there was no way to get this project permit(ted). They gave a recommendation to the Public Advisory Committee that

these three (3) alternatives be dropped because of that reality. The Public Advisory Committee then forwarded that recommendation to the City Council for action by the Public Works Department to approve the recommendation to eliminate those three (3) alternatives to the site. (In November 2001) a recommendation was made for the City to look into establishing a conservation easement for Garcelon Bog. The City Council adopted that and eliminated the bog alternatives.[786]

On June 25, 2002 the Planning Board voted unanimously to send "a favorable recommendation to the City Council and the City Administrator to sign and approve the Garcelon Bog city property conservation easement with the Androscoggin Land Trust, and for the creation of the Garcelon Bog Advisory Committee."[787] For a variety of reasons, the final action for the creation of the conservation easement was not be approved by the city council until February 17, 2009.[788]

This final unanimous action by the city council would protect the 160-acre site where "a thousand-foot boardwalk (with) enough distance from nearby roads to give the place a surprising sense of isolation" could exist in the middle of the city. 150 years ago, it was seen as a potential site for excavating peat for fuel, something that could have resulted in building a railroad operation on the site to haul the material away.[789] This land, once considered as a potential east-west highway connector and a possible railroad siding for a peat mining operation, was an environmental wonder "chock full of black spruce, tamarack and other trees that flourish in wetlands."[790] It is nothing short of miraculous that it all remained largely untouched, and would now be protected under state law and managed by the Androscoggin Land Trust, largely because of Jim's efforts.

Some of Jim's best work was done literally in the last 6 months while he was in office, and they were accomplishments that had enormous impact on the city. Ironically, his vote to approve the Walmart project was the last legislative act of his city council career, and a vote he casted while also expressing his reservations about the future benefits of one of the most important economic development projects in the city's history. That resistance about supporting the Walmart project remained evident when I bumped into Jim in the State Office building in Augusta, several years before his death.

Jim was on his way to a legislative hearing, and we chatted for a moment. For some reason, the Walmart vote came up in discussion. During that discussion, Jim paused. He looked at me and said that of all the votes he had been a part of while serving as a city councilor, the one he most wanted to take back was the Walmart vote. Years later, Jim remained conflicted about supporting a project that had proven itself to be incredibly successful for the city's bottom line, the community's overall economy, and for the employment opportunities it continued to generate. It had also impacted many ancillary companies and non-profit organizations that benefitted in some way from having this distribution center in the community. At the date of this book's publication, Walmart remains the second largest Fortune 500 company employer in Lewiston, while TD Bank remains the first.

I told Jim that it may have been one of his most important votes as a city councilor, and one of the most important in the city's economic development history. He appreciated the compliment, but he also shared that he would continue to feel that the city could have done better and needed to aspire to greater things. That was Jim. I smiled and told him I would continue to respectfully disagree. I shook his hand, wished him well, and told him to give my best to his wife Sally. He reciprocated and wished both my wife and I the same. That would be the last time I would see Dean Carignan. Jim passed away in 2011, and his wife Sally, who had worked with my wife on the Lewiston Housing Authority Board in the early 2000s, passed away in 2020.

# Chapter 6

# Believing, Not Believing, and Listening

# January 2002 – June 2002

### *The Working Group*

2002 would be my third consecutive new year either working in an acting capacity and working with a retired administrator or as the acting city administrator. Being the acting city administrator was beginning to feel "normal" at this juncture. The only difference was I now worked with a new mayor and several new councilors. The Walmart project was approved, and the development planning and negotiating (there were parcels of land that were not under contract yet) was underway with much work ahead. There was also my commitment to get in touch with Jim Cassidy at St. Mary's Regional Medical Center (parent company Sisters of Charity Health System, Inc. or SOCHS) after the New Year.

On January 3rd, I asked my assistant to send a letter[791] to Jim Cassidy apologizing for the delay in responding. I also asked Jim to tell me what exactly he had in mind by pulling together this sizeable group of state and local government agencies, local organizations, the school department, and others. My staff and I had been meeting with many groups already over the course of 2001. We set up a meeting with Cassidy at his office to discuss what he had in mind.

The meeting with Jim was enlightening. He did not intend to simply bring groups together to talk about what was going on with the Somali relocations; he wanted this process to bring together those already involved in what was going on in Lewiston. Jim envisioned that the gathering's purpose find a way to produce a coordinated strategy to address what was not getting done, what more could be done, and to eliminate any duplication of effort to not deplete scarce resources (particularly funding).

Jim was right. The city was spending too much time trying to figure out what we should and should not be doing; learning more about the Somali culture; figuring out how the refugee program works and how it connects to services at the state level; and working with Portland to develop the collaborative refugee program. We simply had not spent time on how this all might work from a more coordinated level.

We set the first meeting for February 5th at the Sisters of Charity Health System's (SOCHS) Fleet Conference Center that was part of St. Mary's hospital. I was present with another 19 participants that reflected the level of activity going on in the Lewiston area. The list included: Sue Charron, Mayor Raymond, and City Council President Rene Bernier who were the attending city officials. Other notables included: James Cassidy, President/CEO, SOCHS; Kaileigh Tara, Director of Healthier Communities, SOCHS (and former Lewiston mayor); Leon "Lee" Levesque, Lewiston School Dept., Superintendent; John Kerry, CEO, Catholic Charities Maine; Pierrot Rugaba, Director of Refugee Resettlement, ME Dept. of Human Services: Kevin Concannon, Commissioner, ME Dept. of Human Services; Jerry Friedman, Executive Director, American Public Human Services Association; and Sue Harlor, Director of Community Services, ME Dept. of Human Services.[792]

The purpose of the meeting was to provide some context for what the current status of things were with the Somali population in Lewiston, such as the estimated current number of arrivals in the city, what was going on in the Lewiston public school system, as well as to let everyone know we had SOCHS as a partner in the effort. There was also agreement on the general categories of things that needed much more discussion: basic city services, social service agency services, what was available from state and local agencies in the city, centralization of services, and funding for refugees that move from their primary resettlement community to another community.[793]

Another meeting was set up for February 28th. Attendees included SOCHS staff, Councilor Bernier, Superintendent Levesque, Catholic Charities staff, and Sue Charron. Discussion revolved around finding ways to better use websites to publish information that interested the public; contacting more agencies such as Central Maine Medical Center and Bates College; contacting benevolent non-profits for funding; producing written handouts from both the city and the school department; trying to assemble Somali community residents identified as their leadership; data collection; outreach to the media and business community; more staffing for General Assistance; and using the local cable government channel for information. The discussion led to the creation of short-term strategies (communications, public health information, city services, school services, etc.) and long-term strategies (grant writing, written handouts, web site utilization, clergy outreach, etc.). Assignments on some of the short and long-term objectives were handed out to several attendees who volunteered their assistance.[794]

At the next meeting on March 7th, some new participants joined the effort including Jere Mauer from Central Maine Medical Center, Dot Meagher from Auburn General Assistance, and Heather Lindkvist, Somali Cultural Advisor to the City of Lewiston, Lecturer and Ph.D. candidate from the University of Chicago. Superintendent Leon "Lee" Levesque reported he would reach out to the Auburn public-school system and that he was going to ask the civil rights team at the high school to find ways to become more engaged with the new Somali students. Levesque also mentioned that there was an article on that very issue in that day's school newspaper. Levesque had been very busy. He also reported that the department was looking to create forums for Somali teachers and parents and that they had already produced a fact sheet for the faculty. Lee also believed that we needed to have a member of the Somali community at these meetings as soon as possible. We all agreed, and the attendees took more assignments on.[795]

The March 7th meeting also resulted in the most important moment in the process. It was decided that while we were working on the various tasks assigned to the committee, we also needed to memorialize the areas of concern, what was being done, who was doing it, and other information into a single "issues" paper. The document would feature the following topics: healthcare, public health, education, General Assistance, housing (public and private), transportation (as it related to jobs, childcare, and healthcare), ESL (public schools and adult education), employment, public safety, public outreach, refugee information, and a Somali communique with their observations and concerns. We also set March 21st as the "drop dead date" to get all drafts for this paper/report before the group for review. There is no record of discussions about who would receive the report, but it would be a document for public release.[796]

We focused the meeting on March 14th on reporting what tasks they had accomplished or were in progress. One task involved our meeting with the Sun Journal staff Executive Editor Rex Rhoades and Managing Editor Carol Coultas to bring them up to speed on what we were working on and to get them additional information about some issues we were discussing. Group member Charles Johnson also reported on his meetings with members of the faith-based community, representing the Catholic, Protestant, Bahai and Islamic faith.

Johnson also reported that LA Arts had contracted with a Somali band to come to the area but was approached by the "Somali elders" and asked not to have them come.[797] There was no further explanation in my notes, but it was becoming a well-known fact that many of the Somali adults that we were getting to know were either very conservative themselves in their religious beliefs or knew many others that were. If the band the Johnson was interested in was recognized to be to 'westernized' and possibly playing any American music (particularly hip-hop/rap music), it would likely not have met with the 'elders' approval. The last note of the March 14th meeting stated that an invitation would go out, likely through Mohamed Abdi, to invite Somali "reps" to the next meeting on March 28th.

The March 28th meeting offered many members of the working group an opportunity to have their first extended conversation with the Somali elders. They had been chosen by the local Somali Al-Noor Mosque in Lewiston, with Mohamed Abdi serving as their translator. The elders shared that possibly 500 to 1,000 more Somali individuals would move to the city over the upcoming months, something that generated concern from city officials.[798]

The in-migration numbers that were being discussed were alarming given the information we had. I decided to create a weekly memo to update the city council and city-school management. It would contain useful data and other information collected by the city, school department, and other sources about our new immigrant residents. I wanted the council to depend on the memo as one of their primary sources of information. It also helped my staff and I to stay on top of our game, given the number of people and agencies that were becoming involved in this unfolding event. The April 4th city council memo showed that as of March 31, 2002, 202 families, representing 568 individuals, [799] had been processed as first-time General Assistance applicants in Lewiston. This represented a 67% family increase since December 31, 2001. At this juncture, the total Somali population in the city was likely over 1,000 individuals.

These General Assistance numbers were a primary topic of conversation at the March 28th meeting. I needed to leave the meeting early and asked Heather Lindkvist to take notes for me. In Heather's March 29, 2002 email summary to me, she shared that General Assistance Director Sue Charron said her office was "stretched to the limit. (Charron) clearly stated her own frustration with the lack of resources (particularly staff) and the increased migration of Somalis in Lewiston. Charron spoke about how busy her office was with the additional traffic being created by the new Somali arrivals, and that they had "resettled more individuals than Catholic Charities of Maine does in a year with a fraction of the staff."[800] Heather added that Sue

> (i)mpressed upon the Somali community leaders... (the) need to inform the (Somali) community at large (i.e., across the U.S.) that immigration to Lewiston, Maine needs to slow down. (Sue said) 'If you get any calls tell them there is no housing at this time'... (In response) (t)he Somali community members offered to provide voluntary services to Sue and her office. The statement 'Sue looks tired' prefaced every

remark (from the elders). Somalis want to help out, but, as Sue pointed out, she does not have the time or personnel to train Somali volunteers... The (Somali elders) discussed how the Somali community can get involved to divert new arrivals from heading to General Assistance: working with landlords to find apartments, providing temporary housing, taking (children) to schools to get enrolled, etc... Members of the (working) group urged the Somali community leaders to get more involved in the resettlement of the new migrants in Maine.[801]

Sgt. James Minkowsky from the Lewiston Police Department also joined the group to speak with the elders. Minkowsky shared with the elders how appreciative he was of the support he and the department had been receiving from Mohamed Abdi and Abdiaziz Ali in the General Assistance Office. Elders reported complaints regarding adults being accused of child abuse and stated that "'if you touch your child you will be taken away.' One woman described the importance of discipline in Somalia: any Somali elder may discipline a child. In the United States though, children are not disciplined as much for fear they will be taken away."[802]

Elders also discussed being stopped by police officers asking them, "what they were doing" and in other cases knocking on their doors to ask them questions. They also shared that some in the Somali community believed that their "American neighbors (were) calling the police because they look different... (and) discussed the tendency to confuse Somali individuals with one another." The elders also asked whether the police department hired Somali officers and what interpretation services were available. Sgt. Minkowsky responded by assuring them that the police were there to protect them and the entire community. He also proposed that the elders organize a meeting that he would attend to discuss "domestic violence... child abuse laws, traffic stops, and answer questions about the role of police officers in the community." Minkowsky went to say that he had made the same proposal in the past but had not received any response to the invitation.[803]

When the working group met again on April 4th, the intent was to focus on the housing situation in Lewiston. Lewiston Housing Authority Executive Director James Dowling spoke to us to provide us some ideas of what the state of affairs was with public housing in Lewiston. He stated that 25% of the 94 housing units at the LHA-managed Hillview Apartment complex were occupied by Somali families who made up 30% of the population. He also shared that 65 Somali families were on a waiting list with other non-immigrant families:

6 Somali families were waiting for 5-bedroom units
18 Somali families were waiting for 4-bedroom units
19 Somali families were waiting for 3-bedroom units
17 Somali families were waiting for 2-bedroom units.[804]

The Section 8 voucher program, also managed by the Lewiston Housing Authority, had been a perennial problem relative to meeting the public housing need in Lewiston over the last 10 years. There were approximately 930 Section 8 vouchers available to Lewiston families for FY 2002. The waiting list as of the meeting date was 430 families (immigrant and non-immigrant families). The LHA had received 700 applicants for Section 8 vouchers since January 2002. Since the demand had already well exceeded the supply, LHA had closed the list to applicants until the numbers on the waiting list warranted adding more families. Aside from the shortage of public housing support, Dowling reported that there were only "2 to 3 events through the summer (of 2001) with PD and Hillview staff" but that there was no "racial problem" at Hillview, except for a few "minor comments, some graffiti, and some unpleasant 'episodes.'"[805]

The April 4th working group was also beginning the process of reviewing the last of the agency "white papers," that according to my April 5th city council memo, would now be a part of a "State report to the Governor." The report would discuss Somali arrival impacts in the city, and though it would not "exhaustively cover every issue," it would "raise awareness in the Governor's Office and within his cabinet on the problems facing the city. Our purpose (was) to engage the state and get them to see (what was happening in Lewiston) as a state policy issue and not just a 'Lewiston/Portland' local issue."[806]

The group's decision to produce this report for the governor is what Jim Cassidy believed could be a difference maker for the city. This process he assembled brought us together to collect, discuss, and exchange information. It was all about assessing needs and capacities, learning more about the situation, and deciding how to move forward. We recognized early on that we were experiencing something that few communities in the U.S. had ever encountered—the rapid relocation of refugee secondary immigrants without the presence of previously resettled refugees (from the same group), and without a major industry or company with jobs that could not be filled by non-immigrant residents. What was happening in Lewiston did not fit the typical refugee community profile that was most familiar to refugee resettlement organizations and the Office of Refugee Resettlement. No one really understood how or why a small community in Maine was the final destination for so many secondary migrant Somalis.

The only explanation that could be offered was that our secondary migration continued to grow because these families saw the community as a good and safe place to raise their families. At that moment in time, we did not have the time to analyze why they were moving. The city had to focus on what we needed to do if they continued to arrive. We had reason to believe that more were coming, and we wanted to have the State of Maine and Governor Angus King working with us every step of the way. The governor's report would be delivered in the not-too-distant future.

**Cheryl Hamilton**

While the working group continued to finalize the report to Governor King, there were many things that we needed to address that were also coming out of the meetings. It may have seemed like a minor matter, but there had been increasing calls from our elected officials to produce some sort of Somali services information sheet that the public could access. I had asked Community Relations Coordinator Dottie Perham-Whittier to do the best she could to monitor what was happening with local social service and non-profit agencies and any activity that was connected to the Somali relocations. That information, along with other relevant news and activity, would be passed along to the city council, city staff, the Somali refugee collaborative, and to the local United Way and the network of agencies that they were supporting. It would all be included in a weekly memo that likely began with my April 5, 2002, weekly memo.[807]

Dottie would also begin assembling a brochure that we could produce in-house and make available publicly. They would be distributed on countertop areas around City Hall and anywhere else we could display them around the city. Dottie's effort would differ from what the school department had produced back in August 2001, which was more heavily weighted towards Somali history, including a brief section on their culture and religion.

Dottie and I were looking for something that would be focused on answering the kinds of "Frequently Asked Questions" we had received in the Administrator's office: Where did the Somalis come from? Why did they move to Lewiston? What do they eat? What is different about their religious beliefs and culture? What challenges are they experiencing? Is anyone paying for them to live in Lewiston?

The final product not only answered those questions, it also provided two language tips: "Iska Waran" means "How are You" and "Fiican" meaning "Fine." The purpose of the brochure was not to make anyone capable of speaking the language or an expert in Somali culture, it was intended only to provide something that would help our residents understand their new neighbors a little more. Dottie would work with Lindkvist and the Portland-Lewiston refugee collaborative's Cultural Skills Trainer Cheryl Hamilton on developing the brochure. Dottie would also be working with our MIS (management information system's) staff to create a "Cultural Diversity Resource" page on our website along with other projects.[808]

Cheryl Hamilton's work as the refugee collaborative's cultural skills trainer came with a wealth of experience for someone who was just out of college a few years prior. An Auburn, Maine native, Cheryl already knew the area. After graduating from Edward Little High School in 1996,[809] Hamilton took a two-year hiatus and was accepted to Clark University in 1998. While attending Clark, she worked for International Services of the American Red Cross and served as the

Coordinator of the World Affairs Council of Boston. Cheryl graduated with a degree in International Studies from Clark in 2001 and attended the SALT Institute for Documentaries Studies for a semester in the fall of 2001. During that time, she was planning a trip to Africa when she came across an ad for the position of Cultural Skills Trainer for the Portland-Lewiston refugee collaborative. Cheryl had done her thesis about the Togolese refugee resettlement in Lewiston and sent that along with her application for the position.[810]

In her thesis, Hamilton had concluded that although she was supportive of the refugee resettlement program in general, she believed the Togolese resettlement demonstrated that Lewiston should not be considered for any future resettlements. In Hamilton's thesis conclusion, she believed that "until there (was) better (cultural) education done (with future refugee populations)... there wasn't enough community integration activities to fully support" another refugee resettlement. That resonated with Sue Charron and the Portland staff. Cheryl was hired in December 2001 and never made it to Africa. Hamilton shared with me that she found it ironic that the person who believed that Lewiston was unprepared to be a refugee resettlement site would now be working on a project to help new refugees who were arriving in the area on their own accord.[811]

Cheryl explained that in the early months of the refugee collaborative, there were demands on her and staff as to what services both Lewiston and Portland wanted for their growing immigrant populations. Hamilton's staff time was, according to the grant, divided as half-time in Lewiston and Portland. Hamilton opined "both cities wanted us more than either city could afford, relative to time." Hamilton added that she and Charron would often say "whichever city (Hamilton) was in was going to be the wrong city, depending on the (city's) perspective."[812]

Hamilton soon discovered that her "cultural skills trainer" position needed to go beyond the life-skills type of training that was originally written into the job description. She understood that these secondary migrants had been exposed to this kind of training already. For most refugees, they managed well enough in their day-to-day activities with what they had already learned while living in the U.S.

225

Sue Charron and the collaborative agreed with Hamilton's emphasis on "community engagement" with Hamilton doing more "education for non-refugee community members, (and) meeting with local refugee leaders," while also working with local agencies and organizations to be better prepared to provide their services.[813]

The agency outreach effort of Hamilton's "community engagement" activities would become part of her "Serving a Multi-Cultural Community Series." These 2002 workshops included "Talking through Translators" in April; "Simply Somali Part Two: From the Women's Perspective" in May; "Cross-Cultural Ethics" in June; "Refugee Related Grants; Finding, Writing and Receiving" in July; and "Addressing Diversity Constructively" in August.[814]

We were still in the process in April of setting up the refugee collaborative's working space, which was wedged into a General Assistance office area that was already approaching its functional capacity with its normal staffing. GA Director Charron was given the green light to hire Omar Ahmed as a part-time GA case worker/translator that would work with refugee collaborative employee Abdiaziz Ali in the GA office. With the addition of the three collaborative employees and a new GA caseworker, space was not the only issue that needed attention (particularly in an environment where confidential conversations were almost always occurring at more than one desk). We also needed more computers, telephones, and lines for staff and for client confidentiality. Even back in 2002, we were cognizant of the potential for problems with the health and safety of the workers by having multiple people handling the same phone receiver.[815]

Although Hamilton would become busier over time with her community outreach endeavors, the grant obligated her to provide a certain number of life-skills training seminars to meet the ORR funding requirements. She wanted to set up a Monday and Tuesday schedule for the seminars and ensure that we had a room to accommodate it. Sue Charon and I wanted to get this done as soon as possible.

Sue and Cheryl found a room, but needed to get some furniture items moved out and moved in. The usual procedure in City Hall was to submit a work order.[816] My role was to move the task along by handling it personally. I was in a position where I could encourage my very talented, and sometimes over-worked maintenance staff to move the task up to the top of the priority pile. They were always accommodating, and we simply could not have repurposed much of that 100-year-old building without their patience and assistance.

We all wanted to ensure that these seminars would become available as soon as possible, but soon discovered that many of the life-skills seminars were often poorly attended. Cheryl shared that in many instances, it was likely that other, more pressing needs may have been competing for the Somalis' time. Hamilton noted that like many people who move into a new community, they needed time to "(find) work or (secure) housing,"[817] health care, school, and a host of other necessities that they needed to address as new residents.

There was also one GA client who had been identified as taking medications for tuberculosis. This was an entirely new experience in the office, and I needed to ensure that we got the best information available from the state on what to do. Denis Jean was our Human Resources Director and would work with Sue on what steps needed to be taken regarding someone who was in the treatment stage for TB.

The bigger issue was that Sue's office was also dealing with 13 asylum cases, none of whom had gone through the medical clearances that refugees are subjected to before they are allowed to enter the U.S. Sue was going to have them tested at St. Mary's hospital. Neither Sue nor I knew what to do if they refused to be tested.[818] Asylum seekers represented an unfamiliar area of the refugee resettlement process that was completely new to us. It would become one of the many things requiring more involvement with the state government in the coming months.

The new city administrator Jim Bennett started working for the city on March 25th and was busy with getting up to speed on the budget and acquainting himself with his staff. A meeting was set up with Jim on April 9th to introduce him to the refugee collaborative staff, as well as to provide him a briefing on what they were doing in Lewiston and Portland. I also set up another meeting on April 12th for Jim, along with Sue Charron and Cheryl Hamilton, to meet with the Somali elders. We were doing what we could to wedge in this time with the Somali elders as Jim was in the throes of the city budget process, something historically undertaken during the first week of April (typically ending at the end of May). Finance Director Dick Metivier was doing the lion's share of assisting Jim with the budget, leaving me time to focus on what was coming around the corner in May. Jim was briefed on that as well, while more families continued to arrive in Lewiston.

## Sue Charron, General Assistance, Adult Ed, Career Center, Meet & Greets

April 2002 would produce several important milestone moments. Our community relations specialist, Dottie Perham-Whittier, was completing the Somali FAQ brochure that would be released about the third week in April. We also posted a "combined schedule/listing of multi-cultural events" on our cultural diversity web page. This posting would be the first attempt to provide the public with an online "central reference point" for all "multi-cultural" events that were brought to our office's attention. We were also tracking the number of Somali ESL student enrollments. As of April 11th, they had grown to approximately 205[819] students.[820]

Our GA office had now grown to eight staff positions, almost double what existed in 2001. Sue Charron and I also began to review our protocols for "TB and blood borne(sic) pathogen exposures." We recognized that GA employees were at a "higher level of risk than other employees within City Hall" given that confidentiality requirements necessitated that staff and clients work within close proximity at desk areas. I asked Human Resources Director Denis Jean to contact our healthcare agency and the state Bureau of Health to establish clear and written protocols. I also asked Denis to review our protocols for the rest of the organization.[821] I had become suddenly aware that the arrival of our 'new Mainers' was exposing a number of areas that revealed either poorly written or non-existent policies that affected many departments and employees. We were suddenly realizing how much more work was required to be compliant with any number of state and federal rules and laws dealing with health, translation and interpretation, and disabilities. That also applied to many agencies and organizations around L-A and the state.

We were also looking to improve how the GA office could improve their Somali clients' experience when seeking employment. A relatively new Department of Labor organization called the Career Center provided many employment services (there were 28 other regional centers throughout the state). Its primary function was to act as a full-service employment organization. It featured self-service access to computers and literature for members of the public seeking to conduct their own work searches. The center also provided staff opportunities for one-on-one meetings if needed and served as the regional center for all Department of Labor functions, including unemployment hearings and other DOL government functions.

The challenge to find work for our immigrant GA clients was obvious. Many Somalis were unfamiliar with the entire concept of using such a facility for a job search, and there were cases where their English-speaking ability was so limited, they would need a translator that was not always be available. Charron and I set up a mid-April meeting with facility director Patti Saarinen to discuss how things could be improved. We learned that the Career Center had been speaking with the Lewiston Adult Education center on how they structured their ESL curriculum, and to collaborate in a way where both operations could improve the opportunities for Somali employment.

During the discussion with Patti, we spoke about employment specialist Rose Hodges and how her work had now positioned Hodges as "the" Somali employment expert. We touched upon how Rose and other center assets could be made available for a population of limited English persons (LEP). The center was looking into new "welfare to work" opportunities and tapping into funding for some sort of "bus/van" or "bus (pass)" program. There were many Somalis who lacked both access to the Career Center and the ability to commute to work.

Saarinen also explained that not having a GED (general education diploma, a certificate confirming the successful completion of a high school level of education) should not prevent someone from getting a job but agreed that having limited English-speaking ability was a barrier. Patti also added that not all Somali clients had a desire to "learn English." [822] In the end, one of our immediate goals from the meeting would be to improve the experience for those who needed and wanted to access Career Center services, and to better serve Somali clients coming into the facility.

After the meeting, the Career Center agreed to set up a weekly Thursday schedule as the day for GA Somali (and other immigrant) clients to meet with staff in person and have an interpreter present and available for job search counseling. They also emphasized that the service was available on other days but may require the client to wait for the interpreter to become available.[823]

The Lewiston Adult Education program was also becoming a bigger part of the service provider equation. By mid-April, the program, located in the high school and the Lewiston Multi-Purpose Center (which also housed the Longley Elementary School), had almost 1,100 individuals enrolled in their "Diploma" program (for student dropouts and adults seeking to receive a fully accredited high school diploma) "and other general population academic and non-academic courses." Another 790 students were working towards their GED or attending other academic or ESL courses. The need for ESL was growing quickly. Of the 790 adult education participants, 123 were ESL students, and 63% of those students were Somali.[824]

Anne Kemper, who served as the Adult Education Coordinator, provided me with information that revealed how overextended the ESL program was with an enrollment of 123 ESL students. Kemper said that ESL students could only receive seven hours of class time due to space limitations; 12 Bates student and staff volunteers were providing 60 hours of service per week, and "some Somali residents (had) also volunteered;" the ESL program was a 5-day per week program, but needed to be restructured to address the various levels of ESL instruction needed for people at different levels of English proficiency; the center had recently received three federal grants for ESL instruction; ESL programs were being conducted "at Hillview Apartments" along with "12 slots" of childcare for ESL students funded through the newly acquired grants; and a new "Somali Community Engagement Projects" program, funded by one of the three new grants, would finance the "curricula focusing on education, health care, civic engagement, and daily living."[825]

It was exciting to see all the work being done by so many of the agencies, non-profits, school, adult education, city, and the collaboration between the organizations. What was noticeably missing in the equation was a qualified ECBO (ethnic community-based organization) and resident and community-driven involvement with the new Mainers. There were so many things that needed the city's attention. We were doing our best to network with as many agencies as we could assemble, and that alone was creating a torrent of tasks and work product. There was literally no time to think about doing anything else, and to focus on what needs were already identified.

Newly elected city councilor Roger Philippon said, "while the city (was doing) its part...the rest of the community need(ed) to pitch in." Roger also believed that the city faced a "historic opportunity" and "hoped (that city residents could) come together." He recognized the challenge ahead of us, but he also believed that we could not do it alone, and that "community organizations need(ed) to come together."[826]

It was gratifying to see one community organization recognize Councilor Philippon's call for community involvement. A few Somali residents met Executive Director Rita Dube at the Franco-American Heritage Center. The meeting between Rita and the Somali residents lead to something special for the Somalis and the community. Rita was accustomed to making things happen in L-A. I had the pleasure of getting to know and working with Rita years earlier when she led the fund-raising efforts for my alma mater, St. Dominic's high school. Dube was hired as the Franco center's first executive director shortly after the Franco board took possession of the old church in 2000. Rita worked "two years without pay" and "'her passion and love of St. Mary's, the parish, the church, (and) the building'" over her 12 years with the facility were directly responsible for the area's "state-of-the-art performance and cultural center."[827]

Dube, her staff, and the Somali resident efforts organized the first free event to the public to meet our new Somali neighbors on April 24th in the center's new banquet center. The evening's primary purpose was to provide everyone an opportunity to meet each other in an informal setting that featured Somali music, food, and some casual conversation.[828] It was a wonderful evening. "More than 300 people attended."[829]

This was clearly a great first step towards the kind of inclusion that Councilor Philippon was thinking about.

The day after the Franco center 'meet-and-greet,' the Lewiston Middle School hosted a "Somali food and fashion (event)" that "shared a program with a student-produced video about preserving Lewiston's 'Little Canada' heritage." Attended by "dozens of families," it was the school's "first 'Cultural Heritage Night.'" Coincidentally, this event, complete with learning about Somali culture, fashion and food, was also an opportunity to view the "award-winning" video titled "'Le Pass au Futur. '" The documentary covered the events leading to the preservation of St. Mary's church,[830] the location now known as the Franco-American Heritage Center where a similar public event was held just the night before. The community was now showing signs of becoming "engaged."

For the rest of the city council, they also believed the city needed more resident involvement. At their city council meeting on April 16th, public questions were directed to the council about the new Somali arrivals. Sharing that they were not equipped to answer many of those questions, some city councilors expressed their interest in "scheduling a forum with city and school officials and members of the Somali community to answer questions and help make the public more familiar with the Somalis." City Council President Rene Bernier said "'I think it's very important to bring the people with the answers before the public" and that there were "'a lot of questions in the community'" and that the city needed to "'get answers out (to the public).'"[831]

The refugee working group, now in the last stages of finishing the governor's report, discussed how to best address the city council's desire for setting up "public information meetings to address concerns relative to Somali arrivals."[832] In May, the city council would have their desire for a public forum fulfilled, and 500 people would be there to take part in a 'town meeting.'

## THERE'S A STORY BREWING AND A TOWN MEETING

We were increasingly finding ourselves under the watchful eye of a very interested news media. A radio station out of Atlanta, Georgia interviewed me on April 18th. "The interviewer was Somali and served as the host of a Somali information radio show" that had a Somali audience in the area. The radio host said the purpose of the show was to "communicate what was happening...in Lewiston." He also said that it was "his intention to urge Somalis not to leave (the Atlanta area) as they may be disappointed with the diminishing lack of (housing and other) resources and (job) choices in this area due to the high number of (Somali refugees) moving into (the Lewiston) area."[833]

I was also contacted by Portland Press Herald journalist Kelley Bouchard who shared that they would run an article in the upcoming weekend's Maine Sunday Telegram. A New York production company that filmed content for the Public Broadcasting for the program "Frontline" also contacted me. They were "considering a story on the Somalis coming to Lewiston." The local radio station WCNN was also doing a daily series "on the Somali population as part of their AM daily programming." For our elected officials, the increased level of media coverage was creating an increasing sense of urgency for a public event sooner rather than later.[834]

By April 26th, the refugee working group discussed what could be assembled for a public meeting soon. There was "consensus" within the group for a single meeting. Facilitators were needed and there was discussion about what kind of person would meet the need. Many names were discussed. Some local and some outside L-A. Others believed it should not be anyone connected with city government. Concerns were expressed to guard against parochial city government bias, as it was the city that would host the event. Where we would hold the event was also important. The middle school[835] had an auditorium that could hold some 800 people, but we also wanted to keep public safety in mind and wanted to ensure that the police department weighed in on what kind of facility would be the most secure.

The question of who would serve on the panel and how large it would be also needed discussion. The working group knew that there were certain services and agencies that required representation: school department, General Assistance, Catholic Charities Maine, public safety, refugee leadership, state agencies like the state refugee office, Department of Human Services, public housing, the Career Center... the list went on.

The format of the meeting would also be important. How would questions be presented to the panel? Would they be oral, written, or both? If written, how would questions be gathered and organized? Would we have roving cordless mics or a single stand mic? We all believed interest was high and that it would be a big turnout, but how many seats were needed? Should the balcony be closed for security purposes? We also looked at dates, and there was a consensus that this should occur as soon as possible. May 14$^{th}$ or 15$^{th}$ appeared to be the most likely date for the public meeting.[836]

It was also likely that this would all occur at about the time Governor King would receive his report. The group charged me with assembling all the working group 'white papers' for the governor's report. I had already begun editing and assembling some papers for the report. I knew it was coming along well, but some information was needed. I believed that we would release it within the next ten days or so; likely before the public town meeting.

Mayor Larry Raymond was also weighing in on the Somali arrivals for perhaps the first time publicly when he was interviewed by Kelley Bouchard for her April 28$^{th}$ Maine Sunday Telegram article.[837] Raymond stated that "(t)here (was) an undercurrent of resentment of people who (were) coming (to Lewiston)." Raymond also commented that he did not believe that the resentment was racial or religious, and that it came down to "dollars and cents." He said that "the citizenry (was) genuinely concerned about the impact on their taxes." He then added that the city should probably "be flattered they've picked Lewiston. Unfortunately, many of them don't come with any money and they don't have jobs, and there is some resentment of that."[838]

The local concerns about the new Mainer arrivals was also acknowledged by "(l)eaders in the Somali community." The newspaper had reported that the city suggested another 500 to 1,000 Somalis could move into the city over the summer. In response to that article, "one Somali leader went on Atlanta's Somali radio station and told (the Somalis) not to come."[839]

Lewiston General Assistance caseworker Abdiaziz Ali also spoke to an Atlanta area radio station "saying that Somalis are welcome in Lewiston, but that they should meter their arrival." GA Director Sue Charron added that the increasingly rapid nature of the relocation could become problematic for the office. Charron said that she had observed an increasing number of people being "vocal about their concern (with the number of Somali relocations). We need to get the word out that we welcome (the Somalis) and we want (them to come to the city)," but Charron also cautioned that arriving in large numbers too quickly made it much more challenging for the city to deliver services.[840]

Bouchard noted in her article that Lewiston officials "have reason to be concerned." Bouchard noted that if a summer surge of some 1,000 Somalis occurred, Lewiston's Somali population could eclipse that of Portland's and that it would have occurred in less than two years compared to the three years they had been arriving in Portland (whose city population was almost twice the size of Lewiston's). Since the first families arrived in Lewiston, over 600 Somalis[841] from 210 families had been processed through General Assistance.

Charron confirmed that of the 210 families, 200 families, or 563 individuals, were "receiving food and housing vouchers." Somali families were now making up "22 percent" of local General Assistance and that number would likely grow[842] until some of those families did the necessary paperwork to qualify more of them for state help through MaineCare (Medicaid) and TANF (Temporary Assistance to Needy Families—previously the Aid to Dependent Families and Children or AFDC program). The State Refugee Coordinator added that 48 Somali families were already receiving TANF.[843]

Lewiston had a remarkable period of growth between 1999 and 2001, but the job market had shrunk over the last year by some 2.9% making it "the ninth largest percentage decline in the country among metropolitan areas." Unemployment was also higher than it was in 2001, and Career Center employment specialist Rose Hodges added that even with higher unemployment, there was a scarcity of available jobs in the area.

Hodges added that those few jobs most likely would require "applicants who speak English and have a high school diploma" or could pass a high school diploma equivalency test. Some Somalis in the community were already attending college,[844] like Ismail Ahmed, who was attending the University of Southern Maine's Lewiston-Auburn College campus.[845] Many other Somalis had little education, or none at all. Hodges said that they were making every effort to work with anyone in the Somali community who wanted to work.[846]

Sue Charron and I also knew, as did other city officials, that some people believed that the Somali relocations were being driven by their desire to enroll in our General Assistance welfare program, funded by both the state and the local governments. In Maine, General Assistance was a state program that mandated participation of all 491 municipalities. In Maine, unlike other parts of the country where social services were county responsibilities, municipal government administered local welfare programs (for those who needed help based on their income, family size, assets, and employment). Not everyone could receive assistance as the eligibility requirements continued to become more stringent over the years. The city also only granted GA based on monthly eligibility. People could qualify for one month and not for the next. Recipients needed to report changes in their income eligibility as soon as it changed, and everyone needed to re-apply every month, even if their status had not changed.

General Assistance was in actuality a state regulated social services program with rigid eligibility guidelines and was rarely understood by most of the public and press. Many people did not believe how difficult it was to qualify for the program, or the rigorous oversight associated with meeting ongoing eligibility to receive program support. For those GA applicants that met the income, assets, and other guidelines of the program, they also had to re-file and re-establish their eligibility that would dictate that month's level of support for the next 30 days.

Receiving GA support would also frequently require a weekly job search. If there were any detected job search or other guidelines violations, the applicant would lose program eligibility for 120 days. For immigrants with little or no English-speaking ability, GA would waive the job search requirement but mandate attendance at ESL classes. Rather than create an impossibly job-search situation for limited-English-speaking applicants to find a job, we required mandatory ESL class attendance. These were people who understood that speaking some English would improve their success in securing a job, the thing that most identified with the kind of "economic self-sufficiency" that was important to them individually, to their families, to their self-worth, and to many people who saw their enrollment in "welfare" as something they desired instead of employment.

But all of that did not stop a woman from calling me one day in early 2003 to complain about the trouble she was having with the water well on her property going dry. According to the Maine Emergency Management Agency, "(a)pproximately 17,000 private wells in Maine went dry in the 9 months prior to April 2002."[847] It was one of the worst droughts in Maine history that had lingering effects for some into 2003.

I asked her exactly where she lived in Lewiston, as I had seen well-drilling trucks passing by my home for months. Our area in Lewiston had no municipal water or sewer service. She gave me the name of a road I did not recognize. I asked her to repeat the name and looked at the city map that hung on the back wall of my office and could not find the road. I was confused and asked her if she lived in Lewiston. The woman told me rather matter-of-factly that she did not live in the city and proceeded to tell me she lived in Hiram, Maine.

At this juncture, I distinctly remember saying to myself, 'so why are you calling me from Hiram, Maine?' Hiram was nearly 50 miles away from Lewiston. I simply just asked her why someone from Hiram would be calling someone from Lewiston for help.

The woman responded that she decided to call me because she read about the Somali relocations to Lewiston. She came to the conclusion that because Somalis were apparently all receiving welfare assistance, there were no funds available to help her with her dry well. When I asked if she had contacted the Hiram town office, she told me that she had called but they were unable to help her.

I told her I would look into it and get back to her. The last thing I wanted to do was to brush her off and tell her that if the Hiram town office was not willing to help her, why should the city of Lewiston. After some phone calls to several state offices, I was able to find someone in state government that was dealing with dry well issues all over the state.

I called the Hiram resident back with the assistance information and assured her that finding help to get the dry well addressed had nothing to do with the Somalis, or welfare. These two programs were funded from different parts of the state budget. I also told her that it was difficult for me to believe that the Hiram town office would not be more helpful, but I did not press her for details. Hiram had a population about 1,500 people. I had worked as a town manager in a small-town office in Richmond, Maine with a population of about 3,000 people. I knew how closely knit these small Maine communities were and doubted that she ever called that town office, as I was certain that they would not have simply dismissed her situation. It was more important for me to let her know that her perceptions of the effects of Somali arrivals anywhere in Maine were incorrect. She was very appreciative to get the information and thanked me. How she felt after the call or whether she ever received help for the well would remain unknown to me.

## The Town Meeting

An advance flyer was prepared by the City Administrator's Office and distributed in various public locations around the city for the May 14$^{th}$ informational meeting with the 6:30 time, location (Lewiston Memorial Armory), and the address of the location. The City Administrator's telephone number was also provided to answer any follow-up questions about the meeting.[848]

The details for the meeting were endless. The Armory was an old building and the city never seemed to have enough money in its budget. This facility had hosted thousands of concerts and public events its history that included championship boxing, high school state-playoff basketball, the "Harlem Globe Trotters," "Allen Freed's Big Beat Show" that featured Buddy Holly and The Crickets, Chuck Berry, and Jerry Lee Lewis (1958), The Jimi Hendrix Experience (1968), and Queen (1975—who opened for the band Kansas).[849] One would think that at some point the city would have equipped the building with an adequate sound system to accommodate large events.

The absence of a PA system required finding an audio company that was available on short notice to provide a system large enough to handle the cavernous Armory space. There was also the matter of a list of endless tasks: table skirts (did not have those either), water for the panelists, a podium (had to move it from City Hall), security, invitations (city officials and legislators from Auburn, Portland, Bangor, the congressional delegation, the governor), posters for our public spaces, sufficient copies of materials, etc.[850]

We finalized the program for what we would call a "Public Informational Meeting." The title selected for the evening's program was "Immigrants & Refugee Arrivals... The Myths & The Facts." The agenda for the May 14, 2002 evening 'town meeting' (what many of us called the information meeting internally) would be uncomplicated: Introductions of the panel; an explanation of the meeting format; opening statements by the panelists; time for public comments and questions; and adjournment after everyone had the opportunity to ask their questions. The moderator for the evening was Chip Morrison, former Auburn City Manager, former state labor commissioner, and current president of the Androscoggin County (formerly Lewiston-Auburn) Chamber of Commerce.[851]

A meeting handout for attendees was available at the Armory entrance so that the public would better understand the evening's format. Opening remarks from panelists would be brief; the facilitator reserved the right to establish ground rules; public comments and questions would be limited to two minutes; people needed to use the microphone provided on the floor; questions would be limited to a single subject; and if they did not want to speak, they could write the comments on a four by six-inch index card and hand it to individuals wearing blue and white name tags that would be located around the floor area.

The panelists were:

Barney Berube, ESL/Bi-lingual Education Specialist, Maine Dept. of Education

Sue Charron, Lewiston General Assistance Administrator (Director)

James Dowling, Executive Director, Lewiston Housing Authority

Sue B. Harlor, Director, Community Services Center, Maine DHS

Leon Levesque, Lewiston Superintendent of Schools

Rhoda Osman, Somali Representative

Pierrot Rugaba, State Refugee Coordinator

Patti Saarinen, Manager, Job Training at the Lewiston Career Center

Said Tani, Somali Representative

Mathew "Matt" Ward, Program Director, Catholic Charities Maine

William Welch, Lewiston Chief of Police[852]

All who took part in putting this town meeting together really did not know what to expect for this event. Our staff had set up approximately 500 chairs on the Armory gym floor and they were almost completely occupied. Several people stood in the back and on the wings of the gym floor. Most people who were in attendance agreed that 500 was a reasonable estimate for the event. Those in attendance, unsurprisingly, were "mostly whit(e)" and "filled with clapping people" either applauding something that was not supportive of immigration or, in the fewer instances that it occurred, for those who said something supportive of the immigrants. "When a Somali man said he loved the city (of Lewiston) and the state of Maine, they clapped." Councilor Philippon who was in the audience said he couldn't tell "'what side (of the issue) people (were) on because they're clapping for everyone.'"[853] My own observations left me to believe that the evening may have been less than evenly divided.

It was not completely surprising to hear the many questions directed to the panel about welfare and General Assistance. Some simply "criticized the city and the state government." Another resident stated "'(f)ine, but what does (qualifying) mean? And does that mean you qualify for life? Do you ever get kicked off? There wasn't an honest person up there.'" Some simply did not believe anything they heard. One woman stated that "(d)espite assurances (from the panel) that Somalis are subject to the same housing and general assistance requirements as other residents," friends told her that "Somalis get preferential treatment."[854]

Another member of the public, who also had believed nothing she heard from the panel, commented that "(w)hen her ancestors came (to Lewiston) three generations ago, they didn't have welfare and general assistance" and that they also "had to work two or three jobs to get by."[855] She was correct in saying that the Irish and the Francos were incredibly industrious people who worked very hard, but she was incorrect in saying that there was no welfare program (similar to General Assistance) available for them. According to James Leamon, after the Irish began to arrive in Lewiston during the 1850s, and

> (w)ithout economic resources of their own, the Irish settled on vacant lots where they built shacks in congested proximity one to another. Here in their various "patches," as their ghettos were called, they were easy prey to sickness and disease. In the cholera epidemic of 1854 two hundred of Lewiston's inhabitants, mostly Irish, died within several weeks. The municipal response to these problems was surprisingly liberal in a 'laissez-faire' age. The town fathers set up a temporary 'pesthouse' for those stricken with disease and provided generous welfare support to the needy. In addition the city government resolved to employ the town's poor on the numerous public projects required by the growing municipality.[856]

It should also be noted that since that initial local welfare program was created in the 1850s, a review of many city annual (and financial) reports after the 1850s suggests that Lewiston had always operated some sort of local welfare service or program for the poor[857] and most at-risk residents.[858]

One panelist emphasized that this entire experience, including this particular evening's meeting, was "all part of the education process." Somali panelist Said Tani said that "(w)hen you put new animals together, and they don't recognize each other, they'll chase each other. People don't get along right off.

But we will." Said, who was a new arrival and had lived in Georgia for 15 years, noted that as different as our respective cultures were, in time the city would see that Somalis were "hard working people."[859]

Sue Charron continued to repeat at the town meeting that anyone, immigrant and non-immigrant, cannot receive General Assistance without meeting the state guidelines (it was a program that was statutorily created with rules promulgated and enforced by the state's Department of Human Services). Some in the audience asked what could be done "to slow down immigration" into the city. State Director of the Community Services Center Sue B. Harlor said that the agency had "put messages on Georgia radio stations asking any people leaving that state" to "meter their arrival." Harlor also stated that doing much more to influence the out-migration from Georgia would be very difficult.[860]

It was interesting to hear Harlor speak about a radio message that advocated for Georgia Somalis to "meter" their arrivals in Lewiston. In the April 30th Bouchard article, Lewiston General Assistance Case Worker Abdiaziz Ali made a statement that revealed he had made a similar plea on the radio station to "meter" the Somali arrival in Georgia at about the same time the Maine DHS was running their radio ad in the Atlanta area. Whether Ali was simply repeating what he had heard on the radio was not important. The question remained: would area Somalis listen to what both DHS and Abdiaziz were saying?

My only discomfort that evening was to provide someone in the audience an answer about how the refugee program worked. It simply was (and is) not a program that only required a three-minute explanation but given his reaction, it appeared as though an entire evening's discussion dedicated on the subject would not have changed his mind. For others, like our new City Administrator Jim Bennett, his memory of the meeting was that there were "a range of emotions" in the room, and that "misinformation" and what Jim interpreted as "not really understanding" much about the Somali relocations, fed into the "fears" that were "driving a lot of the emotions" in the room.[861]

Bennett also shared that at the end of the meeting, someone approached him and proceeded to get "into my face and started yelling at me 'what a disaster this was' and venting in terms of (how) the community (was) changing." Jim said that "over the next 24 hours, I realized that the community building process that we were going to have to go through was going to be a much more intense" effort for it to be successful.[862]

**General Assistance**

Many Somalis would reject the comments made at the May 14th town meeting regarding welfare and how it was driving their relocation choices. State officials also rejected the welfare suspicions expressed by some locals. The state offered that the number of people on receiving welfare (MaineCare) in Maine had dropped from "23,200 (families) to 11,000 because of welfare reform." Bouchard's April 28th article reported that, "Somalis say they want to work and are ashamed to be on welfare." Bouchard went on to say that some non-immigrant residents still wondered why "the city bends over backward to make Somalis feel welcome." The journalist told the story of a resident who "posted two large signs" on the front lawn of his home asking, "why the city helps Somalis when veterans and homeless people go without."[863]

Although how much the city was spending on welfare for Somalis was clearly a topic of conversation at the town meeting, the numbers suggested that the 'problem' did not approach the level of severity that most people suspected. The data below reflects what was being spent between 1990-1992 compared to what was spent in 2002 (using a projected budget number reflecting spending in 2002):[864]

|  | FY90 | FY91 |
|---|---|---|
| GA Exp. | $500,326 | $807,918 |
| CPI Adj.2002 dollars | $686,369 | $1,063,580 |
| CPI Adj.1992 dollars | | |
| Unemployment | 6.7% | 9.3% |

|  | FY92 | FY03(budgeted) |
|---|---|---|
| GA Exp. | $1,155,766 | $425,000 |
| CPI Adj.2002 dollars | $1,477,040 | |
| CPI Adj.1992 dollars | | $332,218 |
| Unemployment | 8.7% | 4.3% (Mar.'02) |

Simply stated, the numbers listed above showed that spending was far less for General Assistance in the projected FY03 budget (reflects FY02 expenditures) compared to what was being spent a decade earlier using expenditures adjusted and not adjusted for inflation. It should also be noted that the above data reflected that the unemployment rate between 1991 and 1992 was also running at nearly twice the rate than it was in 2002. City Hall staff employed with the city during the early 1990s would often say that the lines were so long for General Assistance that chairs lined both sides of City Hall's second floor main hallway to accommodate those who had to wait for hours to receive it.

Two days after the Sun Journal coverage of the May 14$^{th}$ town meeting, Scott Taylor wrote another article specifically focused on the General Assistance program. It did not surprise me that Scott had chosen to do so. It was the subject that clearly dominated much of the evening's discussion both during and after the meeting was over.

Sue Charron once again emphasized in the Taylor article that this "assistance" program was something that every resident in the state could receive, but only if they met the asset and income guidelines for eligibility. This was also confirmed by spokesman Newell Augur from the state DHS, emphasizing that, "most Lewiston Somalis (did) not qualify for (General Assistance) aid." Augur also added that Somalis (at that time) rarely qualified because "their incomes (were) too high" and consequently "earn(ed) enough money that they (were) contributing to the tax base, not taking away from it."[865]

In 2002, the state General Assistance program provided "food or rent vouchers... to low-income families" (no cash is ever paid out to applicants). An example of what a family of four would receive through the program revealed that it offered little more than basic living assistance: A family of four making $700 per month, would qualify for $42 per month (the monthly income limit for eligibility for a family of four needed to be less than $742). A family of four earning less than $371 per month would qualify for $371 per month (all qualifying amounts paid by voucher for needs such as rent or food). Many other qualifying conditions might also apply. If an applicant left their job voluntarily or had other members of the family earning income that put them over the limit, the applicant likely did not qualify.[866]

Help was also available through MaineCare, TANF, and Parents as Scholars. These programs were available to all Maine residents if they qualified with eligible income levels. For a family of four, qualifying for the other Maine assistance programs was roughly in line with the income requirements for General Assistance. Some 11,000 families in Maine were receiving TANF and 1,325 of those families, the majority of which were non-immigrant families, lived in Androscoggin County. There was also public housing support for all income-eligible families, the largest program administered by the Lewiston Housing Authority. Admissibility was based on federal guidelines for families "whose income (was) 80 percent of the area median income." As of May 17th, the "city (had) 169 names on its waiting list for family public housing units." According to LHA Executive Director James Dowling, 68 of those waiting were Somali families.[867]

## The Governor Listens

After three months of countless meetings, phone calls, and emails, the collaboration of some 17 different people on the refugee working group, ten different organizations and agencies, and an "open" letter from the Somali community, the final document was ready for publication. The "Report to Governor Angus King: New Somali Arrivals and Other Issues Relative to Refugee/Secondary Migrants/Immigrants and Cultural Diversity in the City of Lewiston, Maine" was emailed to Governor King on May 9, 2002[868] and release shortly after to the media and the public.

"The purpose of (the) report (was) to provide the Governor's Office with an overview of the refugee/secondary migrant/immigrant (RSI) issues faced by the agencies and citizens of the City of Lewiston." The scope of the report was intentionally broad. The refugee working group wanted to "inform, educate and identify areas of particular concern on a variety of issues," specific to the Somalis and to all RSI residents.[869]

Perhaps the most important element of this undertaking was to ensure that the governor understood Lewiston would not pursue a Portland-style approach to its refugee arrival response. The Portland agencies had chosen to build a very impressive local response to refugee resettlement, with participation from its area agencies going as far back as 1975. The report emphasized that the state needed to "adopt a more active role to address the special needs and challenges" unique to RSI (refugee/secondary migrant/immigrant) populations. The report participants believed that "(t)he immigration story of Portland and Lewiston should serve as the State's opportunity to develop policies and strategies (that) can be applied to other communities throughout the state."[870]

The list of agency reports[871] reflected the working group's opinion of where the state's involvement was needed (listed in no particular order of priority):

    A. The Career Service Center – ESL and (Job) Training Issues (Maine Department of Labor)

B. Refugee Secondary Migrant/Asylee General Information & Services (Catholic Charities Maine)
C. Refugee/Secondary Migrant Facts (Catholic Charities Maine)
D. Impact of Somali Refugee Resettlement on Health Services in the Lewiston-Auburn Area (Central Maine Medical Center)
E. Diversity Impact/Issues at Lewiston High School (Lewiston School Department)
F. Impact of Somali Immigration on Lewiston School System (Lewiston School Department)
G. Lewiston Police Department Observations (Lewiston Police Department)
H. Public and Private Housing – Somali Families Impact and General Information (City Council and Assistant City Administrator's Office)
I. Lewiston General Assistance Services – Other City RSI Activities (Assistant City Administrator's Office and General Assistance Office)
J. DHS Refugee Resettlement Services (State Refugee Coordinator and Community Services Center, Maine Department of Human Services)
K. Open Letter from the Somali Community

The report both reflected the enormous amount of work that was going on in the city and focused on the Somalis and other RSI populations (at the time, there were a handful of other secondary migrant nationalities that were also relocating to the city). The Career Center was doing some work, but there was much more to be done. Job training for LEP populations was difficult to fund and interpretation at the Career Center sometimes fell short with only one interpreter available.[872]

If the governor was not as informed as he needed to be about asylum seekers and the refugee program, Catholic Charities Maine provided that information. CCM explained how federal resettlement funding regulations were limiting their ability to provide secondary migrant services. They also noted that under a separate DHS contract, they were able to provide "employment services" to "100 secondary migrants, but only in the Portland area." It would be an item that would drive much of Lewiston's discussion with CCM, the Department of Labor, and our national efforts to find refugee workforce development funding over the years.[873] CCM also failed to mention in the report that they did not have a permanent office presence in Lewiston, something that Sue Charron and I would pursue in the near future.

Central Maine Medical Center's provided their hospital's perspective of the challenges associated with serving a refugee population with limited English-speaking ability, and a culture that they were only beginning to understand. CMMCs "Family Practice Residency Program" (CMMC had been expanding the number of doctors that worked directly for the hospital over the years) had 250 Somalis registered with the practice back in the "early summer of 2001." By March 2002, the practice had registered double that amount. The CMMC report noted that the rapid arrival of secondary migrants "offered the health community little opportunity to do the necessary pre-planning when it came to decisions on how to allocate limited monies and resources."[874]

Lewiston High School reported that "(a)dministration (had) met with students and faculty to discuss the climate at Lewiston High School" and that "(r)umors reported by the press have been dispelled" (though there was no explanation of what "rumors" were mentioned). Principal Patrick O'Neill also shared that he had met with Somali elders regarding a "student task force" that had was created to generate more student "input." O'Neill was also pursuing "(r)esources from Bates College, the University of Southern Maine (Lewiston-Auburn College), and the Attorney General's Office" in addition to other consulting opportunities.[875]

Lewiston School Superintendent Leon Levesque also weighed in with a report. He noted that the school system's ESL program had grown from 40 students in the 2000-2001 school year to 243 students as of March 2002. Superintendent Levesque also pointed out that of the 243 ESL students in the school system, 203 were Somali, with six of the eight schools in the system providing ESL services. New services, staff, and technology costs were estimated to add another $234,000 to the school budget as of March 2002. In my "Editor's Note," I shared that Adult Education ESL programming and participation was also growing but had limited funding. Finding space and qualified instructors were also becoming an issue.[876]

Perhaps one of the most unique and gut-wrenching parts of the report was the paragraph involving General Assistance services:

> Several weeks ago, a Somali family required GA to provide for the burial (and preparations of the remains for)... their 9-month-old child... Maine state law is not equipped to deal with the probability that any family may make such a request. Its burial permit regulations do not address what occurs in a home environment and the need for Muslims to bury the remains within some 24 hours of death. Burial and emergency GA for burial make not only the issuing of GA challenging (especially on weekends when all agencies are closed), but also requires a level of intervention from local funeral homes and privately operated(sic) cemeteries that, currently, does not exist.[877]

Pierrot Rugaba's report as the State Refugee Coordinator also provided some very useful information regarding Maine's refugee population estimates over the last three federal fiscal years (FFY begins on October 1st and ends on September 30th of each year). In his summary, he reported that in FFY2001, 480 Maine secondary migrant refugees had lived in the state for three years or less and met the federal definition of a secondary migrant (the federal qualifying definition is reserved for those refugees who moved from one state and resided in that state for three continuous years or less while also possessing a Social Security Number).[878]

Rugaba's office tracked federal qualifying secondary migrants in Maine. The data provided by Rugaba was used by the Office of Refugee Resettlement to award additional funding to Maine (and to other states) for qualified secondary migrants receiving MaineCare and other eligible social services. Using that definition, Rugaba also confirmed that 696 refugees had been resettled in Maine over the FFY period between 1999-2001. By the state's accounting, some 1,131 refugees were "presently residing" in the State of Maine by the end of FFY2001.[879]

Rugaba was required to define secondary migrants using the federal definition and to count them using ORR federal guidelines. It also meant that the federal government would not count any secondary migrant refugee living in Maine for over three years. Doing so would generate additional funding for the state. In the eyes of the federal government, after any refugee had been in the country for 3 or more years, that individual should have a lesser need for state services. Rugaba also reported that 4,372 refugees had resettled in Maine between FFY1982-FFY2001 and resettled across 12 cities and "other" towns in Maine. They did not identify Lewiston as a resettlement city, but it was likely listed as a "other" community given the three or four Togolese families that were living in Lewiston by September 30, 2001.[880]

The most interesting part of the report may have been the letter drafted by the Somali community leadership. The letter began with the community expressing its appreciation and "gratitude" for the way they "were welcomed and received" by the city. The letter acknowledged the "sudden influx" of Somali residents who had taken up residence in the city. It also acknowledged that many Somalis left metropolitan areas like "Atlanta, Nashville, Louisville and others" to separate themselves from the "drugs, guns and related violence" they often encountered in those cities.[881]

Although grateful for the community's outreach efforts, the Somalis emphasized they did not want to depend on "welfare and handouts." They wanted to pursue employment opportunities and made a plea to the chamber of commerce and local businesses to "make employment available to our people." They also pointed out areas we already knew needed more attention: more housing choices for people with large families, and more ESL and tutoring programming for Somali K-12 students that might better prepare them for the American system of education. They closed the letter by saying that they wanted to become "useful members" of the community and to have patience with them until they could "stand on (their) feet and be able to support (their) families with minimal assistance."[882]

We closed the report with a number of recommendations based on its many comments and observations. We wanted to ensure there was: intensive job training with an ESL component for adults; transportation for job seekers and families with no transportation alternatives; changing federal funding guidelines that penalized communities such as Lewiston when they experience rapid secondary migrant relocations; translation service support for health care agencies; additional school and police funding for cultural training and translation services; HUD funding that responded to rapid secondary migrant relocations; and more state funding for their own state agencies' cultural training and interpretation needs.

The report was only 24 pages long. We hoped we had accomplished our goal of communicating the urgency of the challenge without overwhelming the governor with more information that could be reasonably processed in a very short amount of time. Only time would reveal how the report with resonate with the governor and the public.

**Lessons Learned**

We were not approaching this report effort with the belief that Governor Angus King might ignore or not take the contents of the report seriously. Many of us knew King and his background in politics both as a staffer and a political analyst. King understood the rigors of the office and also had a close connection to Lewiston. His home was in Brunswick and before he was governor, he was a regular fixture on Maine's public television network for 17 years "when he became host of the progenitor of (the networks program) 'Maine Watch.'" [883] The program was produced and broadcasted from the WCBB studios in Lewiston.

As the nation's second independent governor in history (the first was Governor James Longley of Lewiston), both historically Democratic Lewiston and Republican Auburn voted to support King's first election in a very close race against former Maine Governor Joe Brennan in 1994.[884] King's work as a first-term governor propelled him to a landslide victory for his second term in 1998.[885] Governor King also played a pivotal role in getting the 2001 Walmart project in Lewiston approved by supporting a state tax-relief package that helped to complete the deal.

King had also come to the twin cities area in September 1999 to praise the collaborative efforts of the community's two cities of Lewiston and Auburn. He acknowledged the "positive attitude" of both cities noting that "(i)f you think positive, positive things will happen" and singled out the twin cities' ability to work together unique in that we were doing it "more than any other area in the state."[886]

I was not a personal friend of Governor King, but I knew him. My wife and I were invited to his first inaugural at the Brunswick Naval Air Station (while I was serving as Richmond's town manager). Later in his first term, my brother Greg Nadeau (who was serving as one of his senior policy advisors) and I were invited to the Blaine House to have dinner with King and his wife Mary.

However, my first formal meeting with King did not go particularly well. As Bob Mulready was a few months away from retiring (and putting most of his efforts into the Bates Mill project), I was handling more of the city administrator duties when I traveled with my economic development director and a small delegation of business people in January 2000 to meet with King and several state agency commissioners. I had reached out to my brother Greg, who was also in attendance, to set up the meeting and told him we were going to speak with the governor about the ongoing exodus of state agencies leaving our downtown.

The delegation that came along to the meeting consisted of two Lewiston business leaders, Paul Poliquin and Leighton Cooney, who were both members of the newly created Downtown Development and Management Corporation. Cooney was the president of the DDMC, a member of the Lewiston Downtown Renaissance Task Force, and had also served as the director of the Bureau of General Services that oversaw the facility contracting and leasing activity for the state. The DDMC had discussed the matter of state agencies leaving our downtown with King some eighteen months before our January meeting, [887]likely triggered when the Maine Department of Labor moved its operations to a new business park on the outskirts of the city in 1998.

Once word got out that both the Department of Motor Vehicles and the Workers Compensation Board were looking for new offices in December 1999,[888] both the DDMC and the city council took action to communicate their unhappiness to the Governor. The DDMC wanted a meeting with the Governor. Economic Development Director Greg Mitchell drew up a resolution for the city council, who approved an action to reinforce its message about keeping agencies downtown.

In a December 1999 Sun Journal article announcing that two more state agencies could possibly leave our downtown, King's spokesperson Dennis Bailey stated the governor could implement "urban sprawl" policies to limit the activity by the agencies to leave downtown, but also noted that King had little authority over the bidding and leasing process which was controlled at the agency level. King suggested in the article that the city speak to the commissioners directly about leaving downtown and about our "city's goals." That statement from King seemed a bit disingenuous as the DDMC had already expressed to the governor what the city's goals were regarding state agencies leaving downtown, some 18 months prior.[889]

Leighton Cooney acknowledged in the December 1999 Sun Journal article that King suggesting the city speak directly with the commissioners was "too late" as "bids (had) been submitted and opened." The process was likely too far along to change anything without the governor's direct involvement.[890] That was why the DDMC asked Greg Mitchell and me to arrange the meeting with the governor. It was a last-ditch effort to have him stop a process that was in its last stages of selecting a site, similar to what happened with the U.S. Post Office distribution center. If U.S. Representative Tom Allen could change the mind of those involved with the federally controlled U.S. Post Office to reopen the search process, we had nothing to lose by putting some pressure on King to intervene.

Our January 2000 meeting with King resulted in the Governor taking his message of communicating with the state agency commissioners one step further. With the DMV officials and Workers Compensation commissioner Paul Dionne in the room, he proceeded to ask them how happy their employees were in their current locations. Both commissioners shared the problems they experienced with air quality, repairs, and a host of other issues that they tried to have the owners address, with little success.

Both the DMV and the Workers Compensation offices were in facilities owned by the same group of owners. When King asked the DDMC representatives and Greg Mitchell if anyone had directly spoken with the actual tenants in those facilities, they all acknowledged that they had not, but added that they had spoken to the owners who never reported problems with their tenants. We were basically told by King that if both state organizations left their current buildings, we had only ourselves to blame for not ensuring the tenants were satisfied with their locations.

King could have shared his suggestion about meeting personally with commissioners and tenants back in 1998 so that everyone could do the outreach earlier and possibly convince the agencies to stay downtown. None of us were happy with King's response, but we were all savvy enough to understand that King was not willing to stop or halt the process. This also meant that the departure of both downtown agencies was a strong possibility that, months later, became a reality.

It was hard to understand why Cooney's experience with the Bureau of General Services also did not reveal how easily a state agency could manipulate the leasing process if they were unhappy with their facility. The very reason the Department of Labor left their downtown location back in 1998 was because the agency had reported that they were unhappy with the owner not listening to their concerns about the building.

There was little doubt that such things are never as transparent as one would want them to be and that keeping these agencies in the same long-term leased location is a complex undertaking. It should also be noted that the city was not critical of the Day family who owned the Lewiston business park where all the state agencies eventually landed. They were simply pursuing business opportunities, and the agencies were fair game for the Day's. It was not personal; it was just business.

Immediately following the meeting on the way back to Lewiston, I let everyone in the car know that this would never happen again. The largest state agency operation in our downtown was currently the Maine Department of Human Services regional office. The first order of business when we arrived back in Lewiston was for me and Greg Mitchell to meet with the building's current owner and with the director and Bureau of General Services. Our task would be simple—to discuss how happy DHS was in their current downtown location. DHS had a few years left on their current lease and we had time to head off what happened with the other agencies.

Those meetings with DHS and the Bureau of General Services led to the owner's discovery that he had tenants who were not happy with his building. To owner Roger Michaud's credit, he listened to our advice and to his tenants' concerns. On January 23, 2001,[891] a year after our meeting with King, we had Roger Michaud's new project before the Planning Board. It featured a completely new DHS building that would involve the demolition of a vacant bus terminal, and the construction of a new office building next door to the existing DHS offices. The demolished bus terminal would result in the construction of a new bus terminal integrated into a planned parking garage project one block down from the former bus terminal location. The new terminal would also service our city bus transit operation that never had its own central hub terminal building that would also become the new home for Greyhound Bus (which had previously left the old bus terminal location years prior).

The $6 million DHS project was approved, and the project's groundbreaking ceremony was held on June 26, 2001. The new extension of the old DHS building would be completed by February 2002, and the vacated building would be renovated and completed by the summer of 2002.[892] Our collaborative efforts with the owner and the state kept an incredibly important state social services provider in our downtown and created the synergies needed to properly locate the L-A transit system in its new home. The new DHS building would also become enormously important in assisting our efforts with the new Mainers and other downtown residents that depended on public transportation. The DHS regional office remains in that same location as of the publication of this book.

On the same day of the DHS announcement in 2001, the city reported it had eliminated "eight full-time positions and three part-time position(s)" along with "a number of hiring freezes."

Even with $1 million in budget cuts, the city residents saw an increase of almost one dollar in the property tax mill rate, making it one of the "highest property tax rates in the state."[893] Although Lewiston was doing extraordinarily well with new development projects, any announcement about increasing property taxes would not dampen resident concerns about anything increasing the cost of local government.

There remained much to do in our old Maine city and our continuing efforts to transform its economy, but the rapid arrival of the new Mainers would require an increasing level of our attention.

### Governor Hits the Ground Running

Governor King did not take long to respond to the May 2009 report. Greg Nadeau contacted me from the governor's office within days of receiving the document. A meeting was set up with Greg and King on May 16, 2002, only two days after our public town meeting. My notes about the meeting do not provide the location, nor who attended, but the information in the notes and an email confirmed that King, Greg Nadeau, and I were in attendance along with the following agencies and people: Lewiston School Superintendent Leon Levesque, Sue Charron, Pierrot Rugaba, DHS (possibly Sue Harlor); Maine Bureau of Public Health (possibly Sharon Leahy-Lind); Department of Labor (possibly Paul "Rusty" Cyr); and perhaps Catholic Charities Maine (possibly Matt Ward).[894]

The meeting discussions covered much in the report, but with more detail. The governor was inquisitive and engaged. He inquired about ESL for kids in summer programs asking if "Title 1" federal school funds could be used for ESL and instruction, and inquired about the availability of Bates College and the other colleges to provide ESL volunteers. Pierrot Rugaba's state refugee coordinator position was also discussed. As the state's refugee coordinator working within the DHS, a decision was made that Pierrot would be assigned to the newly renovated DHS Region One office building in Lewiston and would split his time between Augusta and Lewiston as soon as possible. King was making the needle move at the halfway point of our first meeting[895] (my disappointment with his response regarding the exodus of downtown state agencies was now a distant memory).

With DHS now being discussed at the meeting, a decision was made to look into providing another "multi-lingual position in (the) Lewiston (DHS building)." Pierrot would contact ORR for "additional assistance" and the Bureau of Public Health would look into whether MaineCare could be billed for translator services, particularly for health care providers. They would also look into whether MaineCare would cover the children of asylum seekers who needed health/medical services and investigate if there was federal grant funding to assist heads of household who were single women.[896]

The King meeting also produced other ideas that needed follow-up. It was evident that the governor was all in about what he could do and wanted the momentum of the first meeting to carry over into a second meeting. The governor also suggested that we consider a "day long" event attended by city officials and agencies, but also requested that discussing the idea be kept "low key" for the moment. He asked me to contact Mark Fairbrother to schedule the next half-day meeting in Lewiston. That meeting was set for June 11th.[897]

Other things were happening before we all met again on the 11th. Sharon Leahy-Lind, my graduate studies classmate from the Muskie Institute at the University of Southern Maine, was interested in becoming involved with the Somali community.[898] Sharon, like many of the Muskie 'alum' including myself, was a non-traditional student and parent who was also working a full-time job.

Finishing a graduate degree as a non-traditional student was not a simple task. Sharon would complete her graduate studies and I would go on to finish my graduate degree from USM only because Dr. Josephine "Josie" LaPlante had the patience and the confidence in me to finish my studies. It would take me ten years to finish, and that included taking a year off in 1999 to support a family member who had experienced a life-threatening medical illness.

Leahy-Lind contacted my office so that she could be connected with one of the very few up-and-running ECBOs in Lewiston. Sharon met with Azeb Hassan, who was Ethiopian and could speak Somali. Azeb was also one of the co-directors of an organization called the Women's and Children's Advocacy Group [899] (later to become Daryeelka) and co-chaired the organization with a Somali woman named Roda Abdi.

I knew both Azeb and Roda very well. Hassan had already lived in the United States for 12 years, but Abdi had lived in New England "since the late 1980s."[900] Both Azeb and Roda were two of the people I would often call for assistance, particularly when it involved getting information out to the Somali community or to have a group of Somali elders and others invited to a meeting.

Sharon's boss, Dr. Dora Mills was the Director of the Bureau of Health (sister of former Androscoggin District Attorney and current Maine Governor Janet Mills) wanted Sharon to invite Azeb as a "featured expert" in the "Race and Ethnicity Health Disparities section in the Healthy Maine 2010 written report" that Sharon assisted in writing and researching.[901] Azeb agreed to participate.

Our office was also working on the newest challenges associated with General Assistance burial regulations and the matter of actually finding a cemetery in the area that could be made available for people of the Islamic faith. To recruit their help in accommodating our growing Muslim community, Community Relations Coordinator Dottie Perham-Whittier's research on Muslim burial practices was provided to area funeral homes and cemeteries to review. The assembled research group involved Mike Murray from the Evergreen Cemetery in Portland, Somali Advocate for the City Heather Lindkvist, and GA employee Abdiaziz Ali. Perham-Whittier mailed the letter with the researched information to 11 different area funeral homes and cemeteries. The mailing contained four pages of information and instructions covering "body preparation," "funeral," "burial," and "condolences."[902] The result eventually produced a solution for the L-A Muslim when Gracelawn Memorial Park in Auburn contacted our office with an offer to work with the Somali community.

The June 11th governor' group follow-up meeting was scheduled in Lewiston at the Lepage Conference Center at St. Mary's Regional Medical Center. It would take up the entire morning with an early start of 8:00 AM. Greg Nadeau would now serve as the lead contact for the Governor's Office.

This was not Greg's usual role as King's senior policy advisor. For this kind of community matter, the role of representing the governor's office would normally have been assigned to Sue Bell, another senior policy advisor in the governor's office. Bell, the former Republican legislator, had voted against the L-A College funding that then Democratic legislator Greg Nadeau was seeking for Lewiston in 1984.

Politics did indeed make 'strange bedfellows.' Greg stated that "Sue did education (policy) and all the relevant agenc(y) (policy business)" for King at that time. Nadeau added that "(t)he closest thing I would have (been responsible for) was labor (policy)." Both Bell and Nadeau came into the governor's office putting aside partisan party politics to work for the nation's second independent governor from Maine. Greg had great respect for Sue, but in our interview, we both agreed that for all the obvious reasons, King (and very possibly Bell) most likely believed that Greg was the right person for this particular task given our relationship and Greg's residency in Lewiston.[903]

This time around, the school and city elected leaders were present at the June 11th meeting. Mayor Raymond and Councilor Bernier had mutually agreed that she represent the mayor and council for these tasks, given that he was often busy with an expansive law practice and was Judge of Probate for the county. There were also more state agencies and upper agency management present. In attendance at the meeting were: Renee Bernier, President Lewiston City Council; Greg Nadeau, Senior Policy Advisor to Governor King; James Bennett, Lewiston City Administrator; Phil Nadeau, Assistant City Administrator; Leon Levesque, Lewiston Superintendent of Schools; Gail Palmer, DHS; Sue Harlor, DHS; Pierrot Rugaba, DHS; Joyce Benson, State Planning Office; Mary Ellis Crofton, State Planning Office, Rusty Cyr, Department of Labor, Net Porter, Deputy Commissioner, Department of Agriculture; Margaret Bean, Maine State Housing Authority; and Dale Morrell, Sisters of Charity Health System.[904]

Greg Nadeau opened the meeting:

> (Nadeau) stated that the purpose of the meeting was to report where the State agencies were relative to the Governor's request for an immediate

assessment of agency resources both short and long term (a request he made during his meeting with the City of Lewiston and his state agencies on May 16th). Mr. Nadeau stated that the Governor sees the issue of newly arriving immigrants and refugees (IR)... as... a positive development in light of recent census information which shows Maine's population growing at a rate which places it second to last in the nation; the beginning of a process which will see IR populations living in communities beyond the borders of Lewiston and Portland; (and) an opportunity for the state to begin developing policies (that) will assist other Maine municipalities deal more effectively with the fiscal and social challenges associated with some IR population(s).[905]

DHS had been busy and reported that Pierrot Rugaba was about to start his half-time work in Lewiston and would work on pre-assigned days. DHS Commissioner Concannon had met with Division One (Lewiston) and Two (Portland) program deputies in Lewiston "to address the ongoing challenges associated with growing (immigrant-refugee) populations." He found "high levels of commitment with his staff," and planned to build on that. Staff caseloads were "already high and resources limited for hard-to-employ applicants," but DHS was "prepared to do everything" it could to "meet the need." DHS would "commit more resources for cultural diversity training for staff" and would now ensure that "contracting agencies... (would) be required to provide language and assistance via the use of the ATT Language(sic) line, or some similar methods, to meet (interpretation needs) and Title 6 requirements"[906] to enable the agency more efficient access to immediate interpretation, accessing about 100 languages.

DHS would also hire a "position to manage a new multicultural childcare program." The program was originally intended to start at the beginning of FFY2003 (October 1st) but would be moved up to July 1st. This program was important, as it would be the first funding support specifically aimed at assisting the Somali community to develop its own childcare facilities. Rugaba would also work closely with the ORR and the Portland-Lewiston refugee collaborative to secure more funding for two GA case management positions in Lewiston. King offered to write a letter of support, while Commissioner Concannon and his staff had scheduled a meeting with ORR officials.[907]

The DHS Bureau of Health reported that they were looking for "more federal funding for (tuberculosis) testing." As a board member of the American Lung Association, Dale Morell suggested that the state DHS department contact the lung association for a grant. DHS would discuss it further with Dale. DHS also reported that they had been "approached by several Somali women to support a Somali women's center to assist them with a variety of health issues specific to their population." Something similar was also happening through Sisters of Charity.[908]

Joyce Benson shared she would use some of the information shared during the meeting to "develop specific funding opportunities." They were looking for some demographic information about the Somali population: "age, health, professions, education, etc." Much of it was information we simply had not collected. There was no time or resources to do that kind of work at a city staff level. That led to a discussion about doing a "supplemental census" to collect the information. Joyce said she would follow up with me later.[909]

Director Mary Ellis Crofton from the State Planning Office's Community Service Center was looking to "develop and strengthen community service efforts and volunteer operations." She knew that there was a "volunteer managers association" in the L-A area but did not know where they met. This was all made more challenging for Ellis Crofton, given that there was no "central volunteer coordination office" in Lewiston. When I heard her say it, I remember thinking there were possibly only one of those in the 492 municipalities in the state, and it was likely in Portland. Crofton offered to attempt to create a volunteer resource center for our area.[910]

Some of the biggest news updates came from Rusty Cyr at the (state Department of Labor) Career Center, Ned Porter, and Superintendent of Schools Lee Levesque. Cyr announced that the Department of Labor had "identified resources" that would "sufficiently address current intensive job retraining needs for eligible applicants." Although both Rusty and many people in the room understood that this program would not work for all immigrants, Cyr noted that his agency was looking to address ESL demand by working directly with the Lewiston Adult Education program to "meet current needs." Cyr confirmed he would also start "roundtable discussions with local employers" to address ongoing challenges associated with hiring LEP applicants.[911]

Ned Porter had not attended the first meeting, but I was certainly pleased that he had attended this meeting. Ned and I had first met during our May meeting, which was also when he introduced me to Gus Schumacher. I learned at the time that Gus was a consultant for the Kellogg Foundation in Battle Creek, Michigan. Gus shared some of what he was doing with immigrant farms in Massachusetts, and I provided him some information about the Somalis in Lewiston.

Following an exchange of emails between Gus and I on May 16th and May 21st, I learned about the "New Entry Sustainable Farming Program" involving Cambodian, Chinese, Hmong, Khmer, and Hispanic immigrants in western, central, and eastern Massachusetts. I shared during the June 11th governor's meeting that Ned Porter had introduced me to Gus and that our recent communications had produced an opportunity for a meeting to go deeper into what was going on in southern New England. Following the June 11th meeting, it was agreed that we would meet again at Lewiston City Hall on June 20th.[912]

School Superintendent Levesque reported impressive progress since May 16th. He told the group that the school system had received "$50 (thousand) in supplementary ESL funding... for non-labor resources." Although Lee was pleased about the newest grant funding, he also shared that the school funding formula funded expenses two years after they have been realized. Finding funding for anticipated budget gaps was highly problematic when it involved state education funding. He also reported that the school system had installed new "ESL software" in the school library, and that he had contacted "Seeds of Peace"[913] Director Tim Wilson to discuss the possibility of working with immigrant youth in Lewiston. Levesque also spoke about private efforts to raise money for the ESL program.

The Adult Education center's proposal featured many "ESOL" (the Adult Education center used the acronym "ESOL" short for English for Speakers of Other Languages)[914] facts and needs that included staffing levels, anticipated changes in the upcoming FY2003 budget (the city budget year began on July 1st and ended on June 30th of every year), a proposed summer program plan, pre-school childcare, ESOL evening classes, Rosetta Stone licenses, and three different levels of funding for various program costs. Adult education ESOL was a program that continued to rely on volunteer teaching support. Any donations to the program were welcome, and much of that related to the lack of federal or state refugee funding. For immigrant populations like the Somalis who had many adults with low levels of literacy in their own native language, it would likely take several years of ESOL education just to reach a basic 6th grade level of proficiency. By June 2002, the department would receive a $10,000 donation for ESOL adult education programming through the efforts of someone who wished to remain anonymous, but who remained committed to assisting the immigrant population until I retired in 2017.

I was elated by the results of the meeting. I could see that there was a genuine commitment from everyone in the room to raise their games. The meeting also left many of us with multiple tasks that needed follow-up. With the amount of work ahead of us, we agreed to have our next meeting sometime in August. For some, summer and vacations were around the corner. For many, including myself and some city and refugee collaborative staff, there would be plenty more to keep us busy right into fall and winter.

# Chapter 7

# Discovery, Creativity, and Outreach

# July 2002 – September 2002

### The Summer Punch List

In every city government position, there were always moments throughout any given week where you looked at your "punch list" and wondered, 'will any of this actually get done?' Over time, many of us in the public administration profession would learn that, in most cases, it gets done, or as 'done' as it will ever be.

One of those 'punch list' items was finishing the supplementary request for the Office of Refugee Resettlement "unanticipated arrivals" application for the "Portland-Lewiston Secondary Migrant Program," a.k.a. the "Portland and Lewiston Collaborative Refugee Services Program." Like many federal grant programs, there was an enormous amount of paperwork that needed to be created or assembled from many different sources. I had very little to do with the grant application, but I knew that Sue Charron, Cheryl Hamilton, Bob Duranleau (Portland Social Services Director), Gerry Cayer (Portland Human Services Director) and others were doing what needed to be done over the spring. The application was finalized and dated on June 28, 2002.[915] The amount requested from the ORR was

$216,666. The collaborative was given notice the funds request were approved and awarded on August 1, 2002.[916]

This ORR supplementary funding would provide two more case managers, a "Program Coordinator" to manage the program, an "Employment Counselor," and a "unique partnership with the University of Southern Maine's Center for Workplace Learning." The center would serve as the sub-contractor for ESL services and partner with the Lewiston Adult Education center who would "implement(t) a capacity-building model that has proven successful in meeting the ESL needs in Portland over the last decade."[917]

Following the May 14th town meeting, Jim Bennett was also following up on a different and more comprehensive way to go about pursuing community building in Lewiston. Less than a month after the meeting, he began setting up "Municipal Family Meetings" throughout the city. The first was scheduled at L-A College on June 6, 2002. Approximately "40 and 50... residents" attended the city's first such meeting.[918]

The format of these neighborhood meetings intended to have residents work with city staff in smaller groups to discuss the "positives and negatives that Lewiston faces." Bennett wanted to ask resident opinions on "where we're going and what it is we're trying to do" and to "reaffirm why people have chosen to live and work in this community." There may have been more participation from city staff during the evening event, but the first meeting was considered a good first effort. Bennett hoped that word on the first community gathering would fuel more interest in participating in future meetings.[919]

## Collaboration Beyond L-A

L-As collaborative enthusiasm was also providing momentum to reach beyond our communities and to work with other "service center" communities in Maine. The state had some 490 municipalities, but the significant majority of those communities were driving Maine's economy with a legislature that was largely made up with lawmakers who had a minimum of concern for the success of the larger communities in Maine.

According to John Melrose, "the State Planning Office reported (in 1998) that 71% of all jobs, 74% of all services and 77% of all consumer retail sales occurred in just 69 of Maine's nearly 500 municipalities."[920] That really summed it up for many elected officials and public administrators that had to deal with the constant barrage of new state and federal environmental, labor, school, civil rights, tax, and other laws that always had a disproportionate impact on the service center communities. The common refrain from many small communities was that we were the problem, while they enjoyed the comfort of their homes in a community with few services and a low property tax rate.

Neither the people in these smaller communities, nor their legislators, could grasp why our property taxes were so high given 'all the money' we were receiving from the state, federal government, and through our one primary source of raising revenue—property taxes. They enjoyed working, shopping, and recreating in our cities and towns, but they had no interest in paying another cent for any of it or helping us to reduce our dependency on property taxes, the most unpopular form of taxation in most states.[921]

Mayor Kaileigh Tara's efforts to have our city not only work with Auburn, but also to also reach out to Portland and Bangor, was rightly given credit for the idea behind the creation of the Maine Service Center Coalition in 2002. In 2000, she worked with Portland to have both city councils meet to address the tension between the cities involving the Post Office distribution center. She also reached out to Bangor and arranged for our city delegation to meet with their staff and city council.

In the summer of 2001, both the Lewiston and Auburn city councils, led by Mayors Tara and Lee Young, "hosted representatives from Bangor and Augusta." Those efforts led to a larger group of "medium-to-large... municipalities, (that) began meeting (in 2001) to promote a new sales tax plan."[922] Those meetings ultimately led to the creation of the Maine Service Center Coalition, which would be chaired by then Bangor City Manager Ed Barrett who would eventually become the Lewiston City Administrator in 2010.[923] In 2002, John Melrose and his company Maine Tomorrow assisted the MSCC to create and adopt its 2003 strategic plan that would "(guide) its policy and advocacy work"[924] for years to come.

The city of Portland reciprocated with an invitation to host the Lewiston and Auburn elected officials on June 12th in Portland for a meal at a local restaurant. Its purpose would be to discuss property taxes and immigration in our cities,[925] and the timing was ideal. The Portland-Lewiston refugee collaborative was in the final stages of wrapping up our second ORR unanticipated arrivals grant, and I acknowledged at the meeting that "had it not been for the cooperation from Portland, we would not have been as prepared" to handle the unexpectedly large number of secondary Somali immigrants coming into our community.[926]

**Data, Data, Data**

During the governor's June follow-up meetings to his May 9, 2002 report, the matter of collecting data and information on the Somali population came up repeatedly. Many of us understood it was very difficult for state and federal agencies, non-profit foundations, and other groups to develop funding opportunities for Lewiston without data. We were doing the best we could to develop a population tracking method that would use new GA applicant information as a baseline for in-migration of the Somali community. We would use new applicant numbers, including all members of the family, and then add 25% to the total to account for newly arriving Somalis who did not seek GA assistance.

It certainly was not a perfect data collection approach, by neither was tracking jobless numbers for the U.S., state or city. Unemployment rates use sophisticated sampling, statistical modeling, and interviews to produce unemployment data at the national, state, regional, and local level. This method is sometimes criticized for not doing an actual weekly count of the unemployed, and not including people who could not work or were simply no longer looking for employment. The method for estimating unemployment was and continues to be imperfect, but the stability and methodology are consistent over time. This method's consistency also allows the data to be recognized by the public as the most accepted indication of real time and historical unemployment information.

Although our modeling for estimating population was far from sophisticated, it was all we had. The methodology, however, was consistent over time and proved to be fairly reliable when compared to other population data, such as the U.S. Census and Lewiston Public School ELL (English Language Learners) enrollment numbers. School ELL information also included language information that provided some evidence of nationality. This was useful to identify how different student nationalities matched up to our estimated general population numbers (state information about student enrollments did not provide ethnicity and nationality, and only standard demographic identifiers consistent with U.S. Census population surveys.)

The matter of pursuing an updated U.S. Census number was complex. It was certain that the 2000 decennial census did not collect regarding Somali arrivals, given that there were no known Somali families living in Lewiston at that time. We wanted to learn more about what could be done to update our census numbers. We received our answer when Joyce Benson from the State Planning Office briefed us on what it would take to pursue a "special census program" to record new Somali arrivals in Lewiston since 2001.

A supplemental survey required the city to file paperwork and pay a $200 application fee for the U.S. Census Bureau request. The question came down to how large an area would be included in the survey. The larger the area was, the larger the survey population would be. Benson shared the survey sample could involve as little as two of the nine census tracts in the city where most of the Somalis had taken up residence. We could also expand it to three other census tracts that contained most of the public and private housing likely occupied by Somali families over the last two years.[927]

Benson provided several ways that the city could save money. One suggestion involved using AmeriCorps volunteers, but the volunteers would likely have to be trained to conduct the survey and the training would need to be funded.[928] What Benson did not cover was any mention of funding sources. If the city wanted this information, it would need to pay for the costs. Although no cost estimates were provided by the State Planning Office, we knew they would be significant.

We had learned that funding something of this magnitude could involve tens of thousands of dollars, or more. Information from the State of Washington provided some confirmation of the potentially high costs. Their 2013 "Census Administration Manual" estimated that the costs of surveying 5,000 people would be approximately $25,000 survey the population. For 10,000 people, it would be approximately $60,000.[929] Costs would be driven by how many enumerators were needed, weather, housing density (less density, less walking, more transportation costs), callbacks, etc. In our case, the process would require interpreters to both train and to accompany limited English speakers if there were insufficient numbers of Somali census field personnel proficient in English.

Surveying the census tracks where some 1,000 Somalis lived would have likely required surveying an area with an estimated total population 15,000 people. The costs could have been anywhere between $5 to $7 per resident or somewhere between $75,000 or $100,000 or more. The reality was that many agencies were accepting our population estimates and the methodology we were using. Given the costs and logistic complexities, the city continued to focus on immigrant residents outreach, social services, as well as K-12 and adult education school costs.

Towards the end of the summer, we had also received our first communication from Bates College with an offer of assistance. Sue Martin, Assistant Director for the Bates Center for Service Learning, sent out a general mailing to "Service Providers" offering the center's student resources to provide a variety of community services. They would include tutoring for "children and adults," research, planning for community events like "health care forum(s)," conducting surveys and compiling their results.[930]

What was frustrating to me at that time was the lack of college involvement with the new Somali arrivals over the last 17 months. I had visited outgoing Bates President Donald Harward sometime in April or May 2002 to speak with him about what more Bates could do in assisting our rapidly growing Somali population. Harward was leaving Bates College and was in the process of assisting the newly hired president, Elaine Hansen. It was important that Harward work with Hansen so that she would be prepared to assume her responsibilities. He believed it would not be appropriate for him to engage the college in any activities or initiatives that Hansen would need to assume. His preference was to defer to the new president and allow her the opportunity to do what was best for both Bates and the new Somali residents.

I was disappointed with Harward's response and felt that he had made up his mind, and that any further discussion would be a waste of his time and mine. I saw Sue Martin's letter as a genuine first step in the process and could only hope that the new Bates president would position the college to do more to assist the community with its new Mainers.

We would not be disappointed. Before long, Bates would assist the Somali community and the entire city in perhaps its greatest and most vulnerable moment of need.

### E. Howard No. 3

During the summer of 2002, the city was also engaged in restoring its E. Howard No. 3 tower clock, built for the new City Hall in 1891 by Edward Howard, for a cost of "$1,265" (over $34,000 today).[931] According to Rick Balzer of Balzer Family Clock Works in Freeport, Maine, this clock was "'the Cadillac of its time.'"[932] According to Balzer, modifications and poor maintenance had negatively impacted clock's performance. The city had modified the timepiece with an electric motor to eliminate the manual winding of the clock, resulting in mechanical problems affecting the clock's accuracy. Additionally, Balzer told me that it had been improperly maintained and repaired.

I learned much more about our E. Howard clock around the summer of 2001, when I brought my Montgomery Ward wall clock (bought when my wife and I first met in 1974) to be repaired at Rick's Balzer's shop in Freeport. After some discussion at his shop, my being Lewiston's assistant city manager was somehow discussed and triggered Rick's accounting of how the city was improperly maintaining the timepiece. Balzer made this discovery when the city bid out the clock's service sometime in 2001. The city allowed the handful of bidders to conduct a pre-bid inspection of the clock and awarded the contract to another company for a lower price.

It turned out that Rick's expertise in E. Howard clocks was very legitimate. His company had started out as clockmakers and watchmakers in 1970 but later specialized in restoring tower clocks.[933] He also greatly admired E. Howard as one of the best tower clockmakers in the world. Balzer had also trained himself to make parts for these clocks during restoration projects. The inventory of E. Howard clock parts were becoming difficult to find all because replacement parts from older clocks were in short supply or did not exist.

Rick and his wife Linda kept me at the shop for two hours. They explained that tower clock parts from other manufactures were not always interchangeable. He also shared with me that the spokes on a gear that powered these clocks actually served as a unique identifier for the clockmaker. When Rick manufactured new gears that he specifically designed for something like an E. Howard tower clock, the design of the gear spokes exclusively belonged to Balzer. This would serve as a type of "ID" for future generations of clockmakers to help them identify the company responsible for the restored clock.

Rick and his wife Linda also told me about making the first tower clock for the LL Bean store in Freeport and recounted how his company had completely restored an E. Howard clock in Haverhill, Massachusetts, back in 1998. The Haverhill timepiece mechanism had originally been installed inside of an old school and eventually stopped working. It was restored and moved to the third floor of the school, making it available for public viewing, but only by appointment.[934] These time pieces were both durable and beautifully made. Rick said that if we agreed to his proposal, he would not just clean and lubricate the timepiece. He would actually do a complete restoration of the timepiece and return it to its original timepiece design as a clock that required manual re-winding.

He proposed relocating the timepiece to the inside of city hall, as he had done in Haverhill. Moving the timepiece inside would improve its operations by keeping the temperature of the metal constant. He would also remove the timepiece from its current location in the City Hall clock tower and bring the timepiece back to his shop for the restoration, which would include the intricate painted artwork on the timepiece.

To deal with the re-winding of the timepiece, he said that he would outfit the display with an electric motor that would actually mimic the manual re-winding the clock. The motor would be set up with cables, weights, and sensors detecting when re-winding would be needed. For all of this, he would only charge us for the labor and materials to do the project. The Balzers would donate all of their labor needed to relocate the timepiece and charge us only for the materials needed for the restoration. I saw pictures of the Haverhill project and was completely sold. Now I just needed to convince City Manager Vitas, City Engineer Mike Paradis and the Lewiston Finance Board that this was the way we should proceed as the cost of the Balzer proposal would exceed the original repair proposal, that if memory serves me, was about $25,000. This project would cost over $60,000.

Paradis and Vitas agreed to proceed, but on the condition that we needed to seek additional funding for the project. The Finance Committee set aside the original repair bid and approved a new timepiece restoration project. They also approved Balzer's bid to do the work. The timepiece was removed from the City Hall tower on December 14, 2001.[935]

Our efforts to change the scope of work from a 'maintenance' to a 'restoration' project were reaffirmed when the clock was placed on temporary display in the third-floor lobby of City Hall June 18, 2002.[936] It was not functioning, but people who could now see the timepiece for the first time marveled at its simplicity and its beauty. The work then moved into the next phase of finding a location for the timepiece display in the building and determining how to raise the money. One thing was certain, it would be displayed in a location where the public could see "the spectacular piece"[937] anytime they were in the building.

The Lewiston Youth Advisory Council and Councilor Norm Rousseau successfully raised over $25,000, with donations for the clock coming in from as far away as Bristol, Maine. City Engineer Paradis also worked with local contractors and other commercial vendors, who also provided their support and donations for the project, as did the Harrison Associates architectural firm. On July 15, 2004, the city celebrated the clock's unveiling and this wonderful example of community collaboration[938]. Not only was the timepiece now on full public display on the second floor, so was the swinging pendulum and electric re-winding device encased in a glass display in the lower main entry lobby of City Hall.

The Lewiston Youth Advisory Council also came up with the idea of putting an automated information kiosk that would play an audio recording of the history of the timepiece and project when activated. The finished project was a wonderful blend of engineering ingenuity, attractive design, and technology all crafted to highlight this timepiece as a wonderfully artistic display that would otherwise have met its fate in a metal pile, had it not been for the efforts of Rick and Linda Balzer.

When Jim Bennett would eventually move on to become Biddeford, Maine's city manager in 2015, he would also take on the renovation of the city's E. Howard City Hall tower clock in 2019. It would be repaired and restored to its original condition by Balzer Family Clock Works.[939]

## Jim Hanna's Vision

One of the most ambitious and unique parts of my summer 'punch list' would be to see if we could move the immigrant farming idea forward. Unbeknownst to me, Jim Hanna, who was working for the Maine Coalition for Food Security, had traveled to Washington D.C. in the early spring of 2002 to review grants for the USDA Community Food Projects Program. A gentleman named Gus Schumacher, who had previously served as Clinton's Under Secretary of Agriculture, was serving as a consultant for the Kellogg Foundation and invited a number of USDA grant reviewers, who were in Washington D.C. that week, to his house for a social gathering in Georgetown.[940]

Jim Hanna shared in our interview that he and Schumacher spoke that evening about some of the immigrant farming initiatives associated with Schumacher. Hanna said that he also connected with Alison Meares Cohen from Heifer International[941] during that evening in Georgetown. Heifer was involved with environmental sustainability and food security projects that worked with many immigrant farmers.

Gus Schumacher and Hugh Joseph from Tufts University were also doing some terrific work with the "New American Farmer Initiative" with "150 (immigrant) farmers." Some of the farmers were "making a reasonable (full-time) living" and the balance of the other farmers "supplementing other jobs with sales at farmers markets, stores and now to... New York City restaurants and hotels" connected to the immigrant farming initiative.[942] According to Hanna, Joseph was affiliated with a Tufts University program called the "New Entry Sustainable Farming Project"[943] and believed that it was one of the first such projects in the country.[944] Hanna said during that evening in Georgetown, his discussions with Schumacher and Cohen, and the encouragement he received from Gus and Allison, served as the "genesis" for his idea to create a refugee farming project in Maine.[945]

I had the pleasure of meeting Gus on May 13, 2002. It was most likely the first meeting the governor's office had set that up to meet Ned Porter and possibly others from the state Department of Agriculture. During the meeting, I shared the story about the Somali relocations with Gus. He was so interested in what had taken place, he wanted to me to send him more information about the details of the relocations over the past year. Gus emailed me after the meeting with Ned Porter and shared that some chefs were driving up from New York to "meet and plan the sales program for this summer and fall." Gus estimated the deal could be worth some "$200,000 in product sales" for the farmers.[946] He also asked if I could send Hugh Joseph some of the same information that I had shared with Gus.

What I did not know at the time was that Gus had already met with Jim Hanna and that Jim was in the process of doing some research about pulling together a farming project for Maine. The only thing Jim did not know at the time was where the project would be located in Maine, as he also had spoken with people in the Portland area about their interest in a project.[947]

Jim Hanna, who worked with the Maine Coalition for Food security would be at the meeting that Ned Porter and I pulled together on June 20th at Lewiston City Hall. Many in attendance had an interest in the development of a farming project: Abdiaziz Ali, Portland-Lewiston Refugee Collaborative; Dick Brzozowski, Shirley Hager and Vivian Holmes, from the UMaine Cooperative

Extension; Stephanie Gilbert, Maine Dept. of Agriculture; John Piotti, Farms Program Director, Coastal Enterprises, Inc. and State Representative from Unity, Maine; Jose Soto, Executive Director, Maine Rural Workers Coalition; Kirsten Walter, Hillview Community Garden; Mark Hews, Threshold to Maine Resource, Conservation and Development; Ned Porter, Maine Dept. of Agriculture; Russ Libby and Suzie O'Keefe; Maine Organic Farmers and Gardeners Association; and Sue Watson, Time and Tide, USDA.[948]

Multiple subject areas were covered, including: halal meat processing in Guilford, Maine; the predominantly Hispanic temporary migrant workers that come to Maine every year (Jose Soto estimated that the number was approximately 25,000 to 30,000); job opportunities that could be available for Somalis in the seasonal crops industry (such as blueberries) that provide much of the employment for migrant workers; possible farm apprenticeship opportunities; agriculture education programs; the declining workforce interest in the farming industry; partnering with groups to develop markets to sell agricultural products produced by Maine immigrants; and learning from out-of-state models like those in Massachusetts, etc.[949]

Jim Hanna shared that possibly hundreds of migrant farm workers had settled in the greater L-A area at that time, and were "mostly serving as a year round(sic) work force" at a local egg farm. According to Hanna, working conditions "became so bad" that Soto's Maine Rural Workers Coalition sued the egg farm and received "large settlements" that were awarded directly to "many workers."[950]

There was plenty more to do and discuss. Another meeting was set for July 8th at Lewiston City Hall and attended by 27 people.[951] This meeting had local Somali, Latino, and Hispanic residents in attendance, Cheryl Hamilton from the refugee collaborative, Jann Yankauskas from Coastal Enterprises, Inc., and many of the participants had attended the previous meeting in July. The commentary at the beginning of the meeting notes said it all:

> This meeting brought together several groups (as part of a) grassroots, unprecedented effort to strengthen communication and

> present mutual opportunities among Maine's agricultural industry, municipal officials, and immigrants. (With interpretation provided) (d)uring the course of the discussion, four languages were spoken... English, Spanish, Somali and French... There is interest among the different communities and 'generations' of immigrants—Franco-Americans, Hispanic, and Somali—in working together to create productive prospects without the hurdles experienced in past efforts.[952]

Ned Porter began the proceedings by outlining the meeting's purpose. He expressed that the agricultural community had an interest in helping immigrant communities in the L-A area and in Portland. This meeting would serve to "gauge the interest" of those in attendance about such a project. Working with other immigrant groups would follow once they completed the needs assessment. He emphasized that there were many organizations that could provide expertise in several agricultural areas that were discussed on June 20th.[953]

The most important of these undertakings would involve "access to land" as it was the foundation upon which all "agricultural production" was made possible. Ned shared that Jim Hanna, from the Maine Coalition for Food Security "and others would take the lead on a project that may (provide) the means to immigrants to produce farm products... (for) the communities (in their respective areas)." Porter was setting up a meeting with Gus Schumacher and Hugh Joseph and wanted to ensure that the results of the meeting would provide him with the certainty that there was real interest in a project that could become "a pilot site for a national initiative based on the New Entry Sustainable (Farming) Project, or other 'incubator' farm projects."[954]

Jim Hanna wanted to hear from members of the immigrant community about their farming skills and if this kind of project interested them. He emphasized that more planning and discussion was needed, but also wanted to hear what they had to say.[955] What Hanna was not sharing during the meeting was that he was already in the "development phase" of a sustainable refugee farming project, looking at federal grants, talking to other federal agencies, and was already communicating with John Piotti at Coastal Enterprises, Inc. about "what (the project) would look like if we brought the project (to the Lewiston area)."[956]

One Somali "elder" thanked everyone for the effort and shared with the attendees that there was "great diversity or skill and background" within the Somali community. Hispanic attendees asked question about the project. "Would these projects fund individuals or groups? Would land be available for purchase?... Would there be marketing assistance or support? (Was) working capital available?"[957]

The comments from the immigrant attendees tied in nicely with Sue Watson's presentation about the Herron Brothers halal slaughter facility in Guilford, Maine. This was a federally inspected facility that was making "between one and three trips a week with halal product to (Massachusetts)." The facility team wanted to know more about the growing Somali markets in Lewiston and Portland and were looking into how they could assist. Although time was running out, there were "national grant competitions" for the "development and marketing of halal products" that were available. The timing may have excluded any opportunity to put in a competitive proposal, but it was important for those in attendance that these opportunities existed and that there were agencies with the resources to potentially assist them in pursuing similar opportunities.[958]

Kirsten Walter from Hillview Community Garden added she believed the "potential" for this project was "amazing," and reminded the participating organizations that the project should provide "adequate attention... to long-term, sustainable efforts... with each group (identifying) its own barriers (some may be shared, other hurdles may be unique to one group), and then work together to overcome (those barriers)."

Kirsten understood the value of such a project and also believed that challenges could be encountered along the way. As a Bates College student, she was "a recipient of the 2000 national Campus Compact Howard R. Swearer Humanitarian Award and the 2000 Gleistman Foundation's Michael Schwerner Activist Award, both in recognition of the 1999 Hillview Community Garden project she developed in Lewiston."[959] Kirsten was one of many Bates students that took up residency in Lewiston and became actively involved in the community.[960]

There were more questions regarding process and the outreach communication effort. Hanna observed that the Hispanic and Latino community appeared to be represented by a single organization in the Maine Rural Workers Coalition. This ECBO had the support of their community, and the public recognition that they were the organization that would be best suited for outreach to the area's Hispanic and Latino population. Portland-Lewiston collaborative caseworker Abdiaziz Ali was serving as the Somali interpreter for the meeting He expressed that the Somali community had a similar organization through the local Al-Noor Mosque, and that "all news and community announcements" were provided at "Friday prayer" at the mosque.[961]

My experience with the Somali community was that simply going through the mosque would not produce the broadest and quickest way of getting information out to the general Somali community, but it was certainly one organization in the community that needed to be part of any outreach effort. We had often turned to others for outreach efforts, including Mohammed Abid at the school department. We had also turned to Somali residents like Azeb Hassan and Roda Abdi, who were working on creating an ECBO to provide services for Somali women. In August, the city administrator's office would create an ad hoc group of Somali community contacts that we referred to as the "Somali Advisory Committee" that included the mosque and the few ECBOs in the area.

The efforts from this July 8th meeting, and other summer meetings with the stakeholders, would confirm to Jim Hanna that there was interest from the Latino, Hispanic, and Somali communities for a farming project. Jim would secure his first local farming parcel on land owned by a co-operative called the Justice, Equality and Democracy (JED) Center, represented by several Bates College students who were living in a home owned by someone they knew. The parcel was located in Green, Maine and near Sabattus Lake where Bates College had a "row house" storage facility used by the rowing team for the college.[962]

Within two months of the July 8th meeting, Hanna had left his prior employment to become a consultant with Coastal

Enterprises, Inc. With the assistance and funding of CEI and Heifer International, the idea that started with a discussion one evening in Georgetown became the "New American Sustainable Agriculture Project" (NASAP). The first official meeting[963] to introduce NASAP to the Somali community took place in the Daryeelka offices at the Bates Mill Complex on October 12, 2002.[964]

In addition to myself, many of the people like Gus Schumacher, Ned Porter, Kirsten Walter, Hugh Joseph, Abdiaziz Ali, and Azeb Hassan would be present at the meeting. It would also include Bridgett Bartlett and Ethan Miller from JED, the organization that provided the first farming parcel to NASAP. The list of people would also include Alison Meares Cohen from Heifer International, one of the individuals who provided Jim with the encouragement to pursue the project; and Jan Schrock from Heifer International,[965] who was the daughter of Dan West, the founder of Heifer International and the organization that awarded this first-time project $200,000 over a three-year period.[966]

The NASAP program would encounter and overcome the kinds of challenges that Kirsten Walter expressed could happen during the first meetings in the summer of 2002. In 2009, the Cultivating Community organization assumed the responsibility for the NASAP program in Maine. The program continues as of the publication of this book.[967]

Hanna's relationship to Gus Schumacher, whose encouragement at a casual soiree in Georgetown in 2002 contributed to Jim Hanna's efforts to create NASAP, and Schumacher's role as a consultant for the Kellogg Foundation and his interest in Lewiston's immigrants, never directly produced any funding for the Maine sustainable farm project. Schumacher, whose work as a food justice advocate earned him national acclaim, died on September 24, 2017.[968]

## JOCKEYING FOR POSITION

Early in the Somali relocation process, one of the first orders of business for Sue Charron and myself was to identify the leaders of the Somali community who would be willing and capable of working with us. As the number of families slowly increased through 2001, I experienced occasional requests for meetings from newly relocated Somali residents. Many simply wanted to speak with someone "of authority" in city government, or to introduce themselves and to offer their help. Occasionally, the offer would be accompanied with a request to also be paid for their services, most often for interpretation (verbal) services. Translation (written) services were not pursued by the city at this juncture as the number of clients requiring translation was nearly non-existent.

The other issue for City Hall was that we had no way to validate or verify the interpretive qualifications of those who would offer the service. There was no existing certification process at the state level. Catholic Charities Maine were utilizing in-house assessment processes to hire their interpreters/translators, but their in-house certification service was not available for individuals not working for CCM. We effectively were on our own to determine who might be qualified to assist the city in that capacity.

Another development involved Somalis who were coming to see me with requests to provide interpretation and other services. Many would arrive with a copy of their IRS Section 501(c)(3)[969] letter confirming their organization's tax-exempt status. In their eyes, their ECBO was a legitimate non-profit agency certified by the government, and that was enough to demonstrate their ability to provide services in the community. When they were confronted with questions regarding their organization's by-laws, state corporate filing approval, financial statements, a list of their board members, their Form 990 (to be filed annually), and if they had been doing business as a formal organization for more than a year, it was a rare occasion that any of those documents or qualifications could be produced. I would also ask for documented evidence of their ability to provide the services they claimed would be offered, such as interpreting, translation, transportation, or after-school instruction. In all instances, they could not produce anything more than a mission statement.

I empathized with the frustration expressed by many of my Somali visitors when I would explain what they needed to show the city regarding their organization's ability and preparedness. I would often share the stories of Azeb Hassan, Roda Abdi, and Fatuma Hussein. It was important for the aspiring ECBO applicants to know how to prepare and organize their ECBO to become viable organizations. Much of the success for new ECBOs came with having some minor success with providing some sort of public service. The strategy of associating themselves with organizations and people that could support their ECBO dream could also be important. By doing so, they could leverage the administrative and financial expertise of the assisting organization to develop a record of success that could demonstrate a level of credibility and proficiency that could be shared with potential funding agencies.

Without some level of professional guidance and support, it would be incredibly difficult for them to receive any government funding. The level of reporting alone for these agencies would exceed their ability to deal with the mountains of documentation that would be required to support their funding. The city wanted to be inclusive, but we simply could not accept 'their word' that they could provide the service that our government agency needed. I would always extend the opportunity for them to get involved with the city by assisting us to organize meetings and to possibly act as interpreters for their community at public functions. Contributing their time was a way for them to demonstrate who they were, what abilities they had, and how committed and available they were to assist us.

By the summer of 2002, we were beginning to sort out who the "go-to" people and ECBO organizations were. We knew our GA case manager Abdiaziz Ali and Mohammed Abdi, who were hired by the Lewiston school department back in 2001. People like Ali and Abdi would often be the conduit for introducing us to people in the Somali community. Azeb Hassan and Roda Abdi's new women's services ECBO was working with us frequently and we often contacted them for outreach efforts. We understood early on that the Al-Noor Mosque, which had opened in November 2001, was a male-dominant organization, where men received most of the information from the city. Very often, only married men in the mosque would be the likely sources of information provided to females and to others in the general Somali population.

We improved our outreach efforts outside of the mosque by involving the area's two women's organizations: the Women's and Children's Advocacy Group, which would soon be renamed Daryeelka and co-chaired by Azeb Hassan and Roda Abdi; and the United Somali Women of Maine that received their corporation status in May 2002, and was led by Executive Director Fatuma Hussein who had been supported and operating out of the Community Concepts office in Auburn.

One of the most confounding organizations that reached out to me was the African Community and Refugee Center (ACRC) from Clarkston, Georgia. In the paperwork sent to me by mail,[970] it was evident that this organization had become one of the more notable Somali ECBOs in Clarkston and possibly in DeKalb County. Mohammed Maye provided me with a cover "Fact Sheet" about his new Lewiston organization, his corporation certificate from the Georgia Secretary of State's office, and his letter from the "Secretary of State, Corporations Division." Also included was his non-profit status in the state of Georgia, his IRS letter confirming his 501(c)(3) status, and his "Application for Authority to Carry on Activities" form certifying that his corporation could conduct business as a non-profit corporation from the State of Maine. The document listed the organization's business address as "99 Birch Street, #3, Lewiston, ME 04240," situated in an apartment building in Lewiston. Maye also included letters from the "Georgia Citizens Coalition on Hunger," the "Dekalb County, Keep DeKalb Beautiful" office and others.

I recall speaking with Maye by phone and asking him to produce information regarding what kinds of programming they were providing in Clarkston. On May 2, 2002, Maye sent me a fax with attachments that included "Genesis Prevention Coalition Program Review," documenting the work by ACRC. The review reflected the organization had "no negative findings," that the building they were located in was "clean and attractive," that ACRC had "expanded services to better meet the needs of the community," and that the "(q)uantitative goals for social service adjustment services have been exceeded as have quantitative goals in the employment program."[971]

Kelly Bouchard prominently mentioned Maye in a Portland Press Herald article. Bouchard interviewed Maye who had "recently opened a satellite office for the African Community and Refugee Center (ACRC) in Lewiston." Maye explained the difficulties experienced by Somalis living in Clarkston, how older Somalis tend to "cling to their culture's clan," and how many Somali youth and young adults were "leaving tribal ties behind and adopting an individualistic approach more common in the United States." The organization was clearly well established in Georgia and the "Fact Sheet" that he mailed to me said that ACRC had set up offices at "145 Lisbon Street, Suite #504" in Lewiston, confirming that he had opened possibly in early or mid-June 2002 in Lewiston.[972]

For some inexplicable reason, the very organization that appeared to be best positioned as a Lewiston ECBO never established itself with the very people in Lewiston that could promote and use their services. Maye admitted he knew much about Lewiston and that people in the Kenyan and Ethiopian refugee camps also knew about Lewiston bragging, "'(w)e are faster than the Internet.'" His organization had a well-established track record in Georgia, he knew about and was interested in Lewiston, but there was no record of anyone associated with City Hall or the refugee collaborative having any interaction with Mr. Maye after he and I spoke in May. Those interviewed for this book that were City Hall and refugee collaborative staff could not recall the organization, or the name Mohammed Maye. I have no record of any other contacts with Maye after his initial outreach to me in May 2002. I was also unable to locate him for an interview.

The opportunity was within Maye's reach to become a major player for immigrant services in L-A. The only plausible explanation for his inexplicable absence in the many immigrant meetings that took place in City Hall during the summer of 2002 was that they simply did not follow through with his intention to do business in Lewiston. The organization that many state and federal agencies would likely have supported to provide services was soon replaced by other locally created, federally funded ECBOs in Lewiston, which had no prior work record with the state but had one of the most dynamic individuals in the Somali community.

Fatuma Hussein's United Somali Women of Maine organization would soon position themselves for the first federal grant to be awarded to a Lewiston African ECBO (it is possible that the Maine Rural Workers Coalition may have received federal funding before United Somali Women of Maine). A few years after its creation, Hussein's organization would become one of the most recognizable statewide ECBOs in Maine and may now be the longest or one of the longest operating ECBOs in the state.

## United Somali Women of Maine

When Fatuma Hussein left Maine after her first visit in February 2001, she already knew where she and her husband would soon be moving. It was only a matter of putting a plan together to arrange for the relocation to Maine. On March 22, 2001, Fatuma arrived in Maine with her children. Her husband, Muktar, would remain in Atlanta to continue working as a cab driver until Fatuma could resettle their family into a new home.[973]

During this period, Fatuma had a random encounter in the Lewiston area with Abdiaziz Ali, the Lewiston GA case worker who she had previously met in Atlanta. Their bonding experience would take place when Hussein asked Ali to accompany her brother on a trip back to Atlanta. Her brother had recently arrived in the U.S. and the April 2001 trip to Atlanta with Ali would secure the rest of the household belongings.[974]

Before Ali had met Hussein in Lewiston, state officials asked him to make a presentation to the State Refugee Advisory Council about Somali arrivals in Lewiston. Ali saw his re-acquaintance with Hussein as the perfect opportunity to ask her for help. He had not shared with the state council that he had no formal training to do a presentation and Ali was seeking a partner like Hussein who, he believed, could fill in that gap in his skill set.[975]

At some point before or after the move from Atlanta to Maine, Ali told Hussein that he had an opportunity to make the presentation to the state refugee council. Fatuma was dumbstruck. She had never stood in front of a group of people to speak about anything in her life. She was also pregnant with another child, and she needed to learn how to craft this presentation on a computer. Hussein quickly confronted her uncertainties and simply decided that she would somehow get this presentation done. Hussein's intelligence and energy impressed Ali.[976]

This latest encounter with Ali presented Hussein with an opportunity to meet several area people and organizations in the refugee services sector. Hussein admitted in her interview that she knew nothing about immigrant services at that time, but she also saw this as an opportunity that she could not refuse, even if she also did not have any prior experience with assembling a formal presentation.[977]

At some point between June and August 2001, Ali and Hussein stood before the Maine State Refugee Advisory Council, but it would be Hussein's presentation. Those in attendance included the State Refugee Coordinator Pierrot Rugaba who was immediately impressed with this most recent 'new Mainer.' Rugaba and Hussein had never met before, but the presentation was enough for Rugaba to ask if she might be interested in a job working for the state, particularly in Lewiston. Fatuma was appreciative but asked if she might be of value in other ways that could be helpful to Rugaba. Both agreed to meet in Portland two weeks later at the DHS state office building on Marginal Way. At the Portland meeting, and after finally convincing Rugaba that she had no interest in working for the state, Hussein asked him if he could assist her in setting up a childcare service in Lewiston. It struck a chord with Rugaba, who knew that there were childcare service needs for Somali women, and suggested that she speak with Jann Yankauskas, the[978] StartSmart Coordinator at Coastal Enterprises, Inc.[979]

Coastal Enterprises, Inc. (CEI) was a "non-profit community development corporation" that had been in the community for some 15 years. They had recently expanded their operations to the area and because they were an "economic development agency" they could "take more risk than the banks," something that could become an invaluable resource for start-up organization funding that would otherwise be unavailable. They also had a "StartSmart" program that worked with immigrant populations to support and fund business development opportunities "as another way to strengthen the economic fabric of the community." The StartSmart program would provide "1:1 business coaching, assist with feasibility studies for business ideas," and also offer "business classes" and help to secure financing.[980]

Hussein recalled that after her meeting with Rugaba in August 2001, Fatuma and Jann Yankauskas had difficulty connecting with each other for about a month. Hussein's recollection of that first meeting with Yankauskas involved her new apartment that "was all pink... everything was so nice and pretty and clean and organized," something that was difficult to do when you had two kids in the house. After sitting down for some tea, Jann asked Fatuma what she wanted to do. Fatuma had told Rugaba that it was childcare, but Hussein was "confused" as to what exactly she wanted. Jann looked at her and said "'OK Fatuma, if you... close your eyes, and you had a dream, what would be your dream?' and (Fatuma) said 'a women's center, transportation, adult education, employment... and she drew my dream on a piece of paper... and she said 'open your eyes... here's your dream.'"[981]

With the information on that piece of paper, Yankauskas told Hussein to write her proposal. Yankauskas would help her with the process of putting Fatuma's "dream" together. After the meeting, Yankauskas went back to CEI and assisted Hussein in assembling her proposal for a Somali women's ECBO that would provide the kinds of services that Hussein outlined in that meeting with Yankauskas. Once the final proposal was worked out between Yankauskas and Hussein, CEI arranged for eight other organizations to be at a December 2001 meeting. Hussein would meet some new people at this meeting, including newly hired Portland-Lewiston Refugee Collaborative employee Cheryl Hamilton and staff from Community Concepts. Also attending the meeting was Pierrot Rugaba, Jann Yankauskas, and others.

Hussein's presentation was a success and resulted in the approval of a $40,000 Maine DHS grant. The funding would provide the seed money for the new immigrant women's support ECBO and it would result in a new partnership with Community Concepts, Inc., the organization that would act as the fiscal agent for Fatuma's new organization and include donated office space in their Auburn location.⁹⁸²

What Fatuma's new ECBO did not have yet was a name, a board of directors, and an approved non-profit corporation state certificate. There remained much more work to do before Hussein had her new organization up and running. Hussein shared with Rugaba and Yankauskas that she needed some time to do the necessary outreach with the community before she was ready to put the last pieces of the organization together.

In early 2002, Hussein reached out to her friend Amin, who had accompanied her on their first journey to Maine and ultimately to Lewiston in February 2001. As Fatuma was still new to the area, she asked Amin's wife to assist her in pulling together a meeting in their new home in a family development apartment, part of a slowly growing Auburn population of Somalis across the river from Lewiston. It was at this meeting where Hussein had her first opportunity to speak to some 35 Somali women about "culturally appropriate services" and the kind of organization she envisioned that would provide those services.⁹⁸³

The Auburn meeting would also lead to Amin's wife assembling what Hussein described as "the right people." Many were the "elder women, who were the core, the backbone of our community, the backbone of our institutions like the mosque" and "established in the community." Hussein knew her audience and believed that she could connect with them by admitting that she needed their help to get her "dream" off the ground. She told the audience, "'I know I'm young... I don't have a lot of knowledge and wisdom, but I have a vision, and I want you to be a part of that vision, and I want you to drive that vision, and I want you to be the voice of implementing it.'"⁹⁸⁴

Fatuma already had been the primary speaker in two meetings with government and agency officials. Those experiences quickly taught her how to 'read and know your audience.' This meeting was no different. After making her appeal for the group's involvement in the process, Hussein asked the attendees what they thought were the next steps. The Somali women at the meeting told Hussein that they would assemble a "core group" that would "brainstorm" what they envisioned about the new agency and what its name would be. The women in the room then selected the core group that would include

Fatuma and four other women in the room. Everyone also agreed that the core group should keep Jann Yankauskas involved with finalizing the creation of the new ECBO. After instructing the core group to reach out to the Somali women in the area, the women directed the core group to contact several "prominent" Somali women that were already working to support other Somali women in the community. The core group agreed and embarked on working on their assigned tasks.[985]

Over the next several months, the core group began knocking on doors and working with Yankauskas. She assisted the group to select the name "United Somali Women of Maine," and to assemble an agenda for the next meeting. While working with the group, Fatuma prepared herself for a meeting that could ultimately determine the success of her new organization. The meeting that would be the potential beginning of the "dream" she described to Yankauskas was set for May 11, 2002, at the Lewiston Multi-Purpose Center.[986]

Before that meeting took place, one of the Somali women who had been doing some service work with the Somali population in Lewiston contacted Hussein. The woman asked Fatuma if she could come to a meeting in Lewiston to discuss what her plans were for her new organization. The request was to have Hussein meet with her the night before Hussein's meeting at the Multi-Purpose Center. Without first consulting the "core group," Hussein agreed to come to the woman's apartment.[987]

On the way to the Somali woman's apartment, one of the "core group" members spotted Fatuma's car and flagged her down. The woman asked Fatuma what she was doing in Lewiston. Fatuma explained to her friend that a woman had contacted her with a request to meet with her in Lewiston. Hussein's friend became very upset and ordered Hussein to open the car door. She got into the car warning Hussein about what she could be walking into. Fatuma had committed to meet the woman who reached out to her. She remained steadfast about going to the apartment.[988]

Fatuma's friend insisted on accompanying her to the apartment. They both arrived and were greeted by the woman who had called her. As Fatuma's friend suspected, there were also a number of other Somali women who all wanted to speak to Fatuma about her new organization. The meeting was very confrontational as the women in the apartment felt that someone as young and new to the area had no business starting up an organization. They also believe that there were women in Lewiston that were already providing the services that Hussein's organization would offer. Hussein did not want to share much more about the details but expressed that although she left the meeting shaken, but undeterred.[989]

On the following day, May 11, 2002, the day that would forever change Fatuma Hussein's life, she made a point to arrive in Lewiston early that morning. There were many details to attend to for the early evening meeting at the Multi-Purpose Center. Not only were there materials, food, and beverages that were needed, Fatuma had also needed to ensure that the transportation she arranged for some attendees would be available, as would the organized car-pooling.[990]

When the doors of the Multi-Purpose Center cafeteria opened that afternoon, the reward for everyone's hard work produced an attendance that Fatuma estimated at around 100 people. Fatuma had also been called the night before and told that some women that were at the previous evening's meeting were also going to show up to disrupt Fatuma's event in some way. Hussein decided not to share that information with those in attendance. She also decided that the best way to deal with potential disturbance was to start the meeting on time, do the requisite introductions, and get right to the agenda. The sooner things got done, the more productive the event would be, and the less likely that the appearance of the disruptors would cause any significant interruption of meeting business.[991]

The meeting opened and Fatuma's agenda went along flawlessly. She had chairs set up for the elders and for the "core group" that had supported her through the entire process. The participants voted on all the business items that included approving the name "United Somali Women of Maine," as well as a selecting the board of directors. When the disruptors finally appeared, the elegantly dressed women made their way into the meeting room and walked purposefully on the perimeter of the room to attract the attention of the attendees. Shortly after they arrived, some of them began to scream "she's too young for you," intimating that someone Fatuma's age could not possibly be the leader of an organization that could be helpful for them.

The disruption went on for several minutes before security arrived (having and paying for security was always required for weekend events when no city staff were present in the building). The women were asked to leave the meeting and did so, but at that point, the meeting was already over. Fatuma had accomplished her goal. The United Somali Women of Maine was now prepared to become an "official" non-profit agency in Maine.[992]

On Monday, May 13, 2002, Hussein traveled to the Secretary of State's office in Augusta to file her non-profit corporation paperwork. All the pieces were falling into place, but at some point in July 2002, Maine DHS contacted Fatuma and shared they had learned about another women's ECBO in the city. This development would mean that the decision to award the money to the United Somali Women of Maine would now become a competitive award between the two Somali women's organizations.[993]

Maine DHS gave both ECBOs three weeks to prepare their presentations. The meeting was scheduled at the Community Concepts office in Auburn, Maine. Both organizations made their 20-minute presentations and Fatuma went first. Someone from another non-profit agency in Lewiston represented the other organization. In the end, DHS simply believed that United Somali Women of Maine was best prepared to begin working on their project and the $40,000 grant was awarded to them on August 2, 2002. The other ECBO was assured that they would be given time to take part in other future grants and eventually received a $10,000 grant from DHS.[994]

The United Somali Women of Maine would eventually become the Immigrant Resource Center of Maine.[995] Both Fatuma and her organization would also become an increasingly important outreach resource for the city in the months and years to come.

Refugee resettlement in Lewiston had been a local story as far back as Jonathan Van Fleet's 1999 story regarding "how the Twin Cities (could) prepare to accept refugees." [996] That discussion between officials from the city of Portland, St. Mary's hospital and Catholic Charities Maine represented the very first news story that spoke to refugee resettlement in Lewiston. A year later, the Togolese arrived in the city, the very first refugees to be resettled in Lewiston.

The Sun Journal wrote multiple articles covering both the Togolese and the Somali arrivals in Lewiston. The Portland Press Herald/Maine Sunday Telegram also wrote articles about refugees, many from journalist Kelley Bouchard who according to public records, began to write stories about the Lewiston's Somalis in April 2002. The city was also seeing more interest by state radio and television programs for interviews. "1020 Productions," who produced programs for public television's "Frontline" program, shared that they were considering sending staff to the area to check out the Somali story in Lewiston. The state ABC affiliate WMTW would be running a special report as part of their "6:00 report on May 2 and May 3 (2002)."[997]

What had not yet occurred was coverage from any of the national print, radio, or television news media. That all changed in June 2002 when journalist Patrick Reardon came to Maine to interview Pulitzer Prize-winning author Richard Russo to speak to him in Camden, Maine about his book "Empire Falls."

Reardon interviewed me in late May, or early June 2002. He shared with me that while he was in Maine for the Russo interview, his editor suggested he search around for other stories of interest to write about, and that is how he came upon the story of the Somali arrivals in Lewiston. His story "A Yankee Mill Town Globalizes" was published in the Chicago Tribune on June 13, 2002. I always felt that Reardon's very fair and well-written article helped to stimulate the national media's interest in the Lewiston story.

I also felt that it was likely that the Somali story in Lewiston had enough of the necessary ingredients to eventually attract the national media: A small Maine town (Lewiston was the state's second largest city with a population of around 36,000 people) with 1,000 unanticipated refugee relocations in less than one year; people of color moving into the whitest state in the nation; refugees from a very warm climate moving to a colder climate like Maine's; and a large working-class population in a former mill town that was working to shake its undeserved negative image. Most outsiders incorrectly believed that our community remained a 'down-on-its luck' mill town and frequently overlooked the extraordinary run of economic development activity that had occurred for over three years. It all just made good copy.

Following Reardon's June piece in the Tribune, another story "New Arrivals Put a Strain on Lewiston–Influx of Somalis Unparalleled in US" appeared in the Boston Globe on July 16, 2002, and was written by journalist Brian MacQuarrie. The article was filled with unnecessary characterizations of Lewiston, the kind of comments that in many ways led to my writing this book. The Sun Journal's Kathryn Skelton interviewed me regarding the increasing interest in Lewiston by the press and I expressed my disappointment about MacQuarrie and his descriptions of Lewiston as a "'shabby... 'down at the heels'... 'fraying parochial backwater' (town) after spending one morning here.'" I also added that MacQuarrie had "stepped over the line" as a reporter and turned his piece into his own "editorial" about what he thought regarding the appearance and economy of the city,[998] something that I also took exception to given what had taken place over the last 50 years in Lewiston.

I could only imagine what MacQuarrie was writing about other New England textile mill towns that had not received a $40 million gift from the National Park Service like Lowell, Massachusetts. It would have been interesting to see how MacQuarrie felt about places like Fall River and Lynn, Massachusetts. These two communities were similar to Lewiston in that they were on their own in figuring out how to rebuild their economies, and dealing with the aging remnants of a bygone industrial economy.

More objective press coverage was provided by multiple journalists that included Matthew Bell's report of the Lewiston Somalis on his Public Radio International's "The World" program on July 22, 2002; and Douglas Kennedy's segment for "Fox Report with Shepard Smith" on August 6-7, 2002.[999] Also included were the three August 18th "stories about Lewiston (that) appeared in the Atlanta-Journal Constitution." I also met with Ron Claiborne on August 20th to tape a segment for ABC News, and on that same day an article was published on the internet by Newhouse News Service.[1000] Ron Claiborne's "ABC Evening News" report about Lewiston was broadcasted on September 15, 2002.[1001] All that news coverage did not include needless and callous characterizations from those journalists.

Perhaps the most interesting and somewhat puzzling interview occurred with Douglas Kennedy from Fox News. When we first met, there was no conversation about his last name. With everything that was going on at the time, the last thing I had on my mind was to start up a conversation with Kennedy about his last name. I had met my share of Kennedy's over the course of my life. None of them ever shared with me that they were relatives of the Joseph Kennedy family that produced: a war hero, a president, three senators (if you include John) and some extraordinary sisters, brothers and sisters-in-law, and children.

It turned out that Douglas Kennedy was Robert Kennedy's second youngest child. Had I known that Douglas was one of Kennedy's children, it might have been interesting to at least talk to him about his dad's enrollment at Bates College in Lewiston back in 1944-45; or his uncle John speaking in the freezing cold, the day before his election as president in the city park now named after him; or Old Orchard Beach located just south of Lewiston, the place where his grandmother and grandfather both "fell in love."[1002] It was a missed opportunity, and it may have helped to deal with some of the tension that occurred during the interview.

Kennedy had quite a few questions that simply could not be answered in a sentence or two. As we proceeded through the interview, we arrived at a point where Kennedy asked me to simply provide answers with ten second responses. I shared with him that other state and national news media had interviewed me and never asked to "self-edit" my responses. I told him it was his job to ask any question he wanted and for me to provide a complete and reasonably short response. I then told him that if he was not agreeable to what I thought were very reasonable terms for the interview, that we were finished and that he could complete his story without me. We did ultimately agree to continue the interview, and it was one of those brief moments I never forgot. It was all made more memorable when I eventually found out who he was and regretted that I did not speak with him about his father and his extended family's impact on my life as a New Englander.

On January 28, 2016, I was invited to speak as a panelist at the Edward M. Kennedy Institute for the U.S. Senate,[1003] on the subject of "New England's Response to Refugees," part of the institute's "Getting to the Point" series. The institute is unique because it contains a full-scale replica of the U.S. Senate Chambers. It is also located next door to the John F. Kennedy Presidential Library. One of the first papers I remember writing when I attended Lewiston's Bates College was about Ted Kennedy's efforts to pass a comprehensive health insurance plan for all Americans, and the competing plan offered by the Nixon Administration, in 1974.

I grew up in a family that always admired the Kennedy's, understood their imperfections, and mourned the tragedies that affected all of their lives. For my mother and father, they sealed their Kennedy connection in Lewiston's city park when they were given the opportunity to stand on the gazebo (in what would later be Kennedy Park) to meet and listen to a young John Kennedy who was running for president in 1960. I felt I had a connection with Robert Kennedy as both he and I had attended Bates College, and made the connection again when I worked with his son. I made the connection with Kennedy brother Ted when I had been given the honor to speak at the EMK Institute shortly after my birthday. As for Joseph and Rose Kennedy, my entire family shared a deep affection and fond memories of Old Orchard Beach, the place where they fell in love. Although Douglas Kennedy may be the one and only Kennedy that I will ever actually meet, some of us in the Nadeau family can certainly make a case that we have in our way established a personal connection with the Kennedy family whose legacy will live on for generations to come.

## More Outreach

Towards the end of August 2002, the Somali story in Lewiston was now a full-blown national news story. Around the same time, Jim Bennett and I decided it was time for our office to pull together a group of "go-to" Somali representatives who we could quickly turn as circumstances warranted. The combination of local/state/national news media interest; ongoing refugee program and service needs; collaboration with agencies; follow-up with constituent questions; and other city business needed a well-coordinated effort to keep all staff, elected officials, and the Somali community informed given the torrent of information being generated every single day.

Enough time had passed for us to identify Somali individuals who had demonstrated a willingness to assist our office, and to do the follow-up and work that was required to get things done. On August 7, 2002, I sent out an email to a number of people advising them that our office was requesting their participation in an ad hoc committee that would serve as the unofficial "Somali Advisory Committee" (aka Somali Advisory Group) to the City Administrator's Office. The email's message was simple: to seek "more effective ways to get critical information out (to the Somali community) quickly and efficiently."[1004]

Jim and I believed that the way to improve speed and efficiency in our outreach efforts was to work "with those who 'work to speak'" for the Somali community at large."[1005] Filling a room with Somali residents would not be efficient, or fast. We wanted people that could advise us on the best way to get information out to their community. We already knew that people like our GA case worker Abdiaziz Ali would get information to the Al-Noor Mosque congregation, and that school employee Mohammed Abdi would work with the school department to do whatever student outreach could be done through the superintendent's office.

We also wanted to engage the most active ECBOs in the community that could help both our office and the Somalis in getting information out to the broader Somali community. Age differences, gender, clan and/or tribe affiliations could be problematic when you needed to conduct a full outreach effort to the entire area population. We hoped that the email invitations to Azeb Hassan and Roda Abdi from Daryeelka, Fatuma Hussein from United Somali Women of Maine (what had recently been awarded a grant from DHS), and Hassan Ali and Abdihakim Hassan from the Somali Refugee Family Foundation would result in their agreeing to assist us with our outreach effort. We scheduled the first meeting of the advisory committee on August 22$^{nd}$, 4:00 PM at Lewiston City Hall. My email also stated that it would be our intent to hold a meeting at City Hall at the same time on the fourth Thursday of each month and that each person or organization representative could bring one guest (to potentially expand the number of participants).[1006]

I was also beginning to make a practice of providing a 'courtesy copy' email to a growing list of people who also wanted to stay plugged into what was going on in Lewiston and its Somali community. Some 50+ people were listed in my August 7$^{th}$ email to the Somali Advisory Committee, which included the governor's office, the Auburn city manager's office, Catholic Charities Maine, the Chamber of Commerce, the Department of Labor, the Department of Human Services, the state HUD representative, city councilors, state legislators, Lewiston city staff, the school department, and the police department.[1007] It was important for these individuals and organizations to know that we were assembling a group that might provide them access to information they might also need.

It was good to see a reasonably large turnout for the first advisory committee meeting on August 22$^{nd}$. Six Somali individuals representing the city's GA office, the school department, United Somali Women of Maine, the Somali elders, Somali Refugee Family Foundation and Daryeelka were in attendance. I was also pleased that Bill Burney, former Augusta mayor and now the state representative for HUD, was our meeting's first speaker.[1008]

Burney, who also had the distinction of being Maine's first African American mayor, provided a very informal presentation geared around the kind of HUD financing and housing support that generated the most inquiries for him: HUD home financing; Section 8 project-based help for those buildings financed by HUD programming; Section 8 vouchers that are used for eligible apartments that were not located in HUD financed properties;

and traditional public housing. There were already many Somali residents living in the Hillview Apartment complex managed by the Lewiston Housing Authority, but there were other public housing opportunities to discuss with the group. Attendees also directed questions to Bill about how tenants would go about filing a complaint and who could provide them with information about tenant and landlord rights.[1009]

Other conversations during the meeting involved the need for public transportation to areas of the community where there were employers but no available bus service. There were also questions about banking services, senior citizen support organizations, and loan and grant programs available from the city.[1010] Lines of communication were opening, and we were pleased with our first opportunity to work together.

In mid-September, I had been receiving reports from Police Chief Bill Welch that there were incidents going on in the school department that needed to be discussed with his school resource staff, all who were Lewiston police officers. On September 16th, I met with PD resource officers Ron Dumont, Rob Aldrich, Roger Landry, Danielle Lord, Joe Bradeen, and Adam Higgins to discuss what, if anything, was going on in their assigned schools.[1011]

There were a number of youth individuals who were identified. Some were white, some Somali, some older, and some who were already well known to PD staff because of other criminal activity, or for other incidents that had occurred in their assigned school. Resource officers discussed white kids being associated with some loosely organized local groups that they believed were not connected to organized out-of-state gang activity. There was also discussion about one Somali student, believed to be from San Diego, who lived on Knox Street in Lewiston and was possibly "leading a youth group." The officer's description of the term "youth group" was possibly meant to guard against using the "gang" description, as there was no evidence to support the presence of organized gang activity in the city. With that said, there was consensus among the officers that there was tension between some Somali and non-Somali students in the high school. There were a few reports of fighting but no injuries. One officer characterized what he observed as a "general dislike between the groups."[1012]

The day I met with the resource officers, there was a rumor circulating around one school (not identified in my notes) that a fire alarm would be "pulled" (possibly activated on the day we were meeting) and "would result in (the) shooting of white kids." It did not happen, but it did lead to more discussion about officers "chasing down" such rumors that were always immediately investigated. The officers emphasized that "no weapons" had ever been brought to school, and that "even with (a) low incidence of violence, one percent (of the school population was) still getting a disproportionate amount of attention" from PD because of the rumors and allegations.[1013]

These school resource officer reports were consistent with what I was also hearing from the PD about what was happening in the general Somali population of the city. There were few reports of fighting, but there were occasional comments made to the PD about Somalis involving racial epithets and slurs being screamed at them from passing cars, or in places of business and public spaces. In my interview with Fatuma Hussein, she commented that the summer of 2002 was "really hard" for some of the Somali community and that many conflicts and racial incidents, both in the community and in the school system, were simply not being reported. The Somalis were concerned that reporting these incidents to the police would only increase the kind of hateful incidents that they were already experiencing. According to Fatuma Hussein:[1014]

> Our cars were being vandalized, it was difficult to go through Knox Street, there was a lot of tension in the (Somali) community, we had flyers going around... a flyer that had an immigrant family and a white family (that said) how much welfare an immigrant family (was) getting and how much income (a) white family was (making) and they were being posted on our doors.[1015]

Hussein said that what we were seeing in the Sun Journal letters-to-the-editor, and mayor and staff emails over of the summer, was being directed to many Somalis verbally and in actions involving their "car... windows (being) smashed (and)" tires flattened. There were also Somali concerns about reporting to the police for fear that such actions would increase vandalism and other aggressive acts towards one of their clan, tribe, or even a family member.[1016] The lingering effects of the 9/11 attacks were also driving concerns that any complaint filed by a Somali community member might also result in some sort of trouble with federal immigration officials. There was plenty for the city and the Somali Advisory Committee to work on in the coming weeks. What we did not know was that the upcoming October advisory committee agenda would look very different from what we all had planned in September.

# CHAPTER 8

# THE CONVERGENCE
# OCTOBER 2002

### *JUST A COUNTRY LAWYER*

Lewiston's 62nd person[1017] to occupy the position of mayor was Laurier "Larry" Thomas Raymond, Jr. who was born in Lewiston on May 7, 1932 to Lewiston residents Laurier T. Raymond Sr. of Lewiston and Florence (Champoux) Raymond of New Auburn who remained lifelong Lewiston residents. Raymond's grandmothers were both American-born, and both grandfathers were Canadian-born. The Raymond's had two children, Laurier Jr. and a daughter, Jeanine. Larry grew up in a house in the Bates College area of College Street, right next door to his grandparents. Living near the Mt. Davis area of the college had its benefits, as he would often take on Mr. Davis' hill and its large ski "jump they used to have there."[1018]

Larry's father was a 1930 Lewiston High School graduate but never attended college. While Larry was in high school, he worked for his father, who owned "Raymond's Gas and Appliance Company," and delivered propane gas to his father's customers.[1019] Laurier Sr. was also a Democrat who was appointed to the Lewiston School Board, but never ran for office. Laurier Sr. would find work with the city of Lewiston, eventually making his way to becoming the Lewiston City Controller in 1953.[1020] His paternal grandfather was also a Democrat who worked in the shoe industry for over fifty years. Larry also had a great uncle named Patrick Tremblay, who was a Lewiston lawyer. Larry remembered going to Tremblay's Lisbon Street office as a child to sit on the window ledge so he could watch the parades that would often come down Lisbon Street. Larry recalled "smelling the leather of his sofa and the leather books" and at seven years of age, wanting "to become a lawyer."[1021]

While Larry attended Lewiston schools, his father became friendly with Mayor Armand Sansoucy, who appointed Laurier Sr. to the Lewiston School Board. While serving on the school board, Laurier Sr. met and befriended Lewiston attorney Frank Coffin, who was also serving on the school board. Coffin's friendship with Laurier Sr. became something of value to Larry Jr. after he graduated from Lewiston High School in 1950. When Larry had decided that he wanted to go to an out-of-state college,[1022] Raymond's father believed they should both see Frank Coffin for his opinion. Coffin was a Lewiston attorney who was becoming involved in Lewiston and statewide Democratic politics.

Coffin was also the keynote speaker at the 1950 state Democratic convention and was developing a successful law practice. Coffin's reputation contributed to Republican Governor Frederick Payne's decision to recruit Coffin to defend him against "kickback" charges. Coffin would go on to become Democratic party chair during Muskie's first gubernatorial campaign in 1954 and a congressional representative in 1956, serving until 1960.[1023] Laurier Sr. arranged for a meeting so that Larry could speak to Coffin about going to college out-of-state. After speaking with Larry about what he was looking for in a college experience, Coffin recommended Washington and Lee University in Lexington, Virginia.[1024] Larry decided to pursue Coffin's recommendation, a choice that would have a profound impact on the rest of his life.

Larry was the "first generation going to college (and) his parents had to sell their house to be able to afford to send him to college."[1025] He was accepted into the Washington and Lee ROTC (Reserve Officer Training Corps) program, something that also helped to fund his education.[1026] Larry enjoyed the "climate, the different way of speaking, accent, a different way of eating." The college setting and experience was so enjoyable that he received both his undergraduate and law degrees at the university.

During his time at WLU, he joined a band as a "soloist" trumpeter.[1027] Larry had learned to play the trumpet while attending Lewiston Middle School. By the eighth grade, he was such an accomplished musician that he played with an adult Lewiston band called "Vicky Vince and his Orchestra." His musical talent did not happen in isolation. Laurier Sr. was also fond of wind instruments and played the saxophone in such places as the Auburn Music Hall and in the orchestra that played music for movies shown at the Empire Theater in Lewiston in the 1930s.[1028]

Larry would use his trumpet talent to help supplement his income in college, but he also had time to become president of his fraternity, own a "flower concession on campus," and "had a bunch of dance bands on the campus."[1029] According to his long-time friend Chip Morrison, Raymond was truly "a great musician" and "a performer."[1030] The money he made while in college not only helped Larry pay for his expenses, it also helped his sister Jeanine, who was attending the University of Virginia.[1031]

Another close friend, Roger Philippon said Larry "was a big jazz fan" and a "big fan of the big band era."[1032] His daughter Susan Geismar described Larry's musical taste as very "eclectic" with a range that began with Mozart and opera, while also enjoying Ella Fitzgerald, Taj Mahal, and Jimmy Buffett.[1033]

While at WLU, Larry also began a renewed courtship with Constance Lebel, who had been involved with Larry in high school. After the couple broke off the relationship in high school,[1034] Constance became a student at the College of New Rochelle (in New York) when the couple rekindled the relationship. The renewed relationship led to marriage in 1955, one year before Larry finished WLU law school.[1035]

Larry passed the Virginia bar exam in 1956, then spent a brief period as an Army Second Lieutenant at Ft. Sill in Oklahoma where his daughter Susan was born. After leaving Oklahoma to work at a Virginia bank, he and his wife returned to Lewiston with their baby daughter in 1957. Larry's father was now working as the city controller in Lewiston.[1036] The city controller's position at that time was similar to a city manager's position without the ability to hire and fire people, and limited in terms of working directly with the city council.

What the controller's position had was influence with the city's Finance Board. It was the most powerful board/committee in city government, with control over finances and payroll for all city operations. It also opened opportunities to network with influential people in the city like Laurier Sr.'s friend Auburn attorney John Marshall. Marshall was also the former Auburn mayor, and the former deputy attorney general for the state of Maine. Marshall offered Larry Jr. a job and the opportunity for "a partnership if (he) passed (the Maine bar exam)." Raymond thought he might fail the exam but was successful and joined Marshall as a partner in 1958.[1037]

While Larry Jr. was in college, his father's position as city controller (which he left in 1966 and was replaced by Laurier Roy[1038]) also provided Laurier Sr. with the political connections needed for appointed city positions. When Raymond returned from Virginia, Laurier Sr.'s position combined with Larry's stellar academic record, and becoming a Marshall firm lawyer, lined Larry up for a "plum" appointment on the Lewiston Planning Board.[1039] During that time, Larry also worked as counsel for the new Lewiston Urban Renewal Authority. He would not only serve as the Authority's counsel,[1040] he would also take part in transforming a section of downtown Lewiston which would ultimately serve as the future home of the second city parking garage, bus station, and his future law practice many years later.

Raymond had also enlisted in the Army Reserve as a JAG (Judge Advocate General) officer "for eight and a half years." This reserve commitment was the product of his graduating as an ROTC student and a very brief Army experience after law school. Raymond served as an artillery Second Lieutenant for six months at Fort Sill, Oklahoma, and was then discharged as part of military downsizing.[1041]

All of this activity did not seem to slow Raymond down. In 1960, Larry Jr. had begun to make a name for himself and was appointed as the assistant county attorney by County Attorney[1042] Gaston "Gus" Dumais. He would remain as the assistant until Dumais decided to run for county probate judge, a move that opened the door for Larry to run for the upcoming county attorney vacancy. Dumais would go on to lose an opportunity to be probate judge to Patrick Malia in the June 19, 1962 Democratic primary. Raymond won the Democratic primary for county attorney against William Rocheleau [1043] (who would become Lewiston's mayor in 1967) and then won against his Republican opponent Damon Scales on November 6, 1962[1044] for the 1963-64 term. Raymond would quickly make his mark in county attorney's position almost as soon as he started in January 1963.[1045]

According to Raymond, while he was running for the county attorney position in 1962, some of the people he met asked him: "'What are you going to do about that pornography?' And I'd say, 'Well, I don't know what to tell you because I'm not sure what the law is.'" During this period, adult magazines were making their way into the display areas of a number of area stores that typically sold newspapers and magazines. In response to constituent concerns about what some perceived to be a clear violation of the community's standards of morality, Raymond decided to act soon after he was elected. In Raymond's eyes, he needed to do something "because I said I would."[1046]

Raymond did do something. Not long after he assumed the position of the Androscoggin County Attorney, he wrote a letter addressed "to all of the news carriers in town, and there were more than just the few that they have now."[1047] The letter would advise its recipients that it was being sent by his office in response to resident concerns about pornography being publicly displayed in their establishments, and that he planned to bring the matter before the county grand jury that would meet in June 1963.[1048] Raymond would let the grand jury decide if what was being sold on the retailers' shelves met the community standard for pornography or not.[1049]

Two things happened almost immediately after the vendors received the letter from Raymond. The magazines on the shelves of "over 40" vendors[1050] were removed before June 1st because no one "wanted to be indicted." The bigger matter coming out of the vendors' letter involved Larry and his partner William "Bim" Clifford being sued by Playboy and "other" magazines. Playboy had its own "well known" legal representation, while a separate firm represented the other magazines. The lawsuit was looking for "hundreds of thousands of dollars" in damages. Raymond said he was not concerned at the time but understood the gravity of the situation for both himself and Clifford.[1051]

U.S. Federal District Court Judge Edward Gignoux asked Raymond and Clifford to come into his office for a pre-trial conference. Gignoux asked Raymond, who was being represented by John Marshall, if he would be interested in retracting the letter. Raymond said he would not. Raymond told the judge that there were cases before the Maine Supreme Judicial Court and the U.S. Supreme Court that might be helpful in determining the outcome of his case. Gignoux agreed with his assessment.[1052]

Raymond decided to write another letter to the adult magazine publishers and told them "'I don't know what the law is, but whatever the Supreme Court decides, that's what I'm going to follow.'" That letter resulted in Gignoux dismissing the case; the adult magazine publishers withdrawing their lawsuit; and[1053] Raymond being re-elected for a second term as county attorney in November 1964.

He continued to serve into December 1965, but when Androscoggin County Probate Judge Jude Patrick F. Scalia resigned in October 1965[1054], it triggered a process that required the Androscoggin County Democratic Committee to select a candidate to fill the position. Raymond and other Democratic candidates were considered, including William Rocheleau,[1055] who was beaten by Raymond for the County Attorney's seat. The committee selected their candidate and forwarded the recommendation to the governor.

Republican Governor John Reed would accept the county committee's recommendation and appointed Raymond in December 1965 to fill the remainder of Judge Malia's term into 1966. Raymond would run again for the probate position in November 1966 and win a full 4-year term.[1056] Raymond would hold the position for 32 consecutive years until December 1998.[1057]

Becoming a probate judge would not be the only thing that Raymond would do in 1965. He would also play a small role in representing former Lewiston Industrial Development Director and boxing promoter Sam Michael through the process of signing a contract establishing the Central Maine Youth Center as the site for the world heavyweight boxing championship bout between Muhammad Ali and Sonny Liston on May 25, 1965.[1058] As Michael's attorney, Raymond was able to get seats at the fight. Like my father, when he finally had the opportunity to get into his seat, he turned to start watching the fight and it was over.[1059]

This fight would be Michael's last big undertaking in Lewiston. Michael had done a masterful job shepherding the growth of the Lewiston Industrial Park, doing what he could to preserve the textile industry in Lewiston, assisting in the site development and recruitment of the Raytheon Corporation, and almost single-handedly brought the Ali-Liston fight to Lewiston. Michael would go on to be the industrial development and recreational director for Oxford County, Maine.[1060]

**The Player**

Although Raymond was a Democrat and worked in the social and political circles of the Democratic Party, he characterized himself as "more moderate and more conservative than many of my Democratic friends." That did not stop him from immersing himself into the Democratic political-social machine in Lewiston. He worked on local and statewide campaigns, helped to organize fundraisers, made trips to the mills to hand out campaign literature and to organize rides to the polls, and was often asked if he had political aspirations.

At that time, his focus was on his growing legal practice at Marshall, Raymond and Beliveau. Raymond's firm was attracting top attorneys that included John Beliveau (who became a partner, served as Lewiston mayor, county district attorney, and a Maine district court judge), Paul Dionne (who became Lewiston mayor and commissioner of the state Workers Compensation Board), and Tom Delahanty II (who would become a Maine superior court judge and Maine's U.S. Attorney). He was happy with his role in the Democratic Party, as were the Democratic leaders who would often turn to him for assistance.[1061]

One serious offer for a federal position came from Second District U.S. Representative William "Bill" Hathaway. Hathaway and Raymond were friends who had their law offices in the same Lisbon Street building. Hathaway was also an assistant county attorney when he ran for Congress and made Raymond "the chairman of his campaign."[1062] Hathaway lost his first race but was successful in his second attempt in 1964. [1063]

Hathaway had several terms in the U.S. House of Representatives and then became Maine's U.S. Senator by defeating the iconic Maine Republican Margaret Chase Smith in 1972.[1064] His victory over Smith, the friendship with Raymond, and his new position as a U.S. Senator resulted in Hathaway offering Raymond the opportunity to be appointed as a federal judge at some point during his tenure as a Senator. The politics of political appointments became an issue for the freshman Senator's efforts to appoint Raymond, and his defeat to Republican William Cohen in 1978 effectively closed the door for Raymond's opportunity at serving on the federal bench.[1065]

**Renaissance Man**

Larry's personality was often described as a mix of intelligence, civic pride, confidence and enthusiasm. Roger Philippon described Raymond as

> a very, very pro-Lewiston guy, a Lewiston cheerleader. One who was always quick to defend Lewiston from those who might attack it from the outside... Also quick to criticize Lewiston residents who were always down on their city, for whatever reason. That drove him crazy... He was pro-City Hall... pro-education... (and) wanted to see more cooperation with Auburn... Even though I was a far more liberal Democrat than he was, when it came to a lot of Lewiston municipal issues, community issues, we saw eye-to-eye far more often than not.[1066]

Larry also had a very dry, somewhat sarcastic wit. Philippon shared that when people would often ask him why he was running for mayor, he would tell them "I need the money."[1067] Philippon also shared a story back when they were both working in the Androscoggin County building. It was a story that Philippon heard from Raymond when he first started in the registrar's office. It happened during his first year as a probate judge, and it involved the former county attorney Gaston "Gus" Dumais, the person who had hired Raymond as his deputy county attorney.[1068]

As Raymond told it, one day he was walking down the hallway of the county building and Dumais was talking to a woman at the counter window of Larry's office. Dumais did not know that Larry was walking towards him when he told the young woman "Ecoute là, ton nouveau juge, c'est un trou du cul juste comme son père." Translation: "Listen here, your new judge, he's an ass**** just like his father." Philippon said that Larry would laugh every time he told the story and loved sharing it.[1069]

Roger added that after Larry had shared the story about the lawyer, every time Philippon would bring Dumais into chambers to discuss a case with Raymond, Larry would glance over to Philippon with a kind of 'again?' look in his eyes. Roger recalled one time when Dumais was really getting "dressed down" by Raymond who had little tolerance for attorneys who were unprepared for their cases. After hearing what Raymond said to Dumais, Philippon later saw Larry, looked at him, and told him, "ya know Larry, you really are a trot du cul, juste come ton père!"[1070]

Larry was also a true family man. His daughter said he made a point of coming home to sit with his family for dinner. Skiing was a favorite family pastime, as were trips to Florida and Jamaica. Larry was also insistent on taking care of his aging parents and great-grandmother. The entire family would go to his great-grandmother's house, where she would make French-Canadian crêpes[1071] (very different from the more familiar French or Belgian crêpes), and they would often watch the Boston Red Sox on television. Some trips to see the Red Sox at Fenway Park also included his great-grandmother. Larry would also do things like organize the neighborhood fathers to flood the nearby pond with water to create a skating rink that everyone on Buttonwood Lane could enjoy.[1072]

Larry also loved golf and playing with people like Philippon, Chip Morrison, and others. Larry nicknamed Philippon "lefty" both because he played golf from the left side and its appropriateness given Roger's "liberal" leanings. Raymond also liked a bit of 'trash talking' while playing golf. If a player was taking a few too many shots to finish a hole, he would say with sarcastic encouragement "you're getting closer every time!" He would see Roger doing everything to improve his game and would often remind him and others "you're never gonna get any better," insinuating, why keep trying? If you played too well, he would demand urine samples from the player and loved to talk it up in French along with his group, who almost always had one or more French speakers.[1073]

Susan Geismar saw her dad as a real "renaissance man." He loved his family, his work, politics, entertaining, small dogs, enjoyed traveling, played multiple sports including tennis and hockey, had an interest in genealogy, exotic cars, particularly convertibles, and loved to play and to listen to a full range of music styles and artists.[1074] Becoming Lewiston's mayor, possibly the one thing that he had thought about multiple times and not pursued, may have been one of the few things that he had not experienced in a very long and full life. That would all change in 2001.

## Mayor Raymond

Larry's decision to run for mayor in 2001 was not made hastily, according to Roger Philippon. "(Larry and I) worked pretty closely" while Philippon was working as the Register of Probate next to Raymond's Judge of Probate office. Raymond was in his sixth year as probate judge when Philippon started working in the county building. Over the next ten years Philippon worked in that office, the relationship with Larry became a close friendship that lasted the rest of Raymond's life. [1075] This friendship also included their wives (Raymond was divorced in 1980 and re-married his second wife Pauline) and opportunities to socialize as a golf foursome. All were golfers, loved music, and Roger and Larry often golfed together.[1076]

Philippon said that maybe as far back as 1997, Larry had talked to him about the possibility of running for mayor "early in the cycle before Kaileigh (Tara) even announced... (There may have been) some thoughts of running, we might have had coffee over it once or twice".[1077] Ultimately, he decided not to run, but that would all change a few years later. On June 20, 2001, Raymond announced his candidacy for the mayor's position in Lewiston. After decades of working in the community either as an elected county attorney, a probate judge, Planning Board member, Finance Committee member, Chamber president, and almost countless other civic positions, he wished "to continue (serving) his community as he (had) for 40 years." [1078] He persuaded Roger Philippon to get "involved in his mayoral campaign" and also convinced him to run again for city councilor, this time in Ward 1.[1079]

Raymond won with 71% of the vote on November 6, 2001. Raymond was "overwhelmed" at the margin of victory and told the Sun Journal that he wanted to keep the economic development "momentum" moving forward. He also believed that under his administration, "'(t)he perception of Lewiston will not be of a tired old mill town, but a great place to live.'"[1080] Raymond saw himself as a "'consensus builder'" and loved the work he did as a "'country lawyer,'" but felt the call to public service after "'a discussion about (the city's) future and how we get there'" at a Chamber of Commerce luncheon. Raymond also acknowledged the work of the outgoing mayor Kaileigh Tara and applauded her efforts to "'put a happier, more confident face on Lewiston,'" but did not see himself getting as "'personally involved.'"[1081]

Larry believed that upon taking office in early January 2002, the most important business for himself and the city council would be to appoint the next city administrator. I remember the efficiency and urgency of the city administrator search process that effectively began with the interviews that started in early February and resulted in newly appointed Jim Bennett working in his new Lewiston position on March 25, 2002.

Before Jim arrived in March, I had my first opportunity to work with Larry and the city council in their first executive session on January 22, 2002. Under Maine law, the council could have discussions about city business behind closed doors under some fairly narrow guidelines. The purpose for this meeting's executive session would be "to discuss real estate negotiations of which the premature disclosure of the information would prejudice the competitive bargaining position of the City and to discuss real estate negotiations that also involved pending litigation with Legal Counsel."[1082]

The city had also received its share of criticism about how it "conducted closed-door (executive session) meetings and the deals it (had) negotiated to stimulate development." Some of that criticism had been expressed publicly by two people who were now on the city council: Norm Rousseau and Mark Paradis. Another person who had been critical about executive sessions was Nelson Peters,[1083] who had narrowly lost to the new City Council President, Rene Bernier. Peters' brother was also involved in providing either legal service or advice to Norm Rousseau on the library building eminent domain action.

The Rousseau legal proceedings for the 2001 eminent domain city council action involved the building that would house our expanded library. The eminent domain action, that would happen at the end of regular city council business, would be one of the subjects discussed in the executive session. Rousseau was present when we entered the conference room to begin the closed-door portion of the meeting (the matter remained in litigation and was later settled while Rousseau was a city councilor later in 2002).

I cannot specifically remember exactly what Mayor Raymond said, but Raymond began to discuss something that did not pertain to anything that the executive session categories listed on the agenda. There was a legal procedure available for the council to amend the executive session agenda, but it needed to be voted upon in the city council chambers. Once the vote to amend the agenda was completed, we could then move back into executive session and discuss the item.

Listening to Raymond immediately resulted in my remembering what had been said publicly by Rousseau and Paradis, who were now in the room, about our recent executive sessions before Raymond took office. I elected to speak up and to advise the mayor and the council that what was being discussed was not covered by the executive session agenda. Raymond became very agitated and told me that if I was not comfortable with what was being said, I could leave the room. I told him that is what I would do. I had provided the council with the information they needed to know and left the room. I did not want the city councilors to be in a position of not knowing that what was being said violated Maine law, particularly with Rousseau and Paradis now sitting on the council.

The mayor and council finished their business while I sat alone in the council chamber waiting for them to exit and to lock things up (it was rare for any public or press to stay at the end of executive sessions rarely include any other city council votes). When they finished the executive session, they came out of the conference room and entered the chambers to collect their jackets and other personal items. There was not much exchanged between any of us except for "good night," and they all left the building. Ironically, Norm Rousseau had recused himself and left the executive session not long after I excused myself. Rousseau left the executive session because the council would take up the matter of the eminent domain litigation involving his property.

The next day, Raymond called me and proceeded to share, loudly, how unhappy he was about the prior evening's episode. The conversation was pretty heated on both sides. I told him why I did it, that what I said was factual, and that it needed to be heard by the other councilors. After speaking with each other, we both knew where we stood on the issue when we hung up. We never exchanged apologies between us, and it was never discussed again.

After years of looking back on that evening, I believe that I would have handled things differently today. I should have interrupted and asked Larry if I could have a quick word with him in another room. If he would have agreed to speak with me, I would then have explained my concerns about Rousseau and Paradis possibly going public with information about Raymond violating Maine law. Their allegations about violating executive session law in 2001 were not accurate but having the two city councilors witness what he was saying would only confirm their suspicions that such violations had taken place. Had Larry rejected the advice, I would have asked Council President Bernier to come out of the room and have the same conversation with me. If Paradis and Rousseau would not have been in attendance, I may have pursued the option of discussing the matter in the privacy of Larry's office the next day or before the next meeting (he typically went into the office to gather his paperwork for the meeting).

Although my intentions to speak up were solely motivated by my concerns about complying with state law, it was not the ideal way for me to begin the relationship-building process with our new mayor. It should also be said that, to my knowledge, Councilor Rousseau and Councilor Paradis never uttered a word about what happened in that meeting. I will also share that I do not remember another episode of any violation of the Maine executive session law while Larry or anyone else was mayor.

## The Gateway Project

As the months went by, the mayor and council were spending an increasing amount of time answering questions about the Somali relocations. In April, Larry had his first interview about the Somali relocations with Kelley Bouchard from the Portland Press Herald in April. It was also the first time that he shared his concerns about the financial impact of the relocations on the city budget, adding that people had expressed their concern to him "about the impact on their taxes." He also understood that Sue Charron and I had been hearing from Somali community leaders that 500 to 1,000 more Somalis could relocate into the city over the course of the summer. Multiple news agencies would repeatedly report the possibility of these arrivals.

Although the Somali story had become national news over the summer, Sue Charron and I kept the mayor and council informed on what was happening at a city, state agency, and non-profit agency level. What we could not report on was activity by any visible, organized civic group focused on doing community outreach, specifically between non-immigrant residents and the Somali community. Cheryl Hamilton and the refugee collaborative were doing all that they could to ensure that outreach efforts included residents of the Somali community. It was much more of a challenge for the city and refugee collaborative staff to get something organized at the resident community level, much of that difficulty attributable to how much work was happening between agencies and organizations.

There was also the matter of working on other things that needed the mayor and council's attention. We had a very busy summer agenda with other city business that included approving the re-zoning of properties around the Walmart distribution center for a road redesign and to open area for industrial development expansion; the installation of new municipal water tanks to support the Walmart project and industrial expansion; relocating the entrance road for the Walmart project from the south side of the project to the north side; renewal of a five-year joint agreement with Auburn to send our trash to their incinerator waste-to-energy facility in exchange for allowing their ash to be sent to our landfill;[1084] and dealing with the resignation of City Councilor Paul Samson.

Samson's decision to resign was announced by Mayor Raymond at the July 9, 2002[1085] city council meeting. Paul had been dealing with many health issues for a long period of time, and he believed it was time to focus on himself. Raymond spoke with Samson and tried to convince him to stay on without success. This would leave an immediate vacancy on the city council. It would also require the county Democratic Committee to fill the now vacant District 87 House of Representatives' seat. Samson was not only leaving the city council; he was also withdrawing his nomination from a Democratic primary victory over incumbent State Representative William Cote in June.

Under Maine law, the Democratic County Committee could hold a caucus vote to fill the vacant House position and invited only Democrats that lived in District 87 to vote for a new nominee. Fifteen residents came to the county building on a July 21st Sunday afternoon and selected nominee Will Walcott over nominee and current state representative William Cote. On the following day, Cote submitted his resignation to the Secretary of State and left District 87 with no state representative.[1086] As the legislature remained adjourned until January 2003, the city council chose not to conduct a special election for the position and included the District 87 vote as part of the scheduled November 2002 election. On September 10th, Marc Mason, who had lost to Raymond in the 2001 mayor's race, won the City Council Ward 5 special election for the seat vacated by Samson on July 9th.[1087]

The July 9th city council meeting would also include another eminent domain vote regarding a 'gateway' property on Main

Street. Raymond was determined to do something about the busiest gateway location into the city that handled Main Street's (Route 202) northbound traffic coming out of Auburn and into Lewiston. Some 30,000 cars per day used Main Street that included a northern view from the Longley Bridge of the Androscoggin River's "Great Falls" and also a view of some of Lewiston's blighted buildings on the eastern side of Main Street. There was also a building on the corner of Main and Lincoln Street that housed an operating pizza shop and tattoo parlor that in prior years had been one of several strip clubs in the city.

Larry had been discussing the corner with Bennett for months. After some discussion with Raymond, Bennett instructed staff to proceed with an eminent domain process that would permit the city to purchase the property at a market rate price. When the city council received their packet of information for the July 9, 2002 meeting, they were seeing the eminent domain action and the supporting documents for the action for the first time. There was no prior notice to the council that the city administrator would take this action at the request of the mayor.

Prior to the city council eminent domain vote during the July 9th meeting, Councilor Norm Rousseau expressed his support for cleaning up the gateways of the city but was "upset (the) item was put into motion without consulting the Councilors." In addition to Rousseau, "Councilor Jean stated he (was) not pleased with the late notice regarding this topic and (wanted) additional time to review and study the issue." Bennett assured the council "that notices were sent (to the building owner) in consultation with the Mayor." Raymond made it clear that there had been "a public outcry for improvements to the gateway areas, and the eminent domain process (was) fair and fair market value (would) be paid to the owners."[1088]

After discussing the eminent domain action in executive session, the council proceeded to vote on the item. Initially, the council vote was 4-2 approving the eminent domain action, with only Councilors Rousseau and Paradis voting no. Bernier requested that the mayor ask for another vote. When the mayor did so, Bernier changed her vote to "no" resulting in a 3-3 tie on the council. Under the charter, the resulting tie would allow the mayor to vote. Following the very unexpected decision by

Councilor Samson to resign that same day, Raymond would cast the deciding vote, approving the eminent domain action.[1089]

Following the city council's approval of the eminent domain acquisition, property owner Mickey Amlotte filed a court action against the city appealing the city's offer of $160,000. In the end, Mr. Amlotte was awarded $265,000 for the property,[1090] and the demolition of the pizza-tattoo parlor building and several other structures (which had been approved for demolition in 2001) began in late September 2002.[1091] The space created by the demolitions would make room for the city's fourth parking garage that would support parking for Bates Mill complex employees, and the new hotel that would be built years later across the street.

Bennett would also use the occasion of the building demolitions to announce a new city redevelopment initiative that would invest some $25 million into the city and include creating a "cleanup plan for (other) downtown gateways"[1092] that would ultimately lead to other major initiatives described as the "Heritage Initiative" and "Southern Gateway" projects city.

Larry had achieved his first significant goal: to clean up the city's busiest gateway. His priority to address the Main Street gateway into city stimulated more downtown development in future years. Raymond's work would be recognized on July 27, 2004 as part of the newly created Main Street gateway park's grand opening ceremony, the same parcel that included the pizza and tattoo parlors that Raymond selected as the first "gateway" for redevelopment.

Unbeknownst to Raymond back in 2002, this location would eventually host a park that would be dedicated on this July 2004 morning as the "Laurier T. Raymond Gateway Park." Newly elected Mayor Lionel Guay would say at the ceremony that in addition to providing a much nicer gateway entrance into the city, Raymond had spearheaded "much of the downtown redevelopment" in the city. Bennett added that Raymond's "'push (and) pull'" created the momentum for more city involvement in development. Bennett added that, "'change does not occur when someone just stays on the sidelines.'"[1093]

The summer of 2002 had been productive and there was no reason to believe that the fall season would be any different. At the same time, Raymond continued to hear from constituents about their ongoing concerns about the rapid refugee relocations, something he had discussed with the Portland Press Herald in April 2002. The arrivals continued to grow through the summer, although they had begun to decline slightly by late August. Those constituent concerns about the refugee arrivals may have produced the same sense of urgency that Raymond felt in 1963 as a new, young county attorney determined to do something about the growing scourge of men's adult magazines appearing in area stores.

The ongoing concerns expressed about the costs of the relocations, and the city's ability to handle the caseload in the General Assistance office, likely resulted in constituents also asking what Raymond could do about it. Just like he did in 1963, he may have told them that he did not know what he could do but promised them he would do something. Thirty-nine years later, just like in 1963, he may have settled on what many lawyers often do when they elect to take action—he decided to write a letter.

## The Mayor's Letter

Raymond said before his inauguration that he would be a part-time mayor. He would focus on getting involved in the big projects, policy issues, personnel matters, and other business that warranted the full attention of the mayor. As for most of the ceremonial matters like ribbon cuttings and attending the many agency meetings and luncheons that a mayor is often invited to attend, he had asked Council President Bernier to represent the mayor's office and the city in her capacity as the City Council President. Bernier agreed to accommodate Raymond, recognizing that he had a very large law practice. It also helped that Councilor Bernier had the personality that could fit any occasion and was completely comfortable in the role of representing the city at both small and large public events.

The mayor's office was part of the Executive Department suite of offices that included the city administrator, the mayor, the community coordinator, and my assistant administrator's office. The suite also included the administrator's assistant office that was set up to serve as the receptionist and monitor the secured lobby area used by the public. Given Raymond's busy schedule, it was very unusual for him to come into the mayor's office to do business related to the position. Raymond's law office was his base of operations, and he never came into the office to get 'city' work done.

On Monday, September 30, 2002, Larry came into his office in the morning to work at his desk, which was directly in my line-of-sight across of my office desk. I always kept my door open unless I needed privacy for personal or city business. When Larry sat at his desk that morning, I immediately took notice of two very unusual things that Larry had never done before: he was working in the mayor's office, and he appeared to be handwriting a letter or notes. My interviews with Jim Bennett and Dottie Perham-Whittier may have provided information that explained Larry's purpose for coming into the office that morning. I was very likely that he was taking notes from documents we were producing about the Somali arrivals. One source document almost certainly included my weekly memos. It was also possible that he was reviewing the many letters and emails that he had been steadily receiving about the Somali community.

According to Perham-Whittier, who often did most of the administrative work for the city council and the mayor, she never saw Larry or his notes on the morning of September 30th. What she remembered was sending a digital copy of the city's letterhead over to Raymond's secretary, Eleanor Douglas.[1094] When Larry left that morning, it was likely that he had taken his notes back to his law office, dictated a letter, and had his secretary type the letter onto city letterhead. To the best of my recollection, he brought the letter back to City Hall either Monday afternoon, or on Tuesday morning, October 1, 2002, the date that would be on the publicly released letter.

Perham-Whittier remembered that Larry came into her office first and was seeking her opinion about the letter. "He asked me what I thought... he wanted to be sure he was doing the right thing," in addition to sharing any comments she might have about the language in the letter "and the way it was presented." Dottie had come to know Larry well, given her support role to the mayor and council in the office. She did not see the letter as "offensive to me at all." Perham-Whittier also believed that Raymond "was just saying (the city) really worked hard, we're really strapped, (and) we really need some help... (He wanted) to be sure he did the right thing."[1095]

Raymond then proceeded down to my office to show me what he had written. As Larry handed over the letter, he asked for my opinion. I started reading the letter and immediately understood what he was doing. I also remembered the episode between us during the executive session with the city council on January 22, 2002, and the phone call between us the next day. That episode suggested to me that when Larry had his mind set on doing something, and unless you had a very close relationship with him similar to that of Councilor Philippon, you did not question why he is doing something or if he should do it at all.

I felt that, at the very minimum, I needed to provide him with an honest assessment of the letter. I looked at him and said what I have shared with many people privately over the years. I distinctly remember using the word "crucify" but chose never to say that publicly while I was working for the city. I do not remember the exact wording of my response to Larry, but it was something akin to "the press is going to crucify you." I never considered that writing this letter would explode into a national news story. I was reacting to what remained a statewide story, though there had been some national news coverage as recently as September 9, 2002.[1096]

There was no pushback from Larry to my response. To my astonishment, he then invited me to do some editing to the letter requesting that I not change the substance of the message or the letter's intent. I told him I would do my best and proceeded to focus on two paragraphs. I felt I had an obligation to do what I could to make the letter a bit more informational and a little less confrontational. On a separate piece of blank paper (and not on our city administration letterhead), I showed him what I had written, and he thanked me for the effort. He then returned to his office with his letter and mine to have Eleanor type the final letter. I believe that the third and fourth paragraphs of the final letter Larry signed are either entirely or mostly my edits.

At some point between Tuesday, October 1st and Wednesday, October 2nd, Larry returned to City Hall and provided me a copy of his final October 1, 2002 letter[1097] on city letterhead. We discussed precisely what he wanted done with the letter and what I should communicate to the Somali community. He requested I hand carry it over to the Al-Noor Mosque on Lisbon Street around the corner from City Hall, which I did during business hours on October 2nd. He also instructed me to provide the Sun Journal with a copy of his letter the next day, on Thursday, October 3rd.

I prepared my October 2nd cover memo[1098] addressed to the Somali Advisory Group with the mayor's letter. The contents of the memo read:

> I am requesting that you take the appropriate action to forward the enclosed letter from Mayor Raymond to the leadership of the Somali community. I am placing my confidence in our Advisory Group to identify those within your community that should receive a copy of this letter. Please do not hesitate to contact me with any questions. As for

320

> the Mayor, he has expressed his interest to meet with you at our regularly scheduled meeting on October 24th at 4:00 P.M. However, if you feel that a meeting with him should take place prior to that date, I am certain he will make every effort to accommodate an earlier meeting date. Thank you.[1099]

I believe before I hand carried the cover memo and mayor's letter to the mosque, I emailed the letter and memo attachments to all the members of the Somali Advisory Group, and those listed in the memo as a "CC." I then walked the original letter and the memo over to the mosque on Wednesday, October 2nd and presented both documents to someone who was in the building. I do not recall being contacted by anyone from the mosque that day, or the next day, regarding the memo—but it may have happened. I do remember bringing a copy of the mayor's letter to the Sun Journal on Thursday.

In my interview with Jim Bennett, both he and I do not remember if he was present that entire week, or if we discussed the letter that entire week. We surmised it was very possible that he was away on business. It is likely that he received my October 2nd email, as he was CC'd on the memo, but there is clearly a void in our records and memories of any interaction between us that week.

On Friday morning, October 4, 2002, the Sun Journal's Scott Taylor was the first journalist in the country to publish a story about the mayor's letter. The headline read "Mayor Appeals to Somalis to Stem Migration." Taylor opened the article by characterizing the letter as the mayor "hoping" to "appeal to the city's Somali community" for their help in "stemming the tide of new residents." In the article, Taylor reported Raymond stated that General Assistance applications had declined in September, information that Raymond likely pulled from my weekly memo and inserted in his letter. Taylor also characterized the Somali community reaction about the letter as "cautious." One Somali store owner said "(w)hat he is trying to say, it needs to be expressed better. I'd encourage him to meet with us, so we can really determine what the problem is here."[1100]

For Raymond's close friend Roger Philippon, reading about the letter in the Sun Journal that Friday morning came as a complete surprise. Philippon recalled that before the letter, "he had expressed to me some of those concerns that were (written) in the letter and expressed to me that at some point 'I'm gonna' have to do something or say something'" about the Somali relocations to Lewiston.[1101]

Philippon's recollection of his reaction after reading the letter did not initially produce any "shock" or "outrage," and he also remembered thinking "'this is interesting'" and that it "would not go well with some people... and it would go very well with others." What Philippon did not think about or expect was the national and international reaction to the letter.[1102]

Not long after that weekend, Philippon finally met with Raymond and asked "gee Larry, I was surprised (about the letter). Why didn't you tell me about this?" Roger remembers that the response was something like "'ahhh, Christ Philippon, I knew what you were going to tell me about that.'" The discussion pretty much ended there.[1103]

The Portland Press Herald picked up the story on Saturday, October 5th. Kelley Bouchard reported that the Lewiston Somalis she spoke to were either "offended" or "confused" about the letter. She reported the information I had issued publicly about our estimate of "1,060" Somalis living in the city with approximately "280 Somalis" arriving over the summer. Bouchard was also the first reporter in the state to mention what had happened in Holyoke, Massachusetts when their city council had voted to support a resolution rescinding the funding that would support a Somali Bantu resettlement in Holyoke, Massachusetts.[1104] What she did not report was that the Holyoke city council action had taken place on October 1, 2002—the same day Mayor Raymond wrote his letter.[1105]

Bouchard interviewed Raymond, who believed that his letter could not "'be any clearer... We've done a great job trying to deal with the people that have come.'" He also said that "'(t)his large number of new arrivals cannot continue without negative results for all. The Somali community must exercise some discipline and reduce the stress on our limited finances and our generosity.'"[1106]

I heard from somebody over the weekend that the Somali community would not issue any public statements but would likely have a press conference on Monday. The media did not contact me at home and I assumed that the weekend news community was still trying to catch up with the story. I did not receive any Portland newspapers at the time and did not know what they were publishing. I was also committed to referee a Bates College invitational women's volleyball tournament on Friday and Saturday of that weekend. Most of what I saw and heard about the letter appeared confined to state coverage. With no calls coming in on my cell phone and no messages on my pager, I believed we would simply have a busier than normal Monday morning answering state media requests for information and interviews.

What I did not know was that the Associated Press went national with the story on Sunday, October $6^{th}$. I was likely working an out-of-state volleyball tournament that Sunday. As an NCAA volleyball official working multiple Division 1 (and some Division 2 and 3) conferences in and out of New England (there were six Division 1 women's programs), most weekends in the fall were booked in July and August and I was traveling frequently. That same Sunday, the ABC Evening News also ran with the story, which I also did not see.

On Monday morning, October $7^{th}$, I woke up to my usual routine of getting ready for work. In the last stages of putting on my tie, I would typically migrate over to the bedroom and catch a few moments of the NBC morning program "Today." Ann Curry was doing the five-minute news segment that typically aired sometime shortly after the 7AM program began. While I was looking away doing something, I heard her say something like "Mayor Larry Raymond..." or "Lewiston, Maine Mayor..." Whatever it was, it immediately grabbed my attention. It was a short segment, but I knew at that moment the letter had become a national news story. What might have been a 'busier than normal' Monday morning was going to turn into something that would take on a life of its own.

Jim Bennett was an early riser and was in the office when I arrived. He was already working the phones when I came into the office and I settled in quickly to check my emails, voicemails and conference with staff, who just needed to talk about what happened. There was never a sense of panic. I remember that the general office number never stopped ringing, my email box was filling, and the atmosphere was highly energized. Jim and I pulled the staff together and urged everyone to do their best to handle the phones, the emails, and the reception window. It was always a team effort in the office, and we were not going to handle this situation any differently—it would just be five times the effort. The key would be to keep track of who wanted a call back or email response, divvy up the work as needed, and to keep everyone in the Executive Office abreast of what each other team member was doing.

Jim and I were both built pretty much the same way. When there was a big 'moment' or crisis to handle, we just went into crisis mode (both he and I were town managers who had been tested through our own experiences with large weather-related disasters). Jim remembers just how busy and urgent everything felt that morning. "By about 10 or 10:30, we're getting calls from everybody" including CNN and the BBC.[1107] Jim and I eventually got together, and he decided that one of the first things he needed to do was to head over Larry's office located just a block away from City Hall.

Sun Journal reporter Doug Fletcher had interviewed Larry for an article that appeared in that morning's Sun Journal paper. Fletcher was the only reporter that Larry would speak with on Sunday night as Raymond trusted him over the years. Raymond said in the article that he had not heard from anyone in the Somali community, but he had heard from many residents and others who agreed with his sentiments. He stated that some "14 or 15" radio, newspaper and television reporters "from as far off as New York City and Washington's suburbs" had tried to reach him on Sunday alone. Larry went on to say that "'(t)his (was) a local Lewiston family thing,'" and that Lewiston did not "need advice 'from Portland or elsewhere.'"[1108]

Bob Stone, who was running for the state senate seat held by Peggy Rotundo, commented to Fletcher that the Somali arrivals in Lewiston was his "'No. 1 campaign issue,'" and he was "'behind the mayor 100 percent" Stone believed that the city had done well to assimilate 1,000 Somalis, but that they also needed to travel to "'other towns, other states, (and) be better distributed.'" Raymond's close friend City Councilor Roger Philippon was also interviewed for Fletcher's article and said that he intended "to discuss the letter with Raymond privately." Roger also added that there were "'positive aspects'" in the letter and spoke to "'the city's effort in accommodating Somali people'" and the challenges of a rapid refugee relocation "'that we cheerfully accepted.'"[1109]

When Bennett arrived at Raymond's office, he could see that Larry was upset with how things were unfolding publicly and what the press was saying about him. Jim recommended that he stay off the radar for the next few days. Raymond trusted Bennett to pull together a plan for how the city and Larry could best respond to what was happening. Jim would begin by canceling the city council meeting for Tuesday night. He would also reach out to Council President Bernier and Councilor Philippon to have them contact the councilors and recommend that they say nothing to the news media. That would provide Jim and me the time to work on reaching out to the press and the Somali Advocacy Group.[1110]

While Bennett was meeting with Larry, I was doing my best to keep up with a stream of press requests and trying to get other work done. One of those tasks involved working with Omar Ahmed. He was someone I greatly admired and had become an important part of our General Assistance case management staff. Omar was a very thoughtful, intelligent, and very creative individual who had his M.A. in "leadership and organizational studies" and worked for the "Ministry of Education" in Somalia. Ahmed was also seen as a community "elder" and a "poet-playwright."[1111] With all that had been going on in Lewiston, Omar used some of his creative talents to write "A Somali Play," a stage-production about "Somali life to include (Somali) music and culture."[1112]

I wrote a letter that day to the Maine Arts Commission on behalf of the city's Executive Department supporting Omar's efforts to find funding for his play. LA Arts was supporting the play and had "high hopes for its informative impact" in the community. Everyone who saw outreach value in the arts believed that such endeavors were important not only for the Somali community but also as "a much-needed grassroots community awareness effort."[1113] Omar would eventually have his play produced but would also have to deal with his very conservative fellow elders who pushed back on the play's music and dancing, which they did not see as appropriate.

## The Somali Elders Respond

While Bennett and I were occupied with doing the outreach and taking care of other business on Monday, the Somali community leaders were also busily preparing to hold a press conference that afternoon. Over the weekend, a core group of individuals at the Al-Noor Mosque (Masjid Al-Noor) had been working on a letter responding to Raymond's letter, while also setting up the press conference speakers, location, and other details. The letter-writing group had been assembled with the blessing of the elders at the mosque. That group would include a new Somali community member named Abdirizak "Zak" Mahboub.

Mahboub had arrived in the U.S. in 1981 and wanted to pursue a college education. He also quickly discovered how difficult it would be not only to get a college degree, but to simply "start life in a new country." He completed his undergraduate studies, receiving a mechanical engineering degree at the Wentworth Institute of Technology.[1114] After being laid off from his job in 2002, he and his wife set course for Lewiston. She would arrive first and find work with the city of Lewiston in August 2002. He would arrive several weeks before the mayor's letter, still unsure what work was available in the area for his skill sets. In his mind, "'Maine was like the country for me.'"[1115]

After the mosque had received the letter, the group of individuals in the mosque who were involved in its creation were never documented. My work with the Somali community suggested that the group must have comprised those men, not women, who had been the most visible to the public and to the media at that time. That would have included, Mohamed Abdi from the school department, Abdiaziz Ali from the General Assistance Office, elder Awil Bile who represented one of the first families to move into Lewiston, possibly Al-Noor Mosque Imam Ibrahim Ismail, possibly Omar Ahmed, and my list would have ended there. After seeing Mahboub at the mic during the press conference on October 7th, it was highly probable that the group also included Zak Mahboub. The Somali elders would never have allowed Mahboub to speak at the press conference unless they believed that he was a valued part of their community's representation.

On Sunday, the group would approve the final October 6, 2002 letter that was signed with the typewritten signature "Elders of the Somali Community." The letter would also include an attached separate signature page titled "Names of Somali Community Signatories." The page included handwritten signatures of the Somali elders and the likely Somali letter authors. The signatures also included women and other Somalis who had gained the elder's respect as knowledgeable and capable of assisting the community. The letter was addressed to Mayor Raymond with courtesy copies to (Governor) Angus King, (Police Chief) William Welch, Lewiston/Auburn Community Task Force, (State Refugee Coordinator) Pierrot Rugaba, and (City Administrator) Jim(sic) Bennett.[1116]

The contents of the Somali community letter reflected their "dismay" about what was written. They believed that Raymond's timing in writing the letter, after acknowledging that Somali arrivals in Lewiston "dropped... since the end of August 2002," was "untimely." The elders also expressed "astonishment and anger" at Raymond's decision to write the letter, as opposed to meeting with them before its release. Raymond had directed me to say in my memo that he would meet with them at the regularly scheduled meeting of the Somali Advisory Committee on October 24th, or at an earlier date if requested to do so. The Somali community cited examples of other officials, including Governor King and U.S. Representative John Baldacci who had taken the time to meet with them in September.[1117]

The Somali community went on in the letter citing examples of what they had contributed to the community since their arrival, which included helping the city's population grow after experiencing a 10% decline in population during the 2000 Census; helping landlords fill many empty downtown apartments; and stating that more than half of the Somali adults in the city were employed. They also thanked the "general public for their understanding" and acceptance of their arrival and offered that as Somali refugees, they had "renounced (their) Somali citizenship and taken U.S. citizenship" adding "(o)ver 80% of our children are Americans by birth."[1118]

They ended the letter believing that Raymond was an "ill-informed leader who is bent towards bigotry." The Somalis also declared that they would ask "both the state government and law enforcement to guarantee our safety," adding that if any Somali was harmed because of his letter, they would hold Raymond "squarely responsible for any such acts." The last sentence attempted to define Raymond's intent and the letter's potential for harm against the Somali community: "We think your letter is an attempt to agitate and incite the local people and a license to violence against our people physically, verbally and emotionally." The letter ended with the closing: "Hope this is clear and let God show all of us what is right." [1119]

## The Mayor's Opinion

Unsurprisingly, the Somali's Monday press conference reflected some of what was expressed in the Somali community letter. Hawa Kahin spoke and said "'I've been to many, many states... I moved here two months ago and I've never been so outraged.'" At the urging of some people attending the event, she held up a picture of her oldest son who was serving as a U.S. Marine in Japan and said "'(w)e are human beings,' waving the key chain. 'Is it our color, our religion or culture? Which one cannot belong in Maine?'" It was also reported that some of the Somalis attending the event believed that Raymond's letter was a "message from the entire city. Others said they saw it as one man's message."[1120]

It was "one man's message" and Raymond's personal opinion written on his official Lewiston mayor's letterhead. Using official letterhead was available to all city elected officials for a variety of purposes, and there was no prohibition of using city letterhead to express any municipal elected official's opinions on any variety of topics involving the city. The action of expressing oneself on official city letterhead was never a statement of the city's position or its policy. The only way the mayor or city councilor could seek an official city position would be to submit a resolution articulating that position of support, opposition, neutrality, or expression of appreciation before the city council for a formal vote. The council action item would then require an affirmative vote to be accepted as an official city position.

Whether the mayor's letter reflected an official position, or "policy," was covered by the Sun Journal. Bennett shared that "'(j)ust because Larry offered his opinion hasn't changed the resolve this city had held for the past 18 months... We've done a lot, but we're going to continue doing it.'" In that same article I mentioned someone who came to see me about the letter and that she "'demanded we call the mayor and demand he apologize.'" I responded to that person "'(h)e's an elected official, and I can't do that.'"[1121]

The person I was referring to was Kathy Poulos-Minot of the National Limited English Proficient Advocacy Taskforce. Poulos-Minot had come to City Hall on Monday morning while Jim Bennett was out of the office meeting with Larry. She entered the city administrator's lobby and told Dottie Perham-Whittier that she wanted to speak with the mayor. Dottie told her he was not in the office, but suggested she speak with me. Dottie paged me, and I came out of my office and met Poulos-Minot in our reception area.

As soon as we finished the introductions, Poulos-Minot immediately launched into her opinion about what the mayor had done and asked that we pursue his immediate resignation. I explained to her that neither Jim nor I had the authority to demand an elected official to resign, and that Larry's letter was his opinion and not the city's official position. For reasons only she knew, she did not accept or believe the response and made some comment about suing the city. I was somewhat taken aback by her resignation demand and litigation threat. I suggested that in place of litigation, that her organization assist us with improving our services, something that we were actively involved in before the mayor's letter. Poulos-Minot did not seem interested in my proposal and left the office. The entire discussion with her took less than three or four minutes.

I knew little about her organization. As soon as I found out who she and her organization were, I suspected we would from them again. During my meeting with Poulos-Minot, she had failed to tell me she set up "two task force volunteers" to test the effectiveness of the city's interpretation/translation services. One person spoke Somali, and the other was "a Spanish-speaking woman from Portland." As the volunteers went to "every department" (which we disputed), Poulos-Minot alleged that "(i)n each case, the (volunteer) was told that there was no translation nor interpretation available (which we disputed). In every case, they were sent away without getting the help they requested" (which was also disputed).[1122] Once I read the story about her organization's 'sting' operation, it became clearer to me that their only purpose was to find evidence of any compliance shortcomings and then proceed with litigation to correct any violations.

Poulos-Minot later brought her concerns to Jim's attention by email with a list of demands, which again included the mayor's apology for writing the letter and to create a "local task force to monitor the city's treatment of all minorities." Bennett responded by saying that "he felt the (National Limited English Proficient Advocacy) task force was using tensions in Lewiston to get national headlines."[1123] Bennett also stated that he invited Poulos-Minot "to meet with him" saying that "'she won't sit with us...and she isn't interested in working out a solution.'" Poulos-Minot reportedly intended on filing a complaint "as early as (November) 11" but added that the Somali community had requested that she not file the complaint given their reluctance to "'make the situation worse by getting more press coverage.'"[1124]

The Justice Department had become involved with Lewiston by the October 11th weekend, in response to Somali concerns about possible repercussions from the Raymond letter. We would reach out again to the Justice Department on October 29th to request "an audit of the city's processes, procedures and practices" as they related to our civil rights compliance requirements.[1125]

Poulos-Minot and her organization had been responsible for a string of successful cases in places like the Maine Medical Center in Portland, and a nine-year effort against the Maine Department of Health and Human Services to meet the civil rights requirements associated with access to services and programs for limited English speakers.[1126] We knew in the early stages of the Somali arrivals back in 2001 that we were not compliant with federal language interpretation/translation service requirements. Nevertheless, we were frustrated that Poulos-Minot could not see our efforts to be compliant.

In the end, there was no action filed against the city by Poulos-Minot or her organization. Her decision not to file may have been influenced by our outreach directly to the Justice Department. It is also possible that she heeded the Somalis plea not to file, or perhaps it involved both actions that saved the city from yet one more crisis to deal with. Whatever the reason, it was an outcome that gave us the time to be compliant. Regrettably, things would not end there. The letter's collateral damage would be felt again in November, and it would test the entire city's ability to once again come together for the greater good of the entire community.

### Building an Olive Branch

By the end of Monday, Jim and I had set up a meeting for Tuesday, October 8th with several people from the Somali Advocacy Committee. We all needed the opportunity to talk about what we could all do together to avoid having this crisis escalate any further. The consensus was that we needed to bring together many of the people who had signed the Somali community letter sent to Mayor Raymond. Bennett assured people in the meeting that although there were "projections of a $900 million state deficit and a $200 billion federal deficit," the "'day-to-day service delivery'" for the Somalis or anyone else requiring services from the city had not changed.[1127]

Bennett said to the press that we had cut programs for the FY2002 city budget, and eight people were laid off. He added that the Somali arrivals did not cause the cuts; they were merely the realities of a softening economy. Jim also said that General Assistance for the Somalis had dropped from 13% of the total residents receiving GA in August, to 6% in September. Bennett also pointed to federal and state immigration policies that did little to "fully compensate cities and towns that must provide" many of the municipal services that secondary migrant refugees receive, [1128] something that I often shared publicly and in published papers in 2005 and 2011.[1129]

Kelley Bouchard's October 9th article ended with Jim's summation about what the mayor and staff were feeling and experiencing with the unplanned arrival of 1,051 [1130] Somalis. Bennett hoped that the progress that both the city and the Somali community had achieved would not get "bogged down" with inquiries about the "mayor's motivations" in response to allegations that he was a racist, or bigoted. He went on:

> '(Raymond is) suggesting that (the Somali community) let us catch our breath so we can catch up,' Bennett said. 'Staff here feels like we've been running the 100-yard dash for the entire marathon. Two to three years from now, people will remark at the closeness and the compassion of our community... We just need a little time.'[1131]

At the end of the Tuesday meeting, we all agreed that there would be city elected officials present at the next meeting, but that it would not include the mayor. Everyone in the room wanted some resolution, but there was still uncertainty about what kinds of outcomes would start the healing process. We decided to schedule the meeting for Thursday, October 10th at the Lewiston Library, and that the location should not be revealed to the public. Everyone kept their commitment to not discuss details of our Tuesday meeting with the news media, but Jim and I told the group that we would tell the press about scheduling Thursday's follow-up meeting.

In the October 8th Bouchard article, Bennett also spoke about the "'missteps people (had) taken and what'" their impact had on everyone in that day's meeting. In that same story, Raymond's legal secretary Eleanor Douglas also shared with Bouchard that the "mayor (had) no plans to meet earlier (than the October 24th meeting mentioned in my October 2nd cover memo for Raymond's letter) with the Somalis or to respond to their request for an apology and retraction of his letter." [1132] That statement, the day after our Tuesday meeting with Somali representatives, did not provide the Somali community much comfort regarding the prospects for an outcome that they could support any time in the future.

In the interim, the onslaught of media attention was relentless. Jim was doing his best to stay in touch with the mayor.

Jim also recollected that he exchanged many phone calls and personal visits to Raymond's law office down the street, but Jim's efforts to see him in his office required some covert creativity. The constant presence of the press, particularly the local television news reporters and their large well-marked vans, were easily identifiable. Jim shared that he remembered one day when he

> went over to the library (across the street from City Hall) and went out the back door of the library...where (they) used to get the books delivered, to get into the alleyway and used (it) to come up the back way (using the alleyway stairs) to Larry's office.[1133]

It sounded almost silly to hear it from Jim in the interview, but it really had become a bit of a 'cat and mouse' circus with the media. Jim would also go to a local TV studio to be interviewed by Anderson Cooper on Wednesday night, October 9th. Over a three-day period between October 7th and October 9th, we had been contacted by many major U.S. television news organization and programs like "Crossfire" and "60 Minutes," overseas media outlets like the BBC, and many of the nation's major newspapers like the Washington Post, the Los Angeles Times, and the New York Times. CNN also contacted me with an invitation for Mayor Raymond to appear on Anderson Cooper's program with Mayor Michael Sullivan from Holyoke, Massachusetts, whose city council had recently voted to stop the funding for a planned Somali Bantu resettlement. Sullivan did not agree with his council's vote. CNN was looking to do a kind of 'point-counterpoint' between the two mayors. I shared with them I would pass along the invitation to the mayor (I told Jim about it—we never told Larry).

Somehow, Jim and I found a way to split up the press requests while Dottie did her best to keep up with the emails and residents who were just stopping by the office to speak to anyone they could. Because the Executive Office suite was also connected to our Human Resources office, all three staff in that office would also help whenever they could. It was very much an all-hands-on-deck effort. People were doing all that they could, and it was somehow working.

Our staff mantra in the office was simply to follow up on every request for information, whether it was a large news organization, or someone just walking in off the street. If anyone in the office could not answer the request, we would do our best to get the information. Some people would be concerned, some supportive and not supportive, and others just wanted to educate themselves regarding the many issues that were being raised from both sides of the discussion.

Communications were also being sent directly to the mayor and often copied to our office. We received a letter dated October 9th and addressed to the "Dear Members of the Somali Community in Maine" (written in both English and Somali) from state Attorney General G. Steven Rowe, who celebrated the Somali arrivals as important "to our Maine community." He also acknowledged that many of them had left their countries to escape death, war and famine only to now "live with fear and anxiety." Rowe assured them that "the civil rights of all Maine residents are protected" and that he would strive to make Maine "a safe, tolerant and respectful place for everyone to live."[1134]

Thursday, October 10th would bring together a large group of the Somali community representatives and city officials to the Lewiston Library to discuss the mayor's letter. Everyone arrived at the meeting relatively unscathed, as some of the news media began to arrive after noticing the large number of people entering the Lewiston Library (we had originally suggested that we might hold it at City Hall). Many of the Somalis who were in attendance were part of the group of 25 people who had signed the October 6, 2002 Somali community letter responding to the mayor's letter. My recollections of those attending included Awil Bile, Abdirizak Mahboub, Aden Mustafa, Said Mohamed, Abdiaziz Ali, Mohamed Abdi, Roda Abdi, Azeb Hassan and Garaad Dees. Jim Bennett was also there, as was Council President Rene Bernier and City Councilor Roger Philippon.

Roger Philippon, Jim Bennett, and I did not remember the specifics of the meeting, but what we did remember was an outpouring of emotion from many of the Somali representatives in attendance. We were in that room not to speak to the Somalis; we were there to listen and do the best we could to answer their questions. By the end of the meeting, that lasted "more than an hour," they sharded their appreciation that we had listened to their concerns but continued to express their disappointment at not having the opportunity to speak with the mayor. Councilor Philippon told the press that many in the room discussed "'the mayor's letter and other stresses in the community,'" adding that everyone agreed to "'work together and move forward'" and that the "'dialogue between the two groups (needed) to continue.'"[1135]

Bennett also shared with journalist Scott Taylor that while all this was going on, other city business also needed to be addressed. The calendar had been reorganized to allow staff and some elected officials the time to continue working on Somali concerns with the mayor's letter. Large city "gateway" projects, revolving loan fund proposals, and neighborhood meetings were being postponed but needed attention at some point.[1136]

What Bennett did not share was that we had met with Somali representatives shortly after the Thursday meeting to schedule time to speak with Raymond. A small Somali delegation would finally have their private meeting with Mayor Raymond in his law office the next day and there would be no advance public notification that would be issued about the meeting.

### The Mayor's Meeting

As Jim remembered the Friday morning meeting at Raymond's office, there were six men and one woman in the Somali delegation,[1137] but according to Larry Raymond's account of the meeting, there were eight Somali representatives at the meeting.[1138] My interview with Jim Bennett and Susan Geismar confirmed that the delegation included Azeb Hassan, Awil Bile, and Abdirizak Mahboub. A Portland Press Herald article confirmed that Mohamed Abdi was in attendance,[1139] and another Portland Press Herald article confirmed that Abdiaziz Ali was also in attendance.[1140] The meeting was characterized as cordial, honest, and "emotional"[1141] with both sides speaking to their concerns about what had happened during the week.

Before the meeting took place, Bennett recounted that I had worked to set up a meeting with him and Azeb Hassan before the meeting at Raymond's office. Azeb's Daryeelka group was part of our Somali Advisory Group, and Jim and Azeb had become familiar with each other over the last few months.

Jim knew that Raymond's daughter and son-in-law, Susan and John Geismar, had two adopted two black children[1142] from Georgia (who were not Somali) in their family.[1143] Jim also believed that Raymond would not mention his grandchildren during the meeting, as he would not use his grandchildren as a "political" prop to prove that he was neither a racist nor a bigot.[1144] Bennett also knew that Azeb Hassan and Geismar worked together in the Daryeelka organization, and that Azeb knew she had two black children. Bennett had promised to Larry that he would not discuss the children publicly earlier in the week, but there was no mention of someone else not doing so privately. Bennett then asked Hassan if she would share her personal connection with his grandchildren during the meeting, emphasizing how important it would be for the Somali delegation and Larry to hear it from her. Hassan agreed and would find a way to bring it up during the meeting.[1145]

According to Geismar's account of what she knew about the meeting, at some point during the meeting, Azeb was looking at pictures in Raymond's office and noticed a photo of his two black grandchildren. Hassan recognized them as Susan's children and seized the moment to introduce Jim's suggestion into the discussion. Geismar remembers Hassan telling her that after Hassan shared with her father that she knew the kids in the photo, "she just about made my father cry because she said, 'I know your grandchildren and I know your daughter.'"[1146]. Both Bennett and Geismar confirmed how emotional Raymond became regarding the disclosure. There is little doubt about how surprising the revelation about Hassan's connection to Geismar was to Raymond. Geismar shared in her interview that her father never knew that she worked with Hassan, or with Hassan's immigrant services organization Daryeelka. It was likely Bennett did not know that as well.

According to Bennett, the entire tenor of the meeting turned from one where both sides were sharing how they felt about their respective positions, to one of pure emotion for everyone in the room. Bennett said he remembered that immediately following Hassan's revelation about the grandkids, Awil Bile got up from his seat and "hugged" Raymond.[1147] According to Larry Raymond, the "meeting ended with handshakes and words of welcome."[1148]

Raymond confirmed to Sun Journal journalist Doug Fletcher that during the meeting, there were questions from a few Somali delegates about his refusal to apologize for writing the letter. In response, Larry explained why he could not apologize.

> 'We talked about the apology issue. I explained to them that it's impossible for me to apologize for something I still believe was no more than a request. For me to apologize just to placate them, when I didn't believe I did anything wrong, would be an insult. They understand that it would be impossible for me to apologize for something I believed and still believe was a request, and a reasonable request.'[1149]

Raymond also explained that the letter reflected much of what he was hearing from residents about the costs of the relocations, the tensions associated with rapid growth of the relocations, and how he believed it was appropriate for the letter to say "'slow down and let us get on our feet here would be the way to go.'" He also shared that he "'truly believed that (he) did the right thing and... had the best of intentions.'" Raymond went on to say that he had given the letter much thought, with many redrafts, before he released it publicly, as he did not "want his words misconstrued."[1150] Raymond saw the letter this way:

> 'The letter I wrote, to me, was a very simple request. Perhaps I'm a political neophyte, but I expected their response would be sure, you've helped us, and now we'll cooperate. Of course, because of the difficulty they had in seeing what my motive was, it didn't come back that way and that's what started it.'[1151]

Fletcher also spoke to how "personally pained" Raymond was about "accusations that he's racist or bigoted," and how it had affected his ability to "sit with his two black grandchildren to discuss the controversy." Raymond believed he would speak to his grandkids eventually, but also stated that he was having difficulty with what he would say, given the love he had for his grandchildren. "Given his family background, Raymond said 'I couldn't believe that anyone would call me racist.'"[1152]

After the Friday meeting with Raymond, Jim Bennett scheduled a press conference that afternoon to report on what had taken place at the mayor's office. Both Jim and Zak Mahboub would speak at the press conference. Zak started off the press conference by saying that "Raymond (had) impressed the Somalis with an open, honest and emotional discussion that showed he was committed to the city and all of its Somalis" and that Raymond "'really showed us emotions and how we could all move forward'" expressing his gratitude for Raymond agreeing to meet with the Somali delegation and for how the community had received the new Somali residents over the twenty months. [1153]

Raymond would describe his public absence over the week as not "ducking people" but made his only public statements about the letter during his meeting with Doug Fletcher that Friday evening.[1154] His next and last interview involving any in-depth discussion about the letter, his resignation, or anything involving the letter would occur again with Doug Fletcher's SJ interview on January 17, 2003.[1155]

Press releases would also be issued through Raymond's mayoral office[1156] and by the Somali Community on October 11, 2002.[1157] The Somali community press release, issued by "The Elders of the Somali Community of Lewiston," would characterize what happened during the week as "an unfortunate misunderstanding between our Mayor and our Somali community." The press release also drew comparisons between the incident and what could happen between family members who have disagreements and then "draw strength from resolving their issues." The elders also expressed they now had a "deeper appreciation" for being welcomed by the city, and the "social and economic" pressures associated with the rapid growth of the Somali community. They in turn hoped that the community appreciated "the potential richness of opportunity new comers(sic) bring to the city." The Somali press release closed with their acknowledgement of the difficulties that many of its "predecessors faced when coming to Lewiston" and their desire to "repay the welcome of the City and People(sic) of Lewiston," quoting from the Qur'an: "(i)s there a reward for good other than which is better."[1158]

Raymond's press release would begin by saying that all those in attendance at the meeting "agreed the national spotlight that (the) community has been under for the past week, due to misunderstandings, has portrayed our great community and all of its valued citizens in the most erroneous way possible." Raymond would say that he was "'deeply concerned'" that his letter had been interpreted as "'a call to battle,'" and regretted that his "'intentions (had) been so misunderstood and (had) hurt some people,'" emphasizing that it was not his intention to do so. Raymond underscored that his letter requesting that the Somali community "'exercise some discipline, to take a breath, to slow down, and to work collaboratively'" was not a "'call to draw lines in the sand'" as some had implied.[1159]

Raymond also clarified that his comments regarding "'respect for the law and the values that those laws represent'" also meant that the city would pursue anyone harming any Lewiston resident "'to the fullest extent of the law.'" He directed his comments specifically to "'any person who believe(d) that our new Somali residents deserve(d) to be harmed or treated any differently than we treat our own parents, children, or friends.'" He also added that while the city had its fiscal challenges, Raymond would dedicate himself "'to serving the interests of each Lewiston resident in a way that recognize(d) their value to our community.'"[1160]

Raymond closed his press statement by urging everyone to "'place the events of the last week behind us and move forward as a community.'" He also saw his morning meeting with the Somali delegation as the "'next chapter in our relationship,'" and the "'first step'" in dealing with the "'multiple challenges and pressures'" that could not be solved "'in a single sound bite and apparently not in a letter.'"[1161]

Jim Bennett and I also believed that the Friday meeting at Larry's law office was the beginning of the healing process. We both knew there was much work ahead, but there was a palpable sense of relief within the community that the Friday meeting had put its foot on a burning fuse that was becoming uncomfortably shorter. Many of us genuinely hoped that a week filled with community fear, division, angst, national news coverage, multiple Maine newspaper stories, and much state television news coverage might begin to abate. Some evidence of that appeared the day of the meeting with Raymond.

Governor King sent a letter on the day of Raymond's Friday meeting "(t)o the Lewiston community" assuring the Somali community that Maine is a "safe place to live." [1162] He also acknowledged the courage it took for the Somalis to escape civil war in their country, and that it was "the courage and perseverance of refugees and immigrants that enriche(d) us all." King acknowledged the city's struggle to deal with the "rapid absorption" of the new Somali residents and the financial challenges for a city with a "high property tax burden." In that regard, King announced that his office had authorized funding for a new refugee coordinator position to assist our office in dealing with our collaborative outreach efforts. King also announced his interest in developing "a state-wide Task Force on refugee immigration issues" while also recognizing the need to increase Maine's diversity as one approach to offset the economic consequences associated with declining populations.[1163]

There would also be a "friendship walk" on Sunday, October 13th to reinforce the community's support for the new Somali residents, and someone named Mark Schlotterbeck, who was organizing the Sunday event, was about to become a very busy person.

**The Friendship Walk**

On the same day of the mayor's meeting, Sun Journal journalist Lisa Chmelecki wrote an article about the Calvary United Methodist Church inviting everyone to their church to "take a walk Sunday (October 13th) as a way to welcome the city's new Somali community." Chmelecki also reported that the genesis of the idea to organize a walk did not begin with the mayor's letter. It began in the summer of 2002 "when members of the Sabattus Street church gathered with members of the Somali community to make holders for their Bibles and (Qur'an's)." The original plan was to organize a small group on

Sunday to deliver the book holders to the Al-Noor Mosque on Lisbon Street.[1164]

The mayor's letter changed all that. They would deliver the book holders, but they would now have, according to the church's "city missionary" Mark Schlotterbeck, "(k)ids-Muslim, Christian and otherwise... lead the way"[1165] in a walk to support the Somali community. Schlotterbeck would also say that the march's purpose would also serve "'to express our delight that Somalis and Muslims have come to be a part of the community and to enrich it.'"[1166]

In reality, the idea for the friendship walk would go back even further than the summer of 2002. Schlotterbeck had traveled to an "urban theology Center in Sheffield, England" in December 2001. While waiting outside of a coffee shop in the freezing cold for a cab that never arrived, Mark, who loved to carve wood, hailed a taxicab that finally picked him up. The cab was driven by "a young British Muslim," and Schlotterbeck told him he wanted to be taken to a "foundry that makes woodcarving tools." The cab driver told him that, "a 90-year-old Afghan woodcarver (had) just moved to his community and (had) become part of the young driver's mosque." Not only was he a woodcarver, but he had also been making "folding Qur'an holders for the mosque's religious school."[1167]

In the summer of 2002, Mark was sitting outside of his church on Sabattus Street when Imam Ibrahim Ismail, the new and first imam for the first mosque in the twin cities, pulled up in his van to ask him something. During the conversation, Mark told the imam about meeting the cab driver in England and the discussion about the wooden Qur'an holders. He inquired if the imam of the new downtown Lewiston mosque needed Qur'an holders. "'Are you kidding?' Ibrahim says. 'We need about thirty of those things.'"[1168]

Schlotterbeck shared that "(f)or three late afternoons in a row, church kids and mosque kids and neighborhood kids, and grown-ups, (got) together" to make the holders. While doing so, those in attendance spoke to each other, "listened to one another's traditions," ran "around the churchyard," played games and had a "terrific time." They planned to deliver the holders on a Sunday in October during "the hour before worship," and the

Sunday School kids and teachers would deliver the finished holders in "little red wagons" to their "friends at the mosque."[1169]

In reaction to the mayor's letter, the Sunday School walk with "twenty"[1170] or so people would now involve "(a)bout 300 people"[1171] who were invited to what Mark would now call a "Friendship Walk"[1172] to the mosque. The "walk" would actually be a "peaceful march to show support for Somali immigrants."[1173] It would begin at Calvary United Methodist Church and "pass by Trinity Episcopal, where the (church's) parishioners (would) make the Friendship Walk their nine o'clock Mass and (would) join (them)"[1174] on the final leg of the march to the mosque on Lisbon Street.

Calvary's Pastor Ruth Morrison began the walk with a prayer for "healing to our community," and a "new beginning among us." Before the walk could begin, "two young white men, representing a white supremacist organization," stood "across the street with posters" depicting "insulting things about the Somali people."[1175] The message was simple, "How long will it take before Lewiston is like Somalia?" The sign also asked, "Would(sic) you allow this African into your home? Would you accept his demands that you feed him?"[1176]

The two white men were affiliated with an organization called the National Alliance. Andrew Tarsy, the "civil rights director for the New England chapter of the Anti-Defamation League," shared that what was going on in Lewiston clearly had attracted the racist organization's interest. In Tarsy's opinion, it was the "perfect scenario to gain support for ethnic cleansing," and he viewed the organization as "the most dangerous hate group in America."[1177]

The significant majority of "Friendship" marchers walked past, ignored, or moved "right by the (two) men, laughing and shaking their heads." Azeb Hassan took the time to speak with them and to hear them say that they did not hate just Somalis, they were "'against all Africans.'" Don Robitaille asked the two men why they were attending the march and said "(t)hey replied that it was their right to express their views." Robitaille took solace in that "there were only two of them" present at the march.[1178]

The approximately one-mile march included state Attorney General Rowe. He was joined by "marchers (who) were longtime

Lewiston and Auburn residents... some Lewiston School Board members, at least one Auburn city councilor and former Lewiston mayor Kaileigh Tara... (but) Raymond was not present."[1179] The marchers and those that carried a banner with the phrase "'(w)e are all friends,'" arrived at the mosque to a closed Lisbon Street blocked off by the Lewiston Police Department who had also escorted the march to its eventual destination.[1180]

Some marchers took the time to speak to the crowd. Mohamed Abdi was one of the first to speak: "'We are a people who have gone (through) an agonizing pain (in Somalia)... The Somali community pledges to be part of the larger community in Lewiston. There is no better place we could ask for in the whole world.'" Lewiston High School student Hibat Sharif shared that all people were "'human beings and (should be) treated as such no matter what.'" Former Mayor Kaileigh Tara exclaimed she saw this moment in history "'as a wonderful opportunity in our community'" and that the city was "'enriched by all residents in (Lewiston).'" Godfrey Banda captured the moment well, saying that he was surprised and encouraged by the number of people who took part, and was comforted from the speeches adding that "'(t)here (were) more people than I thought who (were) willing to accept diversity'" in Lewiston.[1181]

Before the friendship walk, Schlotterbeck had taken the time to meet with the mayor in private "a number of times... during those intense days" following Raymond's letter. Larry stated he would do so if Mark agreed to keep their meetings private. Schlotterbeck had kept those meetings with Raymond confidential for the last 18 years, and only decided to talk about the meetings after I shared with him that Raymond had died in May 2019.[1182]

During those private meetings, Mark suggested Larry meet with a Somali woman named Zamzam Mohamud, who Schlotterbeck knew well and who was also becoming familiar to many in the Somali community. Larry considered it, but later declined. Mark would look back on those meetings with the mayor and recognized the "difficulty" that Raymond had created with the letter, but also saw a man that was "a kind and genuine person."[1183]

Mark Schlotterbeck had done what he could to help Larry and the community seek a way to heal and to move forward. What Mark did not know was that his actions during the week of October 7$^{th}$ would significantly raise his public profile. Jim and I saw Mark's efforts to organize the October 13th walk as someone the public now recognized as a community leader. Our decision to meet with Mark became a priority when white supremacists announced their intentions to come to Lewiston in November 2002.

With all that was going on, another story involving the actions of elected officials was also unfolding at almost exactly the same time things occurred in Lewiston, and it also involved a New England community's reaction to refugee resettlements. The city was Holyoke, Massachusetts, and the refugees in question were also from Somalia.

## Two Cities and Two Tales

On October 1, 2002, the same day that Mayor Larry Raymond wrote his letter to the Somali community, the city council in Holyoke, Massachusetts addressed an annual $320,577 Office of Refugee Resettlement grant that had been awarded to a local agency. The annual grant was awarded to the Jewish Family Service of Greater Springfield and would assist in the resettlement of "up to 100 Somali Bantus" for each of the next three fiscal years. The funding "would oversee setting up a welcome center in the city, finding housing, arranging social, medical and job training" along with "English-language courses." The city council discussion spoke to its concerns about resettling refugees at a time when its "poor city (was) in a tailspin of economic woes."[1184]

On that October 1st evening, the city council voted 12-2 to oppose the grant, one that was being awarded to an agency that was not under the control of the city of Holyoke.[1185] Mayor Michael Sullivan did not support the council vote. In my interview with Sullivan, he shared that 40% of the Holyoke's population in 2002 was comprised of Puerto Ricans and several other minorities, including Dominicans and African Americans. According to Sullivan, the two Puerto Rican and one African American city councilors were "vehemently against" the funding.[1186]

Sullivan added that during that period, he had also hired African American Police Chief Anthony Scott in 2002. Scott "was a figure bigger than life in newspaper reports (back) then. He was always after judges." On the day after the city council vote appeared in the local newspaper, Sullivan said that Scott came to see him and told him, "'the last thing (Holyoke) needs are more black people around here.'" Sullivan saw that Chief Scott was as "serious as a heart attack" when he said it.[1187]

With a city council and a police chief who both did not support the Bantu relocation, Sullivan did all that he could to garner support for the resettlement. He was the first city official to be approached by the Jewish Family Service organization about the resettlement of the Somali Bantus.[1188] Sullivan also joined the agency in making the first public statement about the resettlement and the Office of Refugee Resettlement grant.[1189] It was reported that Sullivan supported "the idea of helping people start a new life in America and expressed concern about a lack of resources associated with the project."[1190]

Sullivan reached out to every individual of the 15-member city council about the resettlement proposal before the city council vote on October 1st. He also spoke to some of the council constituents "who were really upset" and some in the elderly population believing that Somali arrivals would threaten their services. Sullivan also remembered speaking with a second-generation Puerto Rican family who were "prosperous and were doing well." They told Sullivan that they were selling their home, moving out of Holyoke, and would move to nearby Amherst, Massachusetts.[1191] Incredulous, Sullivan asked why they would take such drastic action to leave the city. The wife of the couple explained to Sullivan why she believed it was necessary to move out of Holyoke:

> '(N)o matter how successful we are in Holyoke, we're still Puerto Rican. And when we move to Amherst, we'll be part of an even smaller minority but (we will be) Puerto Rican in a way that is charming and interesting because of the liberal attitude... the mini-Cambridge attitude that Amherst has (about minorities)... In Holyoke we're Puerto Ricans, in Amherst we're like Ricky Ricardo,'... calling it the 'Ricky Ricardo' effect.[1192]

This kind of immigrant blowback from within his community was not something that Sullivan expected. Sullivan said agreeing to the Bantu resettlement was not "something that I went out and sought... but in my naiveté, I didn't think it would be as hateful as it was."[1193] Faced with a Holyoke city council vote opposing the funding of a Bantu resettlement in the community, the "state Office of Refugees and Immigrants" was insistent that "all the parties" were continuing to discuss Holyoke as a "possible" resettlement site. That did not agree with Sullivan's assessment of the situation. He said that someone (from the Jewish Family Services) had "left a message" on his phone saying that Holyoke was out of the running.[1194]

Sullivan's phone message may have been the product of what was happening in the city of Springfield, located about four miles south of Holyoke. Springfield Mayor Michael J. Albano had already publicly expressed the city's interest in hosting the Bantu refugees. Albano said he would welcome the Bantu to the "City of Homes, where numerous other immigrant groups have settled over the past three centuries," adding "'(t)his is what cities do.'"[1195] Sullivan shared that once it was clear that Holyoke was not the resettlement site, the national news coverage of the story waned significantly.[1196]

By November 2003, Springfield had 29 Somali Bantu resettle into their community. During this time, Cayce, South Carolina had joined Holyoke by publicly rejecting a Somali Bantu refugee resettlement in their community.[1197] Based on a conversation I had with ORR officials on a trip to Washington D.C. in 2007, they believed Holyoke was the first local government in the country to take this kind of local or state legislative action since the passage of the 1980 Refugee Act.

What was notable about the 2002 Holyoke city council's refugee resettlement opposition, was that the refugee resettlement issue resurfaced again 17 years later. President Donald Trump's September 26, 2019 executive order gave state and local governments the opportunity to approve or reject their participation in the refugee resettlement program, putting the issue before the Holyoke City Council once again. President Donald Trump's Executive Order 13888 read:[1198]

> (T)he Secretary of State and the Secretary of Health and Human Services (developed) and implement(ed) a process (allowing)... the State and locality both (to) consent, in writing, to the resettlement of refugees within the State and locality, before refugees are resettled within that State and locality under the (refugee resettlement) Program. The Secretary of State shall publicly release any written consents of States and localities to resettlement of refugees...(Furthermore) the State and the locality's consent to the

resettlement of refugees under the Program is taken into account to the maximum extent consistent with law. In particular, that process shall provide that, if either a State or locality has not provided consent to receive refugees under the Program, then refugees should not be resettled within that State or locality unless the Secretary of State concludes, following consultation with the Secretary of Health and Human Services and the Secretary of Homeland Security, that failing to resettle refugees within that State or locality would be inconsistent with the policies and strategies established under 8 U.S.C. 1522(a)(2)(B) and (C) or other applicable law. If the Secretary of State intends to provide for the resettlement of refugees in a State or locality that has not provided consent, then the Secretary shall notify the President of such decision, along with the reasons for the decision, before proceeding.[1199]

According to Sullivan, in a unanimous vote taken by the Holyoke city council in November 2019, they passed a resolution to support refugee resettlement in response to Trump's executive order.[1200] Holyoke's city council action was supported and signed by Mayor Alex B. Morse who forwarded the city's resolution to Secretary of State Michael R. Pompeo on November 22, 2019.[1201] One of the Holyoke city council members voting to support the resolution was Joseph M. McGiverin, someone who had served on the city council as its president in 2002 and voted against the funding for the Somali Bantu resettlement 17 years prior.[1202]

In Springfield, the city council, who supported Mayor Albano in assisting the Bantu to resettle in Springfield in 2003, also unanimously supported a similar resolution approved by Holyoke, on December 16, 2019. The resolution was forwarded to city mayor Dominic J. Sarno for his signature, but Sarno elected not to issue the "letter of consent" to Secretary Pompeo, a decision that equated to his veto of their action. Sarno had long been an opponent of refugee resettlement in Springfield and believed that the city had done "more than its fair share when it (came) to providing a new home to refugees."[1203]

During that same time, several refugee resettlement organizations came together to file a lawsuit in federal court challenging President Trump's September Executive Order. They believed that states and local governments did not have the authority to approve or disapprove refugee resettlement into their communities under existing federal law. On January 15, 2020, the U.S. District Court in Maryland issued a preliminary injunction setting aside President Trump's Executive Order suspending Mayor Sarno's action. The district court's action would also temporarily preserve the original language of the 1980 Refugee Act that required "actively coordinating" with the states and local governments, and also rejected the requirement for their approval before resettling refugees into a community or state.[1204]

On January 8, 2021, the U.S. Court of Appeals for the Fourth Circuit upheld the U.S. District Court's action to set aside Executive Order 13888 and to leave the refugee resettlement provisions of the 1980 Refugee Act intact.[1205] With a new Democratic president taking office on January 20th, there would be no appeal of the appellate court's decision to the Supreme Court. Consequently, Mayor Sarno, and all other local and state elected officials nationally, no longer had the authority to block or approve a refugee resettlement in their community.

What is somewhat extraordinary about the 2002 events in Holyoke, and in Springfield in 2019, is that neither instance ever resulted in the kind of large-scale public demonstrations, or months of intensive national and international media coverage, that occurred in Lewiston. In both Holyoke and Springfield, municipal officials took official legislative action opposing refugee resettlement. In Lewiston, the mayor wrote a letter expressing his opinion about the impacts of an unplanned, rapid refugee resettlement into the city.

Aside from anyone's opinion regarding the Raymond letter in Lewiston, it was clear that Raymond had not taken an official action. Additionally, no other action or official resolution was ever put before the city council to stop refugee secondary migrant arrivals, or refugee resettlements in Lewiston. Yet somehow, the same media and public who condemned Raymond, and in many cases the city of Lewiston, did not invest nearly the same level of public outrage, scrutiny, or public action against the city officials of either Holyoke or Springfield, Massachusetts.

It should be noted that Holyoke's official 2002 position had clearly changed over time. The same should be said about Holyoke City Councilor McGiverin who changed his position as well. Springfield's Mayor Domenic Sarno continues to serve as its mayor and by all accounts, appears to believe that the city of Springfield remains "closed for business"[1206] when it comes to refugee resettlements.

After being elected in 2007, Mayor Domenic Sarno would continue to serve the city of Springfield into 2021 and remains in office as the longest serving mayor in the city's history.[1207]

# CHAPTER 9

# LA RÉPUDIATION
# NOVEMBER 2002 – MARCH 2003

### HATE BOOKS A MEETING

Following the meeting in Raymond's office on October 11th, the news of the reported 'understanding' between the Somali community and the mayor appeared to be well received by many people in the city. That did not stop many national, state and local news stories from being published during the week of October 14th. There was reporting from the Washington Post,[1208] Associated Press,[1209] New York Times,[1210] Sun Journal,[1211] Portland Press Herald,[1212] and the Maine Sunday Telegram,[1213] but less coverage from the national television and radio news media outlets.

What would also continue was the stream of 'letters to the editor' (called "Your Views") to the Sun Journal. There was no polling done by the media about the mayor's letter, but there was anecdotal evidence of ample support for and against either the content of Raymond's letter or for him as Mayor.

A sampling from different people in support of the mayor's letter and/or Mayor Raymond:

> *Finally, someone, other than local residents whispering around coffee cups in the safety of their homes, says it loud enough to hear: 'We have been overwhelmed....'*[1214]

> A lot of people who read Mayor Raymond's letter understood exactly what the letter said, and it's pretty hard not to. All he is asking is to give the taxpayers of Lewiston a break and is asking this for all to see....[1215]
>
> Mayor Raymond's forebears are probably like mine, immigrants from Canada. In my case, my mother arrived in Lewiston at age 14, lived with relatives for two weeks, got a job in the mill and found an apartment by the third week....[1216]
>
> (T)he continuous and unprecedented migration of the Somalis into our city has now led to a situation of crisis proportions. There are no jobs in Lewiston, even for our own people, and resources are stretched to the breaking point....[1217]
>
> To all who wrote and criticized him and don't contribute to our tax coffers, keep your opinions to yourselves![1218]

Readers who opposed the letter and/or Mayor Raymond wrote:

> The letter's rhetoric of 'us' versus 'you' ('you' being the Somali residents) creates more than what the mayor calls 'breathing room,' it creates a divisive rift that disrupts any hope for harmonious intercultural relations in Lewiston....[1219]
>
> Since he is addressing the letter to the Somali community, Mayor Raymond wants to make each member of that community believe that he or she has a hand in the pocket and wallet of every citizen of Lewiston....[1220]
>
> The mayor of Lewiston said that he waited on the sidelines for 10 months before saying anything about the influx of Somali people to Lewiston. If that letter is the most intelligent thing he could come up with, then I hope that he never writes another one...The mayor should apologize for his badly worded, ill-conceived try at diplomacy....[1221]

> *Instead of thinking what it will cost us financially, let us think about what it will cost us if we don't help... When we aid Somali neighbors to make a smooth transition to a better life, we affirm what is best about our country....*[1222]

There was also the letter from a Lewiston resident that was surprisingly honest and best represented what people on both sides were expressing about the issue, the immigrants, and the mayor:

> *I have watched the migration of Somalis with a mixture of curiosity and apprehension. I am concerned about the stresses on our schools. I am concerned about increases in welfare benefits and property taxes. And, yes, I am somewhat intimidated by an influx of people whose culture and customs and skin color are different than mine... I (also) helped to organize a cultural heritage night at the Lewiston Middle School last spring... I found the Somali-Americans to be delightful people, eager to learn about us and just as eager to talk about themselves... I know our mayor is not a racist... I believe that, in his heart, he feels as I do about our newest residents... (and) will encourage all citizens to work together to solve any perceived problems.*[1223]

Although the news coverage waned in the weeks that followed the mayor's meeting with the Somali delegation, there was much work to be done. We began to finish the details associated with Governor King's offer to provide us with two years of funding for a position. The new refugee coordinator would soon assist my office in doing much of the day-to-day refugee services coordination work that was taking on a life of its own. A job description for the new state funded coordinator position needed to be written soon if we were going to hire someone to be in place for January 1, 2003. Catholic Charities was now operating a satellite refugee office in Lewiston on Westminster Avenue (something we had pursued for months) and wanted to work more closely with our General Assistance office to coordinate services. Additionally, several state agencies, non-profit organizations, and the Department of Justice were all eager to provide assistance.

The Justice Department had already been involved with the Lewiston Somali population and the "Friendship Walk" arranged by the Calvary United Methodist Church on October 13th "at the request of State and local officials, Somali leaders, and the NAACP."[1224] The New England Community Relations Service division of the U.S. Department of Justice and their staff were the lead representatives of the effort. The creation of the CRS was included as part of the 1964 Civil Rights Act: "The (CRS) helps local government and communities develop and implement their own solutions without creating Federal entanglements and in a very real sense the parties retain all of their rights and privileges to address conflicts and disputes peacefully."[1225]

We would also reach out to U.S. Attorney General John Ashcroft on October 29th [1226] to request DOJ compliance assistance with Title 6 of the Civil Rights Act; our level of interpretation and translation compliance; and the Americans with Disabilities Act.

I was also receiving the first of many requests to speak on what was happening in Lewiston around October 15th. The first request came from Professor William Mass at the University of Massachusetts' Lowell campus. It would be part of the Regional Economic and Social Development seminar. My presentation was titled "Profound Change in Lewiston, Maine: The Emerging Somali Community," and my audience would be comprised of "grad students and faculty from RESD and other departments." I saw this opportunity as a city outreach effort and treated all future requests for other speaking engagements the same way. I never sought reimbursement from the city for such travel nor did I seek payment for any appearances (UMass did provide me with some lunch which was greatly appreciated).[1227]

I had complete confidence in my ability to speak on many public policy subjects and had spoken publicly going as far back to 1990s, but this opportunity felt different. I was not simply speaking on any subject. I was speaking about something that was receiving intense scrutiny from the national and international press. Any misspoken word, phrase, or factual error had the potential of feeding the insatiable appetite of the news media. Whatever I would share would be public information and I was very cognizant of not letting down my elected officials, Jim Bennett, or the residents of my community. The October 28th seminar went as well as I could have hoped for, but before long I realized that having the time for this kind of public outreach was simply not available.

There were others that were also doing their own public-outreach efforts. Former Maine Attorney General Jim Tierney was one of them. Following his speech at the University of Maine Orono in April 2002 (see Chapter 4), he spoke again on Maine's population challenges as the keynote speaker at the annual meeting of the Institute of Civic Leadership in Portland during the week of October 21, 2002.[1228]

In his speech, Tierney continued to highlight Maine's lack of diversity, pointing out that "(o)nly 3.5% of residents (were) non-white, compared with roughly 31% nationally" and that by 2025, "one resident in five will be older than 65." Maine was also missing opportunities with minority-based businesses that were "expanding four times faster than U.S. firms overall between 1992 and 1997." The 2000 census had Maine's 2.2% of minority-owned businesses in the state ranked last in the country.[1229]

Tierney shared that the data clearly showed why Maine was growing older and had been experiencing declining growth rates that were also ranking it near the bottom nationally. This had nothing to do with being in the northeast. The difference for the other northeastern states with growing populations was that the "exodus (of people leaving) ha(d) been offset... by people moving in from other countries" (see Chapter 4). In Maine, "(o)nly 3% of (its) residents in the 2000 Census were foreign born, compared with 11% nationally."[1230]

The city also was being presented with opportunities to leverage the outreach help of many outside organizations that were offering program opportunities. One came from the Boston Medical Center, which was seeking the city's support for a project that would "(examine) stigma, environmental stressors, service access and community support, and the effect of these variables on children and adolescent refugee's PTSD (posttraumatic stress disorder) and other mental health symptoms."[1231] We supported the effort.

Another outreach effort involved a weekend forum at Bates College that was being planned by the college's Department of

Philosophy and Religion "in collaboration with the cities of Lewiston and Auburn and local organizations representing the education, business, medical and nonprofit communities of Lewiston-Auburn." The March 2003 conference would focus on the "continued dissemination of information and facilitated discussion of issues surrounding the recent, rapid resettlement of Somali refugees" in the city. I was asked to send a letter to the Maine Humanities Council to request funding for the conference. The "Toward Harmony: Understanding a New Diversity in Lewiston-Auburn Conference" was held in March 2013. In the opinion of many who saw this event as a way to encourage more community dialogue, it was an important first community outreach step following the Many and One rally in January 2003.[1232]

This conference would also mark the second time that Bates College would take a lead support role in assisting a broader community-led effort to work with the Somali community. The first time Bates had come forward to assume a leadership role on behalf of the Somali community involved a white supremacist group, identified at that time as the World Church of the Creator. The city would soon be receiving a communication from the white supremacist organization and our community's response to their arrival would be historic.

## The WCOTC Timeline

Twenty years has dulled the memories of just about everyone involved in dealing with the moment when the city was contacted the World Church of the Creator (WCOTC). They wanted to reserve the Multi-Purpose Center (MPC) for a public meeting on January 11, 2003. What both Jim Bennett and I remembered was the application had come through our Recreation Department. The department managed the side of the MPC building where several small conference rooms could be reserved by any member or group in the community. There was also an open common area and gymnasium in the building that were jointly shared by the city, the school department's K-5

Longley School, as well as the city's senior resident program room.

Everything immediately changed when WCOTC application review determined that the organization was an out-of-state white supremacist group looking to conduct a public meeting in our city. City Administrator Jim Bennett decided that we would reach out Mark Schlotterbeck and other community leaders we had been working with to discuss what we could do as a community in response to the WCOTC meeting.

The absence of city records and fading memories have made it somewhat difficult to firmly establish when the WCOTC application was submitted, and when the first meeting at City Hall was organized with Mark Schlotterbeck and other community representatives in response to the WCOTC application. Through the interviews with Jim Bennett, Mark Schlotterbeck and Sun Journal articles, it is important to establish the timeline from the moment we received the WCOTC application to the point at which the community response to the application became public. The information below provides the research as to how that timeline was established:

1. A Sun Journal article confirmed that the WCOTC application for a meeting on January 11, 2003 was filed with the city sometime in November.[1233]
2. Mark Schlotterbeck suggested that my call inviting him to the first City Hall meeting may have happened either during the week of November 4th or November 11th.[1234]
3. Jim Bennett stated that much of his time prior to the public announcement of the WCOTC meeting was spent speaking with City Attorney Martin Eisenstein discussing the city's legal options regarding the meeting request,[1235] and discussing the event and site safety logistics with Police Chief William "Bill" Welch.[1236]
4. The Sun Journal wrote the first article covering the WCOTC meeting application on November 20th.[1237]
5. Bennett approved the WCOTC application for a meeting originally scheduled at the Multi-Purpose Center on November 22nd but moved the location from the MPC to the Lewiston Armory after the city's

Facility Use Committee made the recommendation.[1238]

6. Mark Schlotterbeck said during a November 25th press conference at City Hall that he had begun discussions with an "interfaith group" about holding a community event a week before his press conference and that the interfaith group decided on Sunday, November 24th "to begin planning the (January) 11 (2003)... diversity celebration."[1239]

7. In our interview, Schlotterbeck also shared that shortly after the first meeting at City Hall with Mark and community leaders, the assembled group selected Mark to lead the "diversity celebration" effort.[1240] The next meeting at Calvary United Methodist Church was also the first meeting of the "interfaith" group that started the first discussions about naming the group. Both Schlotterbeck[1241] and Ahmed[1242] believe that what they discussed was not the final name "Many and One," but possibly a similar sounding name.

Assembling the patchwork of interviews and newspaper articles reveals the WCOTC submitted their application in early November, possibly the week of November 4th. After receiving the application, Bennett spent as much as a week (and possibly into the next week) discussing the city's legal options about the WCOTC with the city attorney. He also discussed security concerns with Chief William "Bill" Welch. Sometime later, likely during the week of November 11th, the first meeting with Schlotterbeck and others was scheduled at City Hall. The meeting provided the momentum for a larger community group, led by their new leader Mark Schlotterbeck, to address how they would respond to the WCOTC.

Schlotterbeck quickly scheduled a meeting at Calvary United Methodist Church during the weekend of November 15-16-17. The newly assembled interfaith group then met during the week of November 18th and decided on Sunday, November 24th that they would hold their yet-to-be-developed January diversity celebration event on January 11, 2003, on the same day that the WCOTC would hold their meeting. The diversity group's announcement of the diversity event would be made at a City

Hall press event on November 25, 2002. This timeline of events will be referenced throughout the rest of this chapter.

## The Threat Assessment

It was not unusual to receive requests from outside organizations to use an MPC conference room, but shortly after the WCOTC submitted their application in the first week of November, Director Maggie Chisholm had the opportunity to review the document. Not recognizing the name of the group, she started looking into who they were and notified Jim and me about what she had found. None of it was good news.

The WCOTC was the second white-supremacist group that was interested in what was going on in Lewiston. The difference was they wanted to conduct a public meeting to promote themselves while using a city building with a K-5 school program. A Portland resident who went by the name of "David Stearns," an alias he used for "security reasons," was the WCOTC point-person handling the details of the meeting. Stearns liked the fact that the organization also embraced the use of "public meetings, unlike some other supremacist groups," as part of their portfolio of outreach methods. His group, however, operated "primarily through the Internet(sic) and via phone."[1243]

It did not take long for Chief Welch to ascertain the seriousness of the WCOTCs request for a meeting. While Jim spoke to City Attorney Marty Eisenstein about our WCOTC legal options, we all began to discuss the suitability of the MPC for their public meeting. The MPC building was in a densely populated section of our downtown with many families and children living in three and four-story tenements throughout that area. There was an elementary school occupying about half of the MPC building. Even though the WCOTC meeting would occur on a Saturday, securing the building for the meeting would potentially disrupt classes and other non-school activities for a portion of the school week. There was ample parking across the street at the Central Maine Youth Center ice arena, with a parking lot that could easily handle up to 400 vehicles. It was also probable that the parking lot would be restricted to law enforcement and press with all on-street parking eliminated (a hardship for most residents living in the area) to minimize property damage. The density of the downtown population was our biggest concern, particularly if violence broke out during the event.

The WCOTC "meeting," that would undoubtedly be directly targeting the new Somali arrivals, would put the entire matter of the Somali's arrival in Lewiston, and the mayor's letter, squarely back on the front page. What was an intensely covered story that appeared to be losing public interest now had the potential to be above-the-fold again nationally and internationally.

Jim believed that the increased interest regarding Somali relocations from the National Alliance possibly triggered the WCOTC application. According to Bennett, police 'intel' suggested that there was no love lost between white supremacist groups and that all the national groups were intent on demonstrating who was the lead organization in the country. The WCOTC's appearance in Lewiston could have been an effort to communicate to the National Alliance that they had their own presence in Maine and were willing to raise the ante on their public profile.

Shortly after the WCOTC application was brought to our attention by Maggie Chisholm during the week of November 4th, Police Chief Bill Welch recalled that Jim asked for his department to begin gathering 'intel' on the group. Bill had access to the FBI, DEA (Drug Enforcement Administration), and the DOJs Community Relations Service (CRS).[1244] CRS had been present for the WCOTC event in Wakefield and had worked with Chief Welch to provide "conciliation assistance"[1245] for the Lewiston October 13th Calvary friendship walk. It was also highly probable that the FBI had an open and active file on the WCOTC and its leader Matt Hale.

According to the New England Chapter of the Anti-Defamation League, the National Alliance, who was actively canvassing the Lewiston-Auburn area and raising their public profile, was "the single most dangerous organized hate group in America." In an Anti-Defamation League report, they accused the group of "plotting violent crimes... murders, bombings and robberies." According to "a civil rights activist who track(ed) the National Alliance," the NAs interest in Lewiston was the "first time" the group had "paid so much attention to a single situation in New England." There was also speculation that a book written by the group's founder had inspired Timothy McVeigh to bomb the federal building in Oklahoma City.[1246]

The WCOTC was no less dangerous. Based in East Peoria, Illinois, the organization "was founded in 1973" as the "Church of the Creator" and struggled in the 1990s when criminal convictions of members, the founder's suicide, and a 1991 lawsuit against the WCOTC destabilized the organization. When Matt Hale came along in 1996, he re-energized the organization throughout the country, openly embracing the founder's 1981 "White Man's Bible" and making it mandatory reading for all of its members. He also supported the organization's violence and racism towards "Jews, Christians, African-Americans and other people of color," openly admitting he was a racist, but rejected the assertion that he was "'irrational.'"[1247]

During late summer 2002, the WCOTC applied for a meeting room at the Wakefield, Massachusetts library. The September 14, 2002 meeting was booked as the "'Emigration Party.'" After staff researched the application and the organization, they discovered that the organization was in fact the WCOTC and discovered they had "recently wreaked its racist havoc" in Wallingford, Connecticut, and York, Pennsylvania. Wakefield Police Chief Stephen Doherty knew that trouble was ahead for the small town of Wakefield.[1248]

Doherty reported that the first thing the WCOTC would do in Lewiston is issue a press release to organizations that oppose their activity. Their goal was to encourage confrontation with their opponents. They had done so in Wakefield and the results produced the result they were seeking. Fifty WCOTC supporters clashed on the sidewalk outside of the Wakefield library with "scores of equally hard-core members of the Progressive Labor Party and (the) Anti-Racist Action (organization)." According to Doherty, some 250 law enforcement personnel[1249] were present in Wakefield to handle approximately 600 anti-white supremacist protestors.[1250]

One female WCOTC member was struck in the head by an opposition group member with a 4-foot wooden club wrapped in cardboard and disguised to look a sign post. The injured female used her blood-covered face as a photo opportunity while also flashing a "Hitler salute" to the press photographer.[1251] It was precisely the kind of 'photo-op' WCOTC hoped for—a visual image intended to generate sympathy for the 'victim' who supported a cause that openly embraced racism and fascism.

## The Community Responds

Within days of receiving the application, Jim and I decided to contact Mark Schlotterbeck at Calvary United Methodist Church, given his now very public profile associated with his October 13th friendship walk. I contacted Mark at the Calvary church during the week of November 11th and asked if he would be interested in attending a meeting at City Hall to discuss an application recently submitted from a white supremacist group.

During my phone call to Schlotterbeck, I also shared with him that I would be reaching out to the Somali Advocacy Group and invite them to bring guests. Mohamed Abdi, Abdiaziz Ali, Azeb Hassan, Roda Abdi, Fatuma Hussein were invited and attended. Mark attended and brought along Tim Griffin and Nasra and Parivash Rohini, and possibly Zamzam Mohamud, who had developed a close friendship with Schlotterbeck.[1252] Jim Bennett and I were both present, and Bennett recalled that someone from the Greek church in Lewiston was also present.

After much discussion during our meeting, there appeared to be some consensus that the goal would be to have a community event that would support the Somali community's arrival in the city and celebrate diversity. This would not be the only activity to pull together a community response to the WCOTC. Immediately after the mayor's letter went public, Jim and I did not know that there was a separate effort involving community individuals who were meeting and discussing how to respond to the mayor's letter. This other undertaking involved residents, faculty and students from the area colleges.

According to Professor Michelle Vazquez Jacobus, who now teaches at the University of Southern Maine, she believed that her participation in this earlier community action coalition activity began at a meeting that was also first organized by Mark Schlotterbeck.[1253] He had pulled the meeting together shortly after the publication of the mayor's letter and it would involve herself and two L-A College students named Ismail Ahmed and Godfrey Banda, who both encouraged her to attend. They also accompanied Michelle to the first meeting.[1254]

Vazquez Jacobus estimated that there were approximately 15 people who attended the meeting.[1255] Michelle also remembered that she and the two L-A College students were the only "academics" representing the area colleges at the meeting. This "grass-roots, community" meeting's purpose was simple—to discuss how to respond to the mayor's letter and to explore the creation of a coalition to deliver that response. It was also decided that the next meeting should include a broader representative group, which would include some representation from students and instructors of the area colleges.[1256]

The next gathering of this early coalition effort would be held at the Bates college "student multicultural center." In attendance were Ahmed, Vazquez Jacobus, Bates College Professor Charles "Val" Carnegie and another male professor who Ahmed could not identify, two "east African" Bates students, one "south African and one Zimbabwean" student, and possibly Bates Dean Jim Carignan.[1257] These early L-A College/Bates College group meetings were taking place before the Schlotterbeck multicultural coalition was formed. These first community coalition assemblies would continue to bring this group of people, organizations, college faculty members, and students together to work in "sub-committees" to discuss the question of "what can we do" about the crisis in the Lewiston-Auburn community.[1258]

Many of the people involved in this early community action/coalition effort, including Vazquez Jacobus, would also become involved with the multicultural coalition led by Schlotterbeck. Some would go on to participate in other "networking" and community action work. One area of interest would include the new city immigrant coordinator's office that would be headed up by Victoria Scott.[1259]

By the time Schlotterbeck spoke at the November 25th press conference to announce the multicultural coalition's decision to hold a "diversity celebration" on January 11, 2003, many of the people who had been meeting before this new coalition was formed were either attending the press conference, committed to working on the event, or would pursue a community response that would be separate from the multicultural coalition's efforts.[1260] One of those people who eventually chose a separate path of community activism would be Ismail Ahmed.

### Ismail Ahmed

Ismail Ahmed (and brother to Zamzam Mohamud) had become a close friend of Schlotterbeck's well before the mayor's letter. Ismail had arrived in Lewiston around December 2001. He soon found work at a call center in Bates Mill and enrolled as a student at the University of Southern Maine's L-A College in the summer of 2002. Ahmed was a new student at L-A College whose focus was on his studies and pursuing a degree. Ismail was already college educated before entering L-A College and eventually became the first Lewiston Somali resident to receive his graduate degree at L-A College.[1261]

Ahmed had little time for anything other than his studies as the fall 2002 semester began. He was not involved with those in the Somali community who were working with the city on a variety of immigrant initiatives. All that changed on the morning of October 4, 2002 when L-A College professor Michelle Vazquez Jacobus walked into class with a copy of that day's Sun Journal edition.

The paper had Scott Taylor's story about Mayor Raymond's letter to the Somali community. Vazquez Jacobus shared it with her class, which included Ahmed. According to Ismail, the news of the mayor's letter changed everything for him that day. "We read (the mayor's letter and) discussed it in class. Then, that whole day there was nothing else to be talked about... Some of the students were furious... we were divided about fifty-fifty."[1262]

According to Vazquez Jacobus, she then moved the open discussion part of the class (about the letter) to a "critical thinking" exercise. Consistent with Ahmed's recollections, she split up the students to debate the issue with half of the randomly selected group defending the mayor's letter, and the other half opposing. Michelle recalled that during the initial discussions about the letter, "there were fewer students that sided with the

Somalis" and supported the mayor's letter. She also remembered placing Ahmed in the group supporting the mayor's letter. Vazquez Jacobus added that by the end of the semester, the entire class was "advocating for the Somalis" and for the multicultural coalition. Some became actively involved in the rally-planning part of the event. One student "who had been very outspoken against Somali people" wrote "her final project on Somali elders" and "became very close to Ismail (Ahmed)."[1263]

Ahmed and Vazquez Jacobus would continue to meet with a group of students and faculty from both colleges regarding the mayor's letter. For Ismail, he would disassociate himself from the Lewiston Somali community's plan to directly respond to Raymond's letter. Ahmed stated that people like Mohamed Abdi and Fatuma Hussein were viewed by him as "pro city," and unable to represent how he felt about the situation. He asked himself "how could they be (impartial)" about the mayor's letter?[1264]

Schlotterbeck and Ahmed both stated that the relationship between the two men was already very close when Jim and I met with Schlotterbeck to discuss the WCOTC and a diversity event. Ahmed knew about the first meeting at City Hall but was unsure why he did not attend. He was taking a full course load at the time and his absence may have involved conflicts with his class schedule. Ahmed also confirmed that he attended the first multicultural coalition meeting at Calvary church and remembers that the name of the organization, or some version of the name ("Many is One" "Many in One")[1265] was discussed at that meeting, something that Schlotterbeck also confirmed.[1266] It should be noted that I was unable to find any public reference to the "Many and One Coalition," the actual name chosen by the organization, until the Sun Journal article "A Course on Beating Bigotry" was published on December 20, 2002.[1267]

As word of the Many and One Coalition's work to develop a multicultural celebration attracted media interest, so did the interest of many organizations representing immigrants, minorities, and the discriminated, oppressed, marginalized and disadvantaged. From Ahmed's perspective, he saw these well-intentioned groups leveraging the diversity celebration event as a platform for their concerns and constituencies. The result was Ahmed's decision to slowly separated himself from the coalition before the rally. Ahmed wanted to focus his efforts specifically on the Somali community and what could be done to raise awareness about Somali concerns and needs. Ahmed said that he "was just a student activist and organizer," and he believed that if the Somali community did not use this event opportunity correctly, the possibility existed that they would never get another opportunity to do so.[1268]

## A Change in Venue

On November 23, 2002, the Sun Journal reported that Jim Bennett had approved the WCTOC application for their meeting but would move the event to the Lewiston Armory on Central Avenue in Lewiston, in close proximity to the Bates College campus.[1269] This city-owned facility was located in a less densely populated residential neighborhood which also included the city's middle school that abutted the property, a large tract of land in back of the Armory that supported a baseball field, practice field, and football field. Chief Welch believed that this site was the next best alternative to the MPC, but still had concerns about the capacity of the building that could hold up to 1,500 or more people. The larger the facility, the greater the ability of the WCOTC to recruit their supporters to fill the site. In Welch's eyes, the smaller the facility, the fewer WCOTC supporters to deal with, inside and outside the property.[1270]

We were guessing about what the attendance would be on January 11th for both events. How many supporters and opponents would be present at both locations? All we could do was plan for the worst-case scenario with an alternative Lewiston Armory site that was not the perfect solution. Chief Welch's concerns about the capacity of the Lewiston Armory were only one of many challenges confronting the city. The neighborhood around the Lewiston Armory was filled with residential single-family homes and some multi-family properties. We also had approximately 1,100 Bates college students[1271] who would be back on campus the weekend before the January 11th event. If a large number of WCOTC sympathizers and opponents attended the WCOTC meeting event, the prospect for a confrontation, significant property damage, and injuries (or worse) would be greater than we all desired.

Bennett insisted the WCOTC purchase liability insurance and pay for additional security costs. It was part of the city policy for non-profits to purchase a liability policy for events that carried higher levels of risk. Recognizing that the WCOTCs history with events was at times violent, Jim's pursuit of insisting that WCOTC pay for both the insurance and security costs began almost immediately after our office had been notified about the application.[1272] Hale rejected our requests and defended his decision not to pay for insurance coverage, or security, as a "free speech" issue, and it appeared that the law would support that opinion.

While all this was going on, Jim Bennett and Chief Bill Welch looked at options about relocating the WCOTC for a second time. Bill stated they had considered several locations, including some of the privately run banquet facilities,[1273] as some were located in fairly remote areas of the city. Jim often took a back-road route between City Hall and his home in a rural section of Lewiston. The trip often took him past a facility that was located in Lewiston's South Park industrial business park. It was the Maine Army National Guard complex at the intersection of Alfred A. Plourde Parkway and Goddard Road in Lewiston near Exit 13 (now Exit 80) off I-95, a.k.a. the Maine Turnpike.[1274]

When Bennett shared his thoughts with Welch about the guard armory complex, Bill thought it was a great idea and it became a pivotal moment in the planning for both the WCOTC and diversity rally on January 11th.[1275] The site was nearly perfect for the WCOTC event, and it would make the Lewiston Armory available to the Many and One Coalition. It was early December, and the coalition had not yet secured a location that would provide them with a facility capable of handling a large event.

What made the national guard armory location most attractive, particularly for an event that had the potential for violence, was its isolation from any housing. There were also many other benefits: many businesses in the area would be uninhabited on a Saturday; it was near I-95 with three optional routes to the interstate to and from the location;[1276] the armory was on the corner of Alfred Plourde Parkway and Goddard Road and both were already restricted for parking; some parking was available in a park-and-ride lot within walking distance; and securing the armory site could be done in advance, given the limited use of a building in the complex that housed a cafeteria that could also be used as a small conference room. Best of all, it was an active Maine Army National Guard facility that was already much more secure than a typical municipal public building.

The challenge would be dealing with the state to secure the armory site on short notice. It was typically not used for any local or non-military events and only supported Army guard reserve activities. To make it a bit more challenging, we would ask the state to let us use this building to permit a racist, white supremacist group with a history of inciting violence, to have a public meeting that could generate significant opposition and result in a confrontation between groups.

Jim could not remember some of the specifics regarding who was involved in the discussion. We remembered that Governor King was still in office at the time, and the authorization to use the national guard armory was granted sometime in mid-December. We also knew that Governor-elect John Baldacci, our outgoing congressional representative, would be our new governor on the day of the event. Both Jim and I agreed that it was almost a certainty that both King, Baldacci, and their staffs were involved in the decision to approve the application.[1277]

Bennett also shared that the people who may have been the likeliest link to connecting us with the final state-level decision makers for the National Guard site may have been State Senator Peggy Rotundo and State Representative John Richardson. Although Rotundo had no memory of being involved with the national guard armory, Jim believed that the first initial contact with the King or Baldacci staff likely involved Rotundo[1278] who was still in her first legislative term and employed at Bates College. Jim understood things would take time and getting a quick response from the state would be an all-hands effort.

Jim also believed that Richardson was likely involved because he was both a well-connected state representative, and the union representative for our police department. Richardson was an up-and-coming Democratic state legislator from Brunswick, who at the end of December, would become the new

House Majority Leader for the 2003-2004 legislative session. Richardson would also become Speaker of the House of Representatives in 2005.[1279]

We knew first-hand how skilled John was as a negotiator from our interactions with him during police contract and personnel interactions. His negotiating skills were also legendary in the legislature. On a trade mission to Cuba, John and his friend, Representative Eddie Duguay, met with Fidel Castro and landed a $20 million trade deal for the state. Regrettably, John died far too soon on June 16, 2020.[1280] Although Richardson's passing would result in my inability to confirm his participation in the site's approval, Jim's recollection of John reminded the two of us that of all the people we knew with a connection to Augusta at that time, John was possibly the best positioned to help strike an agreement with state officials. It is also possible that both King and Baldacci would have worked together to make the decision on their own.

Bennett would announce on December 18th that the WCOTC location would be moved to the national guard facility. The meeting would be held in the "cafeteria of the Lewiston Culinary Arts School" that was housed in a stand-alone building within the national guard complex. The school department leased the building for a program that was part of Lewiston High School's regional vocational programming. Bennett reported that the "guard (would not) be used for security unless (the guard soldiers were) needed." He also said that the guard soldiers would be "drilling" at the facility that weekend, saying that their presence during the event would be nothing more than a "happy coincidence."[1281]

The idea for moving the location out to the guard facility was the product of Chief Welch's instincts, Jim's wisdom, a state administration willing to assist us, and possibly a helping hand from a Lewiston and Brunswick legislator. This development would enhance the safety prospects for the event dramatically. It would put four miles of distance between the two events on January 11th and it also opened the possibility for the diversity event to be held at the Lewiston Armory, or perhaps somewhere else.

## The Birth of the Many and One Coalition

After our efforts to bring together Mark Schlotterbeck and others at City Hall to discuss organizing a diversity event, Mark and his fledgling organization took over the event planning. Communication between their group and our office was largely on an 'as needed' basis for several weeks. Both sides wanted Mark's group to have the freedom to plan whatever kind of assembly that they believed would be best for the Somalis and the community. The city would simply do what it needed to ensure that all the participants and members of the public could all be involved or not involved, and most importantly, be safe.

In the interim, the yet publicly named multicultural coalition was trying to organize an event but was still unsure about what location would best suit their needs. According to Michelle Vazquez Jacobus, she remembered the very first organizational meeting at Calvary church was "chaotic" and "complicated"[1282] as there were not only many people with many opinions, but Michelle also understood that because "it was a church" and that the assembly was "an interfaith meeting," that the "religious... iconography" in the building would be problematic for some Somalis and people of other faiths.[1283]

Vazquez Jacobus said that the group recognized what occurred in that first planning meeting and that the church continued to be used for small groups who were comfortable with the location. For many of the gatherings with a larger attendance, the Lewiston Multi-Purpose Center was most often used. Although they had addressed the discomfort some had experienced with a "culturally inappropriate" setting like a church, two Bates students also had to learn about other religious differences when they brought their dogs to a meeting.

For many Muslims, dogs are seen as unclean or impure, so the appearance of the dogs at the Multi-Purpose Center meeting resulted in the Muslim women leaving the building "visually upset" about the animals.[1284] As in all things, the matter of how much people know about other faiths, and how multiple branches of the Islamic faith define religious practices and restrictions, like dogs, were broad and complex.[1285] In this case, the incident provided another reminder to the organization members of how complex an undertaking it was to bring together people from diverse religions, cultures and ethnicities.

Although the idea for the rally was attributed to the letter's public reaction and the WCOTC meeting announcement, there were people and groups looking to support the idea of a broader diversity-equality-tolerance celebration. Many believed that the event should also include a message that went beyond race, color, and religion. Arguments were being made to also include the physically and mentally challenged populations, and issues associated with gender and sexual orientation, identity, and expression. The heightened intensity of the national news media coverage was signaling to these individuals that they would have more than just a statewide or regional audience watching the events of January 11th in Lewiston. They wanted to show their support for the Somali community in Lewiston, but also sought to leverage the event's potential national coverage to communicate that other groups were also experiencing discrimination, marginalization, inequality, and violence.

Mark Schlotterbeck shared that from the outset, the community response was clear: "Lewiston had something to say about itself" and it was reflected in the local and state-wide interest in participating in the event. After the Many and One's November 25th press conference announcing the January 11th diversity celebration, there were weeks of planning by the event steering committee. "As the process went on... more and more people would say 'well, what about this kind of excluded group of people, or that (excluded group).'"[1286]

Schlotterbeck also understood the concerns that people like Cheryl Hamilton had regarding the growing interests in having representation on the steering committee, and about "enlarging the structure of the organization."[1287] The combination of the growing group interests, the need to find and secure a site, and all the other logistical and media requirements were taking their toll on Schlotterbeck. He recalled that period of time as "an intense seven weeks... I had gone literally weeks with almost no sleep." Mark added that in addition to the growing interest to participate, no one wanted to forget that "there were people that were fearful for their lives... (and) (w)e were trying to do our best."[1288]

Cheryl Hamilton said that the number of groups that were looking for representation on the steering committee became "a little unwieldy and unclear." Hamilton remembers "sort of feeling like some people were coming out of the woodwork" and wondered "why were they suddenly" looking to become part of the event. "It was all happening so fast... It was great to see so much interest, but it was also (the kind of) work that we had been grappling with for months," [1289] seemingly expressing her puzzlement and frustration with the absence of this kind of interest in the Somalis months before the mayor's letter.

Many and One member Matthew Schlobohm also mentioned the high level of interest in the rally, saying that "'a lot of people with different interests and agendas'" were involved and that the organization had "'tried to keep everything open'" in the planning process. Schlobohm felt the process had "'worked well overall. It's been an enormous outpouring from every walk of life." They had an invitation list of some 25 speakers that included "Muhammad Ali and Harry Belafonte," but no one had confirmed. With only 12 days to go, Schlobohm also said that the rally would reflect the local community, with representatives from the "'Franco-Americans, Latinos, Somalis, the gay, lesbian and transgendered community.'"[1290]

Not everyone was supportive of the event's inclusiveness. Doug Taylor, a "leader of the fundamentalist Jesus Party" stated that the event "'should be standing against racism, not muddying the waters'" as he did not support the inclusion of "'sexual politics in the rally.'"[1291] Michelle Jacobus Vazquez also believed that there were problems within the Many and One organization's ability to enable participation from Somalis who were most in need of a voice. Michelle said that for "Somali women, particularly Somali women in Lewiston in 2001 and 2002," the organization needed to be more sensitive to working with women whose culture and religion already made them uncomfortable with "having a high-profile role of any kind."[1292]

In the absence of having someone in the organization who could fill that void for Somali women, there also appeared to be a representation problem with the male Lewiston Somali community. Lewiston resident Kadar Said was one of the few male Somali members to participate in the Many and One organizing process. Another Somali, Omar Jamal, Executive Director of the Somali Justice Advocacy Center, was also able to fill that role but was living in Minneapolis. It was also not out of the realm of possibility that the matter of the Somali's personal safety may have significantly contributed to both their absence in planning participation and their attendance at the Many and One rally

Vazquez Jacobus explained that as the planning process progressed, the "white people in power" began to take over. What had started out as "an organic movement" became increasingly influenced by "liberal academics." She also acknowledged that the primary goal of holding a counter-rally event to support the Somali community, the purpose for which the organization was created, was ultimately successful. She also believed it was important to note the frustrations that she and people like Ismail Ahmed had regarding the process.[1293] The process encountered it share of challenges, but all parties were undeniably working to ensure that this event should be focused on supporting and celebrating the Somali community and everything that diversity was supposed to represent.

The story of the Somali and immigrant population in Lewiston following the Many and One Rally would also reveal that as their perception of safety increased, so did their confidence, opportunities, and abilities to lead. Many more Somali men and women would take on leadership roles that would assist not only immigrants, but the entire community.

Many of us, both at the city level and those associated with the Many and One effort, always tried to remember throughout the rally planning process how frightened, anxious, and fearful many Somalis were about simply being out in public during the period of time between October 2002 and January 2003. We would soon see if the efforts of Many and One and the community would provide them with the kind of peace that they were seeking when they were escaping the terror or civil war and the challenges of living in a refugee camp.

## The 11th Hour

One of the more important tasks for the coalition group would be to select a location. According to both Schlotterbeck and Vazquez Jacobus, there were several locations that were considered. Schlotterbeck stated that he remembered one location included Saints Peter and Paul Church (now the Basilica of Saints Peter and Paul) on Ash Street in downtown Lewiston. It was a location that could hold as many as 1,000 people, but according to Vazquez Jacobus, she and "many" others believed it was a church with the kind of "iconography" that would be just as problematic as the Calvary United Methodist Church was in the very beginning.[1294]

Any further discussion about the basilica became moot after the Portland Diocese gave notice to Schlotterbeck that they would not approve the organization's request.[1295] Given the history of the WCOTC, it would be understandable if the church simply did not want to host an event that could result in violence—outside or inside the church property. The rejection by the Diocese was not unexpected as the WCOTC prided itself in its ability to create a confrontation with those who opposed them. WCOTC and their supporters would have relished the opportunity to confront their opposition outside or inside church property. In their eyes, any confrontation in that kind of setting would have been a public relations success.

Vazquez Jacobus also mentioned that they were looking at both large indoor and outdoor venues and also recognized that there would be challenges associated with Maine winter weather if the event, or even part of the event, were scheduled outside. Michelle said what was certain is that they needed "a big space that didn't have religious material all over it,"[1296] because they already knew that any of the large churches in the area would keep "the religious Jews and the religious Muslims out of the building." Lewiston-Auburn College was also discussed, but ultimately removed from the list because the campus facilities could not accommodate a large crowd.[1297]

Schlotterbeck's leadership, and the commitment of the steering committee and many volunteers, found a way for just about anyone who wanted to be included in an event that was growing by the day. Schlotterbeck commented it was important to note that a significant number of people who assisted the Many and One effort were not part of the steering committee. Volunteers were needed for a variety of tasks associated with the event, but the biggest task facing the event was finding a location.

Without a location, there would be no event for anyone to attend, and time was beginning to run out.

As late as December 18th, Many and One had not yet secured a location. After the city had moved the WCOTC meeting to the Maine Army National Guard facility, the Lewiston Armory location became immediately available for the event. At some point, and likely after Saints Peter and Paul Church was no longer available, someone came up with another idea—to speak with Bates College and inquire about the Merrill Gymnasium on campus.

On December 20th, the Sun Journal published a story about Lewiston-Auburn College hosting the screening of the documentary "Not in Our Town, Not in Our State,"[1298] the 1995 PBS film about hate and racism in Billings, Montana.[1299] The evening was also organized by the diversity group that for the first time publicly was identifying itself as the "Many and One Coalition."

On December 31st, the Sun Journal reported that both the Merrill Gymnasium and the Lewiston Armory were potential sites for the "Many and One Coalition Rally."[1300] The article said that the college would require that the organization, with no funding, purchase liability insurance for the event. Bates would provide the facility at no cost, but Many and One was penniless, had not secured a facility, or booked a single speaker for the event.[1301]

## DIVERSITY MAKES A STAND

The decision by Jim Bennett and Chief Welch to move the WCOTC from the downtown Multi-Purpose Center location allowed the city several weeks to develop its public safety plan for the January 11th rally. Another decision that Jim made in early to mid-December was to meet with the Sun Journal owner Steve Costello and Editor Rex Rhoades to discuss the city's planning for January 11th. Jim understood the complexities confronting the city and wanted to offer the newspaper an opportunity for a Sun Journal reporter to have unlimited access to the planning process. Jim's condition for the proposal would be that nothing confidential would ever be released (such as certain security details that could compromise security planning for future events), and they embargo everything that was printable until after the January 11th events had concluded.

As the intelligence briefings painted an increasingly bleak picture regarding the possibility of violence during the event, Jim believed that having the Sun Journal directly observe the planning process would help to address some of the ensuing criticism that could potentially follow. Although the Sun Journal had no idea about Jim's motives, Rhoades took Jim up on his offer.[1302] Lisa Chmelecki would be offered inside access in a way that few local journalists are rarely granted, and she would remain at Welch and Bennett's side until the day of the rally.

Welch said that the Lewiston Police Department had been working with the federal agencies like the FBI and DEA going back to the September 11, 2001 terrorist attacks.[1303] Information was being shared at the time with communities about a variety of things, particularly in places where there were Muslim populations. Much of the information involved potential threats from anthrax attacks and the safety of Muslim populations in places where they were living in the U.S.

Once the WCOTC announced they were coming to Lewiston, Welch assembled a team of individuals who were tasked with multiple responsibilities. One of Welch's first team leaders was Lt. Roger Landry, who was heading up the criminal investigations division. Landry assembled a group that would include crime analyst Andy Robitaille to research and collect intelligence. That investigative effort helped to build a profile of what they were up against with the WCOTC as the intelligence showed that there was growing interest by other racist organizations to come to Lewiston.[1304] The intelligence also reflected a desire by anti-racist organizations to come to Lewiston to confront those organizations.

Intelligence also revealed that Matt Hale, the WCOTC founder, had a father that was a police officer. Sergeant Michael "Mike" McGonagle was assigned the task of developing a relationship with Hale and was having some success. McGonagle had developed some recognition in the department for his relationship-building skills during investigation interviews and the department needed someone who could connect with Hale. McGonagle worked to find common ground through Hale's relationship with his father. The two men discussed issues that were important to Hale, his organization, and things that mattered to the city, like changing the location of the meeting for a second time.[1305] McGonagle would have to work hard for the information. Hale may have been the head of a white supremacist organization, but he did not lack intelligence.

Hale, who was 31 years old in January 2003, shared with Kelley Bouchard that reading William Shirer's "Rise and Fall of the Third Reich" at the tender age of 12 influenced his "world view" that contributed to being chosen as the WCOTC leader. Bouchard reported Hale wore a "Hitler wristwatch" and used an "Israeli flag as a doormat." He referred to other non-white ethnicities as the "'mud races'", and blamed Jews for "promoting diversity," controlling the media, and subverting "the white race by encouraging racial mixing so they can take over the world."[1306]

Hale was also "an educated man." He graduated with a B.S. in Political Science from an Illinois University, received a "partial (music) scholarship" and passed the Illinois bar in 1998.[1307] In 1999,[1308] the state of Illinois withdrew his license to practice "because of his racist beliefs."[1309] The loss of Hale's license triggered a shooting rampage in 1999 by one of his WCOTC followers who killed two people and injured nine others before taking his own life. Hale knew how to promote his opinions and had been achieving small successes in recruiting interest from other supporters. As an 18-year-old, he created the "American White Supremacist Party at Bradley University" in Illinois.[1310]

Hale knew how to attract attention for his organization and his beliefs. Bennett understood that Hale and his organization were coming to Lewiston to make a statement, as did other organizations on both sides of the issue.

Bennett speculated that the city's original decision to move the WCOTC from the Multi-Purpose Center to the Lewiston Armory likely had some impact on the Many and One's interest in Bates College for the counter-rally.[1311] The Lewiston Armory would not become available until after December 19th, the day the city publicly announced that the WCOTC would be moved, a second time, to the national guard facility. According to my interviews with Michelle Vazquez Jacobus, Mark Schlotterbeck, Jim Bennett, Cheryl Hamilton, Peggy Rotundo, and Bill Welch, the person responsible for making the final decision to select Bates College, and specifically the Merrill Gymnasium,[1312] is unknown.

What is known is that there were multiple people involved at various times in the discussions with Bates College. All the parties that at some point took part in those discussions included Mark Schlotterbeck, Jim Bennett, Bill Welch, Frank Amoroso from the DOJ,[1313] Bates security, and Bates Dean (and former Lewiston city councilor) James Carignan.[1314] On Friday, January 3rd, the public announcement of the successful negotiations completed "late Friday morning" signaled that the Many and One Rally had finally secured their facility for the event.[1315]

The successful negotiations leading to the Bates College approval to host the Many and One Coalition rally on January 11th were a relief to both the coalition and the city. It allowed all parties to focus on the job at hand, and there was much work to be done before the rally. The Many and One's desire to find a large enough facility to handle what Mark Schlotterbeck believed could be "as many as 1,000" people,[1316] would soon attract a crowd that exceeded even their wildest expectations.

There was little time for celebrating their negotiation success. Now, the coalition had to put together a program, confirm speakers, and find donations to pay for expenses that included a $9,000 liability insurance policy. They also had to deal with logistical issues that included room set-up; who would be on stage; materials for the rally; complying with city security requirements; positioning people throughout the facility to answer questions and direct people, and many other tasks. They also needed to finalize the details they had been working on a week-long volunteer training program with events that would begin on Sunday, January 5th, for approximately 200 coalition and non-coalition volunteers.

**Preparation Was Everything**

In a pamphlet produced by the Many and One Coalition titled "Many & One Rally," was an event calendar for the entire week leading up to the rally. These events would include "Training for Nonviolent Marshals" on January 5th; "Pre/Post Rally Committee Meeting and "Many and One Coalition Meeting" on January 6th; "Public Safety Meeting" on January 7th; "Teach-in on Nonviolent Political Action" on January 8th; and "The Ideology of Hate: Past and Present," and a public "Candle Vigil" [1317] and "Bell Tolling" (involving "local churches" that would toll their bells at 8:25pm[1318]) on January 10th.

The origin is uncertain, but there remains an active web page that featured an "Information & Action Resource Page" for the January 11th rally directed at Bates students on campus. At the top of the page are two quotes, including Martin Luther King Jr. who said, "In the end, we will remember not the words of our enemies, but the silence of our friends." The other is from Edmund Burke, who said, "In order for evil to flourish, all that is required is for good men to do nothing." The website provided information about the WCOTC, and also emphasized that "personal discipline and extensive training" was required in order "to stand in peaceful opposition" to groups like the WCOTC. It also reminded students that many of them did not "have the experience and background to do this."[1319]

The web page urged students not to travel to the national guard armory and to attend the rally that would be hosted on campus. The site also urged students to participate in the Many and One events scheduled throughout the week and to volunteer and assist the organization.

Jim Bennett and Chief Welch were busy pulling together many logistical elements of their own. Jim would assemble a "68-

page operational plan"[1320] that he would edit and contribute to for the event. It would involve the assembling of a law enforcement response involving some 230 law enforcement personnel from around the state. The plan was the product of a collaborative effort that would include input from Auburn Police Chief Phil Crowell and his department; Androscoggin County Sheriff Ronald Gagnon and Deputy Sheriff Raymond Lafrance and their department; Lisbon Police Department; Sabattus Police Department; Bangor Police Department; Maine State Police; Frank Amoroso from the Department of Justice Community Relations Services; the Boston Field Office of the FBI; U.S. Drug Enforcement Agency; Attorney General G. Steven Rowe; Androscoggin County District Attorney Norm Croteau; the Maine Army National Guard; a Bates College representative; and the Lewiston Fire Department.[1321]

The details were endless. Lewiston Police Department personnel required training dealing with "armed protestors, tear gas, and even car bombs." Jim had also authorized the expenditure of "$10,000" for the purchase of "brand new riot shields and heavy batons" for Lewiston officers in response to some of what they had learned about WCOTC confrontations in places like Wakefield. The plan would also arrange for issuing press passes to some "200 reporters and photographers;" provide food for all the law enforcement and other staff working for the city;[1322] outline what Lewiston Public Works Director Chris Branch and his personnel would do with staffed dump trucks and other equipment to act as crowd barriers in addition to also setting jersey barriers; developing a list of road closures, setting up barriers and detour signage; removing certain city signs and other landscape items that could become weapons; and trash barrels and other containers that could hide a bomb.[1323]

The Lewiston City Council also took a step that was somewhat uncharacteristic for them. They acted on a resolution supporting the rally and denouncing everything the WCOTC represented and believed. The resolution was part of the Tuesday, January 7th agenda with Lewiston Council President Rene Bernier presiding over the meeting. According to the meeting minutes, Raymond's decision to attend the swearing-in ceremony of Senator Susan Collins in Washington, D.C. necessitated that Bernier preside over the meeting.[1324] On January 3rd, Raymond also told the Sun Journal that he would not be attending the Many and One rally as he would vacation in Florida for the entire week and had made plane reservations "'back in September.'" He would plan to "'ignore (the WCOTC event) wholesale'" and thought that if everyone else "'ignored (the WCOTC) in the first place, they'd just go away.'" Raymond also believed the public "'reaction to his letter was extreme'" and that had "'the response to my letter... been half as responsible as my original request, this would have all gone away.'"[1325]

During the January 7th city council meeting, all seven city councilors approved the resolution. Without equivocation, it stated that the elected officials, city staff, and residents of the community did "not welcome, encourage, or otherwise wish to entertain (white supremacist groups) in our homes, our neighborhood(s), or our community (and that)... our community has grown and evolved through the generations of immigrants and their families." The resolution went on to say that the city council encouraged "all residents to join (the Many and One Coalition) in advocating for unity and harmony to demonstrate to one and all that Lewiston opposed intolerance and embraced diversity."[1326]

Following the public portion of the city council meeting, Jim, Chief Welch, and I joined the city council for an executive session to discuss confidential security plans and some intelligence that we had collected about a variety of groups that could make their way to Lewiston on January 11th.[1327] It was important that the city council knew the depth of the plan and to update them on the latest developments. The council had been briefed often from the very first day we were made aware of the WCOTC. It was clear to the council that the work Jim and Bill had invested in planning of both events was significant, and they understood we were prepared if things became violent. With Raymond in Florida, we would update Council President Bernier and possibly the entire council if circumstances warranted that level of outreach.

## All Was Done but the Waiting

Jim Bennett, Bill Welch, and I were becoming accustomed to the inevitability of having the unexpected happen despite how well things appeared to be coming together. On January 8, 2003, WCOTC founder Matt Hale was arrested in Chicago "as he entered the Dirksen Federal Courthouse in Chicago" for attempting to "hire someone to 'forcibly assault' and murder U.S. District Court Judge Joan H. Lefkow."[1328]

Chief Welch cautioned the press that the law enforcement response to the event would not change with Hale's absence, and cautioned the reporter writing the story that he had concerns "'about (the group's) displaced aggression'" regarding Hale's arrest, and that it could result in their expressing that aggression in Lewiston.[1329]

Bennett and Welch knew about WCOTCs history, and what happened in 1999 when someone went on a shooting rampage in response to Hale being denied his law license in Illinois. Bennett shared with the Sun Journal that "'(i)f anybody thought we were overreacting, well (Hale's actions in Chicago) proves that we're not.'"[1330] Even with the possibility of the WCOTC event being canceled following Hale's arrest, Bennett and Welch's insistence to proceed with all portions of the city's "68-page" operations plan for both events paid off. On Friday, January 10$^{th}$, the city learned that "Hale's second-in-command, Jon Fox, would fill in" for Hale at the WCOTC meeting in the national guard armory.[1331]

The possibility of cancellation involved not only the WCOTC event. Around January 8$^{th}$ or January 9$^{th}$, Bennett stated that he and Chief Welch were in communication with Bates officials who questioned the Merrill security plan. They believed that the city's proposal should not include elements of the plan that were intended to protect the participants and attendees at the event. Bennett's recollection was that both he and Welch went immediately over to meet with Bates officials for "a pretty tense meeting." In effect, Bates requested that the safety plan, drawn up by the Lewiston Police Department, and other law enforcement agencies, be changed to exclude things like the "metal detectors" at the doors along with other important safety measures in the plan.[1332]

Bennett and Welch emphasized at the meeting that they would be unwilling to change any component of the plan. Jim cautioned Bates officials that if the city's plan was not acceptable, the city would not permit the Merrill Gymnasium event to take place on Saturday. Bennett reminded Bates that if the city had to shut down the event, they were "going to have all kinds of other issues" they would have to deal with.[1333]

Bates agreed to the city's requirement, but there was also a Maine Civil Liberties Union (MCLU) filing against the Merrill security plan in Portland's federal court on Friday, January 10$^{th}$, only one or two days after Bates agreed to the safety plan. The MCLU's filing reflected their opposition to the city's requirement banning "graphic words or images" on signs at the rally, and the city's "security measures such as banning cameras and other items from the rallies."[1334] It was unknown whether the filing was the product of the final meeting between the city and Bates officials a few days earlier, or simply a coincidence.

The MCLU claimed such actions were unconstitutional. Welch cautioned the court that if the MCLU prevailed, the city would not have law enforcement in the proximity of either the Merrill gym or the national guard facility events. Welch added that "'75 percent'" of WCOTC rallies have resulted in some sort of violence.[1335]

The judge ruled immediately on January 10$^{th}$ that people were free to write any message they wanted on the signs but agreed with the city on all other security measures. City Attorney Bob Hark considered the ruling a "'fair one.'" Welch would agree with the ruling but cautioned that if any sign message "'riles people up,'" that the police would "'deal with that'" with an appropriate response.[1336]

Another 11$^{th}$ hour announcement included some good news for the rally. Bates College would allow the Many and One Coalition's multicultural celebration to proceed as a supporter came forward with a loan of $9,000 dollars to pay for the liability insurance.[1337]

## Expectations and Opinions

As part of the Many and One events program during the week preceding their rally, the "Public Safety Meeting" was held on January 7th at Lewiston's Multi-Purpose Center. What they originally intended to be "a lively discussion about how Somali immigrants can respond to violence, harassment and hatred," turned quickly into an evening where many Somali residents shared stories of being harassed around the community. Some incidents described by meeting attendees included being "cut off" by an aggressive driver; "followed home" by the same driver; being "jumped and beaten while walking downtown;" and then "waking up in the hospital." Others questioned Deputy Chief Michael Bussiere asking if the "police department really investigated complaints" involving potential hate and harassment crimes, while others expressed fear in dealing with the police.[1338]

Bussiere assured those in the room that the police were "'here to help you'" and urged everyone to call the police with any report of harassment or racist comments being directed at them. He also shared the department's plan on how they would "protect citizens on (January) 11." Mike's comments generated a question about why the department was putting all their attention into a one-day event and "forgetting about day-to-day problems that vex the Somali community."

Maine Attorney General G. Steven Rowe and Assistant A.G. Thomas Harnett were also in attendance. Rowe heard what was being said in the room and assured the audience that he was there "'to listen'" and that he did not come with the purpose of making "'big speech.'"[1339] Both Rowe and Harnett agreed that although the meeting had turned out to be something quite different from what was originally planned, it was an important evening for those in attendance who needed "'to express how they feel.'" According to Deputy Chief Bussiere, the police department had not been originally invited to the meeting, suggesting that he had taken the initiative to be there to show his support for the community. Even after the meeting was over, he continued to converse with some of the Somali attendees following him outside the building who "apologiz(ed) for the tone the gathering had taken."[1340]

Chief Welch understood the complexities of the situation observing that "'(t)hey come from a country where they didn't trust police to begin with, and we understood that.'" He also acknowledged that his department was "'hearing that some things were happening that we weren't aware of – through the elders – so we said, 'Let us know about it.'" Deputy A.G. Harnett's assessment of what came out of the meeting may have summed it up best when he said, "'(s)ometimes you talk at each other before you get around to talking to each other.'" Hartnett added that Tuesday evening's safety meeting could "ultimately lead to improvements in the way Somalis and police communicate with each other."[1341]

As a very busy week of work, meetings, planning, discussions and exhaustion were ending, newly elected Governor John Baldacci was being sworn in as the state's 73rd governor on Wednesday, January 8th. In his inauguration speech, Baldacci told those in attendance that Maine's people and their values would be tested on Saturday in Lewiston. He also declared that Maine "'is not, nor will it ever be, a haven or a headquarters for hate groups and racist organizations'" urging "'all Mainers to firmly embrace diversity and tolerance and oppose bigotry and hatred.'"[1342]

Baldacci knew and acknowledged the history of the two cities and recognized both Lewiston and Auburn for their collaborative work together for economic development. It was very possible that the governor was also banking on L-As collaborative energy to prepare for Saturday's rally.

Both of the community's legislative delegations were also collaborating in Augusta during the week. Lewiston's State Senator Peggy Rotundo, who was re-elected to her second term in the legislature, sponsored a legislative non-binding resolution condemning hate and the WCOTC event. It received the full support of both the Maine House and Senate on January 9, 2003. From the Senate floor, Rotundo said:

> This Saturday, Maine will witness its first official event by a group of white supremacists that promulgates hate and is coming to Maine to build membership in hopes of becoming more active in this state. While it is the right of this group to assemble

peacefully and to exercise its First Amendment right to free speech, the message of this group is so abhorrent to the values of civility, inclusiveness, and justice that have made this state great, that I would ask you to join with me to pass this resolution that is before you. This resolution affirms the fundamental rights of all people whom we represent in this legislature to live with respect and dignity and without fear.[1343]

Senator Neria Douglass from Auburn also spoke to support the resolution:

This resolution was needed because there are those who are attempting to inspire hate, which I think we need to condemn. But more than that, we need to embrace what is good and positive in the people who come here to live. It's part of the growth of our economy, which we so badly need. I urge every member of this body to stand in support and to say welcome to those who would wish to come here.[1344]

The week was also filled with opinions and speculation generated from the media and others about the rally, racism, Mayor Raymond, and what would take place on Saturday. The Sun Journal posted area resident comments throughout the week in the "Your Views" section of the newspaper. It was not surprising that the letters reflected a wide range of opinions.

Some "Your View" contributors called for a spiritual response with a "day of fasting and prayer" ("Day of Prayer", 1/7/03); warned that in the future, people would "either thank the National Alliance (hate group) for acting or wonder why we stood by and did nothing" ("Whites Only," 1/7/03); thanked Jim Bennett and former Lewiston Mayor Kaileigh Tara for "taking a stand and challenging a true monster of mankind" ("Pure Poison," 1/8/03); suggested that groups like the WCOTC were "a vast minority and merely a casualty of free speech" ("Vast Minority," 1/9/03); compared the need for diversity to a healthy forest that required a mix of trees to make it "healthier and stronger" ("Our Forest," 1/9/03); that "too many college and university liberals" were advocating the kind of lies perpetrated by people like "Hitler" and "Joseph Gobbels(sic)" ("Best Defense," 1/11/03); and reminded readers that some resident "disdain and hatred" of Somalis was in reaction to the death of Lisbon, Maine resident SSgt. Thomas Field and explained why "(s)ome people may not be happy about Somalis living up the street" ("Don't Forget," 1/11/03).[1345]

On the Saturday morning of the Many and One Coalition Rally, the January 11, 2003, Sun Journal's front page featured a small, boxed banner near the top of the page that simply said, "Eye of the Storm." This was not meant as a blizzard warning about a 'nor'easter' that can hit our state during any given winter. The giveaway about its true meaning was the large, bold headline below the banner: "Let There be Peace" and its subheading "With Nazis coming, Some Pray for Peace While Police Brace for Trouble." Below the headlines was a picture of people holding lit candles outside of the First Universalist Church in Auburn. The candlelight vigil was part of the Many and One Coalition Friday activities. The vigils would be held throughout the Lewiston-Auburn area and in Maine communities including Augusta, Portland,[1346] and Sabattus.[1347]

The January 11th Sun Journal edition also reported that newly sworn-in Governor Baldacci, while attending a prayer service and luncheon at the Holy Trinity Greek Orthodox Church in Lewiston, shared that he would be at the Saturday rally. Church President Jack Clifford noted that there were "'some 50 different nationalities'" that attended their church and that it had always been "'open to diversity.'"[1348] According to another article, the Governor would also leave his first Blaine House (the official Governor's residence across the street from the State House) public open-house reception early on Saturday morning to attend the Many and One rally.[1349]

The January 11th newspaper also included some notable ads. One was from "Friends International" that was labeled as "Peace and Friendship not Hate and Racism" and was signed by approximately 150 individuals, families, and organizations from around the state.[1350] Another ad featured a picture with a diverse group of L-A residents and was paid for by approximately 70 "businesses, organizations and citizens of Lewiston Auburn." The ad was labeled as "Strength Through Diversity. An L-A Tradition."[1351]

The Many and One Coalition had lined up some 20 speakers for the event [1352] and worked through all the requisite interpersonal/inter-organizational logistics and negotiations. They also had approximately 200 volunteers in place for one of the biggest community demonstrations since the 1937 shoe strikes, which started peacefully in Lewiston, but ended with violence in Auburn.

From the city's perspective, the effort involved over a month of research, staff time, outreach, meetings, negotiations, logistics, intelligence, and some expense. For the Many and One Coalition organizers, many Somali residents, elected officials, and city staff, it was likely that most of us had gone to bed on the eve of the Many and One Rally with one thought on our minds from that morning's paper... "Let There be Peace."

## "UNITED AGAINST HATE"[1353]

I am typically not an early riser but was awake at 7:00 AM, earlier than usual for me on a Saturday morning. For Jim Bennett and Bill Welch, it would be around 4:30 AM, and according to Lisa Chmelecki, "neither Welch or Bennett needed an alarm clock."[1354] Jim not only had the weight of the day ahead of him; he also had to put in some time that morning to help his son put the finishing touches on their Pinewood Derby[1355] car. The Cub Scout annual race event would be held at Montello Elementary school that morning.[1356]

Chief Welch knew he was coming into the day as prepared as his department could be. His department and other agencies had invested possibly thousands of staff hours on researching, discussing, and planning for this day. His first order of business upon leaving the house would be to pick up some bakery items for people coming in early for briefings.[1357] When you live in the northeast, that would usually include heavy doses of Dunkin Donuts coffee as well. Jim would also be at the briefings. Bennett said that he attended every briefing and planning session at the police department from the first day they began back in November.[1358]

For Mark Schlotterbeck, he would also head out to Bates college early that morning. He remembered that "it was a really cold day." [1359] Mark was not exaggerating. The Sun Journal weather information had projected a high temperature of 23 degrees[1360] and there was over a foot of snow on the ground from a storm that had hit the state over the weekend. In actuality, weather data from the National Oceanic and Atmospheric Administration observation platform in Durham, Maine (no temperature data was available from the Lewiston station) said that the high temperature (about 10 miles south of Lewiston) was 20 degrees, most likely at mid-afternoon, on January 11th. The observed 7:00 AM morning temperature was four degrees on January 11th at the Durham station,[1361] and there was some wind throughout the morning and afternoon. Adding a seven mile-per-hour wind to a 20-degree temperature would have meant that the wind chill temperature at mid-afternoon in Lewiston was likely around 11 degrees. It was possible that the wind-chill temperature was below zero and into the single digits most of the morning.

As for that morning's WCOTC meeting at the national guard armory, we knew that Matt Hale's replacement, Jon Fox, was going to present Hale's speech. Sgt. Michael McGonagle had picked up Hale at the Portland International airport the day before. Welch wanted someone from the department to pick him up to ensure that Fox had access to all the "instructions, warnings, and phone numbers that police had given Hale" as they had been confiscated when Hale was arrested in Chicago. After returning from the airport trip, McGonagle told Welch and Bennett that Fox was "'expecting about 30 people from the Connecticut, Massachusetts area'" and that he had received "'about 12 e-mails from local people'" who might attend the meeting. Grinning, Welch said that most of the 12 people were likely "'undercover guys.'"[1362]

After the early morning briefings, Bennett wanted to squeeze in some time to see his son's derby car race. Jim did not believe that he had done his best work helping his son with the car but felt that it would do the job.[1363] Knowing that he could not stay to watch the race for any length of time, Jim made time to be at the event for some father-son support. When Welch came over to pick Bennet up at Montello, he had only spent a short amount of time inside watching the race. Jim got into the car and Bill asked him how things were going with the race. Jim responded he had not seen his son's car in the race adding "'(i)t is what it is.'" Bill and Jim made their way over to Bates College with Jim's bullet-proof "vest (that) waited for him in the trunk."[1364]

Jim said that Welch insisted he wear the vest. Both Jim and former Lewiston mayor John Jenkins (who would be the event host) would be the only two civilians outfitted with vests. Bennett would also wear a "black nylon" police jacket with the words "'Lewiston Police' in bright yellow across the back"[1365] as he would be riding with Chief Welch all day and constantly in close proximity to many law enforcement personnel from all over the state.[1366] Being properly outfitted could avoid any 'mistaken identity' issues if things took a turn for the worse.

When Jim and Bill arrived at Bates College, the Lewiston Public Works Department was busy doing a variety of tasks around a broad area of Bates College. Hundreds of portable no-parking signs and directional signs were needed at Bates and the guard armory. A variety of public works trucks and heavy equipment were used to block intersections preventing any unauthorized vehicles from entering the outer perimeter of the college. The public works equipment would be staffed with PW personnel. The site of the 'Many and One Coalition Rally' was scheduled to open its doors around noontime.

Welch had spoken to Public Works Director Chris Branch and his staff earlier in the week telling them that there were "'going to be things out there that you'll see that you likely have never seen before'" adding that they needed to "'hold (their) temper.'" Welch, always quick on his feet, finished by saying "'(y)ou do not want to be on the 6 o'clock news.'"[1367] Welch wanted to stop and speak with all the Public Works staff one more time to encourage them and to share one last piece of advice telling them "'listen guys, you need to stay in your trucks.'"[1368] Both Welch and Bennett wanted to emphasize that the PW personnel needed to just stay focused on the job at hand with Jim adding "'(i)f everything goes as planned, we'll have you home in time for the second half of the second game.'"[1369]

Bennett and Welch finally made their way over to the Merrill gym. State troopers were already sweeping the facility with bomb-sniffing dogs. Welch took some time to speak with Lt. Butch Pratt, who was in charge of the facility's security. Bill told Pratt that he had been doing a "'great job'" with Pratt replying that he hoped Bill felt the same way at 5:00 PM. It was no small task to secure the facility.[1370]

Jim surveyed the field house area of the gym building where attendees would gather while Bill spoke with Lt. Pratt.[1371] Jim could see the results of the planning inside the field house. Both Jim and Bill had been working with Frank Amoroso from the DOJ Community Relations Service. Frank had been one of the primary consultants on security for both the Merrill site and the national guard armory site. Many of Amoroso's recommendations had been incorporated into the plan. The 3,000 chairs in the facility were all tied together (eliminating the possibility that someone could throw it as a projectile); areas with curtains had been inspected for snipers; rules would be in place to prohibit back packs, boxes, bags (to hide potential weapons), cameras (projectile/weapon), bottled and canned liquids (projectile/weapon), wooden barricades (projectile/weapon), and signs would be allowed but without sticks (projectile/weapon).[1372] It was around 10:30 AM when Jim and Bill headed out to the national guard armory.[1373]

According to Sun Journal reporter Lisa Chmelecki who was embedded with Bennett and Welch for the day, by the time Jim and Bill arrived at the armory's culinary arts cafeteria, there were "(d)ozens of reporters... already waiting behind the barricades outside" the building. Both city officials entered the cafeteria to make a last-minute check of the meeting room.[1374] Kelley Bouchard's reporting for the Portland Press Herald revealed that "(p)olice set up 50 folding chairs tied together in groups of five, so they could not be used as weapons." Windows were taped and covered with "heavy cardboard" to protect the occupants in the event that projectiles were thrown at the windows[1375] (also possibly recommended by Amoroso).

Bennett made another check of the meeting room while Welch spoke to the officers assigned to the site. "More then 50 Lewiston-Auburn police officers, Androscoggin County deputies, state troopers and federal agents" were in an armory garage near the cafeteria. Gear was organized and laid out alongside coffee, baked goods, and "sandwiches and chips were piled on (one) another. But none of the officers were eating. Welch could tell they were antsy." With things at the ready, both Jim and Bill headed back to the police station for some last-minute details. Jim was doing his best to stay in touch with his wife to keep her abreast of developments.[1376]

While at the police station, Bennett took some time to put on his bullet-proof vest saying that it did not make any "sense taking stupid chances." The delay at the station was brief and they returned to Bates College, where a throng of people had already collected in front of the field house doors. Welch, who likely felt the single-digit wind chill temperatures that morning, announced to a relieved and jubilant crowd that the doors would be opening. "Minutes (after Bill's announcement), Welch got word that members of the Progressive Labor Party" were in front of City Hall protesting. Welch and Bennett quickly got into Bill's vehicle and made their way downtown.[1377]

Bennett stated that police intelligence knew that the Progressive Labor Party would come to Lewiston. This was one of the two anti-white supremacist groups that had confronted the WCOTC in Wakefield, Massachusetts back in September 2002. Bennett also said that they had received intelligence on the possible arrival of these anti-racist groups and that a demonstration could occur downtown. That information allowed Welch to modify their operations plan to keep some 20 officers in riot gear inside the Park Street police station (located one short city block down the street from City Hall) in the event they showed up downtown.[1378] When Bennett and Welch arrived, they found "about 50 protestors (chanting "(c)ops, courts, Ku Klux Klan, they are all part of the boss's(sic) plan" in front of City Hall.[1379]

Welch got together with Detective David St. Pierre who was first on scene.[1380] Bill instructed the detective to order that the Progressive Labor Party disperse or be arrested. When St. Pierre used his bullhorn to instruct the protestors to disperse, they did not move. The detective followed up the order with a warning that failing to leave the scene would result in arrest. When the demonstrators ignored the warning, St. Pierre radioed for the arrest team. "In seconds, nine officers in full riot gear walked out of the police station and started marching down Park Street toward the crowd." The protestors spotted the advancing police team and decided not to engage by boarding their bus. Welch got on his phone and advised Deputy Bussiere, who was in the Maine State Police Command vehicle and in command of the WCOTC operations, that he had "'a busload of about 50 headed (his) way'" and that he and Jim would "'be there soon.'"[1381]

By about 12:30, the majority of the crowds attending both the Many and One rally and the WCOTC meeting were arriving.[1382] Most of the news media crowd estimates placed the peak attendance for the Bates College event at somewhere between 4,500 and 5,000 attendees (3,000+ inside and 1,000+ outside), and the WCOTC event at somewhere between 450 and 500 people.[1383] Law enforcement personnel deployed around the city for both events were estimated at approximately 80 Lewiston police officers, with another 150 law enforcement personnel from the other agencies.[1384]

The number of law enforcement that were actively working in Lewiston and part of the Lewiston PD operations plan was very similar to the 250 law enforcement personnel that were on the scene in Wakefield. The major difference was that Wakefield had 600 protestors, about the same sized group that showed up for the WCOTC meeting. What Wakefield did not have was a companion event going on in another part of their city with some 4,000+ people in attendance.

Chief Welch was not certain about the number, but he knew that there were other law enforcement personnel on standby near the Exit 12 (now Exit 75) Maine Turnpike maintenance facility. Bill estimated it could have been as many as 100 or more sworn officers and also believed that this number was not part of the total law enforcement count often reported by the media[1385] (it is important to note that both Lewiston and Auburn needed assistance not only for both Lewiston events but also to cover normal police operations not directly associated with either event).

The presence of the extra personnel at the Maine Turnpike facility reflected the possibility that additional law enforcement could be needed for any confrontations between racist sympathizers and the almost 5,000 people at Bates College, the 500 anti-white supremacists at the guard armory, or to quell any demonstrations or confrontations by opposing sides that might occur again in downtown Lewiston.

There had been reports that the Many and One organizers were planning to march into the street after the Merrill event. There would be nothing to prevent white supremacist sympathizers and anti-white supremacist protestors to leave the WCOTC meeting to take part or confront each other or the Many and One post-rally marchers. It may also explain why Bennett estimated that "half to two-thirds" of the state's law enforcement personnel around the state were prepared to respond if Lewiston needed additional support.[1386] No one really knew what to expect. Lewiston had twice the exposure for violence, with two separate events and sizeable crowds going on at exactly the same time.

## D-Day

When Mark Schlotterbeck decided it was time to leave the Bates campus building and walk over to the field house, he was told by someone that he needed to be "escorted" by police "just to keep us safe." When he and others arrived at Merrill under police escort, his first impression of what he saw when he approached the field house was "there were so many people." Upon entering the building, the sound of "African style drums just throbbing the whole place" was adding to the energy that was filling the room. From Mark's perspective, "it was alive."[1387]

Mark's primary purpose in his role as leader of the Many and One Coalition was to deal with the more complex and larger logistical issues. Mark had navigated matters involving the make-up of the steering committee, finding a rally location, negotiating with the Bates ownership, and paying the bills. On this day, he would need to deal with any last-minute issues that would require an immediate response.

One of those 'last-minute' situations came up almost immediately after Mark had entered the field house. There were several high-profile public officials that made an appearance at the rally. Some were invited as speakers, and some were not. Without naming who was involved, Schlotterbeck stated that there were "(U.S.) Congress people" who attended. Mark remembered "a discussion with someone of the congressional delegation's staff... about where (the elected officials) would be seated" on stage. He shared he was appreciative of their willingness to be present, and that their presence was important to the event and the community. Mark also had to inform the staff member that they would all have to occupy the seats on the gymnasium floor.[1388] The 1:00 start time for the event was approaching, and the speakers were lined up and ready to go. Soon, the event that many had planned since late November was finally going to happen.

During the morning, Sgt. Michael McGonagle and another officer picked up two white vans from a local rental agency that could hold 15 to 20 people each. McGonagle wanted to have vans capable of carrying the 30 or so people that might arrive from the Connecticut-Massachusetts area. The sergeant made his way to Exit 12 to pick up WCOTC representative Jon Fox and "about 20" of his supporters[1389] that had parked their cars in a Maine Turnpike park-and-ride lot. The operations plan specified they did not want Fox or any of their supporters to use their own vehicles.[1390]

The plan wanted to avoid the need for WCOTC members to drive into the armory facility lot and expose themselves to harm or damage to their vehicles (something that the WCOTC would likely find useful as a news media photo-op). There would also be no separate police escort ahead of the vans. The entire idea was to use these fairly innocuous passenger vans to transport the Fox group into the armory parking lot with appropriate police security once they got close to the national guard facility. It was not a long drive from the park-and-ride lot. The distance between Exit 12 and Exit 13 was about three miles to the Maine Army National Guard Armory. The facility was about a quarter mile from the Exit 13 off ramp with roads that were blocked off by police, allowing the vans to enter the armory area without driving through the crowd.

I had already arrived at my assigned position inside the Maine State Police command vehicle earlier in the morning. The WCOTC group had entered the building around 12:30 PM after a very uneventful trip from Exit 12. Shortly after the WCTOCs arrival, Bennett and Welch finally made their way from downtown Lewiston to the command vehicle. The crowd was large, including sixty-five Lewiston police officers[1391] in full riot gear positioned in full view of the spectators, as well as dozens of journalists (and possibly more, as there were 200 press credentials issued that day)[1392].

As the meeting starting time of 1:00 PM drew near, "there were about 40" bystanders and people representing both sides of the issue along the concrete barriers on Goddard Road[1393] when a commotion developed within the bystanders. According to Bennett, there were "20 to 30... state troopers in full riot gear... in one of the garages on the backside" of the armory facility.[1394] "Seconds later (an arrest team comprised of)... four (fully outfitted) officers marched out of the (building near the armory culinary center) in diamond formation. The two on the side used their shields to push back the protestors, while the other two grabbed a man accused of being disorderly"[1395] as he had attempted to "block a racist supporter from attending the meeting."[1396] The lieutenant that ordered the first arrest team then "called for the second arrest team."[1397]

I remember waiting to hear if there would be another arrest and if this would mark the beginning of the confrontations that we expected could happen, but also prayed would not. There was no second arrest, although it was still early.

After the WCOTC meeting began, we noticed from the command vehicle, "about 100 (anti-white supremacists) protestors marching down Alfred Plourde Parkway. Wearing black masks and hooded sweatshirts, they looked organized and dangerous." An undercover officer working inside the crowd reported that the protestors "were members of the radical Anti-Racist Action Network,"[1398] the other anti-white supremacist group that was also involved in the Wakefield violence against the WCOTC. Kelley Bouchard reported that there was another anti-white supremacist group in the crowd named the "NorthEastern(sic) Federation of Anarcho-Communists" and that most of the groups had come "from outside of Maine."[1399]

Some protestors were carrying bats. One person had "a piece of guardrail," and there was talk of "charging the line."[1400] Others "banged on a 5-gallon... make-shift (drum)" and several took turns with a bullhorn yelling "Hey, Nazis, you can't hide! We charge you with genocide!" Someone from the Progressive Party yelled "(w)e will not allow the fascist movement to grow in the U.S.!"[1401] At one point, someone spotted Maine State Police snipers on a building across the street from the armory and started chanting at them.[1402]

As the tension and actions within the crowd showed signs of escalating, Bennett asked "'how long will it take to hook that fire hose up to the hydrant?'" Jim was referring to the hose that was already hooked up to the Lewiston Fire Department's ladder truck that on scene. Bennett had shared that the planning process involved having the state's attorney general office and the county district attorney's office review the operation plans. Use of a fire hose as a crowd-control tactic was discussed. The AG and DA agreed that if the fire hose were used, it would be set to "spray" the crowd as opposed to setting the nozzle to eject a high-pressure stream of water typically used to fight fires. With the frigid temperatures, we hoped that the simple threat of just getting wet might be enough of a deterrent if any violence broke out.[1403]

The hose was hooked to the hydrant, and the order was given to raise the ladder to position the hose above the crowd. As the ladder slowly climbed upward, some in the crowd began to chant, "We're not on fire! We're not on fire!"[1404] Welch remembered the crowd also chanting "Don't spray the f***ing water! Don't spray the f***ing water!"[1405] Journalist Lisa Chmelecki speculated whether the hose threat was "(a) scare tactic... (o)r a real threat?" Welch would not confirm or deny either to Chmelecki.[1406] I knew Bill. He would have kept his options open and would not have hesitated to act if the situation would have called for it.

Inside the armory's culinary arts cafeteria, there were 45 people who would listen to three different speakers. Approximately 20 of those people in the room were the Fox group transported by the Lewiston Police to the meeting, 12 were supporters or observers that arrived on their own,[1407] and the remaining 13 were officers assigned to the meeting room.[1408] Bennett commented he believed that five of the 12 "supporters or observers" were members of the public that were outside the building and were randomly selected by the Lewiston Police Department. Jim added that he also believed that the selection also involved communications between the command vehicle and officers working the crowd to ensure that the five randomly selected people were believed not to be any of the anti-white supremacist protestors or other activists that were expressing aggressive behavior in the crowd.[1409]

## Anxiety and Celebration

From nearly everyone's perspective inside the Merrill field house, the anticipation of the meeting was creating a celebratory atmosphere. The Many and One Coalition's two hundred or more volunteers, who had worked together to create this extraordinary event, were rewarded with an outpouring of positive energy and enthusiasm that was affecting everyone.

When Many and One volunteer Cheryl Hamilton walked into the facility, she "sat in the back of the room" and was immediately overwhelmed. "I ended up going underneath the bleachers and crying." Hamilton was conflicted about the event. On the one hand, she thought that "it was great to see so much interest" in the event. On the other hand, she remained frustrated that the energy and focus that created the support for the rally had not been present in the community sooner.[1410]

The event and possibly the months of work also produced another unexpected result for Hamilton. Being assigned to the door was not seen by her as some menial job but as a "privilege". For Cheryl, it turned out that working the door to provide information to people about what to do and what not to do when they entered the gym, also became an opportunity with an unexpected benefit: It gave her the opportunity to thank "every single person that walked in personally... For me, that was transformative... I had been so sad... and frustrated... for so long...at seeing our clients impacted on a daily basis, that it was nice, at least for that moment, to say thank you."[1411]

State Senator Margaret "Peggy" Rotundo was also at the Many and One rally. Peggy had been in public service since her election to the Lewiston School Committee in 1994, had been working (with a break to raise a new family) for Bates College since she and her husband Dan, who was hired as a professor, arrived around 1970. Peggy had been recently elected to her second term in the state senate, and was also working at the Bates Center for Service Learning[1412] (now called the Harward Center for Community Partnerships [1413]). She was personally and professionally invested in Bates College, the community, and the Lewiston public school system.

Although Rotundo did not have any direct involvement with the Many and One Coalition, she was recognized as a champion for both education and diversity in the community. Peggy's work and collaborative style in the legislature helped to pass the first legislation to support $1,000,000 in ELL funding for schools in the state's 2000-2001 budget. Although there were fewer than 30 ELL students in the Lewiston public school system at the time, [1414] there was a growing population of students in the Portland school system requiring ELL services. She would not only work to increase the statewide ELL funding to two million dollars in the 2002-2003 budget, Rotundo would also become the Co-Chair of the Joint Appropriations Committee after only two years in the Senate, almost unheard of for someone just finishing their freshman year in the legislature.[1415]

When Peggy entered Merrill for the Many and One Rally, she knew that there were some public safety concerns about the presence of white supremacists in the community. She also knew that security inside the gym would be formidable given the large number of people that would be attending, and the number of high-profile government officials who would be present, like newly elected Governor Baldacci, Attorney General G. Steven Rowe, and Senators Susan Collins and Olympia Snowe. What she was witnessing inside and outside the building was a "very uplifting and moving gathering," and felt "very comfortable and safe" when she walked into the building. Before taking her seat, she spotted Governor Baldacci, who had some people around him. She decided to move in his direction to greet him.[1416]

> John (Baldacci) was walking up to the podium, the platform, to speak, and I saw him and he was surrounded by a few people... I sort of walked quickly over to say hi to him before he (spoke)... and I have never seen state police move so quickly as they moved to surround him as I approached him. They clearly were worried about something that could happen, and here was this person, I wasn't running, but I was sort of walking quickly to say hi and I called out his name... and they just immediately surrounded him and walked him quickly away.[1417]

Peggy added that although she felt very safe at the event, the reaction by the state police in protecting the governor, and all that had occurred in Lewiston, produced "a very tense situation within the community, within the state" and for some in the field house. Despite everything that had taken place over the last few months, Peggy was also "proud of the governor being" at the rally and "so proud of the people that came and the statement that we were able to make as a community in Lewiston." For Peggy, "it was such a positive day, such an important day."[1418]

With all that had transpired over the last several months, the bulk of the news media attention was understandably focused on the support for the Somali community. Schlotterbeck had surveyed the crowd and noticed how many non-immigrants were in attendance. Schlotterbeck told me he had been over to the

Lisbon Street mosque many times, and a group of men from the mosque assisted him with a speech that he had worked on for the rally. They also assisted Mark with learning some Somali for the speech. As there were not "many people who spoke Somali that were there," Mark's delivery of his rally speech, partly in Somali, would not be heard by many who spoke the language.[1419] Cheryl Hamilton noted that it should not have been a surprise to anyone that so few Somali residents were attending given how fearful they were about their own safety.[1420]

Schlotterbeck agreed with Hamilton and wanted to ensure that history would see that the rally event came into being because of the events driven by the mayor's letter and the white supremacists coming to Lewiston. Mark believed it was important to understand how the resulting Somali safety concerns impacted them as "human beings" and why "they were afraid."[1421]

## Views from the Floor

Androscoggin County Chamber of Commerce President Chip Morrison attended the Many and One rally. Chip had also recruited chamber board officers and members to attend the event. Morrison shared that the announcement about the WCOTC "skin head rally" meeting scheduled in Lewiston "scared the hell out of me."[1422]

The unfolding events of the last three months had a profound impact on him. It was personal. Chip had "mentored a couple of young entrepreneurs in the African community.' He add that he "liked doing that... Having people who are different from us adds richness to the community in many, many ways." He also believed that the WCOTC event could have been "really awful... and that (it) would have marred our community forever" adding that "(t)he Many and One rally showed us in the light that I would like (it) to be, which is, we value diversity here."[1423]

Although Raymond's daughter Susan Geismar did not attend the rally, she participated in a pre-event march that took place on the morning of the rally. There is no mention of this march in any publication or report that I could find, so Geismar's recollection of the march was one of those rare discoveries that can happen when researching a historical event. Geismar's recollection of the march, which involved "hundreds" of people, began when they assembled on that freezing January 11th morning at the intersection of Sabattus, College, and Horton Street where the Calvary United Methodist Church was located. Geismar remembered several people who were there: Azeb Hassan, Hawa Kahin, Jan Phillips, and Dennis Grafflin.[1424]

Before the march to Bates began, she was conversing with either Hawa or Azeb. At some point, one of them told Geismar that when people looked at her, "'I just think why do you hate me?'" Geismar said she responded by saying "(y)ou know, there are two ways of looking at that... I'm looking at you thinking 'where did you get that gorgeous scarf? I would like to have one like that, you know... (because) you are so beautifully dressed!'" Susan's statement caused Hawa to stop "for a minute and (she) said 'Oh.' Evidently, because of what was going on (in Lewiston), it didn't occur to her that someone would think that the scarf she was wearing... was so striking, that (the scarf) was the cause."[1425]

The morning march would proceed to Bates college and by the time they arrived, "the gym... was completely full." Geismar decided not to go in. Her assessment of her importance to support the marchers and the event's purpose simply came down to producing the best outcome for the event. She remembered telling her fellow marchers that, "nobody needs me here to add fuel to the fire, or to distract (from the) message."[1426] As Raymond's daughter, she was surrounded by people who knew and understood who she was and had witnessed her commitment to the immigrant community. Susan was a Daryeelka board member before her father's letter. Many of the marchers knew her family and her kids as well as her community activism. They needed no further explanation when Susan elected not to go into the building.

Regina Phillips and her sister Rachel Talbot-Ross made the trip to Lewiston from Portland to witness this historic Maine event. For Regina, this event was likely much more personal. She was serving as the supervisor for the city of Portland-owned and operated homeless shelter that had served as the first home for many of the now Lewiston based secondary migrant refugees. They had been arriving at the shelter since she was first employed in her position in 1997. Regina was also the person who would become part of Lewiston's history when she personally transported the first Somali family 'settlers' from the Portland shelter to Lewiston and assisted them with becoming not only the first Somali family ("Family A") at the Hillview apartment complex, but also the first family to take up residence in Lewiston back in February 2001.[1427]

Almost two years later, Phillips was now taking part in an event to welcome the approximately 1,100 Somalis and other immigrants who were now residents in Lewiston. She remembered that "Rachel and I were one of the first people there."[1428] Regina also marveled at how many people attended the event exclaiming

> (t)he place was packed! Not only that, it was in the dead of winter... the entire Bates auditorium was full, and there (were) still people outside trying to get in... they all stayed outside for the entire rally because they said they could hear what was happening inside... it was quite an awesome day.[1429]

For Regina and her sister Rachel, their participation was also a reflection of their family's commitment to fairness, equality, justice and diversity. Their father, Gerald Talbot, had experienced his share of injustice and inequality in his life. In his desire to "fight for civil rights," Talbot became the first "black person elected to the Maine Legislature in 1972." He was also known for bringing his young daughters to "many civil rights events." Talbot was also responsible for re-establishing the Portland NAACP chapter in 1964 after it terminated operations in 1959. He served as its president in "1964-1966, 1970-71 and 1978-1980."[1430]

In October 2002, the Portland NAACP would meet "with a Somali elder... and pledged the organization's support" for the Somali community after the publication of Raymond's letter.[1431] The New England NAACP also "pledged its support" for the Somali refugees. Winston McGill, President of the Portland NAACP chapter spoke at the Many and One rally and made a plea to those in attendance and the public to "'strive to ensure that all citizens regardless of race and ethnicity are guaranteed their God-given right.'"[1432]

41 years after her father had revived Portland's NAACP chapter, Rachel Talbot-Ross would go on to become president of the organization in 2005. Talbot Ross would later be elected to the Maine House of Representatives in 2016, occupying a place next to her father in Maine legislative history as "the first and only Black woman elected to the Maine Legislature and to legislative leadership."[1433]

I had the pleasure of working with both Regina and Rachel. I regret that it took writing this book to better understand the history of their family, and to fully appreciate all the historic contributions made by the Talbot family in Maine.

**Views from the Stage**

The rally finally got underway. "Six children of different faiths quietly offered prayers, accompanied by a flutist from the (Maine) Micmac tribe." The 20-plus speakers were in place to address the supportive and enthusiastic crowd. Lewiston former mayor John Jenkins, the first African American to be elected to the Maine Senate[1434] and as mayor in Lewiston[1435] (would also become Auburn's mayor in 2007),[1436] served as the event host. John, who also worked as a motivational speaker, was the perfect choice to start the proceedings, declaring that the rally was "'a defining moment in history'... as people clapped and pumped their fists in the air." Governor Baldacci then spoke to what people in the state did in response to a threat or a call to action saying that "'we come together as one in Maine'" and respond through "'neighborliness, tolerance,'" and "'respect for one another,'" punctuating the point by exclaiming "'(t)his is not a haven for any hate group!'"[1437]

Mark Schlotterbeck also spoke and continued to expound on his message of inclusiveness for all, reminding everyone that the rally was an opportunity to "come together to say whether you're gay or straight or whether you have this ability or disability, either you're this color, or that color or this religion or that, we say this will be our community!"[1438]

Omar Jamel, the Executive Director of the Somali Advocacy Center in Minneapolis, made note of Raymond's absence and called for the mayor's resignation. Jamal also stated, incorrectly, that the "members of the city council" were also absent from the rally.[1439] In reality, City Councilors Norm Rousseau, Lillian O'Brien and Roger Philippon had attended the rally and were interviewed by Sun Journal reporter Scott Taylor.

Rousseau told Taylor that he believed that Raymond should have attended the rally but "would not encourage" him to resign. Raymond's close friend Councilor Roger Philippon agreed with Rousseau about not supporting any call for the mayor to resign, but also said that "he disagreed with the mayor's letter." Philippon noted that he had disagreed with his friend in the past about the letter, but that both men had "'come to an understanding.'" Philippon also observed that during the rally, calls for the mayor to resign were acknowledged with "'lukewarm applause.'" Not a single city councilor interviewed by Scott Taylor supported calls for Raymond's resignation.[1440]

Many inside the building did not forget mayor Raymond's Florida vacation and his absence at the rally. "Thousands of people wore 'Where's the mayor?' stickers." Omar Jamal from Minneapolis challenged the mayor "'to do the right thing.'"

For most of the speakers, the attention was on the unwelcome WCOTC and all that they represented. Reverend Bill Gordon, "an openly gay pastor of Northern Lights Metropolitan Community Church in Vassalboro, got a standing ovation" after saying that "'(d)iscrimination and hatred are not something that has been imported from outside of this city and state'" underscoring "how discrimination of all kinds must stop" by Maine residents who also needed "to stamp out hate" from those within their own state.[1441]

Almost 38 years after he won his second world championship belt in Lewiston, and almost eight years after his last visit to Lewiston, Muhammad Ali made his presence felt again. Although Parkinson's disease had affected his body, it had not impacted his mind, or his heart. Ali had taken the opportunity to write a letter to the Many and One Coalition in support of the rally and to support peace, justice, and equality for all people. The letter was read to a crowd that knew his connection to Lewiston and listened to his words of support for the Somali community: "'Somali immigrants, like any Americans, have the unalienable right to live anywhere in the United States that they chose... Moreover, they have the responsibility to raise their children in cities and villages that are clean and safe.'"[1442]

Another very compelling and touching moment involved the speech given by Fred Fields, brother of Staff Sergeant Thomas Field who grew up in Lisbon, Maine and was killed in Mogadishu as part of Operation Gothic Serpent, also referred to as the "black hawk down" incident. I had my share of conversations with people who would bring up the incident, suggesting that the death of SSgt. Field was the reason that they rejected the presence of Somalis in the area. Fred Field's willingness to speak at the rally and to welcome "the Somali newcomers" was intended to let the people that spoke to me, and the Somali community, know that "he hoped his words would inspire (the Somalis) to make a good life for themselves (in Lewiston and in Maine)."[1443]

I believe that Fred Field's speech at the Many and One rally had a profound impact on people that extended well beyond the walls of the Merrill field house. I am also certain that since the Many and One rally, I never had another discussion with someone who rejected Somalis or Muslims living in Lewiston because of what happened to SSgt. Field.

When the rally ended, attendees were asked to participate in a symbolic half-mile march of solidarity that would end at the nearby Lewiston Armory. It was getting colder outside, and Bennett and Welch would be arriving as marchers exited the building.

### Hate Has its Say

The WCOTC meeting inside the culinary arts building moved along as planned and was unaffected by the chanting, shouting and banging that was happening outside of the building. Much of what people like David Stearns said was incendiary, racist, and intolerant, although none of it surprised anyone inside the meeting. Stearns declared that the Somalis "'are the enemy—make no mistake... If they get a chance they will probably slit your throat,'" and that they were not bringing "'anything good into our community.'" He also accused the Jews of "'(b)ringing in the Somali immigrants'" as part of a plan to "'divide and conquer... (t)hat's why we are in here and there are demonstrators out there.'"[1444]

Fox attempted to build a more civil picture of the WCOTC, saying that he did not want his children "'to hate someone('s)'" color and to "'love themselves and their race.'" He also explained that their "church" abided by their four principals of "'sound mind, sound body, sound society, and sound environment.'" Fox went on to describe how the WCOTC encouraged living "in small, single-race communities" with self-sustaining farms and eschewing illegal drugs, including pharmaceuticals, because they were provided by "'Jewish doctors.'"[1445]

Fox was told by the Lewiston police in the meeting to "wrap it up by 2:45 (PM)." Welch anticipated that because the crowd outside knew about the scheduled 3:00 ending time, the "protestors would get anxious as the hour approached."[1446] Welch wanted the WCOTC on the road before the protestors could assemble and attempt to confront or block the WCOTCs exit from the building or the area.

Just before 2:45, the officers in the meeting room "gave Fox his five-minute warning" that the meeting would end when one of the white vans that had transported them to the meeting parked itself at the front door of the the meeting room, in plain sight of the crowd. What the protestors did not understand was that any one of the two white vans used to transport the WCOTC delegation from Auburn were large enough to hold Fox's entire group. As "(p)rotestors watched the empty van (parked at the front door)... the white supremacists left through the back door,"[1447] leaving the crowd outside the culinary arts building unaware that the white van parked at the front door was a decoy, allowing the other van to exit the back of the building undetected.

Just as the van left the cafeteria building, "Bennett bit into a whoopie pie as a soft voice came through Welch's earpiece: 'Elvis has left the building,'" confirming that the Fox group had left the guard complex and was on its way back to Auburn.[1448]

Welch told me that they had a "decoy (van) in mind" at some point before the WCOTC meeting. Bill also stated that police did not know how many WCOTC members would be joining Fox[1449] for the meeting at the national guard facility, but both he and Bennett had long forgotten McGonagle's statement to Welch that Fox said he believed as many as 30 WCOTC members could be joining him in Lewiston.

It was very possible that McGonagle took Fox's WCOTC attendance estimate into account when he rented the vans for the Fox group. Welch also noted that they had "other plain vehicles available for multiple uses such as relief vehicles for people on assigned posts"[1450] or something like the Fox group being larger than Fox's estimate. They had built the operations plan with enough flexibility and capacity to handle many unplanned events. We were all grateful that there were very few unplanned events that required a planned, or worse yet, an unplanned response.

Chief Welch's decoy idea worked flawlessly. The opportunity for the van and its WCOTC occupants to leave from the back of the building, allowed the van to exit undetected by the crowd and proceed down Alfred Plourde Parkway away from the crowds near Exit 13. That also allowed the van to use the "back roads" into Auburn and return the WCOTC group back to the Exit 12 park-and-ride lot.[1451] The police officers that brought the group to the park-and-ride lot would also ensure that they were back on the Maine Turnpike heading south towards the Maine border (and likely tracked by state police to ensure no detours were involved).

The other meeting participants that had not traveled with the Fox delegation waited "inside the hall until the demonstration outside dispersed." When police finally went outside to advise the few remaining protestors that the WCOTC participants had vacated the premises, some protestors "demanded proof" that they were no longer in the building. The police brought one protestor into the room to show him that no one was in the building except for a "few reporters and photographers." The man returned to the protestors that remained outside to let them know that the WCOTC participants were no longer in the building or the area.[1452]

For Jim and Bill, the day was not quite over just yet. There was still some concern that the white supremacist sympathizers, their opponents, or both could end up downtown, away from the areas where most of the law enforcement were deployed. "A police team was waiting at the police station" but they were never needed. With the WCOTC now gone and the crowd thinning, Jim and Bill made their way back to the Merrill gym in time to see the beginning of the Many and One march.[1453] I would stay behind until we were ready to shut down the command post.

**A Peaceful Ending**

Mark Schlotterbeck had shared his plan to march with Chief Welch. According to Schlotterbeck, Bill was not pleased that Mark would move what they expected to be several thousand people through the streets of Lewiston. Mark stated that Chief Welch told him that he would be the "first person" Welch would arrest if the crowd marched.[1454]

Welch commented that he did not "recall that conversation" with Schlotterbeck. Welch stated that he typically responded to marching situations as allowable "unless (the march) obstructed traffic or pedestrian flow or incited violence."[1455]

Welch and Bennett made their way to the front door as people were exiting the building. Bill and Jim were both still wearing their police jackets as people were leaving the building to take part in the march down Central Avenue. "Many people stopped to shake their hands" with one woman telling Welch "'(t)hank you. Thank you... I don't admire your work. But I thank you.'"[1456] It was a backhanded compliment, but Welch was probably glad to hear it as opposed to some attack on how police did or did not respond to their event, or to the Somali community.

Welch knew that Central Avenue was completely blocked off and that no action would be needed unless the marchers ventured beyond the public works trucks blocking the intersection. In the end, the brutally cold weather, which was going to become colder as sundown approached, convinced marchers to make it a short walk. The blocked-off portion of Central Avenue,[1457] between the Merrill gym and the Lewiston Armory, easily handled the sizeable crowd exiting Merrill. The combination of the cold, and the city's and Many and One's preparation, delivered everyone a safe event at Merrill and the post-event march. The day would end as a violence-free, celebratory gathering that was part of an incredibly well organized and successful event for participants, residents, law enforcement, city staff, and elected officials.

When I finally arrived at Bates, the march was over and Bates staff had already started cleaning up the field house and putting the chairs and other things away. With students back on campus, staff needed to return the building to a normal, functioning field house and gymnasium. Bill was looking for and finally located Lt. Pratt in the field house congratulating him on a job well done while also acknowledging that "'(e)verybody did a great job.'"[1458] Jim was spending some time with reporters during an impromptu press conference. Afterwards, I congratulated both of them for an incredibly successful day. Welch asked Bennett "'(a)ll right, are we out of here?'" to which Bennett replied to Welch "'(y)es, we are...(n)ice freaking job, big guy.'"[1459]

Before heading home, I went down to my office at City Hall to do one last check of my emails and voicemails to see what had come in since Friday. The entrance used by city administration staff and most employees was the Park Street side-entrance of the building. Downtown seemed empty, but as I made the left off Ash Street and came up to the Park Street intersection where City Hall is located, I could see one lone person standing on the stairs of City Hall and speaking. I saw a few other people I thought may have been with the speaker or might have been listening to what he said. What I saw piqued my curiosity and a desire to speak with him as I entered the City Hall's side entrance. I went into my office to check messages and emails, and then headed up the stairs to the main entrance on Pine Street and opened the door. I did not know who this young man was, but he stopped speaking for a moment and turned around in reaction to my opening the door.

It turned out to be Ismail Ahmed. In our interview, I told Ismail that I believed this was our first encounter. He agreed. Ismail also shared in the interview that although he had separated himself from the Many and One volunteer group, he did attend the rally at the Merrill gym. While no longer a Many and One member, he and a group of fellow Bates and L-A College activists had created a group called "The Bates Takeover Now," a reflection of their belief that Many and One had been "taken over" by "outsiders." Once the rally finished, he had decided to go down to City Hall because he was "not going to be derailed from" his personal agenda and wanted to "hold Raymond accountable" for what he said in the letter.[1460]

During our interview, I also told Ismail that I remembered him speaking to what appeared to be very few people. I believed at the time that he was speaking as a representative of Omar Jamal's Minneapolis based Somali Justice Advocacy Center. I had read years ago that he was identified as one of Jamal's members in an out-of-state paper. Ahmed shared in the interview that, for the most part, he was speaking for himself and was addressing "no one" that day except for a few people from the press. Ismail also stated emphatically that he was never a member of Jamal's organization, saying that he met him briefly when Jamal had come to Lewiston. Not only was Ismail never a member, he said that he had concluded "within two minutes" into their discussion that Jamal was "full of BS" and that he was not "here for the (Somalis)" but only "for the limelight."[1461]

What Ismail and I did not know when we met on that very cold January day in 2003, was that we would meet again at City Hall, and he would be an employee of the Portland-Lewiston refugee collaborative located on the third floor of City Hall, working to assist Somali and other immigrants who had relocated to Lewiston.

## A Little Luck

The Many and One Rally for us represented a significant moment in our city's history. This amazing team effort involving the Many and One Coalition, over 100 city employees (police and non-police staff), many local organizations, law enforcement agencies, and other state and federal agencies was an extraordinary achievement. As the leaders of this historical city event, Police Chief William "Bill" Welch and City Administrator James "Jim" Bennett deservedly received accolades from law enforcement around New England for the outcome both at the national guard armory and the Merrill facility on the Bates College campus.

As for the national news media and their voracious appetite for a story, the day of the Lewiston rally and WCOTC meeting would not produce any national news broadcast or generate any front-page headlines in newspapers. A single arrest, the absence of violence, and the preponderance of peaceful and civil behavior were not enough to hold their attention. There was little to no coverage by most of the national television media after the rally ended. I distinctly remember watching CNN when I returned home, as they were running a simple single news banner at the bottom of the screen mentioning the coalition rally and the WCOTC crowds, and possibly the single arrest that had taken place at the WCOTC event. CNN Headline News ran a story about the Many and One event only after other stories involving pardons of "death row inmates," "troop deployments," and "Iraq's reaction to them."[1462]

The paucity of national news media coverage was precisely what we wanted that day, and what we would have preferred from the very beginning of the publication of the mayor's letter. Great planning, collaboration, teamwork, love of community, unity of purpose, and some luck played into the results. The weather (and possibly the threat of a light "rain" from a fire hose[1463]) had helped to keep the outdoor crowd at Exit 13 a bit more civil and less aggressive. Matt Hale being arrested in Chicago three days earlier also turned out to be a useful development. Jon Fox was there to carry his message, but Matt Hale was the charismatic leader with the ability to 'fire up' the troops.

Bill Welch shared with me in his interview that even with all the meticulous planning, collaboration, and effort, the city was fortunate to only see "one silly arrest" during the entire day. The Many and One Coalition's efforts and the work by the city to host two potentially volatile events on the same day could have produced a very different outcome. Chief Welch was right in his summation of that incredible day, stating, "We were lucky, there (was) no question about that."[1464]

Jim, Bill, me, most public works personnel, local police staff, and others would be able to make it for the "second half of the second game" that day. Bennett would not only be able to get back to the house for some football—he would also have the opportunity to congratulate his son regarding his Pinewood

Derby race. Even with one "out of balance" wheel, Jim remembered that his son either won, or came in second.[1465] I'm uncertain if the derby race or the outcome of the day's events made Jim happier that day, but I am certain that his young son believed it was the former.

## The Fadeaway, Larry Stays, The Catalyst, and the Closer

I slept much better that evening following the Many and One rally. I would not be surprised if most of the people who had worked on producing that day's results had also slept more peacefully and planned to use Sunday as a decompression day. I know I did.

The national news media coverage produced few if any front-page stories that I could remember or locate in my research. The Boston Globe's piece titled "White Supremacy Rally Draws Few in Maine City" found its way below the fold in the City & Religion section of their Sunday, January 12, 2003 edition. Ann Kim's Associated Press piece about the rally titled "Thousands Rally for Diversity in Maine" was in the "Nation" section of "The Missoulian('s)" January 12th edition on page A12. I also do not remember seeing a single story during that Sunday on any of the television news media networks.

Although Scott Taylor's article "Media Frenzy Fades" only described what happened with the limited televised national news coverage on January 11th, it forecasted what would happen with national news interest in the story for months to come. In the absence of any violence or conflict that came out of the event, the peaceful results and the story of the Somali's arrival in Lewiston no longer held their interest. In the minds of the national television news industry, Lewiston's successful day no longer deserved any more 'A Block' [1466] coverage from their network. For those in the national print media, there would be no more stories 'above the fold.'

That did not mean that national news media would completely ignore the story forever, but it meant that the intensity of the coverage would evolve into periodic 'check-ins' on what was going on in our city. Between 2003 and 2010, the only year a national news organization or national publication did not interview me was 2007. However, the Sun Journal published an Associated Press story in May 2007[1467] following an incident[1468] involving a Somali student in the middle school.[1469] Some of the television news networks also covered the incident. National and international coverage regarding the immigrant population would continue through 2020.[1470]

As for our local or state papers and regional television networks, the interest would decrease, but not disappear completely. For both the Somalis and many city officials and community organizations, it would be an unfamiliar environment to work in without the glare and intensity of television and print news journalists wanting to cover every word and every movement we were engaged in throughout the day.

For the Many and One, state agencies, non-profits, and city and school department staff, we all could now focus on what was most important: to continue building on those things that were revealed and discussed publicly through the events leading up to and including January 11th. We had much to celebrate, but we knew that there was much work ahead that needed our immediate attention.

### The Post-Rally Reactions

The mayor and city council would continue to be confronted with local and state news media pressing them for reactions to the post-rally public calls for the mayor's resignation. The Sun Journal ran a story on January 15th with Scott Taylor's interviews with city councilors, who all rejected the suggestion that the mayor resign (see United Against Hate sub-chapter for council reactions).[1471]

In that same Sun Journal edition, Taylor also interviewed community leaders on the matter of Raymond resigning. The leaders included former mayor John Jenkins, former city councilor James Carignan, chamber president Chip Morrison, and former Lewiston mayor Jim Howaniec. Taylor found no support for Raymond to resign from the twin-city leaders, but many qualified their support for Larry to remain as mayor.[1472]

Jenkins believed that the mayor's role in how the community responded to his letter required an "'explanation to the community'" saying that because "'his words helped to fray'" the community, his words might also "'mend and reweave it.'" Jenkins was "'looking to (Raymond) for leadership. He's the one in a position to begin fixing things.'" Carignan spoke to the mayor's absence from the rally and thought that the community was "troubled" by his decision not to attend. Jim saw the decision to leave the state as a "'missed (opportunity) for leadership.'"[1473]

Although Chip Morrison did not feel that he was in a position to judge Raymond about his decision not to be at the field house, he believed Raymond had "been a good leader of the community" and had "'worked for the community, as hard as anybody else.'" Even so, Morrison reflected that from his "'situation,'" being absent from the rally was "'not a decision I would have made.'" Former mayor Howaniec was a bit more direct about the mayor saying that he was "'dismayed by his letter and his subsequent bogus defenses of his position.'" Howaniec said that if Raymond had attended the rally, "'he could have been booed or whatever, made a speech, outlined a plan to move forward, and we could have put this whole thing behind us.'"[1474]

Journalist Mark LaFlamme also did a similar article involving the opinions of some 25 area residents in the January 15th Sun Journal. LaFlamme's informal poll reflected that 10 of the 25 people he interviewed supported Raymond's resignation, while 5 did not. Others had opinions on what he should have done, or not have done, others "did not care," and some had no opinion. Several people did not know much about the situation or had strong opinions but did not want them in the newspaper.[1475]

Raymond weighed in regarding the ongoing controversy of his resignation in a January 18th interview with his favorite Sun Journal journalist Doug Fletcher. It would be the last in-depth interview about resigning, the rally, Florida, his decision not to apologize for the letter, and his relationship with the Somali community. Larry told Fletcher that he had "'plans to resign'" from his position as mayor. He noted that there was work that needed attention, including a "meeting soon with Somali elders" identifying that it would likely involve the same Somali delegation he met with on October 11th in his office and referring to them as "'reasonable people.'" It was Larry's hope that he and the delegation would "'find a middle ground of understanding'" and that he thought they could "'find a solution'" together.[1476]

Mayor Raymond also defended his decision to be absent from the rally, stating that he did not want to "be a lightning rod for racists who Raymond maintain(ed) misread the intent of his

October letter.'" He was also concerned that his presence at the rally might have been disruptive because they were "'unable to accept the reasonableness'" of what he had written in his letter. Raymond said that he respected the hard work of Schlotterbeck and the Many and One organization to organize a successful rally, and the local residents "'who felt that they had to join the Bates event,'" but also wished that all of them would "'respect my decision not to attend'" along with respecting the "'95-percent-plus'" of Lewiston citizens who "'followed'" his instructions not to attend. Raymond saw his leadership approach as someone who built "'consensus,'" not someone who made speeches or had a "'flamboyant'" style like "JFK."[1477]

Raymond would make his last public statement on the issue on February 5, 2003 in an interview with Scott Taylor. Taylor would be the first journalist in the country to break the Raymond story in the Sun Journal, and he would be the last reporter to get a public statement about the Somali story. He spoke with Raymond mayor before the February 4th council meeting, and after his confrontation with a television reporter in the city council chambers. He would tell Taylor that "'(t)he past is the past, and I'm done talking about (anything involving the last several months).'" Larry wanted to get the episode behind him, adding that everyone he talked to wanted to do the same while also blaming "'a few folks, and the media'" for keeping the story alive. He declared that he would "'not be making any more statements about the past.'"[1478]

What Taylor's article did not mention was how one of the television stations did a "60 Minutes" style news media ambush during that February 4th council meeting. When Larry walked behind the council dais to take his seat, the reporter and camera operator sprang off their seats. They both rushed up to the city council dais, simultaneously turning on the camera light while the reporter thrusted his microphone in front of Raymond as he was about to take his seat. The reporter demanded that he make a statement about public calls for his resignation.

Raymond became visibly upset and shut them down by exclaiming "'(t)hat's it. Out of here'" and sending them to the back of the room so he could start the meeting.[1479]

I was so incensed by the reporter's actions that I asked him to come into the hall so I could speak with him privately. I told him I was appalled by this kind of behavior by a Maine television news station. I had never observed this kind of "ambush journalism" before and told him that if he ever did that again, I would tell the station they would have to send another reporter to cover anything at City Hall. If they did not, the news station would not get an interview from any City Hall employee for anything being covered by other news media. He challenged me to go on air and to repeat what I told him. I replied by telling him I would be happy to do so, and that I was certain his station would enjoy having me criticize him and his station on air for embracing the station's new journalism tactics for covering a story.

The reporter, who clearly saw that I was prepared to go on camera with him, decided not to interview me and also elected not to cover the other story that evening. It would involve the city council's approval to support our hockey arena's efforts to bring big-time, semi-professional hockey to our city. This was a major story that was covered by the other TV news stations. It was clear to me that this was the reporter's way of putting me in my place. In return, I called the station the next day to tell the news director about the incident. I also told the news director how disturbing it was to see one of our state's television news station adopting this kind of ambush journalism. The director did not apologize for his reporter's behavior, but I did share with him I preferred they not send him to City Hall to cover another story.

Raymond would never again speak publicly about the letter or anything else regarding the Somali community and related events between October 2002 and February 2003. As for the reporter, I heard the following week that he had been assigned to go to the hockey arena to interview the owner of the facility about the new team that was coming to Lewiston. That reporter never covered another story in Lewiston. He left the station sometime later in 2003.

On Martin Luther King's federal holiday, Sun Journal editorial writer Judy Meyer wrote that "(w)hatever Mayor Larry Raymond may be, he is not a racist" and saw him as a "reputable man" who did not anticipate the "wave and pain and confusion" his letter would produce. In Meyer's opinion, Raymond's resignation "would split this city and that's not what (the city) need(ed)." Judy added that the Sun Journal believed what the city needed was

> to continue the conversation the mayor's letter launched and work to build a city of welcome, with robust culture and a healthy economy. The foundation for our future was established at the Many and One Coalition rally, and we cannot turn back. We—from Lewiston and from away—stood in solidarity, acknowledging that our shared destinies are, as King observed, 'inextricably bound to our freedom... This is our city and we can't let others mold our future. We have to do it ourselves."[1480]

### The Catalyst for Change

I had often said publicly that I would not offer my opinion about Raymond's letter. I did say publicly that I believed his letter to the Somali community had produced unanticipated results that proved beneficial in that it became a catalyst for positive change, community action, and activism. I also shared in this book, that at the time Raymond wrote the letter, our relationship had been impacted by the January 22nd incident between us during a city council meeting. I offered him my honest appraisal of the letter but had the January incident never happened, I would likely have suggested that Raymond speak to the Somali community about his concerns before issuing the letter. If those discussions did not produce the outcome he desired, he could then write and release the letter. It is one of those moments I would love to relive, and one of those regrets that will remain with me for a lifetime.

My opinion about Raymond's letter serving as a catalyst for change has not been universally accepted by everyone. The defense for my hypothesis about the letter serving as a catalyst for change has much to do with my observations of what was happening publicly before October 2002. Prior to the mayor's letter, there were a number of organizations like the City Administrator's Office, Lewiston's General Assistance Office, the Lewiston Police Department, the governor's office, the state attorney general's office, state agencies like the Department of Health and Human Services, the State Refugee Coordinator Office, the Department of Labor, and organizations such as St. Mary's Regional Medical Center, Catholic Charities Maine, Trinity Jubilee Center, Daryeelka, United Somali Women of Maine, the Franco American Heritage Center, Lots to Gardens, Americorps, and many others that were directly involved in working with and assisting the Somali community before the mayor's letter.

Outside of the universe of organizations that included City Hall, there were likely conversations and activities going on in other local agencies, non-profits, local colleges and local schools. Regrettably, the effort to turn any of those organizational conversations and activities into large scale public actions and collaborative efforts were not visible to me, or the many organizations that were working with City Hall.

That all changed with the mayor's letter. What became a local and regional movement through Many and One did not require some high-public-profile, violent altercation or conflict between individuals or groups. There is no dispute that the letter became divisive, generated its share of fear, raised concerns for people's safety and welfare costs, and generated questions about what defined racism and how people felt about inclusivity and immigration. However, I submit that the letter also brought people together and raised awareness within City Hall, multiple local and state organizations, and the community about what was missing to produce a coordinated and direct community response. The letter also made it clear that after the public rally was concluded, as Meyer said in her editorial, the resulting community action produced by Larry's letter would now mean that those "conversations" producing the Many and One Coalition, and the rally, would need to continue if we were to be successful as a community.

I also would often speak about the letter and its impact as a catalyst while also sharing the story of what happened in the city of Minneapolis. This wonderful city had its own moment of truth and awakening at Roosevelt High School, and it would involve their Somali population, but the "conversations" and community action that are so necessary in helping to avoid a crisis, would only happen after some people were injured, and their "catalyst" for change would all happen the day before the 9/11 attacks in September 2001.

**Roosevelt High School**

I was fortunate to be in professions that would permit me to travel around the country. As a member of the International City Managers Association, USA Volleyball, and the Professional Association of Volleyball Officials (who certified officials for NCAA women's volleyball), I had the pleasure of traveling to Minneapolis some six different times for events associated with one profession or the other.

In 2003, the USA Open National Volleyball Championships were in Minneapolis, and I was there to work for the week. I built some extra time into my schedule to meet with city, school, and county officials. Some of those stops would include the Confederation of Somali Community(sic), Roosevelt High School, the Hennepin County Office of Multi-Cultural Services, and the City of Minneapolis Multi-Cultural Services Office. In my 2003 report to Victoria Scott, the Immigrant-Refugee Programs Manager for the city of Lewiston, I spoke about my trip with a focus on my time with a few of the agencies, like the Confederation of Somali Community, which had its office at the Brian Coyle Center in one of the six Pillsbury (as in Pillsbury flour) United Community centers located around the city.[1481]

The Coyle center was in the "Cedar Street neighborhood" that was "one of the more heavily populated (Somali) neighborhoods in Minneapolis." The city's total population was approximately 400,000 at the time, and the Somali population in Hennepin County (Minneapolis is the county seat) was about 40,000 people, the majority living in Minneapolis. The Somalis were not the largest immigrant group in the county. That distinction belonged to the Hispanic community that numbered 50,000 to 60,000 people "(or about 32% of the state's total.)" The Hmong population came in at second. The Coyle center was blessed to have the support of the Pillsbury corporation that

421

provided (for a nominal fee) office space, and if needed, information technology and administrative support for these six centers. That support permitted the Confederation of Somali Communities to focus on their mission, which included "elder intervention... employment, ESL, leadership (and) skill development, housing placement" and much more.[1482]

The Confederation of Somali Community operated under "the guidance of Executive Director Saeed Fahia." Mr. Fahia was an impressive individual and incredibly proud of his organization. He had reason to be. They had started operations back in 1994[1483] and struggled through their early years. Mr. Fahia credited the support and assistance he had received from the Pillsbury funded Coyle center as one factor that helped them stabilize their organization and focus on their mission.[1484]

I was envious. I wondered how much more productive our local community non-profits could be with this kind of corporate support and vision? At the same time, I also had great pride in much of what our city had accomplished without a Fortune 500 corporate headquarters in our community. I often said because we were not a community of great wealth, the only path to success for our community was for everyone to collaborate and outwork everybody else. We all saw what our community could do when we turned back hate. It was hard to believe that we could not direct that energy into a focused community-based effort to improve our overall quality of life as well.

After my meeting with Mr. Fahia, I went over to meet members of the school staff at Roosevelt High School. It was perhaps the most moving and emotional part of the trip. Students were still in session, and they gave me the opportunity to walk around the school with some of the staff. They shared some information with me about their school, something that I shared in my 2003 city report:

> Roosevelt in not the city's largest high school (but) it is one of its most culturally diverse... At Roosevelt, some 50 or more languages (and) dialects are spoken. The staff... clearly understands that this very ethnically, culturally (and) linguistically diverse population in the school is both a

blessing (and) a significant challenge. (The) school possesses wonderful, creative (and) imaginative kids who face the difficulties associate(d) with living in some of the poorest areas of the city. Approximately 75% of the kids live in families that are at or below the federal poverty guidelines in a school that has approximately 35% of its students enrolled in ELL programs (city wide, the numbers are around 21%).

The staff also shared a story that had a significant impact on how they were working on student relations and programming in the school. The story revealed how one incident could have such a profound effect on what they were doing in May 2003. On Monday, September 10, 2001, the day before the 9/11 attacks in New York, Washington D.C., and Pennsylvania, a Roosevelt football coach and a student football player were stabbed in a school bus waiting area for high school students. The football coach was attempting to break up a fight between a group of Somali and African American students when the stabbing occurred. The investigation revealed that the student who stabbed both individuals was Somali.[1485] The student who was stabbed was African American.[1486]

The football player was in "serious condition" in a local hospital on Tuesday, September 11th and police stationed "extra security" in the high school that day (most likely in response to both the stabbings and that morning's terrorist attacks). Police investigators reported that "tensions between Somali and African-American students prompted the fight." The day after the stabbing, the gentleman that I had met in Minneapolis earlier that day during my 2003 trip, Saeed Fahia, commented to the (Minneapolis) Star Tribune on September 12th, that he was "'really saddened about what happened'" at the high school. Fahia also shared that before the stabbings, he took part in meetings between African American and Somali students to discuss their differences.[1487]

The Minneapolis Urban League also weighed in on the story saying that if the altercation between the students resulted from "racial or cultural differences," it made the "stabbings even more troubling." The urban league's president Clarence Hightower also added that the stabbings should not lead people to think that there was a "'huge rift between the African-American and Somali communities'" as he believed it was "'not the case.'"[1488]

Even with the terrorist actions that had taken place that morning, the Roosevelt High School Somali Student Association met with administrators and the school principal, who "agreed to work with other Roosevelt students to promote positive ties." Other steps were taken on Tuesday by "African-American students, peer mediators and a unity group" who all worked on a plan to make Roosevelt a safer place for students and staff. The plan would involve not assigning blame for the stabbing against anyone; promoting a positive narrative about their Tuesday meeting; and speaking positively to anyone speaking negatively. The reaction to the plan was positive, with some students vowing to "'work hard to voice positiveness(sic).'"[1489]

During my visit, it was not surprising for me to hear that the school was in "chaos" for the first few days after the stabbing. Here they were, dealing with this tragic and potentially volatile stabbing incident, while also dealing with the fallout and anxiety of the 9/11 attacks in a large urban center like Minneapolis with the largest population of Somali Muslims in the country.[1490] In response to both events on Tuesday, "social workers circulated throughout the school to make themselves available to whoever wanted to talk, either about the stabbing or (that day's) terrorist attacks."[1491]

The school took additional steps, including not letting the football and soccer teams "hang around the school after practice," and giving out transit bus passes to students involved in other after-school activities in place of waiting for the school bus. Although the school and students were working together and doing many things to respond to all that happened during those first two days, parents remained concerned with the safety of their kids. Some students also felt unsafe in school while others felt safer in class than they did "out in the streets."[1492]

In 2002, as part of the one-year anniversary of the 9/11 attacks and the stabbing in their high school, "more than a thousand (Roosevelt students)... joined hands in a circle around the football field to show their unity. Speakers of different ethnic groups talked about the need for peace." That morning, signs were hung on the school's fencing with "phrases such as 'United We Stand'" while students and staff reflected on what had happened just a year prior. One student fittingly described the one-year anniversary this way: "'It's somewhat sad to say it now, but in order for me to realize how wrong I was (about the significance of peace), it took a massive attack on the heart of our nation and a stabbing in my community (to better understand its significance).'"[1493]

In the eyes of the staff I met in 2003, they saw tangible and beneficial progress being made since the stabbing incident. They expressed what one of their students shared on the one-year anniversary: that the progress with student relations they had observed through 2003, had much to do with the events of those first two days in September 2001, and a student body and community that committed themselves to becoming more involved. Although "cafeteria territoriality" continued to exist in 2003, the staff could see the kind of "interaction between ethnic groups" that had been "largely non-existent in the past." With "drop-out rates, bilingualism, drug abuse, family violence" remaining a constant concern, "I sensed that the staff was very optimistic about the progress that (had) been made" and believed that it would continue.[1494]

I felt back in 2003 that Minneapolis and our city were fortunate. I still feel that way. Thankfully, our wake-up call was not an act of violence, which could have produced more tragic outcomes. What happened in our community was driven by a letter written by our mayor. Fortunately, through the pain and public discussions came hope and a community commitment to action.

Judy Meyer said it best: "(O)ur future was established at the Many and One Coalition rally" and a newly energized level of community activism that would become an important part of the city's trajectory over the next 18 years.

### Raymond's Legacy

In Raymond's October 12, 2002 interview with Doug Fletcher, much of the journalist's focus was spent on having Raymond explain why he wrote the letter, what he was trying to convey, and why he would never apologize for writing what he said. Raymond had written about the city's fiscal condition being challenged, about the pressure it was placing on city staff to keep up with a mushrooming population, and that many of his constituents were concerned for all of those reasons about Somali arrivals. Raymond "regretted" that his letter had been "misunderstood" and "misinterpreted" but would not apologize for writing about something that he believed needed to be said.[1495]

On the evening following the meeting with the Somali elders, Larry Raymond also told Doug Fletcher that he hoped that he "'wouldn't want to be remembered for this.'"[1496] Larry most likely understood that how someone is "remembered" is not easily controlled, by anyone. Raymond had been a wonderful family man with a large social network, a successful attorney that built a well-known and respected legal firm, a well-connected political operative, a public servant with a spotless career as a county attorney and probate judge, and heavily involved in community organizations for decades.

Legacies for those in public service are most often influenced by the sum total of those experiences. They can also be influenced, fairly or unfairly, by a single act. Larry would only serve as mayor for two years and he hoped his service would be "remembered for bringing positive growth... progress, and investment to the city." The reality was that his accomplishments would now have to compete with a letter that took on a life of its own and became an international story. I would likely have never published this book had Larry's mayoral career been "remembered" as he desired and did not include the letter. It is only because of his missive that I know much more about Larry's family, his public service, and how the people closest to Larry saw him and reflected on his life. I would have never known that Mark Schlotterbeck came to know him as "a kind and genuine person" had Larry not written the letter.

What is certain after all the interviews, all the research, and some time to reflect on this book, is that I will not remember Larry only for writing the letter. I also will not only remember Franklin D. Roosevelt for ordering the internment of some 112,000 Japanese residents, approximately 70,000 of them U.S. citizens, during World War II,[1497] or refusing 937 Jews on the SS

St. Louis entry into the U.S. in 1939.[1498] What is also certain is that I will also continue to leave the matter of Laurier T. Raymond Jr.'s and Roosevelt's legacy for others to determine for themselves.

## Raymond's Building and the New Mosque

By late 2002, the Somali community was not only dealing with the fallout from the mayor's letter; they were also a growing community in need of a new building for their place of worship. The Al-Noor Mosque was located at 253 Lisbon Street, in what used to be a small restaurant. It had become too small to support a growing congregation.

The Somali mosque leadership began their search for a building and finally determined that the property that was most affordable and provided the best location for their new mosque was a few blocks away at 23 Lisbon Street.[1499] They also discovered their preferred location was owned by someone named Laurier (Larry) Raymond, Jr.,[1500] who they knew was also the mayor that had written the now infamous letter to their community.

There are no first-hand accounts of the negotiation details, but there was an agreement reached by the mosque leadership and Mayor Raymond to purchase the building. The 2003 agreement between the mosque leaders and Raymond stipulated that they pay the mayor "$50,000 upfront" and then pay an unspecified number of installments totaling "$70,000." Raymond had agreed to structure a purchase agreement that would not include interest fees in the payment,[1501] something that may have been the primary reason for the transaction's success as "Islamic law forbids paying or charging interest on loans."[1502]

The Al-Noor Mosque finished paying the installments in early 2005 and took possession of their new property that continues to serve some of the Somali community to this day. Another mosque was started in another part of the city several years later.

# Chapter 10

## Progress, Peaks, Valleys, and the Unexpected

## March 2003 – December 2020

*March 2003 – 2008*

Our history and the city of Lewiston's ability to forge fresh paths associated with change, in my opinion, had much to do with our community's response to the first waves of immigrants who helped build the most formidable industrial economy in Maine; how those immigrants progressed and grew economically and politically; and the determination of the immigrants and their offspring to affect the transition out of a declining industrial economy. Through the resilience and self-determination of the elected officials and residents who often worked to work together, they changed the economy and the direction of the city at a time when a new wave of immigrants would provide the stimulus needed for a declining population.

This book hopefully demonstrated that it is the arrival of immigrants in the 1800s that built one economy, and their future generations who would contribute the transition into another. Each of those economic transformations involved numerous new people coming into the city, along with new religions, cultures, and ethnicities. In small cities and towns like ours, that kind of change almost always encounters some level of resistance.

Change, particularly ethnic, cultural, and religious change, is rarely easy. When it involves people of color in communities with little diversity, it is almost always more challenging.

This book also spoke to how rapid increases that occurred over a short period of time made the Somali arrivals different. It was unlike anything that many in the refugee resettlement profession and the news media had ever seen anywhere else in the country. Some scholars identify this kind of large and sudden change of ethnicity in a community as 'rapid ethnic diversification.' I often said that our 2001-2002 experience with the unplanned and self-driven relocation of secondary migrants made us the 'poster child' for that kind of sudden ethnic change in a U.S. community. To this day, there is no record of another community in the U.S. having experienced this kind of rapid relocation of secondary migrant. What made this secondary migrant relocation different from all others was the absence of a prior refugee resettlement of that nationality, and the absence of an industry or company recruiting them in the same way the Francos were recruited by the textile mills back in the 19$^{th}$ century.

Lewiston had its share of challenges in responding to this latest large immigration into our community, but the city and the community persevered and re-wrote chapters about the way it could be done. Multiple academic institutions worked together, and individual residents and community action and activism assisted us with outreach. Additionally, state agencies worked with us in ways they had never collaborated with municipalities before; our city partnered with another city 30 miles away to create the first-in-the-nation case management program for secondary migrant refugees; and we then created another first-in-the-country partnership with a faith-based organization to provide refugee services with offices that were set up in City Hall.

Our city residents saw a community rise to the challenge, take action, and continue to evolve over the next 18 years after the Many and One rally. This chapter will review some of L-As most notable moments and people between 2003 and 2020, and will serve as an introduction to what will be covered in more depth in the sequel to this book.

## Post-Many and One Rally, Events, Initiatives, Programs, and the Endless List

For Many and One, they would not become a 'one-hit-wonder' with the success of the coalition's January 11th rally. They would remain a community action and activist organization for years. Not long after the Many and One rally, the organization became a non-profit organization and would pay off their financial obligations incurred with the January rally. That would include the $9,000 loan to the organization for the rally's liability insurance. [1503] Many and One also continued without Mark Schlotterbeck, who resigned from the organization in April 2003.[1504] Their growth eventually involved their participation in areas like "downtown affordable housing."[1505]

Victoria Scott's March 2003 report [1506] was filled with information about what was going on in the L-A area regarding immigrant activities around the community. One of these activities involved Bates College and its staff, many of whom would become a visible and important presence in assisting the immigrant community. During the event-planning stage of the Many and One and WCOTC events, Bates College staff began to plan the "Toward Harmony" conference that was held on campus on March 14-15, 2003. The city donated $500[1507] towards the event which included "(v)isiting lecturer in religion at Bates," and Professor Michael Caspi served as the "lead organizer." The conference "explore(d) the influx of Somalis to the area from myriad angles" which included "schools and social services, the historic view of immigration and the hate-crime phenomenon."[1508]

People outside of the area and the state also wanted to learn more about our refugee story. I was invited to the Loeb Drama Center at Harvard University on January 12, 2003, to participate in a panel discussion about the commonalities of the plight of refugees who arrive in the U.S., and those refugees in the 2,500 year-old Greek American Repertory Theater production "The Children of Herakles."[1509] This very unique play began with a panel discussion of people who would vary with each performance, typically composed of professionals associated with immigration services or policy, and people who arrived in the

U.S. as refugees. The evening's performance and panel discussion took place before a packed audience. It was also the evening I met Holyoke, Massachusetts Mayor Michael Sullivan, who opposed his city council's vote approving a resolution to not fund the Somali Bantu relocation.

In February, I joined other Maine panelists in Camden, Maine at the invitation of the "Camden Conference." The weekend event "included experts who represented a variety of state, national, and international perspectives on matters involving immigrants and immigration policy." The conference, in its 16th year, attracted a national and international audience. The 2003 conference theme "Two Worlds Under Pressure: The Growing Crises of Population and Movement" was timely, necessary, and coincidental given all that occurred in a community just 70 miles west of Camden.[1510]

I would not be the only one invited to speak outside of Lewiston. The "Peer Advisers student organization" of Waterville's Thomas College invited a group of unidentified students and adults from the Somali community. They billed the February 5th event as "Celebrating Somali Culture" featuring a presentation by "Somali junior and senior high school students" including "traditional and contemporary Somali dress, music and dance." It also included a panel discussion made up of Somali adults who spoke and entertained questions from the general public.[1511]

In March 2003, the city continued its partnership with Frank Amoroso and the DOJs Community Relations Division, who assisted us in setting up a series of "community dialogue" meetings over a two-month period. It was called "Lewiston Leads: Community Dialogue for Change" and was "intended to create an environment for an open and honest dialogue among area citizens." The purpose of the dialogues was to "develop policy, processes and ideas which foster and promote healthy community attitudes in a changing cultural and social environment."[1512]

Lewiston would also spend much of 2003 working more closely with: the Portland based Maine Refugee Advisory Council; the Refugee and Mental Health Collaborative; the Career Center; the Governor's Task Force on Immigration and Refugee Policy; Kirsten Walter's Lots to Gardens; Jim Hannah's NASAP

(New American Sustainable Agriculture Project); ECBOs such as Daryeelka, United Somali Women of Maine, Somali Community Justice; and a number of other organizations like Americorps, the Center for Workplace Learning, and Lewiston Adult Education. The Maine Humanities Council was also "assessing its programming to ensure that it is relevant to the concerns of Mainers in the 21$^{st}$ century" and whose January 31$^{st}$ meeting invitation list reflected that assessment goal. The meeting included people like: Fatuma Hussein, director of the new United Somali Women of Maine, Joan Macri, Teacher and Civil Rights Team Coach for Lewiston High School, and Victoria Scott, Lewiston's Immigrant and Refugee Programs Manager.[1513]

## The Maineiacs

The call from Raptor's owner Marc Just would come into my office on December 2, 2002 at the end of the business day. Just and ice hockey rink owner, Roger Theriault, had been talking about bringing his team to Lewiston and Just wanted to know what the city could do to help him. Roger had successfully owned the city's only hockey arena for some 15 or more years, but the kind of money that it would take to land the deal would require the city's involvement.

Jim Bennett and Lewiston Economic Development Director Greg Mitchell would handle the negotiations involving both arena owner Theriault and team owner Marc Just. Landing a Quebec Major Junior Hockey League team in Lewiston would be a significant achievement for the hockey community, for the city, and for the state. The team would be the only CHL (Canadian Hockey League) presence in New England and, at that time, the only QMJHL program in the U.S. The players in this 'major junior' program were considered to be semi-professional players by the NCAA and were not eligible for college play in the U.S. In 2003, the CHL produced most of the players who would eventually play in the professional National Hockey League.

The city council supported the terms of the deal in early 2003[1514] that would include the city's guaranteed $2.2 million loan and tax incentives package which helped Theriault to sign the agreement with team. Just would move his team to Lewiston who would become the "Lewiston Maineiacs" and play their first game in the fall of 2003. The team would win a QMJHL championship in 2007.

## L-A Leads

Lewiston-Auburn was "at the top of the state's business development list for 2002" and ranked second in job creation and "actual dollars invested." Economic Development Director Greg Mitchell said "the last 10 years," represented the "best economic times" the area had experienced. The entire state was doing well. "Maine's economic indicators" had remained "more positive than New England as a whole" according to the state's business development director Jim Nimon. What was notable was that of the 12 major projects that had propelled the twin cities to the top of the state's rankings, only "two were expansions of existing businesses."[1515] There would be more ahead for Lewiston and Auburn.

## The Heritage Initiative and the Visible Community

On June 10, 2004, the city council approved "an ambitious plan to revive about 30 blocks of the city's poorest neighborhood(s)" that would be included in the "Heritage Initiative."[1516] The 10-year initiative would include a downtown revitalization undertaking called the "Southern Gateway"[1517] project, which was announced in May 2003. It would attract $30 million in new investments into one of the primary gateways into downtown Lewiston.

One of the major features of the Heritage plan was a new median-divided, two to four-lane boulevard. The city would integrate the road into some existing roads and create a new entrance and exit for downtown traffic. The $2.5 million dollar boulevard would need $1 to $2 million dollars for property acquisition to create a more direct route for people traveling to and from Main Street (Route 202), the busiest street in the city. It would also provide a direct route for people coming into the city from the Maine Turnpike and bound for the hockey arena and its new Lewiston Maineiacs semi-professional hockey team.

The Heritage Initiative was being introduced at a time when there had already been approximately $10 million dollars in new housing introduced to the area. On November 11, 2004, approximately 100 Bates College students would sleep in outdoor tents on campus to protest the city's lack of resident involvement. Bates sophomore Ben Chin estimated the boulevard project would displace approximately 850 people who "would stand to lose their homes for no good reason." Those involved in this protest would start an organization called "The Visible Community."[1518] The newly created community action group would be primarily responsible for the eventual defeat of the Heritage Initiative's boulevard proposal. The Visible Community would also continue to build on the community activism movement started by the Many and One Coalition almost two years prior to the tent protest at Bates College. Ben Chin would go on to run for mayor of Lewiston, twice.

## The Somali Bantu

The city of Lewiston recorded its first secondary migrant Bantu family arrivals in 2004. By February 2006, the city estimated that approximately "300 Bantu—about 50 families"[1519] had moved into the city, roughly the same number that had been scheduled for resettlement in Holyoke, Massachusetts before their city council opposed their relocation. The Bantu would arrive in Lewiston coming from a "different culture, (speaking) a different language, and (having) a different history" than the indigenous Somalis that had arrived in Lewiston in 2001.[1520]

The Somali Bantu arrivals in Lewiston would be similar to the indigenous Somali arrivals, in that they were also all secondary migrants arriving from other parts of the country. Like their indigenous countrymen and women, it would not begin with refugee resettlement. The relocations would add even more diversity to the community and also mark a transition point when the immigrant make-up of Lewiston's secondary migrant population would begin to see a gradual decline in Somali arrivals and an increase of other African secondary migrants and asylum seekers.

## The Somali Narrative Project

In 2004, I met with four University of Maine professors who had begun a project called the "Somali Narrative Project." Professors Kristin Langellier, Mazie Hough, Kimberly Huisman, and Carol Nordstrom Toner created the project "in response to cultural tensions that arose with the Somalis' mass immigration to Maine."[1521] The project's purpose was to address the "negative images" of both the Somalis and Lewiston through the creation of "'a library of real stories'" that would promote "understanding and improved communication" about who they were, where they came from, and what they experienced in the U.S. and in Maine.[1522]

Kristin Langellier stated that "because generations and children change so quickly in the United States, the elders felt like they were losing their own sense of history. Their children didn't know their history, they didn't know about Somalia or even about immigration."[1523] This effort would lead to the publication of the book "Somalis in Maine: Crossing Cultural Currents" that was published in 2011. The idea for the book "began with a reader's theater performance by members of the Somali Narrative Project at the American Folk Festival"[1524] in Bangor, Maine.

## The Mosque Incident and Middle School Incident

On July 4, 2006, Brent Matthews was arrested by Lewiston police officers for "throwing a (frozen) pig head into the (Al-Noor Mosque) during evening prayers." The animal's head was rolled "'like a bowling ball'" through the building's open door during evening prayers at the mosque. The members of the mosque considered the act "a deliberate insult" as "(p)igs are viewed as unclean by Muslims."[1525]

In addition to local charges from the city, the incident was forwarded to the state attorney general's office for review as a possible "hate-bias crime." Matthews had a criminal record that involved "assault, operating (a vehicle) under the influence and other minor crimes" but no part of his record involved any prior acts involving hate crimes.[1526] Matthews shared with police that he had obtained the pig's head from "a pig roast several days earlier" and described his actions to police "as a joke." Jim Bennett characterized the incident as involving "one idiot" who did "something stupid." Some in the Somali community were more concerned about the incident following "acts of vandalism" that had recently occurred, and a Somali inmate who had died while in custody of the local county jail.

The Matthews incident produced national and "international" media attention. The FBI[1527] would take part in a July 7th city press conference[1528] that reporter Rob Reynolds would also cover for the new Al-Jazeera U.S. news network. They had contacted my office months before and wanted to do a human-interest story[1529] that could be broadcast later in the year after their official U.S. launch. Being in Lewiston for the pig's head incident and the press conference was purely coincidental.

The Many and One Coalition would once again work to pull together another rally to support the Somali community in Kennedy Park on July 12th. The rally would attract some 100 people, including Lewiston Mayor Lionel Guay, Governor John Baldacci, and members of Lewiston-Auburn's interfaith community.[1530]

Nine months later, a middle school student placed a "ham steak in a bag on a lunch table where Somali students were eating." The April 15, 2007 act was reminiscent of the pig head incident and was treated by the school department as a potential hate incident resulting in the student's suspension.[1531] The student's act against his Somali classmate once again placed Lewiston into the national news spotlight.

## The 2008 Recession

The headline in the Sun Journal on February 11, 2008 read "Poll Shows Public Believes Country is in Recession." State economist, and my former professor at the University of Southern Maine, Dr. Charlie Colgan agreed a month earlier that the public was on to something. Colgan believed that the national unemployment rate of 5% and energy costs, which were "killing us" in Maine, all pointed to a recession that he predicted in the first half of the year, noting that "if Maine was lucky," it would be "mild."[1532]

Colgan's note of cautious optimism would prove to be misplaced. In what would become nationally known as "the Great Recession," the economic effects of the recession would produce lasting impacts on the economies of Lewiston and Maine. In 2008, the state employed 33,868 people. Eleven years later, Maine employment would only reach 31,816 and continue to struggle to equal its job numbers before the Great Recession. Also in Maine, unemployment would reach an annual high of 8.3% in 2009. The Lewiston-Auburn Metro rate would hit a high of 8.7%, but a new L-A diversified economy would not produce the double-digit unemployment numbers last seen in the 1980s recession. Maine and Lewiston's housing market would recover in the mid-late 2010s as would the prices for homes, particularly in southern Maine.[1533]

## 2009 - 2014

### The Maine Power Reliability Project

The first mention of the Maine Power Reliability Project (MPRP) may have been in the Maine Public Utilities Commission 2007 Annual Report, which stated that, "The Maine Power Reliability Project (MPRP) involves a proposed broad scale build out of new transmission in the CMP (Central Maine Power) service area, including project components to improve the reliability of particular areas in the CMP system and to upgrade the 345 kV backbone." It was a project that was "under consideration" at that juncture and would eventually become a $1.4 billion project to upgrade Maine and New England's utility grid.[1534]

In Maine, any project that involved power almost always ran into environmental opposition. This project would be no different and Lewiston would run into its own local opposition beginning in 2008.[1535] I served as one of two city liaisons working with the opponents and CMP. Public Works Director David Jones would serve as the city liaison overseeing construction related logistics, while I focused primarily on resident concerns and regulatory/legislative matters. The project would upgrade a portion of the downtown power grid and replace a 100-year-old power sub-station that was recognized by CMP as outdated and a safety concern for workers. The entire project was ultimately approved and made its way through Lewiston as a two-phase project. The $140 million in new investment into the city began in 2010 and saw full completion in 2018.

With the MPRP's downtown Lewiston project phase winding down in 2017, CMP pursued another "massive clean energy project in Massachusetts that could trigger the construction of a 145-mile transmission line" from the Canadian border directly through Lewiston. The estimated investment in Lewiston would approach some $250 million.[1536] They billed the project both as a clean energy project and a project that would help to stabilize the "ever-changing electricity mix" of fuel sources that made electricity rates in New England some of the highest in the country. This project would save New England residents billions of dollars on their utility bills over 20 years.[1537]

Like the MPRP, the project had its opponents. A people's referendum petition was submitted to the Maine Secretary of State's office for the November 2020 election, but was rejected by the Maine Supreme Judicial Court as unconstitutional.[1538] That did not stop the group from putting together another petition drive, which saw the same supporters collecting signatures at polling locations during the 2020 presidential election. The project has not yet received final approval from the U.S. Army Corps of Engineers and may go to referendum.

### The Newsweek Story

Newsweek published a story about Lewiston in its January 26, 2009 edition titled "The Refugees Who Saved Lewiston: A Dying Mill Town Gets a Fresh Burst of Energy."[1539] The article not only drew criticism from city officials such as myself but also from the Chamber of Commerce, as well as residents throughout the area. Brunswick, Maine "freelance writer" Jesse Ellison, who had interviewed Paul Badeau from the Lewiston-Auburn Growth Council, wrote the story.

The article was part of a "magazine-wide piece on the changing face of America" and Badeau reported that "(Ellison) said she was working on a story that was part of a larger package" on President Obama's America, with a "focus on how the Somalis have changed Lewiston." Heather Lindkvist characterized the story as having painted "the city in a much kinder light than previous coverage did."[1540]

What Lindkvist said was partially true only because it did not address the primary criticism leveled by Ellison suggesting the "dying mill town" was transformed by the Somali arrival and not through 50 years of city and community effort that Badeau literally showed her during their tour of the city. There was not "one reason for Lewiston's renaissance." As Badeau said in the article, "many people are responsible for (the renaissance of the city). There's an entire tapestry, and the Somalis are one part of that, one thread."

Badeau's observations were on the mark. The Somali contributions were part of the "thread" that would be needed for any kind of economic renaissance, and that thread would involve the city's population that was growing specifically because of their arrivals. The Sun Journal article also did not credit Ellison for her comments about Somali contributions in occupying many once-vacant storefronts. By 2009, it was an indisputable fact that the Somali relocations, coupled with some of the other immigrant group arrivals, were filling downtown's vacant storefronts and tenements. The 2010 Census would eventually confirm that the city's population grew for the first time in 30 years.

## The Somalis - Storefronts, Employment, General Assistance

Lewiston's downtown in the 1950s was considered to be one of the best retail destinations in the state. The four-story Peck's Department store was the largest department store in Maine[1541] and anchored other major downtown department store retailers like Sears (and Roebuck), J.C. Penney, Woolworths, Montgomery Ward, and Kresges. There were also dozens of locally owned stores like Leblanc's, Ward Brothers, Reid and Hughes, Murphy's (furrier), A.H. Benoit and J. Dostie Jewelers that filled the downtown area. Not a single one of those stores remained downtown by 2010 except for J. Dostie Jewelers.

Paul's Clothing was another long-term downtown retailer, with a clothing store that was once one of Lewiston's busiest retailers originally called "Louie's." Paul Poliquin had worked there for years and was privy to the history of downtown Lewiston, having witnessed the changes along Lisbon Street over several decades. Downtown may not have been the retail center of Maine anymore, but it was also no longer an area filled with social clubs, prostitutes, petty crime, and many empty storefronts. Once vacant spaces were being filled with "25 to 30"[1542] Somali businesses. Many buildings, like Poliquin's, were being renovated and facades being meticulously restored. The once "desolate downtown" was now "bringing people back" to the downtown area. The 2008 recession had largely stopped the progress of renovating the downtown's appearance and infrastructure, but that would also change in the near future.[1543]

Somali employment appeared to be improving in 2011, but the progress would be impeded by the federal government's insistence to disregard the value of work-related ESOL vocational training and education. The Office of Refugee Resettlement would say that much of their programming was intended to "(supplement) and/or (complement) existing employment services to help refugees achieve economic self-sufficiency."[1544]

The problem for refugees in Lewiston and those living in many other small-town U.S. communities was the absence and insufficiency of supplemental or complimentary ESOL vocational programs. In Lewiston, there was very little city capacity to develop and fund such programs, and no county support given their primary functions to provide law enforcement (mainly for communities with no municipal law enforcement), corrections, registry of deeds, district attorney, and judicial functions. Maine law also prohibited counties from collecting their own property taxes and collected their revenues by mandating that municipalities pay them a portion of the property taxes they collect.

At the state level, the federal Workforce Investment Act monies available for job training had little value for immigrant populations who spoke limited English and had education levels below eighth-grade levels. That did not stop the city and the agencies that were working with the city to press forward. With the help of organizations like the Career Center, Lewiston Adult Education, the Center for Workplace Learning, the New Mainers Work Ready project, and the New Mainers Workforce Alliance, some vocational training progress occurred.[1545]

The frustration with U.S. immigrant workforce development policy continued with their refusal not to fully commit to job training for newly arriving refugees who wanted to work. There was ample evidence that many refugees would work once they were equipped to handle the U.S. workplace. Lewiston's increasingly diverse immigrant population wanted what every other immigrant before them wanted: the ability and opportunity to become economically "self-sufficient."

Ten years after the first Somali families arrived in Lewiston, the news media continued to speak to resident concerns about

General Assistance, particularly for immigrant residents who were receiving it. Back in 2002, the immigrant population that was predominantly made up of Somali residents, received 52% of all the assistance provided by the city. That number dropped to 30% by 2006. It continued to drop in 2009 to "less than 16%" for a population of immigrants who were becoming progressively more diverse. Department of Social Services Director Sue Charron reported that the number of immigrants receiving General Assistance increased in 2011 and attributed the percentage increase to a larger number of asylum seekers arriving in Lewiston. In dollars, General Assistance had risen from $180,233 in 2001 to $932,783 in 2011,[1546] with the impacts of the 2008-2009 'Great Recession,' and high unemployment in the area, also contributing to the increase over the last few years.

### The Lepage Years

Paul LePage had a childhood that would have broken most people. He grew up in Lewiston's Little Canada in a "tall tenement with 12 apartments" on Lincoln Street[1547] (another newspaper reports it was a 4-room house on Lisbon Street)[1548] with 17 other siblings (possibly 15 or 17)[1549] in a household where his alcoholic father mistreated just about everyone.

There were stories of violence, no hot water, outhouses, and LePage going to the hospital "with a broken nose." That episode led to him running away from home, never to return.[1550] He had the good fortune of being taken in by a family, received his undergraduate degree at Lewiston's Husson College, and completed his MA in Business Administration at the University of Maine.[1551]

With a successful political career as a Waterville city councilor and mayor, and business career for the Lewiston-based bargain department store chain Marden's, he ran as an unlikely and unknown Republican contender against six other primary candidates and became the surprise winner for Governor in November 2010. The governor was a fiscal and social conservative with a focus on the state's budget and its welfare programs.

LePage's first term was at times tumultuous with Democrats and other progressives, and he was re-elected for a second term in 2014. His impact on state policy in a number of areas was notable, particularly on the state's social services and immigrant programs. It was a sudden turn of events in Vietnam that prompted the nation's first fiscally Independent governor, Lewiston resident James Longley, to become the first state leader to authorize the creation of the first Maine refugee program with the successful resettlement 166 Vietnamese between 1975 and 1977. Forty years later, it would become a collection of unlikely political events that would come together when Republican conservative Paul LePage, the next Lewiston native to become governor, officially ended the state's participation with refugee resettlement on March 4, 2017.[1552]

After the five-year administration of termed-out Democratic Mayor Laurent "Larry" Gilbert, and his activism as an avid supporter of diversity and Lewiston's growing refugee community, Republican Robert "Bob" Macdonald would be elected mayor in 2011 after his own unlikely campaign. Macdonald would become not only a LePage supporter, but also write his own chapter in Lewiston's immigrant history that would attract national attention.

### The First Elected Official

Mayor Robert Macdonald had appointed Zamzam Mohamud to fill the vacant school committee position earlier in 2013 and would become the first Somali resident to hold a public office in the city's history. Jama Mohamed would become the first Somali and Bantu resident to be elected to a city office. Mohamed would accomplish this historic achievement as a write-in school board candidate for a Ward 5 seat that had no candidate on the ballot.[1553]

Mohamed arrived in Lewiston in 2008 and had helped in the founding of the Somali Bantu Youth Association, a very active ECBO in the community. Jama had started the organization in response to the Bantu community's concerns regarding the paucity of summer activities for Bantu youth. His ECBO reached out to the Lewiston school department, who assisted Mohamed with setting up a summer program. That collaboration contributed to his decision to run for the school committee.[1554]

Zamzam Mohamud failed in her bid to be elected for her the at-large seat, but Jama Mohamed was only one vote shy of receiving the required 50 write-in votes to win the seat. In a ballot recount, Mohamed picked up 10 more votes to become the first "African immigrant" to be elected to office in the city's history. When asked by the Sun Journal why he ran, Mohamed simply replied, "'it is my duty to serve.'"[1555]

## The Merger

Through a procedure outlined in Maine law, a petition drive was organized during the years 2013 and 2014 to create a Lewiston-Auburn joint charter commission. The elected commission would be charged with the responsibility of producing a new charter that would merge the two cities. The 2,500 petition signatures were collected as required by Maine law. The primary election for Democratic and Republican candidates was scheduled for June 10, 2014. Voters elected a slate of joint charter commission candidates for three positions representing Auburn and three in Lewiston.[1556]

Maine law did not mandate a timeline for the completion of the final charter that would eventually require a vote of support from both cities. The effort was the culmination of many joint commissions and studies that had been conducted over many years. Creating the merger proposal involved dozens of public meetings and many more between the two city staffs and the commission. It would involve almost four years of work before the charter commission would bring it before the two cities for a vote.

## The Safest City

There were suggestions and concerns expressed by a few residents and many non-residents that crime would increase with the arrival of the refugees. The crime data said differently. Back in 1988, the FBI's Uniform Crime Reporting data stated that Lewiston's crime rate was 77.15 per 100,000 of population. It had declined to 27.27 per 100,000 by 2014, "a drop of 24 percent from 2013."[1557]

"According to FBI statistics, Bangor... had a higher rate (than Lewiston's) since 1996." Portland's crime rate had also "been higher than Lewiston('s) since 2002," and Auburn's had been "higher than Lewiston('s) since 2007." With an increasing focus on community outreach, the Lewiston Police Department had been making progress on the city's crime rate "over the past three decades." Department officials specifically focused much of the credit on "the department's active and engaged community policing team." Officer Joe Philippon would credit the department's "increasing contact with children and following up with social service agencies when they see a child a need."[1558]

In 2000, "there were 678 juveniles charged with various crimes" spiking "to 747 in 2001." By 2014, there were "168 juvenile arrests—a 35.63% drop from 2013 and a 77.51% decrease since 2001."[1559]

## 2015 – 2020

### The Asylum Seekers

Asylum seekers began to arrive in Lewiston as far back as 2001. The numbers were initially tiny, typically less than a dozen or two per year. That changed in 2007 when the numbers ticked upward. In FY 2013, Lewiston processed 83 asylum seekers. By FY 2014, that number had increased to 103 within the first 6 months of the fiscal year.[1560]

Asylum seeker General Assistance applications began to dominate the total number of immigrants applying for GA in FY 2014. In that fiscal year, the 416 asylum seekers applied for GA. In FY 2016, the number increased to 762 people and would be eclipsed by the 522 people who applied in the first six months of FY 2017. In February 2017, asylum seeker "'intakes'" were being scheduled at a rate of 30 per month.[1561]

The challenge with asylum seekers had much to do with their status in the U.S. They were not here as part of the refugee resettlement process. Because the U.S. had not yet approved them for asylum, under federal law, they were not eligible for any federal assistance of any kind. However, under Maine law, they could be eligible for social services if they qualified based on their income. The administration of Governor Paul LePage would challenge what they received for state social services after Donald Trump was elected president in 2016.

Between the years 2015 and 2018, "African asylum seekers made up, on average, about 83(%) of all new immigrant arrivals"[1562] processed in the Lewiston Social Services department. Asylum seekers would also become a significant topic of conversation in Portland, Maine in 2018.

### A 40-Year First

Lewiston had been called a "hockey town" for decades. Hockey was a Canadian sport imported into our city when the French-Canadians arrived to work in our textile mills. The city high schools had won multiple state boys Class A championships with both of its high schools, St. Dominic Regional High School ("St. Dom's")[1563] and Lewiston High School. Between 1938 and 2000, the two programs won 66% of the (boys) state hockey championships. That success established the city as a high school and youth hockey powerhouse. That was not the case with other sports, with the exception of Class A tennis. The arrival of new immigrants into the city would make Class A soccer the next exception.

The 2015 Lewiston High School boys' soccer team had been ranked nationally as the 22nd best team in the country and was led by Mike McGraw, who had been coaching the team for 33 years. When it came to the more competitive Class A bracket, Lewiston had never won a championship in 40 years. That all changed in 2015. With a roster that was predominantly made up of African immigrant boys, the team won its first state soccer championship since becoming a varsity program in 1975.[1564]

This interesting story was not only covered as a national news story but was also featured on "HBO Real Sports with Bryant Gumbel." "Real Sports" would make their second trip to Maine since their 2005 interview with Neil Leifer about his photo of Muhammad Ali in the 1965 fight against Sonny Liston.[1565] The boys' soccer team victory would also become the book "One Goal," written by Amy Bass in 2018[1566] and later optioned by Netflix as "a film or TV series."[1567]

## The Trailblazers

Following the footsteps of Zamzam Mohamud and Jama Mohamed, three more Somali residents ran for office in 2017. Candidates Safiya Khalid, Hassan Abdi and Ahmed Sheikh would toss their hat into the ring for Lewiston's school board. Like the Franco Americans before them, the three "political newcomer(s)" would look to build upon Jama Mohamed's 2013 victory run and pursue public office.[1568]

According to Rilwan Osman of the Maine Immigrant and Refugee Services, with more former refugees gaining citizenship "(s)ome 2,500 members of the immigrant community were eligible to vote" in the 2017 election. For refugees to qualify for citizenship, they would need to remain in the U.S. for no less than five years.[1569]

None of the three Somali candidates would win in 2017, but Osman believed that simply running for office and taking part in democracy from their "community's perspective" made everyone "winners." Former City Councilor Roger Philippon would accurately predict that a Somali resident would win election again "in the near future."[1570] Safiya Khalid would lose her race by the largest margin of the three candidates in 2017 but would fulfill Philippon's prediction by becoming a candidate for city office in 2019. In that election, Safiya would set her sights on something different. She would run for a seat on the Lewiston City Council, and win.

There would also be a new wave of city department position retirements held by employees with double-digit careers. Their replacements injected a number of younger administrative staff into some of the city's top positions. It had started to some degree in 2009 with the departures of 33-year employee Police Chief Bill Welch and Finance Director Richard Metivier, who ended his 40-year career. Their departures were followed by 40-year employee and Human Resource Director Denis Jean in 2010. Recreation Director Maggie Chisholm's departure occurred after 25 years with the city in 2014. Tax Assessor Joe Grube left his position after almost 40 years with the city in 2015. Police Chief Mike Bussiere would leave the city for Texas after 26 years.

The largest turnover began in 2017 with the retirement of Fire Chief Paul LeClair whose 36-year career would end in January 2017 to become the jointly operated 911 center director. I would retire in June 2017 after 18 years as the deputy city administrator and be replaced by former Auburn assistant city manager Denis D'Auteuil who would eventually become Lewiston's city administrator in July 2020. City purchasing director Norm Beauparlant would also leave as a 43-year employee and retire in 2017, as would Library director Rick Speer after 34 years. The next year would see three major department heads retire. It would include Public Works director David Jones retiring after 19 years; Social Services director Sue Charron leaving after 25 years; and City Code Enforcement and Planning director Gil Arsenault who retired after 34 years with the city.

Including upper management staff like tax collectors Paul Labrecque and Nancy Meneally with some 80 years between them, in the years between 2009 and 2018, almost 500 years of combined experience would no longer be working with elected officials and residents to guide their city. I never saw this as a 'brain drain.' I believed that it was more of a 'brain gain' and a necessary injection of creativity and new ideas for the city. This was the case during the 1980s Gosselin and 1990s Mulready administrations, when their new wave of younger, talented people would be hired and promoted internally by the city. The real question is whether this newest group of department leaders remain committed to lengthy city careers in the same way that many of their predecessors were. Many of today's employees see a career as less of a stepping stone and more as an opportunity to prepare them for a better position, anywhere. Only time will tell.

## The Immigrant and Refugee Working Group

City Councilor and Democrat Kristen Cloutier quickly distinguished herself on the city council as someone who could work "both sides of the aisle." After serving only one term, the council elected Cloutier as its president in 2015. During her two terms, she would work to keep property tax rates lower, support economic development, address the state-leading high rates of lead poisoning in Lewiston's downtown children, and advocate for the immigrant community. In 2016, she received Republican mayor Macdonald's support to create an ad hoc group to form the "Immigrant and Refugee Integration and Policy Development Working Group" who would conduct their first meeting in September 2016. The working group's purpose was articulated in their report:

- Identify and inventory immigrant and refugee services available in the community, including referral and support mechanisms for new arrivals;
- Identify the needs of the current immigrant and refugee community that are not being met by service providers or advocacy or community

groups; • Identify possible funding streams from Federal and State agencies that can address ongoing and unmet immigrant and refugee needs; • Identify and utilize city, school, and community resources, including those of the business community, to encourage employment/entrepreneurship within the immigrant and refugee community... Make recommendations to the Lewiston City Council; and to assist with policy development in relation to the tasks identified above.[1571]

This kind of undertaking had not taken place since the city assembled its immigrant report sent to Governor Angus King in May 2002. The difference was that the Lewiston community had built far more organizational capacity at the non-governmental and community level. It was time to take stock of what we had and what we needed in 2016 and 2017. The report would be delivered to the city council in December 2017 and would recommend city and state support for a welcoming center and that more community services be provided by the immigrant organizations in the community.

### The Continuing Renaissance

Boston based WCVB TVs "Chronicle" program had visited Lewiston frequently. For a small city like Lewiston, much of what you do is often not recognizable or notable until someone "from away" talks about it. In 2018, Chronicle looked at the history of the Bates Mill, celebrating the work of the Androscoggin Land Trust and the cleanliness of the Androscoggin River,[1572] and met with the owners of "Bourgeois Guitars" located in the privately owned Hill Mill (at one time owned by Bates Manufacturing) and the locally owned "Bob's Peanuts" that was located not too far from where I grew up.

Many were also pleasantly surprised to see that "Thrillist" had selected Lewiston as the state's "most underrated" city. In their eyes, Lewiston's underrated "renaissance" was worth directing their readers "to head inland to hit up the fully repurposed mill town of Lewiston and its sister city across the Androscoggin River, Auburn." Quoddy Inc., handmade shoemakers located in Lewiston's Pepperell Mill and Labadie's Bakery and their "whoopie pies," would also be singled out as reasons for visiting the city.[1573]

Quoddy President and CEO John Andreliunas would add that the "pop culture website" could easily have listed "Bates College, mill redevelopment, lots of good dining, and the annual "Dempsey (bike and running) Challenge"[1574] created and led by actor (born in Lewiston's Central Maine Medical Center) Patrick Dempsey[1575] as additional reasons to visit the city.[1576] Much of what they discussed spoke directly to the work invested by the city over the last 6 decades. It was reaffirming for many locally (and away) who had been working so diligently for so long to achieve precisely these results.

It may not have seemed like anything of significance to many residents when it happened, but the city's 10-year effort to take possession of 1.5 miles of canals in March 2018 was another seminal economic development moment for the city.[1577] As the mills began to shut down and vacate, ownership and maintenance of the canals, which belonged to several utility companies over many decades, declined over time.

The once lushly landscaped areas that bordered both sides of the canals were becoming overrun with wild bushes and untrimmed areas of tall wild grasses and weeds. The city also had concerns about the potential for catastrophic canal wall failures if maintenance was not completed as needed. With city control of the canals and their abutting rights-of-way, the community could now discuss next steps relating to use, design, lighting, access, etc. The absence of control and ownership would not allow any of that to happen.

The official March 2018 transaction was finalized when the canal ownership was transferred to the city. Administration and the city council knew it could take years for results, but the city was accustomed to being patient and knew that great planning had the potential for producing great results. Leveraging the canals as another asset to enhance its downtown was something that did not exist in most U.S. cities. These canals had the potential to create new "waterfront" properties in a downtown area of development that was already growing and achieving real economic development success.

## The Kennedy Park Incident

Internally as a city staff, we would always discuss where we were as a community, relative to how things were back in 2001 and 2002 with our new immigrant experience. We could see the progress, but we knew much more needed to be done. Much of what the city needed was in the immigrant working group report that was published in December 2017.

The city was well positioned to do the work with several immigrant ECBOs who were willing and capable of getting things done. City Councilor and newly elected State Representative Kristen Cloutier, who would remain as the council president, would now embark on the hard work ahead. As 2018 unfolded, the moment we feared might occur someday happened. According to witness statements, "30 Somali and Congolese people" became embroiled in a brawl with "15 white people"[1578] during an early summer evening on June 12, 2018 after some "teens in a car drove past the park and shot pellets and BBs at a group... striking several people."[1579]

The group alleged to have been involved in the "pellet" shooting, reportedly targeted Donald Giusti and others who proceeded to chase down the assailants and the brawl ensued. During the fight, someone threw a rock, striking Giusti[1580] who succumbed to multiple injuries sustained by the rock and other internal injuries on June 14th.[1581] Three people would be arrested; two were minors. The city would once again become embroiled in controversy, hateful acts, and racist speech. City, community leaders, residents, and family members of the deceased responded with messages of calm and peace, as would Kristen Cloutier, who become the interim mayor following Shane Bouchard's resignation in 2019.

The venue of the trial involving the alleged assailant accused of causing Giusti's death was moved to Cumberland County. No trial had been scheduled as of this writing.

## New Developments, the Auburn spotlight, and Khalid Wins

The voters in Auburn "overwhelmingly" approved the construction of a new state-funded high school in a June 11, 2019 city referendum. It became the "most expensive high school in Maine" with "geothermal heating and cooling," and a "top-notch athletic stadium." The new school's $10.5 million dollar "1,200-seat performing arts center" funding would depend on local property taxes and fundraising, as it would not receive any state funding.[1582]

It would also feature a "trades wing" that would become the "Auburn campus of the Lewiston Regional Technical Center." The LRTC served as the vocational training program for six area high schools (that included Auburn) who shared 375 of the 750 available seats in the Lewiston based program. It all[1583] started modestly back in 1967 as one of the first regional vocational programs in the state (see the Appendix, Item 51). The demand for seats in the program now required a waiting list. The new Auburn campus would reduce the waiting list and feature "10 programs" that would include precision and composite manufacturing, "engineering with robotics, and two exploratory programs in construction trades and health careers."[1584]

The new LRTC campus would also open another 425 seats in the technical school and set aside approximately 50% of the seating for Auburn students. This $30 million undertaking[1585] was all accomplished through the cooperation of the two public school systems, and once again spotlight L-As ability to collaborate on significant and beneficial programs and services for all area residents.

The euphoria of the school vote would not last long following the Boston Globe's story involving "The Teacher Project at Columbia Journalism School('s)" investigation of "racism at Edward Little High School." The "Teacher Project" had done a story as "part of a series focusing on the experiences of immigrant children trying to get an education." It began as a Lewiston-Auburn story, but the reporters' focused on "Auburn's administration" as they believed they "didn't seem as responsive to student (racism) concerns and didn't get the same level of scrutiny" as Lewiston's school system had received.[1586]

The "starting point" of the investigation had begun back in November 2018 and was the product of a "report" written and submitted to the American Civil Liberties Union by a former ELHS student. The Teacher Project story stated that "administrators and teachers at Edward Little showed 'a lack of accountability'" in dealing with complaints raised by immigrants and students of color" in a school that was 85% white, compared to Lewiston's high school that was 63% white. Interviews with students and parents revealed that racism had "gone unchecked and festered," and becoming increasingly worse since President Trump's election in 2016.[1587]

Mayor Jason Levesque's reaction to the Globe story may have summed up the community's response best, stating that what happened at ELHS highlighted "the issues of acceptance, toleration and diversity that every community in America must deal with." Levesque said Auburn was a very welcoming community for all of its residents, but he shared that there was more work to do and "that (the) work will never end. It's an ever-changing process."[1588]

Although Mayor Levesque lived in Auburn, he had an investment history in Lewiston. Before he became Auburn's mayor, he had purchased and renovated a former downtown Lewiston department store in 2013 to house a telemarketing business that he owned. He sold the business and later sold the building in January 2019. In May 2019, the Auburn mayor would invest again in Lewiston and purchased the iconic Peck's department store building that housed an L.L. Bean call center and a law firm.[1589]

The economic development activity in both cities was also seeing another wave of investment. Walmart was looking to fill 100 jobs and add to its existing staff of 500 employees. Wages started at $16.90 per hour and increased to $19.50 per hour for some weekend workers. Benefits included "16 weeks of paid maternity leave." Another Lewiston company, Grand Rounds, announced it would also hire another 100 employees.[1590]

In 2014, Safiya Khalid became a Lewiston High School graduate who would get her degree from the University of Southern Maine in 2018. During her senior year at USM, she launched an unsuccessful bid for a seat on the Lewiston School Committee in November 2017.[1591] Undaunted, she would decide to run in 2019 for the open Ward 1 Lewiston City Council seat held by Jim Lysen. In what the press described as a "contentious race" with her Republican opponent, Khalid won by 70% of the vote in her ward.[1592]

In the words of Abigail Fisher Williamson, who wrote "Welcoming New Americans?" featuring Lewiston, Maine as one of the four U.S. cities in the book, Khalid's win was "'a real milestone' for the city." Williams' observation of Safiya's victory was not hyperbole. Khalid would become the youngest city councilor, the city's first Muslim and Somali American,[1593] and the only first-generation African immigrant to be elected to a municipal government office in the city's history. Her victory was "covered by CNN, Washington Post, Fortune (magazine), Christian Science Monitor" and the BBC "in addition to every major news outlet in Maine."[1594]

In took only 13 years from the date of the first Somali family's arrival in Lewiston to elect Lewiston's first Somali to a city position on the school board. It would take just 18 years for the city to elect its second Somali resident to a Lewiston elected office. From the date of the first Franco arrivals in 1860, it took the Francos twenty years to experience their first municipal election success. It would take another 34 years to elect their first mayor.

## Choice Neighborhoods

The community group "Healthy Neighborhoods Planning Council" and its coordinator Shana Cox (who would later become President and CEO of the L-A Metropolitan Chamber of Commerce) had been working with the community "to identify the single biggest issue that impacts health" in Lewiston since 2012. For those who took part in the process, it was not surprising to learn that housing was the single biggest issue, particularly in downtown Lewiston. That "housing" was chosen meant issues of affordability, "access to medical care," food security, exposure to lead, and "employment and schools" would also need to be part of the downtown area housing discussion. The targeted downtown census areas had levels of poverty affecting almost half the population in two of its nine census tracts.[1595]

In 2017, the city would seek a highly competitive $1.3 million U.S. Department of Housing and Urban Development "Choice Neighborhood Planning and Action Grant." According to former city councilor and co-op housing coordinator Craig Saddlemire, the grant would "really (support) community-driven change." [1596] In addition to Lewiston, only two other cities received the 2018 grant—Los Angeles and Philadelphia. Lewiston became the "first city of its size" in the program's 10-year history.[1597]

Some 400 residents took part in a series of "mapping workshops, public pop-up sessions, (and) focus groups" in a yearlong effort that began in the summer of 2018. The 250-page "'transformation plan'" would create proposals for new "mixed-use" housing that would create some 160 new units of housing in the target area. The plan, and the partnership between the city, Healthy Neighborhoods, Community Concepts, [1598] and the Lewiston Housing Authority, Inc. would form the foundation of the city's December 2020 application for a HUD grant of up to $30 million dollars that would be matched with $1.5 million from the city.[1599]

## The Year That was 2020

*-The Pandemic-*

When I outlined what I hoped to cover in this book back in January 2020, I envisioned I would finish the last chapter of the book with a somewhat brief summary of 2020s most publicly significant moments, projects, or developments. By the end of 2019, I felt reasonably certain that it would involve the community's new economic development wave that appeared poised for something big in 2020.

That all changed by March 2020. The press covered the coronavirus pandemic every day. In some way, the disease would affect almost every individual and community in the country. Few U.S. communities escaped the ravages of the deadly COVID-19 illness produced by the virus. It impacted people's health, employment, finances, and their politics. There were many deaths, tragedies, and struggles that affected millions.

Maine would record its first confirmed COVID-19 case on March 10, 2020. The case involved an Auburn, Maine, U.S. Navy reserve female who flew into the Portland (Maine) Jetport on March 6th and later developed "respiratory" and "flu-like symptoms." The woman was picked up at the airport by Lewiston resident Michelle Roberts,[1600] sister of Phil Nadeau. The state ordered both women to quarantine, but neither became ill from the virus. The World Health Organization would officially declare "the COVID-19 outbreak a pandemic" on March 11, 2020.[1601]

Both Lewiston[1602] and Auburn[1603] would declare emergencies in their cities before the state's "shelter-in-place" order in April, and it would challenge both cities to approve their FY 2021 budgets that would begin on July 1, 2020. Both cities were left to guess on how badly shutting down a city, state, and basically the entire country would skew revenue and expenditure projections at all levels of government.

The cities would struggle with questions about reopening not only government, but every public activity, business, and service within their communities. They would be confronted with rules set up by the state, federal agencies, congress, the president, and had to completely re-envision how to educate their kids. Both cities would also struggle with outreach to their immigrant populations. These challenges would persist through 2020 while COVID-19 rates rose. Maine would eventually rank as the "third-lowest" new case ratio in the country at the end of 2020 behind Vermont and Hawaii.[1604]

As I write the last lines in this book in late February 2021, 500,000+ Americans have died from COVID-19, and national vaccine distributions have begun, albeit at a slower pace than was first projected in early December 2020. According to the Maine CDC, as of late February 2021, some 44,000 cases and 670 deaths had been reported in Maine. Hopefully, this nightmare will be under control sooner rather than later. It will likely be looked upon as this country's greatest public security threat since the

1962 Cuban missile crisis, its greatest public health threat since the 1917 pandemic, and its greatest economic challenge since the Great Depression. It will also hopefully be largely behind us in 2021.

*-Black Lives Matter-*

The story has been told numerous times by the national media. As the result of a police call response involving a forged check report, Minneapolis Police arrested George Floyd on May 25, 2020. During that police arrest, there were allegations involving four police officers who may have contributed to Floyd's death. Someone posted a video of the incident on social media that produced protests in Minneapolis on May 26, 2020. The incident fueled a national reaction with protests around the country and in Lewiston-Auburn on May 31, 2020.[1605]

The protest in Lewiston-Auburn involved "a few dozen people" who marched from Auburn's Festival Plaza near Auburn City Hall. They proceeded across the Vietnam Veterans Memorial Bridge, stopping at the Lewiston and Auburn Police Stations along the way. The "largely peaceful" march's only incident involved the blocking of a truck "flying a 'Trump 2020' flag," and the protestors ripping the flag "from the truck."[1606] More protests would ensue, but it would not involve any violence, arrests, or destruction of property.

The community protests were followed by newly elected Lewiston City Councilor Safiya Khalid's June 16th resolution she submitted to the Lewiston City Council. The resolution would condemn "racial profiling and excessive force by police and (commit) the Lewiston Police Department to achieving equality in its practices." After some lengthy discussion, the council's 6-1 vote approved the resolution. The resolution would also commit the city to "conduct anti-bias and de-escalation training for police personnel." The police union would support much of the resolution, but also criticized the comments of "the majority" of city councilors who "openly and covertly associate our officers with current national events, disputable studies and historical incidents."

The union would also support the use of body cameras for police officers that would receive a city council resolution approval on July 7th. The police would also encourage city councilor to participate in "ridealongs" and attend "police training" sessions.[1607]

Other actions would follow, including Mayor Mark Cayer's creation of the "Equity and Diversity Committee" and his committee appointments announced on July 7th. The committee would review police "policies and procedures;" how police complaints are handled; the "type and nature" of police training; and police "recruiting and hiring practices."[1608] The police union would react to the new committee by pulling its resolution support in August, with the exception of the body-camera system. The city council would approve the funding for the body cameras on October 21st [1609] and the Equity and Diversity Committee would meet on December 16th and submit its final recommendations and support for the report with a unanimous affirmative vote.[1610]

### -Ed Barrett-

After 22 years as Bangor's city manager, Ed Barrett was told by his city council that they wanted to move the city in a different direction. In late 2009, the city council invited Ed to stay until the end of his contract, but Ed believed it was in the best interest of the city that he leave. He did not want his presence to be a distraction for a council who believed that they wanted someone else to lead their city in a new direction.

At about the same time, Lewiston's city council had selected three city administrator candidates as the last group being considered for the vacant position. I was one of those candidates. When Barrett's departure from Bangor made state-wide news, the Lewiston council invited Ed to be the fourth and final candidate. The council did not select me as the city administrator, but the decision gave me the opportunity to work with one of the best city managers in the state. Ed would come into the job on January 1, 2010, with a post-recession budget that we projected would produce some 40 job vacancies in the FY 2011 city budget. In his 35-year career, he had never dealt with employee layoffs. Ed would call the FY 2011 budget "'the most difficult budget I've ever had to do'" and he would be confronted with more layoffs in 2014.[1611]

There would be other challenges in his term as the city's administrator, but Ed also had many successes. Those would include: more economic development; the "Legacy Lewiston Comprehensive Plan and the Choice Neighborhood Plan;" the "Riverfront Island Master Plan" (covering the 100+ acre area abutting Bates Mill complex); reducing the city's debt, increasing the city code enforcement staff; the canal ownership agreement; the Franklin Corporation agreement for residential leased-land; staffing for Lewiston's lead-grant initiative; the completion of the 4$^{th}$ Bates Mill garage; and other accomplishments that would cap off his 10 plus years with the city. When Barrett retired in June 2020, he would become the longest serving administrator since the creation of the city administrator's position in 1980.

-*The Election*-

In the middle of a pandemic that had already claimed the lives of some 300,000 Americans, U.S. citizens demonstrated a level of democracy that some believed could not happen during a pandemic that had claimed hundreds of thousands of American lives. The turnout generated the largest vote for a presidential victory in U.S. history, and the largest vote for the loser in U.S. history.

The vote would also yield other surprising results. It would increase the number of Republican seats in the U.S. House of Representatives despite a Democratic win in the White House. It would also produce perhaps the most unexpected result of the 2020 elections: a runoff election for both Georgia U.S. Senate seats resulting in victory for both Democratic candidates. The outcome would create a 50/50 split in the Senate that would enable the Democrats to assume the majority for the first time since 2015. It was just one more reminder of how fickle and unpredictable people, polls, elections, and politics can be.

The electoral vote would be contested by some in congress, by some state legislators, and by others who attempted to use force to change the voting result on the very day it was to be certified on January 6, 2021. For me and many Americans, it would be one of the saddest days in our democracy's history. There have been moments that were far more violent and certainly the Civil War was the most painful and deadly episode in our democratic experiment. But the sight of U.S. citizens storming the U.S. Capital to overturn what had always been a symbolic, peaceful transfer of power, was heartbreaking.

The attack on the U.S. Capital by its own citizens was not a protest by individuals disgruntled about policy; this was a violent act of insurrection against the U.S. government to halt a constitutional process that would formally install a new president. Fifty Republican and Democratic states had all certified the vote, with some states only proceeding after the unproven accusations of voter fraud and theft had been determined to be without merit in state courts, federal courts, and the U.S. Supreme Court. Some of those courts were staffed with judges nominated by a Republican President and approved by a Republican Senate. The U.S. Supreme Court had three justices nominated by President Trump and appointed by Republican Senators. This did not stop many congressional legislators from insisting that votes in certain states be challenged. They did so even after the very chambers they were voting in had just been invaded by a seditious mob that same night, incited to act by nothing more than unproven conspiracy theories.

Ultimately, democracy prevailed, and congress approved the electoral vote establishing Joseph Biden as the next president. The sight of what happened January 6, 2021 will forever remain in my mind, and likely in the minds of many Americans who still remember where they were during the assassinations of John and Robert Kennedy, Martin Luther King, Jr., as well as the 9/11 attacks. I will forever remember where I was and what I was doing during that fateful day in January 2021. I was writing these very paragraphs of the book while it was taking place.

# Epilogue

David Vermette closed his book "A Distinct Alien Race" speaking with his Franco-American ancestors. The graveyard conversation in the area where some of his family had been buried included a declaration of his purpose in writing his book. He told them he had written the book in recognition of their commitment to leave Quebec and to make a new life for themselves in Brunswick, Maine. That commitment also required working long hours for minimal pay in mills that could often be dangerous. It also necessitated that they work in a community where their presence was often met with disdain, marginalization, and discrimination. Vermette's ancestors explained to him that they no longer had needs that required fulfillment or recognition. What they had done in coming to America, they did for him. Their reply to David was unequivocal—"'(n)ow, it is up to you.'"[1612]

David went on to do what he believed needed to be done for himself on behalf of those that had come before him. One of those things was to write about their experiences and its impact on David and other Francos. I embraced his ancestors' reply and wanted to contribute something to Lewiston's story. In some ways, Lewiston's immigrant story is not unlike any community whose historical roots go back some 170 years, particularly in small towns like Brunswick and Lewiston, Maine. My decision was to write a book providing the reader with some context about Lewiston's small-town response to its immigration history. I also wanted readers to understand how immigration influenced its residents, elected officials, our economy, and the cultural trajectory of those experiences over time.

When the Somalis first arrived in 2001 and 2002, the national media ignored the actual history of L-A's transformation that was influenced by so many people. The city and community invested hundreds of millions of dollars in new businesses, schools, new jobs, new commercial and residential construction, and new infrastructure. Many in the national media (and occasionally the state media) elected to paint Lewiston as a city that was rundown, declining, and a "former" textile mill town that had remained unchanged for decades. The state recognized our economic development progress, yet the news media persisted with their woeful depictions of a failing city.

Down East magazine provided historic coverage of L-As transformation 1999, and many including Inc. Magazine, also recognized the progress of both cities. National and state recognition also came from organizations including the International City Manager's Association, the National Civic League, the Rockefeller Foundation, the state's economic development office, and several governors. The local government and community efforts of Lewiston and Auburn to transform their cities happened through decades of increased community action and activism, determination, collaboration, and a commitment to policy continuity.

Lewiston and Auburn, a community that was once the economic center of Maine, had experienced an economic development renaissance of historic proportions between the years of 1999 and 2003 that was made possible by the 50 years of effort that preceded the renaissance. It continued well into 2007 before the 'Great Recession' of 2008 slowed down the entire national economy.

Had the Somali arrivals occurred in a community that had not pursued the political, economic, collaborative policies and efforts that helped to transform both cities, the results of those first refugee arrivals in 2001 and 2002 may have produced a very different outcome.

What years of work produced for the Somali arrivals was a city's capability to harness its resilience and adaptive creativity to elevate the discussion of diversity and immigration in Maine to a state-wide, national, and international level. Lewiston's resulting community response included a rally for the Somali refugees that ranks as one of the largest community actions in the state's history, and the successful rejection of a white supremacist message of hate that was managed by community and law enforcement response that left only peace and celebration in its wake.

More importantly, the community response continued after the rally and spawned a level of community action and activism that continues to this day. There was also another period of potentially significant growth that produced notable results until the events of 2020 delivered a historic blow to the national economy. As 2021 begins, there appears to be optimism that what began in 2018 may happen again, and that will be part of the focus of the sequel to this book.

Finally, the events that ushered in 2021 inside the U.S. Capital on January 6, 2021 would remind everyone that our democracy is not to be taken for granted. Someone on television spoke about how the structure of the U.S. Capitol building projects an image of strength in its construction. The "Architect of the Capitol" states that the building evokes "the ideals that guided the nation's founders as they framed their new republic."[1613]

Although the building's structural strength was no match for the insurrectionists who dared to desecrate this historic and noble place, the intrusion also symbolized the fragility of our democracy. The day's events proved that democracy could prevail if that is what the people of this country want, but it also revealed once more that a democracy can only endure if it is the will of its people to preserve and protect its existence.

We all want what the founders envisioned when they worked to create this republic, and I have seen first-hand how democracy can work in a place like Lewiston-Auburn. As for democracy's prospects for the rest of our country, we may best explain its fragility through American Theologian Reinhold Neibuhr's vision of our democracy's importance. Taking some minor liberties to update Niebuhr's quote, he said "(hu)mankind's capacity for justice makes democracy possible, but (hu)mankind's inclination to injustice makes democracy necessary."[1614]

As for our nation's future and what we see as a free, fair, equitable, and inclusive system of governing, I will choose to believe in our capacity to make democracy possible. I will also believe that our better angels will always find a way to minimize our lapses to embrace justice as we continue to build our "more perfect union."

# Acknowledgements

There were a number of people who suggested through my tenure in Lewiston that I "should write a book." My most recent memory involved several email exchanges with former Maine State Senator Peggy Rotundo. Peggy is one of those elected officials that simply do not come along all that frequently. We had many wonderful, capable, and important elected officials I had the pleasure of knowing personally, but Peggy was always in a class of her own. Incredibly intelligent, thoughtful, insightful, patient, capable of connecting with both sides of the aisle, and committed to public service for all the right reasons; Peggy was the person who finally convinced me to write this book. After I shared with my wife Marcia that I was going to write a book, Peggy was the second person to know that I would take on this project. She continues to be involved in our community, even after leaving elected office, and our community will always be a better place with her involvement.

I also understood early in my research how important our state newspapers would be in writing this book. I directed my first permission request to Executive Editor Judy Meyer of the Sun Journal in Lewiston, who I knew early in my Lewiston career. Not only did Judy agree to let me cite the newspaper, but she also provided me unrestricted use of all of their publications, only asking for proper attribution for anything I would use in those articles. When those articles were not available through Google Newspaper Archives, she dug through her "back door" to get me the articles that were not available online. Judy went the extra mile when she did not need to, and so did the Sun Journal. She and the newspaper are the most cited source in this book, and I am indebted to SJ and their journalists, past and present, and some of the best in their profession.

I was also blessed to have both Steve Greenlee of the Portland Press Herald/Maine Sunday Telegram, Dan Macleod of the Bangor Daily News, and Laurie Steele of the Twin City Times agree to unrestricted access with the same conditions for attribution requested by the Sun Journal. There were instances where the reporting from their journalists added important and otherwise unreported information about Lewiston or information that was germane to a chapter in the book. Maine is blessed with news media staff that work hard and take great pride in their craft. Like those of us in government, people sometimes stumble and occasionally fail, but few in the media do not care about reporting the facts and the truth. This book simply would not have been possible without the news media. Other newspapers also provided permission to use their publications. They included the Star Tribune in Minneapolis and The Republican that covers news in the Springfield and Holyoke, Massachusetts area.

I also interviewed over 30 people from this book. Some agreed to be interviewed but would later decide not to take part in this book. I remain indebted to all who agreed to be interviewed. Those who allowed the use of their interviews for this book included: Ismail Ahmed, Edward "Ed" Barrett, Sue Charron, State Representative Kristen Cloutier, Shana Cox, Paul Dionne, Susan Geismar, Mike Gotto, James "Jim" Hanna, Mary LaFontaine, Richard Metivier, Greg Mitchell, Charles "Chip" Morrison, Bernard "Bernie" Murphy, Regina Philipps, Dottie Perham-Whittier, Peggy Rotundo, Mark Schlotterbeck, Harry Simones, Michael Sullivan, and William "Bill" Welch.

I interviewed some people more than once. My friend Fatuma Hussein led the list of multiple interviews and her contributions to this book were incredibly useful and important. I am forever grateful for the time she invested in this project and her friendship. Lucien Gosselin was the second longest set of interviews. His career with the city and the Lewiston-Auburn Economic Growth Council spanned the years between 1963 and 2014 and cover a significant part of this book. Lucien's contributions as a city employee, public administrator, and community leader are unmatched in city history. His interviews and the material he provided have added new and important information to the historical record of several important stories in this book. I cannot imagine how different the stories involving the Rockland Experience, L-A College and the city's economic development history would have been without Lucien's help.

Jim Bennett was another multiple interview contributor. He and his wife Debbie became our friends. We got to know his young children while watching them grow into adults, and the years we worked together will always be special. Jim remains one of the busiest and best managers in the state who will soon become the Maine Municipal Association president. His time was greatly appreciated and an incredibly important part of this book. Other multiple interview contributors included Cheryl Hamilton, Lincoln "Linc" Jeffers, my brother Greg Nadeau, Roger Philippon, Alan Turgeon and Michelle Vazquez Jacobus. To everyone who set aside their time to be interviewed, thank you for your invaluable contributions.

Most of my experience in being published involved research and professional publications, and I have never self-published before. Doing this kind of book commercially will very often require copyright permissions, sometimes from both the author and the publishing entity. It was a pleasure working with all who agreed to allow me to use their material with no associated costs. The major national newspapers, news services, magazines, many non-profit organizations, and publishing houses will most often require payment for citing their material. Many of them appear disinterested in supporting authors who want to self-publish commercially and have a well-documented history of doing published research. Hopefully, as the growing self-publishing industry continues to build a credible cadre of proven historical authors who are not publishing to make a living, those organizations will recognize the value of supporting people like myself who do not have the financial support that comes with landing a "big publishing deal."

I also want to thank and recognize those publishers, authors, and websites who supported a first-time commercial historical and non-fiction author and have authorized the use of their material: Andrew Laverdiere, LivingNewDeal.org; Erin Best, author; David Chittim, Androscoggin Historical Society; Dan Macleod, Bangor Daily News; Jay Burns, Bates Magazine and Communications; Pat Webber, Edmund Muskie Archives at Bates College; Leslie Choquette, author; Paul Carnahan, Vermont Historical Society; Claude Belanger and Damien-Claude Belanger, authors; John Belshaw, author; BC Campus, publisher; Anna Feherty, University of Southern Maine Franco-Heritage Collection; Sarah D'Antonio, Robert and Elizabeth Dole Archive; Manjit Kaur, University of Nebraska Press; Sharon

Gaber, Darcy Boellstorff, Jeff Vincent, John Gaber, authors; Shari Garmise, Shari Nourick, Elizabeth Thorstensen, authors; International Economic Development Council; Greg Leroy, Phil Mattera, Arlene Martinez, Good Jobs First; Douglas Hodgkin, author; Nancy Randolph, Just Write Books, LLC; Rick Morris, Lewiston Historical Commission; Mazie Hough, Kristin Langellier, Kim Huisman, Carol Nordstrom Toner, editors and authors; Sarah Serafimidis, North Atlantic Books; James Leamon, author; Dierdre Maagean, Gillian AvRuskin, authors; Barbara Harrity, Maine Policy Review; Ray Kelly, The Republican (Springfield, Holyoke, Chicopee, MA area); Garrett Martin and Mario Moretto, Maine Center for Economic Policy; Colleen Stoxen, Star Tribune of Minneapolis; Eric Conrad, Maine Municipal Association; Mnopedia.org and Confederation of Somali Community in Minnesota; Jay Newberry, author; Andy O'Brien, author; Ethan Andrews, The Free Press; Paul Pare, author; Pew Research Center; Central Intelligence Agency; U.S. Army; U.S. Government departments and agencies; State of Maine; City of Lewiston; Androscoggin Historical Society; Lewiston Historic Preservation Commission; John Rand, author; Larry Wold, Market President, TD Bank-Maine; Douglas Rooks, author; James Myall and Mary Rice-DeFosse, authors; Katie Parry, History Press; Andrew Murray, McGill-Queen's University Press; Mikayla Mislak, Rowman and Littlefield; Rob Sneddon, author; James Tierney, author; Peter Temin, author; David Vermette, author; Robin Philpot, Baraka Books; and Alex DeWall, World Peace Foundation.

Other authors: Mason Wade, Madelaine Giguere, Lesa Scholl, A.M.Myhrman, J.A. Rademaker, Charlotte Michaude, Adelard Janelle, James Allen, J.K.L. LaFlamme, David E. Lavigne, Arthur J. Favreau, Heinz Kloss, Yili Chien, Paul Morris, John P. Deeben, James Pritchard, Lucien Gosselin, Reginald C. Barrows, Dennis J. Palumbo, Lucy Salyer, Diana Briton Putnam, Mohamood Cabdi Noor, Mary T. Sarnecky, Richard W. Stewart, Jason M. Alexander, Marshall V. Ecklund, and Michael A. McNerney. If I have overlooked anyone, my apologies, as I do appreciate your support in making this book possible.

I would also like to acknowledge the city of Lewiston staff who were involved with coordinating and assisting my research requests during some very difficult and challenging times. A pandemic and an administration change certainly made the business of working with my information requests more challenging as well. Also, I would like to express my deepest appreciation to all the contributors involved in the publications produced by the Lewiston Historical Preservation Commission. The work of legendary city historians Gridley Barrows, Geneva Kirk, James Leamon, Douglas Hodgkin, and others provided me with material and direction for much of my research into the city's prior history. It is my hope that they will see this book as contributing value to that historical record in some meaningful way.

Finally, I would like to recognize the work and patience of my editor, Jules Fox. He was a constant source of information and encouragement. His guidance, steady hand, and keen eye were invaluable in my completing this book. I also would like to recognize Les at 'germancreative.com' for her creative and insightful work on the book cover. Jules and Les made a great team, and I was fortunate to have them both in my corner. I would be remiss if I also did not recognize photographer Denis Tangney, Jr. who produced the iStock Lewiston photo used for the front cover, and Russ Dillingham for his back cover photo.

# APPENDIX

## LA Joint Agreements, Initiatives, Projects, Mergers, Committees(1)
11/23/20

| | YEAR | NAME | COMMENTS | REMAINS ACTIVE |
|---|---|---|---|---|
| 1 | 1849 | LEWISTON FALLS VILLAGE CORPORATION | A Fire Department for Lewiston, a portion of Auburn and Danville, and continued until 1856 when the legislature passed an act creating the Lewiston Village Corporation and the Auburn Village Corporation | NO |
| 2 | 1872 | LEWISTON-AUBURN RAILROAD COMPANY | The railroad line was opened in 1874. The railroad continues to be jointly owned and operated by both cities. | YES |
| 3 | 1880 | ELECTRIC FIRE ALARM COMPANY | This company installed fire alarm telegraph boxes in Lewiston and in 1882 the system was extended to Auburn and operated jointly until 1920. | NO |
| 4 | 1881 | LEWISTON AND AUBURN HORSE RAILROAD | A horse drawn trolley system. | NO |
| 5 | 1925 | AUBURN WATER DISTRICT AND LEWISTON WATER DEPARTMENT JOINT LAKE PATROL | The two cities have been working together to protect the Lake Auburn water source for over 100 years. See Andrew Rice, "The Future of Lake Auburn: More Recreation and Development?" (Lewiston) Sun Journal, February 4, 2019. | YES |
| 6 | 1937 | AUBURN-LEWISTON MUNICIPAL AIRPORT | Construction was jointly funded and began in 1935. The airport, originally named the "Lewiston-Auburn Airport," was opened in 1937 and operations were jointly funded. The Department of Defense utilized the airport as early as 1942 and assumed control of the airport and officially naming it the ""Lewiston Naval Auxiliary Air Facility (NAAF), Site Number: D01ME0009" on April 15, 1943. The airport was deeded back to the cities in 1946. For attribution, see Endnotes. | YES |
| 7 | 1962 | ANDROSCOGGIN VALLEY REGIONAL PLANNING COMMITTEE (AVRPC) | The creation of the regional AVRPC was made possible when both Lewiston and Auburn agreed to become members. As the largest contributors to the effort, they were a critical source of funding and support for the regional effort that included multiple communities in the greater Lewiston-Auburn area. The AVRPC later became the Androscoggin Valley Council of Governments (AVCOG) in 1981 and continues to operate to this day. For attribution, see Endnotes. | YES |
| 8 | 1963 | LEWISTON-AUBURN CHAMBER OF COMMERCE | The Lewiston Chamber of Commerce was founded in 1887. The Auburn Chamber of Commerce was in existence as far back as 1919 and ceased to exist sometime after 1951. As far back as 1932, there were public discussions about merging the two organizations. The Lewiston Chamber of Commerce moved from its 56 Park Street location to the new First-Manufacturers National Bank Building on the corner of Ash and Park Streets in 1963. The Lewiston Chamber approved the new name, the Lewiston-Auburn Chamber of Commerce, on January 30, 1963. The organization name was later changed to the Androscoggin County Chamber of Commerce and is now called the LA Metropolitan Chamber of Commerce. For attribution see Endnotes. | YES |
| 9 | 1964 | ANDROSCOGGIN STATE VOCATIONAL INSTITUTE | The vocational school was spearheaded by then Lewiston State Representative Louis Jalbert and received the support from elected officials in both cities. The Auburn location was selected as the best suited site for the school and supported by both cities. Approved by voters in 1963, the vocational school was renamed the Central Maine Vocational Institute in 1965 and would be relocated to its existing location. It was renamed in 1989 as the Central Maine Technical College and in 2003 received its current name the Central Maine Community College. For attribution, see Endnotes. | YES |
| 10 | 1965 | LEWISTON AUBURN TRANSPORTATION COMPREHENSIVE STUDY policy committee (LACTS) | Now called the Androscoggin Transportation Resource Center (ATRC) and has served as the Metropolitan Planning Organization (MPO) going back to federal legislation created in 1962. Its members are comprised of a Policy Committee of elected and appointed officials from the Cities of Lewiston and Auburn, the Towns of Lisbon and Sabattus, the Androscoggin Valley Council of Governments (AVCOG), as well as the Androscoggin County Chamber of Commerce, the Maine Turnpike Authority (MTA), Western Maine Transportation Services, the Maine Department of Transportation (MaineDOT), and the federal funding agencies of the United States Department of Transportation (USDOT). See https://www.avcog.org/888/About-ATRC. | YES |
| 11 | 1967 | LEWISTON-AUBURN WATER POLLUTION CONTROL AUTHORITY (LAWPCA) | The charter was approved by a legislative act in 1967, the first such charter to be approved for municipalities in the state. The sewage treatment plant opened in 1974 and is jointly owned and operated by the City of Lewiston and the Auburn Sewer District. It was the first municipally/district owned tertiary sewage treatment plant opened in the state. It continues to be operated by both entities to this day. For attribution, see Endnotes. | YES |
| 12 | 1968 | LEWISTON AND AUBURN FIRE DEPARTMENTS | Mutual aid agreement. | YES |
| 13 | 1973 | LEWISTON PUBLIC LIBRARY "LPL plus" PROGRAM | The Lewiston Library efforts to bring more cultural and artistic events to the city resulted in the creation of the "LPL plus" program in 1973. That program soon led to a joint effort with Auburn creating "LPL Plus APL" program eventually leading to the creation of LA Arts in 1988 that remains active to this day. For attribution see Endnotes. | YES |
| 14 | 1975 | THE ROCKLAND EXPERIENCE | City staffs from both cities meet at the Samoset hotel on a weekend in April 1975 to discuss the relationship between the two cities. This weekend produces renewed commitments for cooperation between the two cities. | N/A |
| 15 | 1975 | LEWISTON AND AUBURN POLICE DEPARTMENTS | Mutual aid agreement. | YES |
| 16 | 1976 | LEWISTON AUBURN TRANSIT COMMITTEE (LATC) | Following the near demise of the transit system in 1975, the two cities agreed to provide the first public subsidies in 1975 to assist privately owned Hudson Bus Lines maintain public transit for both cities. In 1976, both cities agree to create LATC and to continue to subsidize public transportation in both cities. For attribution see Endnotes. | YES |

| | | | | |
|---|---|---|---|---|
| 17 | 1976 | LEWISTON AUBURN JOINT PURCHASING INTIATIVE | This agreement was created as a direct result of the "Rockland Experience" weekend meeting in 1975. | YES |
| 18 | 1978 | LEWISTON AUBURN 9-1-1 CENTER | The consolidation of emergency services for both cities. Formerly located in the new Lewiston Central Fire Station built in 1973, the center is relocated to Auburn Central Fire Station in the 1990s and remains in operation. | YES |
| 19 | 1979 | AUBURN LEWISTON INDUSTRIAL PARK AND TAX SHARING AGREEMENT | First tax sharing agreement between two Maine municipalities in state history. | YES |
| 20 | 1980 | LEWISTON AUBURN SOLID WASTE STUDY COMMITTEE | | NO |
| 21 | 1980 | LEWISTON AUBURN CABLE TV NEGOTIATION CMTEE | This was the first effort for both cities to negotiate a franchise agreement with the local cable tv provider (there was only one service at the time) as a single joint agreement. All future cable tv agreements were negotiated jointly. I was associated with all cable TV franchise negotiations since 1999 and knew the history of all prior franchise agreements and the cable TV committee. | YES |
| 22 | 1980 | LEWISTON AUBURN TURNPIKE COMMITTEE | | NO |
| 23 | 1981 | LEWISTON AUBURN ECONOMIC GROWTH COMMITTEE (LAEGC) | The Lewiston Development Corporation was instrumental in creating the Lewiston Economic Growth Council in 1976 and dissolved upon the creation of the LAEGC. The agreement for this organization has morphed over time. Once funded by both cities as a stand alone organization, it now receives its funding and administrative support through the LA Metropolitan Chamber of Commerce.* | *YES |
| 24 | 1982 | LEWISTON AUBURN COLLEGE ADVOCACY COMMITTEE (for the purpose of creating L-A College. | The joint committee was created as part of the effort to create a Lewiston-Auburn College in the area. The college was funded by the legislature in 1987 and built in Lewiston in 1988. For attribution see Endnotes. | YES |
| 25 | 1984 | CHARLES MONTY HYDRO DAM PROJECT | This was the second time both cities would come together to create a joint revenue agreement. The dam was owned by a state electric utility company but agreed to a revenue sharing agreement with both cities in place of Lewiston building its own (competing) hydro electric dam. | YES |
| 26 | 1984 | LEWISTON-AUBURN UNIFIED EMERGENCY MANAGEMENT AGENCY (EMA) | Both cities pay for costs associated with Androscoggin EMA services that serves as one of 16 county EMA agencies affiliated with the state EMA and FEMA. | YES |
| 27 | 1988 | JOINT "THE RIGHT MOVE, THE TWIN CITIES" MARKETING CAMPAIGN | This was the first joint marketing effort, administered by LAEGC, focused on economic development in the area during the 1988-89 time period. See https://www.iedcevents.org/Downloads/Conferences/annual_16/holden.pdf. | NO |
| 28 | 1992 | JOINT "CITIES OF THE ANDROSCOGGIN" BRANDING CAMPAIGN | A collaborative image branding effort involving the Lewiston-Auburn Economic Growth Council, the L-A Chamber of Commerce, LA Arts, and WCSH TV in Portland, ME. Broader in scope than "Right Move," the campaign would focus on quality of life assets in the area involving health care, arts, education with a focus on natural resources including the improving water quality and recreational value of the Androscoggin River. See https://www.iedcevents.org/Downloads/Conferences/annual_16/holden.pdf. | NO |
| 29 | 1993 | LEWISTON AUBURN LAKE WATERSHED PROTECTION COMMITTEE | Created to protect the watershed area of Lake Auburn, the only drinking water source for both cities. Both Lewiston and the Auburn Water District also operate and fund the water treatment facility at Lake Auburn. | YES |
| 30 | 1994 | LEWISTON AUBURN CABLE ADVISORY COMMITTEE | An informal agreement was reached in 1994 but was finally adopted as a formal agreement between both cities in 2016. See https://www.lewistonmaine.gov/ArchiveCenter/ViewFile/Item/3581. | YES |
| 31 | 1995 | LEWISTON AUBURN WATER AND SEWER CONSOLIDATION STUDY | | NO |
| 32 | 1996 | L-A TOGETHER | Initiative launched by both cities to study and encourage more cooperation between both cities. See https://www.iedcevents.org/Downloads/Conferences/annual_16/holden.pdf. | NO |
| 33 | 1998 | L-A EXCELS | Follow up effort to L-A Together to implement and improve upon the work of L-A Together | NO |
| 34 | 1998 | JOINT L-A ECONOMIC DEVELOPMENT PROTOCOL | A formal agreement outlining how both cities would handle inquiries from businesses looking to locate in either Lewiston or Auburn. All administration for the protocols would be the responsibility of LAEGC | YES |
| 35 | 1999 | JOINT L-A TAX INCREMENT FINANCING (TIF) AGREEMENT | A formal agreement outlining how both cities would craft TIFs for prospective businesses looking to locate or expand in either city. | YES |
| 36 | 1999 | US POST OFFICE CENTER RELOCATION TO LEWISTON | Effort by both cities to work together to locate a US Post Office distribution center from Portland to L-A. The search process resulted in the L-A area's selection but was changed through efforts launched by the Post Office union, the City of Portland, the Portland Chamber of Commerce and political pressure to re-open the search process. The project location was changed to Scarborough and the new center opened in 2006. For attribution see Endnotes. | N/A |
| 37 | 2001.99 | LEWISTON AUBURN JOINT PURCHASING INTIATIVE | This agreement was created as a direct result of the "Rockland Experience" weekend meeting in 1975. | YES |
| 38 | 2003.35 | LEWISTON AUBURN 9-1-1 CENTER | The consolidation of emergency services for both cities. Formerly located in the new Lewiston Central Fire Station built in 1973, the center is relocated to Auburn Central Fire Station in the 1990s and remains in operation. | YES |
| 39 | 2004.7 | LEWISTON AUBURN JOINT PURCHASING INTIATIVE | This agreement was created as a direct result of the "Rockland Experience" weekend meeting in 1975. | YES |

| # | Year | Name | Description | Implemented |
|---|---|---|---|---|
| 40 | 2003 | L-A CASH COALITION | Developed as an area intiative in cooperation with the IRS, it returns millions of federal dollars to area eligible families. The project began during my tenure with the City of Lewiston. | YES |
| 41 | 2003 | ANDROSCOGGIN VALLEY PINE TREE ZONE | Developed as a collaborative effort by area counties, its purpose is to created tax incentives for companies that exist or want to locate into the designated zone. | NO |
| 42 | 2004 | L-A COMMISSION ON JOINT SERVICES | Purpose was to explore more cooperative opportunities between the two cities. | NO |
| 43 | 2006 | CITIZENS COMMISSION ON LEWISTON AUBURN COOPERATION | Purpose was to implement some or all of the findings from the 2004 joint commission. | NO |
| 44 | 2008 | L-A PUBLIC HEALTH COMMITTEE (LAPHC) | Agreement was jointly approved by both cities to help coordinate public health policy and to make recommendations on new health policy in both cities. Auburn formally left the committee in 2016 but the committee was renamed the *"Lewiston Area Public Health Committee" to allow for participation from Auburn officials, agencies or residents. I assisted in creating the committee and the revised committee in 2016. | *YES |
| 45 | 2009 | L-A JOINT CODE ENFORCEMENT SOFTWARE PURCHASE | Both cities agree to jointly purchase and collaborate on new code enforcement software system that will share a single server. The system had its share of technical problems and was eventually designed and set up as two independently operating system's. I assisted with the purchase and implementation of the software. | NO |
| 46 | 2012 | L-A BIKE PED COMMITTEE | Committee was formed through a joint resolution of both city councils. The committee created the first "Complete Streets Policy" in 2013 that was adopted by both city councils. | YES |
| 47 | 2012 | JOINT ULTRAVIOLET LIGHT DISINFECTION TREATMENT FACILITY | THE $12 million project was completed in 2012. A number of drinking water projects have been undertaken between the two cities for decades. Of the "50,000-plus municipal water system's in the country, the Lake Auburn watershed is one of only 50 or 60 protected" bodies of water that do not require "expensive" filtration. See Richard Burnham, "Lewiston-Auburn Joint Lake Auburn Ultraviolet Light Drinking Water Treatment Facility Nears Completion," *(Lewiston) Sun Journal*, June 7, 2011. | |
| 48 | 2013 | LAWPCA ANAEROBIC DIGESTER PROJECT | The Lewiston-Auburn Water Polloution Control Authority $15.5 million anaerobic digester/co-generation project was one of the single largest public sector projects in the history of the two communities. **For attribution see Endnotes.** | YES |
| 49 | 2014 | LEWISTON AUBURN JOINT CHARTER COMMISSION | Created following a vote by both cities to create a commission for the purpose of creating a new charter to formally merge the two cities. | NO |
| 50 | 2017 | VOTE TO MERGE THE CITIES OF LEWISTON AND AUBURN | The November 2017 vote failed to be approved in both Lewiston and Auburn. Joint collaboration between the cities continues to this day. | NO |
| 51 | 2019 | NEW (AUBURN) EL HIGH SCHOOL & LEW REG TECH SCHOOL (LRTC) WING | The LRTC was created through enabling state legislation in 1965, and by the State Board of Education in 1966 designating 14 school districts as locations for regional technical and vocational centers. The LRTC began in the 1967-68 school year at the former LHS school building on Central Avenue in Lewiston.(2) The new LRTC wing to be located in the new ELHS is scheduled for completion in 2023. The LRTC expansion and new wing was jointly agreed to by the Lewiston and Auburn public school systems in 2018(3) and approved by voters on June 11, 2019.(4) | YES |

(1) For attribution, see Lucien B. Gosselin, "Lewiston/Auburn College Chronology," August 6, 1995, 1, paper unless otherwise noted. All "Endnotes" refer to book endnotes.

(2) Subcommittee on Education of the Committee on Labor and Public Welfare United States Senate, "S. 3099, To Amend the Higher Education Act of 1965...and Related Acts (and) S.3099, To Amend the Vocational Act of 1963, and for Other Purposes and Related Bills," Hearings, Ninetieth Congress, Second Session, U.S. Government Printing Office, Washington: 1968, 5749-5754, https://www.google.com/books/edition/Education_Legislation_1968/AFhFAQAAMAAJ?hl=en&gbpv=1&dq=lewiston+regional+technical+center+created&pg=PA5747&printsec=frontcover, last accessed December 1, 2020.

(3) Bonnie Washuk, "LRTC Expanding to Auburn," *(Lewiston) Sun Journal (online)*, November 14, 2018.

(4) Bonnie Washuk, "Auburn Votes Big For New Edward Little High School," *(Lewiston) Sun Journal (online), June 11, 2019.*

# Notes

[1] Justin Pelletier, "Empty Arena's Weren't a Concern," *(Lewiston) Sun Journal,* May 25, 2005, C4, https://news.google.com/newspapers?nid=bcT4vkklUMwC&dat=20050525&printsec=frontpage&hl=en, last accessed April 20, 2020.

[2] Rob Sneddon, *The Phantom Punch: The Story Behind Boxing's Most Controversial Bout* (Camden: Down East Books, 2016), 121-127.

[3] Ibid., 122.

[4] Ibid., 97-104 & 124-127.

[5] Ibid., 48-51.

[6] Kalle Oakes, "Ali-Liston: The 'Phantom Punch' turns 50," *(Lewiston) Sun Journal(online),* May 15, 2015, https://www.sunjournal.com/2015/05/15/ali-liston-phantom-punch-turns-50/, last accessed April 20, 2020.

[7] Ibid.

[8] Mark Emmert, "The Maine Moment that Made Muhammad Ali," *Portland Press Herald(online),* May 24, 2015, https://www.pressherald.com/2015/05/24/may-25-1965-the-maine-moment-that-made-muhammad-ali/, last accessed January 9, 2021.

[9] Ibid.

[10] Rob Sneddon, "The Phantom Punch," 142-143.

[11] *The Lewiston Daily Sun,* "Kennedy and the Crowds,"(photos by Philbrick and Houghton), November 7, 1960, 1.

[12] Edward C. Schlick, "Tells Shivering Throng Need for U.S. Action," *The Lewiston Daily Sun,* November 7, 1960, 1.

[13] Bob Hoobing (AP), "Ali Confused at Fight Site," *The Lewiston Daily Sun,* May 24, 1965, 16, https://news.google.com/newspapers?nid=IT5EXw6i2GUC&dat=19650524& printsec=frontpage&hl=en, last accessed July 5, 2020.

[14] *The Lewiston Daily Sun,* "Clay-Liston Fight Definitely Slated at Lewiston CMYC," May 8, 1965, https://news.google.com/newspapers?nid=IT5EXw6i2GUC&dat=19650508&printsec=frontpage&hl=en, last accessed July 5, 2020.

[15] Rob Sneddon, "The Phantom Punch," 190.

[16] Ibid., 212.

[17] Ibid., 184 & 188-189.

[18] Ibid., 192-197.

[19] Robert and Elizabeth Dole Archive and Special Collections. Robert J. Dole Institute of Politics, University of Kansas. Dole Archives Collection, Kansas State University. 1995. Speeches. File c019_097_013_all.pdf. "Lewiston Bicentennial Committee 1795-1995: Lewiston Bicentennial Mission Statement," 2, "Banquet '200'"

(program), 3, retrieved at: http://dolearchivecollections.ku.edu/collections/speeches/097/c019_097_013_all.pdf, last accessed July 3, 2020.

[20] What was not mentioned in any of the news coverage of Ali's return to Lewiston with Floyd Patterson, was that prior to the November 22, 1965 Ali-Patterson match, Patterson wrote an article for Sports Illustrated attacking Ali's stating that his choice to be a Muslim was a "disgraces the sport and the nation. Cassius Clay must be beaten and the Black Muslims' scourge removed from boxing."(Sneddon, 215) It was a lost opportunity by the media to report on the strength in the character of both Ali and Patterson, and how they had demonstrated that that history between them was long forgotten.

[21] Steve Cherlock, "Ali Showed He Was 'The Greatest' During 1995 Visit to Lewiston," *(Lewiston) Sun Journal(online)*, June 11, 2016, https://www.sunjournal.com/2016/06/11/ali-showed-the-greatest-1995-visit-lewiston/, last accessed July 5, 2020.

[22] For more information about Neil Leifer, see https://www.esquire.com/entertainment/books/a35252752/neil-leifer-boxing-photos-book-60-years-fights-fighters/, last accessed March 17, 2021.

[23] Randy Whitehouse, "Deford: Picture is Why Fight is Remembered," *(Lewiston) Sun Journal*, May 25, 2005, https://news.google.com/newspapers?nid=bcT4vkklUMwC&dat=20050525&printsec=frontpage&hl=en, last accessed June 22, 2020.

[24] James S. Leamon, *Historic Lewiston: A Textile City in Transition*, (Auburn, ME: The Lewiston Historical Commission and Graphics Department, (Auburn, ME: Central Maine Vocational Technical Institute, 1976), v, https://www.lewistonmaine.gov/DocumentCenter/View/1191/Historic-Lew-A-Textile-City-in-Transition-1976?bidId=, last accessed June 22, 2020.

[25] Peter Temin, "The Industrialization of New England: 1830-1880," National Bureau of Economic Research Working Paper Series on Historical Factors in Long Run Growth. Historical Paper 114, 1999, 8-9, paper presented at Boston Federal Reserve Bank conference, October 2, 1998. Copyright 1999 by Peter Temin. https://www.nber.org/papers/h0114.pdf, last accessed June 22, 2020.

[26] Ibid., 23-24.

[27] Ibid.,16.

[28] James Leamon, "Historic Lewiston: A Textile City in Transition," 8.

[29] John A. Rand, *"The Peoples Lewiston-Auburn Maine 1875-1975,"* (Freeport, ME: The Bond Wheelwright Company), 1975, 3.

[30] Ibid., 3; Leamon, "Historic Lewiston: A Textile City in Transition," 10.

[31] David Vermette, *A Distinct Alien Race: The Untold Story of Franco-Americans. Industrialization, Immigration, Religious Strife*, (Montreal, QC: Baraka Books, 2018), 98.

[32] *Lewiston Falls Journal*, May 11, 1860, notes in BMCHF; Margaret J. Buker, "The Irish in Lewiston, Maine: A Search for Security on the Urban Frontier, 1850-1880," Maine Historical Society Quarterly, XIII, No. 1/A (Special, 1973), 8-9, cited in Leamon, "Historic Lewiston: A Textile City in Transition," 15.

[33] Temin, "The Industrialization of New England," 35.

[34] Patrick Connors, "Culture Clash Out of Strife," *(Lewiston) Sun Journal*, October 13, 2002, source document Judy Meyer email to Phil Nadeau, June 11, 2020. **(NOTE: Many of the Lewiston newspaper articles cited prior to 2003, were found through Google Newspaper Archives. There were no Lewiston newspapers available for October 2002 and for all Sunday editions. Through the assistance of Sun Journal Executive Editor Judy Meyer, I was able to obtain articles that were printed in the Sun Journal in the month of October 2002 and for several Sundays in 2002 and 2003 that were also not available through Google Newspaper Archives. All articles obtained provided by Judy Meyer are noted in the Endnotes of this book.)**

[35] Ibid.

[36] James Leamon, "Historic Lewiston: A Textile City in Transition," 15.

[37] *Lewiston Falls Journal*, Buker, 18, cited in Leamon, "Historic Lewiston: A Textile City in Transition," 15.

[38] Patrick Connors, "Culture Clash Out of Strife."

[39] *The Free Press* (Camden, ME), "When the Irish Refugees Came to Maine: Poverty, Discrimination & Bitter Struggle," Andy O'Brien, May 12, 2015, https://freepressonline.com/Content/Features/Andy-O-Brien-Historical-Articles/Article/When-the-Irish-Refugees-Came-to-Maine/52/796/37396, last accessed June 22, 2020.

[40] Lesa Scholl, "Irish Migration to London During the c.1845-52 Famine: Henry Mayhew's Representation in London Labour and the London Poor," BRANCH: Britain, Representation and Nineteenth-Century History, Ed. Dino Franco Felluga, Extension of Romanticism and Victorianism on the Net, http://creativecommons.org/licenses/by/3.0/, retrieved from http://www.branchcollective.org/?ps_articles=lesa-scholl-irish-migration-to-london-during-the-c-1845-52-famine-henry-mayhews-representation-in-london-labour-and-the-london-poor, last accessed September 23, 2020.

[41] James Myall, "The Year Maine Went Mad – the Know Nothingism of 1854-5," *Bangor Daily News(online)*, April 7, 2019, http://myall.bangordailynews.com/2019/04/07/home/the-year-maine-

went-mad-the-know-nothingism-of-1854-5/, last accessed on June 25, 2020.

[42] Ibid.

[43] Douglas I. Hodgkin, *"Frontier to Industrial City: Lewiston Town Politics, 1768-1863."* (Topsham: Just Write Books, 2008), 177, https://www.amazon.com/Frontier-Industrial-City-Lewiston-1768-1863/dp/1934949108, last accessed June 22, 2020.

[44] James Leamon, "Historic Lewiston: A Textile City in Transition," 24.

[45] Damien-Claude Belanger and Claude Belanger, "French Canadian emigration to the United States 1840-1930," August 23, 2000 (revised), in *Quebec History,* Montreal, QC: Marianopolis College, http://faculty.marianopolis.edu/c.belanger/quebechistory/readings/leaving.htm, last accessed June 22, 2020.

[46] Ibid.

[47] Charlotte Michaud, Adelard Janelle, and James Leamon, "Historic Lewiston: Franco-American Origins," (Auburn, ME: Central Maine Technical College, 1974), 12, https://www.lewistonmaine.gov/DocumentCenter/View/1190/Historic-Lew-Franco-American-Origins-1974?bidId=, last accessed September 9, 2020.

[48] Mary Rice-DeFosse and James Myall, *"The Franco-Americans of Lewiston-Auburn,"* (Charleston, SC: The History Press, 2015), 14.

[49] A. M. Myhrman and J. A. Rademaker, *"The Second Colonization Process in an Industrial Community,"* unpublished manuscript in LPL, cited in Leamon, "Historic Lewiston: A Textile City in Transition," 17.

[50] Mason Wade, "French and French-Canadians in the United States," 1967, in *A Franco-American Overview: Volume 3, New England (Part One),* ed. Madelaine Giguère (Cambridge: National Assessment and Dissemination Center for Bilingual/Bicultural Education, 1981), 41.

[51] Ibid., 42.

[52] James Leamon, "Historic Lewiston: A Textile City in Transition," 17.

[53] Using Leamon's 70% textile workforce number, the estimate of 5,000 textile wage earners is based on total wage earners information of 7,159 for Lewiston in the 1900 U.S. Census. See Department of the U.S. Census Office, "Bulletins of the Twelfth Census of the United States: Published between November 1, 1901, and April 29, 1902, Numbers 107-163," 1902, 127, 8, https://books.google.com/books?id=O2QUAQAAMAAJ&pg=RA19-PA1&lpg=RA19-PA1&dq=lewiston+maine+1900+employment+census&source=bl&ots=op4O-WHOQT&sig=ACfU3U3Ct4YrsbKNF2htzCnmDtdqKYsoBw&hl=en&sa=X&ved=2ahUKEwjP99WmlsjqAhXQhOAKHVFMBfkQ6AEwDXo

ECAcQAQ#v=onepage&q=lewiston%20maine%201900%20employment%20census&f=false, last accessed July 12, 2020.
[54] Ibid., 14.
[55] Rice-DeFosse and James Mayall, "The Franco-Americans of Lewiston-Auburn," 13.
[56] James Leamon, "Historic Lewiston: A Textile City in Transition," 17.
[57] David Vermette, "A Distinct Alien Race," 30.
[58] J.D. Belshaw, *"Canadian History: Pre-Confederation,"* (Victoria, BC: BCcampus, 2015), CC by 4.0, retrieved at: https://opentextbc.ca/preconfederation/, last accessed June 23, 2020.
[59] *The New York Times,* "The French Canadians," July 5, 1889, 4, https://timesmachine.nytimes.com/timesmachine/1889/07/05/109321342.html?pageNumber=4, last accessed July 5, 2020.
[60] *The New York Times,* "The French Canadians in New England," June 6, 1892, 4.
[61] Leslie Choquette, "French Canadian Immigration to Vermont and New England (1840-1930)," in *Vermont History.* Vol. 86, No. 1, Winter/Spring 2018, 1-8, https://vermonthistory.org/journal/86/VH8601FrenchCanadianImmigration.pdf, last accessed on June 22, 2020
[62] Egbert C. Smyth, "The French-Canadians in New England," paper from Proceedings of the American Antiquarian Society at the annual meeting, October 21,1891, published 1892, 319-322, https://digicom.bpl.lib.me.us/books_pubs/171 ,last accessed June 25, 2020.
[63] James Allen, "Franco-Americans in Maine: A Geographical Perspective," 1974, in *A Franco-American overview: New England (part one),* 3, edited by Madeleine Giguère, (Cambridge: Evaluation, Dissemination and Assessment Center, 1981), 95.
[64] One hundred years ago, the three largest population in Maine were found in Portland, Lewiston and Bangor respectively. The same three remain the largest cities in that same order. For more information about these cities see https://www.mainememory.net/sitebuilder/site/907/page/1318/print, last accessed February 22, 2021.
[65] J.K.L. Laflamme, David E. Lavigne and Arthur J. Favreau, "The French Catholics in the United States," in *A Franco-American overview: New England (part one),* 3, edited by Madeleine Giguère. (Cambridge: Evaluation, Dissemination and Assessment Center, 1981), 28.
[66] Donna Rousseau, "The History of Catholic Education in Lewiston-Auburn," *(Lewiston) Sun Journal(online),* January 29, 2011, https://www.sunjournal.com/2011/01/29/history-catholic-education-lewiston-auburn/, last accessed July 5, 2020.
[67] James Allen, "Franco-Americans in Maine," 95.

[68] Ibid., 95.

[69] Heinz Kloss, *Les Droits Linguistiques des Franco-Américains aux Etats-Unis*, (Quebec, 1970), 52, cited in James Allen, "Franco-Americans in Maine," 95-96.

[70] "Under city government the executive authority went to two bodies. The Mayor presided over the Board of Aldermen (composed of one from each of seven wards), while the Common Council was composed of three per ward. These two bodies had a veto over each other and served without compensation. All were elected annually on the first Monday of March and then proceeded to name the sub-officers. The work was done by joint standing committees of the Council and Aldermen: Finance, Accounts, Public Property, Highways, Drains and Sewer Fire Department, Schools, Engrossed Bills and Ordinances, and Printing. Many of the titles of officials were the same as in town government. However, the Selectmen were replaced by Assessors and Overseers of the Poor and the following were added: city physician, engineer and four assistants, poundkeeper (in place of hog reaves), school committee, street commissioner, liquor agent, superintendent of burials, and city solicitor...(T)he Common Council was abolished in 1920...," see Geneva Kirk and Gridley Barrows, "Historic Lewiston: Its Government," Lewiston Historical Commission, (Auburn, ME: Central Maine Technical College, 1981-82), 3, https://www.lewistonmaine.gov/DocumentCenter/View/1188/Historic-Lew-Its-Government-1982?bidId=, last accessed July 1, 2020.

[71] Charlotte Michaud, Adelard Janelle, and James Leamon, "Historic Lewiston: Franco-American Origins," 25.

[72] Geneva Kirk and Gridley Barrows, "Historic Lewiston: Its Government," 34.

[73] City of Lewiston, "National Register of Historic Places Registration Form," Historic Preservation Review Board, Agenda, December 6, 2018, 13, http://www.lewistonrecreation.com/Archive/ViewFile/Item/3889, last accessed November 30, 2020.

[74] Ibid., 17.

[75] David Vermette, "A Distinct Alien Race," 232.

[76] City of Lewiston, "National Register of Historic Places Registration Form," 17.

[77] Ibid., 17-18.

[78] Ibid., 18.

[79] Erin Best, "The Klan Issue: How French Canadians Combatted Nativism Through 1920 Maine Local Politics," 2019. In *Undergraduate Review*, **14**, 38-44, retrieved at: https://vc.bridgew.edu/undergrad_rev/vol14/iss2/8, last accessed June 23, 2020.

⁸⁰ David Vermette, "A Distinct Alien Race," 284.
⁸¹ David Vermette, "A Distinct Alien Race," 274-275.
⁸² Ibid., 281-282.
⁸³ Erin Best, "The Klan Issue," 43.
⁸⁴ Paul H. Mills, "The Man Who Beat Both Baxter and the Klan," *(Lewiston) Sun Journal(online),* December 30, 2007, https://www.sunjournal.com/2007/12/30/man-beat-baxter-klan/, last accessed July 6, 2020.
⁸⁵ Lewiston Historical Commission, "Historic Lewiston: Its Government," 13.
⁸⁶ Lewiston Historical Commission, "Historic Lewiston: Franco-American origins," 25.
⁸⁷ David Vermette, "A Distinct Alien Race," 112-113.
⁸⁸ *The Lewiston Daily Sun,* "Rioting Brings Guardsmen Here," April 22, 1937, 1, https://news.google.com/newspapers?nid=IT5EXw6i2GUC&dat=19370422&printsec=frontpage&hl=en, last accessed July 1, 2020
⁸⁹ The Lewiston Daily Sun, "Slingshots Hurl Stones at Three Lewiston Homes." *The Lewiston Daily Sun,* April 23, 1937, 1, https://news.google.com/newspapers?nid=IT5EXw6i2GUC&dat=19370423&printsec=frontpage&hl=en, last accessed July 1, 2020
⁹⁰ Kathryn Skelton, "Nobel Peace Prize Winner and Former Lewiston Resident Bernard Lown," *(Lewiston) Sun Journal(online),* August 31, 2008, https://www.sunjournal.com/2008/08/31/nobel-peace-prize-winner-former-lewiston-resident-bernard-lown/, last accessed November 11, 2020.
⁹¹ Ibid.
⁹² Ibid.
⁹³ Ibid.
⁹⁴ *(Lewiston) Sun Journal(online),* "Bridge Honors Cardiologist," May 11, 2009, https://www.sunjournal.com/2009/05/11/bridge-honors-cardiologist/, last accessed November 11, 2020.
⁹⁵ Kathryn Skelton, "Bernard Lown Peace Bridge," *(Lewiston) Sun Journal(online),* October 18, 2008, https://www.sunjournal.com/2008/10/18/bernard-lown-peace-bridge/, last accessed February 22, 2021.
⁹⁶ U.S. Department of Homeland Security, "RAIO Combined Training Program: Refugee Definition," U.S. Citizenship and Immigration Services, December 20, 2019, https://www.uscis.gov/sites/default/files/document/foia/Refugee_Definition_LP_RAIO.pdf, last accessed January 10, 2021.
⁹⁷ For more information about Dr. Lown's receipt of the Nobel Peace Prize, see https://www.nytimes.com/1985/10/12/world/nobel-peace-

prize-given-to-doctors-opposed-to-war.html, last accessed February 22, 2021.

[98] *Bangor Daily News(online)*, "1937 Shoe Worker Strike Hits Milestone," Associated Press, June 24, 2002, https://archive.bangordailynews.com/2002/06/24/1937-shoe-worker-strike-hits-milestone/, last accessed July 6, 2020.

[99] Lewiston Historical Commission, "Historic Lewiston: Its Government," 4.

[100] Mary Rice-DeFosse and James Myall, "The Franco-Americans of Lewiston-Auburn," 90.

[101] Ibid., 90.

[102] See endnote 68. The common council's termination in 1920 left only the board of aldermen as the sole legislative body.

[103] Geneva Kirk and Gridley Barrows, "Historic Lewiston: Its Government," 4-5.

[104] New York Public Library, "Index to Municipal Reference Library Notes," IV, September 5, 1917-June 26, 1918, 352.132Au1, archived at the Library of the University of California, see https://drive.google.com/file/d/1UFO6xp1w1Q3wbZKWhzwwicUuKqisbEX7/view?usp=sharing, link created December 26, 2020.

[105] The Lewiston Daily Sun, "Rioting Brings Guardsmen Here," 12.

[106] *The Lewiston Daily Sun*, "Walton to Succeed Ford as Auburn City Manager; Fogg Slated New Head of Fire Dep't(sic); Police Chief Unsettled," January 3, 1938, 1, (NOTE: The January 1, 1938 edition is embedded in the URL for the January 3, 1938 edition), https://news.google.com/newspapers?nid=IT5EXw6i2GUC&dat=19380101&printsec=frontpage&hl=en, last accessed July 6, 2020.

[107] *The Lewiston Daily Sun*, "Walton Manager; May Go to Court: Blocked by Green, Majority Rallies, Forces Balloting," January 4, 1938. 9 (NOTE: The January 4, 1938 edition is embedded in the URL for the January 1, 1938 edition), https://news.google.com/newspapers?nid=IT5EXw6i2GUC&dat=19380101&printsec=frontpage&hl=en, last accessed on July 7, 2020.

[108] *The Lewiston Daily Sun*, "Seek Injunction Against Walton: Court Order Restrains Council from Acting on Any Appointment, Salary," January 12, 1938. 1, https://news.google.com/newspapers?nid=IT5EXw6i2GUC&dat=19380112&printsec=frontpage&hl=en, last accessed July 7, 2020.

[109] *The Lewiston Daily Sun*, "Dismiss Petition for Injunction on Walton as Manager," January 29, 1938. 1, https://news.google.com/newspapers?nid=IT5EXw6i2GUC&dat=19380129&printsec=frontpage&hl=en, last accessed July 7, 2020.

[110] John Beliveau, interview with Andrea L'Hommedieu, "Beliveau, John Oral History Interview," The Edmund S. Muskie Archives and

Special Collections Library, Edmund S. Muskie Oral History Collection, Bates College, August 25, 1999, 23, http://scarab.bates.edu/muskie_oh/23, last accessed July 6, 2020.

[111] Douglas Rooks, *Rise, Decline, and Renewal: The Democratic Party in Maine,* (Lanham: The Rowan & Littlefield Publishing Group, 2018), Kindle eBook, 4, https://www.amazon.com/Rise-Decline-Renewal-Democratic-Party-ebook/dp/B079YY2XYG, last accessed July 7, 2020.

[112] *The Lewiston Daily Sun,* "Aliberti Ousts Jalbert by 15 Votes," Joe O'Connor, June 13, 1984, 10, https://news.google.com/newspapers?nid=IT5EXw6i2GUC&dat=19840613&printsec=frontpage&hl=en, last accessed July 6, 2020.

[113] Douglas Rooks, "Rise, Decline, and Renewal," 24.

[114] Ibid., 18.

[115] The Lewiston Daily Sun, "Aliberti Ousts Jalbert by 15 Votes," 10.

[116] William C. Harkins, "Malenfant, Jalbert in Run-Off," *The Lewiston Daily Sun,* February 16, 1954, 1, https://news.google.com/newspapers?nid=IT5EXw6i2GUC&dat=19540216&printsec=frontpage&hl=en, last accessed November 9, 2020.

[117] R. Bruce Huntington, "Malenfant Says He Has Promised No Appointments," *Lewiston Evening Journal,* March 2, 1954, 1-6.

[118] Ibid., 6.

[119] Ed Kisonak, "Gagne Whips Dube; Jalbert 'Out,'" *Lewiston Evening Journal,* June 22, 1954, 1, https://news.google.com/newspapers?nid=oQQVFBP0nzwC&dat=19540622&printsec=frontpage&hl=en, last accessed July 6, 2020.

[120] Maine State Legislature, "Legislative Record of the Ninety-Eighth Legislature of the State of Maine," 1, 53, January 8, 1957, http://lldc.mainelegislature.org/Open/LegRec/_98/House/LegRec_1957-01-08_HP_p0051-0056.pdf, last accessed December 7, 2020.

[121] All information confirming the Appropriations Committee appointment were confirmed through the Maine State Legislature, Legislative Record, Index to Regular Session, see https://www.maine.gov/legis/lawlib/lldl/legisrecord.htm, last accessed November 9, 2020.

[122] Douglas Rooks, "Rise, Decline, and Renewal," 24-25, 72.

[123] *The Lewiston Daily Sun,* "Aliberti Ousts Jalbert by 15 Votes," 10.

[124] Douglas Rooks, "Rise, Decline, and Renewal," 81.

[125] *The Lewiston Daily Sun,* "Aliberti Ousts Jalbert by 15 Votes," 10.

[126] *The Lewiston Daily Sun,* "Bitter Jalbert Blames Media, Seeks Ballot Inspection," Glen Chase, June 16, 1984, 1, https://news.google.com/newspapers?nid=IT5EXw6i2GUC&dat=19840616&printsec=frontpage&hl=en, last accessed July 7, 2020.

[127] *The Lewiston Daily Sun,* "Aliberti Ruled Winner Over Jalbert," Joe O'Connor, July 19, 1984, 1,

https://news.google.com/newspapers?nid=IT5EXw6i2GUC&dat=19840719&printsec=frontpage&hl=en, last accessed July 7, 2020.

[128] *The Lewiston Daily Sun*, "Brennan Rules Aliberti is Winner Over Jalbert," Staff and wire reports. August 22, 1984, 1, https://news.google.com/newspapers?nid=IT5EXw6i2GUC&dat=19840822&printsec=frontpage&hl=en, last accessed July 7, 2020.

[129] Douglas Rooks, "Rise, Decline, and Renewal," 26.

[130] Denis Blais, interviewed by Madelaine Giguere, February 28, 1994, University of Southern Maine, Franco-American Collection, Oral Histories, https://digitalcommons.usm.maine.edu/fac-interviews-and-lectures/6/, last accessed July 6, 2020.

[131] Ibid.

[132] According to Denis Blais, "Anne Marie Dugas" became the first woman to be elected to the Lewiston City Council, see Ibid. According to the Lewiston Evening Journal, "Mrs. Marie A. Dugas" defeated "Mrs. Doris M. Bergeron" for the Ward 1 seat on Lewiston the city council, see R. Bruce Huntington, "Boisvert Wins Lewiston Mayoralty: Clinches Victory with 6,106 Votes," *Lewiston Evening Journal,* February 18, 1958, (NOTE: The February 18, 1958 Lewiston Evening Journal issue is embedded within the URL for the February 13, 1958 issue), https://news.google.com/newspapers?nid=oQQVFBP0nzwC&dat=19580213&printsec=frontpage&hl=en,m, last accessed March 18, 2021.

[133] Ibid.

[134] John Beliveau, interview with Andrea L'Hommedieu, "Beliveau, John Oral History Interview."

[135] Kalle Oakes, "Maine Events," (*Lewiston*) *Sun Journal(online)*, May 22, 2005, https://www.sunjournal.com/2005/05/22/maine-events/, last accessed July 7. 2020.

[136] David Sargent, "River Views: Record-Fast Fight Fought in Lewiston in 1946," *(Lewiston) Sun Journal(online)*, January 29, 2013, https://www.sunjournal.com/2013/01/29/river-views-record-fast-fight-fought-lewiston-1946/, last accessed July 7, 2020.

[137] John Beliveau, interview with Andrea L'Hommedieu, "Beliveau, John Oral History Interview."

[138] *The Lewiston Daily Sun,* (picture) "New Police Commission," April 5, 1961, 2.

[139] Geneva Kirk and Gridley Barrows, "Historic Lewiston: Its Government," 52.

[140] Ibid.

[141] Paul H. Mills, "A Political Pioneer's Life Recounted in New Book," *(Lewiston) Sun Journal(online),* December 4, 2005, https://www.sunjournal.com/2005/12/04/political-pioneers-life-recounted-new-book/, last accessed February 24, 2021.

[142] Ibid.

[143] Maine State Legislature, "Legislative Record of the One Hundred and Fifth Legislature," State of Maine, 1971, January 6, 1971, 3-4, http://lldc.mainelegislature.org/Open/LegRec/105/House/LegRec_1971-01-06_HP_p0003-0021.pdf, last accessed February 24, 2021.

[144] Bonnie Washuk, "Female Lawmakers Stand Out," *(Lewiston) Sun Journal(online),* March 13, 2005.

[145] Rebekah Metzier, "Berube, Rodrigue Honored on Franco Day," *(Lewiston) Sun Journal(online),* March 26, 2009, https://www.sunjournal.com/2009/03/26/berube-rodrigue-honored-franco-day/, last accessed February 24, 2021.

[146] It is often reported that Georgette Berube was the first woman in state history to run for governor. In 1982, Berube ran in the Democratic primary for governor and lost to incumbent Joseph Brennan. In that same year, Sherry Huber ran in the Republican primary and also lost to Charles Cragin, see Paul Mills, "Franco-Americans, Woman(sic) and the Gubernatorial Arena," *(Lewiston) Sun Journal(online),* June 27, 2010, https://www.sunjournal.com/2010/06/27/franco-americans-woman-gubernatorial-arena/, last accessed March 17, 2021.

[147] Ibid.

[148] Cynthia Mendros, "Cynthia Mendros: Lewiston, Maine: Leading the Way For Women," *(Lewiston) Sun Journal(online),* October 5, 2014, https://www.sunjournal.com/2014/10/05/cynthia-mendros-lewiston-maine-leading-way-women/, last accessed February 24, 2021.

[149] Rebekah Metzier, "Berube, Rodrigue Honored on Franco Day."

[150] "The district—one of two in Maine—covered the rural northern two-thirds of the state. Snowe's principal opponent was Democrat Markham Gartley, Maine's secretary of state who had gained notoriety for being the first prisoner of war released from North Vietnam in 1972," retrieved from United States House of Representatives, "Snowe, Olympia Jean," Biography, see https://history.house.gov/People/Detail/21955, last accessed November 9, 2020.

[151] Ibid.

[152] Mark LaFlamme, "Former Lewiston and Auburn Mayor John Jenkins Dies," *(Lewiston) Sun Journal (online),* September 30, 2020, https://www.sunjournal.com/2020/09/30/former-lewiston-auburn-mayor-john-jenkins-dies/, last accessed November 9, 2020.

[153] Jenkins ran against opponent Tammy Grieshaber and won a one-year seat as mayor so that Auburn could align its municipal election cycle to Lewiston's (see Scott Taylor, "Jenkin's Part II," *(Lewiston) Sun Journal,* November 7, 2006, B1). Jenkin's ran again in 2007 and became the first Auburn "city-wide" official to win as a write-in candidate (see Steve Collins, "John Jenkins Eyeing Possible Gubernatorial Race," *(Lewiston) Sun Journal (online),* September 1, 2017,

https://www.sunjournal.com/2017/09/01/john-jenkins-eyeing-possible-gubernatorial-race/, last accessed November 9, 2020).

[154] Lindsay Tice, "Lewiston Mayor Abruptly Resigns," *(Lewiston) Sun Journal(online)*, March 8, 2019, https://www.sunjournal.com/2019/03/08/shane-bouchard-to-hold-11-a-m-press-conference/, last accessed November 9, 2020.

[155] Stanley B. Attwood, "1938 Marks Seventy-Fifth Anniversary of the City of Lewiston," *The Lewiston Daily Sun, Annual Review Edition*, January 5, 1938, 11A, https://news.google.com/newspapers?nid=IT5EXw6i2GUC&dat=19380101&printsec=frontpage&hl=en, last accessed July 7, 2020.

[156] YiLi Chien and Paul Morris, "On the Economy Blog," Federal Reserve Bank of St. Louis, April 11, 2017, https://www.stlouisfed.org/on-the-economy/2017/april/us-manufacturing-really-declining, last accessed July 12, 2020.

[157] John A. Rand, "The Peoples Lewiston-Auburn Maine 1875-1975," 99-110

[158] City of Auburn, "A Report of Commission Activities and Lessons Learned, November 2006 – February 2009," August 26, 2009, 3, http://www.auburnmaine.gov/CMSContent/Boards_and_Committees/Joint%20Charter%20Commission/CCLAC%20%20A%20Report%20of%20Commission%20Activities%20and%20Lessons%20Learned.pdf, last accessed July 16, 2020.

[159] Lewiston was incorporated and chartered as a town in 1795. It would become incorporated as a city in 1861. Auburn was incorporated as a town in 1842 and as a city in 1869.

[160] Douglas I. Hodgkin, "Frontier to Industrial City," 173.

[161] Ibid., 177.

[162] *Lewiston Evening Journal*, "Auburn Wants Airport but How Can It be Had?" August 26, 2930, 12 (NOTE: The August 26, 1930 edition is embedded in the URL for the August 27, 1930 edition), https://news.google.com/newspapers?nid=oQQVFBP0nzwC&dat=19300827&printsec=frontpage&hl=en, last accessed November 10, 2020.

[163] Ibid.

[164] The Living New Deal, "Auburn-Lewiston Municipal Airport – Auburn ME", web site. https://livingnewdeal.org/projects/auburn-lewiston-municipal-airport-auburn-me/, last accessed July 9, 2020.

[165] John P. Deeben, "Family Experiences and New Deal Relief: The Correspondence Files of the Federal Emergency Relief Administration, 1933–1936," *Prologue Magazine,* The U.S. National Archives and Records Administration, Washington, D.C., https://www.archives.gov/publications/prologue/2012/fall/fera.html#nt2, last accessed July 9, 2020

[166] City of Lewiston (Me.), "Seventy-Second Annual Report of the Receipts and Expenses of the City of Lewiston Maine," February 28, 1935, Maine Town Documents, 4804, 9-13, https://digitalcommons.library.umaine.edu/cgi/viewcontent.cgi?article=5967&context=towndocs, last accessed July 9, 2020.
[167] Ibid.
[168] City of Lewiston (Me.), "Annual Municipal Report Fiscal Year Ending February 28, 1937, Lewiston Maine," 1937, Maine Town Documents, 4806, 16-17, https://digitalcommons.library.umaine.edu/cgi/viewcontent.cgi?article=5969&context=towndocs, last accessed July 9, 2020.
[169] City of Lewiston, Maine, "Annual Municipal Report Fiscal Year Ending February 28, 1938," Lewiston, Maine" (1938), Maine Town Documents, 4807, 12, https://digitalcommons.library.umaine.edu/towndocs/4807, last accessed September 10, 2020.
[170] Ralph B. Skinner, "Boston to Lewiston in 53 Mins.," *The Lewiston Evening Journal*, December 1, 1937, 1-17, https://news.google.com/newspapers?nid=oQQVFBP0nzwC&dat=19371201&printsec=frontpage&hl=en, last accessed February 21, 2021.
[171] Ibid.
[172] The Living New Deal, "Auburn-Lewiston Municipal Airport."
[173] U.S. Army Corps of Engineers, Rock Island District, "Archives Search Report: Conclusions and Recommendations for the Former Lewiston Naval Auxiliary(sic) Air Facility," December 1995, Project Fact Sheet, cited in Wikipedia, "Auburn/Lewiston Municipal Airport," last edited February 11, 2020, https://web.archive.org/web/20120426002211/http://naelibrary.nae.usace.army.mil/dp192/ned95082.pdf .
[174] Ibid, 2.
[175] Bonnie Washuk, "George H.W. Bush Called Lewiston-Auburn Home During WWII," *(Lewiston) Sun Journal(online)*, December 1, 2018, https://www.sunjournal.com/2018/12/01/george-h-w-bushs-ties-to-lewiston-auburn/, last accessed July 9, 2020.
[176] U.S. Army Corps of Engineers, Rock Island District, "Archives Search Report: Conclusions and Recommendations for the Former Lewiston Naval Auxiliary(sic) Air Facility," 5.
[177] *(Lewiston) Sun Journal(online)*, "Roland Marcotte: 1918-2003," August 23, 2003. https://www.sunjournal.com/2003/08/23/roland-l-marcotte/, last accessed July 9, 2020.
[178] *Lewiston Evening Journal*, "Charter Committee Continues Discussion of Proposed Changes," December 11, 1948, 12, https://news.google.com/newspapers?nid=oQQVFBP0nzwC&dat=19481211&printsec=frontpage&hl=en, last accessed July 11, 2020.

[179] *The Lewiston Daily Sun*, "Lewiston Aldermen Recommend Hiring of Salesman for City," June 17, 1949, 2, https://news.google.com/newspapers?nid=1928&dat=19490617&id=OZggAAAAIBAJ&sjid=QmgFAAAAIBAJ&pg=708,7609099, last accessed July 11, 2020.

[180] *The Lewiston Daily Sun*, "On Making Lewiston Grow," 4.

[181] *Lewiston Evening Journal*, "Complete Text of Mayor Marcotte's Inaugural Address," March 16, 1953, 10, https://news.google.com/newspapers?nid=oQQVFBP0nzwC&dat=19530316&printsec=frontpage&hl=en, last accessed July 11, 2020.

[182] *The Lewiston Evening Journal*, "The Full Text of Mayor Marcotte's Inaugural Address," March 17, 1952, 12, https://news.google.com/newspapers?nid=oQQVFBP0nzwC&dat=19520317&printsec=frontpage&hl=en, last accessed July 16, 2020.

[183] *Lewiston Evening Journal*, "Lewiston Officially Opens New Industrial Department," July 1, 1952, 16, https://news.google.com/newspapers?nid=oQQVFBP0nzwC&dat=19520702&printsec=frontpage&hl=en, (NOTE: The URL will show July 2, 1952 but page 16 of the July 1, 1952 issue is located to the left of the July 2, 1952 front page), last accessed July 11, 2020.

[184] R. Bruce Huntington, "Raytheon Plant to Employ 2,000; New $8 Million Lewiston Payroll: Construction to Start This Fall," *Lewiston Evening Journal*, July 1, 1959, 1, https://news.google.com/newspapers?nid=oQQVFBP0nzwC&dat=19590701&printsec=frontpage&hl=en, last accessed July 11, 2020.

[185] Ibid.

[186] Ibid.

[187] Ibid.

[188] *Lewiston Evening Journal*, "Means Big Economic Boost for Community," July 1, 1959, 15.

[189] R. Bruce Huntington, "Raytheon to Halt Operations Here: 'Phased Out' Over Next Ten Months," *Lewiston Evening Journal*, March 1, 1963, 1, https://news.google.com/newspapers?nid=oQQVFBP0nzwC&dat=19630301&printsec=frontpage&hl=en, last accessed July 11, 2020.

[190] *The Lewiston Daily Sun*, "Report Raytheon is Ending Its Diode Production Here," February 27, 1963, 14 (NOTE: Page 14 of the February 27, 1963 edition is located to the left front page of the February 28, 1963 edition), https://news.google.com/newspapers?nid=IT5EXw6i2GUC&dat=19630228&printsec=frontpage&hl=en, last accessed October 28, 2020.

[191] R. Bruce Huntington, "Raytheon to Halt Operations Here: 'Phased Out' Over Next Ten Months," 5.

[192] United States of America Congressional Record, "Proceeding and Debates of the 88th Congress, Second Edition," April 21, 1964 to May 2, 1964, 110, 7, 8925-8926, https://books.google.com/books?id=sB-N4xsoJFAC&pg=PA8926&lpg=PA8926&dq=raytheon+plants+in+california+1963&source=bl&ots=CQ3JzR1xO4&sig=ACfU3U3SMmW3AEGbKQfUtgeZskEBezihuA&hl=en&sa=X&ved=2ahUKEwj3uJbFp8jqAhVJUt8KHeVRBRsQ6AEwAHoECAkQAQ#v=onepage&q=raytheon%20plants%20in%20california%201963&f=false, last accessed July 12, 2020.

[193] R. Bruce Huntington, "Raytheon to Halt Operations Here: 'Phased Out' Over Next Ten Months," 5.

[194] *Lewiston Evening Journal,* "Editorials: Raytheon's Decision," March 1, 1963, 4.

[195] Lewiston's water and sewer system was municipally owned while Auburn's water and sewer system was owned and operated by a legislatively created special district, separate from Auburn municipal government, that also possessed bonding authority.

[196] Paul Marcotte, "Mayor Urges Patience, Teamwork: Joblessness Termed the No. 1 Task," *Lewiston Evening Journal,* January 6, 1964, 6, https://news.google.com/newspapers?nid=oQQVFBP0nzwC&dat=19640104&printsec=frontpage&hl=en, last accessed July 11, 2020.

[197] The original list of Lewiston-Auburn collaborative ventures was provided by Lucien Gosselin. That list was amended and, in some cases, corrected to reflect information researched for this book. All of this is reflected in the Appendix. The new collaborative list is not intended to be exhaustive or all inclusive. It has been expanded to cover other collaborative efforts between the two cities. See original collabortive document: Lucien Gosselin, "Lewiston-Auburn Collaboration," (no date), emailed to Phil Nadeau on July 23, 2020, see https://drive.google.com/file/d/1hKH8iMC9uX9Xx9l0OF7r4jv7Q5roe3UJ/view?usp=sharing, link created December 26, 2020.

[198] *Lewiston Evening Journal,* "Regional Planner Would Cost $10,700 First Year," July 18, 1962, 9, https://news.google.com/newspapers?nid=oQQVFBP0nzwC&dat=19620718&printsec=frontpage&hl=en, last accessed July 11, 1962.

[199] *(Lewiston) Sun Journal(online),* "Roland Marcotte: 1918-2003."

[200] *(Lewiston) Sun Journal(online), advertising supplement,* "Central Maine Community College: Celebrating 50 Years, 1964-2014," November 12, 2014, 5, https://www.mccs.me.edu/wp-content/uploads/2014CMCC50thsmaller.pdf, last accessed July 12, 2020.

[201] Dick Plante, "'Voc' School Won't Be As Costly To City Of Auburn," *Lewiston Evening Journal,* March 10, 1964, 1,

https://news.google.com/newspapers?nid=oQQVFBP0nzwC&dat=19640310&printsec=frontpage&hl=en, last accessed July 12, 2020.

[202] *Lewiston Evening Journal*, "Jalbert Calls For Broader Vocational Training Program On the High School Level," March 9, 1964, 16 (NOTE: page 16 is attached to Google Newspaper file for March 10, 1964 edition), https://news.google.com/newspapers?nid=oQQVFBP0nzwC&dat=19640310&printsec=frontpage&hl=en, last accessed July 16, 2020.

[203] Lewiston-Auburn Water Pollution Control Authority, "About Us: Summary of the Organization," 2020, http://www.lawpca.org/?page_id=237, last accessed July 16, 2020.

[204] Ibid.

[205] Dottie Perham-Whittier, "City of Lewiston Press Release," September 11, 2013, http://me-lewiston.civicplus.com/Archive/ViewFile/Item/1991, last accessed October 24, 2020.

[206] Federal Reserve Bank of Minneapolis, "Consumer Price Index 1913...," web site, https://www.minneapolisfed.org/about-us/monetary-policy/inflation-calculator/consumer-price-index-1913-, last accessed August 1, 2020.

[207] Tom Robustelli, "How did Hudson Bus Lines Come About?'," *Lewiston Journal*, July 6, 1981, 1.

[208] Ibid.

[209] Ibid.

[210] Tom Robustelli. "Why the Bus Line is Going Broke," *Lewiston Journal*, July 8, 1981, cited in Phil Nadeau, "Report to the Maine Department of Transportation and the Federal Transit Administration: Blue Bird L4RE Low-Floor Transit Bus Reliability and Parts-Support Inadequacy," July 2014, Auburn, Maine: Lewiston-Auburn Transit Committee, 2014, 8.

[211] Tom Robustelli. "Hudson Proposes End to All Bus Subsidies," *Lewiston Journal,* November 23, 1981, cited in Phil Nadeau, "Report to the Maine Department of Transportation and the Federal Transit Administration: Blue Bird L4RE Low-Floor Transit Bus Reliability and Parts-Support Inadequacy," July 2014, Auburn, Maine: Lewiston-Auburn Transit Committee, 2014, 8.

[212] U.S. Department of Housing and Urban Development, Office of Policy Development and Research, "SOCDS Census Date: Output for Lewiston City, ME: Labor Percent of Families in National Income Brackets," MSA table produced from web site on July 19, 2020, https://www.socds.huduser.gov, last accessed July 19, 2020.

[213] *The Lewiston Daily Sun,* "Gosselin, Nolin, LaBrecque Get New CD Appointments," February 18, 1963, 14.

[214] Lucien Gosselin email to Phil Nadeau, "Bio," November 26, 2020.

[215] Lucien Gosselin, interview #1 with Phil Nadeau.
[216] Bernard J. Murphy, Jr., interviewed by Phil Nadeau, September 19, 2020.
[217] Ibid.
[218] Ibid.
[219] James Pritchard, "The Rockland Experience: Lewiston and Auburn, Maine Confront Some Tough Intercity Issues," Case Study, Bureau of Public Administration, University of Maine Orono, paper undated, 3, copy provided by Lucien Gosselin on July 27, 2020.
[220] James Pritchard, "The Rockland Experience," 3.
[221] *Lewiston Evening Journal,* "Editorials: Twin City Pow Wow," 4, April 16, 1975, cited in James Pritchard, "The Rockland Experience," 4.
[222] James Pritchard, "The Rockland Experience," 7.
[223] The address and building have always been in Rockport, but the property is partially located in the larger city of Rockland. The facility has been renamed the Samoset Resort.
[224] James Pritchard, "The Rockland Experience," bid., 8.
[225] *Lewiston Evening Journal,* "Conference of Twin City Officials Will be Held," 6, April 5, 1975.
[226] James Pritchard, "The Rockland Experience,", 8.
[227] Ibid., 9.
[228] Glen Burgess, "Bury-the-Hatchet Session Buried, For Now at Least," *Lewiston Evening Journal,* March 27, 1975, cited in James Pritchard, "The Rockland Experience," 10.
[229] James Pritchard, "The Rockland Experience," 9-10.
[230] Ibid., 10-11.
[231] Paul Pare, "Rockland 'Peace Talks' Productive," *Lewiston Evening Journal,* 1, April 14, 1975. https://news.google.com/newspapers?nid=oQQVFBP0nzwC&dat=19750414&printsec=frontpage&hl=en, last accessed August 2, 2020.
[232] James Pritchard, "The Rockland Experience," 11.
[233] Auburn attendees: City Manager Bernard Murphy, Police Chief Peter Mador, Public Works Director Jack Berman, Acting School Superintendent Richard Babb, Finance Director George Kehoe, Assistant City Manager John Spita, Assistant to the Manager Kirsten Larson Turley. Lewiston attendees: Controller Lucien Gosselin, Public Works Director Roger Pruneau, Police Chief Lucien Longtin, Planning and Community Development Director Nathanial Bowdith, City Engineer Harland Hatch, Assistant Controller Richard Metivier, City Auditor Robert Reny, Intergovernmental Coordinator Leslie Stevens, see Paul Pare, "Rockland 'Peace Talks' Productive," 1-9.
[234] Paul Pare, "Rockland 'Peace Talks' Productive," 1.
[235] Ibid, 1.
[236] James Pritchard, "The Rockland Experience," 12.

237 Ibid., 12.
238 Ibid.
239 Ibid., 8.
240 Paul Pare, "'Eyes of Texarkana Upon Them,'" *Lewiston Evening Journal*, 1, April 16, 1975, https://news.google.com/newspapers?nid=oQQVFBP0nzwC&dat=19750416&printsec=frontpage&hl=en, last accessed August 2, 2020.
241 Paul Pare, "'Eyes of Texarkana Upon Them,'" 1-10.
242 James Pritchard, "The Rockland Experience,"21.
243 Ibid.
244 Bernard J. Murphy, Jr., interviewed by Phil Nadeau.
245 Steve Sherlock, "Auburn: A celebration 150 years in the Making," *(Lewiston) Sun Journal(online)*, February 17, 2019, https://www.sunjournal.com/2019/02/17/auburn-a-celebration-150-years-in-the-making-2/, last accessed June 27, 2020.
246 Lori Valigra, "One of Maine's Last Shoemakers Uses Yankee Ingenuity to Fulfill Ambitious Growth Plans," *Bangor Daily News(online)*, November 4, 2019, https://bangordailynews.com/2019/11/04/news/one-of-maines-last-shoemakers-uses-yankee-ingenuity-to-fulfill-ambitious-growth-plans/, last accessed July 5, 2020.
247 John A. Rand, "The Peoples Lewiston-Auburn Maine 1875-1975," 55.
248 Leamon, "Historic Lewiston: A Textile City in Transition," 30.
249 U.S Department of Commerce, Bureau of the Census, "1970 Census of Population: Advance Report (Maine)", PC(V1)-21, December 1970, 3, ftp://ftp.census.gov/library/publications/decennial/1970/pc-v1/26084397v1ch2.pdf, last accessed July 12, 2020.
250 . Lori Valigra, "One of Maine's Last Shoemakers Uses Yankee Ingenuity to Fulfill Ambitious Growth Plans," November 4, 2019, https://bangordailynews.com/2019/11/04/news/one-of-maines-last-shoemakers-uses-yankee-ingenuity-to-fulfill-ambitious-growth-plans/, last accessed July 12, 2020.
251 Denis Blais, interviewed by Madelaine Giguere.
252 Leamon, "Historic Lewiston: A Textile City in Transition," 43.
253 Lori Valigra, "The Old Lewiston Mill Could Get a New Life as a Hub for Maine Businesses," *Bangor Daily News(online)*, October 13, 2019, https://bangordailynews.com/2019/10/13/news/this-old-lewiston-mill-could-get-a-new-life-as-a-hub-for-maine-businesses/, last accessed July 20, 2020.
254 Lewiston Historical Commission, *"Historic Lewiston: Bales to Bedspreads,"* (Auburn, ME: Central Maine Technical College, 2000), 6, https://www.lewistonmaine.gov/DocumentCenter/View/1194/Historic-Lew-Bales-to-Bedspreads-2000?bidId=, last accessed June 27, 2020.

[255] The Historical Commission's estimate of 6,000 workers at Bates Mill (Endnote 66) may be somewhat inflated or may reflect an increase in hiring after March 1952. According to a March 1952 Associated Press survey, Lewiston's total textile worker numbers were around 5,600 as of December 31, 1951 and declined in March 1952 to 4,800 wage earners. See *Lewiston Evening Journal*, "Textile Employment Still on Downgrade in New England," April 18, 1952, 2, https://news.google.com/newspapers?nid=oQQVFBP0nzwC&dat=19520418&printsec=frontpage&hl=en, last accessed July 12, 2020.

[256] Before 1951, my research confirms that both Auburn and Lewiston had their own Chamber of Commerce. Lewiston's was established in 1887. A newspaper article confirmed the 75th anniversary year in 1962 (*Lewiston Evening Journal*, "Lewiston Chamber Office at New Location Feb. 1," December 14, 1962, 1, https://news.google.com/newspapers?nid=oQQVFBP0nzwC&dat=19621213&printsec=frontpage&hl=en );

Auburn's organization dates back as far as 1919 (unable to confirm the actual date it was established, see *The Lewiston Daily Sun*, October 21, 1919, 10, https://news.google.com/newspapers?nid=IT5EXw6i2GUC&dat=19191021&printsec=frontpage&hl=en );

The first chamber merger attempt failed in 1932 (*Lewiston Evening Journal*, "Chamber Merger Not Practical at This Time," July 19, 1932, 1, https://news.google.com/newspapers?nid=oQQVFBP0nzwC&dat=19320718&printsec=frontpage&hl=en );

A Lewiston newspaper urged more cooperation between the chambers of commerce of both cities in 1951. No further research was done to establish when the Auburn Chamber ceased to exist but it appears to be sometime between 1951 and 1962 (*Lewiston Daily Sun*, "On Making Lewiston Grow," March 7, 1951, 4, https://news.google.com/newspapers?nid=IT5EXw6i2GUC&dat=19510307&printsec=frontpage&hl=en );

The Lewiston Chamber announced its relocation to the new Ash Street location in February 1963. (*Lewiston Evening Journal*, "Lewiston Chamber Office at New Location Feb. 1," December 14, 1962, 1, https://news.google.com/newspapers?nid=oQQVFBP0nzwC&dat=19621213&printsec=frontpage&hl=en );

The Lewiston Chamber announced that it would vote to change the name to "Lewiston-Auburn Chamber of Commerce" at its annual meeting on January 30, 1963 after Auburn residents petitioned the chamber for the name change. The need for a Auburn citizen petition would only have been necessary if the Auburn Chamber was not in existence at the time of the proposed name change (*Lewiston Evening*

*Journal,* "Chamber Members to Vote on Change of Name as Annual Meeting Held January 30," January 19, 1963, 16, https://news.google.com/newspapers?nid=oQQVFBP0nzwC&dat=19630119&printsec=frontpage&hl=en );
No article mentioned the actual January 30th vote to approve the chamber name change but an article about the January 30, 1963 annual meeting speaker made reference to the new name confirming that the name change occurred on January 30, 1963 (*The Lewiston Daily Sun,* "Chamber Hears Sergio Rojas," January 31, 1963, 2, https://news.google.com/newspapers?nid=IT5EXw6i2GUC&dat=19630131&printsec=frontpage&hl=en )

[257] *The Lewiston Daily Sun,* "On Making Lewiston Grow," March 7, 1951, 4, https://news.google.com/newspapers?nid=IT5EXw6i2GUC&dat=19510307&printsec=frontpage&hl=en, last accessed July 16, 2020.

[258] Paul Badeau, "LDC a Major Force in Lewiston's Growth," *(Lewiston) Sun Journal(online),* September 30, 2003, https://www.sunjournal.com/2003/09/30/ldc-major-force-lewistons-growth-2/, last accessed July 16, 2020.

[259] *(Lewiston) Twin City Times,* "Lewiston Development Corporation Celebrates 60 years of Community Improvements," September 27, 2012, https://twincitytimes.com/news/lewiston-development-corporation-celebrates-60-years-of-community-improvements, last accessed June 27, 2020.

[260] John A. Rand, "The Peoples Lewiston-Auburn Maine 1875-1975," 86.

[261] William C. Harkins, "Geiger Assured City to Have a 'Great Future,'" *The Lewiston Daily Sun,* December 2, 1954, 1.

[262] Paul Badeau, "LDC a Major Force in Lewiston's Growth."

[263] William C. Harkins, "Geiger Assured City to Have a 'Great Future,'" 1.

[264] Bonnie Washuk, "New School Will Honor Ray Geiger," May 27, 2008, https://www.sunjournal.com/2008/05/27/new-school-will-honor-ray-geiger/, last accessed November 13, 2020.

[265] lbaillargeon@sunjournal.com, "Geiger Family Bio," September 9, 2009, https://www.sunjournal.com/2009/09/09/geiger-family-bio/, last accessed November 13, 2020.

[266] lbaillargeon@sunjournal.com, "Geiger Family Bio."

[267] Ibid.

[268] Ibid.

[269] Ibid.

[270] Scott Taylor, "Geiger Announces Expansion, Move to Solar Power, " *(Lewiston) Sun Journa(online)l,* September 29, 2016,

https://www.sunjournal.com/2016/09/29/geiger-announces-expansion-move-solar-power/, last accessed November 13, 2020.

[271] *(Lewiston) Sun Journal(online)*, "Lewiston Development Corporation historical highlights." September 30, 2003, https://www.sunjournal.com/2003/09/30/lewiston-development-corporation-historical-highlights-2/, last accessed June 27, 2020.

[272] John A. Rand, "The Peoples Lewiston-Auburn Maine 1875-1975," 91.

[273] Ibid., 93.

[274] U.S. Department of Transportation, Federal Highway Administration, Eisenhower Interstate Highway System, Previous Facts of the Day. Update June 27, 2017, https://www.fhwa.dot.gov/interstate/previousfacts.cfm, last accessed July 6, 2020.

[275] Reggie Bouchard, "Huge Cookie Baking Plant is Erected in Auburn," *The Lewiston Daily Sun,* January 29, 1963, https://news.google.com/newspapers?nid=IT5EXw6i2GUC&dat=19630130&printsec=frontpage&hl=en, last accessed October 25, 2020.

[276] John A. Rand, "The Peoples Lewiston-Auburn Maine 1875-1975," 93-99.

[277] Leamon, "Historic Lewiston: A Textile City in Transition," 43.

[278] Lucien Gosselin, interview #1 with Phil Nadeau, July 22, 2020.

[279] Paul Badeau, "LDC a Major Force in Lewiston's Growth."

[280] Reginald C. Barrows, *"Maine Turnpike Story,"* 1955, Books and Publications, 5, Digital Commons@bpl. https://digicom.bpl.lib.me.us/books_pubs/5, last accessed July 6, 2020.

[281] John A. Rand, "The Peoples Lewiston-Auburn Maine 1875-1975," 99.

[282] Ibid., 87-110.

[283] U.S Department of Commerce, Bureau of the Census, "1970 Census of Population and Housing: Census Tracts, Lewiston-Auburn, Maine, Standard Metropolitan Statistical Area." PHC(1)-111, H-4, February 1972.

[284] Ibid.

[285] Ibid., P-4.

[286] Ibid.

[287] *Lewiston Evening Journal,* "URA Takes Steps to Begin Second Phase of Project," September 28, 1962, 11.

[288] Ibid., P-7.

[289] U.S. Department of Commerce, Bureau of the Census, "Median Income Up in 1970," Current Population Reports: Consumer Income, May 20, 1971, P-60, 78, 1, https://www2.census.gov/library/publications/1971/demographics/p60-78.pdf, last accessed July 13, 2020.

²⁹⁰ U.S. Department of Commerce, Bureau of the Census, "Statistical Abstract of the United States, 1980: National Data Book and Guide to Sources," ed. 101, 455, (Washington D.C., U.S. Government Printing Office, 1980), https://books.google.com/books?id=V078gsXXzBMC&pg=PA455&lpg=PA455&dq=us+census+maine+median+family+income+1970&source=bl&ots=6OfhEubV-6&sig=ACfU3U02TZ8Ll7wJQ_HV-WLDA88WOEX_tw&hl=en&sa=X&ved=2ahUKEwiJzd6LosvqAhUlmeAKHYw6BQA4FBDoATAAegQIChAB#v=onepage&q=us%20census%20maine%20median%20family%20income%201970&f=false, last accessed July 13, 2020.

²⁹¹ U.S. Department of Housing and Urban Development, Office of Policy Development and Research, "SOCDS Census Date: Output for Lewiston City, ME: Labor Force," MSA table produced from web site on July 19, 2020, https://www.socds.huduser.gov, last accessed July 19, 2020.

²⁹² U.S. Department of Housing and Urban Development, Office of Policy Development and Research, "SOCDS Census Date: Output for Lewiston City, ME: Employed Residents by Industry (SIC Classification)," MSA table produced from web site on July 19, 2020, https://www.socds.huduser.gov, last accessed July 19, 2020

²⁹³ *Lewiston Evening Journal*, "URA Takes Steps to Begin Second Phase of Project," September 28, 1962, 11.

²⁹⁴ *Lewiston Evening Journal*, "Auburn URA to Meet With Council, APB," September 28, 1962, 11.

²⁹⁵ Ibid.

²⁹⁶ Larry Raymond, interview with Mike Richard, "Raymond, Larry Oral History Interview," The Edmund S. Muskie Archives and Special Collections Library, Edmund S. Muskie Oral History Collection, Bates College, June 30, 1999, 336, http://scarab.bates.edu/muskie_oh/336, last accessed October 22, 2020.

²⁹⁷ Richard Kisonak, "Contracts are voted by URA," *The Lewiston Daily Sun*, January 25, 1963, 24 (NOTE: The URL is for the January 26, 1963 edition. Page 24 of the January 25, 1963 edition is located to the left of the January 25, 1963 edition), https://news.google.com/newspapers?nid=IT5EXw6i2GUC&dat=19630126&printsec=frontpage&hl=en, last accessed October 25, 2020.

²⁹⁸ *Lewiston Evening Journal*, "URA Takes Steps to Begin Second Phase of Project," 11.

²⁹⁹ U.S. Department of Housing and Urban Development, "Opportunities to Improve the Model Cities Program in Kansas City and St. Louis, Missouri, and New Orleans, Louisiana," Report to Congress, Comptroller General of the United States, B-171500, 093485, January 1, 1973, 5-6.

[300] Hearings Before the Special Committee on Aging, "Usefulness of the Model Cities Program to the Elderly," Part 1, July 23, 1968, 97-98, Washington, D.C.: U.S. Government Printing Office, 1968, https://books.google.com/books?id=hP8jwvdTx3sC&pg=PA98&lpg=PA98&dq=lewiston+maine+selected+for+model+cities+program&source=bl&ots=qumIdRbdP8&sig=ACfU3U3fSoSvbzsL24e8nBtQYtwXOj6bfg&hl=en&sa=X&ved=2ahUKEwiP1o7o9crqAhXHMd8KHTkqBcsQ6AEwAnoECAoQAQ#v=onepage&q=lewiston%20maine%20selected%20for%20model%20cities%20program&f=false, last accessed July 13, 2020.

[301] Henry Bourgeois, interview with Andrea L'Hommedieu, "Bourgeois, Henry Oral History Interview," The Edmund S. Muskie Archives and Special Collections Library, Edmund S. Muskie Oral History Collection, Bates College, September 19, 2000, 45, http://scarab.bates.edu/muskie_oh/45, last accessed July 13, 2020.

[302] Mike Boehmer and Jason Wolfe, "Bartlett Street Has a Long History," *The Lewiston Journal*, February 13, 1989, 3A, https://news.google.com/newspapers?nid=zCpYd49hD24C&dat=19890213&printsec=frontpage&hl=en, last accessed December 16, 2020.

[303] Shari Garmise Ph.D, Shari Nourick, and Elizabeth Thorstensen, "Forty Years of Urban Economic Development: A Retrospective," The International Economic Development Council, Washington, D.C., Feburary 2008, 12, http://www.iedconline.org/clientuploads/Downloads/history/Forty_Years_Urban_Economic_Development.pdf, last accessed July 12, 2020.

[304] Lucien Gosselin, interview #1 with Phil Nadeau.

[305] Helene Lapointe, "Lewiston's $750,000 Central Fire Station Should Be Ready in April," *Lewiston Evening Journal*, February 6, 1973, 56A, (NOTE: Page 56A, February 6, 1973 edition is included in URL for February 7, 1973 edition), https://news.google.com/newspapers?nid=oQQVFBP0nzwC&dat=19730207&printsec=frontpage&hl=en, last accessed July 12, 2020.

[306] *Lewiston Evening Journal*, "At Kennedy Park Dedication (picture)," August 23, 1973, 32, (NOTE: Page 32, August 23, 1973 edition is included in URL for August 24, 1973 edition), https://news.google.com/newspapers?nid=1913&dat=19730824&id=p3xhAAAAIBAJ&sjid=p2gFAAAAIBAJ&pg=917,3392500, last accessed July 14, 2020.

[307] *Lewiston Evening Journal*, "(Picture) The Fire Department Finally Relocates," August 22, 1973, p.36, (issue is erroneously included in URL for August 23, 1973 edition), https://news.google.com/newspapers?nid=oQQVFBP0nzwC&dat=19730823&printsec=frontpage&hl=en, last accessed July 14, 2020.

308 Mayor John Orestis would become the first mayor in its 112-year history to be elected to a two-year term from 1974-1975. Lewiston voters approved a charter amendment in 1972 changing both the mayor and seven members of the Board of Alderman to two-year terms. Orestis was elected for his first term in 1972 and served a one-year term in 1973, see Paul Pare, "Lewiston to Go Without Inauguration Next Year," December 11, 1974, 25.

309 John Orestis, interview with Mike Richard, "Orestis, John Oral History Interview," The Edmund S. Muskie Archives and Special Collections Library, Edmund S. Muskie Oral History Collection, Bates College, August 29, 1999, 313, http://scarab.bates.edu/muskie_oh/313, last accessed July 14, 2020.

310 Henry Bourgeois, interview with Andrea L'Hommedieu, "Bourgeois, Henry Oral History Interview."

311 John Orestis, interview with Mike Richard, "Orestis, John Oral History Interview."

312 Paul Pare, "Model Cities Agency Staff Due to Dwindle," *Lewiston Evening Journal*, June 7, 1973, 5.

313 I was born in Lewiston but was not a resident from mid-1972 to mid-1976 and again from mid-1994 to mid-1999. I was also a local business owner from 1987 to 1991 and a member of the Lewiston Finance Committee from 1989 to 1994. I resigned from the Finance Committee to accept the appointment as Richmond, Maine's Town Manager in May 1994.

314 Limited Liability Company, for information about the purpose of an LLC (can vary by state), see https://www.irs.gov/businesses/small-businesses-self-employed/limited-liability-company-llc, and https://www.leg.state.nv.us/nrs/nrs-086.html#NRS086Sec361, last accessed December 16, 2020.

315 U.S Department of Commerce, Bureau of the Census, "1970 Census of Population and Housing: Census Tracts, Lewiston-Auburn, Maine, Standard Metropolitan Statistical Area." PHC(1)-111, H-4, February 1972.

316 Ibid.

317 *The Lewiston Daily Sun*, "Lewiston Studies Code Enforcement," February 12, 1982, 13.

318 Sharon Deveau, "Dozens Homeless in $1 million Blaze," *The Lewiston Journal*, February 13, 1989, 1A, https://news.google.com/newspapers?nid=zCpYd49hD24C&dat=19890213&printsec=frontpage&hl=en, last accessed December 26, 2020.

319 Tess Nacelewicz, "Fire Victim Suffers Attack," *The Lewiston Daily Sun*, February 14, 1989, 9, https://news.google.com/newspapers?nid=IT5EXw6i2GUC&dat=19890214&printsec=frontpage&hl=en, last accessed December 16, 2020.

[320] *The Lewiston Journal*, "Major Fires in the Twin Cities Area," February 13, 1989, 3A.
[321] Bates College website, "July 1943: The Navy Arrives," 2004, retrieved at: https://www.bates.edu/150-years/months/july/navy-arrives/, last accessed July 19, 2020.
[322] For more information about the G.I. Bill, technically the "Servicemen's Readjustment Act of 1944," see U.S. Department of Veterans Affairs, "Education and Training" web site: https://www.benefits.va.gov/gibill/history.asp, last accessed August 2, 2020.
[323] The Lewiston-Auburn Metropolitan Statistical Area (MSA) is defined by the U.S. Census as the entirety of Androscoggin County.
[324] All data from the U.S. Department of Housing and Urban Development, "SOCDS Census Data: Output for Lewiston city, ME: Percent of Persons Aged 25 or more by Highest Educational Attainment"; "Percent of Employed Residents by Industry"; "Percent of Families in National Income Brackets," HUD User, Office of Policy Development and Research, SOCDS Census and American Community Survey Data, Lewiston-Auburn MSA, https://socds.huduser.gov/Census/Census_Home.html, last accessed July 29, 2020.
[325] Dionne served two terms in 1980-81 and 1982-83 becoming the first two-term, four-year mayor in Lewiston history, and the first mayor under the city's new charter that went into effect in 1980.
[326] Lucien Gosselin, interview #3 with Phil Nadeau, October 20, 2020.
[327] Ibid.
[328] Ibid.
[329] Paul Dionne, interview with Phil Nadeau, August 18, 2020.
[330] Tammy Eves, "Peck's Announces Closing after 101 Years," *The Lewiston Daily Sun,* November 11, 1981, 1, https://news.google.com/newspapers?nid=IT5EXw6i2GUC&dat=19811111&printsec=frontpage&hl=en, last accessed September 9, 2020.
[331] Lucien Gosselin, interview #3 with Phil Nadeau.
[332] Paul Dionne, interview with Phil Nadeau, and Lucien B. Gosselin and Dr. Richard J. Maiman, "A Legislative College at Lewiston/Auburn," December 21, 1993, University of Southern Maine paper, 2, source document provided by Lucien Gosselin.
[333] Lucien Gosselin, interview #3 with Phil Nadeau.
[334] Kendall Holmes, "Cities must pay to establish UM-Lewiston," *Maine Sunday Telegram,* February 27, 1983, 1, as cited in Lucien B. Gosselin and Dr. Richard J. Maiman, "A Legislative College at Lewiston/Auburn," 3.
[335] Ibid.
[336] Ibid.

[337] Douglas Rooks, "Rise, Decline, and Renewal," 80-81.
[338] Kendall Holmes, "Cities must pay to establish UM-Lewiston."
[339] Dennis J. Palumbo, *Public Policy in America, Government in Action*, (Orlando: Harcourt Brace Jovanovich College Publishers, 1988), 35, cited in Lucien B. Gosselin and Dr. Richard J. Maiman, "A Legislative College at Lewiston/Auburn," 4.
[340] Greg Nadeau, interview #1 with Phil Nadeau, May 28, 2020.
[341] Greg Nadeau, interview #1 with Phil Nadeau.
[342] Lucien B. Gosselin, "Lewiston/Auburn College Chronology," paper, August 6, 1995, 1, source document provided by Lucien Gosselin.
[343] Ursula Albert, "LDC Purchases Former Sears Building," *Lewiston Journal*, July 29, 1983, cited in Lucien Gosselin, "Lewiston-Auburn College Chronology," August 6, 1995, 1.
[344] Greg Nadeau, Interview with Phil Nadeau.
[345] Ursula Albert, "Dionne: The City Will Pay its UM Share: Lewiston has Two Options Under Plan" *Lewiston Journal*, February 23, 1983, 1. https://news.google.com/newspapers?nid=zCpYd49hD24C&dat=19830223&printsec=frontpage&hl=en, last accessed July 28, 2020.
[346] Tom Robustelli, "GOP Opposes Peck's Campus," *Lewiston Journal*, March 1, 1983, 1.
[347] *Bangor Daily News*, "Editorial: State of the State," February 24, 1983, 14, https://news.google.com/newspapers?nid=3yMDF_cvnR8C&dat=19830224&printsec=frontpage&hl=en, last accessed July 28, 2020.
[348] John Hale, "Proposed Lewiston Campus Would Affect One-Third of UMA Students," *Kennebec Journal*, February 25, 1983, cited in Lucien Gosselin, "Lewiston/Auburn College Chronology," August 6, 1995, 1, paper.
[349] Joseph McGonigle, "Opponents of UMaine-Lewiston Plan Are Invited to Twin Cities," *The Lewiston Daily Sun*, March 2, 1983, 9.
[350] Ibid.
[351] U.S. Department of Housing and Urban Development, "SOCDS Census Data: Output for Lewiston city, ME: Unemployment Rate."
[352] ALFRED Archival Economic Data, St. Louis Fed, "Unemployment Rate in Maine," Federal Reserve Bank of St. Louis, web site, Seasonally Adjusted, https://alfred.stlouisfed.org/series?seid=MEUR&utm_source=series_page&utm_medium=related_content&utm_term=related_resources&utm_campaign=alfred, last accessed July 29, 2020.
[353] U.S. Bureau of Labor Statistics, Monthly Labor Review, "Unemployment Continued to Rise as Recession Deepened," February 1983, 4, https://www.bls.gov/opub/mlr/1983/02/art1full.pdf, last accessed July 29, 2020.
[354] Ibid.

355 ALFRED Archival Economic Data, St. Louis Fed, "Unemployment Rate in Maine."
356 Ibid.
357 The average rate produced by Phil Nadeau utilizing Freddie Mac data, see Freddie Mac, "30-Year Fixed Rate Mortgages Since 1971," web site. http://www.freddiemac.com/pmms/pmms30.html, last accessed July 29, 2020.
358 Joseph McGonigle, "Lewiston, State Officials Agree on UML Financing," *The Lewiston Daily Sun,* March 7, 1983, 1.
359 Joe O'Connor, "Council Pledges $3.1M for UM Campus," *The Lewiston Daily Sun,* March 22, 1983, 1.
360 Tom Robustelli, "UML: Towns Are Not Enthused," *Lewiston Journal,* March 22, 1983, 1.
361 Joe O'Connor, "Council Pledges $3.1M for UM Campus," *The Lewiston Daily Sun,* 1.
362 Glen Chase, "New UML-A Vote OK'd in Lewiston: Council Vote Follows Plea by Brennan to Try Again," *The Lewiston Daily Sun,* March 13, 1985, 1, https://news.google.com/newspapers?nid=IT5EXw6i2GUC&dat=19850313&printsec=frontpage&hl=en last accessed August 21, 2020.
363 Lucien B. Gosselin and Dr. Richard J. Maiman, "A Legislative College at Lewiston/Auburn," 8.
364 Tom Robustelli, "UML: Lewiston Isn't United on Plans," *Lewiston Journal,* April 26, 1983, 1.
365 Tom Robustelli, "Mr. D Still no Fan: Brennan, Jalbert Meet on Funding for UML," *Lewiston Journal,* May 2, 1983, retrieved from Lucien B. Gosselin, "Lewiston/Auburn College Chronology," 3.
366 Lucien Gosselin, "Lewiston/Auburn College Chronology," 4-5.
367 Peter Jackson, "UML Campus Suffers Blow in Legislature, Plan Tentatively Axed by Panel," *The Lewiston Daily Sun,* June 14, 1983, 1.
368 Joseph McGonigle, "Lewiston Officials Still Hopeful," *The Lewiston Daily Sun,* June 14, 1983, 1.
369 Edmund A. MacDonald, "Budget: Jalbert to Fight UML Funding," *The Lewiston Daily Sun,* June 22, 1983, 1.
370 Ibid., 8.
371 Ibid.
372 Charles Morrison, interview with Phil Nadeau, August 12, 2020.
373 Ibid.
374 Ibid.
375 Edmund A. MacDonald, "UM Campus in Lewiston Approved," *The Lewiston Daily Sun,"* June 23, 1983, 1.
376 James Allen, "Franco-Americans in Maine: A Geographical Perspective," 87.
377 Edmund A. MacDonald, "UM Campus in Lewiston Approved," 12.

[378] Lucien Gosselin, interview #3 with Phil Nadeau
[379] Lucien Gosselin, interview #3 with Phil Nadeau.
[380] Greg Nadeau, interview with Phil Nadeau.
[381] Lucien Gosselin, interview #3 with Phil Nadeau.
[382] Ibid.
[383] Paul Dionne, interview with Phil Nadeau.
[384] Ibid.
[385] Greg Nadeau, interview with Phil Nadeau.
[386] Douglas Rooks, "Rise, Decline, and Renewal," 25.
[387] Glen Chase, "Questions About UML Plan Remain Unanswered," *The Lewiston Daily Sun,* September 15, 1983, 9.
[388] Lucien B. Gosselin and Dr. Richard J. Maiman, "A Legislative College at Lewiston/Auburn," 9.
[389] Ibid., 10.
[390] Peter Jackson, "UML Saga: Another Chapter Ends," *The Lewiston Daily Sun,* October 31, 1983, 19.
[391] Lucien B. Gosselin and Dr. Richard J. Maiman, "A Legislative College at Lewiston/Auburn," 10.
[392] Greg Nadeau, interview with Phil Nadeau.
[393] Lucien Gosselin, interview #3 with Phil Nadeau.
[394] Glen Chase, "Council Postpones Referendum on UML," *The Lewiston Daily Sun,"* November 2, 1983, 13.
[395] Glen Chase, "UM Trustees Okay Site Plan; Funding Vote Next," *The Lewiston Daily Sun,* July 10, 1984, 1.
[396] Bonnie Washuk, "Auburn Voters to Decide UML-A Funding," *The Lewiston Daily Sun,* August 21, 1984.
[397] J.R. Sirkin, "Auburn Officials Mum on Hydro Stance," *The Lewiston Daily Sun,* July 24, 1984.
[398] Glen Chase, "Twin Cities, CMP Agree to Build Hydro Project: Lewiston to get $1M a Year, Auburn $200,000 from 24 Megawatt Plant," *The Lewiston Sun Journal,* December 4, 1984, 1.
[399] Glen Chase, "Hydroelectric Project Resulted from Closer Cooperation of Cities," *The Lewiston Daily Sun,* December 4, 1984, 1.
[400] Glen Chase, "Solid Support for UML-A Campus is Indicated in a Poll of Voters," *The Lewiston Daily Sun,* November 2, 1984, 1.
[401] Glen Chase, "UML-A Finally Stirs Opposition," *The Lewiston Daily Sun,* November 6, 1984, 15.
[402] Glen Chase, "New UML-A Vote in Lewiston," *The Lewiston Daily Sun,* March 13, 1985, 1.
[403] Greg Nadeau, interview with Phil Nadeau.
[404] Maine State Legislature, "Legislative Record of the One Hundred and Twelfth Legislature," State of Maine, Vol. 1, December 5, 1984 – June 20, 1985,

http://lldc.mainelegislature.org/Open/LegRec/112/House/LegRec_1985-01-03_HP_p0045-0047.pdf, last accessed November 9, 2020.

[405] Lucien B. Gosselin, "Lewiston/Auburn College Chronology," 12.

[406] Lucien B. Gosselin and Dr. Richard J. Maiman, "A Legislative College at Lewiston/Auburn," 13.

[407] Lucien B. Gosselin, "Lewiston/Auburn College Chronology," 11-12.

[408] Lucien B. Gosselin and Dr. Richard J. Maiman, "A Legislative College at Lewiston/Auburn," 13.

[409] Ibid., 13-14.

[410] Edmund A. MacDonald, "UMLA Takes Another Step Ahead in the State House," *The Lewiston Daily Sun*, June 12, 1987, A1-A12.

[411] Lucien B. Gosselin and Dr. Richard J. Maiman, "A Legislative College at Lewiston/Auburn,"13.

[412] For more information about John Martin see: John Martin, interview with Don Nicoll, "Martin, John Oral History Interview," The Edmund S. Muskie Archives and Special Collections Library, Edmund S. Muskie Oral History Collection, Bates College, October 10, 1998, 238, http://scarab.bates.edu/muskie_oh/238, last accessed August 22, 2020.

[413] Maine State Legislature, "Legislative Record of the One Hundred and Sixteenth Legislature of the State of Maine," First Regular Session, House of Representatives, 1, H-4, December 2, 1992, retrieved from http://lldc.mainelegislature.org/Open/LegRec/116/House/LegRec_1992-12-02_HP_pH0001-0031.pdf, last accessed August 22, 2020.

[414] Greg Nadeau, interview with Phil Nadeau.

[415] Ibid.

[416] Edmund A. MacDonald, "State Budget Includes $1.1 Million in UMLA Funding," *The Lewiston Daily Sun,"* June 18, 1987, 13. https://news.google.com/newspapers?nid=IT5EXw6i2GUC&dat=19870618&printsec=frontpage&hl=en, last accessed August 22, 2020.

[417] Mark Hayward and Michael Lopez, "University Center to Expand Program," *The Lewiston Journal,* June 18, 1987, 1, https://news.google.com/newspapers?nid=zCpYd49hD24C&dat=19870618&printsec=frontpage&hl=en, last accessed August 22, 2020.

[418] Lucien B. Gosselin and Dr. Richard J. Maiman, "A Legislative College at Lewiston/Auburn," 15-16.

[419] Jonathan Van Fleet, "Twin Cities Ponder Ways to Help Refugees," *(Lewiston) Sun Journal,* April 6, 1999, 1.

[420] Katarina Bugarski, "Belgrade is in Flames," *(Lewiston) Sun Journal,* April 6, 1999, 1, https://news.google.com/newspapers?nid=bcT4vkklUMwC&dat=19990406&printsec=frontpage&hl=en, last accessed August 22, 2020.

[421] Jonathan Van Fleet, "Twin Cities Ponder Ways to Help Refugees," 1.

[422] Ibid., 1-7.

[423] "In 1891, Congress created the Bureau of Immigration to oversee the admission of immigrants, including those considered "refugees." Because early U.S. immigration laws did not restrict the number of immigrants the U.S. would accept, no separate laws existed for refugee admissions and refugees could resettle in the U.S. as long as they met the regular requirements for immigrant admissions" cited in Department of Homeland Security, U.S. Citizenship and Immigration Services, "Refugee Timeline," retrieved from https://www.uscis.gov/about-us/our-history/history-office-and-library/featured-stories-from-the-uscis-history-office-and-library/refugee-timeline, last accessed August 8, 2020.

[424] Catholic Charities Refugee and Immigration Services, "FAQs: Frequently Asked Questions," retrieved from https://www.ccmaine.org/refugee-immigration-services/faqs, last accessed August 8, 2020.

[425] United States General Accounting Office, Comptroller General of the United States, "Report to the Congress: U.S. Provides Safe Haven for Indochinese Refugees," ID-75-71, GAO Library System No. 097003, June 16, 1975, 1.

[426] Linda White, "Viet Refugees Arrive in Maine," *Bangor Daily News*, July 28, 1975, 1, https://news.google.com/newspapers?nid=3yMDF_cvnR8C&dat=19750728&printsec=frontpage&hl=en, last accessed September 9, 2020.

[427] "The Division of Economic Opportunity was established in 1964 as an administrative unit of the Executive Department… Effective September 19, 1975, the Division was renamed Division of Community Services…
In carrying out its responsibilities and functions, the Division…provided technical assistance to Maine's thirteen Community Action Agencies and to provide information and advice to the Governor…(F)rom September 1975 to September 1977, (i)ts purpose (was) to help 166 Vietnamese resettle successfully in the state. Resettlement include(d)finding homes, jobs, English language training and in general trying to ease the cultural shock. In addition, however, the program offere(d) its services to all 400 Indo-Chinese who (were resettled) in the state," see Maine State Legislature, Law and Legislative Digital Library, "Maine State Government Annual Report 1976-1977," 1978, 73-75, http://lldc.mainelegislature.org/Open/Rpts/jk2835_b87a_1977.pdf, last accessed August 9, 2020.

[428] *Bangor Daily News*, "Vietnamese Tell Why They Came," July 28, 1975, 8.

[429] Linda White, "Viet Refugees Arrive in Maine," 8.

[430] Ibid.

[431] Ibid.

[432] Linda White, "Viet Refugees Arrive in Maine," *Bangor Daily News),* 8.
[433] Ibid.
[434] "Because of the anticipated volume of refugees, (President Gerald Ford)…appointed Ambassador L. Dean Brown on April 18 (1975) to head a special Interagency Task Force for coordinating all U.S. activities for evacuating Indochina refugees. (Ambassador Brown resigned and Julia Vadala Taft of the Department of Health, Education, and Welfare began serving as Acting Director on May 27 (1975)," cited from United States General Accounting Office, Comptroller General of the United States, "Report to the Congress: U.S. Provides Safe Haven for Indochinese Refugees," 1.
[435] United States General Accounting Office, Comptroller General of the United States, "Report to the Congress: Evacuation and Temporary Care Afforded Indochinese Refugees – Operation New Life," 15, ID-76-63, GAO Library System No. 098163, June 1, 1976, https://www.gao.gov/assets/120/115626.pdf, last accessed December 25, 2020.
[436] United States General Accounting Office, Comptroller General of the United States, "Report to the Congress: Domestic Resettlement of Indochinese Refugees – Struggle for Self-Reliance," May 10, 1977, i, HRD-77-35, B133001, https://www.gao.gov/assets/120/118759.pdf, last accessed December 25, 2020.
[437] Ibid., 5.
[438] Ibid.
[439] The term "new Mainer" has been used by many agencies in Maine who work with immigrant and refugee populations for years. How old the term is or its origins are unknown.
[440] United States General Accounting Office, Comptroller General of the United States, "Report to the Congress: Evacuation and Temporary Care Afforded Indochinese Refugees – Operation New Life," 40.
[441] 94th Congress, Senate, Report 94-119, "Indochina Migration and Refugee Assistance Act of 1975," May 12, 1975, 6, retrieved from https://www.cia.gov/library/readingroom/docs/CIA-RDP77M00144R001100130006-3.pdf, last accessed August 9, 2020.
[442] Linda White, "Viet Refugee Program is Curtailed," *Bangor Daily News,* August 6, 1975, 1-2, https://news.google.com/newspapers?nid=3yMDF_cvnR8C&dat=19750806&printsec=frontpage&hl=en, last accessed August 9, 2020.
[443] United States General Accounting Office, Comptroller General of the United States, "Report to the Congress: Domestic Resettlement of Indochinese Refugees – Struggle for Self-Reliance," 32, 42.
[444] United States General Accounting Office, Comptroller General of the United States, "Report to the Congress: Evacuation and Temporary Care

Afforded Indochinese Refugees – Operation New Life," 40, https://www.gao.gov/assets/120/115626.pdf, last accessed August 9, 2020.

[445] United States General Accounting Office, Comptroller General of the United States, "Report to the Congress: Domestic Resettlement of Indochinese Refugees – Struggle for Self-Reliance," 7.

[446] Jonathan Van Fleet, "City Said Nearly Ready for Refugees," *(Lewiston) Sun Journal*, August 14, 1999, B1 (NOTE: The August 14, 1999 edition is embedded in the URL for the August 13, 1999 edition), https://news.google.com/newspapers?nid=bcT4vkklUMwC&dat=19990813&printsec=frontpage&hl=en, last accessed October 13, 2020.

[447] Ibid., B1-B2.

[448] Ibid.

[449] Lucy Salyer, "Chew Heong v. United States: Chinese Exclusion and the Federal Courts," Federal Trials and Great Debates in United States History, Federal Judicial Center Federal Judicial History Office, Washington, D.C. 2006, 1, https://www.fjc.gov/sites/default/files/trials/exclusion.pdf, last accessed October 13, 2020.

[450] Ibid.

[451] Ibid., 16.

[452] Ibid., 28.

[453] Ibid., 73.

[454] Congressional Bills 112th Congress, "Expressing the Regret of the Senate for the Passage of Discriminatory Laws Against the Chinese in America, Including the Chinese Exclusion Act," May 26, 2011, U.S. Government Publishing Office, S. Res. 201 Introduced in Senate (IS), https://www.govinfo.gov/content/pkg/BILLS-112sres201is/html/BILLS-112sres201is.htm, last accessed August 14, 2020.

[455] Ibid.

[456] *The New York Times*, "The Chinese of the Eastern States," May 1, 1881, 6.

[457] Damien-Claude Belanger and Claude Belanger, "French Canadian emigration to the United States 1840-1930."

[458] *The New York Times*, "The Chinese of the Eastern States," 6.

[459] Damien-Claude Belanger and Claude Belanger, "French Canadian emigration to the United States 1840-1930."

[460] *The New York Times*, "The Chinese of the Eastern States," 6.

[461] Damien-Claude Belanger and Claude Belanger, "French Canadian emigration to the United States 1840-1930."

[462] U.S. Senate of the United States, "Expressing the Regret of the Senate for the Passage of Discriminatory Laws Against the Chinese in America," 112th Congress, 1st Session, May 26, 2011,

https://www.govinfo.gov/content/pkg/BILLS-112sres201ats/pdf/BILLS-112sres201ats.pdf, last accessed August 15, 2020.

[463] "Togo is a (West African) republic dominated by President General Gnassingbe Eyadema, who has ruled since 1967, when he came to power in a military coup. Although opposition political parties were legalized following widespread protests in 1991, Eyadema and his Rally of the Togolese People (RPT), strongly backed by the armed forces, have continued to dominate the exercise of political power. Eyadema used his entrenched position to repress genuine opposition and to secure another 5-year term in an election held in June 1998, which, like previous multiparty elections, was marred by systematic fraud…The Government's human rights record continued to be poor; while there were some improvements in a few areas, serious problems remain…An Amnesty International (AI) report issued in May stated that hundreds of bodies-presumably many members of the opposition-were thrown into the sea around the time of the June 1998 Presidential election," see U.S. Department of State, Bureau of Democracy, Human Rights, and Labor, "1999 Country Reports on Human Rights Practices: Togo," February 25, 2000, retrieved from https://19972001.state.gov/global/human_rights/1999_hrp_report/togo.html, last accessed August 15, 2020.

[464] Michael Gordon, "Refugee Issue Stirs Questions," *(Lewiston) Sun Journal,* December 21, 1999, A8, https://news.google.com/newspapers?nid=bcT4vkklUMwC&dat=19991221&printsec=frontpage&hl=en, last accessed August 15, 2020.

[465] Michael Gordon, "Refugee Issue Stirs Questions," A8.

[466] John Gaber, Sharon Gaber, Jeff Vincent, Darcy Boellstorff, "Analysis of Refugee Resettlement in the Great Plains," Great Plains Research: A Journal of Natural and Social Sciences, 719, Fall 2004, Vol 14, No. 2, 173, https://digitalcommons.unl.edu/greatplainsresearch/719, last accessed August 15, 2020.

[467] People from the country of Togo are identified by the UNHCR as "Togolese," see UNHCR report https://www.refworld.org/country,,COI,,UNHCR,,COMMENTARY,,TGO,,5a12bd322,0.html, last accessed February 27, 2021.

[468] Michael Gordon, "Refugee Issue Stirs Questions," A8.

[469] Ibid.

[470] Michael Gordon, "Lessons in Hospitality," *(Lewiston) Sun Journal,* January 24, 2000, B1.

[471] Ibid., B1-B2.

[472] Michael Gordon, "Spreading the Word," *(Lewiston) Sun Journal,* February 29, 2000, B1.

[473] Michael Gordon, "Fascist Says Refugees Not Welcome," *(Lewiston) Sun Journal,* March 23, 2000, A1-A8, https://news.google.com/newspapers?nid=bcT4vkklUMwC&dat=20000323&printsec=frontpage&hl=en, last accessed August 15, 2020.

[474] Kathryn Skelton, "Togo Refugees to Keep Coming," *(Lewiston) Sun Journal,* November 21, 2000, B1.

[475] For more information about Bates Manufacturing and how it lives on through Maine Heritage Weavers, see https://www.batesmillstore.com/pages/our-story, last accessed February 27, 2021.

[476] Town of Richmond, Maine, "Comprehensive Plan," Draft for State Review, February 2016, 12, https://www.maine.gov/dacf/municipalplanning/comp_plans/Richmond_2016.pdf, last accessed December 5, 2020.

[477] Scott Taylor, "As L-A's Slogan Ages, 'It's Happening' Everywhere," *(Lewiston) Sun Journal,* November 10, 2012, https://www.sunjournal.com/2012/11/10/l-as-slogan-ages-its-happening-everywhere/, last accessed August 16, 2020.

[478] David A Sargent, "Auburn Council Adopts Development Plan," *(Lewiston) Sun Journal,* February 2, 1999, B1.

[479] Jonathan Van Fleet, "Plan Maps Big Changes," *(Lewiston) Sun Journal,* July 21, 1999, A1.

[480] Jonathan Van Fleet, "No Room at the Inn," *(Lewiston) Sun Journal,* August 19, 1999, B1, https://news.google.com/newspapers?nid=bcT4vkklUMwC&dat=19990819&printsec=frontpage&hl=en, last accessed August 16, 2020.

[481] Jonathan Van Fleet, "Platz, Peoples Boost Mill, Developer: Deal Has No Down Side, " and "Tenant to Double its People," *(Lewiston) Sun Journal,* August 24, 1999, A1.

[482] For the purposes of this book, all references to the retail or corporate "Wal-Mart" entities shall be listed as the new legal name "Walmart" that became effective on February 1, 2008. For more information about the name change, see https://corporate.walmart.com/newsroom/2017/12/05/walmart-changes-its-legal-name-to-reflect-how-customers-want-to-shop, last accessed March 2, 2021.

[483] Daniel Hartill, "Developer Eyes 90 Acres in Auburn," *(Lewiston) Sun Journal,* October 13, 1999, B1.

[484] Jonathan Van Fleet, "Nine-Acre Park Planned on Riverbank in Lewiston," *(Lewiston) Sun Journal,* May 17, 1999, B1, https://news.google.com/newspapers?nid=bcT4vkklUMwC&dat=19990517&printsec=frontpage&hl=en, last accessed August 16, 2020.

[485] Daniel Hartill, "Smart Development," *(Lewiston) Sun Journal,* January 7, 2000, A1.

[486] Daniel Hartill, "Auburn's Secret: More Stores May Be Coming," *(Lewiston) Sun Journal,* August 5, 1999, B1.
[487] Jonathan Van Fleet, "Court Going to Lisbon St.," *(Lewiston) Sun Journal,* October 11, 1999., A1.
[488] Jonathan Van Fleet, "Johnson Sees Preservation, Economic Rebirth," April 14, 1999, B1.
[489] Construction of the bridge began in 1973, see *(Lewiston) Sun Journal(online),* "Updated L-A Vietnam Veterans Memorial to be Dedicated Aug. 10," August 4, 2014, https://www.sunjournal.com/2014/08/04/updated-l-a-vietnam-veterans-memorial-dedicated-aug-10/, last accessed August 16, 2020. The "third bridge" proposal over the Androscoggin River had been discussed as far back as 1945, see Arch Soutar, "Through State Traffic and Local Traffic Will Face Pre-War Intolerable Delays Unless Bottleneck Caused by Inadequate Bridges is Corrected After the War," *Lewiston Sun-Journal,* January 17, 1945, 1.
[490] Daniel Hartill, "Bottleneck Threatens Store Plan," *(Lewiston) Sun Journal,* February 28, 2000, A1-A5, https://news.google.com/newspapers?nid=bcT4vkklUMwC&dat=20000228&printsec=frontpage&hl=en, last accessed August 10, 2020.
[491] David A. Sargent, "Councilors Face Joint Action on Tax Financing Policies," *(Lewiston) Sun Journal,* February 22, 1999, B1.
[492] Daniel Hartill, "CMMC Seeks Heart Support," *(Lewiston) Sun Journal,* January 18, 2000, A1.
[493] Jonathan Van Fleet, "Post Office Delivers: Postal Service Decides to Put New Mail Center in Twin Cities," *(Lewiston) Sun Journal,* October 21, 1999, A1.
[494] Lisa Giguere, "Jobless Rate Hits New Low," *(Lewiston) Sun Journal,* April 19, 1999, A1.
[495] Liz Chapman, "State Tops Nation in Job Growth," *(Lewiston) Sun Journal,* May 6, 1999, A1.
[496] In my interview with Allan Turgeon on September 8, 2020, we discussed the matter of how many structures were part of the Bates complex when the city of Lewiston assumed ownership in 1992. Over time, there have been multiple descriptions of how many buildings were in existence: 10, 11, etc. The literature suggests that 10 buildings was most often identified. According to a document Turgeon sent to me by email on September 22, 2020, it was determined that there were 18 separate buildings (some connected with covered walkways) on the mill property in 1992: Mill # 1; Mill # 1 Wing; Mill # 1 Storehouse; Mill #2; Mill #2 Wing A; Mill #2 Wing B; Mill #2 Storehouse; Mill # 3; Mill #3 Annex East and Mill #3 Annex West (both demolished after 1992); Mill #4; Mill #5; Mill #6; Mill #7; Mill #8 (demolished after 1992); Mill #9 (boiler building); Mill #10 (ash storage building demolished after 1992);

Executive Office building (demolished after 1992). The total estimated number of square feet in the entire Bates Mill complex in 1992 was approximately 1.24 million sf. Following the demolition of approximately 171.3 thousand sf, the complex now has approximately 1.07 million sf.

[497] Allan Turgeon, interview with Phil Nadeau, September 8, 2020.

[498] Committee on Energy and Natural Resources United States Senate, "Hearing Before the Subcommittee on Public Lands, National Parks, and Forests," July 30, 1987, 44, One Hundredth Congress, First Session.

[499] Committee on Natural Resources U.S. House of Representatives, "Legislative Hearing Before the Subcommittee on National Parks, Forests and Public Lands," statement of the Hon. Niki Tsongas, January 24, 2012, Serial No. 112-91, One Hundred Twelfth Congress, Second Session, https://www.govinfo.gov/content/pkg/CHRG-112hhrg72506/html/CHRG-112hhrg72506.htm, last accessed August 17, 2020.

[500] Ibid., statement of Adam Baacke, Assistant City Manager and Director of Planning and Development, Lowell, Massachusetts.

[501] The United States Mint, H.I.P Pocket Change Kids Site, "Lowell National Historic Park Quarter," retrieved at https://www.usmint.gov/learn/kids/library/america-the-beautiful-quarters/lowell, last accessed August 17, 2020.

[502] Allan Dowd, "Bates: No Fraud in Loom Sale," *(Lewiston) Sun Journal,* May 15, 1992, 12.

[503] Martha C. Dumais, "Bates Mill Future Remains Up in Air," *(Lewiston) Sun Journal,* April 11, 1992, 1, https://news.google.com/newspapers?nid=bcT4vkklUMwC&dat=19920411&printsec=frontpage&hl=en, last accessed August 23, 2020.

[504] Jennifer Sullivan, "Union Rejects Bates Contract Offer," *(Lewiston) Sun Journal,* May 30, 1987, 1.

[505] Carolyn Magnuson, "Bank Fights City Over Bates Mill," *(Lewiston) Sun Journal,* April 25, 1992, 13.

[506] Martha C. Dumais, "Bates-City Agreement Allows Firm to Operate," *(Lewiston) Sun Journal,* August 13, 1992, 11, https://news.google.com/newspapers?nid=bcT4vkklUMwC&dat=19920813&printsec=frontpage&hl=en, last accessed August 23, 2020.

[507] Heather A. Hunter, "Comprehensive Annual Financial Report," City of Lewiston, June 30, 2008, 51.

[508] Lincoln Jeffers, "City History with Bates Mill," City of Lewiston, Economic and Community Development memo to the Honorable Mayor and Members of the City Council, February 7, 2018, 1, retrieved from City of Lewiston Workshop Agenda, February 18, 2018, retrieved at: https://www.lewistonmaine.gov/ArchiveCenter/ViewFile/Item/3732, last accessed August 23, 2020.

509 Ibid.

510 Ibid.

511 Jonathan Van Fleet, "Platz Still Committed to Twin Cities Growth," *(Lewiston) Sun Journal*, August 17, 1998, 1, https://news.google.com/newspapers?nid=bcT4vkklUMwC&dat=19980817&printsec=frontpage&hl=en, last accessed August 23, 2020.

512 Lincoln Jeffers, "City History with Bates Mill," 4.

513 *(Lewiston) Sun Journal*, "Bates Mill, Elections Top Stories of '97," January 1, 1998, B1.

514 It should be noted that since 1992, the most controversial element of the city's ownership of the Bates Mill complex was the prospect for a convention center that had been recommended in at least two more published reports after 1997. In response, the city council approved an ordinance change that prohibited the building of a convention center unless approved by a voter referendum. A convention center was never built in any portion of the Bates Mill complex.

515 Randy Whitehouse, "City Council Expected to Vote on Bates Mill Grant Application," *(Lewiston) Sun Journal*, November 18, 1997, B1.

516 Jonathan Van Fleet, "Council: No Sale for Mill," August 12, 1998, A1.

517 *(Lewiston) Sun Journal*, "Mill Panel to Answer Questions," September 9, 1998, B1, and Allan Turgeon, "Bates Mill Redevelopment Strategy," Power-Point presentation to The Maine Conference for Technical Assistance to Brownfield Communities, June 14, 2012, file provided by Allan Turgeon email September 22, 2020.

518 Jonathan Van Fleet, "City Councilor Calls 'No' Vote a Mandate," *(Lewiston) Sun Journal*, November 4, 1998, A1.

519 Jonathan Van Fleet, "Group Threatens Legal Action," *(Lewiston) Sun Journal*, January 8, 1999, B1.

520 Jonathan Van Fleet, "Council Oks $5M Mill Bond," *(Lewiston) Sun Journal*, January 20, 1999, B1.

521 Jonathan Van Fleet, "Council to Act on Bates Mill Expansion," *(Lewiston) Sun Journal*, January 5, 1999, B1, https://news.google.com/newspapers?nid=bcT4vkklUMwC&dat=19990105&printsec=frontpage&hl=en, last accessed August 24, 2020.

522 Jonathan Van Fleet, "Platz, Peoples Boost Mill: Tenant to Double its People," *(Lewiston) Sun Journal*, August 24, 1999, A1.

523 Jonathan Van Fleet, "Peoples Poised to Grow," *(Lewiston) Sun Journal*, August 23, 1999, A1 (NOTE: The URL is for the August 21, 1999 edition and includes the August 23, 1999 edition), https://news.google.com/newspapers?nid=bcT4vkklUMwC&dat=19990821&printsec=frontpage&hl=en, last accessed August 25, 2020

524 Glen Bolduc, "Bates Buildings Sale OK'd," *(Lewiston) Sun Journal*, February 7, 2001, A1.

525 Michael Gordon, "Mainers Stock Up as a Precaution," *(Lewiston) Sun Journal,* January 1, 2000, B1.

526 Jonathan Van Fleet, "Post Office Delivers," *(Lewiston) Sun Journal,* October 21, 1999, A11, https://news.google.com/newspapers?nid=bcT4vkklUMwC&dat=19991021&printsec=frontpage&hl=en, last accessed August 25, 2020.

527 Jonathan Van Fleet, "Post Office Drops Portland Site," *(Lewiston) Sun Journal,* January 23, 1999, A1.

528 Ibid, A9.

529 Jonathan Van Fleet, "Post Office Delivers," *(Lewiston) Sun Journal,* A11.

530 Daniel Hartill and Michael Gordon, "Mail Job's Impact Uncertain," *(Lewiston) Sun Journal,* October 22, 1999, A1.

531 Charlie Pomerleau, "Union Workers Picket Against Postal Move to L-A," *(Lewiston) Sun Journal,* December 2, 1999, A1.

532 Mark LaFlamme, "Postal Service Eyeing Other Sites," *(Lewiston) Sun Journal,* December 4, 1999, A1.

533 Charlie Pomerleau, "Local Site Sacked: Lewiston Officials Moving On," May 26, 2000, A1, https://news.google.com/newspapers?nid=bcT4vkklUMwC&dat=20000526&printsec=frontpage&hl=en, last accessed August 26, 2000.

534 Erica Thoits, "Scarborough Mail Processing Center Opens," *Portland Press Herald(online),* July 12, 2006, (NOTE: Many Portland Press Herald/Maine Sunday Telegram articles were retrieved through the paid subscription service NewsLibrary.com).

535 Kathryn Skelton, "Togo Refugees to Keep Coming," *(Lewiston) Sun Journal,* November 21, 2000, A1.

536 Douglas Rooks, "The New Mainers: Somalis are the Latest Wave of Immigrants," Maine Townsman, December 2002, https://www.memun.org/DesktopModules/Bring2mind/DMX/Download.aspx?EntryId=4885&Command=Core_Download&language=en-US&PortalId=0&TabId=119, last accessed August 26, 2020.

537 Ibid.

538 Phil Nadeau, "The Somalis of Lewiston: Effects of Rapid Immigration to a Homogeneous Maine City," Portland, Maine: The Southern Maine Review, 2005, 110.

539 For the purposes of this book, a refugee identified as a "secondary migrant" shall be defined in accordance with the Catholic Charities Maine definition: "a person who entered the United States as a refugee and was resettled in one state, but then chose to move to another state. For example, a refugee who was resettled in Chicago, IL, but then chose to move to Portland, Maine, would be considered a secondary migrant when arriving in Maine," see Catholic Charities Maine web site:

https://www.ccmaine.org/refugee-immigration-services/faqs#Fact4, last accessed August 26, 2020.

[540] Garrett Martin Ed., "Asians in the Maine Economy," Maine Center for Economic Policy, 2011, 8 , https://www.mecep.org/wp-content/uploads/2014/09/MECEP_Asians-in-Maine_Report-4-20-2011.pdf, last accessed August 26, 2020.

[541] Douglas Rooks, "The New Mainers: Somalis are the Latest Wave of Immigrants."

[542] Maine State Housing Authority, "The State of Maine's Housing 2002," September 2002, 18, https://mainehousing.org/docs/default-source/housing-reports/state-of-maine%27s-housing-2002---presented-@-the-2002-governor%27s-affordable-housing-conference.pdf?sfvrsn=4&sfvrsn=4, last accessed August 26, 2020.

[543] From the City of Portland: "State law requires municipalities to administer General Assistance (GA) provides immediate aid to individuals who meet eligibility requirements and are unable to provide basic necessities essential to maintain themselves or their family. Maine law states that municipalities have the responsibility to provide General Assistance to all eligible residents of the municipality and non-residents (including transients) who intend to reside in the municipality. GA provides a specific amount and type of aid for basic needs during a limited time period and is not intended to be a categorical welfare program. GA provides basic needs in the areas of shelter/housing, utilities, food, medication, and other essential goods and services. All assistance is issued in vouchers and no cash is authorized. Each applicant for GA is assigned to a Financial Eligibility Specialist (similar approach in Lewiston) who determines eligibility and refers applicants to in-house employment and self-sufficiency programs as a requirement for future eligibility," see City of Portland, Maine, Health and Human Services Department, Social Services Division, "General Assistance Program: Year End Report, FY 2015," 2, retrieved at http://www.ci.portland.me.us/ArchiveCenter/ViewFile/Item/726, last accessed September 9, 2020.

[544] Application for Federal Assistance, Supplemental Grant, Category 2: Unanticipated Arrivals, Portland-Lewiston Secondary Migrant Program, signatory Joseph E. Gray, Portland City Manager, date of signature, June 28, 2002, 3.

[545] Daniel Hartill, "County Pumps Heart Unit," *(Lewiston) Sun Journal,* January 20, 2000, B1.

[546] Daniel Hartill, "CMMC Seeks Heart Support," *(Lewiston) Sun Journal,* January 18, 2000, B1, https://news.google.com/newspapers?nid=bcT4vkklUMwC&dat=20000118&printsec=frontpage&hl=en, last accessed September 9, 2020.

[547] Daniel Hartill, "County Pumps Heart Unit."

548 Charlie Pomerleau, "CMMC Critical of MMC Ad," *(Lewiston) Sun Journal,* June 22, 2000, A2.
549 Lisa Chmelecki, "MMC Files Attack," *(Lewiston) Sun Journal,* August 22, 2000, A7.
550 Ibid.
551 Lisa Chmelecki, "State Delays Cardiac Decision," *(Lewiston) Sun Journal,* August 25, 2000, A1.
552 Ibid., A8.
553 Lisa Chmelecki, "'A Team Effort: Maine Med Won't Contest Ruling,'" *(Lewiston) Sun Journal,* October 3, 2000, A1-A5.
554 Charlie Pomerleau, "Refugees Adjusting to Lewiston," *(Lewiston) Sun Journal,* March 2, 2000, A1.
555 Andorra Bruno, "U.S. Refugee Resettlement Assistance," Congressional Research Service, January 4, 2011, 1, 7-5700, R41570, https://fas.org/sgp/crs/row/R41570.pdf, last accessed August 28, 2020.
556 Doug Fletcher, "Jobless Rate Down," *(Lewiston) Sun Journal,* May 19, 2000, B1.
557 Doug Fletcher, "L-A Area Booming," *(Lewiston) Sun Journal,* August 2, 2000, A1.
558 Lisa Giguere, "'Banner year' for Jobs,'" *(Lewiston) Sun Journal,* December 27, 1999, B1.
559 Daniel Hartill, "En Francais: "Togolese(sic) Refugee Brings Culture to Classrooms," *(Lewiston) Sun Journal,* May 26, 2001, A1.
560 Diana Briton Putman and Mohamood Cabdi Noor, *The Somalis: Their History and Culture,* Refugee Service Center, Center for Applied Linguistics: Washington, D.C., 1993, 7, retrieved at https://files.eric.ed.gov/fulltext/ED377254.pdf, last accessed August 30, 2020.
561 Ibid.
562 Central Intelligence Agency, "The World Factbook: Africa, Somalia," Somalia, Background, last updated August 17, 2020, https://www.cia.gov/the-world-factbook/countries/somalia/#military-and-security, last accessed January 9, 2021.
563 Ibid.
564 Office of Refugee Resettlement, "FY 1999 Annual Report to the Congress," U.S. Department of Health and Human Services, Administration for Children and Families, U.S. Government Printing Office: Washington, D.C., 2001-615-032/24276, A-2, https://www.acf.hhs.gov/sites/default/files/orr/annual_orr_report_to_congress_1999.pdf, last accessed August 30, 2020.
565 Ibid., 41.
566 Jay L. Newberry, "Somali Refugee Resettlement and Locational Determinants in the United States," Dissertation, Michigan State University, 2011, 1.

[567] For more information about the 1980 Refugee Act see https://www.congress.gov/bill/96th-congress/senate-bill/643.

[568] Kimberly A. Huisman, et al., ed., *Somalis in Maine: Crossing Cultural Currents*, (Berkeley: North Atlantic Books, 2011) V, 256., https://www.amazon.com/Somalis-Maine-Crossing-Cultural-Currents/dp/1556439261, last accessed August 30, 2020.

[569] Department of Homeland Security, "Table 1: Persons Obtaining Lawful Permanent Residence Status – 1820 to 2017," October 2, 2018, https://www.dhs.gov/immigration-statistics/yearbook/2017/table1, last accessed September 5, 2020.

[570] Committee on the Judiciary, United States Senate, "Review of U.S. Refugee Resettlement Programs and Policies," A Report Prepared at the Request of Senator Edward. M. Kennedy, Chairman, Congressional Research Service, Library of Congress, Ninety-Sixth Congress, U.S. Government Printing Office: Washington, D.C., 1980, 1, retrieved from https://files.eric.ed.gov/fulltext/ED206779.pdf, last accessed September 5, 2020.

[571] FOR ITEMS ONE THROUGH SEVEN – Ibid., 7-11.

[572] Ibid., Table III, 15.

[573] Ibid., Table II, 12.

[574] Ibid., Table III, 15.

[575] 96th Congress, Public Law 96-212, March 17, 1980. 94 STAT.102, https://www.govinfo.gov/content/pkg/STATUTE-94/pdf/STATUTE-94-Pg102.pdf, last accessed September 5, 2020.

[576] Ibid.

[577] Daniel Hartill, "Bottleneck Threatens Store Plan," A1-A5.

[578] Ibid.

[579] Daniel Hartill, "Auburn Seeks Input on Overpass," *(Lewiston) Sun Journal,* February 28, 2000, A1.

[580] Daniel Hartill, "City Council Oks Overpass," *(Lewiston) Sun Journal,* May 3, 2000, A1.

[581] Application for Federal Assistance, Supplemental Grant, Category 2, "Unanticipated Arrivals," 1.

[582] Sue Charron, interview with Phil Nadeau, April 21, 2020.

[583] There were two applications to the Office of Refugee resettlement for "Unanticipated Arrivals" funding. One that was submitted in June 2001 and approved September 2001 for $250,000, and a supplementary application submitted on June 28, 2002 for another $250,000. The June 2001 meeting schedule document was listed as "Appendix 10" in the June 2002 unanticipated arrivals grant application. I did not have a copy of the entire June 2001 application document.

[584] Application for Federal Assistance, Supplemental Grant, Category 2, June 2001, Appendix 10

[585] Ibid.

586 Sue Charron, interview with Phil Nadeau.
587 Daniel Hartill, "Portland Somalis Eye Lewiston," *(Lewiston) Sun Journal,* February 13, 2001, B1, https://news.google.com/newspapers?nid=bcT4vkklUMwC&dat=20010213&printsec=frontpage&hl=en, last accessed September 6, 2020.
588 Ibid., B2.
589 Ibid., B2.
590 It should be noted that this did not represent the first efforts of the city's school system to provide ESL services to its students. "In 1894, The Lewiston public schools were conducting (English) language classes at Lincoln and Bates street schools for French, Irish and German students," see Patrick Connors, "Culture Clash Out of Strife," *(Lewiston) Sun Journal,* October 13, 2002, source document Judy Meyer email to Phil Nadeau, June 11, 2020.
591 Daniel Hartill, "Portland Somalis Eye Lewiston," B2.
592 Fatuma Hussein, interview #1 with Phil Nadeau, September 5, 2020
593 Andrew Cullen, "Struggle and Progress: 10 Years of Somalis in Lewiston," *(Lewiston) Sun Journal(online),* December 18, 2011, https://www.sunjournal.com/2011/12/18/struggle-progess-10-years-somalis-lewiston/, last accessed September 6, 2020.
594 Ibid.
595 Regina Phillips, interview with Phil Nadeau, September 9, 2020.
596 Fatuma Hussein, interview #1 with Phil Nadeau.
597 Ibid.
598 Ibid.
599 Ibid.
600 Ibid.
601 Ibid.
602 City of Clarkston, Georgia, "Clarkston Comprehensive Plan 2025: Community Assessment and Public Participation Strategy," December 2005, 7, https://www.dca.ga.gov/sites/default/files/clarkstonci.community_assessment_plan_2006.pdf, last accessed September 6, 2020.
603 Kelley Bouchard, "A Thousand Miles," *Portland Press Herald(online),* June 30, 2002.
604 Fatuma Hussein, interview #1 with Phil Nadeau.
605 Ibid.
606 The Somali word "sahan" is often used to describe the practice of someone traveling to explore or do reconnaissance of other areas to determine if they are more suitable and/or meet the needs and desires of a particular family, group, or community of individuals and typically report back to those who need the information.
607 Ibid.

608 "'Halal' means prepared under and maintained in strict compliance with the laws and customs of the Islamic religion including but not limited to those laws and customs of zabiha/zabeeha (slaughtered according to appropriate Islamic code), and as expressed by reliable recognized Islamic entities and scholars," see Illinois General Assembly, Illinois Compiled Statutes, "Public Health: (410 ILCS 637/), Halal Food Act," https://www.ilga.gov/legislation/ilcs/ilcs3.asp?ActID=1581&ChapterID=35, last accessed September 10, 2020.

609 Fatuma Hussein, interview #1 with Phil Nadeau.

610 Ibid.

611 Regina Phillips, interview with Phil Nadeau.

612 Lisa Chmelecki, "Census 2000: Twin Cities Lose People During '90s," March 30, 2001, A1, https://news.google.com/newspapers?nid=bcT4vkklUMwC&dat=20010330&printsec=frontpage&hl=en, last accessed September 10, 2020.

613 *(Lewiston) Sun Journal*, (table) "Census: Figures for Sun Journal Area," A9.

614 Doug Fletcher, "Business, Jobs Rolling In: Millions in New Development Coming to Tri-County Region," March 5, 2001, B1.

615 The 2000 average national rate of inflation was 3.4%, the highest average since 1991, see Federal Reserve Bank of Minneapolis, Inflation Calculator, "Consumer Price Index 1913 - ...," retrieved from https://www.minneapolisfed.org/about-us/monetary-policy/inflation-calculator/consumer-price-index-1913-, last accessed September 12, 2020.

616 National unemployment average increased from 4.0% in 2000 to 4.8% in 2001(numbers may have been revised in later reports), see U.S. Bureau of Labor Statistics, "Current Labor Statistics, Monthly Labor Review, January 2003," retrieved at https://www.bls.gov/opub/mlr/2003/01/cls0301.pdf, last accessed September 12, 2020.

617 Lisa Chmelecki, "Census 2000: Twin Cities Lose People During '90s," March 30, 2001, A9.

618 *(Lewiston) Sun Journal*, "Maine Becomes Fourth-Oldest State," May 23, 2001, A9.

619 Maine.gov, "Maine: Geography and Demography, 2000, retrieved at https://www.google.com/url?sa=t&rct=j&q=&esrc=s&source=web&cd=&ved=2ahUKEwjmop36nOfrAhXHt1kKHdE5BrIQFjACegQIChAE&url=https%3A%2F%2Fwww.maine.gov%2Fdhhs%2Fmecdc%2Fpublic-health-systems%2Fdata-research%2Fdata%2Fdocuments%2Fword%2Fdemo-2000.rtf&usg=AOvVaw0YwWY-j2Q5t0qcmdkrW_0V, last accessed September 13, 2020.

[620] Deirdre A. Mageean, et al., "Whither Maine's Population," Maine Policy Review 9.1, 2000, 31, https://digitalcommons.library.umaine.edu/mpr/vol9/iss1/69, last accessed September 14, 2020.

[621] Kevin Miller, "Census: Maine Oldest, Whitest State in Nation," *Bangor Daily News(online),* May 13, 2009, https://bangordailynews.com/2009/05/13/news/bangor/census-maine-oldest-whitest-state-in-nation/, last accessed September 14, 2020.

[622] University of Southern Maine, Muskie School of Public Service, "Changing Maine: Maine's Changing Population and Housing 1990-2010," September 2012, 6, https://umaine.edu/mitchellcenter/wp-content/uploads/sites/293/2013/08/Census_Report_1012121.pdf, last accessed November 27, 2020.

[623] Deirdre A. Mageean, et al., "Whither Maine's Population," 29.

[624] Ibid., 30.

[625] Ibid.

[626] Ibid., 31.

[627] Teachers Insurance and Annuity Association of America (TIAA) and College Retirement Equities Fund (CREF) Insurance Company.

[628] James Tierney, "Diversity in Maine: An Opportunity," University of Maine, Orono, TIAA/CREF Distinguished Honors Graduate Lecture, April 22, 2002, see https://drive.google.com/file/d/1v2qdwpXkk6_f2Vzn3_1-EPiWl3GAI2Qj/view?usp=sharing, link created January 2, 2021.

[629] Ibid.

[630] Ibid.

[631] Ibid.

[632] Portland's population growth between 1990 and 2000 was essentially flat would have likely declined without refugee resettlements in the city (see City of Portland, Maine, "Portland's Plan 2030," June 2017, 95). Consider that between only FFY1999 and FFY2001, over 1,100 secondary migrant refugees have moved into Portland. Add an average of 125 annual refugee resettlements in Portland over the three FFY 1999-2001 period (average for 30-year period going back to 1982 was 125), the absence of those foreign-born individuals in the city would likely have resulted in a 2000 census population decrease, see Phil Nadeau, ed., "Report to Governor Angus King: New Somali Arrivals and Other Issues Relative to Refugee/Secondary Migrants/Immigrants and Cultural Diversity in the City of Lewiston," City of Lewiston, Office of the City Administrator and Assistant City Administrator, May 9, 2002, 19, source document available from Phil Nadeau.

[633] Pew Research Center, "Facts on U.S. Immigrants, 2018," Washington, D.C. (August 20, 2020),

https://www.pewresearch.org/hispanic/2020/08/20/facts-on-u-s-immigrants-trend-data/, last accessed September 14, 2020.

[634] Pew Research Center, "Share of Foreign-Born Population, By State: 1960-2018," (downloaded Excel spreadsheet), Washington, D.C. (August 20, 2020), https://www.pewresearch.org/hispanic/2020/08/20/facts-on-u-s-immigrants-trend-data/, last accessed September 14, 2020.

[635] Sue Charron, interview with Phil Nadeau.

[636] Regina Phillips, interview with Phil Nadeau.

[637] Ibid.

[638] Phil Nadeau, "The Somalis of Lewiston: Effects of Rapid Immigration to a Homogeneous Maine City," 110.

[639] Sue Charron, interview with Phil Nadeau.

[640] Regina Phillips, interview with Phil Nadeau.

[641] Glen Bolduc, "Lewiston Watches Somali Impact," *(Lewiston) Sun Journal,* July 17, 2001, B2, https://news.google.com/newspapers?nid=bcT4vkklUMwC&dat=20010717&printsec=frontpage&hl=en, last accessed September 16, 2020.

[642] Phil Nadeau, "The Somalis of Lewiston: Effects of Rapid Immigration to a Homogeneous Maine City," Table 3., 112.

[643] Application for Federal Assistance, Supplemental Grant, Category 2, "Unanticipated Arrivals," Appendix 10.

[644] Ibid., 1.

[645] Ibid., 3.

[646] Ibid., Appendix 2.

[647] Phil Nadeau memo to Mayor Laurier Raymond, Lewiston City Council, and James Bennett, "Weekly Update: Somali Secondary Migrant/Cultural Diversity Activity," April 5, 2002, 2.

[648] The General Assistance data was extrapolated to produce an estimated number of GA applicants processed by the end of December 2001, see Phil Nadeau memo to Mayor Laurier Raymond, Lewiston City Council, and James Bennett, "Weekly Update: Somali Secondary Migrant/Cultural Diversity Activity," April 5, 2002, 2.

[649] U.S. Department of Defense, "The National 9/11 Pentagon Memorial," https://www.defense.gov/Experience/Pentagon-Memorial/, last accessed September 18, 2020.

[650] *(Lewiston) Sun Journal,* "'An Act of War,'" September 12, 2001, A1.

[651] Daniel Hartill, "'It's Very Surreal,'" *(Lewiston) Sun Journal,* September 12, 2001, A1.

[652] Rex Rhoades, "Staying Human in Spite of Fear," *(Lewiston) Sun Journal,* September 12, 2001, A6.

[653] Lisa Chmelecki, "On Terror's Trail: Lewiston High Grad a Victim," *(Lewiston) Sun Journal,* September 13, 2001, A1.

654 Scott Taylor, "Somalis Upset Over Attacks," *(Lewiston) Sun Journal,* September 13, 2001, B1.

655 Ibid.

656 Mark LaFlamme, "Former Sun Writer Missing," *(Lewiston) Sun Journal,* September 14, 2001, A1, https://news.google.com/newspapers?nid=bcT4vkklUMwC&dat=20010914&printsec=frontpage&hl=en, last accessed September 17, 2020.

657 Jesse Tisch, "Bates Students Offended by Link of Islam, Terrorism," *(Lewiston) Sun Journal,* September 14, 2001, B4.

658 Glen Bolduc, "We are More United Than Ever Before," *(Lewiston) Sun Journal,* September 17, 2001, A1.

659 *(Lewiston) Sun Journal,* "Minorities Feel Backlash," September 17, 2001, A2.

660 Bonnie Washuk, "Maine Muslims Feel Sadness, Fear, Loyalty," *(Lewiston) Sun Journal,* September 21, 2001, A1.

661 Bonnie Washuk, "Somali: Islam is About Peace," *(Lewiston) Sun Journal,* September 21, 2001, A7.

662 Christopher Williams, "Hijackers in Maine," *(Lewiston) Sun Journal,* October 5, 2001, A1-A8, https://news.google.com/newspapers?nid=bcT4vkklUMwC&dat=20011005&printsec=frontpage&hl=en, last accessed September 19, 2020.

663 U.S. Department of Justice, "Amerithrax Investigation Summary," February 13, 2010, 3, https://www.justice.gov/archive/amerithrax/docs/amx-investigative-summary.pdf, last accessed September 19, 2020.

664 U.S. Commission on Civil Rights, "Bioterrorism and Health Care Disparities," briefing paper, March 8, 2002, retrieved at https://www.usccr.gov/pubs/archives/biotrbrf/paper.htm, last accessed September 19, 2020.

665 Mark LaFlamme, "Mystery Powder Found at Bank," *(Lewiston) Sun Journal,* October 12, 2001, A9.

666 *(Lewiston) Sun Journal,* "NBC Employee Contracts Anthrax; FBI Says No Known Connections," October 13, 2001, A1.

667 Scott Taylor, "L-A Emergency Officials Limited in Face of Terrorist Threat," *(Lewiston) Sun Journal,* October 13, 2001, B1.

668 Bonnie Washuk, "State Fights Fear, Stress," *(Lewiston) Sun Journal,* October 17, 2001, A1-A9.

669 Scott Taylor, "Lewiston's Top Employee Resigns Post," *(Lewiston) Sun Journal,* October 18, 2001, A1.

670 This expression was used somewhat colloquially by people who worked in the immigrant and refugee services industry to identify new immigrants coming into Maine. I was unable to find a source of any kind that could confirm when the expression had first been employed but in my May 26, 2020 interview with Cheryl Hamilton, she stated that

it was certainly used prior to 2001 and was likely an extension of the expression 'new Americans' that was part of the immigrant services lexicon of the 1990s and used to identify immigrants coming into the U.S.

[671] Bonnie Washuk, "Students Show Passion for Fashion," *(Lewiston) Sun Journal(online),* May 17, 2008, https://www.sunjournal.com/2008/05/17/students-show-passion-fashion/, last accessed September 19, 2020.

[672] Scott Taylor, "Auburn Not Bracing for Refugees," *(Lewiston) Sun Journal,* September 27, 2001, B1.

[673] Phil Nadeau memo to Mayor Laurier Raymond, Lewiston City Council, and James Bennett, "Weekly Update: Somali Secondary Migrant/Cultural Diversity Activity," April 5, 2002, 2.

[674] Scott Taylor, "City Search Goes Back to 'Square One,'" *(Lewiston) Sun Journal,* November 27, 2001, A1-A7.

[675] Scott Taylor, "Council Considers Next Move," *(Lewiston) Sun Journal,* November 30, 2002, B1.

[676] Scott Taylor, "Search Continues for Administrator," *(Lewiston) Sun Journal,* December 5, 2001, B1.

[677] Scott Taylor, "Top Job Search Nearing Deadline," *(Lewiston) Sun Journal,* January 24, 2002, B1.

[678] James Bennett, interview #1 with Phil Nadeau, August 25, 2020.

[679] Jonathan Van Fleet, "Lewiston Expands Job Search," *(Lewiston) Sun Journal,* March 1, 2000, B1.

[680] Jonathan Van Fleet, "Back to the Start," *(Lewiston) Sun Journal,* March 9, 2000, B1.

[681] Lisbon, Maine had a 'town manager' form of government. Generally, under Maine law the manager is typically responsible for all hiring and firing of personnel, managing the budget, and implementation of policies and other matters that are approved by the voters who approve all policy and major purchases at a 'town meeting.' The manager also works with a board of selectmen who hire/fire the town manager, oversee all town operations, create ad hoc committees, develop the document with items to be voted on at the town meeting (the 'warrant'), and set the date for the town meeting.

[682] James Bennett, interview #1 with Phil Nadeau.

[683] Ibid.

[684] Ibid.

[685] Ibid.

[686] Scott Taylor, "Top Job Search Nearing Deadline," *(Lewiston) Sun Journal,* January 24, 2002, B1-B2.

[687] Ibid.

[688] Scott Taylor, "New Administrator Starts Today," *(Lewiston) Sun Journal,* March 25, 2002, A1.

[689] James Bennett, interview #1 with Phil Nadeau.
[690] Scott Taylor, "Top Job Search Nearing Deadline," A1.
[691] Mary T. Sarnecky, *A Contemporary History of the U.S. Army Nurse Corps,* Office of the Surgeon General, Borden Institute, Washington, D.C., 2010, 483, retrieved at: https://ke.army.mil/bordeninstitute/other_pub/nurse/NurseCorpsch21.pdf, last accessed September 21, 2020.
[692] Dr. Richard W. Stewart, "The United States Army in Somalia, 1992-1994," 6.
[693] Major Jason M. Alexander, "Operation Restore Hope: Strengthening Multilateral Operations," U.S. Army Command and General Staff College, Fort Leavenworth, KS, Master's Thesis, 2013, 1, https://apps.dtic.mil/sti/pdfs/ADA598979.pdf, last accessed September 21, 2020.
[694] Ibid., 1-2.
[695] Ibid., 5.
[696] Ibid., 5.
[697] Dr. Richard W. Stewart, "The United States Army in Somalia, 1992-1994," 5.
[698] Ibid., 5.
[699] Ibid., 8.
[700] Ibid., 9.
[701] Ibid., 10.
[702] For more information on how broadly "casualty" is defined by the military, see https://www.hrc.army.mil/content/Army%20Casualty%20and%20Mortuary%20Affairs%20Frequently%20Asked%20Questions, last accessed February 27, 2021.
[703] Ibid., 10.
[704] Ibid., 11.
[705] Marshall V. Ecklund and Michael A. McNerney, "Personnel Recovery Operations for Special Operations Forces in Urban Environments: Modeling Successful Overt and Clandestine Methods of Recovery," Master's Thesis, Naval Postgraduate School, Monterey, California, June 2004, 39, https://apps.dtic.mil/dtic/tr/fulltext/u2/a425043.pdf, last accessed September 22, 2020.
[706] Ibid.
[707] Dr. Richard W. Stewart, "The United States Army in Somalia, 1992-1994," 13.
[708] *(Lewiston) Sun Journal,* "New Hampshire Native Captured After Helicopter Crash in Somalia," October 5, 1993, 1.
[709] *(Lewiston) Sun Journal,* "U.S. Deaths Rise in Somalia, More Troops Ordered to Go," October 5, 1993, 3.

710 Tim Hanson, "Carthage Man Injured in Somalia on Sunday," *(Lewiston) Sun Journal,* October 6, 1993, 1.
711 *(Lewiston) Sun Journal,* "Missing Man Was in Same Helicopter as N.H. Native," 1, October 6, 1993.
712 Susan Johns, "Wages of War: Local Opinion Turns Against Aid to Somalia," *(Lewiston) Sun Journal,* October 7, 1993, 1.
713 Ibid.
714 Ibid., 7.
715 Ibid.
716 *(Lewiston) Sun Journal,* "Lisbon Soldier is Reported Killed in Action," October 8, 1993, 1.
717 Susan Johns, "Family Mourns Lisbon Soldier Killed in Somalia," *(Lewiston) Sun Journal,* October 9, 1993, 1.
718 Ibid., 7.
719 Maine State Legislature, "Resolve, to Designate Route 196 through Lisbon in Memory of Staff Sargeant(sic) Thomas Field," 116th Maine Legislature, Second Regular Session-1994, Legislative Document No. 1779, H.P. 1317, House of Representatives, January 25, 1994, 1, retrieved from the Maine Law and Legislative Digital Library at http://lldc.mainelegislature.org/Open/LDs/116/116-LD-1779.pdf, last accessed September 28, 2020.
720 World Peace Foundation, Mass Atrocity Endings Research, "Somalia: Fall of Siad Barre and the Civil War," August 7, 2015, retrieved at https://sites.tufts.edu/atrocityendings/2015/08/07/somalia-fall-of-siad-barre-civil-war/#_ednref1, last accessed September 28, 2020.
721 Doug Fletcher, "City Eyes Mega-Deal," November 1, 2001, A1-A5.
722 Greg Mitchell, interview with Phil Nadeau, October 12, 2020.
723 Lincoln Jeffers, interview #1 with Phil Nadeau, September 29, 2020.
724 Mike Gotto, interview with Phil Nadeau (not taped-interview notes in Phil Nadeau email to Mike Gotto, October 20, 2020), October 20, 2020.
725 Mike Gotto email to Phil Nadeau, subject "Today's Interview," October 30, 2020, 8:20AM.
726 Lucien Gosselin, interview #3 with Phil Nadeau.
727 Mike Gotto email to Phil Nadeau, October 30, 2020, 8:20AM.
728 Lincoln Jeffers, interview #1 with Phil Nadeau.
729 Mike Gotto email to Phil Nadeau, subject "Today's Interview," October 30, 2020, 3:47PM.
730 Ibid.
731 Mike Gotto, interview with Phil Nadeau, October 20, 2020.
732 Mike Gotto email to Phil Nadeau, October 30, 2020, 8:20AM.
733 Mike Gotto, interview with Phil Nadeau.
734 Mike Gotto email to Phil Nadeau, October 30, 2020, 8:20AM.
735 Mike Gotto, interview with Phil Nadeau.

736 Lucien Gosselin, interview #3 with Phil Nadeau.
737 Mike Gotto, interview with Phil Nadeau.
738 Mike Gotto email to Phil Nadeau, October 30, 2020, 8:20AM.
739 Mike Gotto, interview with Phil Nadeau.
740 Ibid.
741 Mike Gotto email to Phil Nadeau, October 30, 2020, 8:20AM.
742 Mike Gotto, interview with Phil Nadeau.
743 Ibid.
744 Daniel Hartill, "'It Changed People's Lives.' The Wal-Mart Distribution Center 10 Years Later," *(Lewiston) Sun Journal(online)*, December 14, 2014.
745 Lincoln Jeffers, email to Phil Nadeau, December 20, 2020.
746 Greg Mitchell, interview with Phil Nadeau.
747 Ibid.
748 Doug Fletcher, "City Eyes Mega-Deal," A1.
749 Doug Fletcher, "City Offers Wal-Mart Deal," *(Lewiston) Sun Journal*, December 20, 2001, 1.
750 James Carignan email to Kaileigh Tara, "Walmart Stuff," December 26, 2001, source document available from Phil Nadeau.
751 Greg Mitchell, interview with Phil Nadeau.
752 Scott Taylor, "Wal-Mart Looks Away for General Contractor," *(Lewiston) Sun Journal (online)*, March 20, 2004.
753 City of Lewiston, "Regular Meeting Held in the Council Room at 5:00PM," December 28, 2001, 1, http://www.lewistonmaine.gov/ArchiveCenter/ViewFile/Item/616, last accessed January 11, 2021.
754 Ibid.
755 Doug Fletcher, "City Offers Wal-Mart Deal,"A1-A9.
756 City of Lewiston, "Regular Meeting Held in the Council Room at 5:00PM," December 28, 2001, 1.
757 Ibid., 2.
758 Doug Fletcher, "Wal-Mart a Winner," *(Lewiston) Sun Journal*, December 29, 2001, A9.
759 City of Lewiston, "Regular Meeting Held in the Council Room at 5:00PM," December 28, 2001, 1.
760 Doug Fletcher, "Wal-Mart a Winner," A1.
761 Mike Gotto, interview with Phil Nadeau.
762 *(Lewiston) Sun Journal*, "City Celebrates," January 4, 2002, A1-A7.
763 Daniel Hartill, "'It Changed People's Lives.' The Wal-Mart Distribution Center 10 Years Later."
764 Carol Coultas, "Mood Festive as Wal-Mart Shows Off Massive Facility," *(Lewiston) Sun Journal(online)*, August 4, 2005, https://www.sunjournal.com/2005/08/04/mood-festive-wal-mart-shows-massive-facility/, last accessed November 1, 2020.

765 Mark LaFlamme and Lisa Chmelecki, "Lewiston Gets Scare," November 1, 2001, A1.
766 Ibid., A7.
767 Lisa Chmelecki, "CMMC Cardiac Center On Its Way," *(Lewiston) Sun Journal,* October 23, 2001, B1.
768 Scott Taylor, "$2.5M Needed," *(Lewiston) Sun Journal,* November 9, 2001, B1.
769 Jonathan Van Fleet, "Court Going to Lisbon St.," A1.
770 Ibid., B2.
771 Scott Taylor, "City Staff Discusses Contracts," *(Lewiston) Sun Journal,* November 9, 2001, B1.
772 "Established in 1965, Western Maine Community Action (WMCA) is a social service agency that has been providing assistance to low and mid-income families living in the western mountain region of Maine," see Western Maine Community Action web site https://wmca.org/about/, last accessed September 20, 2001.
773 Doug Fletcher, "Somalis Discuss Needs and Traditions," *(Lewiston) Sun Journal,* November 22, 2001, B1-B2.
774 Scott Taylor, "Council Moved to Take Over Pilsbury Block," *(Lewiston) Sun Journal,* B1.
775 LA Arts website, "History," see https://laarts.org/about/#history, last accessed September 26, 2020.
776 City of Lewiston, "Regular Meeting Held in the Council Room at 6:00PM," City Council, November 13, 2001.
777 For more information about the National Civic League's "All-America City" award, see https://www.nationalcivicleague.org/america-city-award/, last accessed February 27, 2021.
778 Daniel Hartill, "Franco Group to Celebrate New Center," November 23, 2000, B7.
779 Gendron Franco Center web site, "History," retrieved from https://www.francocenter.org/about-the-franco-center/mission-history/, last accessed October 1, 2020.
780 Andie Hannon, "Former Bates Dean Dies," *(Lewiston) Sun Journal(online),* August 15, 2011, https://www.sunjournal.com/2011/08/15/former-bates-dean-dies/, last accessed September 26, 2020.
781 Ibid.
782 *Bates Magazine,* "Dean Emeritus James Carignan '61, Man of 'High Energy, Principled Action and Unwavering Commitment,' Dies at 72," August 15, 2011, https://www.bates.edu/news/2011/08/15/james-carignan-obit/, last accessed September 27, 2020.
783 Scott Taylor, "Council Spends on Center," December 13, 2001, B1-B4.

[784] City of Lewiston, "Planning Board Minutes," June 25, 2002 (revised July 30, 2002), 1, retrieved at https://www.lewistonmaine.gov/ArchiveCenter/ViewFile/Item/1025, last accessed September 29, 2020.

[785] City of Lewiston, "Regular Meeting Held in the Council Room at 6:00PM," City Council minutes of November 13, 2001, 6-7, retrieved at https://www.lewistonmaine.gov/ArchiveCenter/ViewFile/Item/611, last accessed September 29, 2020.

[786] City of Lewiston, "Planning Board Minutes," 3.

[787] Ibid., 5.

[788] City of Lewiston, "Regular Meeting Held in the Council Room at 7:00PM," February 17, 2009, 3-4, retrieved at https://www.lewistonmaine.gov/ArchiveCenter/ViewFile/Item/404, last accessed September 29, 2020.

[789] Steve Collins, "Lewiston's Garcelon Bog: From 'Disease-Ridden Swamp to Protected Refuge," *(Lewiston) Sun Journal(online)*, July 12, 2020, https://www.sunjournal.com/2020/07/12/lewistons-garcelon-bog-from-disease-ridden-swamp-to-protected-refuge/, last accessed September 26, 2020.

[790] Ibid.

[791] Dot Perham-Whittier, letter to James E. Cassidy, January 3, 2002, source document available from Phil Nadeau.

[792] Dot Perham-Whittier, "Revised List of Participants for 2/5 Mtg(sic)," fax with attached list of participants, January 22, 2002, source documents available from Phil Nadeau.

[793] Phil Nadeau notes from working group meeting, Lepage Conference Center, February 7, 2002, source document available from Phil Nadeau.

[794] Phil Nadeau notes from working group meeting, Lepage Conference Center, February 28, 2002, source document available from Phil Nadeau.

[795] Phil Nadeau notes from working group meeting, Lepage Conference Center, March 7, 2002, source document available from Phil Nadeau.

[796] Ibid.

[797] Phil Nadeau notes from working group meeting, Lepage Conference Center, March 14, 2002, source document available from Phil Nadeau.

[798] Phil Nadeau notes from working group meeting, Lepage Conference Center, March 28, 2002, source document available from Phil Nadeau.

[799] Phil Nadeau memo to Mayor Laurier Raymond, Lewiston City Council, and James Bennett, "Weekly Update: Somali Secondary Migrant/Cultural Diversity Activity," April 5, 2002, 2.

[800] Heather Lindkvist email to Phil Nadeau, "Working Group," March 29, 2002.

[801] Ibid.

[802] Ibid.

[803] Ibid.
[804] Phil Nadeau notes from working group meeting, Lepage Conference Center, April 4, 2002, source document available from Phil Nadeau.
[805] Ibid.
[806] Ibid.
[807] Phil Nadeau memo to Mayor Laurier Raymond, Lewiston City Council, and James Bennett, "Weekly Update: Somali Secondary Migrant/Cultural Diversity Activity," April 5, 2002, 2.
[808] Ibid.
[809] Cheryl Hamilton, interview #1 with Phil Nadeau, May 26, 2020.
[810] Ibid.
[811] Ibid.
[812] Ibid.
[813] Ibid.
[814] Cheryl Hamilton email to RIMIS@yahoogroups.com, April 3, 2002, source document available from Phil Nadeau.
[815] Sue Charron email to Phil Nadeau and Denis Jean (Human Resources Director), April 2, 2002.
[816] Sue Charron email to Denis Jean and Phil Nadeau, April 9, 2002.
[817] Cheryl Hamilton, interview #1 with Phil Nadeau.
[818] Sue Charron email to Denis Jean and Phil Nadeau, April 2, 2002.
[819] The State of Maine did not track student populations by ethnicity or nationality. They did track the languages spoken by students identifying those languages by nationality. The immigrant numbers reported in all city school reports reflect how many students were enrolled in English Language Learner programs. In the early years of 2001-2002, the significant majority of Somali students in the Lewiston public school system were enrolled in ELL programs at some point in their academic school experience. ELL numbers correlated closely to the number of immigrant students in the school system. In 2001-2002, the ELL enrollments were predominantly Somali students.
[820] Phil Nadeau memo to Mayor Laurier Raymond, Lewiston City Council, Lewiston Legislative Delegation, and James Bennett, "Weekly Update: Somali Secondary Migrant/Cultural Diversity Activity," April 11, 2002, 3.
[821] Ibid.
[822] Phil Nadeau notes from meeting with Patti Sarineen, Career Center, April 18, 2002, source document available from Phil Nadeau.
[823] Phil Nadeau memo to Mayor Laurier Raymond, Lewiston City Council, Lewiston Legislative Delegation, and James Bennett, "Weekly Update: Somali Secondary Migrant/Cultural Diversity Activity," April 26, 2002, 3.

[824] Phil Nadeau, "New Somali Arrivals, General Refugee/Secondary Migrant & Other Cultural Diversity Issues, "April 16, 2002, 3, source document available from Phil Nadeau.
[825] Ibid.
[826] Scott Taylor, "City Mulls Somali Issues," *(Lewiston) Sun Journal*, April 18, 2002, B2.
[827] Bonnie Washuk, "Franco Center Says 'Merci' to Rita Dube," *(Lewiston) Sun Journal(online)*, January 12, 2013, https://www.sunjournal.com/2013/01/13/franco-center-says-merci-rita-dube/, last accessed March 13, 2021.
[828] Phil Nadeau memo to Mayor Laurier Raymond, Lewiston City Council, Lewiston Legislative Delegation, and James Bennett, "Weekly Update: Somali Secondary Migrant/Cultural Diversity Activity," April 18, 2002, 2.
[829] Kelley Bouchard, "Lewiston's Somali Surge," *Portland Press Herald(online)*, April 28, 2002.
[830] David A. Sargent, "Colorful, Tasteful, Diverse," *(Lewiston) Sun Journal*, April 26, 2002, B1.
[831] Scott Taylor, "City Mulls Somali Issues," B2.
[832] Phil Nadeau memo to Mayor Laurier Raymond, Lewiston City Council, Lewiston Legislative Delegation, and James Bennett, "Weekly Update: Somali Secondary Migrant/Cultural Diversity Activity," April 26, 2002, 3.
[833] Ibid., 2.
[834] Ibid.
[835] Phil Nadeau working group notes, Lepage Conference Center, April 26, 2002, source document available from Phil Nadeau.
[836] Ibid.
[837] Kelley Bouchard, "Lewiston's Somali Surge."
[838] Ibid.
[839] Ibid.
[840] Ibid.
[841] It is important to note that I began to estimate overall Somali population numbers by taking the number of new General Assistance applications and adding 25% to that number, the estimate of how many Somalis were not coming into the General Assistance office for services. The 25% number was based on anecdotal evidence only. That would have placed total number of Somalis in Lewiston as of April 30, 2002, at approximately 750 but could have been as high as 1,000..
[842] Kelley Bouchard, "Lewiston's Somali Surge."
[843] Ibid.
[844] Ibid.
[845] Ismail Ahmed, interview with Phil Nadeau, August 5, 2020.
[846] Kelley Bouchard, "Lewiston's Somali Surge."

847 U.S. Department of the Interior, "The 1999-2002 Drought in Maine- How Bad is It?" U.S. Geological Survey, November 29, 2016, https://pubs.usgs.gov/fs/2004/3021/, last accessed October 4, 2020.
848 City of Lewiston, "Please Join Us!" Public Informational Meeting flyer, undated, source document available from Phil Nadeau.
849 For more Lewiston Armory concert information, see https://www.setlist.fm/search?query=lewiston+armory+lewiston+maine, and Central Maine Youth Center/Colisee concert information https://www.setlist.fm/search?page=3&query=Central+Maine+youth+center+lewiston+maine, last accessed March 13, 2021.
850 Phil Nadeau notes for "Public Meeting," unknown location, undated, source document available from Phil Nadeau.
851 City of Lewiston, "Public Informational Meeting: Immigrants & Refugee Arrivals, The Myths & The Facts," handout, no date (Note: date of meeting was May 14, 2002), source document available from Phil Nadeau.
852 Ibid.
853 Scott Taylor, "Roomful, Earful," *(Lewiston) Sun Journal,* May 15, 2002, A1, https://news.google.com/newspapers?nid=bcT4vkklUMwC&dat=20020515&printsec=frontpage&hl=en, last accessed October 4, 2020.
854 Ibid., A1-A8.
855 Ibid., A8.
856 James Leamon, "Historic Lewiston: A Textile City in Transition," 15.
857 City of Lewiston, Me., "Twenty-Fourth Annual Report of the Receipts and Expenditures of the City of Lewiston for the Fiscal Year Ending February 28, 1887 Together with Other Annual Reports and Papers Relating to the Affairs of the City," 1887, 7, Maine Town Documents 4617, https://digitalcommons.library.umaine.edu/cgi/viewcontent.cgi?article=5780&context=towndocs, last accessed October 4, 2020.
858 City of Lewiston, Me., "Sixty-first Annual Report of the Receipts and Expenses of the City of Lewiston for the Fiscal Year Ending February 28, 1924 Together with Annual Reports and Papers Relating to the Affairs of the City," 1924, 57, Maine Town Documents, 4796, https://digitalcommons.library.umaine.edu/cgi/viewcontent.cgi?article=5959&context=towndocs, last accessed October 4, 2020.
859 Scott Taylor, "Roomful, Earful," A8.
860 Ibid.
861 James Bennett, interview #1 with Phil Nadeau.
862 Ibid.
863 Kelley Bouchard, "Lewiston's Somali Surge."

[864] Phil Nadeau memo to Mayor Laurier Raymond, Lewiston City Council, Lewiston Legislative Delegation, and James Bennett, "Weekly Update: Somali Secondary Migrant/Cultural Diversity Activity," May 2 2002, 3.
[865] Scott Taylor, "Officials: Somalis Get Equal Treatment," *(Lewiston) Sun Journal,* May 17, 2002, A8.
[866] Ibid.
[867] Ibid.
[868] Phil Nadeau, ed., "Report to Governor Angus King: New Somali Arrivals and Other Issues Relative to Refugee/Secondary Migrants/Immigrants and Cultural Diversity in the City of Lewiston," City of Lewiston, Office of the City Administrator and Assistant City Administrator, May 9, 2002, 19, see https://drive.google.com/file/d/1roAh2WN6HZ6ugyhtyRWdVXt2-kp7Uw_A/view?usp=sharing, link created December 26, 2020.
[869] Ibid., 1.
[870] Ibid., 2-3.
[871] Ibid., 3-22.
[872] Ibid., 3-4.
[873] Ibid., 4-8.
[874] Ibid., 8.
[875] Ibid., 10.
[876] Ibid., 10-12.
[877] Ibid., 16.
[878] Ibid., 19.
[879] Ibid.
[880] Ibid.
[881] Ibid., 20-22.
[882] Ibid.
[883] Colin Woordward, "The Making of a Man Without a Party," *Portland Press Herald(online),* September 22, 2012, https://www.pressherald.com/2012/09/22/the-making-of-a-man-without-a-party_2012-09-23/, last accessed October 7, 2020.
[884] Susan Johns, "King Starts 'Team' Work," *(Lewiston) Sun Journal,* November 10, 1994, 1-15.
[885] Liz Chapman, "King Wins Big," *(Lewiston) Sun Journal,* November 4, 1998, 1.
[886] Bonnie Washuk, "King Sings City's Praises," *(Lewiston) Sun Journal,* September 29, 1999, A1.
[887] Jonathan Van Fleet, "City: Don't Move Offices," *(Lewiston) Sun Journal,* December 28, 1999, A1.
[888] Jonathan Van Fleet, "City: Don't Move Offices," A1.
[889] Ibid., A7.
[890] Ibid.

[891] City of Lewiston, "Planning Board Meeting Minutes for January 23, 2001," 1-3.
[892] Glen Bolduc, "DHS Expansion Dedicated," *(Lewiston) Sun Journal,* June 28, 2001, B1.
[893] Glen Bolduc, "Lewiston Budget Cuts Mean Less Staffing," *(Lewiston) Sun Journal,* June 28, 2001, B1.
[894] Phil Nadeau, notes for meeting with Governor Angus King, Blaine House, May 16, 2002, source document available from Phil Nadeau.
[895] Ibid.
[896] Ibid.
[897] Ibid.
[898] Sharon Leahy-Lind email to Dottie Perham-Whittier, subject "HM 2010 Memo to Ms. Hassan," May 31, 2002, source document available from Phil Nadeau.
[899] Daniel Hartill, "Somali Women Aim to Help Themselves," *(Lewiston) Sun Journal,* May 20, 2002, B1.
[900] Ibid.
[901] Sharon Leahy-Lind email to Dottie Perham-Whittier.
[902] Dottie Perham-Whittier, cover letter with instructions for "Muslim Body Preparation, Funeral, Burial & Condolences," June 14, 2002, source document available from Phil Nadeau.
[903] Greg Nadeau, interview with Phil Nadeau.
[904] Phil Nadeau, "Joint City and State Staff Meeting on Refugee and Immigration Matters," City of Lewiston, Executive Summary, June 11, 2002, 1, source document available from Phil Nadeau.
[905] Ibid., 1.
[906] Ibid., 2.
[907] Ibid.
[908] Ibid.
[909] Ibid., 3.
[910] Ibid.
[911] Ibid.
[912] Gus Schumacher email to Phil Nadeau, "New Immigrant Potential in Lewiston, ME for Future Farming Operations," May 16, 2002, source document available from Phil Nadeau.
[913] For more on "Seeds of Peace" in Poland, Maine see https://www.seedsofpeace.org/programs/developing-leaders/camp/., last accessed October 8, 2020.
[914] Teaching methods and programming for teaching English to limited or non-English speakers has changed over time and will continue to change as methods, technology the science of learning change over time. A quick summary of acronyms provided by the Maine Department of Education: "EL (English learner) – noun, a student who speaks a primary or home language other than English and has not yet achieved

English language proficiency; the preferred term, as "English language learner" is seen as redundant by some; ELL (English language learner) – noun, a student who speaks a primary or home language other than English and has not yet achieved English language proficiency; no longer the preferred term (see EL); ESOL (English for speakers of other languages) – adjective, describes a type of class, student, teacher, program, etc.; it is perceived as more inclusive and is therefore the preferred term; ESL (English as a second language) – adjective, describes a type of class, student, teacher, program, etc.; in recent years many perceive this acronym as pejorative, so it is being replaced with ESOL; "second" refers to the non-primary status of a language rather than the chronological order of acquisition (for example, a person may speak three languages before learning English, and English would still be referred to as a "second" language); DLL (dual language learner) – noun, generally used to mean a student who is learning a second language while continuing to develop his/her primary language; often refers to young learners developing dual literacy from early childhood; in this country the term generally implies that one of the two languages is English, but this is not necessarily the case," see Maine Department of Education, "Serving Maine's English Learners," Policy and Resource Guide, ESOL and Bilingual Programs, (updated) March 11, 2020, retrieved at https://www.maine.gov/doe/learning/englishlearners/resources, last accessed October 7, 2020.

[915] Application for Federal Assistance, Supplemental Grant, Category 2: "Unanticipated Arrivals," 1.

[916] Department of Health and Human Services, "Financial Assistance Award," Office of Refugee Resttlement (Awarding Office), Award No. 90RU0041/01, Cat. No. 93576, August 1, 2002.

[917] Application for Federal Assistance, Supplemental Grant, Category 2: "Unanticipated Arrivals."

[918] Ethan Austin, "Residents See Positive Side of Lewiston," *(Lewiston) Sun Journal,* June 7, 2002, B1-B2.

[919] Ibid.

[920] John Melrose, "Revitalizing Maine's Service Centers," Maine Policy Review, 2003, 12, 3, 49, https://digitalcommons.library.umaine.edu/mpr/vol12/iss3/9, last accessed October 8, 2002.

[921] For more information about why property taxes are "unpopular," see https://www.governing.com/news/headlines/why-are-property-taxes-so-unpopular-in-many-states.html, last accessed March 13, 2021.

[922] Scott Taylor, "City Officials to Discuss Issues," *(Lewiston) Sun Journal,* June 11, 2002, B1.

[923] The relationship between Ed Barrett and myself first began with our interactions through the Maine Municipal Association's Legislative Policy Committee between 1994-2002. That relationship continued through our work together on the Maine Service Center Coalition. Following Ed's departure as Chair of the MSCC, I was elected as the organization's second Chair in 2007.

[924] John Melrose, "Revitalizing Maine's Service Centers," 51.

[925] Scott Taylor, "City Leaders Talk Taxes, Immigrations(sic)," *(Lewiston) Sun Journal,* June 13 2002, B1.

[926] Ibid.

[927] Joyce Benson email to Phil Nadeau, subject "Update on Special Census for Lewiston," July 29, 2002.

[928] Ibid.

[929] State of Washington, "Census Administrator Manual," Office of Financial Management, Forecasting Division, February 2013, 1-2, https://www.ofm.wa.gov/sites/default/files/public/legacy/pop/annex/forms/administrator.pdf, last accessed on October 10, 2020.

[930] Sue Martin, letter to "Service Providers," Bates College, Center for Service Learning, August 21, 2002, source document available from Phil Nadeau.

[931] Estimate for value based on inflation information between January 2013 and January 2021, see U.S. Bureau of Labor Statistics, "CPI Inflation Calculator," https://www.bls.gov/data/inflation_calculator.htm, last accessed February 28, 2021.

[932] Chelsea Conaboy, "City's Historic Clock Goes on Exhibit," *(Lewiston) Sun Journal,* June 19, 2002, B1.

[933] Balzer Family Clock Works, "About the Balzers," retrieved at https://balzerclockworks.com/Portfolio/about.htm, last accessed on October 10, 2020.

[934] City of Haverhill, "One Hundred Years of Teaching and Learning: Beneath the Tower Clock, 1898-Rebirth of a Monument-1998," Tower Clock Foundation, retrieved at https://www.cityofhaverhill.com/visitors/city_history/tower_clock_foundation.php, last accessed on October 10, 2020.

[935] Chelsea Conaboy, "City's Historic Clock Goes on Exhibit," B1.

[936] Ibid., B1

[937] Ibid., B2.

[938] City of Lewiston, "1891 E. Howard Clock – A Lewiston Treasure," History of Lewiston, retrieved at https://www.lewistonmaine.gov/423/1891-E-Howard-Clock, last accessed October 10, 2020.

[939] City of Biddeford, Maine, "Restoration Work on City Hall Clock Begins," April 2, 2019,

https://www.biddefordmaine.org/DocumentCenter/View/4867/040219-Clock-Restoration-Press-Release, last accessed November 2, 2020.

[940] Jim Hanna, interview with Phil Nadeau, October 28, 2020.

[941] For more information about Heifer International see https://www.heifer.org.

[942] Gus Schumacher email to Phil Nadeau, "New Immigrant Potential in Lewiston, ME for Future Farming Operations," May 16, 2002, source document available from Phil Nadeau.

[943] The project began in 1998. For more information see https://nesfp.org/about, last accessed November 20, 2020.

[944] Jim Hanna, interview with Phil Nadeau.

[945] Ibid.

[946] Gus Schumacher email to Phil Nadeau.

[947] Jim Hanna, interview with Phil Nadeau.

[948] Bonnie Simcock email to (email group including Phil Nadeau), subject "Agenda Somali Agriculture Meeting June 20 – Lewiston, ME," June 19, 2002.

[949] Phil Nadeau, notes from Somali Agricultural Meeting, Lewiston City Hall, June 20, 2002, source document available from Phil Nadeau.

[950] James Hanna email to Phil Nadeau, December 8, 2020.

[951] Phil Nadeau, "minutes" from "Immigrant Agriculture Project Meeting," Lewiston City Hall, July 8, 2002.

[952] Ibid.

[953] Ibid.

[954] Ibid.

[955] Ibid.

[956] Jim Hanna, interview with Phil Nadeau.

[957] Phil Nadeau, "minutes" from "Immigrant Agriculture Project Meeting."

[958] Ibid.

[959] *Bates News*, "Bates College Senior Wins Two National Awards for Lewiston Community Garden Project," Bates College Communication Office, March 10, 2000, https://www.bates.edu/news/2000/03/10/national-awards-garden-project/, last accessed October 12, 2020.

[960] Phil Nadeau, "minutes" from "Immigrant Agriculture Project Meeting."

[961] Ibid.

[962] Jim Hanna, interview with Phil Nadeau.

[963] The very first NASAP meeting happened sometime in September 2002 when Jim Hanna made the presentation to the Maine Rural Workers Coalition, see Jim Hanna, interview with Phil Nadeau.

[964] Jim Hanna, email to group (includes Phil Nadeau), subject "Meeting on Lewiston Farming Project," October 3, 2002.

965 Ibid.
966 Jim Hanna, interview with Phil Nadeau.
967 For more information on Cultivating Community and NASAP, see https://www.cultivatingcommunity.org/contact-us/, last accessed November 20, 2020.
968 For more information about Gus Schumacher, see https://foodtank.com/news/2017/09/gus-schumacher-obituary/, last accessed November 20, 2020.
969 "To be tax-exempt under section 501(c)(3) of the Internal Revenue Code, an organization must be organized and operated exclusively for exempt purposes set forth in section 501(c)(3), and none of its earnings may inure to any private shareholder or individual," see Internal Revenue Service, "Exemption Requirements – 501(c)(3) Organizations," retrieved at https://www.irs.gov/charities-non-profits/charitable-organizations/exemption-requirements-501c3-organizations, last accessed October 12, 2020.
970 Phil Nadeau, mailed documents referenced in the paragraph are all available from Phil Nadeau.
971 Genesis Prevention Coalition Program Review, "Program Summary," February 2, 2002, source document available from Phil Nadeau.
972 Kelley Bouchard, "A Thousand Miles."
973 Fatuma Hussein, interview #1 with Phil Nadeau.
974 Fatuma Hussein, interview #4 with Phil Nadeau, December 30, 2020.
975 Ibid.
976 Ibid.
977 Fatuma Hussein, interview #1 with Phil Nadeau.
978 Ibid.
979 Donna Keene Rousseau, "CEI - Positive Impact on Business and Home Ownership," *(Lewiston) Sun Journal(online)*, March 8, 2003, https://www.sunjournal.com/2003/03/08/cei-positive-impact-business-home-ownership/, last accessed October 13, 2020.
980 Ibid.
981 Fatuma Hussein, interview #1 with Phil Nadeau.
982 Ibid.
983 Ibid.
984 Ibid.
985 Ibid.
986 Ibid.
987 Ibid.
988 Ibid.
989 Ibid.
990 Ibid.
991 Ibid.

992 Ibid.
993 Ibid.
994 Ibid.
995 For more information about the Immigrant Resource of Maine, see https://www.ircofmaine.org/about-us, last accessed October 15, 2020.
996 Jonathan Van Fleet, "Twin Cities Ponder Ways to Help Refugees," 1.
997 Phil Nadeau memo to Mayor Laurier Raymond, Lewiston City Council, Lewiston Legislative Delegation, and James Bennett, "Weekly Update: Somali Secondary Migrant/Cultural Diversity Activity," May 2, 2002, 2.
998 Kathryn Skelton, "Somalis in Spotlight," *(Lewiston) Sun Journal*, August 21, 2002, A1.
999 Phil Nadeau, "The Somalis of Lewiston: Effects of Rapid Immigration to a Homogenous Maine City," 122 (see Footnote 104).
1000 Kathryn Skelton, "Somalis in Spotlight," A8.
1001 . Phil Nadeau, "The Somalis of Lewiston: Effects of Rapid Immigration to a Homogenous Maine City," 122 (see Footnote 104).
1002 Paul Mills, "The JFK Centennial: When Camelot Came to Maine," *(Lewiston) Sun Journal(online)*, May 28, 2017, https://www.sunjournal.com/2017/05/28/the-jfk-centennial-when-camelot-came-to-maine/, November 2, 2020.
1003 For more information on the EMK Institute, see https://www.emkinstitute.org/resources/what-youll-experience?gclid=CjwKCAiA-f78BRBbEiwATKRRBGce007_nvvqT2GwzFoerg1UTRk9K8BOAn01ir-QAzeYGVGuhxfjQBoCPvAQAvD_BwE, last accessed November 2, 2020.
1004 Phil Nadeau email to Mohammed Abdi, Omar Ahmed, Abdiaziz Ali, Daryeelka, Somali Refugee Foundation, United Somali Women of Maine, subject "Creation of Somali Advisory Committee," August 7, 2002.
1005 Ibid.
1006 Ibid.
1007 Ibid.
1008 Phil Nadeau, notes from Somali Advisory Committee meeting, August 22, 2002, source document available from Phil Nadeau.
1009 Ibid.
1010 Phil Nadeau, supplemental notes from Somali Advisory Committee meeting, (undated but believed to be from the August 22, 2002 meeting), source document available from Phil Nadeau.
1011 Phil Nadeau, notes from "City/School Meeting" with PD Resource Officers Ron Dumont (High School); Rob Aldrich (High School); Roger Landry (DARE, High School, Hillview Apartments); Danielle Lord (Lewiston Middle School); Joe Bradeen (elementary schools); Adam

Higgins (Lewiston Middle School), September 19, 2002, redacted source document available from Phil Nadeau.

[1012] Ibid.

[1013] Ibid.

[1014] Fatuma Hussein, interview #2 with Phil Nadeau, September 19, 2020.

[1015] Ibid.

[1016] Ibid.

[1017] From 1863 to 1973, all elected Lewiston mayors served one-year terms. John Orestis would become the first mayor to serve a two-year term in 1974-1975. A charter change in 2012 allowed for the mayor to serve three consecutive terms. Mayor Robert Macdonald would become the first mayor in Lewiston history to serve three consecutive two-year terms from 2012 to 2017 (the mayor who served the most years as mayor was Lewiston's first Franco mayor Robert J. Wiseman who served as mayor for 9 years over 9 different years between 1914 and 1935, see Geneva Kirk and Gridley Barrows, "Historic Lewiston: Its Government," 13.)

[1018] Larry Raymond, interview with Mike Richard, "Raymond, Larry Oral History Interview."

[1019] Susan Geismar, interview with Phil Nadeau, November 4, 2020.

[1020] Laurier T. Raymond Sr. filled the City Controller's position (see *The Lewiston Daily Sun*, "New Lewiston School Supt. To Receive Salary of $7,520," October 23, 1953, 22, [NOTE: URL for this article is listed as October 24, 1953], https://news.google.com/newspapers?nid=IT5EXw6i2GUC&dat=19531024&printsec=frontpage&hl=en, last accessed November 8, 2020.) after H.R. Gosselin left the position sometime in 1953 (see *The Lewiston Daily Sun*, "City Officials and Teachers Confer; Salary Plan Secret," January 22, 1953, 14).

[1021] Larry Raymond, interview with Mike Richard, "Raymond, Larry Oral History Interview."

[1022] Ibid.

[1023] Douglas Rooks, "Rise, Decline, and Renewal," 31-35.

[1024] Larry Raymond, interview with Mike Richard, "Raymond, Larry Oral History Interview."

[1025] Susan Geismar, interview with Phil Nadeau.

[1026] Ibid.

[1027] Larry Raymond, interview with Mike Richard, "Raymond, Larry Oral History Interview."

[1028] Susan Geismar, interview with Phil Nadeau.

[1029] Larry Raymond, interview with Mike Richard, "Raymond, Larry Oral History Interview."

[1030] Charles Morrison, interview with Phil Nadeau.

[1031] Larry Raymond, interview with Mike Richard, "Raymond, Larry Oral History Interview."
[1032] Roger Philippon, interview #2 with Phil Nadeau, September 2, 2020.
[1033] Susan Geismar, interview with Phil Nadeau.
[1034] Ibid.
[1035] Larry Raymond, interview with Mike Richard, "Raymond, Larry Oral History Interview."
[1036] Susan Geismar, interview with Phil Nadeau and *The Lewiston Daily Sun*, "Doherty and Finance Board Settle Behind Close Doors," August 28, 1956, 14 (NOTE: URL for page 14 of the August 28, 1956 edition is on the left side of the front page image for August, 29, 1956 edition), https://news.google.com/newspapers?nid=IT5EXw6i2GUC&dat=19560829&printsec=frontpage&hl=en, last accessed November 2, 2020.
[1037] Scott Taylor, "From Country Lawyer to Mayor," *(Lewiston) Sun Journal*, January 2, 2002, B1, https://news.google.com/newspapers?nid=bcT4vkklUMwC&dat=20020102&printsec=frontpage&hl=en, last accessed October 28, 2020.
[1038] Laurier T. Raymond, Sr. left the City Controller position in 1966 as noted through articles in the Lewiston Daily Sun on May 2, 1966 confirming he was in the position at that time ("Finance Board Will Review City's Annual Audit Report") and confirming that Laurier E. Roy was in the position on December 13, 1966 ("FB Recommends $3.5 Million 1967 Tax Anticipation Loan").
[1039] Larry Raymond, interview with Mike Richard, "Raymond, Larry Oral History Interview."
[1040] Richard Kisonak, "Contracts are voted by URA," *The Lewiston Daily Sun*, January 25, 1963, 24.
[1041] Larry Raymond, interview with Mike Richard, "Raymond, Larry Oral History Interview."
[1042] The position was the equivalent of the county "District Attorney" position that has been in place for years in Androscoggin County.
[1043] *The Lewiston Daily Sun*, "Raymond Defeats Rocheleau for County Nod," June 19, 1962, 2, https://news.google.com/newspapers?nid=IT5EXw6i2GUC&dat=19620619&printsec=frontpage&hl=en, last accessed January 11, 2020.
[1044] *The Lewiston Daily Sun*, "Androscoggin County Posts Taken by Demo Candidates," November 7, 1962, 2.
[1045] Larry Raymond, interview with Mike Richard, "Raymond, Larry Oral History Interview."
[1046] Ibid.
[1047] Ibid.
[1048] Cliff Hodgman, "Atty. Raymond Says Expects to Make Move Soon in Debate with Playboy Magazine," *Lewiston Evening Journal*, September 11, 1963, 22 (NOTE: the URL is for the September 12, 1963

edition. Page 22 of the September 11, 1963 edition is found to the left of the front page of the September 12, 1963 edition), https://news.google.com/newspapers?nid=oQQVFBP0nzwC&dat=19630912&printsec=frontpage&hl=en, last accessed on October 28, 2020.

[1049] Larry Raymond, interview with Mike Richard, "Raymond, Larry Oral History Interview."

[1050] Cliff Hodgman, "Atty. Raymond Says Expects to Make Move Soon in Debate with Playboy Magazine," 22.

[1051] Larry Raymond, interview with Mike Richard, "Raymond, Larry Oral History Interview."

[1052] Ibid.

[1053] Ibid.

[1054] *The Lewiston Daily Sun*, "Judge Naiman to Preside in County Probate Court, October 16, 1965, 2.

[1055] *The Lewiston Daily Sun*, "County Group Will Discuss Vacancy on Probate Court," October 21, 1965.

[1056] *The Lewiston Daily Sun*, "Raymond Renamed Judge of Probate by County Voters," November 9, 1966, 32 (NOTE: The URL is for the November 10, 1966 edition. Page 32 of the November 9, 1966 edition is found to the left of the front page of the November 10, 1966), https://news.google.com/newspapers?nid=IT5EXw6i2GUC&dat=19661110&printsec=frontpage&hl=en, last accessed October 28, 2020.

[1057] J. Craig Anderson, "Former Lewiston Mayor Laurier T. Raymond Jr. Dies at 87," *(Lewiston) Sun Journal(online),* May 27, 2019, https://www.sunjournal.com/2019/05/27/laurier-t-raymond-former-lewiston-mayor-dies-at-87/, last accessed October 28, 2020.

[1058] R. Bruce Huntington, "No Question Any More: Clay-Liston Scrap Will be Held at Youth Center," *Lewiston Evening Journal,* May 12, 1965, 1, https://news.google.com/newspapers?nid=oQQVFBP0nzwC&dat=19650512&printsec=frontpage&hl=en, last accessed October 28, 2020.

[1059] Susan Geismar, interview with Phil Nadeau.

[1060] Rob Sneddon, *The Phantom Punch,* 116.

[1061] Larry Raymond, interview with Mike Richard, "Raymond, Larry Oral History Interview."

[1062] Ibid.

[1063] Douglas Rooks, "Rise, Decline, and Renewal," 71.

[1064] Ibid.

[1065] Larry Raymond, interview with Mike Richard, "Raymond, Larry Oral History Interview."

[1066] Roger Philippon, interview #1 with Phil Nadeau, May 26, 2020.

[1067] Ibid.

[1068] Roger Philippon, interview #2 with Phil Nadeau.

[1069] Ibid.

1070 Ibid.

1071 For many Franco American families like mine, the crêpes would be made with shortening that often produced enough smoke to set off a fire alarm. For more information about French Canadian crêpes, see https://snappygourmet.com/french-canadian-breakfast-crepes/, last accessed January 11, 2021.

1072 Susan Geismar, interview with Phil Nadeau.

1073 Roger Philippon, interview #2 with Phil Nadeau.

1074 Susan Geismar, interview with Phil Nadeau.

1075 Roger Philippon, interview #1 with Phil Nadeau.

1076 Roger Philippon, interview #2 with Phil Nadeau.

1077 Roger Philippon, interview #1 with Phil Nadeau.

1078 *(Lewiston) Sun Journal,* "Raymond Announces Candidacy for Mayor," June 21, 2001, B1.

1079 Roger Philippon, interview #1 with Phil Nadeau.

1080 Scott Taylor, "Lewiston Loves Raymond," *(Lewiston) Sun Journal,* November 7, 2001, A1-A7, https://news.google.com/newspapers?nid=bcT4vkklUMwC&dat=20011107&printsec=frontpage&hl=en, last accessed December 24, 2002.

1081 Scott Taylor, "From Country Lawyer to Mayor," B1-B2.

1082 City of Lewiston, "Regular Meeting Held in the City Council Room at 7:00 PM," City Council (minutes), January 22, 2002.

1083 Rex Rhoades, "Our View: Going in the Right Direction," *(Lewiston) Sun Journal,* November 9, 2001, A6, https://news.google.com/newspapers?nid=bcT4vkklUMwC&dat=20011109&printsec=frontpage&hl=en, last accessed January 11, 2021

1084 City of Lewiston, "Regular Meeting Held in the City Council Room at 7:00 PM," City Council (minutes), June 4, 2002.

1085 City of Lewiston, "Regular Meeting Held in the City Council Room at 7:00 PM," City Council (minutes), July 9, 2002.

1086 Scott Taylor, "Cote Steps Down," *(Lewiston) Sun Journal,* July 24, 2002, B1.

1087 Scott Taylor, Mason, Prevost Post Wins," *(Lewiston) Sun Journal (online),* September 11, 2002.

1088 City of Lewiston, "Regular Meeting Held in the City Council Room at 7:00 PM," City Council (minutes), July 9, 2002.

1089 Ibid.

1090 Scott Taylor, "Raymond Honored with Gateway Park," *(Lewiston) Sun Journal,* July 28, 2004, B1, https://news.google.com/newspapers?nid=bcT4vkklUMwC&dat=20040728&printsec=frontpage&hl=en, last accessed January 11, 2021.

1091 Laura Segall, "Demolition," (picture) *(Lewiston) Sun Journal,* September 26, 2002, A1.

[1092] Scott Taylor, "Administration Aims High," *(Lewiston) Sun Journal,* September 25, 2002, A1-A5, https://news.google.com/newspapers?nid=bcT4vkklUMwC&dat=20020925&printsec=frontpage&hl=en, last accessed January 13, 2021.
[1093] Scott Taylor, "Raymond Honored with Gateway Park."
[1094] Dottie Perham-Whittier, interview with Phil Nadeau, May 5, 2002.
[1095] Ibid.
[1096] Jonathan Tilove, "Somali Migration Transforms Lewiston," *Kennebec Journal Morning Sentinel,* September 8, 2002.
[1097] Mayor Laurier T. Raymond, Jr., "Letter to the Somali Community," October 1, 2002, available at https://drive.google.com/file/d/1UbDFKiDuOcY-TIcejNNF55tjxE20aa9i/view?usp=sharing, link created on December 24, 2020.
[1098] Phil Nadeau, "Transmittal of Mayor's Letter to Somali Leadership," October 2, 2002, Memorandum, Somali Advisory Group, see https://drive.google.com/file/d/1yGv1EH4Ytde2K37jAGqLQdPv7xQRUQ4D/view?usp=sharing, link created December 26, 2020.
[1099] Ibid.
[1100] Scott Taylor, "Mayor Appeals to Somalis to Stem Migration," *(Lewiston) Sun Journal,* October 4, 2002, source Judy Meyer email to Phil Nadeau, June 11, 2020.
[1101] Roger Philippon, interview #1 with Phil Nadeau.
[1102] Ibid.
[1103] Ibid.
[1104] Kelley Bouchard, "Closing the door: Mayor's Request Disconcerts Somalis," *Portland Press Herald(online),* October 5, 2002
[1105] David Reid, "City Council Opposes Somali Resettlement," *The Republican,* October 2, 2002, A01.
[1106] Kelley Bouchard, "Closing the door: Mayor's Request Disconcerts Somalis."
[1107] James Bennett, interview #1 with Phil Nadeau.
[1108] Doug Fletcher, "Somali Letter Draws Spotlight," *(Lewiston) Sun Journal,* October 7, 2002, source Judy Meyer email to Phil Nadeau, June 11, 2020.
[1109] Ibid.
[1110] James Bennett, interview #1 with Phil Nadeau.
[1111] *Bates News,* "Speaker Biographies for African Refugee Health: Best Practices," September 17, 2010, https://www.bates.edu/news/2010/09/17/arh-biographies/, last accessed November 2, 2020.
[1112] Phil Nadeau, (so subject) letter to Artist and Community Panel, Maine Arts Commission, City of Lewiston Executive Department, October 7, 2002, source document available from Phil Nadeau.

[1113] Ibid.
[1114] John Richardson, "Six Mainers Who Made an Impact in 2003," *Portland Press Herald,* December 28, 2003, 1A.
[1115] Ibid.
[1116] Somali Community Services, Inc., "Your Letter Dated October 1st(sic), 2002. Somalis in Lewiston," letter to Mr. (Laurier) Raymond, Mayor, City of Lewiston, October 6, 2002, see https://drive.google.com/file/d/18SloDOddHy21AxIY9vgG4Kr_yFMsv-vd/view?usp=sharing, link created December 26, 2020.
[1117] Ibid.
[1118] Ibid.
[1119] Ibid.
[1120] Lisa Chmelecki, "Immigrants Say Letter Was a Bigoted Act," *(Lewiston) Sun Journal,* October 8, 2002, source document Judy Meyer email to Phil Nadeau, June 11, 2020.
[1121] Scott Taylor, "Officially, City Still Has Open Door Policy," *(Lewiston) Sun Journal,* October 8, 2002, source Judy Meyer email to Phil Nadeau, June 11, 2020.
[1122] Scott Taylor, "Group Alleges Discrimination," *(Lewiston) Sun Journal,* November 8, 2002, B1.
[1123] Ibid.
[1124] Ibid.
[1125] Ibid.
[1126] Gregory D. Kesich, "Agency Agrees to Interpreters for its Clients," *Portland Press Herald(online),* April 3, 2006.
[1127] Kelley Bouchard, "Lewiston Officials Talk With Somalis About 'Missteps,'" *Portland Press Herald(online),* October 9, 2002, 1A.
[1128] Ibid.
[1129] See Phil Nadeau, "The Somalis of Lewiston: Effects of Rapid Immigration to a Homogeneous Maine City," in *The Southern Maine Review,* eds. Jeremiah. P. Conway, et al., (Portland: The University of Southern Maine, 2005), 1, Spring, 102-147; Phil Nadeau, "A Work in Progress: Lewiston Responds to the Rapid Migration of Somali Refugees," in Kimberly A. Huisman, et al., ed., *Somalis in Maine: Crossing Cultural Currents,* (Berkeley: North Atlantic Books, 2011) 1, 3, 53-72.
[1130] The number 1,051 was the official number I was reporting out as of October 7, 2002 to multiple news agencies and was often reported as a rounded-up number of 1,060 or simply "over 1,000," see Scott Taylor, "Officially, City Still Has Open-Door Policy."
[1131] Kelley Bouchard, "Lewiston Officials Talk with Somalis About 'Missteps,'" 1A.
[1132] Ibid.
[1133] James Bennett, interview #2 with Phil Nadeau, August 8, 2020.

[1134] State of Maine Office of the Attorney General, (to the "Members of the Somali Community," October 9, 2002, see https://drive.google.com/file/d/1Kmb_vxdQ7DP1qd_Z5aAtMFIQbHM5deNV/view?usp=sharing, link created January 7, 2021.

[1135] Scott Taylor, "Somali, City Leaders Meet," *(Lewiston) Sun Journal*, October 11, 2002, source document Judy Meyer email to Phil Nadeau, June 11, 2020.

[1136] Ibid.

[1137] James Bennett, interview #2 with Phil Nadeau.

[1138] Doug Fletcher, "Mayor Reflects on Painful Week," *(Lewiston) Sun Journal*, October 12, 2002, source document available from Phil Nadeau.

[1139] Tom Bell, "Lewiston Marchers Welcome Somalis," *Portland Press Herald(online)*, October 14, 2002, 1A.

[1140] David Connery-Marin, "Complaints of Racism Soften After Somalis Meet Mayor," *Portland Press Herald*, October 12, 2002, 1A.

[1141] Scott Taylor, "Raymond Meets Honestly, Openly with Somalis," *(Lewiston) Sun Journal*, October 12, 2002, source document available from Phil Nadeau.

[1142] James Bennett, interview #1 with Phil Nadeau.

[1143] Doug Fletcher, "Mayor Reflects on Painful Week."

[1144] James Bennett, interview #2 with Phil Nadeau.

[1145] Ibid.

[1146] Susan Geismar, interview with Phil Nadeau.

[1147] James Bennett, interview #1 with Phil Nadeau.

[1148] Doug Fletcher, "Mayor Reflects on Painful Week."

[1149] Ibid.

[1150] Ibid.

[1151] Ibid.

[1152] Ibid.

[1153] Scott Taylor, "Raymond Meets Honestly, Openly with Somalis," *(Lewiston) Sun Journal*, October 12, 2002, source document Judy Meyer to Phil Nadeau, June 11, 2020.

[1154] Doug Fletcher, "Mayor Reflects on Painful Week.

[1155] Doug Fletcher, "Mayor Looks Ahead," *(Lewiston) Sun Journal*, January 18, 2003, A1-A11, https://news.google.com/newspapers?nid=bcT4vkklUMwC&dat=20030118&printsec=frontpage&hl=en, link created July 3, 2021.

[1156] Mayor Laurier T. Raymond, "Press Release," October 11, 2002, available at https://drive.google.com/file/d/1K4cejgmK294BAkw7uWFe-09zeNr8YImM/view?usp=sharing, link created December 24, 2020.

[1157] The Elders of the Somali Community of Lewiston, "Press Release," October 11, 2002, available at https://drive.google.com/file/d/1MKq8oNsdqI3lEazkav4frO3zdeCIZCfj/view?usp=sharing, link created December 24, 2020.

[1158] Ibid.

[1159] Mayor Laurier T. Raymond, "Press Release."

[1160] Ibid.

[1161] Ibid.

[1162] Angus S. King, Jr., letter to the Lewiston community, October 11, 2002, Office of the Governor, State of Maine, August, Maine, see https://drive.google.com/file/d/1nMYdJGGKcE7Zux9_Mk2VSMb6S9coWWw_/view?usp=sharing, link created December 26, 2020.

[1163] Ibid.

[1164] Lisa Chmelecki, "Walk Planned to Welcome Somalis," *(Lewiston) Sun Journal,* October 11, 2002, source document Judy Meyer email to Phil Nadeau, June 11, 2002.

[1165] Mark Schlotterbeck, "Many & One: Let Us Be That City," Many & One Rally 10th Anniversary, Callahan Hall/Lewiston Public Library, Lewiston, Maine, January 11, 2013, 3, source document provided by Mark Schlotterbeck to Phil Nadeau.

[1166] Lisa Chmelecki, "Walk Planned to Welcome Somalis."

[1167] Mark Schlotterbeck, "Many & One: Let Us Be That City.".

[1168] Ibid.

[1169] Ibid.

[1170] Mark Schlotterbeck, interview with Phil Nadeau, May 3, 2020.

[1171] Tom Bell, "Lewiston Marchers Welcome Somalis."

[1172] Mark Schlotterbeck, interview with Phil Nadeau.

[1173] Tom Bell, "Lewiston Marchers Welcome Somalis."

[1174] Mark Schlotterbeck, "Many & One: Let Us Be That City,"

[1175] Ibid.

[1176] Lisa Chmelecki, "Neo-Nazi Group Eyes Somali Situation," *(Lewiston) Sun Journal,* October 15, 2002, source document Judy Meyer email to Phil Nadeau, June 11, 2020.

[1177] Ibid.

[1178] Ibid.

[1179] Tom Bell, "Lewiston Marchers Welcome Somalis."

[1180] Seth Golden, "Walkers Unite", *(Lewiston) Sun Journal,* October 15, 2002, source document Judy Meyer email to Phil Nadeau, June 11, 2020.

[1181] Ibid.

[1182] Mark Schlotterbeck, interview with Phil Nadeau.

[1183] Ibid.

[1184] David Reid, "City Council Opposes Somali Resettlement," *The Republican,* October 2, 2002, A01.

[1185] David Reid, "Proposal to Resettle Somalis Appears to be Stuck in Neutral," *The Republican,* November 1, 2002, A01.

[1186] Michael Sullivan, interview with Phil Nadeau, May 18, 2020.
[1187] Ibid.
[1188] For more information about the Somali Bantu resettlements in 2002, see http://www.donatellaorch.com/articles/following_freedom.html, last accessed November 18, 2020.
[1189] Ibid.
[1190] David Reid, "Proposal to Resettle Somalis Appears to be Stuck in Neutral."
[1191] Michael Sullivan, interview with Phil Nadeau.
[1192] Ibid.
[1193] Ibid.
[1194] David Reid, "Proposal to Resettle Somalis Appears to be Stuck in Neutral."
[1195] David Reid, "Somali Refugees Plan Incomplete," *The Republican*, February 20, 2003, B01.
[1196] Michael Sullivan, interview with Phil Nadeau.
[1197] Stephanie Barry, "Bantus 'Capable' Residents," *The Republic*, November 7, 2003, B01.
[1198] Federal Register, "Enhancing State and Local Involvement in Refugee Resettlement," A Presidential Document by the Executive Office of the President 10/1/19, Executive Order 13888 of September 26, 2019, https://www.federalregister.gov/documents/2019/10/01/2019-21505/enhancing-state-and-local-involvement-in-refugee-resettlement, last accessed November 16, 2020.
[1199] Ibid.
[1200] Michael Sullivan, interview with Phil Nadeau.
[1201] Mayor Alex B. Morse, letter to Secretary of State Michael R. Pompeo, November 22, 2019, Mayor's Office, City of Holyoke, MA, https://www.state.gov/wp-content/uploads/2019/12/Holyoke_MA-City-of-Initial-Resettlement-Consent-Letter.pdf, last accessed March 15, 2021.
[1202] Michael Sullivan, interview with Phil Nadeau.
[1203] Jim Kinney, "Springfield mayor Domenic Sarno Won't Grant Refugee Consent, Defies Unanimous City Council Vote," *The Republic*, December 19, 2019.
[1204] United States Court of Appeals for the Fourth Circuit, "HIAS, Inc. et al. Plaintiffs/Appellees v. Donald Trump et al., Defendants/Appellees," Appeal from the U.S. District Court for the District Court of Maryland, Amicus brief of the States of California, et al., in support of affirmance of the preliminary injunction issued in favor of the appellees, USCA4 Appeal: 20-1160, DOC 29-1, June 1, 2020, retrieved at https://ago.vermont.gov/wp-content/uploads/2020/06/29-1-Filed-Amicus-Brief.pdf, last accessed November 18, 2020.

[1205] United States Court of Appeals for the Fourth Circuit, "Hias, Inc, Church World Service, Lutheran Immigration & Refugee Service, Inc., V. Donald J. Trump, in his official capacity as President of the United States; Michael R. Pompeo, in his official capacity as Secretary of State; Alex M, Azar, II, in his official capacity as Secretary of Health and Human Services, Chad Wolf, in his official capacity as Acting Secretary of Homeland Security, No, 20-1160, January 8, 2021, https://www.ca4.uscourts.gov/opinions/201160.P.pdf, last accessed March 15, 2021.

[1206] Stephanie Barry, "Springfield City Officials Decry Housing for Refugees, Ask for Accountability," *The Republican,* March 24, 2019.

[1207] For more information about the Mayor of City of Springfield, Massachusetts, see https://www.springfield-ma.gov/cos/index.php?id=mayor, last accessed November 18, 2020.

[1208] Michael Powell, "Maine Town, Sudden Diversity and Controversy," *The Washington Post,* October 14, 2002.

[1209] *Bangor Daily News,* "Lewiston Mayor Not Apologizing," Associated Press, October 15, 2002.

[1210] Pam Belluck, "Mixed Welcome as Somalis Settle in Maine City," *The New York Times,* October 15, 2002.

[1211] Lisa Chmelecki, "Neo-Nazi Group Eyes Somali Situation," *(Lewiston) Sun Journal,* October 15, 2002.

[1212] *Portland Press Herald(online),* "Refugees Add Too Much to be Turned Away," October 19, 2002.

[1213] Meredith Goad, "Somalis' Strain on Lewiston Disputed," *Maine Sunday Telegram(online),* October 20, 2002.

[1214] *(Lewiston) Sun Journal,* "Thank You," *Your Views,* October 8, 2002, source document Judy Meyer email to Phil Nadeau, June 11, 2020.

[1215] *(Lewiston) Sun Journal,* "Open Debate," *Your Views,* October 8, 2002, source document Judy Meyer email to Phil Nadeau, June 11, 2020.

[1216] *(Lewiston) Sun Journal,* "Our Tolerance," *Your Views,* October 10, 2002, source document Judy Meyer email to Phil Nadeau, June 11, 2020.

[1217] *(Lewiston) Sun Journal,* "Generosity," *Your Views,* October 11, 2002, source document Judy Meyer email to Phil Nadeau, June 11, 2020.

[1218] *(Lewiston) Sun Journal,* "Walk the Walk," *Your Views,* October 15, 2002, source document Judy Meyer email to Phil Nadeau, June 11, 2020.

[1219] *(Lewiston) Sun Journal,* "Rise Above," *Your Views,* October 9, 2002, source document Judy Meyer email to Phil Nadeau, June 11, 2020.

1220 *(Lewiston) Sun Journal,* "Irresponsible," *Your Views,* October 10, 2002, source document Judy Meyer email to Phil Nadeau, June 11, 2020.

1221 *(Lewiston) Sun Journal,* "An Apology," *Your Views,* October 11, 2002, source document Judy Meyer email to Phil Nadeau, June 11, 2020.

1222 *(Lewiston) Sun Journal,* "Our Kindness," *Your Views,* October 11, 2002, source document Judy Meyer email to Phil Nadeau, June 11, 2020.

1223 *(Lewiston) Sun Journal,* "Our Mayor," *Your Views,* October 15, 2002, source document Judy Meyer email to Phil Nadeau, June 11, 2020.

1224 U.S. Department of Justice, "Community Relations Service FY 2003 Annual Report," Community Relations Service, Case Profiles, Lewiston, Maine – CRS Intervention Through Collaboration, https://www.justice.gov/archive/crs/pubs/fy2003/annualreport2003.htm#profiles_1, last accessed December 7, 2020.

1225 Ibid., "Message from the Director."

1226 Scott Taylor, "Group Alleges Discrimination," B1.

1227 William Mass email to Phil Nadeau, "UMass Lowell Seminar – Oct 28," October 15, 2002, source document available from Phil Nadeau.

1228 Tux Turkel, "Give Us Your Young, Your Smart, Your Energetic Masses...," *Maine Sunday Telegram(online),* October 27, 2002.

1229 Ibid.

1230 Ibid.

1231 Heidi Ellis email to Phil Nadeau, "Refugee Mental Health Project," October 31, 2002.

1232 Phil Nadeau, "Grant Application: 'Toward Harmony: Understanding a New Diversity in Lewiston-Auburn,'" City of Lewiston, Executive Department, November 11, 2002, source document available from Phil Nadeau.

1233 Scott Taylor, "Racist Rally Moved," *(Lewiston) Sun Journal,* December 19, 2002, A8.

1234 Mark Schlotterbeck, interview with Phil Nadeau.

1235 James Bennett, interview #2 with Phil Nadeau.

1236 William Welch, interview with Phil Nadeau, July 27, 2020.

1237 Lisa Chmelecki, "Second Racist Group Targets City," *(Lewiston) Sun Journal,* November 20, 2002, B1.

1238 Kathleen Skelton, "Officials: Racists' Meeting Approved," *(Lewiston) Sun Journal,* November 23, 2002, A1.

1239 Scott Taylor, "Diversity Makes Stand," *(Lewiston) Sun Journal,* November 26, 2002, A1, https://news.google.com/newspapers?nid=bcT4vkklUMwC&dat=20021126&printsec=frontpage&hl=en, last accessed December 4, 2020.

[1240] Mark Schlotterbeck, interview with Phil Nadeau.
[1241] Ibid.
[1242] Ismail Ahmed, interview with Phil Nadeau.
[1243] David Connerty-Marin, "Maine Not Immune to Intolerance," *Maine Sunday Telegram,* December 22, 2002, 1A.
[1244] William Welch, interview with Phil Nadeau.
[1245] U.S. Department of Justice, "Community Relations Service FY 2003 Annual Report."
[1246] *(Lewiston) Sun Journal,* "Hate Group's Web Site Targets L-A," November 8, 2002, A1.
[1247] Lisa Chmelecki, "Second Racist Group Targets City," B2.
[1248] Bill Nemitz, "One Way to Foil Hate Group: Just Leave it Alone," *Portland Press Herald(online),* November 22, 2002, 1B.
[1249] Ibid.
[1250] Kathleen Skelton, "Officials: Racists' Meeting Approved."
[1251] Ibid.
[1252] Mark Schlotterbeck, interview with Phil Nadeau.
[1253] Michelle Vazquez Jacobus, interview #1 with Phil Nadeau, December 14, 2020.
[1254] Michelle Vazquez Jacobus, interview #2 with Phil Nadeau, December 28, 2020.
[1255] Michelle Vazquez Jacobus, interview #1 with Phil Nadeau.
[1256] Michelle Vazquez Jacobus, interview #3 with Phil Nadeau, January 1, 2021.
[1257] Ismail Ahmed, interview with Phil Nadeau
[1258] Michelle Vazquez Jacobus, interview #1 with Phil Nadeau.
[1259] Ibid.
[1260] Ibid.
[1261] Ismail Ahmed, interview with Phil Nadeau.
[1262] Ibid.
[1263] Michelle Vazquez Jacobus, interview #3 with Phil Nadeau.
[1264] Ibid.
[1265] Schlotterbeck was speculating and was unsure what the other iterations of the final name "Many and One" were, in Mark Schlotterbeck, interview with Phil Nadeau.
[1266] Mark Schlotterbeck, interview with Phil Nadeau.
[1267] Lisa Chmelecki, "A Course on Beating Bigotry," *(Lewiston) Sun Journal,* December 20, 2002, A5.
[1268] Ismail Ahmed, interview with Phil Nadeau.
[1269] Kathleen Skelton, "Officials: Racists' Meeting Approved."
[1270] William Welch, interview with Phil Nadeau.
[1271] Bates College "Bates Facts," Bates Institutional Research, Analysis and Planning, 2002-2003, https://www.bates.edu/research/bates-facts/, last accessed January 12, 2021.

[1272] James Bennett, interview #2 with Phil Nadeau.
[1273] William Welch, interview with Phil Nadeau.
[1274] James Bennett, interview #2 with Phil Nadeau.
[1275] William Welch, interview with Phil Nadeau.
[1276] Ibid.
[1277] James Bennett, interview #2 with Phil Nadeau.
[1278] Ibid.
[1279] Maine State Legislature, Legislators' Biographical Database, http://legislature.maine.gov/lawlibrary/legis-biog-testpage/9428, last accessed December 4, 2020.
[1280] Nick Sambides, Jr., "Former Maine House Speaker John Richardson Dies at Age 62," *Bangor Daily News (online)*, June 16, 2020, https://bangordailynews.com/2020/06/16/politics/former-maine-house-speaker-john-richardson-dies-at-age-62/, last accessed December 4, 2020.
[1281] Scott Taylor, "Racist Rally Moved," A8.
[1282] Michelle Vazquez Jacobus, interview #3 with Phil Nadeau.
[1283] Michelle Vazquez Jacobus, interview #1 with Phil Nadeau.
[1284] Michelle Vazquez Jacobus, interview #3 with Phil Nadeau.
[1285] For more information about Islam and dog/pet ownership, see https://www.humanesociety.org/sites/default/files/docs/pets-and-muslims-factsheet.pdf, last accessed December 14, 2020.
[1286] Mark Schlotterbeck, interview with Phil Nadeau.
[1287] Ibid.
[1288] Ibid.
[1289] Cheryl Hamilton, interview #2 with Phil Nadeau.
[1290] Scott Taylor, "Rally Details Taking Shape," *(Lewiston) Sun Journal*, December 31, 2002, B1-B2, (NOTE: The December 31, 2002 edition is embedded in the URL for the December 30, 2002 edition), https://news.google.com/newspapers?nid=bcT4vkklUMwC&dat=20021230&printsec=frontpage&hl=en, last accessed March 16, 2021.
[1291] Ibid., B2.
[1292] Michelle Vazquez Jacobus, interview #2 with Phil Nadeau.
[1293] Ibid.
[1294] Michelle Vazquez Jacobus, interview #1 with Phil Nadeau.
[1295] Mark Schlotterbeck, interview with Phil Nadeau.
[1296] Michelle Vazquez Jacobus, interview #3 with Phil Nadeau.
[1297] Michelle Vazquez Jacobus, interview #1 with Phil Nadeau.
[1298] Lisa Chmelecki, "A Course on Beating Bigotry," A1.
[1299] For more information about "Not in Our Town, Not in Our Country" see https://www.niot.org/about-us, last accessed December 1, 2020.
[1300] Many and One-Hall & Inkabadan, "Many and One Rally," handout, January 11, 2003, source document available from Phil Nadeau.
[1301] Scott Taylor, "Diversity Makes Stand."

[1302] James Bennett, interview #2 with Phil Nadeau.
[1303] William Welch, interview with Phil Nadeau.
[1304] Ibid.
[1305] James Bennett, interview #2 with Phil Nadeau.
[1306] Kelley Bouchard, "Racist, and Proud of It," *Portland Press Herald(online),* January 5, 2003, 1A.
[1307] Ibid.
[1308] Scott Taylor, "Lewiston Gets Ready for Whatever Happens," *(Lewiston) Sun Journal,* A1-A7.
[1309] Kelley Bouchard, "Racist, and Proud of It," A1.
[1310] Ibid.
[1311] James Bennett, interview #2 with Phil Nadeau.
[1312] For more information about the Merrill Gymnasium, see https://www.bates.edu/campus-tour/athletics-buildings/merrill-indoor-gymnasium/, last accessed December 15, 2020.
[1313] William Welch, interview with Phil Nadeau.
[1314] Mark Schlotterbeck, interview with Phil Nadeau.
[1315] Scott Taylor, "Location Chosen for Diversity Rally," *(Lewiston) Sun Journal,* January 4, 2002, B1.
[1316] Ibid.
[1317] Many and One Coalition, "Many & One Rally,"(undated), pamphlet, source document available from Phil Nadeau.
[1318] Scott Taylor, "Location Chosen for Diversity Rally," B1.
[1319] See http://abacus.bates.edu/admin/offices/doc/action/response.htm, last accessed December 5, 2020.
[1320] Lisa Chmelecki, "In Command," *(Lewiston) Sun Journal,* January 18, 2003, source document Judy Meyer email to Phil Nadeau, November 16, 2020.
[1321] James Bennett, interview #2 with Phil Nadeau.
[1322] Lisa Chmelecki, "In Command."
[1323] William Welch, interview with Phil Nadeau.
[1324] City of Lewiston, "Regular Meeting Held in the Council Room at 7:00PM," City Council (minutes), January 7, 2003, 7, http://www.lewistonmaine.gov/ArchiveCenter/ViewFile/Item/560, last accessed December 6, 2020.
[1325] Scott Taylor, "Mayor Set to Leave Town," *(Lewiston) Sun Journal,* January 4, 2003, B1-B2, https://news.google.com/newspapers?nid=bcT4vkklUMwC&dat=20030104&printsec=frontpage&hl=en, last accessed January 12, 2021.
[1326] City of Lewiston, "Regular Meeting Held in the Council Room at 7:00PM," City Council (minutes), January 7, 2003, 7, http://www.lewistonmaine.gov/ArchiveCenter/ViewFile/Item/560, last accessed January 12, 2021.
[1327] Ibid., 9.

[1328] Scott Taylor, "Hale Arrest Means Little for Lewiston," *(Lewiston) Sun Journal,* January 9, 2003, A7.
[1329] Ibid.
[1330] Ibid.
[1331] Lisa Chmelecki, "In Command."
[1332] James Bennett, interview #2 with Phil Nadeau.
[1333] Ibid.
[1334] Mark LaFlamme, "MCLU Wins Partial Injunction," *(Lewiston) Sun Journal,* January 11, 2003, A1.
[1335] Ibid., A11.
[1336] Ibid.
[1337] Mark Schlotterbeck, interview with Phil Nadeau.
[1338] Mark LaFlamme, "Somalis Share Stories," *(Lewiston) Sun Journal,* January 8, 2003, B1-B2, https://news.google.com/newspapers?nid=bcT4vkklUMwC&dat=20030108&printsec=frontpage&hl=en, last accessed December 7, 2020.
[1339] Ibid.
[1340] *(Lewiston) Sun Journal,* "Complaints Against Police Officers Shift Meeting on Safety," January 9, 2003, A3.
[1341] Ibid.
[1342] Bonnie Washuk, "'Time for Action,'" *(Lewiston) Sun Journal,* January 9, 2003, A1-A5.
[1343] Maine State Legislature, "Senate Legislative Record, One Hundred and Twenty-First Legislature, State of Maine," January 9, 2003, 1, S-37, http://lldc.mainelegislature.org/Open/LegRec/121/Senate/LegRec_2003-01-09_SP_pS0033-0041.pdf, last accessed December 7, 2020.
[1344] Ibid.
[1345] *(Lewiston) Sun Journal,* "Your Views", A6, all titles and published dates listed.
[1346] Daryn Slover (photographer), "Standing Together" (photograph), *(Lewiston) Sun Journal,* January 11, 2003, A1.
[1347] Seth Golden, "Residents Unite Against Hate Groups," *(Lewiston) Sun Journal,* January 11, 2003, B4.
[1348] Scott Taylor, "Governor Calls for Solidarity," *(Lewiston) Sun Journal,* January 11, 2003, A11.
[1349] *(Lewiston) Sun Journal,* "Baldacci to Leave Reception for Rally," January 11, 2003, B4.
[1350] Ibid., A9.
[1351] Ibid., A11.
[1352] Kelley Bouchard, "Two Worlds Collide in Lewiston," *Maine Sunday Telegram,* January 12, 2003 (corrections published February 6, 2003), 1A.
[1353] Lisa Chmelecki, "United Against Hate," *(Lewiston) Sun Journal,* November 26, 2002, A1.

1354 Lisa Chmelecki, "In Command."
1355 For more information about the Pinewood Derby, see https://www.abc-pinewood-derby.com/pinewood_derby_rules.php, last accessed December 9, 2020.
1356 James Bennett, interview #2 with Phil Nadeau.
1357 Lisa Chmelecki, "In Command."
1358 James Bennett, interview #2 with Phil Nadeau.
1359 Mark Schlotterbeck, interview with Phil Nadeau.
1360 *(Lewiston) Sun Journal,* "Regional Weather Forecast," January 11, 2003, A12.
1361 U.S. Department of Commerce, National Oceanic and Atmospheric Administration, "Record of Climatological Observations," January 2003, Durham, Maine, US, USCOO172048, https://www.ncdc.noaa.gov/cdo-web/datasets/GHCND/stations/GHCND:USC00172048/detail, last accessed December 9, 2020.
1362 Lisa Chmelecki, "In Command."
1363 James Bennett, interview #2 with Phil Nadeau.
1364 Lisa Chmelecki, "In Command."
1365 Ibid.
1366 James Bennett, interview #2 with Phil Nadeau.
1367 Lisa Chmelecki, "In Command."
1368 William Welch, interview with Phil Nadeau.
1369 Lisa Chmelecki, "In Command."
1370 Ibid.
1371 Ibid.
1372 William Welch, interview with Phil Nadeau.
1373 Lisa Chmelecki, "In Command."
1374 Ibid.
1375 Kelley Bouchard, "Two Worlds Collide in Lewiston," 1A.
1376 Lisa Chmelecki, "In Command."
1377 Ibid.
1378 James Bennett, interview #2 with Phil Nadeau.
1379 Lisa Chmelecki, "In Command."
1380 James Bennett, interview #2 with Phil Nadeau.
1381 Lisa Chmelecki, "In Command."
1382 Ibid.
1383 Kelley Bouchard, "Two Worlds Collide in Lewiston," 1A.
1384 James Bennett, interview #2 with Phil Nadeau.
1385 William Welch, interview with Phil Nadeau.
1386 Ibid.
1387 Mark Schlotterbeck, interview with Phil Nadeau.
1388 Ibid.
1389 Kelley Bouchard, "Two Worlds Collide in Lewiston," 1A.

1390 Lisa Chmelecki, "In Command."
1391 Ibid.
1392 Ibid.
1393 Kelley Bouchard, "Two Worlds Collide in Lewiston," 1A.
1394 James Bennett, interview #2 with Phil Nadeau.
1395 Lisa Chmelecki, "In Command."
1396 Kelley Bouchard, "Two Worlds Collide in Lewiston," 1A.
1397 Lisa Chmelecki, "In Command."
1398 Ibid.
1399 Ibid.
1400 Lisa Chmelecki, "In Command."
1401 Kelley Bouchard, "Two Worlds Collide in Lewiston," 1A.
1402 William Welch, interview with Phil Nadeau.
1403 James Bennett, interview #2 with Phil Nadeau.
1404 Lisa Chmelecki, "In Command."
1405 William Welch, interview with Phil Nadeau.
1406 Lisa Chmelecki, "In Command."
1407 Kelley Bouchard, "Two Worlds Collide in Lewiston," 1A.
1408 Lisa Chmelecki, "In Command."
1409 James Bennett, interview #2 with Phil Nadeau.
1410 Cheryl Hamilton, interview #2 with Phil Nadeau.
1411 Ibid.
1412 Margaret "Peggy" Rotundo, interview with Phil Nadeau, November 6, 2020.
1413 For more information on the Harward Center for Community Partnerships, see https://www.bates.edu/harward/, last accessed December 11, 2020.
1414 Michael Gordon, "Spreading the Word," *(Lewiston) Sun Journal*, February 29, 2000, B1.
1415 Margaret "Peggy" Rotundo, interview with Phil Nadeau
1416 Ibid.
1417 Ibid.
1418 Ibid.
1419 Mark Schlotterbeck, interview with Phil Nadeau.
1420 Cheryl Hamilton, interview #2 with Phil Nadeau.
1421 Mark Schlotterbeck, interview with Phil Nadeau.
1422 Charles Morrison, interview with Phil Nadeau.
1423 Ibid.
1424 Susan Geismar, interview with Phil Nadeau.
1425 Ibid.
1426 Ibid.
1427 Regina Phillips, interview with Phil Nadeau.
1428 Ibid.
1429 Ibid.

[1430] Kelley Bouchard, "An NAACP Family Legacy is Handed Down," *Maine Sunday Telegram,* January 2, 2005, B1.
[1431] Meredith Goad and Kelley Bouchard, "Officials Meet with Somalis to Boost Ties," *Portland Press Herald,* October 11, 2002, 1A.
[1432] Kelley Bouchard, "Two Worlds Collide in Lewiston," 1A.
[1433] Maine House Democrats, "Representative Rachel Talbot Ross," retrieved at https://legislature.maine.gov/housedems/talbotrossr/index.html, last accessed December 11, 2020.
[1434] Mark LaFlamme, "Former Lewiston and Auburn Mayor John Jenkins Dies."
[1435] William Burney was elected as Augusta's, and the state's, first African American mayor in 1988.
[1436] Scott Taylor, "Jenkins Part II: Auburn Mayor-John Jenkins is First to Serve Both Twin Cities," *(Lewiston) Sun Journal,* November 7, 2006, B1, https://news.google.com/newspapers?nid=bcT4vkklUMwC&dat=20061107&printsec=frontpage&hl=en, last accessed January 12, 2021.
[1437] Kelley Bouchard, "Two Worlds Collide in Lewiston," 1A.
[1438] Ibid.
[1439] Ibid.
[1440] Scott Taylor, "Council Backs Mayor," *(Lewiston) Sun Journal,* January 15, 2003, A7, https://news.google.com/newspapers?nid=bcT4vkklUMwC&dat=20030115&printsec=frontpage&hl=en, last accessed December 15, 2020.
[1441] Kelley Bouchard, "Two Worlds Collide in Lewiston," 1A.
[1442] Ibid.
[1443] Bonnie Washuk, "10-Year Anniversary of 'Many and One Rally' to be Celebrated Friday," *(Lewiston) Sun Journal(online),* January 8, 2013, https://www.sunjournal.com/2013/01/08/10-year-anniversary-many-one-rally-celebrated-friday/, last accessed December 15, 2020.
[1444] Kelley Bouchard, "Two Worlds Collide in Lewiston," 1A.
[1445] Ibid.
[1446] Lisa Chmelecki, "In Command."
[1447] Ibid.
[1448] Ibid.
[1449] William Welch, text message to Phil Nadeau, December 10, 2020.
[1450] William Welch, text message to Phil Nadeau, December 16, 2020.
[1451] Lisa Chmelecki, "In Command."
[1452] Kelley Bouchard, "Two Worlds Collide in Lewiston," 1A.
[1453] Lisa Chmelecki, "In Command."
[1454] Mark Schlotterbeck, interview with Phil Nadeau.
[1455] William Welch, text to Phil Nadeau, December 14, 2020.
[1456] Lisa Chmelecki, "In Command."

1457 James Bennett, interview #2 with Phil Nadeau.
1458 Lisa Chmelecki, "In Command."
1459 Ibid.
1460 Ismail Ahmed, interview with Phil Nadeau.
1461 Ibid.
1462 Scott Taylor, "Media Frenzy Fades," *(Lewiston) Sun Journal,* January 13, 2002, A1.
1463 James Bennett, interview #2 with Phil Nadeau.
1464 William Welch, interview with Phil Nadeau.
1465 Ibid.
1466 Television news broadcast jargon for stories that warrant being featured at the beginning section of the news broadcast. For more information about news producing, see https://press.rebus.community/writingforelectronicmedia/chapter/producing/, last accessed December 15, 2020.
1467 Jerry Harkevy, "Somalis Find New Lives, Adjustments in Lewiston," *(Lewiston) Sun Journal (online),* May 12, 2007, https://www.sunjournal.com/2007/05/12/somalis-find-new-lives-adjustments-lewiston/, last accessed December 17, 2020.
1468 Bonnie Washuk, "Somalis, Others Reflect on High-Tension Week in Community Relations," *(Lewiston) Sun Journal (online),* April 24, 2007, https://www.sunjournal.com/2007/04/24/somalis-others-reflect-high-tension-week-community-relations/, last accessed December 17, 2020.
1469 The middle school incident was also covered by the national television news media. For more information, see Nicholas Plagman, "Naivete, and an Innocent Mistake," *(Lewiston) Sun Journal (online),* May 20, 2007, https://www.sunjournal.com/2007/05/20/naivete-innocent-mistake/, last accessed December 17, 2020.
1470 For more information about Lewiston immigrant national news coverage, see https://www.washingtonpost.com/nation/2020/07/18/im-scared/?arc404=true, last accessed January 12, 2021.
1471 Scott Taylor, "Council Backs Mayor," A1-A7.
1472 Scott Taylor, "Leaders Say Raymond Must Act," *(Lewiston) Sun Journal,* January 15, 2003, A7, https://news.google.com/newspapers?nid=bcT4vkklUMwC&dat=20030115&printsec=frontpage&hl=en, last accessed January 12, 2021.
1473 Ibid.
1474 Ibid.
1475 Mark LaFlamme, "Residents Take Sides on Resignation Issue," *(Lewiston) Sun Journal,* January 15, 2003, A7.
1476 Doug Fletcher, "Mayor Looks Ahead," A1-A11.
1477 Ibid.

1478 Scott Taylor, "Raymond Mum on Race Issue," *(Lewiston) Sun Journal,* February 6, 2003, B2.
1479 Ibid.
1480 Judy Meyer, "Creating a City of Welcome," *(Lewiston) Sun Journal,* January 20, 2003, A6, https://news.google.com/newspapers?nid=bcT4vkklUMwC&dat=20030120&printsec=frontpage&hl=en, January 12, 2021.
1481 Victoria Scott, "Immigrant and Refugee/Multicultural Activity Report," City of Lewiston, Executive Department, report to Mayor Laurier Raymond, et al., June 10, 2003, 3, source document available from Phil Nadeau.
1482 Ibid.
1483 For more information about the Confederation of Somali Community, see https://www.mnopedia.org/place/confederation-somali-community-minnesota, last accessed December 18, 2020.
1484 Victoria Scott, "Immigrant and Refugee/Multicultural Activity Report," June 10, 2003, 3.
1485 This information was provided to me by the Roosevelt High School staff in May 2003.
1486 Jim Adams Howie Padilla, Norman Draper, "High School Tries to Calm Tensions," *(Minneapolis) Star Tribune,* September 12, 2001, B1.
1487 Ibid.
1488 Ibid., B2.
1489 Ibid.
1490 This information was provided to me by the Roosevelt High School staff in May 2003.
1491 Jim Adams Howie Padilla, Norman Draper, "High School Tries to Calm Tensions," B2.
1492 Ibid.
1493 Norman Draper, Allie Shah, "Schools Mark Day That Held the Hardest Possible Lessons," *(Minneapolis) Star Tribune,* September 12, 2002, A23.
1494 Victoria Scott, "Immigrant and Refugee/Multicultural Activity Report," June 10, 2003, 3.
1495 Doug Fletcher, "Mayor Reflects on Painful Week."
1496 Ibid.
1497 The National Archives and Record Administration, "Japanese-American Internment During World War II," see http://www.archives.gov/education/lessons/japanese-relocation, last accessed December 24, 2020.
1498 For more information about the Jewish refugees and the SS St. Louis, see http://www.fdrlibrary.marist.edu/archives/pdfs/holocaust.pdf, and https://www.history.com/news/wwii-jewish-refugee-ship-st-louis-1939, last accessed on December 28, 2020.

[1499] Scott Taylor, "Mosque May be Forced to Move," *(Lewiston) Sun Journal (online),* August 20, 2005.

[1500] Andrew Cullen, "Struggle and Progress: 10 Years of Somalis in Lewiston," *(Lewiston) Sun Journal (online),* December 18, 2011.

[1501] Scott Taylor, "Mosque May be Forced to Move."

[1502] Ibid.

[1503] Mark Schlotterbeck, interview with Phil Nadeau.

[1504] Scott Taylor, "Schlotterbeck Steps Down," *(Lewiston) Sun Journal (online),* April 4, 2003.

[1505] Scott Taylor, "Many and One Targets Housing," *(Lewiston) Sun Journal (online),* February 9, 2005.

[1506] Victoria Scott, "Immigrant and Refugee/Multicultural Activity Report," City of Lewiston, Executive Department, report to Mayor Laurier Raymond, et al., March 2003, source document available from Phil Nadeau.

[1507] Scott Taylor, "Council Aids Diversity Conference," *(Lewiston) Sun Journal,* February 19, 2003, B2.

[1508] Ibid., 8.

[1509] For more about the "Children of Herakles," see https://americanrepertorytheater.org/shows-events/the-children-of-herakles/, last accessed December 23, 2020.

[1510] Ibid., 4.

[1511] *(Lewiston) Sun Journal,* "Somali Culture Featured at Thomas," February 3, 2003, B2.

[1512] Ibid., 3.

[1513] Ibid., 4-6.

[1514] Scott Taylor, "Hockey Plan Advances," *(Lewiston) Sun Journal,* February 5, 2003, A1, https://news.google.com/newspapers?nid=bcT4vkklUMwC&dat=20030205&printsec=frontpage&hl=en, last accessed December 30, 2020.

[1515] Scott Taylor, "Leading Edge of Development," *(Lewiston) Sun Journal,* February 15, 2003, A1-A10, https://news.google.com/newspapers?nid=bcT4vkklUMwC&dat=20030215&printsec=frontpage&hl=en, last accessed December 30, 2020.

[1516] Carol Coultas, "City Revival," *(Lewiston) Sun Journal,* June 11, 2004, A1, https://news.google.com/newspapers?nid=bcT4vkklUMwC&dat=20040611&printsec=frontpage&hl=en, last accessed December 30, 2020.

[1517] Daniel Hartill, "City Attacks Urban Blight," *(Lewiston) Sun Journal,* May 30, 2003, A1, https://news.google.com/newspapers?nid=bcT4vkklUMwC&dat=20030530&printsec=frontpage&hl=en, December 30, 2020.

[1518] Mark LaFlamme and Lisa Chmelecki, "Bates Students Tenting in Protest," *(Lewiston) Sun Journal,* November 12, 2004, A1-A5, https://news.google.com/newspapers?nid=bcT4vkklUMwC&dat=20041112&printsec=frontpage&hl=en, last accessed December 30, 2020.

[1519] Scott Taylor, "A New Life in Maine," *(Lewiston) Sun Journal (online)*, February 13, 2006.

[1520] Ibid.

[1521] University of Maine, "New Book Chronicles Somali Experiences in Maine," January 13, 2011, see https://umaine.edu/news/blog/2011/06/13/new-book-chronicles-somali-experiences-in-maine/, last accessed December 30, 2020.

[1522] Ibid.

[1523] Roxanne Moore Saucier, "Somalis in Maine Topic of Book," *Bangor Daily News(online)*, June 21, 2011, https://bangordailynews.com/2011/06/21/news/bangor/somalis-in-maine-topic-of-new-book/, last accessed December 30, 2020.

[1524] Ibid.

[1525] Lindsay Tice, "Mosque Incident Suspect Arrested," *(Lewiston) Sun Journal*, July 5, 2006, https://news.google.com/newspapers?nid=bcT4vkklUMwC&dat=20060705&printsec=frontpage&hl=en, last accessed December 31, 2020.

[1526] Ibid.

[1527] Scott Taylor, "Somalis Feel Wary," *(Lewiston) Sun Journal*, July 6, 2006, A1.

[1528] Christopher Williams, "Pig's Head Roller was Fired by City in 2002," *(Lewiston) Sun Journal*, July 8, 2006, A1-A9, https://news.google.com/newspapers?nid=bcT4vkklUMwC&dat=20060708&printsec=frontpage&hl=en, last accessed March 17, 2021.

[1529] For more information about the Al-Jazeera Lewiston news story, see https://www.youtube.com/watch?v=H0g-h_aL458, last accessed December 31, 2020.

[1530] Scott Taylor, "Community Stands as One," *(Lewiston) Sun Journal*, July 13, 2006, A1.

[1531] Bonnie Washuk, "'Hate Incident' in City," *(Lewiston) Sun Journal*, April 19, 2007, A1 (NOTE: The April 19, 2007 Sun Journal issue is embedded in the URL for the April 16, 2007 issue), https://news.google.com/newspapers?nid=bcT4vkklUMwC&dat=20070416&printsec=frontpage&hl=en, last accessed December 31, 2020.

[1532] Carol Coultas, "Dreary Forecast," *(Lewiston) Sun Journal(online)*, January 11, 2008.

[1533] *(Lewiston) Sun Journal(online)*, "The Decade in Maine Business and Economy," December 29, 2019, https://www.sunjournal.com/2019/12/29/the-decade-in-maine-business-and-economy/, last accessed January 2, 2021.

[1534] State of Maine Public Utilities Commission, "2007 Annual Report," February 1, 2008, 49.

[1535] *(Lewiston) Sun Journal(online)*, "Opponents of Power Line Plan Lewiston Meeting," December 1, 2008.

[1536] Kathryn Skelton, "If Bid is Approved, CMP to Invest Millions in Lewiston Converter Station," *(Lewiston) Sun Journal(online)*, November 28, 2017.

[1537] Kathryn Skelton, "CMP Bids for Project That Would Create 145-Mile Transmission Line," *(Lewiston) Sun Journal(online)*, July 28, 2017.

[1538] Megan Gray, "Supreme Court Rules CMP Corridor Referendum Unconstitutional," *Portland Press Herald(online)*, August 13, 2020.

[1539] Scott Taylor, "Newsweek Article Draws Criticism," *(Lewiston) Sun Journal(online)*, January 24, 2009.

[1540] Ibid.

[1541] City of Lewiston Historic Preservation Review Board, "Historic Lewiston: A Self-Guided Tour of our History, Architecture and Culture," Historic Buildings and Sites, No. 3, http://www.lewistonmaine.gov/DocumentCenter/View/1141/Walking-Tour-Brochure?bidId=, last accessed January 2, 2021.

[1542] Bonnie Washuk, "Somali Stores Bring People Back to Lisbon Street," *(Lewiston) Sun Journal(online)*, August 29, 2010.

[1543] Ibid.

[1544] Phil Nadeau, "A Work in Progress: Lewiston Responds to the Rapid Immigration of Somali Refugees," 69.

[1545] Ibid., 71-72.

[1546] Andrew Cullen, "A Decade Later: The City, Somalis, and Spending," *(Lewiston) Sun Journal*, December 18, 2011, https://www.google.com/url?client=internal-element-cse&cx=004498235353933368441:ukh7f6idvka&q=https://www.sunjournal.com/2011/12/18/decade-later-city-somalis-spending/&sa=U&ved=2ahUKEwitkeuF1I3uAhWFuVkKHYOBA3UQFjAAegQIABAC&usg=AOvVaw3w8FshawejW9nBkyuvNiBO, last accessed January 2, 2021.

[1547] Mark LaFlamme, "Lepage Wows Franco Crowd in Lewiston," *(Lewiston) Sun Journal(online)*, March 17, 2011.

[1548] Tom Bell (Portland Press Herald), "Lepage Family Bonds Survive Troubling Upbringing in Lewiston," *(Lewiston) Sun Journal(online)*, January 5, 2011.

[1549] Ibid.

[1550] Ibid.

[1551] Ibid.

[1552] Rosie Hughes (Bangor Daily News), "Maine to End Its Role in Refugee Resettlement," *(Lewiston) Sun Journal(online)*, January 26, 2017.

1553 Bonnie Washuk, "Mohamed Seeking School Committee Seat as a Write-In," *(Lewiston) Sun Journal(online)*, October 29, 2013.
1554 Ibid.
1555 Bonnie Washuk, "Lewiston Elects First African Immigrant to Public Office," *(Lewiston) Sun Journal(online)*, November 21, 2013.
1556 Gene Geiger, "Charter Commission Will Not Seek Vote on Merger in November," *Twin City Times*, August 11, 2016, 1, https://twincitypub.pageflip.site/editions/TCT11016, last accessed January 3, 2021.
1557 Judith Meyer, "Lewiston Police Chief Deputizes Chamber to Counter City's Rough Operation," *(Lewiston) Sun Journal(online)*, November 12, 2015, https://www.sunjournal.com/2015/11/12/lewiston-police-chief-deputizes-chamber-counter-citys-rough-reputation/?sid=1818577, last accessed January 12, 2021.
1558 Ibid.
1559 Ibid.
1560 Kathryn Skelton, "Pastor Helps Settle Asylum-Seekers Moving to Twin Cities," *(Lewiston) Sun Journal(online)*, February 9, 2014.
1561 Andrew Rice, "Lewiston Seeing Increased Number of Asylum-Seekers," *(Lewiston) Sun Journal(online)*, January 31, 2017.
1562 Phil Nadeau, "Phil Nadeau: African Migrants and the US/Mexican Border," *(Lewiston) Sun Journal(online)*, July 21, 2019.
1563 St. Dominic's Regional High School moved from its original Lewiston location to a newly constructed facility in Auburn in January 2002.
1564 Kevin Mills, "Lewiston Celebrates First Class A State Soccer Title," *(Lewiston) Sun Journal(online)*, November 7, 2015.
1565 For more information about the Lewiston High School 2015 Soccer Championship, see HBO Real Sports with Bryant Gumbel, "Coming to America," Season 22, Episode 10, October 2016, https://www.hbo.com/real-sports-with-bryant-gumbel/2016/october, last accessed January 3, 2021.
1566 Amy Bass, *One Goal*, (New York: Hachette Books, 2018).
1567 Ray Routhier (Portland Press Herald), "Book About Lewiston Soccer Team is Optioned by Netflix," *(Lewiston) Sun Journal(online)*, June 20, 2018.
1568 Bonnie Washuk, "Somali Community Producing More Voters, Candidates," *(Lewiston) Sun Journal(online)*, November 11, 2017, https://www.sunjournal.com/2017/11/11/somali-community-producing-more-voters-candidates/, last accessed January 7, 2021.
1569 Ibid.
1570 Ibid.
1571 Immigrant and Refugee Integration and Policy Development Working Group, "Final Report," December 2017, see

https://drive.google.com/file/d/1pyqRFZ18oedGxo00ufwdYMRuZ_f2jqH3/view?usp=sharing, link created January 4, 2021.

[1572] For more information, see "Chronicle" at https://www.youtube.com/watch?v=ujj7NLmaBD0m, last accessed January 4, 2021.

[1573] Kathryn Skelton, "Thrillist Picks Lewiston as Most Underrated City in Maine," *(Lewiston) Sun Journal(online)*, March 2, 2018.

[1574] For more about the Dempsey Challenge, see https://www.newscentermaine.com/article/news/outreach/dempsey/dempsey-challenge-in-10th-year-assembles-thousands-for-charity/97-477759841, last accessed January 12, 2021.

[1575] For more about the Dempsey Center, see https://www.dempseycenter.org/patrick-dempsey/, last accessed January 12, 2021.

[1576] Ibid.

[1577] *(Lewiston) Sun Journal(online)*, "Lewiston Now Owns the Canals and Will Start Cleaning Them Up," March 23, 2018.

[1578] Christopher Williams, "State Seeks to Try Lewiston Teen as Adult on Manslaughter Charge," *(Lewiston) Sun Journal(online)*, March 24, 2019.

[1579] Mark LaFlamme and Christopher Williams, "Three Arrested in Donald Guisti's Killing," *(Lewiston) Sun Journal(online)*, April 11, 2019.

[1580] Christopher Williams, "State Seeks to Try Lewiston Teen as Adult on Manslaughter Charge."

[1581] *(Lewiston) Sun Journal(online)*, "Lewiston Man Dies from Injuries Sustained in Tuesday Night Fight," June 15, 2018.

[1582] Bonnie Washuk, "Auburn Votes Big for New Edward Little High School," *(Lewiston) Sun Journal(online)*, June 11, 2019, https://www.sunjournal.com/2019/06/11/turnout-is-light-as-auburn-votes-on-new-edward-little-high-school/, last accessed January 5, 2021.

[1583] Bonnie Washuk, "Lewiston Regional Technical Center Wing at Edward Little Would Expand Career, Technical Offerings," *(Lewiston) Sun Journal(online)*, June 8, 2019, https://www.sunjournal.com/2019/06/08/lrtc-wing-at-edward-little-would-expand-career-technical-offerings/, last accessed January 5, 2021.

[1584] Ibid.

[1585] Ibid.

[1586] Steve Collins, "Racism at Edward Little Highlighted in The Boston Globe," *(Lewiston) Sun Journal(online)*, August 19, 2019, https://www.sunjournal.com/2019/08/16/racism-at-edward-little-highlighted-in-the-boston-globe/, last accessed January 5, 2021.

[1587] Ibid.

[1588] Ibid.

[1589] Kathryn Skelton, "Auburn Mayor Levesque Buys Former Peck Building in Lewiston," *(Lewiston) Sun Journal(online),* May 9, 2019, https://www.sunjournal.com/2019/05/09/auburn-mayor-jason-levesque-buys-former-peck-building-in-lewiston/, last accessed January 5, 2021.

[1590] Kathryn Skelton, "Walmart Looks to Fill 100 Jobs at Lewiston Distribution Center," *(Lewiston) Sun Journal(online),* June 10, 2019, https://www.sunjournal.com/2019/06/10/walmart-looks-to-fill-100-jobs-at-lewiston-distribution-center/, last accessed January 5, 2021.

[1591] Kathryn Skelton, "Safiya Khalid: A Calling to Make Change," *(Lewiston) Sun Journal(online),* October 7, 2018,

[1592] Andrew Rice, "Safiya Khalid Elected First Somali-American to Lewiston City Council," *(Lewiston) Sun Journal(online),* November 5, 2019, https://www.sunjournal.com/2019/11/05/safiya-khalid-elected-first-somali-american-to-lewiston-city-council/, last accessed January 5, 2021.

[1593] Ibid.

[1594] Ibid.

[1595] Andrew Rice, "Lewiston Seeks Grant to Transform Tree Streets Neighborhood," *(Lewiston) Sun Journal(online),* August 23, 2017, https://www.sunjournal.com/2017/08/23/city-seeks-grant-to-transform-tree-streets-neighborhood/?rel=related, last accessed January 5, 2021.

[1596] Ibid.

[1597] Andrew Rice, "City Oks Bid For Redevelopment Grant," *(Lewiston) Sun Journal(online),* November 25, 2020, C1.

[1598] Andrew Rice, " 'Transformation' Plan for Downtown Lewiston Includes Two Ambitious Redevelopment," *(Lewiston) Sun Journal(online),* June 28, 2019, https://www.sunjournal.com/2019/06/28/transformation-plan-for-downtown-lewiston-includes-two-ambitious-redevelopments/, last accessed January 5, 2021.

[1599] Andrew Rice, "City Oks Bid For Redevelopment Grant," C1.

[1600] Mark LaFlamme, "Maine's First Presumed COVID-19 Case is a Navy Reservist Tested at CMMC," *(Lewiston) Sun Journal(online),* March 12, 2020, https://www.sunjournal.com/2020/03/12/janet-mills-says-androscoggin-county-woman-is-states-first-presumptive-case-of-covid-19/, last accessed February 24, 2021.

[1601] Center for Disease Control and Prevention, "Severe Outcomes Among Patients with Coronavirus Disease, 2019 (COVID-19) – United States, February 12 – March 16, 2020," March 27, 2020, https://www.cdc.gov/mmwr/volumes/69/wr/mm6912e2.htm, last accessed March 11, 2021.

[1602] Andrew Rice, "Lewiston Declares City Emergency," *(Lewiston) Sun Journal(online),* March 18, 2020, https://www.sunjournal.com/2020/03/17/lewiston-declares-city-emergency/, last accessed January 5, 2021.

[1603] Andrew Rice, "Auburn Declares Emergency Prior to Statewide Shelter-in-Place," *(Lewiston) Sun Journal(online)*, April 1, 2020, https://www.sunjournal.com/2020/04/01/auburn-declares-emergency-prior-to-statewide-shelter-in-place/, last accessed January 5, 2021.

[1604] Jim Lawlor (Portland Press Herald), "Dr. Shah Warns: 'Let's Not Forget the Storm, Even as the Sun is Emerging," *(Lewiston) Sun Journal(online)*, December 14, 2020, https://www.sunjournal.com/2020/12/14/maine-reports-426-cases-of-covid-19-two-more-deaths/, last accessed January 5, 2021.

[1605] Jon Bolduc, "Video: Many Turn Out in Lewiston-Auburn to Oppose Police Brutality Nationwide," *(Lewiston) Sun Journal(online)*, May 31, 2020, https://www.google.com/url?client=internal-element-cse&cx=004498235353933368441:ukh7f6idvka&q=https://www.sunjournal.com/2020/05/31/video-many-protesters-turnout-in-lewiston-auburn-to-support-black-lives-matter/&sa=U&ved=2ahUKEwjR4pac94fuAhVBmVkKHTCSAncQFjAAegQIARAC&usg=AOvVaw3bvLfP3T0sL0EbsK3lIlCe, last accessed January 6, 2021.

[1606] Ibid.

[1607] Andrew Rice, "Lewiston Council Passes Resolution on Policing, Equal Justice," *(Lewiston) Sun Journal(online)*, June 16, 2020, https://www.sunjournal.com/2020/06/16/lewiston-council-passes-resolution-on-policing-equal-justice/, last accessed January 6, 2021.

[1608] Andrew Rice, "Lewiston Mayor Announces Appointments to Equity and Diversity Committee," *(Lewiston) Sun Journal(online)*, July 7, 2020, https://www.sunjournal.com/2020/07/07/lewiston-mayor-announces-membership-of-equity-and-diversity-committee/, last accessed January 6, 2021.

[1609] Andrew Rice, "Council Approves Funds for Police Body Cameras," *(Lewiston) Sun Journal(online)*, October 21, 2020.

[1610] Andrew Rice, "Lewiston Equity and Diversity Committee Finalizes Recommendations for City," *(Lewiston) Sun Journal(online)*, December 17, 2020, https://www.sunjournal.com/2020/12/17/lewiston-equity-and-diversity-committee-finalizes-recommendations/, last accessed January 6, 2021.

[1611] Andrew Rice, "Lewiston City Administrator Ed Barrett Announces Retirement this Year," *(Lewiston) Sun Journal(online)*, February 4, 2020, https://www.sunjournal.com/2020/02/04/lewiston-city-administrator-ed-barrett-announces-retirement-this-year/, last accessed January 6, 2021.

[1612] David Vermette, "A Distinct Alien Race," 337.

[1613] The Architect of the Capitol, "U.S. Capitol Building," https://www.aoc.gov/explore-capitol-campus/buildings-grounds/capitol-building, last accessed January 8, 2021.

[1614] Congressional Record, "Proceedings and Debates of the 89th Congress," United States of America, Second Session, Vol. 112, Part 4, February 28, 1966 – March 9, 1966, 4504, https://www.google.com/books/edition/Congressional_Record/tvCi8PB_yS0C?hl=en&gbpv=1&dq=mankind's+capacity+for+justice+makes+democracy+possible,+but+mankind's+inclination+to+injustice+makes+democracy+necessary&pg=PA4504&printsec=frontcover, last accessed February 28, 2021.

www.ingramcontent.com/pod-product-compliance
Lightning Source LLC
Chambersburg PA
CBHW022041200426
43209CB00072B/1919/J